MODERN OPERATING SYSTEMS

MODERN OPERATING SYSTEMS

ANDREW S. TANENBAUM

Vrije Universiteit
Amsterdam, The Netherlands

PRENTICE HALL
UPPER SADDLE RIVER, NJ 07458

Tanenbaum, Andrew S.
    Modern operating systems / Andrew S. Tanenbaum.
        p.   cm.
    Includes bibliographical references and index.
    ISBN 0-13-588187-0
    1. Operating systems (Computers)   I. Title.
QA76.76.O63T359 1992
005.4'3--dc20   91-45010
                                                 CIP

Acquisitions editor: Tom McElwee
Production supervisor: Bayani Mendoza de Leon
Cover designer: Bruce Kenselaar
Prepress buyer: Linda Behrens
Manufacturing buyer: Dave Dickey
Supplements editor: Alice Dworkin
Interior designer: Andrew S. Tanenbaum

 © 1992 by Prentice Hall, Inc.
A Simon & Schuster Company
Upper Saddle River, New Jersey 07458

The author and publisher of this book have used their best efforts in preparing this book. These
efforts include the development, research, and testing of the theories and programs to determine their
effectiveness. The author and publisher make no warranty of any kind, expressed or implied, with
regard to these programs or the documentation contained in this book. The author and publisher
shall not be liable in any event for incidental or consequential damages in connection with, or arising
out of, the furnishing, performance, or use of these programs.

Printed in the United States of America
10 9 8 7

ISBN 0-13-588187-0

Prentice-Hall International (UK) Limited, *London*
Prentice-Hall of Australia Pty. Limited, *Sydney*
Prentice-Hall Canada Inc., *Toronto*
Prentice-Hall Hispanoamericana. S.A., *Mexico*
Prentice-Hall of India Private Limited, *New Delhi*
Prentice-Hall of Japan, Inc., *Tokyo*
Simon & Schuster Asia Pte. Ltd., *Singapore*
Editora Prentice-Hall do Brasil, Ltda., *Rio de Janeiro*

TRADEMARK INFORMATION

IBM PC is a registered trademark of
    International Business Machines
    Corporation.
UNIX is a registered trademark of AT&T
    (Bell Laboratories.).
PDP ll and VAX are registered
    trademarks of Digital Equipment
    Corporation.
MS-DOS is a trademark of Microsoft
    Corporation.
Atari is a trademark of Atari
    Corporation.
SPARC is a trademark of Sun
    Microsystems.
Macintosh is a trademark of Apple
    Computer, Inc.
Intel is a registered trademark of Intel
    Corporation.

To Suzanne, Barbara, Marvin and Little Bram

CONTENTS

PART 2: DISTRIBUTED OPERATING SYSTEMS

9 INTRODUCTION TO DISTRIBUTED SYSTEMS   **362**

15 CASE STUDY 4: MACH   637

A READING LIST AND BIBLIOGRAPHY   682

PREFACE

In the past, most computers ran standalone, and most operating systems were designed to run on a single processor. This situation is rapidly changing into one in which computers are networked together, making distributed operating systems more important. This book is unusual for an undergraduate text in that it recognizes this transition and gives as much attention to distributed operating systems as to traditional single CPU operating systems.

During the past 15 years, I have personally helped design and implement three different operating systems: TSS-11 (PDP-11), MINIX (IBM PC, Atari, Amiga, Macintosh, and SPARC), and Amoeba (80386, Sun-3, SPARC, and VAX). I have drawn on this long experience to emphasize those topics that actually matter in real systems. All the subjects that are expected in an undergraduate text on operating systems are included here, including processes, interprocess communication, semaphores, monitors, message passing, classical IPC problems, scheduling, swapping, virtual memory, paging algorithms, segmentation, file systems, security, protection mechanisms, I/O hardware and software, and deadlocks. The amount of space devoted to some of these topics is different than in some other books, however, reflecting my belief that students should learn about concepts that are of practical value in real systems, rather than those that are just of theoretical interest. For example, CPU scheduling is worth a section, not a whole chapter. Many complicated scheduling algorithms have been proposed and analyzed in the literature, but most real systems just use some kind of simple priority or round robin scheme.

The second half of the book deals with distributed systems. After an introductory chapter on the hardware and software of distributed systems, we go on to look at layered protocols, the client-server model, remote procedure call, group communication, clock synchronization, mutual exclusion, election algorithms, atomic transactions, threads, and distributed file systems, among many other topics. Although including so much material on distributed systems in an undergraduate course is perhaps unusual, developments in the computer industry make it essential that all students be familiar with these important systems as they will soon dominate the scene.

To reinforce the fundamental concepts presented in the text, four detailed examples, two traditional and two distributed, are presented. The traditional (i.e., nondistributed) systems are UNIX and MS-DOS. The distributed ones are Amoeba and Mach. In addition to these four examples, each of which rates an entire chapter, other systems are also covered more briefly, including NFS, AFS, and ISIS. By the end of the book, the reader should have a good idea of the range of possibilities available in modern operating systems.

For the record, I would like to point out that this book began as an attempt to edit my earlier book, *Operating Systems: Design and Implementation*, and remove all the material on MINIX from it to make it suitable for traditional "theory," as opposed to "laboratory" courses. While I was doing this editing, I became convinced that distributed systems are becoming so important, that I added seven chapters on the subject. It is my intention, however, to update the MINIX book in the foreseeable future, so as to have two up-to-date books: one for "hands on" and one for "hands off" readers.

Each chapter concludes with problems for the reader. A solutions manual for these problems is available from Prentice-Hall.

I would like to thank the following people for scrutinizing the manuscript and making many valuable suggestions for improvement: Henri Bal, Brian Bershad, Ralf Brown, Rich Draves, Ken Birman, Phyllis Bregman, Scott Carson, Fadi Deek, Daniel Duchamp, Philip Homburg, Frans Kaashoek, Ed Keizer, Darrell Long, Richard Newman-Wolfe, Eugene Pinsky, Donna Quammen, Rick Rashid, Greg Riccardi, Dennis Ritchie, Vince Russo, Andrew Schulman, Greg Sharp, Charles Shub, Jennifer Steiner, Daniel Stodolsky, Mary Thompson, Hans van Staveren, Leendert van Doorn, Kees Verstoep, and Victor Wallace. My editor at Prentice-Hall, Tom McElwee, did a fine job in numerous ways.

Despite all this help, no doubt some errors remain. That seems to be inevitable, no matter how many people read the manuscript. People who wish to report errors should contact me by electronic mail via the Internet at ast@CS.VU.NL. Also, universities or companies interested in obtaining Amoeba (see Chap. 14) should contact me the same way.

Finally, I would like to thank Suzanne again for her continuing patience. Without her support and understanding I would never have made it. I also want to thank Barbara and Marvin for using the 286 and leaving the 386 for me. I would especially like to thank them for turning off the sound upon request, just like Bram.

Andrew S. Tanenbaum

PART
1

TRADITIONAL OPERATING SYSTEMS

1

INTRODUCTION

Without its software, a computer is basically a useless lump of metal. With its software, a computer can store, process, and retrieve information, find spelling errors in manuscripts, play adventure, and engage in many other valuable activities to earn its keep. Computer software can be roughly divided into two kinds: the system programs, which manage the operation of the computer itself, and the application programs, which solve problems for their users. The most fundamental of all the system programs is the **operating system**, which controls all the computer's resources and provides the base upon which the application programs can be written.

A modern computer system consists of one or more processors, some main memory (often known as "core memory," even though magnetic cores have not been used in memories for over a decade), clocks, terminals, disks, network interfaces, and other input/output devices. All in all, a complex system. Writing programs that keep track of all these components and use them correctly, let alone optimally, is an extremely difficult job. If every programmer had to be concerned with how disk drives work, and with all the dozens of things that could go wrong when reading a disk block, it is unlikely that many programs could be written at all.

Many years ago it became abundantly clear that some way had to be found to shield programmers from the complexity of the hardware. The way that has gradually evolved is to put a layer of software on top of the bare hardware, to manage all parts of the system, and present the user with an interface or **virtual machine** that is easier to understand and program. This layer of software is the operating system, and forms the subject of this book.

The situation is shown in Fig. 1-1. At the bottom is the hardware, which in many cases is itself composed of two or more layers. The lowest layer contains physical devices, consisting of integrated circuit chips, wires, power supplies, cathode ray tubes, and similar physical devices. How these are constructed and how they work is the province of the electrical engineer.

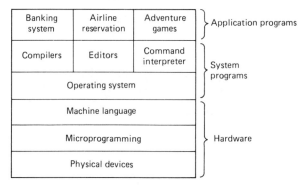

Fig. 1-1. A computer system consists of hardware, system programs, and application programs.

Next comes a layer of primitive software that directly controls these devices and provides a cleaner interface to the next layer. This software, called the **microprogram**, is usually located in read-only memory. It is actually an interpreter, fetching the machine language instructions such as ADD, MOVE, and JUMP, and carrying them out as a series of little steps. To carry out an ADD instruction, for example, the microprogram must determine where the numbers to be added are located, fetch them, add them, and store the result somewhere. The set of instructions that the microprogram interprets defines the **machine language**, which is not really part of the hard machine at all, but computer manufacturers always describe it in their manuals as such, so many people think of it as being the real "machine." On some machines the microprogram is implemented in hardware, and is not really a distinct layer.

The machine language typically has between 50 and 300 instructions, mostly for moving data around the machine, doing arithmetic, and comparing values. In this layer, the input/output devices are controlled by loading values into special **device registers**. For example, a disk can be commanded to read by loading the values of the disk address, main memory address, byte count, and direction (READ or WRITE) into its registers. In practice, many more parameters are needed, and the status returned by the drive after an operation is highly complex. Furthermore, for many I/O devices, timing plays an important role in the programming.

A major function of the operating system is to hide all this complexity and give the programmer a more convenient set of instructions to work with. For example, READ BLOCK FROM FILE is conceptually simpler than having to worry about the details of moving disk heads, waiting for them to settle down, and so on.

On top of the operating system is the rest of the system software. Here we find the command interpreter (shell), compilers, editors and similar applicationindependent programs. It is important to realize that these programs are definitely not part of the operating system, even though they are typically supplied by the computer manufacturer. This is a crucial, but subtle, point. The operating system is that portion of the software that runs in **kernel mode** or **supervisor mode**. It is protected from user tampering by the hardware (ignoring for the moment some of the older microprocessors that do not have hardware protection at all). Compilers and editors run in **user mode**. If a user does not like a particular compiler, he† is free to write his own if he so chooses; he is not free to write his own disk interrupt handler, which is part of the operating system and is normally protected by hardware against attempts by users to modify it.

Finally, above the system programs come the application programs. These programs are written by the users to solve their particular problems, such as commercial data processing, engineering calculations, or game playing.

1.1. WHAT IS AN OPERATING SYSTEM?

Most computer users have had some experience with an operating system, but it is difficult to pin down precisely what an operating system is. Part of the problem is that operating systems perform two basically unrelated functions, and depending on who is doing the talking, you hear mostly about one function or the other. Let us now look at both.

1.1.1. The Operating System as an Extended Machine

As mentioned earlier, the **architecture** (instruction set, memory organization, I/O and bus structure) of most computers at the machine language level is primitive and awkward to program, especially for input/output. To make this point more concrete, let us briefly look at how floppy disk I/O is done using the NEC PD765 controller chip, which is used on the IBM PC and many other personal computers. (Throughout this book we will use the terms "floppy disk" and "diskette" interchangeably.) The PD765 has 16 commands, each specified by loading between 1 and 9 bytes into a device register. These commands are for reading and writing data, moving the disk arm, and formatting tracks, as well as initializing, sensing, resetting, and recalibrating the controller and the drives.

The most basic commands are READ and WRITE, each of which requires 13 parameters, packed into 9 bytes. These parameters specify such items as the address of the disk block to be read, the number of sectors per track, the recording mode used on the physical medium, the intersector gap spacing, and what to do with a deleted-data-address-mark. If you do not understand this mumbo jumbo, do not worry, that is precisely the point—it is rather esoteric. When the operation is completed, the controller chip returns 23 status and error fields packed into 7 bytes. As if this were not enough, the floppy disk programmer must also be constantly aware of whether the

---

† "He" should be read as "he or she" throughout the book.

motor is on or off. If the motor is off, it must be turned on (with a long start-up delay) before data can be read or written. The motor cannot be left on too long, however, or the floppy disk will wear out. The programmer is thus forced to deal with the trade-off between long start-up delays versus wearing out floppy disks (and losing the data on them).

Without going into the *real* details, it should be clear that the average programmer probably does not want to get too intimately involved with the programming of floppy disks (or Winchester disks, which are just as complex and quite different). Instead, what the programmer wants is a simple, high-level abstraction to deal with. In the case of disks, a typical abstraction would be that the disk contains a collection of named files. Each file can be opened for reading or writing, then read or written, and finally closed. Details such as whether or not recording should use modified frequency modulation and what the current state of the motor is should not appear in the abstraction presented to the user.

The program that hides the truth about the hardware from the programmer and presents a nice, simple view of named files that can be read and written is, of course, the operating system. Just as the operating system shields the programmer from the disk hardware and presents a simple file-oriented interface, it also conceals a lot of unpleasant business concerning interrupts, timers, memory management, and other low-level features. In each case, the abstraction presented to the user of the operating system is simpler and easier to use than the underlying hardware.

In this view, the function of the operating system is to present the user with the equivalent of an **extended machine** or **virtual machine** that is easier to program than the underlying hardware. How the operating system achieves this goal is a long story, which we will study in detail throughout this book.

1.1.2. The Operating System as a Resource Manager

The concept of the operating system as primarily providing its users with a convenient interface is a top-down view. An alternative, bottom-up, view holds that the operating system is there to manage all the pieces of a complex system. Modern computers consist of processors, memories, timers, disks, terminals, magnetic tape drives, network interfaces, laser printers, and a wide variety of other devices. In the alternative view, the job of the operating system is to provide for an orderly and controlled allocation of the processors, memories, and I/O devices among the various programs competing for them.

Imagine what would happen if three programs running on some computer all tried to print their output simultaneously on the same printer. The first few lines of printout might be from program 1, the next few from program 2, then some from program 3, and so forth. The result would be chaos. The operating system can bring order to the potential chaos by buffering all the output destined for the printer on the disk. When one program is finished, the operating system can then copy its output from the disk file where it has been stored to the printer, while at the same time the other program can continue generating more output, oblivious to the fact that the output is not really going to the printer (yet).

When a computer has multiple users, the need for managing and protecting the memory, I/O devices, and other resources is even more apparent. This need arises because it is frequently necessary for users to share expensive resources such as tape drives and phototypesetters. Economic issues aside, it is also often necessary for users who are working together to share information. In short, this view of the operating system holds that its primary task is to keep track of who is using which resource, to grant resource requests, to account for usage, and to mediate conflicting requests from different programs and users.

1.2. HISTORY OF OPERATING SYSTEMS

Operating systems have been evolving through the years. In the following sections we will briefly look at this development. Since operating systems have historically been closely tied to the architecture of the computers on which they run, we will look at successive generations of computers to see what their operating systems were like. This mapping of operating system generations to computer generations is crude, but it does provide some structure where there would otherwise be none.

The first true digital computer was designed by the English mathematician Charles Babbage (1792-1871). Although Babbage spent most of his life and fortune trying to build his "analytical engine," he never got it working properly because it was a purely mechanical design, and the technology of his day could not produce the wheels, gears, cogs and other mechanical parts to the high precision that he needed. Needless to say, the analytical engine did not have an operating system.

1.2.1. The First Generation (1945-1955): Vacuum Tubes and Plugboards

After Babbage's unsuccessful efforts, little progress was made in constructing digital computers until World War II. Around the mid-1940s, Howard Aiken at Harvard, John von Neumann at the Institute for Advanced Study in Princeton, J. Presper Eckert and William Mauchley at the University of Pennsylvania, and Konrad Zuse in Germany, among others, all succeeded in building calculating engines using vacuum tubes. These machines were enormous, filling up entire rooms with tens of thousands of vacuum tubes, but were much slower than even the cheapest home computer available today.

In these early days, a single group of people designed, built, programmed, operated, and maintained each machine. All programming was done in absolute machine language, often by wiring up plugboards to control the machine's basic functions. Programming languages were unknown (not even assembly language). Operating systems were unheard of. The usual mode of operation was for the programmer to sign up for a block of time on the signup sheet on the wall, then come down to the machine room, insert his or her plugboard into the computer, and spend the next few hours hoping that none of the 20,000 or so vacuum tubes would burn out during the run. Virtually all the problems were straightforward numerical calculations, such as grinding out tables of sines and cosines.

By the early 1950s, the routine had improved somewhat with the introduction of punched cards. It was now possible to write programs on cards and read them in, instead of using plugboards; otherwise the procedure was the same.

1.2.2. The Second Generation (1955-1965): Transistors and Batch Systems

The introduction of the transistor in the mid-1950s changed the picture radically. Computers became reliable enough that they could be manufactured and sold to paying customers with the expectation that they would continue to function long enough to get some useful work done. For the first time, there was a clear separation between designers, builders, operators, programmers, and maintenance personnel.

These machines were locked away in specially air conditioned computer rooms, with staffs of professional operators to run them. Only big corporations, or major government agencies or universities could afford the multimillion dollar price tag. To run a **job** (i.e., a program or set of programs), a programmer would first write the program on paper (in FORTRAN or assembler), then punch it on cards. He would then bring the card deck down to the input room and hand it to one of the operators.

When the computer finished whatever job it was currently running, an operator would go over to the printer and tear off the output and carry it over to the output room, so that the programmer could collect it later. Then he would take one of the card decks that had been brought from the input room and read it in. If the FORTRAN compiler was needed, the operator would have to get it from a file cabinet and read it in. Much computer time was wasted while operators were walking around the machine room.

Given the high cost of the equipment, it is not surprising that people quickly looked for ways to reduce the wasted time. The solution generally adopted was the **batch system**. The idea behind it was to collect a tray full of jobs in the input room, and then read them onto a magnetic tape using a small, (relatively) inexpensive computer, such as the IBM 1401, which was very good at reading cards, copying tapes, and printing output, but not at all good at numerical calculations. Other, much more expensive machines, such as the IBM 7094, were used for the real computing. This situation is shown in Fig. 1-2.

After about an hour of collecting a batch of jobs, the tape was rewound and brought into the machine room, where it was mounted on a tape drive. The operator then loaded a special program (the ancestor of today's operating system), which read the first job from tape and ran it. The output was written onto a second tape, instead of being printed. After each job finished, the operating system automatically read the next job from the tape and began running it. When the whole batch was done, the operator removed the input and output tapes, replaced the input tape with the next batch, and brought the output tape to a 1401 for printing **off line** (i.e., not connected to the main computer).

The structure of a typical input job is shown in Fig. 1-3. It started out with a $JOB card, specifying the maximum run time in minutes, the account number to be charged, and the programmer's name. Then came a $FORTRAN card, telling the operating system to load the FORTRAN compiler from the system tape. It was

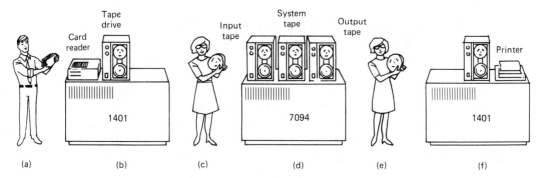

Fig. 1-2. An early batch system. (a) Programmers bring cards to 1401. (b) 1401 reads batch of jobs onto tape. (c) Operator carries input tape to 7094. (d) 7094 does computing. (e) Operator carries output tape to 1401. (f) 1401 prints output.

followed by the program to be compiled, and then a $LOAD card, directing the operating system to load the object program just compiled. (Compiled programs were often written on scratch tapes and had to be loaded explicitly.) Next came the $RUN card, telling the operating system to run the program with the data following it. Finally, the $END card marked the end of the job. These primitive control cards were the forerunners of modern job control languages and command interpreters.

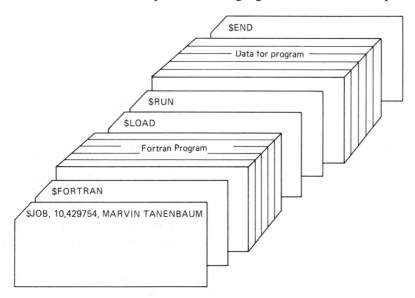

Fig. 1-3. Structure of a typical FMS job.

Large second generation computers were used mostly for scientific and engineering calculations, such as solving partial differential equations. They were largely programmed in FORTRAN and assembly language. Typical operating systems were FMS (the Fortran Monitor System) and IBSYS, IBM's operating system for the 7094.

1.2.3. The Third Generation (1965-1980): ICs and Multiprogramming

By the early 1960s most computer manufacturers had two distinct, and totally incompatible, product lines. On the one hand there were the word-oriented, large-scale scientific computers, such as the 7094, which were used for numerical calculations in science and engineering. On the other hand, there were the character-oriented, commercial computers, such as the 1401, which were widely used for tape sorting and printing by banks and insurance companies.

Developing and maintaining two completely different product lines was an expensive proposition for the manufacturers. In addition, many new computer customers initially needed a small machine, but later outgrew it and wanted a bigger machine that would run all their old programs, but faster.

IBM attempted to solve both of these problems at a single stroke by introducing the System/360. The 360 was a series of software-compatible machines ranging from 1401-sized to much more powerful than the 7094. The machines differed only in price and performance (maximum memory, processor speed, number of I/O devices permitted, and so forth.). Since all the machines had the same architecture and instruction set, at least in theory, programs written for one machine could run on all the others. Furthermore, the 360 was designed to handle both scientific and commercial computing. Thus a single family of machines could satisfy the needs of all customers. In subsequent years, IBM has come out with compatible successors to the 360 line, using more modern technology, known as the 370, 4300, 3080, and 3090 series.

The 360 was the first major computer line to use (small-scale) integrated circuits (ICs), thus providing a major price/performance advantage over the second generation machines, which were built up from individual transistors. It was an immediate success, and the idea of a family of compatible computers was soon adopted by all the other major manufacturers. The descendants of these machines are still in use at large computer centers today.

The greatest strength of the "one family" idea was simultaneously its greatest weakness. The intention was that all software, including the operating system, had to work on all models. It had to run on small systems, which often just replaced 1401s for copying cards to tape, and on very large systems, which often replaced 7094s for doing weather forecasting and other heavy computing. It had to be good on systems with few peripherals and on systems with many peripherals. It had to work in commercial environments and in scientific environments. Above all, it had to be efficient for all of these different uses.

There was no way that IBM (or anybody else) could write a piece of software to meet all those conflicting requirements. The result was an enormous and extraordinarily complex operating system, probably two to three orders of magnitude larger than FMS. It consisted of millions of lines of assembly language written by thousands of programmers, and contained thousands upon thousands of bugs, which necessitated a continuous stream of new releases in an attempt to correct them. Each new release fixed some bugs and introduced new ones, so the number of bugs probably remained constant in time.

One of the designers of OS/360, Fred Brooks, subsequently wrote a witty and incisive book (Brooks, 1975) describing his experiences with OS/360. While it would be impossible to summarize the book here, suffice it to say that the cover shows a herd of prehistoric beasts stuck in a tar pit. The cover of Silberschatz et al.'s book (1991) makes a similar point.

Despite its enormous size and problems, OS/360 and the similar third-generation operating systems produced by other computer manufacturers actually satisfied most of their customers reasonably well. They also popularized several key techniques absent in second generation operating systems. Probably the most important of these was **multiprogramming**. On the 7094, when the current job paused to wait for a tape or other I/O operation to complete, the CPU simply sat idle until the I/O finished. With heavily CPU-bound scientific calculations, I/O is infrequent, so this wasted time is not significant. With commercial data processing, the I/O wait time can often be 80 or 90 percent of the total time, so something had to be done to avoid having the CPU be idle so much.

The solution that evolved was to partition memory into several pieces, with a different job in each partition, as shown in Fig. 1-4. While one job was waiting for I/O to complete, another job could be using the CPU. If enough jobs could be held in main memory at once, the CPU could be kept busy nearly 100 percent of the time. Having multiple jobs in memory at once requires special hardware to protect each job against snooping and mischief by the other ones, but the 360 and other third generation systems were equipped with this hardware.

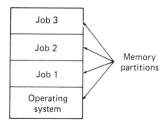

Fig. 1-4. A multiprogramming system with three jobs in memory.

Another major feature present in third-generation operating systems was the ability to read jobs from cards onto the disk as soon as they were brought to the computer room. Then, whenever a running job finished, the operating system could load a new job from the disk into the now-empty partition and run it. This technique is called **spooling** (from Simultaneous Peripheral Operation On Line) and was also used for output. With spooling, the 1401s were no longer needed, and much carrying of tapes disappeared.

Although third-generation operating systems were well-suited for big scientific calculations and massive commercial data processing runs, they were still basically batch systems. Many programmers pined for the first generation days when they had the machine all to themselves for a few hours, so they could debug their programs quickly. With third generation systems, the time between submitting a job and getting back the output was often several hours, so a single misplaced comma could cause a compilation to fail, and the programmer to waste half a day.

This desire for quick response time paved the way for **timesharing**, a variant of multiprogramming, in which each user has an on-line terminal. In a timesharing system, if 20 users are logged in and 17 of them are thinking or talking or drinking coffee, the CPU can be allocated in turn to the three jobs that want service. Since people debugging programs usually issue short commands (e.g., compile a five-page program) rather than long ones (e.g., sort a million-record tape), the computer can provide fast, interactive service to a number of users and perhaps also work on big batch jobs in the background when the CPU is otherwise idle. Although the first serious timesharing system (CTSS) was developed at MIT on a specially modified 7094 (Corbato et al., 1962), it did not really become popular until the necessary protection hardware became widespread during the third generation.

After the success of the CTSS system, MIT, Bell Labs, and General Electric (then a major computer manufacturer) decided to embark on the development of a "computer utility," a machine that would support hundreds of simultaneous timesharing users. Their model was the electricity distribution system—when you need electric power, you just stick a plug in the wall, and within reason, as much power as you need will be there. The designers of this system, known as **MULTICS** (MULTiplexed Information and Computing Service), envisioned one huge machine providing computing power for everyone in Boston. The idea that machines as powerful as their GE-645 would be sold as personal computers for a few thousand dollars only 20 years later was pure science fiction at the time.

To make a long story short, MULTICS introduced many seminal ideas into the computer literature, but building it was a lot harder than anyone had expected. Bell Labs dropped out of the project, and General Electric quit the computer business altogether. Eventually MULTICS ran well enough to be used in a production environment at MIT and a few dozen sites elsewhere, but the concept of a computer utility fizzled out. Still, MULTICS had an enormous influence on subsequent systems. It is described in (Corbato et al., 1972; Corbato and Vyssotsky, 1965; Daley and Dennis, 1968; Organick, 1972; Saltzer, 1974).

Another major development during the third generation was the phenomenal growth of minicomputers, starting with the DEC PDP-1 in 1961. The PDP-1 had only 4K of 18-bit words, but at $120,000 per machine (less than 5 percent of the price of a 7094), they sold like hotcakes. For certain kinds of nonnumerical work, it was almost as fast as the 7094, and gave birth to a whole new industry. It was quickly followed by a series of other PDPs (unlike IBM's family, all incompatible) culminating in the PDP-11.

One of the computer scientists at Bell Labs who had worked on the MULTICS project, Ken Thompson, subsequently found a small PDP-7 minicomputer that no one was using and set out to write a stripped-down, one-user version of MULTICS. This work later developed into the UNIX† operating system, which now dominates the minicomputer, workstation, and other markets. We will study UNIX in detail in Chap. 7, and give its history there.

---

† UNIX is a registered trademark of AT&T.

1.2.4. The Fourth Generation (1980-1990): Personal Computers

With the development of LSI (Large Scale Integration) circuits, chips containing thousands of transistors on a square centimeter of silicon, the age of the personal computer dawned. In terms of architecture, personal computers were not that different from minicomputers of the PDP-11 class, but in terms of price they certainly were different. Where the minicomputer made it possible for a department in a company or university to have its own computer, the microprocessor chip made it possible for a single individual to have his or her own personal computer. The most powerful personal computers used by businesses, universities, and government installations are usually called **workstations**, but they are really just large personal computers. Usually they are connected together by a network.

The widespread availability of computing power, especially highly interactive computing power usually with excellent graphics, led to the growth of a major industry producing software for personal computers. Much of this software was **user-friendly**, meaning that it was intended for users who did not know anything about computers, and furthermore had absolutely no intention whatsoever of learning. This was certainly a major change from OS/360, whose job control language, JCL, was so arcane that entire books have been written about it (e.g., Cadow, 1970).

Two operating systems have dominated the personal computer and workstation scene: Microsoft's MS-DOS and UNIX. MS-DOS is widely used on the IBM PC and other machines using the Intel 8088 CPU and its successors, the 80286, 80386, and 80486 (which we will refer to henceforth as the 286, 386, and 486, respectively). Although the initial version of MS-DOS was relatively primitive, subsequent versions have included more advanced features, including many taken from UNIX. This development is not entirely surprising given that Microsoft is a major UNIX supplier. We will study MS-DOS in detail in Chap. 8.

The other major contender is UNIX, which is dominant on non-Intel computers and workstations, especially those powered by high-performance RISC chips. These machines usually have the computing power of a minicomputer, even though they are dedicated to a single user, so it is logical that they are equipped with an operating system originally designed for minicomputers, namely UNIX.

An interesting development that began taking place during the mid-1980s is the growth of networks of personal computers running **network operating systems** and **distributed operating systems**. In a network operating system, the users are aware of the existence of multiple computers, and can log in to remote machines and copy files from one machine to another. Each machine runs its own local operating system and has its own user (or users).

A distributed operating system, in contrast, is one that appears to its users as a traditional uniprocessor system, even though it is actually composed of multiple processors. In a true distributed system, users should not be aware of where their programs are being run or where their files are located; that should all be handled automatically and efficiently by the operating system.

Network operating systems are not fundamentally different from single-processor operating systems. They obviously need a network interface controller and some low-level software to drive it, as well as programs to achieve remote login and remote file access, but these additions do not change the essential structure of the operating system.

True distributed operating systems require more than just adding a little code to a uniprocessor operating system, because distributed and centralized systems differ in critical ways. Distributed systems, for example, often allow programs to run on several processors at the same time, thus requiring more complex processor scheduling algorithms in order to optimize the amount of parallelism achieved.

Communication delays within the network often mean that these (and other) algorithms must run with incomplete, outdated, or even incorrect information. This situation is radically different from a single-processor system in which the operating system has complete information about the system state. We will examine distributed systems in considerable detail in the second part of this book.

1.3. OPERATING SYSTEM CONCEPTS

The interface between the operating system and the user programs is defined by the set of "extended instructions" that the operating system provides. These extended instructions are known as **system calls**. The system calls create, delete, and use various software objects managed by the operating system. The most important of these are processes and files, which will be introduced in this section. For the sake of being specific, our discussion is somewhat oriented towards UNIX and MS-DOS, which are superficially somewhat similar, but most of the principles apply equally well to other systems, with some of the details different.

1.3.1. Processes

A key concept in all operating systems, is the **process**. A process is basically a program in execution. It consists of the executable program, the program's data and stack, its program counter, stack pointer, and other registers, and all the other information needed to run the program.

We will come back to the process concept in much more detail in Chap. 2, but for the time being, the easiest way to get a good intuitive feel for a process is to think about timesharing systems. Periodically, the operating system decides to stop running one process and start running another, for example, because the first one has had more than its share of CPU time in the past second.

When a process is temporarily suspended like this, it must later be restarted in exactly the same state it had when it was stopped. This means that all information about the process must be explicitly saved somewhere during the suspension. For example, if the process has several files open, the exact position in the files where the process was must be recorded somewhere, so that a subsequent READ given after the process is restarted will read the proper data. In many operating systems, all the information about each process, other than the contents of its own address space, is stored in an operating system table called the **process table**, which is an array (or linked list) of structures, one for each process currently in existence.

Thus, a (suspended) process consists of its address space, usually called the **core image** (in honor of the magnetic core memories used in days of yore), and its process table entry, which contains its registers, among other things.

The key process management system calls are those dealing with the creation and termination of processes. Consider a typical example. A process called the **command interpreter** or **shell** reads commands from a terminal. The user has just typed a command requesting that a program be compiled. The shell must now create a new process that will run the compiler. When that process has finished the compilation, it executes a system call to terminate itself.

If a process can create one or more other processes (referred to as **child processes**) and these processes in turn can create child processes, we quickly arrive at the process tree structure of Fig. 1-5.

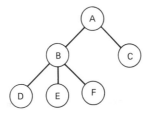

Fig. 1-5. A process tree. Process *A* created two child processes, *B* and *C*. Process *B* created three child processes, *D*, *E*, and *F*.

Other process system calls are available to request more memory (or release unused memory), wait for a child process to terminate, and overlay its program with a different one.

Occasionally, there is a need to convey information to a running process that is not sitting around waiting for it. For example, a process that is communicating with another process on a different computer does so by sending messages over a network. To guard against the possibility that a message or its reply is lost, the sender may request that its own operating system notify it after a specified number of seconds, so that it can retransmit the message if no acknowledgement has been received yet. After setting this timer, the program may continue doing other work.

When the specified number of seconds has elapsed, the operating system sends a **signal** to the process. The signal causes the process to temporarily suspend whatever it was doing, save its registers on the stack, and start running a special signal handling procedure, for example, to retransmit a presumably lost message. When the signal handler is done, the running process is restarted in the state it was just before the signal. Signals are the software analog of hardware interrupts, and can be generated by a variety of causes in addition to timers expiring. Many traps detected by hardware, such as executing an illegal instruction or using an invalid address, are also converted into signals to the guilty process. Signals are also used for process-to-process communication, when one process wants to communicate something to another process in a hurry.

In a multiprogramming system, it is important to keep track of which user owns which process. In such a system, each authorized user is assigned a **uid** (**user identification**), typically a 16-bit or 32-bit integer. Each process is assigned the uid of its owner. When a process sends a signal to another process, a check can be made to see that the sender and receiver have the same uid. Similarly, people can be divided into groups (project teams, departments, etc.), each with its own **gid** (**group identification**). The uids and gids also play a role in protecting information in the computer (e.g., sometimes you may look at reports written by people in your group, but not at strangers' reports).

1.3.2. Files

The other broad category of system calls relates to the file system. As noted before, a major function of the operating system is to hide the peculiarities of the disks and other I/O devices, and present the programmer with a nice, clean abstract model of device-independent files. System calls are obviously needed to create files, remove files, read files, and write files. Before a file can be read, it must be opened, and after it has been read it should be closed, so calls are provided to do these things.

In order to provide a place to keep files, most operating systems support the concept of a **directory** as a way of grouping files together. A student, for example, might have one directory for each course he was taking (for the programs needed for that course), another directory for electronic mail, and still another directory for computer games. System calls are then needed to create and remove directories. Calls are also provided to put an existing file in a directory, and to remove a file from a directory. Directory entries may be either files or other directories. This model also gives rise to a hierarchy—the file system, as shown in Fig. 1-6.

The process and file hierarchies both are organized as trees, but the similarity stops there. Process hierarchies usually are not very deep (more than three levels is unusual), whereas file hierarchies are commonly four, five, or even more levels deep. Process hierarchies are typically short-lived, generally a few minutes at most, whereas the directory hierarchy may exist for years. Ownership and protection also differ for processes and files. Typically, only a parent process may control or even access a child process, but mechanisms nearly always exist to allow files and directories to be read by a wider group than just the owner.

Every file within the directory hierarchy can be specified by giving its **path name** from the top of the directory hierarchy, the **root directory**. Such absolute path names consist of the list of directories that must be traversed from the root directory to get to the file, with slashes separating the components. In Fig. 1-6, the path for file *CS101* is */Faculty/Prof.Brown/Courses/CS101*. The leading slash indicates that the path is absolute, that is, starting at the root directory.

At every instant, each process has a current **working directory**, in which path names not beginning with a slash are looked for. In Fig. 1-6, if */Faculty/Prof.Brown* were the working directory, then use of the path name *Courses/CS101* would yield

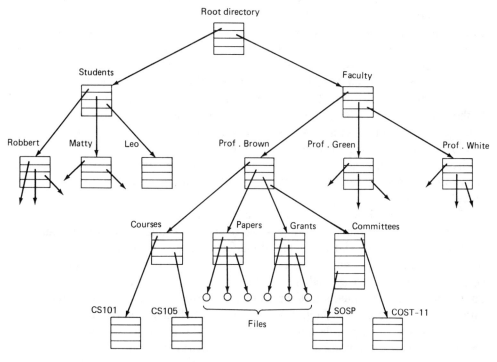

Fig. 1-6. A file system for a university department.

the same file as the absolute path name given above. Processes can change their working directory by issuing a system call specifying the new working directory. As an aside, some systems use \ instead of / as the separator in path names.

If several people have access to the same computer, it is important to provide a means for protecting the privacy of each person's files. Different systems have different schemes. In UNIX, for example, files and directories are protected by assigning each one a 9-bit binary protection code. The protection code consists of three 3-bit fields, one for the owner, one for other members of the owner's group (users are divided into groups by the system administrator), and one for everyone else. Each field has a bit for read access, a bit for write access, and a bit for execute access. These 3 bits are known as the **rwx bits**. For example, the protection code *rwxr-x--x* means that the owner can read, write, or execute the file, other group members can read or execute (but not write) the file, and everyone else can execute (but not read or write) the file. For a directory, *x* indicates search permission. A dash means that the corresponding permission is absent.

Before a file can be read or written, it must be opened, at which time the permissions are checked. If the access is permitted, the system returns a small integer called a **file descriptor** or **handle** to use in subsequent operations. If the access is prohibited, an error code is returned.

Many operating systems, including UNIX and MS-DOS, provide an abstraction to allow users to perform input/output without getting buried in all the details of the hardware. This abstraction represents each I/O device as a **special file**. Special files are provided in order to make I/O devices look like files. That way, they can be read and written using the same system calls as are used for reading and writing files. Two kinds of special files exist: **block special files** and **character special files**. Block special files are used to model devices that consist of a collection of randomly addressable blocks, such as disks. By opening a block special file and reading, say, block 4, a program can directly access the fourth block on the device, without regard to the structure of the file system contained on it. Programs that do system maintenance often need this facility. Access to special files is controlled by the same protection mechanism used to protect other files, so the power to directly access I/O devices can be restricted to the system administrator, for example. For security reasons, limiting access to I/O devices such as the raw disk and the network is frequently necessary.

Character special files are used to model devices that consist of character streams, rather than fixed-size randomly addressable blocks. Terminals, line printers, and network interfaces are typical examples of character special devices. The normal way for a program to read and write on the user's terminal is to read and write the corresponding character special file. In UNIX and MS-DOS, when a process is started up, file descriptor 0, called **standard input**, is normally arranged to refer to the terminal for the purpose of reading. File descriptor 1, called **standard output**, refers to the terminal for writing. File descriptor 2, called **standard error**, also refers to the terminal for output, but normally is used only for writing error messages.

The last feature we will discuss in this overview is one that relates to both processes and files: pipes. A **pipe** is a sort of pseudo-file that can be used to connect two processes together, as shown in Fig. 1-7. When process *A* wants to send data to process *B*, it writes on the pipe as though it were an output file. Process *B* can read the data by reading from the pipe as though it were an input file. Thus, communication between processes looks very much like ordinary file reads and writes. Stronger yet, the only way a process can discover that the output file it is writing on is not really a file, but a pipe, is by making a special system call. Both UNIX and MS-DOS support pipes.

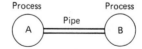

Fig. 1-7. Two processes connected by a pipe.

1.3.3. System Calls

User programs communicate with the operating system and request services from it by making **system calls**. Corresponding to each system call is a library procedure that user programs can call. This procedure puts the parameters of the system call in a specified place, such as the machine registers, and then issues a TRAP instruction (a kind of protected procedure call) to start the operating system. The purpose of the library procedure is to hide the details of the TRAP instruction and make system calls look like ordinary procedure calls.

When the operating system gets control after the TRAP, it examines the parameters to see if they are valid, and if so, performs the work requested. When it is finished, the operating system puts a status code in a register, telling whether it succeeded or failed, and executes a RETURN FROM TRAP instruction, to return control back to the library procedure. The library procedure then returns to the caller in the usual way, returning the status code as a function value. Sometimes additional values are returned in the parameters.

To make the system call mechanism clearer, let us take a quick look at a simple example, the READ system call used in UNIX and MS-DOS. It has three parameters, the first one specifying the file to be read, the second one specifying a buffer to put the file's data, and the third one telling how many bytes to read. A call to READ from a C program might look like this:

```
count = read(file, buffer, nbytes);
```

Note that there is a subtle difference between the user-callable library procedure, *read*, and the actual system call, READ, which is invoked by *read*. To try to make these concepts clearer, system call names will be printed in small caps (e.g., READ) while procedure names will be printed in italics (e.g., *read*). In many contexts they are effectively interchangeable, however.

The effect of calling the *read* procedure (and thus making the READ system call) is to cause data from the specified file to be copied into the buffer, where the program can get at it. The procedure returns the number of bytes actually read in *count*. This value is normally the same as *nbytes*, but may be smaller, if, for example, the end-of-file is encountered while reading.

If the system call cannot be carried out, either due to an invalid parameter or a disk error, *count* is set to −1, and the error number is put in a global variable, where the program can inspect it. Programs should always check the results of their system calls to see if errors occurred.

The number and type of system calls varies from operating system to operating system. In Chaps. 7 and 8, we will look at some of the UNIX and MS-DOS system calls, respectively. For the time being, it is sufficient to say that there are usually system calls to create processes, manage memory, read and write files, and do input/output, such as reading from the terminal and printing on the printer.

1.3.4. The Shell

The operating system is the code that carries out the system calls. Editors, compilers, assemblers, linkers, and command interpreters are definitely not part of the operating system, even though they are important and useful. At the risk of confusing things somewhat, in this section we will look briefly at the UNIX command interpreter, called the **shell**, which, although not part of the operating system, makes heavy use of many operating system features and thus serves as a good example of how the system calls can be used. It is also the primary interface between a user sitting at his terminal and the operating system.

When any user logs in, a shell is started up. The shell has the terminal as standard input and standard output. It starts out by typing the **prompt**, a character such as a dollar sign, which tells the user that the shell is waiting to accept a command. If the user now types

```
date
```

for example, the shell creates a child process and runs the *date* program as the child. While the child process is running, the shell waits for it to terminate. When the child finishes, the shell types the prompt again and tries to read the next input line.

The user can specify that standard output be redirected to a file by typing, for example,

```
date >file
```

Similarly, standard input can be redirected, as in

```
sort <file1 >file2
```

which invokes the sort program with input taken from *file1* and output sent to *file2*.

The output of one program can be used as the input for another program by connecting them with a pipe. Thus

```
cat file1 file2 file3 | sort >/dev/lp
```

invokes the *cat* program to concatenate three files and send the output to *sort* to arrange all the lines in alphabetical order. The output of *sort* is redirected to the file */dev/lp*, which is a typical name for the special character file for the line printer. (By convention, all the special files are kept in the directory */dev*, at least in UNIX systems).

If a user puts an ampersand after a command, the shell does not wait for it to complete. Instead it just gives a prompt immediately. Consequently,

```
cat file1 file2 file3 | sort >/dev/lp &
```

starts up the sort as a background job, allowing the user to continue working normally while the sort is going on. The shell has a number of other interesting features, some of which we will look at in Chap. 7.

1.4. OPERATING SYSTEM STRUCTURE

Now that we have seen what operating systems look like on the outside (i.e, the programmer's interface), it is time to take a look inside. In the following sections, we will examine four different structures that have been tried, in order to get some idea of the spectrum of possibilities. These are by no means exhaustive, but they give an idea of some designs that have been tried in practice.

1.4.1. Monolithic Systems

By far the most common organization, this approach might well be subtitled "The Big Mess." The structure is that there is no structure. The operating system is written as a collection of procedures, each of which can call any of the other ones whenever it needs to. When this technique is used, each procedure in the system has a well-defined interface in terms of parameters and results, and each one is free to call any other one, if the latter provides some useful computation that the former needs.

To construct the actual object program of the operating system when this approach is used, one compiles all the individual procedures, or files containing the procedures, and then binds them all together into a single object file with the linker. In terms of information hiding, there is essentially none—every procedure is visible to every other one (as opposed to a structure containing modules or packages, in which much of the information is local to a module, and only officially designated entry points can be called from outside the module).

Even in monolithic systems, however, it is possible to have at least a little structure. The services (system calls) provided by the operating system are requested by putting the parameters in well-defined places, such as in registers or on the stack, and then executing a special trap instruction known as a **kernel call** or **supervisor call**.

This instruction switches the machine from **user mode** to **kernel mode** (also known as **supervisor mode**), and transfers control to the operating system, shown as event (1) in Fig. 1-8. (Most CPUs have two modes: kernel mode, for the operating system, in which all instructions are allowed; and user mode, for user programs, in which I/O and certain other instructions are not allowed.)

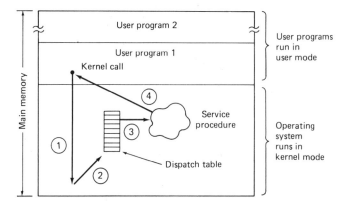

Fig. 1-8. How a system call can be made: (1) User program traps to the kernel. (2) Operating system determines service number required. (3) Operating system locates and calls service procedure. (4) Control is returned to user program.

The operating system then examines the parameters of the call to determine which system call is to be carried out, shown as (2) in Fig. 1-8. Next, the operating system indexes into a table that contains in slot k a pointer to the procedure that carries out system call k. This operation, shown as (3) in Fig. 1-8, identifies the service procedure, which is then called. Finally, the system call is finished and control is given back to the user program.

This organization suggests a basic structure for the operating system:

1. A main program that invokes the requested service procedure.

2. A set of service procedures that carry out the system calls.

3. A set of utility procedures that help the service procedures.

In this model, for each system call there is one service procedure that takes care of it. The utility procedures do things that are needed by several service procedures, such as fetching data from user programs. This division of the procedures into three layers is shown in Fig. 1-9.

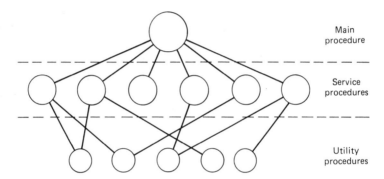

Fig. 1-9. A simple structuring model for a monolithic system.

1.4.2. Layered Systems

A generalization of the approach of Fig. 1-9 is to organize the operating system as a hierarchy of layers, each one constructed upon the one below it. The first system constructed in this way was the THE system built at the Technische Hogeschool Eindhoven in the Netherlands by E. W. Dijkstra (1968) and his students. The THE system was a simple batch system for a Dutch computer, the Electrologica X8, which had 32K of 27-bit words (bits were expensive in those days).

The system had 6 layers, as shown in Fig. 1-10. Layer 0 dealt with allocation of the processor, switching between processes when interrupts occurred or timers expired. Above layer 0, the system consisted of sequential processes, each of which could be programmed without having to worry about the fact that multiple processes were running on a single processor. In other words, layer 0 provided the basic multiprogramming of the CPU.

Layer 1 did the memory management. It allocated space for processes in main memory and on a 512K word drum used for holding parts of processes (pages) for

5	The operator
4	User programs
3	Input/output management
2	Operator-process communication
1	Memory and drum management
0	Processor allocation and multiprogramming

Fig. 1-10. Structure of the THE operating system.

which there was no room in main memory. Above layer 1, processes did not have to worry about whether they were in memory or on the drum; the layer 1 software took care of making sure pages were brought into memory whenever they were needed.

Layer 2 handled communication between each process and the operator console. Above this layer each process effectively had its own operator console. Layer 3 took care of managing the I/O devices and buffering the information streams to and from them. Above layer 3 each process could deal with abstract I/O devices with nice properties, instead of real devices with many peculiarities. Layer 4 was where the user programs were found. They did not have to worry about process, memory, console, or I/O management. The system operator process was located in layer 5.

A further generalization of the layering concept was present in the MULTICS system. Instead of layers, MULTICS was organized as a series of concentric rings, with the inner ones being more privileged than the outer ones. When a procedure in an outer ring wanted to call a procedure in an inner ring, it had to make the equivalent of a system call, that is, a TRAP instruction whose parameters were carefully checked for validity before allowing the call to proceed. Although the entire operating system was part of the address space of each user process in MULTICS, the hardware made it possible to designate individual procedures (memory segments, actually) as protected against reading, writing, or executing.

Whereas the THE layering scheme was really only a design aid, because all the parts of the system were ultimately linked together into a single object program, in MULTICS, the ring mechanism was very much present at run time and enforced by the hardware. The advantage of the ring mechanism is that it can easily be extended to structure user subsystems. For example, a professor could write a program to test and grade student programs and run this program in ring n, with the student programs running in ring $n + 1$ so that they could not change their grades.

1.4.3. Virtual Machines

The initial releases of OS/360 were strictly batch systems. Nevertheless, many 360 users wanted to have timesharing, so various groups, both inside and outside IBM decided to write timesharing systems for it. The official IBM timesharing system, TSS/360, was delivered late, and when it finally arrived it was so big and slow that few sites converted over to it. It was eventually abandoned after its development had consumed some 50 million dollars (Graham, 1970). But a group at IBM's Scientific Center in Cambridge, Mass., produced a radically different system that IBM eventually accepted as a product, and which is now widely used.

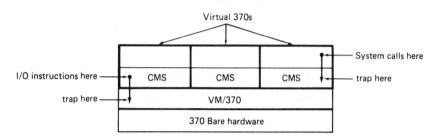

Fig. 1-11. The structure of VM/370 with CMS.

This system, originally called CP/CMS and now called VM/370 (Seawright and MacKinnon, 1979), was based on an astute observation: a timesharing system provides (1) multiprogramming and (2) an extended machine with a more convenient interface than the bare hardware. The essence of VM/370 is to completely separate these two functions.

The heart of the system, known as the **virtual machine monitor**, runs on the bare hardware and does the multiprogramming, providing not one, but several virtual machines to the next layer up, as shown in Fig. 1-11. However, unlike all other operating systems, these virtual machines are not extended machines, with files and other nice features. Instead, they are *exact* copies of the bare hardware, including kernel/user mode, I/O, interrupts, and everything else the real machine has.

Because each virtual machine is identical to the true hardware, each one can run any operating system that will run directly on the hardware. Different virtual machines can, and usually do, run different operating systems. Some run one of the descendants of OS/360 for batch processing, while other ones run a single-user, interactive system called CMS (Conversational Monitor System) for timesharing users.

When a CMS program executes a system call, the call is trapped to the operating system in its own virtual machine, not to VM/370, just as it would if it were running on a real machine instead of a virtual one. CMS then issues the normal hardware I/O instructions for reading its virtual disk or whatever is needed to carry out the call. These I/O instructions are trapped by VM/370, which then performs them as part of its simulation of the real hardware. By making a complete separation of the functions of multiprogramming and providing an extended machine, each of the pieces can be much simpler, more flexible, and easier to maintain.

1.4.4. Client-Server Model

VM/370 gains much in simplicity by moving a large part of the traditional operating system code (implementing the extended machine) into a higher layer, CMS. Nevertheless, VM/370 itself is still a complex program because simulating a number of virtual 370s is not *that* simple (especially if you want to do it reasonably efficiently).

A trend in modern operating systems is to take this idea of moving code up into higher layers even further, and remove as much as possible from the operating system, leaving a minimal **kernel**. The usual approach is to implement most of the operating system functions in user processes. To request a service, such as reading a block of a file, a user process (now known as the **client process**) sends the request to a **server process**, which then does the work and sends back the answer.

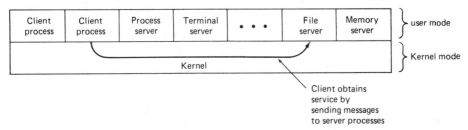

Fig. 1-12. The client-server model.

In this model, shown in Fig. 1-12, all the kernel does is handle the communication between clients and servers. By splitting the operating system up into parts, each of which only handles one facet of the system, such as file service, process service, terminal service, or memory service, each part becomes small and manageable. Furthermore, because all the servers run as user-mode processes, and not in kernel mode, they do not have direct access to the hardware. As a consequence, if a bug in the file server is triggered, the file service may crash, but this will not usually bring the whole machine down.

Another advantage of the client-server model is its adaptability to use in distributed systems (see Fig. 1-13). If a client communicates with a server by sending it messages, the client need not know whether the message is handled locally in its own machine, or whether it was sent across a network to a server on a remote machine. As far as the client is concerned, the same thing happens in both cases: a request was sent and a reply came back.

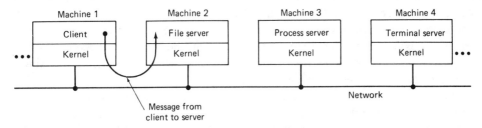

Fig. 1-13. The client-server model in a distributed system.

The picture painted above of a kernel that handles only the transport of messages from clients to servers and back is not completely realistic. Some operating system

functions (such as loading commands into the physical I/O device registers) are difficult, if not impossible, to do from user-space programs. There are two ways of dealing with this problem. One way is to have some critical server processes (e.g., I/O
device drivers) actually run in kernel mode, with complete access to all the hardware,
but still communicate with other processes using the normal message mechanism.

The other way is to build a minimal amount of **mechanism** into the kernel, but
leave the **policy** decisions up to servers in user space. For example, the kernel might
recognize that a message sent to a certain special address means to take the contents
of that message and load it into the I/O device registers for some disk, to start a disk
read. In this example, the kernel would not even inspect the bytes in the message to
see if they were valid or meaningful; it would just blindly copy them into the disk's
device registers. (Obviously some scheme for limiting such messages to authorized
processes only must be used.) The split between mechanism and policy is an important concept; it occurs again and again in operating systems in various contexts.

1.5. OUTLINE OF THE REST OF THIS BOOK

Operating systems have come a long way since the 1950s. Originally designed to
control a single computer, they are now frequently used to run a large collection of
machines connected together by a network. These new operating systems are called
network or distributed operating systems, as mentioned earlier, but the old ones do
not really have a generic name. Various terms are in use, including **centralized**,
single-processor, **single-CPU**, or even **traditional** operating systems. In all cases,
what is meant is an operating system that manages a single computer on its own.

As an aside, we should mention that there are also **multiprocessor operating
systems**, which control tightly integrated systems containing two or more CPUs.
Since these are intermediate in form to the single-processor systems and the distributed systems, having aspects of both, we will not study them further in this book.

Both single-processor and distributed systems are important. The former are still
more numerous, but that is rapidly changing. By the year 2000, it is expected that
essentially all computers in industry, academia, and government will be networked.
For this reason, we believe that distributed operating systems are the way of the
future, and that belief is reflected in the structure of this book. The first part of the
book is about single-processor operating systems; the second part is about distributed
systems. It is possible to read the first part without the second, but the chapters on
distributed systems presume the reader is familiar with the material on single-
processor operating systems presented in Part 1.

Operating systems typically have four major components: process management,
memory management, file management, and I/O device management. The next four
chapters deal with these four topics, one topic per chapter. In Chap. 2, we will deal
with processes, interprocess communication, and process scheduling. In Chap. 3, we
will study memory management, including both swap-based systems and virtual
memory systems. In Chap. 4 we will examine the file system, including design,

security, and protection aspects. In Chap. 5, we will look at input/output. Deadlocks are the subject of Chap. 6.

The next two chapters are detailed case studies. Chap. 7 is about UNIX. Chap. 8 is about MS-DOS. Both chapters start with the history of the system, followed by an overview. Then comes a section showing how the concepts of processes, memory management, file system, and I/O are handled by the example system. After that we look at some of the system calls supported by the system. Finally, we examine how the system is implemented internally.

Part 2, on distributed operating systems, begins with Chap. 9. This chapter forms an introduction to the subject, and goes into some detail into what is and what is not a distributed system. Both hardware and software aspects are covered.

Probably the single most important issue that separates single-processor operating systems from distributed ones is the role of communication. Accordingly, we have devoted an entire chapter (10) to communication in distributed systems. Numerous models are explained here.

Communication over an unreliable network introduces synchronization problems. These are examined in Chap. 11. We will also look at deadlocks in distributed systems here too.

Chap. 12 discusses processes and processors in distributed systems. Among the topics covered are threads, system models, processor allocation, and scheduling.

Chap. 13 discusses the design and implementation of distributed file systems, which differ from their centralized cousins in various ways.

Just as we had two detailed examples of single-processor operating systems, we conclude this part of the book with two detailed examples of distributed operating systems, namely Amoeba (Chap. 14) and Mach (Chap. 15).

Appendix A contains a list of suggested readings and a bibliography of all references cited in the book. To continue your study of operating systems, this chapter provides some pointers on where to get started.

Appendix B is a brief introduction to the C programming language, which may help readers not familiar with this language to understand the example programs given in this book. The examples are simple enough, however, that they should be understandable to Pascal or Modula 2 programmers with little help.

1.6. SUMMARY

In this chapter we started out by looking at operating systems from two viewpoints: resource managers and extended machines. In the resource manager view, the operating system's job is to efficiently manage the different parts of the system. In the extended machine view, the job of the system is to provide the users with a virtual machine that is more convenient to use than the actual machine.

We then briefly glanced back at the history of computers and their operating systems, to see how we got where we are now. Four eras were surveyed, from vacuum tubes to personal computers. Then we introduced two major operating system concepts, the process and the file. Both of these will play a major role throughout the book. We also briefly described system calls, and gave a simple example, READ.

Finally, we examined different ways of structuring an operating system: as a monolithic system, as a hierarchy of layers, as a virtual machine system and as a client-server model.

PROBLEMS

1. What are the two main functions of an operating system?

2. What is multiprogramming? Give two reasons for having it.

3. What is spooling? Do you think that advanced personal computers will have spooling as a standard feature in the future?

4. On early computers, every byte of data read or written was directly handled by the CPU (i.e., there was no DMA—Direct Memory Access). What implications does this organization have for multiprogramming?

5. Why was timesharing not widespread on second generation computers?

6. Which of the following instructions should be allowed only in kernel mode?

    (a) Disable all interrupts.
    (b) Read the time-of-day clock.
    (c) Set the time-of-day clock.
    (d) Change the memory map.

7. List some differences between personal computer operating systems and mainframe operating systems.

8. How does the operating system generally tell whether the path name for a file is absolute or relative to the working directory?

9. Why is the shell not part of the operating system itself?

10. Give an example of how mechanism and policy can be separated with respect to scheduling. Suggest a mechanism that could allow a parent process to control the scheduling policy for its children.

11. The client-server model is popular in distributed systems. Can it also be used in a single-computer system?

12. Why is the process table needed in a timesharing system? Is it also needed in personal computer systems in which only one process exists, that process taking over the entire machine until it is finished?

13. What is the essential difference between a block special file and a character special file?

2

PROCESSES

We are now about to embark on a detailed study of how operating systems are designed and constructed. The most central concept in any operating system is the *process*: an abstraction of a running program. Everything else hinges on this concept, and it is important that the operating system designer (and student) know what a process is as early as possible. In this chapter we will sometimes use UNIX as an example, as it has a simple, but powerful, method for managing processes.

2.1. INTRODUCTION TO PROCESSES

All modern computers can do several things at the same time. While running a user program, a computer can also be reading from a disk and printing on a terminal or printer. In a multiprogramming system, the CPU also switches from program to program, running each for tens or hundreds of milliseconds. While, strictly speaking, at any instant of time, the CPU is running only one program, in the course of 1 second, it may work on several programs, thus giving the users the illusion of parallelism. Sometimes people speak of **pseudoparallelism** to mean this rapid switching back and forth of the CPU between programs, to contrast it with the true hardware parallelism of the CPU computing while one or more I/O devices are running. Keeping track of multiple, parallel activities is hard to do. Therefore, operating system designers over the years have evolved a model that makes parallelism easier to deal with. That model is the subject of this chapter.

2.1.1. The Process Model

In this model, all the runnable software on the computer, often including the operating system, is organized into a number of **sequential processes**, or just **processes** for short. A process is just an executing program, including the current values of the program counter, registers, and variables. Conceptually, each process has its own virtual CPU. In reality, of course, the real CPU switches back and forth from process to process, but to understand the system, it is much easier to think about a collection of processes running in (pseudo) parallel, than to try to keep track of how the CPU switches from program to program. This rapid switching back and forth is called **multiprogramming**, as we saw in the previous chapter. In Fig. 2-1(a) we see a computer multiprogramming four programs in memory.

In Fig. 2-1(b) we see how this is abstracted into four processes, each with its own flow of control (i.e., its own program counter), and each one running independent of the other ones. In Fig. 2-1(c) we see that viewed over a long enough time interval, all the processes have made progress, but at any given instant only one process is actually running.

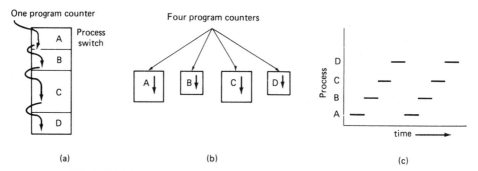

Fig. 2-1. (a) Multiprogramming of four programs. (b) Conceptual model of four independent, sequential processes. (c) Only one program is active at any instant.

With the CPU switching back and forth among the processes, the rate at which a process performs its computation will not be uniform, and probably not even reproducible if the same processes are run again. Thus, processes must not be programmed with built-in assumptions about timing. Consider, for example, an I/O process that starts a magnetic tape in motion, executes an idle loop 1000 times to let the tape get up to speed, and then issues a command to read the first record. If the CPU decides to switch to another process during the idle loop, the tape process might not run again until after the first record was already past the read head. When a process has critical real-time requirements like this, that is, certain events absolutely must occur within a specified number of milliseconds, special measures must be taken to ensure that they do occur. Normally, however, most processes are not affected by the underlying multiprogramming of the CPU or the relative speeds of different processes.

The difference between a process and a program is subtle, but crucial. An analogy may help make this point clearer. Consider a culinary-minded computer scientist who is baking a birthday cake for his daughter. He has a birthday cake recipe and a kitchen well-stocked with the necessary input: flour, eggs, sugar, extract of vanilla and so on. In this analogy, the recipe is the program (i.e., an algorithm expressed in some suitable notation), the computer scientist is the processor (CPU), and the cake ingredients are the input data. The process is the activity consisting of our baker reading the recipe, fetching the ingredients, and baking the cake.

Now imagine that the computer scientist's son comes running in crying, saying that he has been stung by a bee. The computer scientist records where he was in the recipe (the state of the current process is saved), gets out a first aid book, and begins following the directions in it. Here we see the processor being switched from one process (baking) to a higher priority process (administering medical care), each having a different program (recipe vs. first aid book). When the bee sting has been taken care of, the computer scientist goes back to his cake, continuing at the point where he left off.

The key idea here is that a process is an activity of some kind. It has a program, input, output, and a state. A single processor may be shared among several processes, with some scheduling algorithm being used to determine when to stop work on one process and service a different one.

Process Hierarchies

Operating systems that support the process concept must provide some way to create all the processes needed. In very simple systems, or in systems designed for running only a single application, it may be possible to have all the processes that will ever be needed be present when the system comes up. In most systems, however, some way is needed to create and destroy processes as needed during operation.

In UNIX, processes are created by the FORK system call, which creates an identical copy of the calling process. After the FORK call, the parent continues running, in parallel with the child. The parent can then fork off more children, so at any instant it may have several executing children. The children can also execute FORK, so it is possible to get a whole tree of processes, arbitrarily deep.

In MS-DOS a system call exists to load a specified binary file into memory and execute it as a child process. In contrast to UNIX, in MS-DOS this call suspends the parent until the child has finished execution, so the parent and child do not run in parallel.

Process States

Although each process is an independent entity, with its own program counter and internal state, processes often need to interact with other processes. One process may generate some output that another process uses as input. In the shell command

```
cat chapter1 chapter2 chapter3 | grep tree
```

the first process, running *cat*, concatenates and outputs three files. The second process, running *grep*, selects all lines containing the word "tree." Depending on the relative speeds of the two processes (which depends on both the relative complexity of the programs and how much CPU time each one has had), it may happen that *grep* is ready to run, but there is no input waiting for it. It must then **block** until some input is available.

When a process blocks, it does so because logically it cannot continue, typically because it is waiting for input that is not yet available. It is also possible for a process that is conceptually ready and able to run to be stopped because the operating system has decided to allocate the CPU to another process for a while. These two conditions are completely different. In the first case, the suspension is inherent in the problem (you cannot process the user's command line until it has been typed). In the second case, it is a technicality of the system (not enough CPUs to give each process its own private processor). In Fig. 2-2 we see a state diagram showing the three states a process may be in:

1. Running (actually using the CPU at that instant).

2. Ready (runnable; temporarily stopped to let another process run).

3. Blocked (unable to run until some external event happens).

Logically, the first two states are similar. In both cases the process is willing to run, only in the second one, there is temporarily no CPU available for it. The third state is different from the first two in that the process cannot run, even if the CPU has nothing else to do.

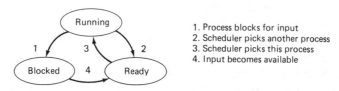

1. Process blocks for input
2. Scheduler picks another process
3. Scheduler picks this process
4. Input becomes available

Fig. 2-2. A process can be in running, blocked, or ready state. Transitions between these states are as shown.

Four transitions are possible among these three states, as shown. Transition 1 occurs when a process discovers that it cannot continue. In some systems the process must execute a system call, BLOCK, to get into blocked state. More commonly, when a process reads from a pipe or special file (e.g., a terminal) and there is no input available, the process is automatically blocked.

Transitions 2 and 3 are caused by the process scheduler (a part of the operating system), without the process even knowing about them. Transition 2 occurs when the scheduler decides that the running process has run long enough, and it is time to let another process have some CPU time. Transition 3 occurs when all the other processes have had their share and it is time for the first process to run again. The subject of scheduling, that is, deciding which process should run when and for how long, is an important one; we will look at it later in this chapter. Many algorithms have been devised to try to balance the competing demands of efficiency for the system as a whole and fairness to individual processes.

Transition 4 occurs when the external event for which a process was waiting (such as the arrival of some input) happens. If no other process is running at that instant, transition 3 will be triggered immediately, and the process will start running. Otherwise it may have to wait in *ready* state for a little while until the CPU is available.

Using the process model, it becomes much easier to think about what is going on inside the system. Some of the processes run programs that carry out commands typed in by a user. Other processes are part of the system and handle tasks such as carrying out requests for file services or managing the details of running a disk or a tape drive. When a disk interrupt occurs, the system makes a decision to stop running the current process and run the disk process, which was blocked waiting for that interrupt. Thus, instead of thinking about interrupts, we can think about user processes, disk processes, terminal processes, and so on, which block when they are waiting for something to happen. When the disk block has been read or the character typed, the process waiting for it is unblocked and is eligible to run again.

This view gives rise to the model shown in Fig. 2-3. Here the lowest level of the operating system is the scheduler, with a variety of processes on top of it. All the interrupt handling and details of actually starting and stopping processes are hidden away in the scheduler, which is actually quite small. The rest of the operating system is nicely structured in process form.

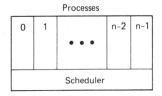

Fig. 2-3. The lowest layer of a process-structured operating system handles interrupts and does scheduling. The rest of the system consists of sequential processes.

2.1.2. Implementation of Processes

To implement the process model, the operating system maintains a table (an array of structures), called the **process table**, with one entry per process. This entry contains information about the process' state, its program counter, stack pointer, memory allocation, the status of its open files, its accounting and scheduling information, and everything else about the process that must be saved when the process is switched from *running* to *ready* state so that it can be restarted later as if it had never been stopped.

Although the exact fields contained in the process table vary from system to system, in general some will deal with process management, others with memory management, and still others with the file system. Figure 2-4 shows some of the more common fields present in UNIX systems.

Process management	Memory management	File management
Registers	Pointer to text segment	UMASK mask
Program counter	Pointer to data segment	Root directory
Program status word	Pointer to bss segment	Working directory
Stack pointer	Exit status	File descriptors
Process state	Signal status	Effective uid
Time when process started	Process id	Effective gid
CPU time used	Parent process	System call parameters
Children's CPU time	Process group	Various flag bits
Time of next alarm	Real uid	
Message queue pointers	Effective uid	
Pending signal bits	Real gid	
Process id	Effective gid	
Various flag bits	Bit maps for signals	
	Various flag bits	

Fig. 2-4. Some typical process table fields.

Now that we have looked at the process table, it is possible to explain a little more about how the illusion of multiple sequential processes is maintained on a machine with one CPU and many I/O devices. Associated with each I/O device class (e.g., floppy disks, hard disks, timers, terminals) is a location near the bottom of memory called the **interrupt vector**. It contains the address of the interrupt service procedure. Suppose user process 3 is running when a disk interrupt occurs. The program counter, program status word, and possibly one or more registers are pushed onto the stack by the interrupt hardware. The computer then jumps to the address specified in the disk interrupt vector. That is all the hardware does. From here on, it is up to the software.

The interrupt service procedure starts out by saving all the registers in the process table entry for the current process. The current process number and a pointer to its entry are kept in global variables so they can be found quickly. Then the information deposited by the interrupt is removed from the stack, and the stack pointer is set to a temporary stack used by the process handler. Actions such as saving the registers and setting the stack pointer cannot even be expressed in C (or any other high-level language) so they are performed by a small assembly language routine. When this routine is finished, it calls a C procedure to do the real work of processing the interrupt.

The next step is to determine which process started the disk request. Normally this process will have gone to sleep after starting the request, so it must now be awakened. The state of this process is now changed from *blocked* to *ready* and the scheduler called.

Whether that process is run next depends on the scheduling algorithm. We know for sure at least two processes are now ready: the process that started the disk I/O and the one that was interrupted. It is up to the scheduler to choose the most important one. In UNIX, for example, an I/O-bound process is given higher priority than a CPU-bound process, so it can issue its next I/O request quickly. This strategy maximizes the amount of parallelism, keeping both the disk and the CPU busy. However, other systems use different schemes, for example, emphasizing fairness over efficiency.

To return to the newly selected process, the C procedure called by the assembly language interrupt code now returns, and the assembly language code loads up the registers and memory map for the now-current process and starts it running. The interrupt handling and scheduling are summarized in Fig. 2-5.

```
1. Hardware stacks program counter, etc.
2. Hardware loads new program counter from interrupt vector.
3. Assembly language procedure saves registers.
4. Assembly language procedure sets up new stack.
5. C procedure marks service process as ready.
6. Scheduler decides which process to run next.
7. C procedure returns to the assembly code.
8. Assembly language procedure starts up current process.
```

Fig. 2-5. Skeleton of what the operating system does when an interrupt occurs.

2.2. INTERPROCESS COMMUNICATION

Processes frequently need to communicate with other processes. For example, in a shell pipeline, the output of the first process must be passed to the second process, and so on down the line. Thus there is a need for communication between processes, preferably in a well-structured way not using interrupts. In the following sections we will look at some of the issues related to this **InterProcess Communication** or **IPC**.

2.2.1. Race Conditions

In some operating systems, processes that are working together often share some common storage that each one can read and write. The shared storage may be in main memory or it may be a shared file; the location of the shared memory does not change the nature of the communication or the problems that arise. To see how interprocess communication works in practice, let us consider a simple but common example, a print spooler. When a process wants to print a file, it enters the file name in a special **spooler directory**. Another process, the **printer daemon**, periodically checks to see if there are any files to be printed, and if there are it prints them and then removes their names from the directory.

Imagine that our spooler directory has a large (potentially infinite) number of slots, numbered 0, 1, 2, ..., each one capable of holding a file name. Also imagine that there are two shared variables, *out*, which points to the next file to be printed, and *in*, which points to the next free slot in the directory. These two variables might well be kept on a two-word file available to all processes. At a certain instant, slots 0 to 3 are empty (the files have already been printed) and slots 4 to 6 are full (with the names of files queued for printing). More or less simultaneously, processes A and B decide they want to queue a file for printing. This situation is shown in Fig. 2-6.

In jurisdictions where Murphy's law is applicable, the following might happen. Process A reads *in* and stores the value, 7, in a local variable called *next_free_slot*. Just then a clock interrupt occurs and the CPU decides that process A has run long enough, so it switches to process B. Process B also reads *in*, and also gets a 7, so it

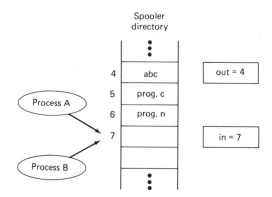

Fig. 2-6. Two processes want to access shared memory at the same time.

stores the name of its file in slot 7 and updates *in* to be an 8. Then it goes off and does other things.

Eventually process *A* runs again, starting from the place it left off. It looks at *next_free_slot*, finds a 7 there, and writes its file name in slot 7, erasing the name that process *B* just put there. Then it computes *next_free_slot* + 1, which is 8, and sets *in* to 8. The spooler directory is now internally consistent, so the printer daemon will not notice anything wrong, but process *B* will never get any output. Situations like this, where two or more processes are reading or writing some shared data and the final result depends on who runs precisely when, are called **race conditions**. Debugging programs containing race conditions is no fun at all. The results of most test runs are fine, but once in a rare while something weird and unexplained happens.

2.2.2. Critical Sections

How do we avoid race conditions? The key to preventing trouble here and in many other situations involving shared memory, shared files, and shared everything else, is to find some way to prohibit more than one process from reading and writing the shared data at the same time. Put in other words, what we need is **mutual exclusion**—some way of making sure that if one process is using a shared variable or file, the other processes will be excluded from doing the same thing. The difficulty above occurred because process *B* started using one of the shared variables before process *A* was finished with it. The choice of appropriate primitive operations for achieving mutual exclusion is a major design issue in any operating system, and a subject that we will examine in great detail in the following sections.

The problem of avoiding race conditions can also be formulated in an abstract way. Part of the time, a process is busy doing internal computations and other things that do not lead to race conditions. However, sometimes a process may be accessing shared memory or files, or doing other critical things that can lead to races. That part of the program where the shared memory is accessed is called the **critical section**. If we could arrange matters such that no two processes were ever in their critical sections at the same time, we could avoid race conditions.

Although this requirement avoids race conditions, this is not sufficient for having parallel processes cooperate correctly and efficiently using shared data. We need four conditions to hold to have a good solution:

1. No two processes may be simultaneously inside their critical sections.

2. No assumptions may be made about speeds or the number of CPUs.

3. No process running outside its critical section may block other processes.

4. No process should have to wait forever to enter its critical section.

2.2.3. Mutual Exclusion with Busy Waiting

In this section we will examine various proposals for achieving mutual exclusion, so that while one process is busy updating shared memory in its critical region, no other process will enter *its* critical region and cause trouble.

Disabling Interrupts

The simplest solution is to have each process disable all interrupts just after entering its critical region and re-enable them just before leaving it. With interrupts disabled, no clock interrupts can occur. The CPU is only switched from process to process as a result of clock or other interrupts, after all, and with interrupts turned off the CPU will not be switched to another process. Thus, once a process has disabled interrupts, it can examine and update the shared memory without fear that any other process will intervene.

This approach is generally unattractive because it is unwise to give user processes the power to turn off interrupts. Suppose one of them did it, and never turned them on again? That could be the end of the system. Furthermore, if the computer has two or more CPUs, disabling interrupts affects only the CPU that executed the disable instruction. The other ones will continue running and can access the shared memory.

On the other hand, it is frequently convenient for the kernel itself to disable interrupts for a few instructions while it is updating variables or lists. If an interrupt occurred while the list of ready processes, for example, was in an inconsistent state, race conditions could occur. The conclusion is: disabling interrupts is sometimes a useful technique within the kernel, but is not appropriate as a general mutual exclusion mechanism for user processes.

Lock Variables

As a second attempt, let us look for a software solution. Consider having a single, shared, (lock) variable, initially 0. When a process wants to enter its critical region, it first tests the lock. If the lock is 0, the process sets it to 1 and enters the critical region. If the lock is already 1, the process just waits until it becomes 0.

Thus, a 0 means that no process is in its critical region, and a 1 means that some process is in its critical region.

Unfortunately, this idea contains exactly the same fatal flaw that we saw in the spooler directory. Suppose one process reads the lock and sees that it is 0. Before it can set the lock to 1, another process is scheduled, runs, and sets the lock to 1. When the first process runs again, it will also set the lock to 1, and two processes will be in their critical regions at the same time.

Now you might think that we could get around this problem by first reading out the lock value, then checking it again just before storing into it, but that really does not help. The race now occurs if the second process modifies the lock just after the first process has finished its second check.

Strict Alternation

A third approach to the mutual exclusion problem is shown in Fig. 2-7. This program fragment, like nearly all the others in this book, is written in C. The competition was between C, Modula 2, and Pascal. Each one has its supporters and detractors. C was chosen here because real operating systems are often written in C, rarely in Modula 2, and never in Pascal. If you are not familiar with C, please read the introduction to it in Appendix B.

```
while (TRUE) {                          while (TRUE) {
   while (turn != 0) /* wait */ ;          while (turn != 1) /* wait */ ;
   critical_section();                     critical_section();
   turn = 1;                               turn = 0;
   noncritical_section();                  noncritical_section();
}                                       }

              (a)                                     (b)
```

Fig. 2-7. A proposed solution to the critical section problem.

In Fig. 2-7, the integer variable *turn*, initially 0, keeps track of whose turn it is to enter the critical region and examine or update the shared memory. Initially, process 0 inspects *turn*, finds it to be 0, and enters its critical region. Process 1 also finds it to be 0, and therefore sits in a tight loop continually testing *turn* to see when it becomes 1. Continuously testing a variable waiting for some value to appear is called **busy waiting**. It should usually be avoided, since it wastes CPU time. Only when there is a reasonable expectation that the wait will be short is busy waiting used.

When process 0 leaves the critical section, it sets *turn* to 1, to allow process 1 to enter its critical section. Suppose process 1 finishes its critical section quickly, so both processes are in their noncritical sections, with *turn* set to 0. Now process 0 executes its whole loop quickly, coming back to its noncritical section with *turn* set to 1. At this point, process 0 finishes its noncritical section and goes back to the top of its loop. Unfortunately, it is not permitted to enter its critical section now, because *turn* is 1 and process 1 is busy with its noncritical section. Put differently, taking turns is not a good idea when one of the processes is much slower than the other.

This situation violates condition 3 set out above: process 0 is being blocked by a process not in its critical section. Going back to the spooler directory discussed above, if we now associate the critical section with reading and writing the spooler directory, process 0 would not be allowed to print another file because process 1 was doing something else.

In fact, this solution requires that the two processes strictly alternate in entering their critical regions, for example, in spooling files. Neither one would be permitted to spool two in a row. While this algorithm does avoid all races, it is not really a serious candidate as a solution.

Peterson's Solution

By combining the idea of taking turns with the idea of lock variables and warning variables, a Dutch mathematician, T. Dekker, was the first one to devise a software solution to the mutual exclusion problem that does not require strict alternation. For a discussion of Dekker's algorithm, see Dijkstra (1965).

In 1981, G.L. Peterson discovered a much simpler way to achieve mutual exclusion, thus rendering Dekker's solution obsolete. Peterson's algorithm is shown in Fig. 2-8. This algorithm consists of two procedures written in ANSI C, which means that function prototypes should be supplied for all the functions defined and used. Conventionally, such prototypes are grouped together in header files. The first line of Fig. 2-8 includes all these prototypes. The details are not really important here, so they are not listed in the book.

```c
#include "prototypes.h"

#define FALSE   0
#define TRUE    1
#define N       2                       /* number of processes */

int turn;                               /* whose turn is it? */
int interested[N];                      /* all values initially 0 (FALSE) */

void enter_region(int process)          /* process: who is entering (0 or 1) */
{
  int other;                            /* number of the other process */

  other = 1 - process;                  /* the opposite of process */
  interested[process] = TRUE;           /* show that you are interested */
  turn = process;                       /* set flag */
  while (turn == process && interested[other] == TRUE) /* null statement */ ;
}

void leave_region(int process)          /* process: who is leaving (0 or 1) */
{
  interested[process] = FALSE;          /* indicate departure from critical region */
}
```

Fig. 2-8. Peterson's solution for achieving mutual exclusion.

Before using the shared variables (i.e., before entering its critical region), each process calls *enter_region* with its own process number, 0 or 1, as parameter. This call will cause it to wait, if need be, until it is safe to enter. After it has finished with the shared variables, the process calls *leave_region* to indicate that it is done and to allow the other process to enter, if it so desires.

Let us see how this solution works. Initially neither process is in its critical region. Now process 0 calls *enter_region*. It indicates its interest by setting its array element, and sets *turn* to 0. Since process 1 is not interested, *enter_region* returns immediately. If process 1 now calls *enter_region*, it will hang there until *interested*[0] goes to *FALSE*, an event that only happens when process 0 calls *leave_region*.

Now consider the case that both processes call *enter_region* almost simultaneously. Both will store their process number in *turn*. Whichever store is done last is the one that counts; the first one is lost. Suppose process 1 stores last, so *turn* is 1. When both processes come to the `while` statement, process 0 executes it zero times, and enters its critical region. Process 1 loops and does not enter its critical region.

The TSL Instruction

Now let us look at a proposal that requires a little help from the hardware. Many computers, especially those designed with multiple processors in mind, have an instruction TEST AND SET LOCK (TSL) that works as follows. It reads the contents of the memory word into a register and then stores a nonzero value at that memory address. The operations of reading the word and storing into it are guaranteed to be indivisible—no other processor can access the word until the instruction is finished. The CPU executing the TSL instruction locks the memory bus to prohibit other CPUs from accessing memory until it is done.

To use the TSL instruction, we will use a shared variable, *flag*, to coordinate access to shared memory. When *flag* is 0, any process may set it to 1 using the TSL instruction and then read or write the shared memory. When it is done, the process sets *flag* back to 0 using an ordinary MOVE instruction.

How can this instruction be used to prevent two processes from simultaneously entering their critical regions? The solution is given in Fig. 2-9. There a four-instruction subroutine in a fictitious (but typical) assembly language is shown. The first instruction copies the old value of *flag* to a register and then sets *flag* to 1. Then the old value is compared with 0. If it is nonzero, the lock was already set, so the program just goes back to the beginning and tests it again. Sooner or later it will become 0 (when the process currently in its critical section is done with its critical section), and the subroutine returns, with the lock set. Clearing the lock is simple. The program just stores a 0 in *flag*. No special instructions are needed.

One solution to the critical section problem is now straightforward. Before entering its critical section, a process calls *enter_region*, which does busy waiting until the lock is free, then it acquires the lock and returns. After the critical section the process calls *leave_region*, which stores a 0 in *flag*. As with all solutions based on

```
enter_region:
        tsl register,flag    | copy flag to register and set flag to 1
        cmp register,#0      | was flag zero?
        jnz enter_region     | if it was non zero, lock was set, so loop
        ret                  | return to caller; critical region entered

leave_region:
        mov flag,#0          | store a 0 in flag
        ret                  | return to caller
```

Fig. 2-9. Setting and clearing locks using TSL.

critical regions, the processes must call *enter_region* and *leave_region* at the correct times for the method to work. If a process cheats, the mutual exclusion will fail.

2.2.4. Sleep and Wakeup

Both Peterson's solution and the solution using TSL are correct, but both have the defect of requiring busy waiting. In essence, what these solutions do is this: when a process wants to enter its critical section, it checks to see if the entry is allowed. If it is not, the process just sits in a tight loop waiting until it is.

Not only does this approach waste CPU time, but it can also have unexpected effects. Consider a computer with two processes, H, with high priority and L, with low priority. The scheduling rules are such that H is run whenever it is in ready state. At a certain moment, with L in its critical region, H becomes ready to run (e.g., an I/O operation completes). H now begins busy waiting, but since L is never scheduled while H is running, L never gets the chance to leave its critical region, so H loops forever. This situation is sometimes referred to as the **priority inversion problem**.

Now let us look at some interprocess communication primitives that block instead of wasting CPU time when they are not allowed to enter their critical sections. One of the simplest is the pair SLEEP and WAKEUP. SLEEP is a system call that causes the caller to block, that is, be suspended until another process wakes it up. The WAKEUP call has one parameter, the process to be awakened. Alternatively, both SLEEP and WAKEUP each have one parameter, a memory address used to match up SLEEPs with WAKEUPs.

The Producer-Consumer Problem

As an example of how these primitives are used, let us consider the **producer-consumer** problem (also known as the **bounded buffer** problem). Two processes share a common, fixed-size buffer. One of them, the producer, puts information into the buffer, and the other one, the consumer, takes it out.

Trouble arises when the producer wants to put a new item in the buffer, but it is already full. The solution is for the producer to go to sleep, to be awakened when the consumer has removed one or more items. Similarly, if the consumer wants to remove an item from the buffer and sees that the buffer is empty, it goes to sleep until the producer puts something in the buffer and wakes it up.

This approach sounds simple enough, but it leads to the same kinds of race conditions we saw earlier with the spooler directory. To keep track of the number of items in the buffer, we will need a variable, *count*. If the maximum number of items the buffer can hold is *N*, the producer's code will first test to see if *count* is *N*. If it is, the producer will go to sleep; if it is not, the producer will add an item and increment *count*.

The consumer's code is similar: first test *count* to see if it is 0. If it is, go to sleep; if it is nonzero, remove an item and decrement the counter. Each of the processes also tests to see if the other should be sleeping, and if not, wakes it up. The code for both producer and consumer is shown in Fig. 2-10.

```
#include "prototypes.h"

#define N 100                        /* number of slots in the buffer */

int count = 0;                       /* number of items in the buffer */

void producer(void)
{
  int item;

  while (TRUE) {                     /* repeat forever */
       produce_item(&item);          /* generate next item */
       if (count == N) sleep();      /* if buffer is full, go to sleep */
       enter_item(item);             /* put item in buffer */
       count = count + 1;            /* increment count of items in buffer */
       if (count == 1) wakeup(consumer);        /* was buffer empty? */
  }
}


void consumer(void)
{
  int item;

  while (TRUE) {                     /* repeat forever */
       if (count == 0) sleep();      /* if buffer is empty, go to sleep */
       remove_item(&item);           /* take item out of buffer */
       count = count - 1;            /* decrement count of items in buffer */
       if (count == N-1) wakeup(producer);      /* was buffer full? */
       consume_item(item);           /* print item */
  }
}
```

Fig. 2-10. The producer-consumer problem with a fatal race condition.

To express system calls such as SLEEP and WAKEUP in C, we will show them as calls to library routines. They are not part of the standard C library, but presumably would be available on any system that actually had these system calls. The procedures *enter_item* and *remove_item*, which are not shown, handle the bookkeeping of putting items into and taking items out of the buffer.

Now let us get back to the race condition. It can occur because access to *count* is unconstrained. The following situation could possibly occur. The buffer is empty and the consumer has just read *count* to see if it is 0. At that instant, the scheduler decides to stop running the consumer temporarily and start running the producer. The producer enters an item in the buffer, increments *count*, and notices that it is now 1. Reasoning that *count* was just 0, and thus the consumer must be sleeping, the producer calls *wakeup* to wake the consumer up.

Unfortunately, the consumer is not yet logically asleep, so the wakeup signal is lost. When the consumer next runs, it will test the value of *count* it previously read, find it to be 0, and go to sleep. Sooner or later the producer will fill up the buffer and also go to sleep. Both will sleep forever.

The essence of the problem here is that a wakeup sent to a process that is not (yet) sleeping is lost. If it were not lost, everything would be all right. A quick fix is to modify the rules to add a **wakeup waiting bit** to the picture. When a wakeup is sent to a process that is already awake, this bit is set. Later, when the process tries to go to sleep, if the wakeup waiting bit is on, it will be turned off, but the process will stay awake. The wakeup waiting bit is really a piggy bank for wakeup signals.

While the wakeup waiting bit saves the day in this simple example, it is easy to construct examples with three or more processes in which one wakeup waiting bit is insufficient. We could make another patch, and add a second wakeup waiting bit, or maybe 8 or 32 of them, but in principle the problem is still there.

2.2.5. Semaphores

This was the situation in 1965, when E. W. Dijkstra (1965) suggested using an integer variable to count the number of wakeups saved for future use. In his proposal, a new variable type, called a **semaphore**, was introduced. A semaphore could have the value 0, indicating that no wakeups were saved, or some positive value if one or more wakeups were pending.

Dijkstra proposed having two operations, DOWN and UP (generalizations of SLEEP and WAKEUP, respectively). The DOWN operation on a semaphore checks to see if the value is greater than 0. If so, it decrements the value (i.e., uses up one stored wakeup) and just continues. If the value is 0, the process is put to sleep. Checking the value, changing it, and possibly going to sleep is all done as a single, indivisible, **atomic action**. It is guaranteed that once a semaphore operation has started, no other process can access the semaphore until the operation has completed or blocked. This atomicity is absolutely essential to solving synchronization problems and avoiding race conditions.

The UP operation increments the value of the semaphore addressed. If one or more processes were sleeping on that semaphore, unable to complete an earlier DOWN operation, one of them is chosen by the system (e.g., at random), and is allowed to complete its DOWN. Thus, after an UP on a semaphore with processes sleeping on it, the semaphore will still be 0, but there will be one fewer process sleeping on it. The operation of incrementing the semaphore and waking up one process is also indivisible. No process ever blocks doing an UP, just as no process ever blocks doing a WAKEUP in the earlier model.

As an aside, in Dijkstra's original paper, he used the names P and V instead of DOWN and UP, respectively, but since these have no mnemonic significance to people who do not speak Dutch (and only marginal significance to those who do), we will use the terms DOWN and UP instead. These were first introduced in Algol 68.

Solving the Producer-Consumer Problem using Semaphores

Semaphores solve the lost-wakeup problem, as shown in Fig. 2-11. It is essential that they be implemented in an indivisible way. The normal way is to implement UP and DOWN as system calls, with the operating system briefly disabling all interrupts while it is testing the semaphore, updating it, and putting the process to sleep, if necessary. As all of these actions take only a few instructions, no harm is done in disabling interrupts. If multiple CPUs are being used, each semaphore should be protected by a lock variable, with the TSL instruction used to make sure that only one CPU at a time examines the semaphore. Be sure you understand that using TSL to prevent several CPUs from accessing the semaphore at the same time is quite different from busy waiting by the producer or consumer waiting for the other to empty or fill the buffer. The semaphore operation will only take a few microseconds, whereas the producer or consumer might take arbitrarily long.

This solution uses three semaphores: one called *full* for counting the number of slots that are full, one called *empty* for counting the number of slots that are empty, and one called *mutex* to make sure the producer and consumer do not access the buffer at the same time. *Full* is initially 0, *empty* is initially equal to the number of slots in the buffer, and *mutex* is initially 1. Semaphores that are initialized to 1 and used by two or more processes to ensure that only one of them can enter its critical region at the same time are called **binary semaphores**. If each process does a DOWN just before entering its critical region and an UP just after leaving it, mutual exclusion is guaranteed.

Now that we have a good interprocess communication primitive at our disposal, let us go back and look at the interrupt sequence of Fig. 2-5 again. In a system using semaphores, the natural way to hide interrupts is to have a semaphore, initially set to 0, associated with each I/O device. Just after starting an I/O device, the managing process does a DOWN on the associated semaphore, thus blocking immediately. When the interrupt comes in, the interrupt handler then does an UP on the associated semaphore, which makes the relevant process ready to run again. In this model, step 5 in Fig. 2-5 consists of doing an UP on the device's semaphore, so that in step 6 the scheduler will be able to run the device manager. Of course, if several processes are now ready, the scheduler may choose to run an even more important process next. We will look at how scheduling is done later in this chapter.

In the example of Fig. 2-11, we have actually used semaphores in two different ways. This difference is important enough to make explicit. The *mutex* semaphore is used for mutual exclusion. It is designed to guarantee that only one process at a time will be reading or writing the buffer and the associated variables. This mutual exclusion is required to prevent chaos.

```
#include "prototypes.h"

#define N 100                    /* number of slots in the buffer */

typedef int semaphore;           /* semaphores are a special kind of int */

semaphore mutex = 1;             /* controls access to critical region */
semaphore empty = N;             /* counts empty buffer slots */
semaphore full = 0;              /* counts full buffer slots */

void producer(void)
{
  int item;

  while (TRUE) {                 /* TRUE is the constant 1 */
       produce_item(&item);      /* generate something to put in buffer */
       down(&empty);             /* decrement empty count */
       down(&mutex);             /* enter critical region */
       enter_item(item);         /* put new item in buffer */
       up(&mutex);               /* leave critical region */
       up(&full);                /* increment count of full slots */
  }
}


void consumer(void)
{
  int item;

  while (TRUE) {                 /* infinite loop */
       down(&full);              /* decrement full count */
       down(&mutex);             /* enter critical region */
       remove_item(&item);       /* take item from buffer */
       up(&mutex);               /* leave critical region */
       up(&empty);               /* increment count of empty slots */
       consume_item(item);       /* do something with the item */
  }
}
```

Fig. 2-11. The producer-consumer problem using semaphores.

The other use of semaphores is for **synchronization**. The *full* and *empty* semaphores are needed to guarantee that certain event sequences do or do not occur. In this case, they ensure that the producer stops running when the buffer is full, and the consumer stops running when it is empty. This use is different from mutual exclusion.

2.2.6. Event Counters

The solution to the producer-consumer problem using semaphores relied on mutual exclusion to avoid race conditions. It is also possible to program a solution without requiring mutual exclusion. In this section we will describe such a method.

It uses a special kind of variable called an **event counter** (Reed and Kanodia, 1979). Three operations are defined on an event counter E:

1. *Read(E)*: Return the current value of E.

2. *Advance(E)*: Atomically increment E by 1.

3. *Await(E, v)*: Wait until E has a value of v or more.

The producer-consumer problem does not use READ, but it is needed for other synchronization problems.

Notice that event counters only increase, never decrease. They always start at 0. Figure 2-12 shows the producer-consumer problem once more, this time using event counters.

```c
#include "prototypes.h"

#define N 100                  /* number of slots in the buffer */

typedef int event_counter;     /* event_counters are a special kind of int */

event_counter in = 0;          /* counts items inserted into buffer */
event_counter out = 0;         /* counts items removed from buffer */

void producer(void)
{
  int item, sequence = 0;

  while (TRUE) {                /* infinite loop */
        produce_item(&item);    /* generate something to put in buffer */
        sequence = sequence + 1; /* count items produced so far */
        await(out, sequence - N); /* wait until there is room in buffer */
        enter_item(item);       /* put item in slot (sequence-1) % N */
        advance(&in);           /* let consumer know about another item */
  }
}


void consumer(void)
{
  int item, sequence = 0;

  while (TRUE) {                /* infinite loop */
        sequence = sequence + 1; /* number of item to remove from buffer */
        await(in, sequence);    /* wait until required item is present */
        remove_item(&item);     /* take item from slot (sequence-1) % N */
        advance(&out);          /* let producer know that item is gone */
        consume_item(item);     /* do something with the item */
  }
}
```

Fig. 2-12. The producer-consumer problem using event counters.

Two event counters are used. The first one, *in*, counts the cumulative number of items that the producer has put into the buffer since the program started running. The other one, *out*, counts the cumulative number of items that the consumer has removed from the buffer so far. It is clear that *in* must be greater than or equal to *out*, but not by more than the size of the buffer.

When the producer has computed a new item, it checks to see if there is room in the buffer, using the AWAIT system call. Initially, *out* will be 0 and *sequence − N* will be negative, so the producer does not block. If the producer generates $N + 1$ items before the consumer has begun, the AWAIT statement will wait until *out* becomes 1, something that will only happen after the consumer has removed one item.

The consumer's logic is even simpler. Before trying to remove the *k*-th item, it just waits until *in* has reached *k*, that is, the producer has put *k* items into the buffer.

2.2.7. Monitors

With semaphores and event counters, interprocess communication looks easy, doesn't it? Forget it. Look closely at the order of the DOWNs before entering or removing items from the buffer in Fig. 2-11. Suppose the two DOWNs in the producer's code were reversed in order, so *mutex* was decremented before *empty* instead of after it. If the buffer were completely full, the producer would block, with *mutex* set to 0. Consequently, the next time the consumer tried to access the buffer, it would do a DOWN on *mutex*, now 0, and block too. Both processes would stay blocked forever and no more work would ever be done. This unfortunate situation is called a **deadlock**. We will study deadlocks in detail in Chap. 6.

This problem is pointed out to show how careful you must be when using semaphores. One subtle error and everything comes to a grinding halt. It is like programming in assembly language, only worse, because the errors are race conditions, deadlocks, and other forms of unpredictable and irreproducible behavior.

To make it easier to write correct programs, Hoare (1974) and Brinch Hansen (1975) proposed a higher level synchronization primitive called a **monitor**. Their proposals differed slightly, as described below. A monitor is a collection of procedures, variables, and data structures that are all grouped together in a special kind of module or package. Processes may call the procedures in a monitor whenever they want to, but they cannot directly access the monitor's internal data structures from procedures declared outside the monitor. Figure 2-13 illustrates a monitor written in an imaginary language, pidgin Pascal.

Monitors have an important property that makes them useful for achieving mutual exclusion: only one process can be active in a monitor at any instant. Monitors are a programming language construct, so the compiler knows they are special and can handle calls to monitor procedures differently from other procedure calls. Typically, when a process calls a monitor procedure, the first few instructions of the procedure will check to see if any other process is currently active within the monitor. If so, the calling process will be suspended until the other process has left the monitor. If no other process is using the monitor, the calling process may enter.

It is up to the compiler to implement the mutual exclusion on monitor entries, but a common way is to use a binary semaphore. Because the compiler, not the programmer, is arranging for the mutual exclusion, it is much less likely that something will

```
monitor example
  integer i;
  condition c;

  procedure producer(x);
    .
    .
    .
  end;

  procedure consumer(x);
    .
    .
    .
  end;
end monitor;
```
                                            Fig. 2-13. A monitor.

go wrong. In any event, the person writing the monitor does not have to be aware of how the compiler arranges for mutual exclusion. It is sufficient to know that by turning all the critical sections into monitor procedures, no two processes will ever execute their critical sections at the same time.

Although monitors provide an easy way to achieve mutual exclusion, as we have seen above, that is not enough. We also need a way for processes to block when they cannot proceed. In the producer-consumer problem, it is easy enough to put all the tests for buffer-full and buffer-empty in monitor procedures, but how should the producer block when it finds the buffer full?

The solution lies in the introduction of **condition variables**, along with two operations on them, WAIT and SIGNAL. When a monitor procedure discovers that it cannot continue (e.g., the producer finds the buffer full), it does a WAIT on some condition variable, say, *full*. This action causes the calling process to block. It also allows another process that had been previously prohibited from entering the monitor to enter now.

This other process, for example, the consumer, can wake up its sleeping partner by doing a SIGNAL on the condition variable that its partner is waiting on. To avoid having two active processes in the monitor at the same time, we need a rule telling what happens after a SIGNAL. Hoare proposed to let the newly awakened process run, suspending the other one. Brinch Hansen proposed finessing the problem by requiring that a process doing a SIGNAL *must* exit the monitor immediately. In other words, a SIGNAL statement may appear only as the final statement in a monitor procedure. We will use Brinch Hansen's proposal because it is conceptually simpler and is also easier to implement. If a SIGNAL is done on a condition variable on which several processes are waiting, only one of them, determined by the system scheduler, is revived.

Condition variables are not counters. They do not accumulate signals for later use the way semaphores do. Thus if a condition variable is signaled with no one waiting on it, the signal is lost. The WAIT must come before the SIGNAL. This rule makes the implementation much simpler. In practice it is not a problem because it is easy to keep track of the state of each process with variables, if need be. A process that might otherwise do a SIGNAL can see that this operation is not necessary by looking at the variables.

A skeleton of the producer-consumer problem with monitors is given in Fig. 2-14 in pidgin Pascal.

You may be thinking that the operations WAIT and SIGNAL look similar to SLEEP and WAKEUP, which we saw earlier had fatal race conditions. They *are* very similar, but with one crucial difference: SLEEP and WAKEUP failed because while one process was trying to go to sleep, the other one was trying to wake it up. With monitors, that cannot happen. The automatic mutual exclusion on monitor procedures guarantees that if, say, the producer inside a monitor procedure discovers that the buffer is full, it will be able to complete the WAIT operation without having to worry about the possibility that the scheduler may switch to the consumer just before the WAIT completes. The consumer will not even be let into the monitor at all until the WAIT is finished and the producer has been marked as no longer runnable.

By making the mutual exclusion of critical regions automatic, monitors make parallel programming much less error-prone than with semaphores. Still, they too have some drawbacks. It is not for nothing that Fig. 2-14 is written in a strange kind of pidgin Pascal rather than in C, as are the other examples in this book. As we said earlier, monitors are a programming language concept. The compiler must recognize them and arrange for the mutual exclusion somehow. C, Pascal, and most other languages do not have monitors, so it is unreasonable to expect their compilers to enforce any mutual exclusion rules. In fact, how could the compiler even know which procedures were in monitors and which were not?

These same languages do not have semaphores either, but adding semaphores is easy: all you need to do is add two short assembly language routines to the library to issue the UP and DOWN system calls. The compilers do not even have to know that they exist. Of course, the operating systems have to know about the semaphores, but at least if you have decided to write a semaphore-based operating system, you can write the user programs for it in C or Pascal or even BASIC if you are masochistic enough. With monitors, you need a language that has them built in. A few languages, such as Concurrent Euclid (Holt, 1983) have them, but they are rare.

Another problem with monitors, and also with semaphores, is that they were designed for solving the mutual exclusion problem on one or more CPUs that all have access to a common memory. By putting the semaphores (or event counters) in the shared memory and protecting them with TSL instructions, we can avoid races. When we go to a distributed system consisting of multiple CPUs, each with its own private memory, connected by a local area network, these primitives become inapplicable. The conclusion is that semaphores are too low level and monitors are not usable except in a few programming languages. Furthermore, none of the primitives provide for information exchange between machines. Something else is needed.

```
monitor ProducerConsumer
condition full, empty;
integer count;

  procedure enter;
  begin
    if count = N then wait (full);
    enter_item;
    count := count + 1;
    if count = 1 then signal (empty);
  end;

  procedure remove;
  begin
    if count = 0 then wait (empty);
    remove_item;
    count := count - 1;
    if count = N - 1 then signal (full);
  end;

  count := 0;
end monitor;

procedure producer;
begin
  while true do
  begin
    produce_item;
    ProducerConsumer.enter;
  end
end;

procedure consumer;
begin
  while true do
  begin
    ProducerConsumer.remove;
    consume_item;
  end
end;
```

Fig. 2-14. An outline of the producer-consumer problem with monitors. The buffer has N slots.

2.2.8. Message Passing

That something else is **message passing**. This method of interprocess communication uses two primitives SEND and RECEIVE, which, like semaphores and unlike monitors, are system calls rather than language constructs. As such, they can easily be put into library procedures, such as

```
send(destination, &message);
```

and

```
receive(source, &message);
```

The former sends a message to a given destination and the latter receives a message from a given source (or from *ANY*, if the receiver does not care). If no message is available, the receiver could block until one arrives.

Design Issues for Message Passing Systems

Message passing systems have many challenging problems and design issues that do not arise with semaphores or monitors, especially if the communicating processes are on different machines connected by a network. For example, messages can be lost by the network. To guard against lost messages, the sender and receiver can agree that as soon as a message has been received, the receiver will send back a special **acknowledgement** message. If the sender has not received the acknowledgement within a certain time interval, it retransmits the message.

Now consider what happens if the message itself is received correctly, but the acknowledgement is lost. The sender will retransmit the message, so the receiver will get it twice. It is essential that the receiver can distinguish a new message from the retransmission of an old one. Usually this problem is solved by putting consecutive sequence numbers in each original message. If the receiver gets a message bearing the same sequence number as the previous message, it knows that the message is a duplicate that can be ignored.

Message systems also have to deal with the question of how processes are named, so that the process specified in a SEND or RECEIVE call is unambiguous. Often a naming scheme such as *process@machine* or *machine:process* is used.

If the number of machines is very large, and there is no central authority that allocates machine names, it may happen that two organizations give their machine the same name. The problem of conflicts can be reduced considerably by grouping machines into **domains**, and then addressing processes as *process@machine.domain*. In this scheme there is no problem if two machines have the same name, provided that they are in different domains. The domain names must also be unique, of course.

Authentication is also an issue in message systems: how can the client tell that he is communicating with the real file server, and not with an imposter? How can the file server tell which client has requested a file? Encrypting the messages with a key known only to authorized users can often be helpful here.

At the other end of the spectrum, there are also design issues that are important when the sender and receiver are on the same machine. One of these is performance. Copying messages from one process to another is always slower than doing a semaphore operation or entering a monitor. Much work has gone into making message passing efficient. Cheriton (1984), for example, has suggested limiting message size to what will fit in the machine's registers, and then doing message passing using the registers.

The Producer-Consumer Problem with Message Passing

Now let us see how the producer-consumer problem can be solved with message passing and no shared memory. A solution is given in Fig. 2-15. We assume that all messages are the same size and that messages sent but not yet received are buffered automatically by the operating system. In this solution, a total of N messages is used, analogous to the N slots in a shared memory buffer. The consumer starts out by sending N empty messages to the producer. Whenever the producer has an item to give to the consumer, it takes an empty message and sends back a full one. In this way, the total number of messages in the system remains constant in time, so they can be stored in a given amount of memory.

If the producer works faster than the consumer, all the messages will end up full, waiting for the consumer; the producer will be blocked, waiting for an empty to come back. If the consumer works faster, then the reverse happens: all the messages will be empties waiting for the producer to fill them up; the consumer will be blocked, waiting for a full message.

Many variants are possible with message passing. For starters, let us look at how messages are addressed. One way is to assign each process a unique address and have messages be addressed to processes. An alternative way is to invent a new data structure, called a **mailbox**. A mailbox is a place to buffer a certain number of messages, typically specified when the mailbox is created. When mailboxes are used, the address parameters in the SEND and RECEIVE calls are mailboxes, not processes. When a process tries to send to a mailbox that is full, it is suspended until a message is removed from that mailbox.

For the producer-consumer problem, both the producer and consumer would create mailboxes large enough to hold N messages. The producer would send messages containing data to the consumer's mailbox, and the consumer would send empty messages to the producer's mailbox. When mailboxes are used, the buffering mechanism is clear: the destination mailbox holds messages that have been sent to the destination process but have not yet been accepted.

The other extreme from having mailboxes is to eliminate all buffering. When this approach is followed, if the SEND is done before the RECEIVE, the sending process is blocked until the RECEIVE happens, at which time the message can be copied directly from the sender to the receiver, with no intermediate buffering. Similarly, if the RECEIVE is done first, the receiver is blocked until a SEND happens. This strategy is often known as a **rendezvous**. It is easier to implement than a buffered message scheme but is less flexible since the sender and receiver are forced to run in lockstep.

The interprocess communication between user processes in UNIX is via pipes,

```
#include "prototypes.h"

#define N 100                    /* number of slots in the buffer */
#define MSIZE 4                  /* message size */

typedef int message[MSIZE];

void producer(void)
{
  int item;
  message m;                     /* message buffer */

  while(TRUE) {
        produce_item(&item);     /* generate something to put in buffer */
        receive(consumer, &m);   /* wait for an empty to arrive */
        build_message(&m, item); /* construct a message to send */
        send(consumer, &m);      /* send item to consumer */
  }
}

void consumer(void)
{
  int item, i;
  message m;

  for (i = 0; i < N; i++) send(producer, &m);     /* send N empties */
  while (TRUE) {
        receive(producer, &m);   /* get message containing item */
        extract_item(&m, &item); /* take item out of message */
        send(producer, &m);      /* send back emptry reply */
        consumer_item(item);     /* do something with item */
  }
}
```

Fig. 2-15. The producer-consumer problem with N messages.

which are effectively mailboxes. The only real difference between a message system with mailboxes and the pipe mechanism is that pipes do not preserve message boundaries. In other words, if one process writes 10 messages of 100 bytes to a pipe and another process reads 1000 bytes from that pipe, the reader will get all 10 messages at once. With a true message system, each READ should return only one message. Of course, if the processes agree always to read and write fixed-size messages from the pipe, or to end each message with a special character (e.g., line feed), no problems arise.

2.2.9. Equivalence of Primitives

Reed and Kanodia (1979) described a different interprocess communication method called **sequencers.** Campbell and Habermann (1974) discussed a method called **path expressions.** Atkinson and Hewitt (1979) introduced **serializers.** While the list of different methods is not endless, it is certainly pretty long, with new ones being dreamed up all the time. Fortunately, space limitations prevent us from looking at all of them. Furthermore, many of the proposed schemes are similar to other ones.

In the previous sections we have studied four different interprocess communication primitives. Over the years, each one has accumulated supporters who maintain that their favorite way is the best way. The truth of the matter is that all these methods are essentially semantically equivalent (at least as far as single CPU systems are concerned). Using any of them, you can build the other ones.

We will now show the essential equivalence of semaphores, monitors, and messages. Not only is this interesting in its own right, but it also provides more insight and understanding about how the primitives work and how they can be implemented. Lack of space prevents us from dealing with event counters as well, but the general approach should be clear from the other examples.

Using Semaphores to Implement Monitors and Messages

Let us first see how we can build monitors and messages using semaphores. If the operating system provides semaphores as a basic feature, any compiler writer can easily implement monitors in his language as follows. First a small runtime collection of procedures for managing monitors is constructed and put in the library. These are listed in Fig. 2-16. Then, whenever generating code involving monitors, calls are made to the appropriate runtime procedure to perform the necessary function.

Associated with each monitor is a binary semaphore, *mutex*, initially 1, to control entry to the monitor, and an additional semaphore, initially 0, per condition variable. When a process enters a monitor, the compiler generates a call to the runtime procedure *enter_monitor*, which does a DOWN on the *mutex* associated with the monitor being entered. If the monitor is currently in use, the process will block.

Although it might seem logical that the code for exiting a monitor simply do an UP on *mutex*, this simple solution does not always work. When the process has not signaled any other processes, then it can, indeed, just UP *mutex* and exit the monitor. This case is shown as *leave_normally* in Fig. 2-16.

The complication comes from the condition variables. WAIT on a condition variable, *c*, is carried out as a sequence of two semaphore operations. First comes an UP on *mutex*, to allow other processes to enter the monitor. Then comes a DOWN on *c* to block on the condition variable.

Remember that SIGNAL must always be done as the last operation before leaving a monitor. This rule is needed to be able to combine signaling and exiting into the library procedure *leave_with_signal*. All it does is an UP on the condition variable. Then it leaves the monitor without releasing *mutex*. The trick here is that since *mutex* is still 0, no other process can enter the monitor at this point. However, the just-awakened process is now active in the monitor, and will do an UP on *mutex* when it leaves. In this manner, the signaling process effectively passes the mutual exclusion to the signaled process to make sure no competitors get it.

Let us now see how this mechanism works with the producer-consumer problem. The *mutex* semaphore guarantees that each process has exclusive access to the

```
#include "prototypes.h"

typedef int semaphore;

semaphore mutex = 1;              /* to control access to the monitor */

void enter_monitor(void)          /* code to execute upon entry to monitor */
{
  down(mutex);                    /* only one at a time inside please */
}


void leave_normally(void)         /* leave monitor without signaling */
{
  up(mutex);                      /* allow other processes to enter */
}


void leave_with_signal(c)         /* signal on c and leave monitor */
semaphore c;                      /* which condition variable to signal */
{
  up(c);                          /* release one process waiting on c */
}


void wait(c)                      /* go to sleep on a condition */
semaphore c;                      /* which condition */
{
  up(mutex);                      /* allow another process to enter */
  down(c);                        /* go to sleep on the condition */
}
```

Fig. 2-16. Library procedures for implementing monitors with semaphores.

monitor for its critical section. Suppose the consumer starts first and discovers that there is no work for it in the buffer. It does a WAIT *empty*, which causes an UP on *mutex* and a DOWN on *empty*. The consumer goes to sleep, and the producer is allowed to enter as soon as it wants to. When the producer discovers that *count* (see Fig. 2-14) is 1, it will do SIGNAL *empty* to wake up the consumer. At this point both producer and consumer are active in the monitor, but since one of our rules of programming with monitors is that after doing SIGNAL a process must leave the monitor immediately, no harm is done.

Note that if the producer does its UP on *mutex* and leaves the monitor before the consumer has done its DOWN on *mutex*, it is possible that the producer could try to enter the monitor again quickly. However, this attempt will fail because *mutex* is 0. Only when the consumer leaves the monitor can the producer enter it again.

Now let us look at how to implement message passing with semaphores. Associated with each process is a semaphore, initially 0, on which it will block when a SEND or RECEIVE must wait for completion. A shared buffer area will be used to hold mailboxes, each one containing an array of message slots. The slots in each mailbox are chained together in a linked list, so messages are delivered in the order received. Each mailbox has integer variables telling how many slots are full and how many are empty. Finally, each mailbox also contains the start of two queues, one queue for processes that are unable to send to the mailbox and one queue for processes that are unable to receive from the mailbox. These queues need to supply only the process numbers of the waiting processes so an UP can be done on the relevant semaphore. The whole shared buffer is protected by a binary semaphore, *mutex*, to make sure that only one process can inspect or update the shared data structures at once. It is shown in Fig. 2-17.

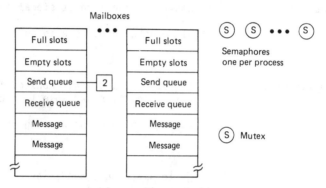

Fig. 2-17. The shared buffer for implementing message passing with semaphores.

When a SEND or RECEIVE is done on a mailbox containing at least one empty or full slot, respectively, the operation inserts or removes a message, updates the counters and links, and exits normally. The use of *mutex* at the start and end of the critical region ensures that only one process at a time can use the counters and pointers, in order to avoid race conditions.

When a RECEIVE is done on an empty mailbox, the process trying to receive a message first enters itself on the receive queue for the mailbox and then does an UP on *mutex* and a DOWN on its own semaphore, thus putting itself to sleep. Later, when it is awakened, it will immediately do a DOWN on *mutex* just as in the case of using semaphores to construct monitors.

When a SEND is done, if room exists in the destination mailbox, the message is put there and the sender checks to see if the receiving queue for that mailbox has any waiting processes. If so, the first one is removed from the queue, and the sender does an UP on its semaphore. The sender then exits the critical region and the newly awakened receiver can continue. Their respective DOWN and UP on *mutex* cancel (in whatever order they occur) and no problems occur, provided that just as with monitors, a process that wakes up another process always does the WAKEUP as the very last thing before leaving the critical region.

When a SEND cannot complete due to a full mailbox, the sender first queues itself on the destination mailbox, then does an UP on *mutex* and a DOWN on its own semaphore. Later, when a receiver removes a message from the full mailbox and notices that someone is queued trying to send to that mailbox, the sender will be awakened.

Using Monitors to Implement Semaphores and Messages

Implementing semaphores and messages using monitors follows roughly the same pattern as what we have just described, but is simpler, because monitors are a higher level construct than semaphores. To implement semaphores, we need a counter and a linked list for each semaphore to be implemented, as well as a condition variable per process. When a DOWN is done, the caller checks (inside the monitor) to see if the counter for that semaphore is greater than zero. If it is, the counter is decremented and the caller simply exits the monitor. If the counter is zero, the caller adds its own process number to the linked list for that semaphore and does a WAIT on its condition variable.

When an UP is done on a semaphore, the calling process increments the counter (inside the monitor, of course) and then checks to see if the linked list for that semaphore has any entries. If the list has entries, the calling process removes one of them and does a SIGNAL on the condition variable for that process. Note that the calling process is not required to choose the first process on the linked list. In a more sophisticated implementation, each process could put its priority on the list along with its process number, so that the highest priority process would be awakened first.

Implementing messages using monitors is essentially the same as with semaphores, except that instead of a semaphore per process we have a condition variable per process. The mailbox structures are the same for both implementations.

Using Messages to Implement Semaphores and Monitors

If a message system is available, it is possible to implement semaphores and monitors using a little trick. The trick is to introduce a new process, the *synchronization process*. Let us first look at how this process can be used to implement semaphores. The synchronization process maintains a counter and a linked list of waiting processes for each semaphore. To do an UP or DOWN, a process calls the corresponding (library) procedure, *up* or *down*, which sends a message to the synchronization process specifying the operation desired and the semaphore to be used. The library procedure then does a RECEIVE to get the reply from the synchronization process.

When the message arrives, the synchronization process checks the counter to see if the required operation can be completed. UPs can always complete, but DOWNs will block if the value of the semaphore is 0. If the operation is allowed, the synchronization process sends back an empty message, thus unblocking the caller. If, however, the operation is a DOWN and the semaphore is 0, the synchronization process enters the caller onto the queue and does not send a reply. The result is that the process doing the DOWN is blocked, just as it should be. Later, when an UP is done, the synchronization process picks one of the processes blocked on the semaphore, either in first-come-first-served order, priority order, or some other order, and sends it a reply. Race conditions are avoided here because the synchronization process handles only one request at a time.

Monitors can be implemented using messages using the same trick. We showed earlier how monitors can be implemented using semaphores. Now we have shown how semaphores can be implemented using messages. By combining the two, we get monitors from messages. One way to achieve this goal is to have the compiler implement the monitor procedures by calling the library procedures *up* and *down* for the *mutex* and per-process semaphores, as described at the beginning of this section. These procedures would then be implemented by sending messages to the synchronization process. Other implementations are also possible.

2.3. CLASSICAL IPC PROBLEMS

The operating systems literature is full of interesting problems that have been widely discussed and analyzed. In the following sections we will examine three of the better-known problems.

2.3.1. The Dining Philosophers Problem

In 1965, Dijkstra posed and solved a synchronization problem called the **dining philosophers problem**. Since that time, everyone inventing yet another synchronization primitive has tried to demonstrate how wonderful the new primitive is by showing how elegantly it solves the dining philosophers problem. The problem can be stated as follows. Five philosophers are seated around a table. Each philosopher has a plate of spaghetti. The spaghetti is so slippery that a philosopher needs two forks to eat it. Between each plate is a fork. The table is shown in Fig. 2-18.

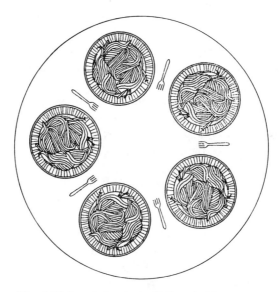

Fig. 2-18. Lunch time in the Philosophy Department.

The life of a philosopher consists of alternate periods of eating and thinking. (This is something of an abstraction, even for philosophers, but the other activities are irrelevant here.) When a philosopher gets hungry, she tries to acquire her left and right fork, one at a time, in either order. If successful in acquiring two forks, she eats for a while, then puts down the forks and continues to think. The key question is: can you write a program for each philosopher that does what it is supposed to do and never gets stuck? (It has been pointed out that the two-fork requirement is somewhat artificial; perhaps we should switch from Italian to Chinese food, substituting rice for spaghetti and chopsticks for forks.)

Figure 2-19 shows the obvious solution. The procedure *take_fork* waits until the specified fork is available and then seizes it. Unfortunately, the obvious solution is wrong. Suppose that all five philosophers take their left forks simultaneously. None will be able to take their right forks, and there will be a deadlock.

```
#include "prototypes.h"

#define N 5                     /* number of philosophers */

void philosopher(int i)         /* i: which philosopher (0 to N-1) */
{
  while (TRUE) {
        think();                /* philosopher is thinking */
        take_fork(i);           /* take left fork */
        take_fork((i+1) % N);   /* take right fork; % is modulo operator */
        eat();                  /* yum-yum, spaghetti */
        put_fork(i);            /* put left fork back on the table */
        put_fork((i+1) % N);    /* put right fork back on the table */
  }
}
```

Fig. 2-19. A nonsolution to the dining philosophers problem.

We could modify the program so that after taking the left fork, the program checks to see if the right fork is available. If it is not, the philosopher puts down the left one, waits for some time, and then repeats the whole process. This proposal too, fails, although for a different reason. With a little bit of bad luck, all the philosophers could start the algorithm simultaneously, picking up their left forks, seeing that their right forks were not available, putting down their left forks, waiting, picking up their left forks again simultaneously, and so on, forever. A situation like this, in which all the programs continue to run indefinitely but fail to make any progress is called **starvation**. (It is called starvation even when the problem does not occur in an Italian or a Chinese restaurant.)

Now you might think, "If the philosophers would just wait a random time instead of the same time after failing to acquire the right-hand fork, the chance that everything would continue in lockstep for even an hour is very small." This observation is true, but in some applications one would prefer a solution that always works and cannot fail due to an unlikely series of random numbers. (Think about safety control in a nuclear power plant.)

One improvement to Fig. 2-19 that has no deadlock and no starvation is to protect the five statements following the call to *think* by a binary semaphore. Before starting to acquire forks, a philosopher would do a DOWN on *mutex*. After replacing the forks, she would do an UP on *mutex*. From a theoretical viewpoint, this solution is adequate. From a practical one, it has a performance bug: only one philosopher can be eating at any instant. With five forks available, we should be able to allow two philosophers to eat at the same time.

The solution presented in Fig. 2-20 is correct and also allows the maximum parallelism for an arbitrary number of philosophers. It uses an array, *state*, to keep track of whether a philosopher is eating, thinking, or hungry (trying to acquire forks). A philosopher may move only into eating state if neither neighbor is eating. Philosopher i's neighbors are defined by the macros *LEFT* and *RIGHT*. In other words, if i is 2, *LEFT* is 1 and *RIGHT* is 3.

The program uses an array of semaphores, one per philosopher, so hungry philosophers can block if the needed forks are busy. Note that each process runs the procedure *philosopher* as its main code, but the other procedures, *take_forks*, *put_forks*, and *test* are ordinary procedures and not separate processes.

2.3.2. The Readers and Writers Problem

The dining philosophers problem is useful for modeling processes that are competing for exclusive access to a limited number of resources, such as tape drives or other I/O devices. Another famous problem is the readers and writers problem (Courtois et al., 1971), which models access to a data base. Imagine a big data base, such as an airline reservation system, with many competing processes wishing to read and write it. It is acceptable to have multiple processes reading the data base at the same time, but if one process is writing (i.e., changing) the data base, no other processes may have access to the data base, not even readers. The question is how do you program the readers and the writers? One solution is shown in Fig. 2-21.

In this solution, the first reader to get access to the data base does a DOWN on the semaphore *db*. Subsequent readers merely increment a counter, *rc*. As readers leave, they decrement the counter and the last one out does an UP on the semaphore, allowing a blocked writer, if there is one, to get in.

Implicit in this solution is that readers have priority over writers. If a writer appears while several readers are in the data base, the writer must wait. If new readers keep appearing, so that there is always at least one reader in the data base, the writer must keep waiting until no more readers are interested in the data base. Courtois et al. also presented a solution that gives priority to writers. For details, we refer you to their paper.

2.3.3. The Sleeping Barber Problem

Another classical IPC problem takes place in a barber shop. The barber shop has one barber, one barber chair, and n chairs for waiting customers, if any, to sit in. If there are no customers present, the barber sits down in the barber chair and falls asleep, as illustrated in Fig. 2-22. When a customer arrives, he has to wake up the sleeping barber. If additional customers arrive while the barber is cutting a customer's hair, they either sit down (if there are empty chairs) or leave the shop (if

```
#include "prototypes.h"

#define N              5         /* number of philosophers */
#define LEFT     (i-1)%N         /* number of i's left neighbor */
#define RIGHT    (i+1)%N         /* number of i's right neighbor */
#define THINKING       0         /* philosopher is thinking */
#define HUNGRY         1         /* philosopher is trying to get forks */
#define EATING         2         /* philosopher is eating */

typedef int semaphore;          /* semaphores are a special kind of int */
int state[N];                   /* array to keep track of everyone's state */
semaphore mutex = 1;            /* mutual exclusion for critical regions */
semaphore s[N];                 /* one semaphore per philosopher */

void philosopher(int i)         /* i: which philosopher (0 to N-1) */
{
  while (TRUE) {                /* repeat forever */
        think();               /* philosopher is thinking */
        take_forks(i);         /* acquire two forks or block */
        eat();                 /* yum-yum, spaghetti */
        put_forks(i);          /* put both forks back on table */
  }
}

void take_forks(int i)          /* i: which philosopher (0 to N-1) */
{
  down(&mutex);                /* enter critical region */
  state[i] = HUNGRY;           /* record fact that philosopher i is hungry */
  test(i);                     /* try to acquire 2 forks */
  up(&mutex);                  /* exit critical region */
  down(&s[i]);                 /* block if forks were not acquired */
}

void put_forks(int i)           /* i: which philosopher (0 to N-1) */
{
  down(&mutex);                /* enter critical region */
  state[i] = THINKING;         /* philosopher has finished eating */
  test(LEFT);                  /* see if left neighbor can now eat */
  test(RIGHT);                 /* see if right neighbor can now eat */
  up(&mutex);                  /* exit critical region */
}

void test(int i)                /* i: which philosopher (0 to N-1) */
{
  if (state[i] == HUNGRY && state[LEFT] != EATING && state[RIGHT] != EATING) {
        state[i] = EATING;
        up(&s[i]);
  }
}
```

Fig. 2-20. A solution to the dining philosophers problem.

```
#include "prototypes.h"

typedef int semaphore;              /* use your imagination */

semaphore mutex = 1;                /* controls access to 'rc' */
semaphore db = 1;                   /* controls access to the data base */
int rc = 0;                         /* # of processes reading or wanting to */

void reader(void)
{
  while (TRUE) {                    /* repeat forever */
       down(&mutex);                /* get exclusive access to 'rc' */
       rc = rc + 1;                 /* one reader more now */
       if (rc == 1) down(&db);      /* if this is the first reader ... */
       up(&mutex);                  /* release exclusive access to 'rc' */
       read_data_base();            /* access the data */
       down(&mutex);                /* get exclusive access to 'rc' */
       rc = rc - 1;                 /* one reader fewer now */
       if (rc == 0) up(&db);        /* if this is the last reader ... */
       up(&mutex);                  /* release exclusive access to 'rc' */
       use_data_read();             /* noncritical section */
  }
}


void writer(void)
{
  while (TRUE) {                    /* repeat forever */
       think_up_data();             /* noncritical section */
       down(&db);                   /* get exclusive access */
       write_data_base();           /* update the data */
       up(&db);                     /* release exclusive access */
  }
}
```

Fig. 2-21. A solution to the readers and writers problem.

all chairs are full). The problem is to program the barber and the customers without getting into race conditions.

Our solution uses three semaphores: *customers*, which counts waiting customers (excluding the customer in the barber chair, who is not waiting), *barbers*, the number of barbers who are idle, waiting for customers (0 or 1), and *mutex*, which is used for mutual exclusion. We also need a variable, *waiting*, which also counts the waiting customers. It is essentially a copy of *customers*. The reason for having *waiting* is that there is no way to read the current value of a semaphore, and in this solution, a customer entering the barber shop has to count the number of waiting customers. If it is less than the number of chairs, he stays, otherwise, he leaves.

Our solution is shown in Fig. 2-23. When the barber shows up for work in the morning, he executes the procedure *Barber*, causing him to block on the semaphore *customers* until somebody arrives. He then goes to sleep as shown in Fig. 2-22.

When the first customer arrives, he executes *Customer*, starting by acquiring *mutex* to enter a critical region. If another customer enters shortly thereafter, the

Fig. 2-22. The sleeping barber.

second one will not be able to do anything until the first one has released *mutex*. The customer then checks to see if the number of waiting customers is less than the number of chairs. If not, he releases *mutex* and leaves without a haircut.

If there is an available chair, the customer increments the integer variable, *waiting*. Then it ups the semaphore *customers*, thus waking up the barber. At this point, the customer and barber are both awake. When the customer releases *mutex*, the barber grabs it, does some housekeeping, and begins the haircut.

When the haircut is over, the customer exits the procedure and leaves the shop. Unlike our earlier examples, there is no loop for the customer because getting a haircut is idempotent. The barber loops, however, and tries to get the next customer. If one is present, another haircut is given. If not, the barber goes to sleep.

2.4. PROCESS SCHEDULING

In the examples of the previous sections, we have often had situations in which two or more processes (e.g., producer and consumer) were logically runnable. When more than one process is runnable, the operating system must decide which one to

```
#include "prototypes.h"

#define CHAIRS 5                    /* # chairs for waiting customers */

typedef int semaphore;             /* use your imagination */

semaphore customers = 0;           /* # of customers waiting for service */
semaphore barbers = 0;             /* # of barbers waiting for customers */
semaphore mutex = 1;               /* for mutual exclusion */
int waiting = 0;                   /* customers are waiting (not being cut) */

void Barber(void)
{
  while (TRUE) {
        down(customers);           /* go to sleep if # of customers is 0 */
        down(mutex);               /* acquire access to 'waiting' */
        waiting = waiting - 1;     /* decrement count of waiting customers */
        up(barbers);               /* one barber is now ready to cut hair */
        up(mutex);                 /* release 'waiting' */
        cut_hair();                /* cut hair (outside critical region) */
  }
}


void Customer(void)
{
  down(mutex);                     /* enter critical region */
  if (waiting < CHAIRS) {          /* if there are no free chairs, leave */
        waiting = waiting + 1;     /* increment count of waiting customers */
        up(customers);             /* wake up barber if necessary */
        up(mutex);                 /* release access to 'waiting' */
        down(barbers);             /* go to sleep if # of free barbers is 0 */
        get_haircut();             /* be seated and be serviced */
  } else {
        up(mutex);                 /* shop is full; do not wait */
  }
}
```

Fig. 2-23. A solution to the sleeping barber problem.

run first. That part of the operating system concerned with this decision is called the **scheduler**, and the algorithm it uses is called the **scheduling algorithm**.

Back in the old days of batch systems with input in the form of card images on a magnetic tape, the scheduling algorithm was simple: just run the next job on the tape. With multi-user timesharing systems, often combined with batch jobs in the background, the scheduling algorithm is more complex. Invariably there are multiple users waiting for service, and there may well be batch or other background jobs as well. Even in pure timesharing systems there are often background jobs, such as the electronic mail system, which often is running all the time, sending or receiving mail or network news.

Before looking at specific scheduling algorithms, we should think about what the scheduler is trying to achieve. After all, the scheduler is concerned with deciding on policy, not providing a mechanism. Various criteria come to mind as to what constitutes a good scheduling algorithm. Some of the more obvious possibilities include:

1. Fairness: make sure each process gets its fair share of the CPU.

2. Efficiency: keep the CPU busy 100 percent of the time.

3. Response time: minimize response time for interactive users.

4. Turnaround: minimize the time batch users must wait for output.

5. Throughput: maximize the number of jobs processed per hour.

A little thought will show that some of these goals are contradictory. To minimize response time for interactive users, the scheduler should not run any batch jobs at all (except maybe between 3 A.M. and 6 A.M., when all the interactive users are snug in their beds). The batch users probably will not like this algorithm, however; it violates criterion 4. It can be shown (Kleinrock, 1975) that any scheduling algorithm that favors some class of jobs hurts another class of jobs. The amount of CPU time available is finite, after all. To give one user more you have to give another user less. Such is life.

A complication that schedulers have to deal with is that every process is unique and unpredictable. Some spend a lot of time waiting for file I/O, while others would use the CPU for hours at a time if given the chance. When the scheduler starts running some process, it never knows for sure how long it will be until that process blocks, either for I/O, or on a semaphore, or for some other reason. To make sure that no process runs too long, nearly all computers have an electronic timer or clock built in, which causes an interrupt periodically. A frequency of 50 or 60 times a second (called 50 or 60 **Hertz** and abbreviated **Hz**) is common, but on many computers the operating system can set the timer frequency to anything it wants. At each clock interrupt, the operating system gets to run and decide whether the currently running process should be allowed to continue, or whether it has had enough CPU time for the moment and should be suspended to give another process the CPU.

The strategy of allowing processes that are logically runnable to be temporarily suspended is called **preemptive scheduling**, and is in contrast to the **run to completion** method of the early batch systems. Run to completion is also called **nonpreemptive scheduling**. As we have seen throughout this chapter, a process can be suspended at an arbitrary instant, without warning, so another process can be run. This leads to race conditions and necessitates semaphores, event counters, monitors, messages, or some other sophisticated method for preventing them. On the other hand, a policy of letting a process run as long as it wanted to would mean that somebody computing π to a billion places could deny service to all other users indefinitely.

Thus although nonpreemptive scheduling algorithms are simple and easy to implement, they are usually not suitable for general-purpose systems with multiple competing users. On the other hand, for a dedicated system, such as a data base system, it may well be reasonable for the master process to start a child process working on a request and let it run until it completes. The difference with the general-purpose system is that all processes in the data base system are under the control of a single master, which knows what each child is going to do and about how long it will take.

2.4.1. Round Robin Scheduling

Now let us look at some specific scheduling algorithms. One of the oldest, simplest, fairest, and most widely used algorithms is **round robin**. Each process is assigned a time interval, called its **quantum**, which it is allowed to run. If the process is still running at the end of the quantum, the CPU is preempted and given to another process. If the process has blocked or finished before the quantum has elapsed, the CPU switching is done when the process blocks, of course. Round robin is easy to implement. All the scheduler needs to do is maintain a list of runnable processes, as shown in Fig. 2-24(a). When the quantum runs out on a process, it is put on the end of the list, as shown in Fig. 2-24(b).

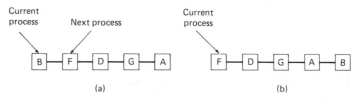

Fig. 2-24. Round robin scheduling. (a) The list of runnable processes. (b) The list of runnable processes after *B*'s quantum runs out.

The only interesting issue with round robin is the length of the quantum. Switching from one process to another requires a certain amount of time for doing the administration—saving and loading registers and memory maps, updating various tables and lists, etc. Suppose this **process switch** or **context switch**, as it is sometimes called, takes 5 msec. Also suppose that the quantum is set at 20 msec. With these parameters, after doing 20 msec of useful work, the CPU will have to spend 5 msec on process switching. Twenty percent of the CPU time will be wasted on administrative overhead.

To improve the CPU efficiency, we could set the quantum to, say, 500 msec. Now the wasted time is less than 1 percent. But consider what happens if ten interactive users hit the carriage return key at roughly the same time. Ten processes will be put on the list of runnable processes. If the CPU is idle, the first one will start immediately, the second one may not start until about 1/2 sec later, and so on. The unlucky last one may have to wait 5 sec before getting a chance, assuming all the others use their full quanta. Most users will perceive a 5-sec response to a short command as terrible.

The conclusion can be formulated as follows: setting the quantum too short causes too many process switches and lowers the CPU efficiency, but setting it too long may cause poor response to short interactive requests. A quantum around 100 msec is often a reasonable compromise.

2.4.2. Priority Scheduling

Round robin scheduling makes the implicit assumption that all processes are equally important. Frequently, the people who own and operate computer centers have different ideas on that subject. At a university computer center, the pecking order may be deans first, then professors, secretaries, janitors, and finally students. The need to take external factors into account leads to **priority scheduling**. The basic idea is straightforward: each process is assigned a priority, and the runnable process with the highest priority is allowed to run.

To prevent high-priority processes from running indefinitely, the scheduler may decrease the priority of the currently running process at each clock tick (i.e., at each clock interrupt). If this action causes its priority to drop below that of the next highest process, a process switch occurs.

Priorities can be assigned to processes statically or dynamically. On a military computer, processes started by generals might begin at priority 100, processes started by colonels at 90, majors at 80, captains at 70, lieutenants at 60, and so on. Alternatively, at a commercial computer center, high-priority jobs might cost 100 dollars an hour, medium priority 75 dollars an hour, and low priority 50 dollars an hour. The UNIX system has a command, *nice*, which allows a user to voluntarily reduce the priority of his process, in order to be nice to the other users. Nobody ever uses it.

Priorities can also be assigned dynamically by the system to achieve certain system goals. For example, some processes are highly I/O bound and spend most of their time waiting for I/O to complete. Whenever such a process wants the CPU, it should be given the CPU immediately, to let it start its next I/O request, which can then proceed in parallel with another process actually computing. Making the I/O bound process wait a long time for the CPU will just mean having it around occupying memory for an unnecessarily long time. A simple algorithm for giving good service to I/O bound processes is to set the priority to $1/f$, where f is the fraction of the last quantum that a process used. A process that used only 2 msec of its 100 msec quantum would get priority 50, while a process that ran 50 msec before blocking would get priority 2, and a process that used the whole quantum would get priority 1.

It is often convenient to group processes into priority classes and use priority scheduling among the classes but round robin scheduling within each class. Figure 2-25 shows a system with four priority classes. The scheduling algorithm is as follows: as long as there are runnable processes in priority class 4, just run each one for one quantum, round robin fashion, and never bother with lower priority classes. If priority class 4 is empty, then run the class 3 processes round robin. If classes 4 and 3 are both empty, then run class 2 round robin, and so on. If priorities are not adjusted from time to time, lower priority classes may all starve to death.

2.4.3. Multiple Queues

One of the earliest priority schedulers was in CTSS (Corbato et al., 1962). CTSS had the problem that process switching was very slow because the 7094 could hold only one process in memory. Each switch meant swapping the current process to

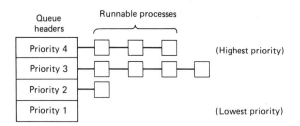

Fig. 2-25. A scheduling algorithm with four priority classes.

disk and reading in a new one from disk. The CTSS designers quickly realized that it was more efficient to give CPU-bound processes a large quantum once in a while, rather than giving them small quanta frequently (to reduce swapping). On the other hand, giving all processes a large quantum would mean poor response time, as we have already seen. Their solution was to set up priority classes. Processes in the highest class were run for one quantum. Processes in the next highest class were run for two quanta. Processes in the next class were run for four quanta, and so on. Whenever a process used up all the quanta allocated to it, it was moved down one class.

As an example, consider a process that needed to compute continuously for 100 quanta. It would initially be given one quantum, then swapped out. Next time it would get two quanta before being swapped out. On succeeding runs it would get 4, 8, 16, 32, and 64 quanta, although it would have used only 37 of the final 64 quanta to complete its work. Only 7 swaps would be needed (including the initial load) instead of 100 with a pure round robin algorithm. Furthermore, as the process sank deeper and deeper into the priority queues, it would be run less and less frequently, saving the CPU for short, interactive processes.

The following policy was adopted to prevent a process that needed to run for a long time when it first started, but became interactive later, from being punished forever. Whenever a carriage return was typed at a terminal, the process belonging to that terminal was moved to the highest priority class, on the assumption that it was about to become interactive. One fine day some user with a heavily CPU-bound process discovered that just sitting at the terminal and typing carriage returns at random every few seconds did wonders for his response time. He told all his friends. Moral of the story: getting it right in practice is much harder than getting it right in principle.

Many other algorithms have been used for assigning processes to priority classes. For example, the influential XDS 940 system (Lampson, 1968), built at Berkeley, had four priority classes, called terminal, I/O, short quantum, and long quantum. When a process that was waiting for terminal input was finally awakened, it went into the highest priority class (terminal). When a process waiting for a disk block became ready, it went into the second class. When a process was still running when its quantum ran out, it was initially placed in the third class. However, if a process used up its quantum too many times in a row without blocking for terminal or other

I/O, it was moved down to the bottom queue. Many other systems use something similar to favor interactive users.

2.4.4. Shortest Job First

Most of the above algorithms were designed for interactive systems. Now let us look at one that is especially appropriate for batch jobs for which the run times are known in advance. In an insurance company, for example, people can predict quite accurately how long it will take to run a batch of 1000 claims, since similar work is done every day. When several equally important jobs are sitting in the input queue waiting to be started, the scheduler should use **shortest job first**. Look at Fig. 2-26. Here we find four jobs A, B, C, and D, with run times of 8, 4, 4, and 4 minutes, respectively. By running them in that order, the turnaround time for A is 8 minutes, for B is 12 minutes, for C is 16 minutes, and for D is 20 minutes, for an average of 14 minutes.

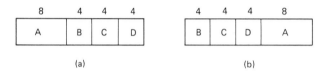

Fig. 2-26. An example of shortest job first scheduling.

Now let us consider running these four jobs using shortest job first, as shown in Fig. 2-26(b). The turnaround times are now 4, 8, 12, and 20 minutes, for an average of 11 minutes. Shortest job first is provably optimal. Consider the case of four jobs, with run times of a, b, c, and d, respectively. The first job finishes at time a, the second finishes at time $a+b$, and so on. The mean turnaround time is $(4a + 3b + 2c + d)/4$. It is clear that a contributes more to the average than the other times, so it should be the shortest job, with b next, then c and finally d as the longest as it affects only its own turnaround time. The same argument applies equally well to any number of jobs.

Because shortest job first always produces the minimum average response time, it would be nice if it could be used for interactive processes as well. To a certain extent, it can be. Interactive processes generally follow the pattern of wait for command, execute command, wait for command, execute command, and so on. If we regard the execution of each command as a separate "job," then we could minimize overall response time by running the shortest one first. The only problem is figuring out which of the currently runnable processes is the shortest one.

One approach is to make estimates based on past behavior and run the process with the shortest estimated running time. Suppose the estimated time per command for some terminal is T_0. Now suppose its next run is measured to be T_1. We could update our estimate by taking a weighted sum of these two numbers, that is, $aT_0 + (1 - a)T_1$. Through the choice of a we can decide to have the estimation process forget old runs quickly, or remember them for a long time. With $a = 1/2$, we get successive estimates of

$$T_0, \quad T_0/2 + T_1/2, \quad T_0/4 + T_1/4 + T_2/2, \quad T_0/8 + T_1/8 + T_2/4 + T_3/2$$

Thus, after three new runs, the weight of T_0 in the new estimate has dropped to 1/8.

The technique of estimating the next value in a series by taking the weighted average of the current measured value and the previous estimate is sometimes called **aging**. It is applicable to many situations where a prediction must be made based on previous values. Aging is especially easy to implement when $a = 1/2$. All that is needed is to add the new value to the current estimate and divide the sum by 2 (by shifting it right 1 bit).

It is worth pointing out that the shortest job first algorithm is only optimal when all the jobs are available simultaneously. As a counterexample, consider five jobs, A through E, with run times of 2, 4, 1, 1, and 1, respectively. Their arrival times are 0, 0, 3, 3, and 3.

Initially, only A or B can be chosen, since the other three jobs have not arrived yet. Using shortest job first we will run the jobs in the order A, B, C, D, E, for an average wait of 4.6. However, running them in the order B, C, D, E, A has an average wait of 4.4.

2.4.5. Guaranteed Scheduling

A completely different approach to scheduling is to make real promises to the user about performance and then live up to them. One promise that is realistic to make and easy to live up to is this: If there are n users logged in while you are working, you will receive about $1/n$ of the CPU power.

To make good on this promise, the system must keep track of how much CPU time a user has had for all his processes since login, and also how long each user has been logged in. It then computes the amount of CPU each user is entitled to, namely the time since login divided by n. Since the amount of CPU time each user has actually had is also known, it is straightforward to compute the ratio of actual CPU had to CPU time entitled. A ratio of 0.5 means that a process has only had half of what it should have had, and a ratio of 2.0 means that a process has had twice as much as it was entitled to. The algorithm is then to run the process with the lowest ratio until its ratio has moved above its closest competitor.

A similar idea can be applied to real-time systems, in which there are absolute deadlines that must be met. Here one looks for the process in greatest danger of missing its deadline, and runs it first. A process that must finish in 10 seconds gets priority over one that must finish in 10 minutes.

2.4.6. Policy versus Mechanism

Up until now, we have tacitly assumed that all the processes in the system belong to different users and are thus competing for the CPU. While this is often true, sometimes it happens that one process has many children running under its control. For example, a data base management system process may have many children. Each child might be working on a different request, or each one might have some specific function to perform (query parsing, disk access, etc.). It is entirely possible that the main process has an excellent idea of which of its children are the most important (or time critical) and which the least. Unfortunately, none of the schedulers discussed above accept any input from user processes about scheduling decisions. As a result, the scheduler rarely makes the best choice.

The solution to this problem is to separate the **scheduling mechanism** from the **scheduling policy**. What this means is that the scheduling algorithm is parametrized in some way, but the parameters can be filled in by user processes. Let us consider the data base example again. Suppose that the kernel uses a priority scheduling algorithm, but provides a system call by which a process can set (and change) the priorities of its children. In this way the parent can control in detail how its children are scheduled, even though it itself does not do the scheduling. Here the mechanism is in the kernel but the policy is set by a user process.

2.4.7. Two-level Scheduling

Up until now we have more or less assumed that all runnable processes are in main memory. If insufficient main memory is available, some of the runnable processes will have to be kept on the disk. This situation has major implications for scheduling, since the process switching time to bring in and run a process from disk is orders of magnitude more than switching to a process already in main memory.

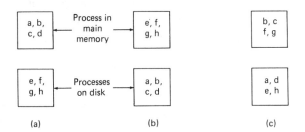

Fig. 2-27. A two-level scheduler must move processes between disk and memory, and also choose processes to run from among those in memory. Three different instants of time are represented by (a), (b), and (c) .

A more practical way of dealing with swapped out processes is to use a two-level scheduler. Some subset of the runnable processes is first loaded into main memory, as shown in Fig. 2-27(a). The scheduler then restricts itself to only choosing processes from this subset for a while. Periodically, a higher-level scheduler is invoked to remove processes that have been in memory long enough and to load processes that have been on disk too long. Once the change has been made, as in Fig. 2-27(b), the lower-level scheduler again restricts itself to only running processes that are actually in memory. Thus, the lower-level scheduler is concerned with making a choice among the runnable processes that are in memory at that moment, while the higher-level scheduler is concerned with shuttling processes back and forth between memory and disk.

Among the criteria that the higher-level scheduler could use to make its decisions are the following ones:

1. How long has it been since the process was swapped in or out?

2. How much CPU time has the process had recently?

3. How big is the process? (Small ones do not get in the way.)

4. How high is the priority of the process?

Again here we could use round robin, priority scheduling, or any of various other methods.

2.5. SUMMARY

To hide the effects of interrupts, operating systems provide a conceptual model consisting of sequential processes running in parallel. Each process has its own state, and can be thought of as running on its own virtual processor.

Sometimes processes have to interact, for example, sharing a common buffer area. This interaction can lead to race conditions, situations in which the exact timing determines the result. Race conditions lead to behavior that is not reproducible.

To avoid race conditions, we introduced the concept of a critical region, which is a section of code in which a process is doing something to the shared state, and does not want other processes working there too. Critical sections provide mutual exclusion.

Processes can communicate with each other using interprocess communication primitives. These primitives are used to ensure that no two processes are ever in their critical sections at the same time, that is, to guarantee mutual exclusion. A process can be running, runnable, or blocked, and can change state when it or another process executes one of the interprocess communication primitives.

Various interprocess communication primitives have been proposed. Among these are semaphores, monitors, event counters, and message passing. Theoretically, they are equivalent, in that each one can be used to implement the others. In actual systems, semaphores and message passing are the most widely used.

A number of classical problems have been solved using these and other primitives. In fact, the first test of any new proposed primitive is to see how well it solves the classical problems. These include the producer-consumer, dining philosophers, readers and writers, and sleeping barber problems. Even with proper primitives, care has to be taken to avoid errors and deadlocks.

Many scheduling algorithms are known. The job of a scheduling algorithm is to determine which process to run next, taking into consideration factors such as response time, efficiency, and fairness. Well-known scheduling algorithms include round robin, priority scheduling, multilevel queues, shortest job first, and guaranteed scheduling. In some systems, the scheduling mechanism and the scheduling policy are split, allowing increased flexibility.

PROBLEMS

1. Suppose you were to design an advanced computer architecture that did process switching in hardware, instead of having interrupts. What information would the CPU need? Describe how the hardware process switching might work.

2. What is a race condition?

3. Explain the difference between busy waiting and blocking.

4. Does the busy waiting solution using the *turn* variable (Fig. 2-7) work when the two processes are running on two CPUs, sharing a common memory?

5. Consider a computer that does not have a TEST AND SET LOCK instruction, but does have an instruction to swap the contents of a register and a memory word in a single indivisible action. Can that be used to write a routine *enter_region* such as the one found in Fig. 2-8?

6. It is not uncommon for a computer to have and use both a TSL instruction and another synchronization primitive, such as semaphores or monitors. These two types play a different role, however, and do not compete with each other. Explain why this is so.

7. Figure 2-10 has a fatal race condition discussed in the text, namely, if either process decides to go to sleep and is descheduled just before it calls *sleep*, a wakeup can be lost. Actually, there is a second race condition in the program as well. What is it? (Hint: look at the variable *count*.)

8. Give a sketch of how an operating system that can disable interrupts could implement semaphores.

9. In Sec. 2.2.4, a situation with a high-priority process, H, and a low-priority process, L, was described, which led to H looping forever. Does the same problem occur if round robin scheduling is used instead of priority scheduling? Discuss.

10. Synchronization within monitors uses condition variables and two special operations, WAIT and SIGNAL. A more general form of synchronization would be to have a single primitive, WAITUNTIL that had an arbitrary Boolean predicate as parameter. Thus, one could say, for example,

WAITUNTIL $x < 0$ **or** $y + z < n$

The SIGNAL primitive would no longer be needed. This scheme is clearly more general than that of Hoare or Brinch Hansen, but it is not used. Why not? (Hint: think about the implementation.)

11. A fast food restaurant has four kinds of employees: (1) order takers, who take customers' orders; (2) cooks, who prepare the food; (3) packaging specialists, who stuff the food into bags; and (4) cashiers, who give the bags to customers and take their money. Each employee can be regarded as a communicating sequential process. What form of interprocess communication do they use?

12. Suppose we have a message-passing system using mailboxes. When sending to a full mailbox or trying to receive from an empty one, a process does not block. Instead, it gets an error code back. The process responds to the error code by just trying again, over and over, until it succeeds. Does this scheme lead to race conditions?

13. The implementation of monitors using semaphores did not use an explicit linked list of blocked processes, whereas the implementation of semaphores using monitors did. Explain. (Hint: think about the differences between semaphores and condition variables.)

14. In the solution to the dining philosophers problem (Fig. 2-20), why is the state variable set to *HUNGRY* in the procedure *take_forks*?

15. Consider the procedure *put_forks* in Fig. 2-20. Suppose the variable *state*[*i*] was set to *THINKING after* the two calls to *test*, rather than *before*. How would this change affect the solution for the case of 3 philosophers? For 100 philosophers?

16. The readers and writers problem can be formulated in several ways with regard to which category of processes can be started when. Carefully describe three different variations of the problem, each one favoring (or not favoring) some category of processes. For each variation, specify what happens when a reader or a writer becomes ready to access the data base, and what happens when a process is finished using the data base.

17. Does the solution to the sleeping barber problem formulated in Fig. 2-23 generalize to multiple barbers?

18. The CDC 6600 computer could handle up to 10 I/O processes simultaneously using an interesting form of round robin scheduling called **processor sharing**. A process switch occurred after each instruction, so instruction 1 came from process 1, instruction 2 came from process 2, etc. The process switching was done by special hardware, and the overhead was zero. If a process needed T sec to complete in the absence of competition, how much time would it need if processor sharing was used with n processes?

19. Round robin schedulers normally maintain a list of all runnable processes, with each process occurring exactly once in the list. What would happen if a process occurred twice in the list? Can you think of any reason for allowing this?

20. Measurements of a certain system have shown that the average process runs for a time T before blocking on I/O. A process switch requires a time S, which is effectively wasted (overhead). For round robin scheduling with quantum Q, give a formula for the CPU efficiency for each of the following.

    (a) $Q = \infty$
    (b) $Q > T$
    (c) $S < Q < T$
    (d) $Q = S$
    (e) Q nearly 0

21. Most round robin schedulers use a fixed size quantum. Give an argument in favor of a small quantum. Now give one in favor of a large quantum.

22. Five batch jobs *A* through *E*, arrive at a computer center at almost the same time. They have estimated running times of 10, 6, 2, 4, and 8 minutes. Their (externally determined) priorities are 3, 5, 2, 1, and 4, respectively, with 5 being the highest priority. For each of the following scheduling algorithms, determine the mean process turnaround time. Ignore process switching overhead.

  (a) Round robin.
  (b) Priority scheduling.
  (c) First-come, first served (run in order 10, 6, 2, 4, 8).
  (d) Shortest job first.

For (a), assume that the system is multiprogrammed, and that each job gets its fair share of the CPU. For (b) through (d) assume that only one job at a time runs, until it finishes. All jobs are completely CPU bound.

23. Five jobs are waiting to be run. Their expected run times are 9, 6, 3, 5, and *X*. In what order should they be run to minimize average response time? (Your answer will depend on *X*.)

24. The aging algorithm with $a = 1/2$ is being used to predict run times. The previous four runs, from oldest to most recent are 40, 20, 40, and 15 msec. What is the prediction of the next time?

25. Explain why two-level scheduling is commonly used.

26. Assume that you have an operating system that provides semaphores. Implement a message system. Write the procedures for sending and receiving messages.

27. Solve the dining philosophers problem using monitors instead of semaphores.

28. Solve the sleeping barber problem for the case of a shop with multiple barbers.

29. Another classic problem is the cigarette smoker's problem (Patil, 1971). Three chain smokers are together in a room with a vendor of cigarette supplies. To make and use a cigarette, each smoker needs three ingredients: tobacco, paper, and matches, all of which the vendor has in ample supply. One smoker has his own tobacco, a second has his own paper, and the third has her own matches. The action begins when the vendor puts two of the ingredients on a table, to allow one of the smokers to commit an unhealthy act. When the appropriate smoker is done, he or she wakes up the vendor, who then puts down two more ingredients (at random), thus unblocking another smoker. Try to write programs for the smokers and the agent that solve this problem. What problems do you encounter? (The author *very* seriously considered rephrasing this problem with carpenters needing hammers, nails and wood, or gardeners needing seeds, earth, and manure, but even in computer science there is such a thing as tradition.)

30. Another classical problem is Lamport's (1974) bakery problem. In this problem, a bakery has a variety of breads and cakes being sold by *n* salespeople. Every entering customer takes a number. Until that number is called, the customer waits. Whenever a salesperson is free, the next number is called. Write a procedure for the salespeople to execute and another one for the customers.

3

MEMORY MANAGEMENT

Memory is an important resource that must be carefully managed. While the average home computer nowadays has ten times as much memory as the IBM 7094, the largest computer in the world in the early 1960s, programs are getting bigger just as fast as memories. To paraphrase Parkinson's law, "Programs expand to fill the memory available to hold them." In this chapter we will study how operating systems manage their memory.

The part of the operating system that manages memory is called the **memory manager**. Its job is to keep track of which parts of memory are in use and which parts are not in use, to allocate memory to processes when they need it and deallocate it when they are done, and to manage swapping between main memory and disk when main memory is not big enough to hold all the processes.

In this chapter we will investigate a number of different memory management schemes, ranging from very simple to highly sophisticated. We will start at the beginning and look first at the simplest possible memory management system, and then gradually progress to more and more elaborate ones.

3.1. MEMORY MANAGEMENT WITHOUT SWAPPING OR PAGING

Memory management systems can be divided into two classes: those that move processes back and forth between main memory and disk during execution (swapping and paging), and those that do not. The latter are simpler, so we will study them first. Later in the chapter we will examine swapping and paging. Throughout this chapter the reader should keep in mind that swapping and paging are largely artifacts caused by the lack of sufficient main memory to hold all the programs at once. As main memory gets cheaper, the arguments in favor of one kind of memory management scheme or another may become obsolete.

3.1.1. Monoprogramming without Swapping or Paging

The simplest possible memory management scheme is to have just one process in memory at a time, and to allow that process to use all of memory. The user loads the entire memory with a program from disk or tape, and it takes over the whole machine. Although this approach was common up until about 1960, it is not used any more, not even on inexpensive home computers, mostly because it implies that every process must contain within it a device driver for each I/O device it uses.

The usual technique used on simple microcomputers is shown in Fig. 3-1. The memory is divided up between the operating system and a single user process. The operating system may be at the bottom of memory in RAM (Random Access Memory), as shown in Fig. 3-1(a), or it may be in ROM (Read Only Memory) at the top of memory, as shown in Fig. 3-1(b), or the device drivers may be at the top of memory in a ROM and the rest of the operating system in RAM at the bottom of memory, as shown in Fig. 3-1(c). The IBM PC, for example, uses the model of Fig. 3-1(c), with the device driver ROM located in the highest 8K block of the 1M address space. The program in the ROM is called the **BIOS** (Basic Input Output System).

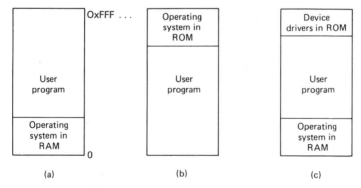

Fig. 3-1. Three ways of organizing memory with an operating system and one user process.

When the system is organized in this way, only one process at a time can be running. The user types a command on the terminal, and the operating system loads the requested program from disk into memory and executes it. When the process finishes, the operating system types a prompt character on the terminal and then waits for a command from the terminal to load another process, overwriting the first one.

3.1.2. Multiprogramming and Memory Usage

Although monoprogramming is sometimes used on small computers, on larger computers with multiple users it is rarely used. In Chap. 2 we already saw one reason for multiprogramming—to make it easier to program an application by splitting it up into two or more processes. Another motivation is that large computers often provide interactive service to several people simultaneously, which requires the ability to have more than one process in memory at once in order to get reasonable performance. Loading a process, running it for 100 msec, and then spending a few hundred milliseconds swapping it to disk is inefficient. But if the quantum is set too much above 100 msec, the response time will be poor.

Another reason for multiprogramming a computer (also applicable to batch systems) is that most processes spend a substantial fraction of their time waiting for disk I/O to complete. It is common for a process to sit in a loop reading data blocks from a disk file and then doing some computation on the contents of the blocks read. If it takes 40 msec to read a block, and the computation takes 10 msec, with monoprogramming the CPU will be idle waiting for the disk 80 percent of the time.

Modeling Multiprogramming

When multiprogramming is used, the CPU utilization can be improved. Crudely put, if the average process computes only 20 percent of the time it is sitting in memory, with five processes in memory at once, the CPU should be busy all the time. This model is unrealistically optimistic, however, since it assumes that all five processes will never be waiting for I/O at the same time.

A better model is to look at CPU usage from a probabilistic viewpoint. Suppose that a process spends a fraction p of its time in I/O wait state. With n processes in memory at once, the probability that all n processes are waiting for I/O (in which case the CPU will be idle) is p^n. The CPU utilization is then given by the formula

$$\text{CPU utilization} = 1 - p^n$$

Figure 3-2 shows the CPU utilization as a function of n, which is called the **degree of multiprogramming**.

From the figure it is clear that if processes spend 80 percent of their time waiting for I/O, at least 10 processes must be in memory at once to get the CPU waste below 10 percent. When you realize that an interactive process waiting for a user to type something at a terminal is in I/O wait state, it should be clear that I/O wait times of 80 percent and more are not unusual. But even in batch systems, processes doing a lot of disk or tape I/O will often have this percentage or more.

For the sake of complete accuracy, it should be pointed out that the probabilistic model just described is only an approximation. It implicitly assumes that all n processes are independent, meaning that it is quite acceptable for a system with five processes in memory to have three running and two waiting. But with a single CPU, we cannot have three processes running at once, so a process becoming ready while

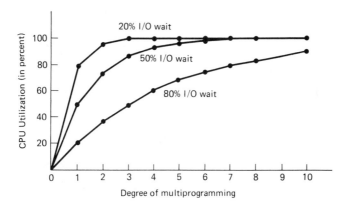

Fig. 3-2. CPU utilization as a function of the number of processes in memory.

the CPU is busy will have to wait. Thus the processes are not independent. A more accurate model can be constructed using queueing theory, but the point we are making—multiprogramming lets processes use the CPU when it would be otherwise idle—is, of course, still valid, even if the true curves of Fig. 3-2 are slightly different.

Even though the model of Fig. 3-2 is simple-minded, it can still be used to make specific, although approximate, predictions about CPU performance. Suppose, for example, that a computer has 1M of memory, with the operating system taking up 200K and each user program also taking up 200K. These sizes allow four user programs to be in memory at once. With an 80 percent average I/O wait, we have a CPU utilization (ignoring operating system overhead) of about 60 percent. Adding another megabyte of memory allows the system to go from four-way multiprogramming to nine-way multiprogramming, thus raising the CPU utilization to 87 percent. In other words, the second megabyte will raise the throughput by 45 percent.

Adding a third megabyte would only increase CPU utilization from 87 percent to 96 percent, thus raising the throughput by only another 10 percent. Using this model the computer's owner might decide that a second megabyte was a good investment, but that a third megabyte was not.

Analysis of Multiprogramming System Performance

This model can also be used to analyze batch systems. Consider, for example, a computer center whose jobs average 80 percent I/O wait time. On a particular morning, four jobs are submitted as shown in Fig. 3-3(a). The first job, arriving at 10:00 A.M., requires 4 minutes of CPU time. With 80 percent I/O wait, the job uses only 12 seconds of CPU time for each minute it is sitting in memory, even if no other jobs are competing with it for the CPU. The other 48 seconds are spent waiting for I/O to complete. Thus the job will have to sit in memory for at least 20 minutes in order to get 4 minutes of CPU work done, even in the absence of competition for the CPU.

From 10:00 A.M. to 10:10 A.M., job 1 is all by itself in memory and gets 2 minutes

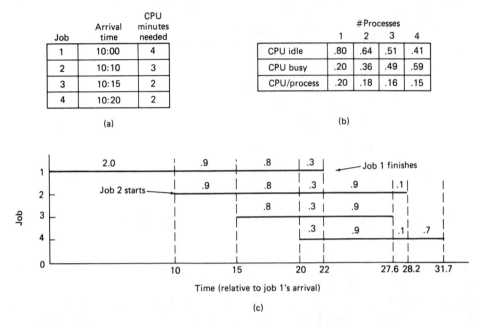

Fig. 3-3. (a) Arrival and work requirements of four jobs. (b) CPU utilization for 1 to 4 jobs with 80 percent I/O wait. (c) Sequence of events as jobs arrive and finish. The numbers above the horizontal lines show how much CPU time, in minutes, each job gets in each interval.

of work done. When job 2 arrives at 10:10 A.M., the CPU utilization increases from 0.20 to 0.36, due to the higher degree of multiprogramming (see Fig. 3-2). However, with round robin scheduling, each job gets half of the CPU, so each job gets 0.18 minutes of CPU work done for each minute it is in memory. Notice that the addition of a second job costs the first job only 10 percent of its performance (from 0.20 to 0.18 minutes of CPU per minute of real time).

At 10:15 A.M. the third job arrives. At this point job 1 has received 2.9 minutes of CPU and job 2 has had 0.9 minutes of CPU. With three-way multiprogramming, each job gets 0.16 minutes of CPU time per minute of real time, as shown in Fig. 3-3(b). From 10:15 A.M. to 10:20 A.M. each of the three jobs gets 0.8 minutes of CPU time. At 10:20 A.M. a fourth job arrives. Fig. 3-3(c) shows the complete sequence of events.

3.1.3. Multiprogramming with Fixed Partitions

By now it should be clear that it is often useful to have more than one process in memory at once. The question is then: "How should memory be organized to achieve this goal?" The easiest way is simply to divide memory up into *n* (possibly unequal) partitions. This partitioning can, for example, be done manually by the operator when the system is started up.

When a job arrives, it can be put into the input queue for the smallest partition large enough to hold it. Since the partitions are fixed in this scheme, any space in a partition not used by a job is lost. In Fig. 3-4(a) we see how this system of fixed partitions and separate input queues looks.

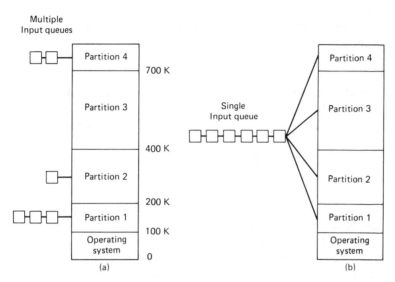

Fig. 3-4. (a) Fixed memory partitions with separate input queues for each partition. (b) Fixed memory partitions with a single input queue.

The disadvantage of sorting the incoming jobs into separate queues becomes apparent when the queue for a large partition is empty but the queue for a small partition is full, as is the case for partitions 1 and 4 in Fig. 3-4(a). An alternative organization is to maintain a single queue as in Fig. 3-4(b). Whenever a partition becomes free, the job closest to the front of the queue that fits in it could be loaded into the empty partition and run. Since it is undesirable to waste a large partition on a small job, a different strategy is to search the whole input queue whenever a partition becomes free and pick the largest job that fits. Note that the latter algorithm discriminates against small jobs as being unworthy of having a whole partition, whereas usually it is desirable to give the smallest jobs (assumed to be interactive jobs) the best service, not the worst.

One way out is to have at least one small partition around. Such a partition will allow small jobs to run without having to allocate a large partition for them.

Another approach is to have a rule stating that a job that is eligible to run not be skipped over more than k times. Each time it is skipped over, it gets one point. When it has acquired k points, it may not be skipped again.

This system, with fixed partitions set up by the operator in the morning and not changed thereafter, was used by OS/360 on large IBM mainframes for many years. It was called MFT (Multiprogramming with a Fixed number of Tasks or OS/MFT). It is simple to understand and equally simple to implement: incoming jobs are queued until a suitable partition is available, at which time the job is loaded into that partition and run until it terminates.

Relocation and Protection

Multiprogramming introduces two essential problems that must be solved—relocation and protection. Look at Fig. 3-4. From the figure it is clear that different jobs will be run at different addresses. When a program is linked (i.e., the main program, user-written procedures, and library procedures are combined into a single address space), the linker must know at what address the program will begin in memory.

For example, suppose that the first instruction is a call to a procedure at relative address 100 within the binary file produced by the linker. If this program is loaded in partition 1, that instruction will jump to absolute address 100, which is inside the operating system. What is needed is a call to 100K + 100. If the program is loaded into partition 2, it must be carried out as a call to 200K + 100, and so on. This problem is known as the **relocation** problem.

One possible solution is to actually modify the instructions as the program is loaded into memory. Programs loaded into partition 1 have 100K added to each address, programs loaded into partition 2 have 200K added to addresses, and so forth. To perform relocation during loading like this, the linker must include in the binary program a list or bit map telling which program words are addresses to be relocated and which are opcodes, constants, or other items that must not be relocated. OS/MFT worked this way. Some microcomputers also work like this.

Relocation during loading does not solve the protection problem. A malicious program can always construct a new instruction and jump to it. Because programs in this system use absolute memory addresses rather than addresses relative to a register, there is no way to stop a program from building an instruction that reads or writes any word in memory. In multiuser systems, it is undesirable to let processes read and write memory belonging to other users.

The solution that IBM chose for protecting the 360 was to divide memory into blocks of 2K bytes and assign a 4-bit protection code to each block. The PSW contained a 4-bit key. The 360 hardware trapped any attempt by a running process to access memory whose protection code differed from the PSW key. Since only the operating system could change the protection codes and key, user processes were prevented from interfering with one another and with the operating system itself.

An alternative solution to both the relocation and protection problems is to equip the machine with two special hardware registers, called the **base** and **limit** registers. When a process is scheduled, the base register is loaded with the address of the start of its partition, and the limit register is loaded with the length of the partition. Every memory address generated automatically has the base register contents added to it before being sent to memory. Thus if the base register is 100K, a CALL 100 instruction is effectively turned into a CALL 100K+100 instruction, without the instruction itself being modified. Addresses are also checked against the limit register to make sure that they do not attempt to address memory outside the current partition. The hardware protects the base and limit registers to prevent user programs from modifying them. The IBM PC uses a weaker version of this scheme—it has base registers (the segment registers), but no limit registers.

An additional advantage of using a base register for relocation is that a program can be moved in memory after it has started execution. After it has been moved, all that needs to be done to make it ready to run is change the value of the base register. When the relocation is done by modifying the program as it is loaded, it cannot be moved without going through the entire modification process again.

3.2. SWAPPING

With a batch system, organizing memory into fixed partitions is simple and effective. As long as enough jobs can be kept in memory to keep the CPU busy all the time, there is no reason to use anything more complicated. With timesharing, the situation is different: there are normally more users than there is memory to hold all their processes, so it is necessary to keep excess processes on disk. To run these processes, they must be brought into main memory, of course. Moving processes from main memory to disk and back is called **swapping**, and is the subject of the following sections.

3.2.1. Multiprogramming with Variable Partitions

In principle, a swapping system could be based on fixed partitions. Whenever a process blocked, it could be moved to the disk and another process brought into its partition from the disk. In practice, fixed partitions are unattractive when memory is scarce because too much of it is wasted by programs that are smaller than their partitions. A different memory management algorithm is used instead. It is known as **variable partitions**.

When variable partitions are used, the number and size of the processes in memory vary dynamically throughout the day. Figure 3-5 shows how variable partitions work. Initially only process *A* is in memory. Then processes *B* and *C* are created or swapped in from disk. In Fig. 3-5(d) *A* terminates or is swapped out to disk. Then *D* comes in and *B* goes out. Finally *E* comes in.

The main difference between the fixed partitions of Fig. 3-4 and the variable partitions of Fig. 3-5 is that the number, location, and size of the partitions vary dynamically in the latter as processes come and go, whereas they are fixed in the former. The flexibility of not being tied to a fixed number of partitions that may be too large or too small improves memory utilization but it also complicates allocating and deallocating memory, as well as keeping track of it.

It is possible to combine all the holes into one big one by moving all the processes downward as far as possible. This technique is known as **memory compaction**. It is usually not done because it requires a lot of CPU time. For example, on a 1 megabyte machine that can copy 1 byte per microsec (1 megabyte/sec), it takes 1 sec to compact all of memory. The old CDC Cybers compacted, however, because they had special hardware and could compact at a rate of 40 megabytes/sec.

A point that is worth making concerns how much memory should be allocated for a process when it is created or swapped in. If processes are created with a fixed size

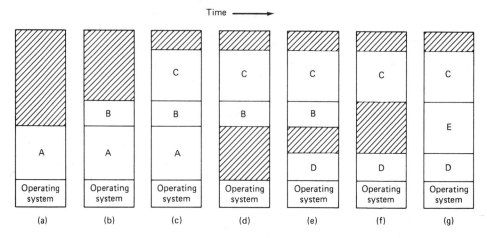

Fig. 3-5. Memory allocation changes as processes come into memory and leave it. The shaded regions are unused memory.

that never changes, then the allocation is simple: you allocate exactly what is needed, no more and no less.

If, however, processes' data segments can grow, for example, by dynamically allocating memory from a heap, as in many programming languages, a problem occurs whenever a process tries to grow. If a hole is adjacent to the process, it can be allocated and the process allowed to grow into the hole. On the other hand, if the process is adjacent to another process, the growing process will either have to be moved to a hole in memory large enough for it, or one or more processes will have to be swapped out to create a large enough hole. If a process cannot grow in memory and the swap area on the disk is full, the process will have to wait or be killed.

If it is expected that most processes will grow as they run, it is probably a good idea to allocate a little extra memory whenever a process is swapped in or moved, to reduce the overhead associated with moving or swapping processes that no longer fit in their allocated memory. However, when swapping processes to disk, only the memory actually in use should be swapped; it is wasteful to swap the extra memory as well. In Fig. 3-6(a) we see a memory configuration in which space for growth has been allocated to two processes.

If processes can have two growing segments, for example, the data segment being used as a heap and the stack, an alternative arrangement suggests itself, namely that of Fig. 3-6(b). In this figure we see that each process has a stack at the top of its allocated memory growing downward, and a data segment just beyond the program text, growing upward. The memory between them can be used for either segment. If it runs out, either the process will have to be moved to a hole with enough space, swapped out of memory until a large enough hole can be created, or killed.

In general terms, there are three ways that operating systems use to keep track of memory usage: bit maps, lists, and buddy systems. In the following sections we will look at each of these three methods in turn.

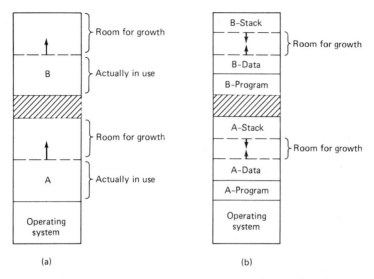

Fig. 3-6. (a) Allocating space for a growing data segment. (b) Allocating space for a growing stack and a growing data segment.

3.2.2. Memory Management with Bit Maps

With a bit map, memory is divided up into allocation units, perhaps as small as a few words and perhaps as large as several kilobytes. Corresponding to each allocation unit is a bit in the bit map, which is 0 if the unit is free and 1 if it is occupied (or vice versa). Figure 3-7 shows part of memory and the corresponding bit map.

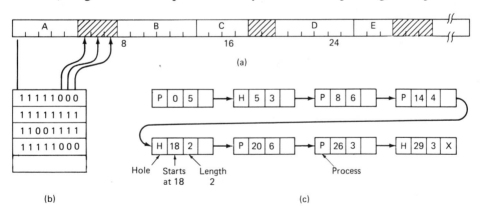

Fig. 3-7. (a) A part of memory with five processes and 3 holes. The tick marks show the memory allocation units. The shaded regions (0 in the bit map) are free. (b) The corresponding bit map. (c) The same information as a linked list.

The size of the allocation unit is an important design issue. The smaller the allocation unit, the larger the bit map. However, even with an allocation unit as small as 4 bytes, 32 bits of memory will require only 1 bit of the map. A memory of $32n$ bits will use *n* map bits, so the bit map will take up only 1/33 of memory. If the allocation unit is chosen large, the bit map will be small, but appreciable memory may be wasted in the last unit if the process size is not an exact multiple of the allocation unit.

A bit map provides a simple way to keep track of memory words in a fixed amount of memory because the size of the bit map depends only on the size of memory and the size of the allocation unit. The main problem with it is that when it has been decided to bring a *k* unit process into memory, the memory manager must search the bit map to find a run of *k* consecutive 0 bits in the map. Searching a bit map for a run of a given length is a slow operation, so in practice, bit maps are not often used.

3.2.3. Memory Management with Linked Lists

Another way of keeping track of memory is maintaining a linked list of allocated and free memory segments, where a segment is either a process or a hole between two processes. The memory of Fig. 3-7(a) is represented in Fig. 3-7(c) as a linked list of segments. Each entry in the list specifies a hole (H) or process (P), the address at which it starts, the length, and a pointer to the next entry.

In this example, the segment list is kept sorted by address. Sorting this way has the advantage that when a process terminates or is swapped out, updating the list is straightforward. A terminating process normally has two neighbors (except when it is at the very top or bottom of memory). These may be either processes or holes, leading to the four combinations of Fig. 3-8. In Fig. 3-8(a) updating the list requires replacing a P by an H. In Fig. 3-8(b) and Fig. 3-8(c), two entries are coalesced into one, and the list becomes one entry shorter. In Fig. 3-8(d), three entries are merged and two items are removed from the list. Since the process table slot for the terminating process will normally point to the list entry for the process itself, it may be more convenient to have the list as a double-linked list, rather than the single-linked list of Fig. 3-7(c). This structure makes it easier to find the previous entry and to see if a merge is possible.

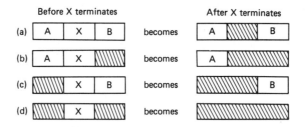

Fig. 3-8. Four neighbor combinations for the terminating process, *X*.

When the processes and holes are kept on a list sorted by address, several algorithms can be used to allocate memory for a newly created or swapped in process. We assume that the memory manager knows how much memory to allocate. The simplest algorithm is **first fit**. The memory manager scans along the list of segments until it finds a hole that is big enough. The hole is then broken up into two pieces, one for the process and one for the unused memory, except in the unlikely case of an exact fit. First fit is a fast algorithm because it searches as little as possible.

A minor variation of first fit is **next fit**. It works the same way as first fit, except that it keeps track of where it is when it finds a suitable hole. The next time it is called, it starts searching from where it left off, instead of always at the beginning, as first fit does. Simulations by Bays (1977) show that next fit gives slightly worse performance than first fit.

Another well-known algorithm is **best fit**. Best fit searches the entire list and takes the smallest hole that is adequate. Rather than breaking up a big hole that might be needed later, best fit tries to find a hole that is close to the actual size needed.

As an example of first fit and best fit, consider Fig. 3-7 again. If a block of size 2 is needed, first fit will allocate the hole at 5, but best fit will allocate the hole at 18.

Best fit is slower than first fit because it must search the entire list every time it is called. Somewhat surprisingly, it also results in more wasted memory than first fit or next fit because it tends to fill up memory with tiny, useless holes. First fit generates larger holes on the average.

To get around the problem of breaking up nearly exact matches into a process and a tiny hole, one could think about **worst fit**, that is, always take the largest available hole, so that the hole broken off will be big enough to be useful. Simulation has shown that worst fit is not a very good idea either.

All four algorithms can be speeded up by maintaining separate lists for processes and holes. In this way, all of them devote their full energy to inspecting holes, not processes. The price paid for this speedup on allocation is the additional complexity and slowdown when deallocating memory, since a freed segment has to be removed from the process list and inserted into the hole list.

If distinct lists are maintained for processes and holes, the hole list may be kept sorted on size, to make best fit faster. When best fit searches a list of holes from smallest to largest, as soon as it finds a hole that fits, it knows that the hole is the smallest one that will do the job, hence the best fit. With a hole list sorted by size, first fit and best fit are equally fast, and next fit is pointless.

When the holes are kept on separate lists from the processes, a small optimization is possible. Instead of having a separate set of data structures for maintaining the hole list, as is done in Fig. 3-7(c), the holes themselves can be used. The first word of each hole could be the hole size, and the second word a pointer to the following entry. The nodes of the list of Fig. 3-7(c), which require three words and one bit (P/H), are no longer needed.

Yet another allocation algorithm is **quick fit**, which maintains separate lists for some of the more common sizes requested. For example, it might have a table with n entries, in which the first entry was a pointer to the head of a list of 4K holes, the second entry was a pointer to a list of 8K holes, the third entry a pointer to 12K holes, and so on. Holes of say, 21K, could either be put on the 20K list or on a special list of odd-sized holes. With quick fit, finding a hole of the required size is extremely fast, but it has the same disadvantage as all schemes that sort by hole size, namely, when a process terminates or is swapped out, finding its neighbors to see if a merge is possible is expensive. If merging is not done, memory will quickly fragment into a large number of small, useless holes.

If we drop our implicit assumption that nothing is known in advance about the probability distribution of requested sizes and process lifetimes, then various other algorithms become applicable. The work of Oldehoeft and Allan (1985), Stephenson (1983), and Beck (1982) describes some of the possibilities.

3.2.4. Memory Management with the Buddy System

We saw in the previous section that keeping all the holes on one or more lists sorted by hole size made allocation very fast, but deallocation slow because all the hole lists had to be searched to find the deallocated segment's neighbors. The buddy system (Knuth, 1973; Knowlton, 1965) is a memory management algorithm that takes advantage of the fact that computers use binary numbers for addressing in order to speed up the merging of adjacent holes when a process terminates or is swapped out.

It works like this. The memory manager maintains a list of free blocks of size 1, 2, 4, 8, 16, etc., bytes, up to the size of memory. With a 1M memory, for example, 21 such lists are needed, ranging from 1 byte to 1 megabyte. Initially, all of memory is free, and the 1M list has a single entry containing a single 1M hole. The other lists are empty. The initial memory configuration is shown in Fig. 3-9 in the top row.

	0	128 K	256 K	384 K	512 K	640 K	768 K	896 K	1 M	Holes
Initially										1
Request 70	A	128		256			512			3
Request 35	A	B	64	256			512			3
Request 80	A	B	64	C	128		512			3
Return A	128	B	64	C	128		512			4
Request 60	128	B	D	C	128		512			4
Return B	128	64	D	C	128		512			4
Return D	256			C	128		512			3
Return C	1024									1

Fig. 3-9. The buddy system. The horizontal axis represents memory addresses. The numbers are the sizes of unallocated blocks of memory in K. The letters represent allocated blocks of memory.

Now let us see how the buddy system works when a 70K process is swapped into an empty 1M memory. As the hole lists are only for powers of 2, 128K will be requested, that being the smallest power of 2 that is big enough. No 128K block is available, nor are blocks for 256K or 512K. Thus the 1M block is split into two 512K blocks, called **buddies,** one at memory address 0 and the other at memory address 512K. One of these, the one at 0, is then split into two 256K buddy blocks, one at 0 and one at 256K. The lower of these is then split into two 128K blocks, and the one at address 0 (marked A in Fig. 3-9) is allocated to the process.

Next, a 35K process is swapped in. This time we round 35K up to a power of 2 and discover that no 64K blocks are available, so we split the 128K block into two 64K buddies, one at 128K and one at 192K. The block at 128K is allocated to the process, marked as B in Fig. 3-9. The third request is for 80K.

Now let us see what happens when a block is returned. Imagine that 128K block A (of which only 70K is used) is freed at this point. It just goes on the free list for 128K blocks at this point. Now a 60K block is needed, so a check is made to see if any sufficiently large blocks are available. The 64K block located at address 192K will do so it is allocated.

Now block B is returned. At this point we have a 128K block at 0 and a 64K block at 128K that are free. No merging is possible yet. Note that even if the 128K block at 0 had been split into a 64K block at 0 that was in use and a free block at 64K, no merging could occur. When block D is returned, we can reconstruct the 256K block at address 0. Finally, when block C is returned, we return to the initial configuration of a single hole of 1M.

Buddy systems have an advantage over algorithms that sort blocks by size but not necessarily at addresses that are multiples of the block size. The advantage is that when a block of size 2^k bytes is freed, the memory manager has to search only the list of 2^k holes to see if a merge is possible. With other algorithms that allow memory blocks to be split in arbitrary ways, all the hole lists must be searched. The result is that the buddy system is fast.

Unfortunately, it is also extremely inefficient in terms of memory utilization. The problem comes from the fact that all requests must be rounded up to a power of 2. A 35K process must be allocated 64K. The extra 29K is just wasted. This form of overhead is known as **internal fragmentation** because the wasted memory is internal to the allocated segments. In Fig. 3-5 we have holes *between* the segments, but no wasted space *within* the segments. This form of waste is called **external frag-mentation** or **checkerboarding**.

Various authors (e.g., Peterson and Norman, 1977; Kaufman, 1984) have modified the buddy system in various ways to try to get around some of its problems.

3.2.5. Allocation of Swap Space

The algorithms presented above are for keeping track of main memory so that when processes are swapped in, the system can find space for them. In some systems, when a process is in memory, no disk space is allocated to it. When it must be swapped out, space must be allocated in the disk swap area for it. On each swap, it may be placed somewhere else on disk. The algorithms for managing swap space are the same ones used for managing main memory.

In other systems, when a process is created, swap space is allocated for it on disk (using one of the algorithms we have studied). Whenever the process is swapped out, it is always swapped to its allocated space, rather than going to a different place each time. When the process exits, the swap space is deallocated.

The only difference is that disk space for a process must be allocated as an integral number of disk blocks. Therefore, a process of size 13.5K using a disk with 1K blocks will be rounded up to 14K before the free disk space data structures are searched.

3.2.6. Analysis of Swapping Systems

The free list and bit map algorithms lead to a form of external fragmentation that is easy to analyze. Imagine a simulation run to determine how much memory is wasted in holes at any instant. The simulator might start at 0, generating segment sizes at random, and marking them as process or hole, also at random. This simulation would lead to as many holes as processes. However, if adjacent holes were then merged, the number of holes would become smaller than the number of segments.

The ratio of holes to processes can be found by the following analysis (Knuth, 1973). Consider an average process in the middle of memory after the system has come to equilibrium. During its stay in memory, half of the operations on the segment just above it will be process allocations and half will be process deallocations. Thus, half the time it has another process as upper neighbor, and half the time it has a hole as upper neighbor. Averaged over time, there must be half as many holes as processes. In other words, if the mean number of processes in memory is n, the mean number of holes is $n/2$. This result is known as the **fifty percent rule**.

The fifty percent rule has its origin in a fundamental asymmetry between processes and holes. When two holes are adjacent in memory, they are merged into a single hole. Adjacent processes are not merged. This mechanism systematically reduces the number of holes.

Another useful result is the **unused memory rule**. Let f be the fraction of memory occupied by holes, s be the average size of the n processes, and ks be the average hole size for some $k > 0$. With a total memory of m bytes, the $n/2$ holes occupy $m - ns$ bytes. Algebraically,

$$(n/2) \times ks = m - ns$$

Solving this equation for m, we get

$$m = ns(1 + k/2)$$

The fraction of memory in holes is just the number of holes, $n/2$, times the average hole size, ks, divided by the total memory, m, or

$$f = \frac{nks/2}{m} = \frac{nks/2}{ns(1 + k/2)} = \frac{k}{k + 2}$$

As an example, if holes are 1/2 as large as processes, $k = 1/2$, and 20 percent of the memory will be wasted in holes. If we reduce the average hole size to 1/4 of the average process size, for example, by using best fit instead of first fit, the wastage will drop to about 11 percent. As long as the average hole size is an appreciable fraction of the average process size, a substantial amount of memory will be wasted.

3.3. VIRTUAL MEMORY

Many years ago people were first confronted with programs that were too big to fit in the available memory. The solution usually adopted was to split the program into pieces, called **overlays**. Overlay 0 would start running first. When it was done, it would call another overlay. Some overlay systems were highly complex, allowing multiple overlays in memory at once. The overlays were kept on the disk and swapped in and out of memory by the operating system.

Although the actual work of swapping overlays in and out was done by the system, the work of splitting the program into pieces had to be done by the programmer. Splitting up large programs into small, modular pieces was time consuming and boring. It did not take long before someone thought of a way to turn the whole job over to the computer.

The method that was devised (Fotheringham, 1961) has come to be known as **virtual memory**. The basic idea behind virtual memory is that the combined size of the program, data, and stack may exceed the amount of physical memory available for it. The operating system keeps those parts of the program currently in use in main memory, and the rest on the disk. For example, a 1M program can run on a 256K machine by carefully choosing which 256K to keep in memory at each instant, with pieces of the program being swapped between disk and memory as needed.

Virtual memory can also work in a multiprogramming system. For example, eight 1M programs can each be allocated a 256K partition in a 2M memory, with each program operating as though it had its own, private 256K machine. In fact, virtual memory and multiprogramming fit together very well. While a program is waiting for part of itself to be swapped in, it is waiting for I/O and cannot run, so the CPU can be given to another process.

3.3.1. Paging

Most virtual memory systems use a technique called **paging**, which we will now describe. On any computer, there exists a set of memory addresses that programs can produce. When a program uses an instruction like

MOVE REG,1000

it is copying the contents of memory address 1000 to REG (or vice versa, depending on the computer). Addresses can be generated using indexing, base registers, segment registers, and other ways.

These program-generated addresses are called **virtual addresses** and form the **virtual address space**. On computers without virtual memory, the virtual address is put directly onto the memory bus and causes the physical memory word with the same address to be read or written. When virtual memory is used, the virtual addresses do not go directly to the memory bus. Instead, they go to a **memory management unit** (MMU), a chip or collection of chips that maps the virtual addresses onto the physical memory addresses as illustrated in Fig. 3-10.

An example of how this mapping works is shown in Fig. 3-11. In this example,

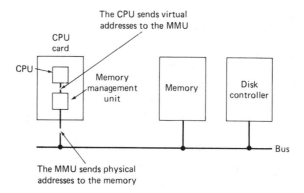

Fig. 3-10. The position and function of the MMU.

we have a computer that can generate 16-bit addresses, from 0 up to 64K. These are the virtual addresses. This computer, however, has only 32K of physical memory, so although 64K programs can be written, they cannot be loaded into memory in their entirety and run. A complete copy of a program's core image, up to 64K, must be present on the disk, however, so that pieces can be brought in as needed.

The virtual address space is divided up into units called **pages**. The corresponding units in the physical memory are called **page frames**. The pages and page frames are always the same size. In this example they are 4K, but page sizes from 512 bytes to 8K are commonly used. With 64K of virtual address space and 32K of physical memory, we have 16 virtual pages and 8 page frames. Transfers between memory and disk are always in units of a page.

When the program tries to access address 0, for example, using the instruction

MOVE REG,0

the virtual address 0 is sent to the MMU. The MMU sees that this virtual address falls in page 0 (0 to 4095), which according to its mapping is page frame 2 (8192 to 12287). It thus transforms the address to 8192 and outputs address 8192 onto the bus. The memory board knows nothing at all about the MMU, and just sees a request for reading or writing address 8192, which it honors. Thus, the MMU has effectively mapped all virtual addresses between 0 and 4095 onto physical addresses 8192 to 12287.

Similarly, an instruction

MOVE REG,8192

is effectively transformed into

MOVE REG,24576

because virtual address 8192 is in virtual page 2 and this page is mapped onto physical page frame 6 (physical addresses 24576 to 28671). As a third example, virtual address 20500 is 20 bytes from the start of virtual page 5 (virtual addresses 20480 to 24575) and maps onto physical address 12288 + 20 = 12308.

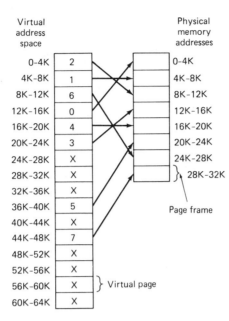

Fig. 3-11. The relation between virtual addresses and physical memory addresses is given by the page table.

By itself, this ability to map the 16 virtual pages onto any of the eight page frames by setting the MMU's map appropriately does not solve the problem that the virtual address space is larger than the physical memory. Since we have only eight physical page frames, only eight of the virtual pages in Fig. 3-11 are mapped onto physical memory. The others, shown as a cross in the figure, are not mapped. In the actual hardware, a **Present/absent bit** in each entry keeps track of whether the page is mapped or not.

What happens if the program tries to use an unmapped page, for example, by using the instruction

MOVE REG,32780

which is byte 12 within virtual page 8 (starting at 32768)? The MMU notices that the page is unmapped (indicated by a cross in the figure), and causes the CPU to trap to the operating system. This trap is called a **page fault**. The operating system picks a little-used page frame and writes its contents back to the disk. It then fetches the page just referenced into the page frame just freed, changes the map, and restarts the trapped instruction.

For example, if the operating system decided to evict page frame 1, it would load virtual page 8 at physical address 4K and make two changes to the MMU map. First, it would mark virtual page 1's entry as unmapped, to trap any future accesses to virtual addresses between 4K and 8K. Then it would replace the cross in virtual page 8's entry with a 1, so that when the trapped instruction is re-executed, it will map virtual address 32780 onto physical address 4108.

Now let us look inside the MMU to see how it works and why we have chosen to use a page size that is a power of 2. In Fig. 3-12 we see an example of a virtual address, 8196 (0010000000000100 in binary), being mapped using the MMU map of Fig. 3-11. The incoming 16-bit virtual address is split up into a 4-bit page number and a 12-bit offset. With 4 bits for the page number, we can represent 16 pages, and with 12 bits for the offset, we can address all 4096 bytes within a page.

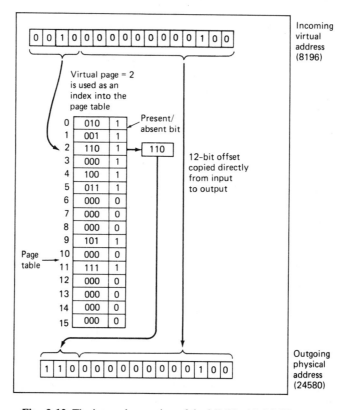

Fig. 3-12. The internal operation of the MMU with 16 4K pages.

The page number is used as an index into the **page table**, yielding the number of the page frame corresponding to that virtual page. If the *Present/absent* bit is 0, a trap to the operating system is caused. If the bit is 1, the page frame number found in the page table is copied to the high-order 3 bits of the output register, along with the 12-bit offset, which is copied unmodified from the incoming virtual address. Together they form a 15-bit physical address. The output register is then put onto the memory bus as the physical memory address.

3.3.2. Page Tables

In theory, the mapping virtual addresses onto physical addresses is as we have just described it. The virtual address is split into a virtual page number (high-order bits) and an offset (low-order bits). The virtual page number is used as an index into the page table to find the entry for that virtual page. From the page table entry, the page frame number (if any) is found. The page frame number is attached to the high-order end of the offset, replacing the virtual page number, to form a physical address that can be sent to the memory.

The purpose of the page table is to map virtual pages onto page frames. Mathematically speaking, the page table is a function, with the virtual page number as argument and the physical frame number as result. Using the result of this function, the virtual page field in a virtual address can be replaced by a page frame field, thus forming a physical memory address.

Despite this simple description, two major issues must be faced:

1. The page table can be extremely large.

2. The mapping must be fast.

The first point follows from the fact that modern computers use virtual addresses of at least 32 bits. With, say, a 4K page size, a 32-bit address space has 1 million pages, and a 64-bit address space has more than you want to contemplate. With 1 million pages in the virtual address space, the page table must have 1 million entries. And remember that each process needs its own page table.

The second point is a consequence of the fact that the virtual-to-physical mapping must be done on every memory reference. A typical instruction has an instruction word, and often a memory operand as well. Consequently, it is necessary to make 1, 2, or sometimes more page table references per instruction. If an instruction takes, say, 10 nsec, as it does on high-end workstations, the page table lookup must be done in a few nanoseconds to avoid becoming a major bottleneck.

The need for large, fast page mapping, is a significant constraint on the way computers are built. Although the problem is most serious with top-of-the-line machines, it is also an issue at the low end as well, where cost and price/performance are critical. In this section and the following ones, we will look at page table design in detail, and show a number of hardware solutions that have been used in actual computers.

The simplest design (at least conceptually), is to have a single page table consisting of an array of fast hardware registers, with one entry for each virtual page, indexed by virtual page number. When a process is started up, the operating system loads the registers with the process' page table, taken from a copy kept in main memory. During process execution, no more memory references are needed for the page table. The advantages of this method are that it is straightforward and requires no memory references during mapping. A disadvantage is that it is potentially expensive (if the page table is large). Having to load the page table at every context switch can also hurt performance.

At the other extreme, the page table can be entirely in main memory. All the hardware needs then is a single register that points to the start of the page table. This design allows the memory map to be changed at a context switch by reloading one register. Of course it has the disadvantage of requiring one or more memory references to read page table entries during the execution of each instruction. For this reason, this approach is rarely used in its most pure form, but below we will study some variations that have much better performance.

Multilevel Page Tables

To get around the problem of having huge page tables in memory all the time, many computers use a multilevel page table. A simple example is shown in Fig. 3-13. In Fig. 3-13(a) we have a 32-bit virtual address that is partitioned into a 10-bit *PT1* field, a 10-bit *PT2* field, and a 12-bit *Offset* field. Since offsets are 12 bits, pages are 4K, and there are a total of 2^{20} of them.

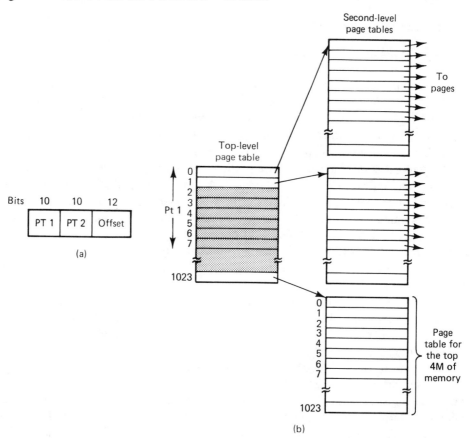

Fig. 3-13. (a) A 32-bit address with two page table fields. (b) Two-level page tables.

The secret to the multilevel page table method is to avoid keeping all the page tables in memory all the time. In particular, those that are not needed should not be kept around. Suppose, for example, that a process needs 12 megabytes, the bottom 4 megabytes of memory for program text, the next 4 megabytes for data, and the top 4 megabytes for the stack. In between the top of the data and the bottom of the stack is a gigantic hole that is not used.

In Fig. 3-13(b) we see how the two-level page table works in this example. On the left we have the top-level page table, with 1024 entries, corresponding to the 10-bit *PT1* field. When a virtual address is presented to the MMU, it first extracts the *PT1* field, and uses it as an index into the top-level page table. Each of these 1024 entries represents 4M because the entire 4 gigabyte (i.e., 32-bit) virtual address space has been chopped into 1024 chunks.

The entry located by indexing into the top-level page table yields the address or the page frame number of a second level page table. Entry 0 of the top-level page table points to the page table for the program text, entry 1 points to the page table for the data, and entry 1023 points to the page table for the stack. The other (shaded) entries are not used. The *PT2* field is now used as an index into the selected second-level page table to find the page frame number for the page itself.

As an example, consider the 32-bit virtual address 0x00403004 (4,206,596 decimal), which is 12292 bytes into the data. This address corresponds to $PT1 = 1$, $PT2 = 3$, and *Offset* = 4. The MMU first uses *PT1* to index into the top-level page table and obtain entry 1, which corresponds to address 4M to 8M. It then uses *PT2* to index into the second-level page table just found, and extract entry 3, which corresponds to addresses 12288 to 16383 within its 4M chunk (i.e., absolute addresses 4,206,592 to 4,210,687). This entry contains the page frame number of the page containing virtual address 0x00403004. If that page is not in memory, the *Present/absent* bit in the page table entry will be zero, causing a page fault. If the page is in memory, the page frame number taken from the second-level page table is combined with the offset (4) to construct a physical address. This address is put on the bus and sent to memory.

The interesting thing to note about Fig. 3-13 is that although the address space contains over a million pages, only four page tables are actually needed: the top-level table, and the second level tables for 0 to 4M, 4M to 8M, and the top 4M. The *Present/absent* bits in 1021 entries of the top-level page table are set to 0, forcing a page fault if they are ever accessed. Should this occur, the operating system will notice that the process is trying to reference memory that it is not supposed to, and will take appropriate action, such as sending it a signal or killing it. In this example we have chosen round numbers for the various sizes and have picked *PT1* equal to *PT2* but in actual practice other values are also possible, of course.

The two-level page table system of Fig. 3-13 can be expanded to three, four, or more levels. Additional levels give more flexibility, but it is doubtful that the additional complexity is worth it beyond three levels.

Let us now turn from the structure of the page tables in the large, to the details of a single page table entry. The exact layout of an entry is highly machine dependent, but the kind of information present is roughly the same from machine to machine. In Fig. 3-14 we give a sample page table entry. The size varies from computer to computer, but 32 bits is a common size. The most important field is the *Page frame number*. After all, the goal of the page mapping is to locate this value. Next to it we have the *Present/absent* bit. If this bit is 1, the entry is valid and can be used. If it is 0, the virtual page to which the entry belongs is not currently in memory. Accessing a page table entry with this bit set to 0 causes a page fault.

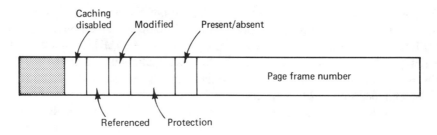

Fig. 3-14. A typical page table entry.

The *Protection* bits tell what kinds of access are permitted. In the simplest form, this field is 1 bit, with 0 for read/write and 1 for read only. A more sophisticated arrangement is 3 bits, one each for enabling reading, writing, and executing the page.

The *Modified* and *Referenced* bits keep track of page usage. When a page is written to, the hardware automatically sets the *Modified* bit. This bit is of value when the operating system decides to reclaim a page frame. If the page in it has been modified, it must be written back to the disk. If it has not been modified, it can just be abandoned, since the disk copy is still valid. The *Referenced* bit is set whenever a page is referenced, either for reading or writing. Its value is to help the operating system choose a page to evict when a page fault occurs. Pages that are not being used are better candidates than pages that are, and this bit plays an important role in several of the page replacement algorithms that we will study later in this chapter.

Finally, the last bit allows caching to be disabled for the page. This feature is important for pages that map onto device registers rather than memory. If the operating system is sitting in a tight loop waiting for some I/O device to respond to a command it was just given, it is essential that the hardware keep fetching the word from the device, and not use an old cached copy. With this bit, caching can be turned off. Machines that have a separate I/O space and do not use memory mapped I/O do not need this bit.

Note that the disk address used to hold the page when it is not in memory is not part of the page table. The reason is simple. The page table holds only that information the hardware needs to translate a virtual address to a physical address. Information the operating system needs to handle page faults is kept in software tables inside the operating system.

3.3.3. Examples of Paging Hardware

Although the design of paging hardware might be considered belonging to the subject of computer architecture rather than to the subject of operating systems, the relationship between paging hardware (i.e., MMU) and operating systems is so intimate that we will take a brief look at some actual paging hardware in this section. We will look at four examples, representing, one, two, three, and four-level paging systems, respectively.

One-level Paging: The PDP-11

Let us start with a particularly simple paging system, that of the DEC PDP-11, a 16-bit minicomputer popular during the 1970s and still being manufactured and used for industrial process control applications. The PDP-11 has 16-bit virtual addresses and up to 4M of memory on some models. Page size is 8K.

On the smaller models, the page table consists of eight slots, in hardware, each one controlling one of the eight pages. Since the PDP-11 has memory-mapped I/O, the page table entries can be written (and read) by using addresses in the top 4K of memory. When the operating system starts up a user process, it loads the page table for this process by directly copying a shadow copy of the page table in main memory to the actual hardware registers.

The larger PDP-11 models use a trick to double the virtual address space. They have separate virtual address spaces for instructions and data. Each one goes from 0 to 64K, and each one is divided into eight pages, as shown in Fig. 3-15. Furthermore, each one has its own page table. When the computer wants to fetch an instruction, the MMU looks up the virtual address in the instruction space page table to map the instruction space page onto a physical page frame. Similarly, when fetching or storing a data word, the data space page table is used. In this way, processes have access to 64K of program text and an additional 64K of data space (including the stack), even though addresses are only 16 bits.

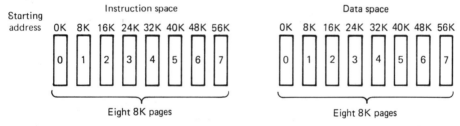

Fig. 3-15. Virtual address space on the PDP-11/70 and some other PDP-11 models. Separate address spaces are provided for instructions and data.

With a 16-bit address and an 8K page, the virtual addresses are split into a 3-bit virtual page number and a 13-bit offset. The 3-bit virtual page number is used as an index into the appropriate (instruction space or data space) page table to yield a page frame number. With 4M of memory, the page frame numbers are 9 bits, since it takes 2^9 8K pages to fill up 4M. Because a single process has a maximum size of 128K, in 4M there is sufficient room for 31 processes. Even with 31 processes, there is still 128K left over for the operating system. PDP-11 timesharing systems often had more processes than this, and had to swap.

The advantages of the PDP-11 system are obvious. The scheme is simple, and because it is entirely in hardware, fast. With only 16 page table entries, loading them all when a process starts does not take long. While the idea works fine on the PDP-11, unfortunately, it does not scale well to larger machines.

Two-level Paging: The VAX

The successor to the PDP-11 is the VAX, one of the first true 32-bit minicomputers. The VAX has 16 32-bit registers and a 32-bit virtual address space. Although many features of the VAX are taken from the PDP-11, the paging hardware is quite different.

Pages on the VAX are fixed at 512 bytes, a size that was probably too small when it came out, and is certainly too small now. Virtual addresses are split up into three fields, as shown in Fig. 3-16. The high-order 2 bits of the virtual address indicate the space to be used. Bits 00 indicate user program text and data, 01 indicate user stack, and 10 indicate system space, where the operating system resides. The fourth combination, 11, is reserved for future use.

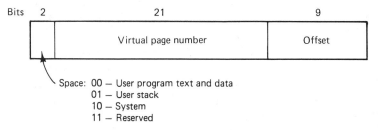

Fig. 3-16. A VAX virtual address.

This use of the top 2 bits means that the 4 gigabyte virtual address space possible with 32-bit addresses is partitioned into 4 sections, starting at 0, 1, 2, and 3 gigabytes, respectively. The bottom quarter is for user programs, starting at 0 and extending up as far as necessary, usually far below 1G though. The stack uses the second quarter, starting at address $2^{31} - 1$ and running downward, usually for not more than a few megabytes at most. As is normally the case, each process has its own program text and its own stack.

However, the third quarter, which contains the operating system, is shared among all processes. Thus the contents of the word at address 2^{31} is the same in every process on the machine, and contains the first word of the operating system. This architecture is shown in Fig. 3-17.

The paging structure of the VAX works like this. With 21-bit virtual page numbers, every process has over 2 million pages in its address space. Page table entries are 4 bytes, so each process needs an 8M page table. With a dozen or so processes, the amount of memory needed quickly gets out of hand, especially since the smaller VAXes only have a total memory of 2M. Consequently, the designers opted for a two-level page table method that allows user page tables to be themselves paged out.

Slightly simplified, each process is assigned a chunk of virtual address space in the 2G to 3G range for its page table. At most it might need 8M, but most processes need far less. The pages in this range are in the virtual memory of each process, and need not always be present. They can be brought in as needed, like any other pages.

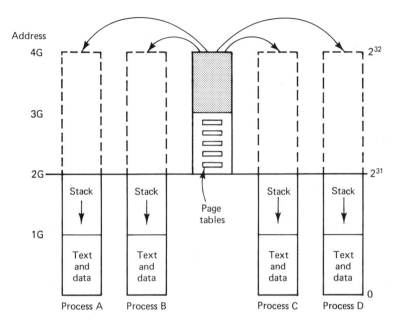

Fig. 3-17. Four processes on the VAX.

This design allows user page tables to be paged themselves. Only the pages for the operating system itself are locked in memory, as is the page table for system space.

The physical address of the system space page table is permanently kept in a special MMU register so the hardware can always find it. When the operating system starts up a user process, it loads a second MMU register with the *virtual* address of that process' page table (an address between 2G and 3G). Using these two registers, address translation works as follows. When a virtual address is presented to the MMU, it extracts the virtual page number and shifts it left 2 bits, because page table entries are 4 bytes. The resulting offset and the virtual address of the process' page table are then added to get the virtual address, A, in the process address space where the corresponding page table entry is located. This virtual address is always in the 2G to 3G range, because that is where all the user page tables are located, as shown in Fig. 3-17.

Using the MMU register that contains the physical address of the system space page table, virtual address A is looked up. If its page is present, the instruction can be executed. If, however, a page fault occurs, the missing page table page must first be brought in and the instruction restarted.

Although this paging structure is far more complicated than the PDP-11's it does allow multiple processes to have page tables each of which is larger than all of physical memory. It also puts the operating system into each process' address space, to make it easier for the system to access user data structures efficiently. Furthermore, it makes context switching highly efficient, since the only thing that has to be changed on a context switch is the one register giving the virtual address of the current process' page table.

An obvious disadvantage of this method is that two memory references are needed to the page tables on each user memory reference. The first one is to the system page table and the second is to the user page table. If this algorithm were actually carried out all the time, the VAX would be very slow. Fortunately, special hardware (an associative memory, described later) bypasses this path most of the time. We will discuss such hardware later in this chapter.

Three-level Paging: The SPARC

Since the early 1980s, many computer manufacturers have been building machines based on high-performance RISC chips. Sun Microsystems has been basing their machines on the SPARC chip, a derivative of work done at Berkeley (Patterson and Séquin, 1981). Sun has also defined a reference paging MMU for the SPARC, although not all models use it. It uses three-level page tables, as shown in Fig. 3-18.

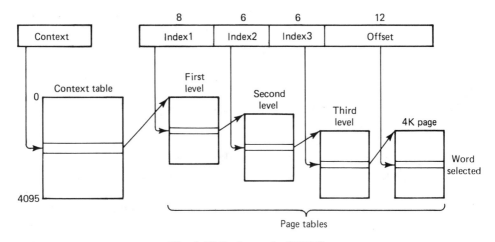

Fig. 3-18. Paging on the SPARC.

To avoid having to reload the tables when process switching occurs, the hardware can support multiple **contexts**, one per process. When a process is loaded into the machine, the operating system assigns it a unique context number. That context number is reserved for the process until it terminates. Current MMU chips have 4096 contexts.

On every memory reference, the context number and the virtual address are presented to the MMU. Conceptually, the MMU uses the context number as an index into its (hardware) context table to find the top-level page table for that context (i.e., the process currently running). It then uses *Index1* to select an entry from the top-level page table. That entry points to the next level of page table, and so on until the page is found. As usual in paging systems, to speed up the lookup, an associative memory is present.

Four-level Paging: The 68030

Paging on the 68030 is highly sophisticated, to provide just about anything the operating system writers might need. The number of levels of page tables is programmable, from 0 and 4, controlled by the operating system. Furthermore, the number of bits at each level is also programmable, in Fig. 3-18. The 68030's field widths are determined by the value written to a global register, the **TCR (Translation Control Register)**. Furthermore, since many programs need far less than 2^{32} bytes of memory, it is possible to tell the MMU to ignore the uppermost n bits.

As a (somewhat simplified) example, consider Fig. 3-19(a), which shows one of the many ways of breaking up 32-bit virtual addresses. Here we have decided to ignore the upper 10 bits (meaning that virtual addresses must be below 4M), followed by four levels of table lookup, A, B, C, and D. Page sizes can be set by the operating system. All the powers of two from 256 bytes to 32K are permitted. In this example, we have chosen to allocate 11 bits to *Offset*, which implies a page size of 2K.

In Fig. 3-19(b) we show a virtual address, 0x002B8806, split up according to the division of Fig. 3-19(a). In this format, 4 bits are allocated to the first table, which has up to 16 entries. The first entry in this table applies to virtual addresses in the range 0x00000000 to 0x0003FFFF The second one maps addresses in the range 0x00040000 to 0x0007FFFF, and so on. When presented with the virtual address of Fig. 3-19(b), the 68030's on-chip MMU ignores bits 22 through 31, and uses bits 18 through 21 as an index into the A table, as shown in Fig. 3-19(c).

The result of this lookup is a pointer to a B table, with eight entries (because the B fields of Fig. 3-19(a) and (b) are 3 bits). Next, the contents of the B field, bits 15 through 17 (with binary value 111) are used as an index into the B table, to get a pointer to one of the four-entry C page tables. This time we select entry 00, which contains a pointer to the D table. The D entry is a page descriptor, giving the page frame number and other information. By combining the page frame number and the contents of the *Offset* field, we can construct the physical address of the byte or word needed. It should be noted that the operating system does not have to use all four levels if the job can be done with fewer.

3.3.4. Associative Memory

In all the paging schemes we have discussed so far, except the PDP-11's, the page tables are kept in memory, due to their large size. Potentially, this design has an enormous impact on performance. Consider, for example, an instruction that copies one register to another. In the absence of paging, this instruction makes only one memory reference, to fetch the instruction. With paging, additional memory references will be needed to access the page table. On the VAX, two page table references are needed for the instruction fetch, for a total of three. Since execution speed is generally limited by the rate the CPU can get instructions and data out of the memory, with paging enabled the 68030 might run at 20 percent of the speed it could achieve with paging turned off. Under these conditions, no one would use it.

Computer designers have known about this problem for years, and have come up

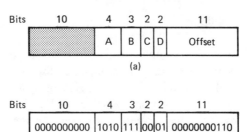

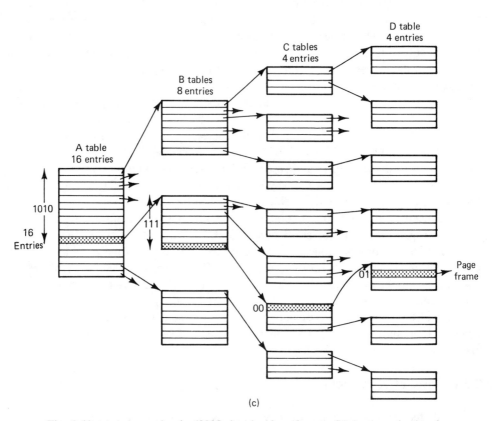

Fig. 3-19. (a) An example of a 68030 virtual address format. (b) An example virtual address. (c) Page tables corresponding to (a) and (b).

with a solution. Their solution is based on the observation that most programs tend to make a large number of references to a small number of pages, and not the other way around. Thus only a small fraction of the page table entries are heavily read; the rest are barely used at all.

The solution that has been devised is to equip computers with a small hardware device for mapping virtual addresses to physical addresses without going through the page table. The device, called an **associative memory** (or sometimes a **translation**

lookaside buffer), is illustrated in Fig. 3-20. It is usually inside the MMU and consists of a small number of entries, eight in this example, but rarely more than 32. Each entry contains information about one page, in particular, the virtual page number, a bit that is set when the page is modified, the protection code (read/write/execute permissions), and the physical page frame in which the page is located. These fields have a one-to-one correspondence with the fields in the page table. Another bit indicates whether the entry is valid (i.e., in use) or not.

Valid
entry

	Virtual page	Modified	Protection	Page frame
1	140	1	RW	31
1	20	0	R X	38
1	130	1	RW	29
1	129	1	RW	62
1	19	0	R X	50
1	21	0	R X	45
1	860	1	RW	14
1	861	1	RW	75

Fig. 3-20. An associative memory to speed up paging.

In our example, the process is in a loop that spans virtual pages 19, 20, and 21, so these entries are present in the associative memory, with a protection code for reading and executing. The main data currently being used (say, an array being processed) is on pages 129 and 130. Page 140 contains the indices used in the array calculations. Finally, the stack is on pages 860 and 861.

Let us now see how the associative memory functions. When a virtual address is presented to the MMU for translation, the hardware first checks to see if its virtual page number is present in the associative memory by comparing it to all the entries simultaneously (i.e., in parallel). If a valid match is found and the access does not violate the protection bits, the page frame is taken directly from the associative memory, without going to the page table. If the virtual page number is present in the associative memory but the instruction is trying to write on a read-only page, a protection fault is generated, the same way as it would be from the page table itself.

The interesting case is what happens when the virtual page number is not in the associative memory. The MMU detects the miss, and does an ordinary page table lookup. It then evicts one of the entries from the associative memory, and replaces it with the page table entry just looked up. Thus if that page is used again soon, the second time it will result in a hit rather than a miss. When an entry is purged from the associative memory, the modified bit is copied back into the page table entry in memory. The other values are already there. When the associative memory is loaded from the page table, all the fields are taken from memory.

The fraction of memory references that can be satisfied from the associative memory is called the **hit ratio**. The higher the hit ratio, the better the performance. A hit ratio of almost 100 percent means that essentially all memory references are being translated by the associative memory, and that the page table is hardly being used at all. On the other hand, a process accessing long linked lists threaded through dozens of pages will have a hit ratio of close to 0 percent and will be using the page table on almost every memory reference.

As an example, suppose that it takes 100 nsec to access the page table and 20 nsec to access the associative memory. With a 90 percent hit ratio, the average access time is $0.9 \times 20 + 0.1 \times 100$, which is 28 nsec. For other hit ratios with these parameters, the average access times are shown in Fig. 3-21.

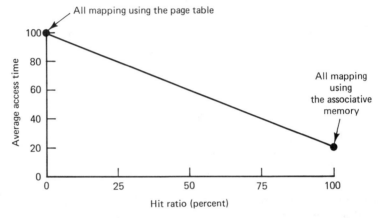

Fig. 3-21. Average access time for a 100 nsec page table access and a 20 nsec associative memory access.

In the general case, the average performance depends on three factors: the page table access time, the associative memory access time, and the hit ratio. The hit ratio depends on the mean number of pages referenced over a short interval and the associative memory size. Since the number of pages referenced depends on program behavior, something outside the control of the MMU designers, their only way to increase the hit ratio is to increase the number of entries in the associative memory. Needless to say, this also increases the cost.

Before leaving this topic, a few subtle details are worth mentioning. When the virtual address consists of multiple fields, as in Fig. 3-19, the associative memory must hold all of them in the virtual page number field. A match only counts when the entire virtual address (excluding the offset) is a hit. Matching only the first one is of no use.

Another issue is how the associative memory functions in a system with multiple processes. Each process has its own page table and its own mapping, of course. When a new process runs, it is essential that it not attempt to use the entries in the associative memory that pertain to the previous process. In general, there are two solutions. The simplest is to provide a machine instruction to invalidate the associative memory, that is, clear all the validity bits. When starting a new process, the operating system can execute this instruction to ensure that the new process does not see any of the old entries.

The other solution is to extend the associative memory with a process or context identifier field, and add a hardware register to the machine to hold the identifier for the current process. In this way, the hardware can compare not only the virtual page number, but also the process identifier. Entries for processes other than the current one are then just ignored. This approach requires additional hardware, but saves time on every context switch. Since context switches also include clock and other interrupts, if the associative memory is large, the time can be appreciable.

Zero-level Paging: The MIPS R2000

The MIPS R2000 is a RISC machine that has taken the associative memory idea to its limit: the page tables have been completely eliminated (at least as far as the hardware goes). The R2000 has a conventional addressing scheme, with 32-bit addresses and 4K pages. Each 32-bit virtual address consists of a 20-bit virtual page number and a 12-bit offset. Physical memory addresses are also 32 bits.

The CPU contains a 64-entry associative memory on the CPU chip. Each entry holds the virtual page number, the page frame number, a process identifier (as discussed above), and some flag bits, as shown in Fig. 3-22. When the CPU generates a virtual address, the hardware automatically compares its virtual page number to all the entries in the associative memory at once. If a match is found, the translation occurs, and the chip outputs the physical address needed onto the bus.

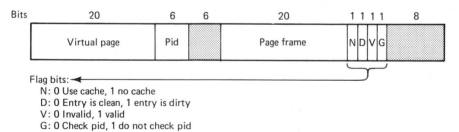

Fig. 3-22. The MIPS R2000 associative memory entry.

So far, everything is normal. All associative memories work this way. The interesting part is what happens on a miss. Unlike all other machines we have studied, the hardware does not look up the virtual page table. Instead it causes a trap to the operating system. The operating system must then determine which virtual page is needed, by looking in certain hardware registers. It must then choose an entry to evict from the associative memory. Finally it must load the new page entry into the associative memory, and restart the instruction. Of course, if the page is not in memory, then it must also execute the code for a normal page fault as well.

The unusual part is that a kernel trap is caused not only on page faults, but on associative memory misses as well. The reason for this unusual design is to keep the machine as simple as possible, in order to make it very fast. The designers felt that handling misses in hardware would take up too much chip area, which they could more profitably devote to other features, such as an on-chip cache controller and an on-chip MMU.

Before building the chip, the designers performed numerous simulation studies to see (1) how often a miss would occur with a 64-entry table, and (2) how fast they could evict an entry and load the new one. The results showed that the performance was as good as conventional designs with a more complex, but off-chip MMU and associative memory.

3.3.5. Inverted Page Tables

On early computers, the virtual address space was usually quite small. The PDP-11, for example, had only 8 or 16 pages, depending on whether or not the particular model had separate instruction and data spaces. Physical memory, however, was larger, up to 512 page frames on models with a 4M memory. Under these conditions it made sense to organize the page table as entries indexed by virtual page number. The page table could even be kept in hardware in some cases.

Nowadays, many computers have a 32-bit virtual address space and a 32-bit physical memory. With a 4K page size, each process needs 2^{20} entries in its page table. With 4 bytes per entry, each process needs 4 megabytes for its page table. Although this amount is large, it is not unmanageable. The various multilevel paging schemes we have discussed show how these tables can be stored and used. As on the PDP-11, these tables are always accessed by indexing with the virtual page number.

With the advent of RISC chips having 64-bit virtual address spaces, the situation changes drastically. For the first time, the amount of virtual address space dwarfs the amount of physical memory (a 64-bit address space can hold 20 million terabytes of information). With a 4K page size, such a machine needs 2^{52} or about 4 quadrillion page table entries. Four quadrillion is a big number. It exceeds the number of stars in the galaxy. It is even larger than the U.S. National Debt. Organizing the page tables as linear arrays of 4 quadrillion entries per process may require some rethinking.

The one saving grace here is that although the virtual address space is immense, the number of physical page frames is not, since current memories are still only in the gigabyte range or less. This observation has led designers to build machines (e.g., IBM System/38 and HP Spectrum) in which the page table is organized around physical memory instead of virtual memory.

As an example, consider the two page tables shown in Fig. 3-23. The one on the left is a conventional per-process page table sorted by virtual page number. The hardware extracts the virtual page number from the virtual address and uses it as an index into the page table. With virtual page k, the k-th entry is selected, and its page frame is used to build the physical address.

Unlike the page table on the left, the one on the right is not sorted by virtual address. Instead, the i-th entry contains information about the page currently occupying page frame i. The number of entries in this table is thus equal to the number of

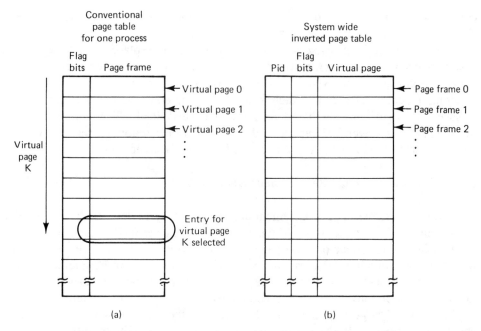

Fig. 3-23. (a) A conventional page table. (b) An inverted page table.

page frames in physical memory, independent of the number of pages in the virtual address space. The page table of Fig. 3-23(b) is called an **inverted page table**.

An inverted page table is always used with an associative memory. On a hit, the inverted page table is not needed. On a miss, the page table must be searched for an entry whose virtual page number matches the virtual page in the current memory address. This search can be speeded up by maintaining a hash table of all the page table entries. The hash table lookup can be done either in hardware or by the operating system, analogous to the way the R2000 works. If the lookup is done in software, it is essential that this not happen too often.

If the page needed is not in memory, it must be looked up by the operating system. For this purpose, a conventional page table is needed, although it may be stored on disk instead of in memory. Of course, storing the page table on disk means that the page fault handler will need to make one or more extra disk references before bringing in the needed page. This overhead is probably unavoidable given the large size of the page table, hence the large amount of information required.

3.4. PAGE REPLACEMENT ALGORITHMS

When a page fault occurs, the operating system has to choose a page to remove from memory to make room for the page that has to be brought in. If the page to be removed has been modified while in memory, it must be rewritten to the disk to bring the disk copy up to date. If, however, the page has not been changed (e.g., a page contains program text), the disk copy is already up to date, so no rewrite is needed. The page to be read in just overwrites the page being evicted.

While it would be possible to pick a random page to replace at each page fault, system performance is much better if a page that is not heavily used is chosen. If a heavily used page is removed, it will probably have to be brought back in quickly, resulting in extra overhead. Much work has been done on the subject of page replacement algorithms, both theoretical and experimental. The bibliography by Smith (1978) lists over 300 papers on the subject. In the following sections we will describe some of the more interesting algorithms that have been found.

3.4.1. The Optimal Page Replacement Algorithm

The best possible page replacement algorithm is easy to describe but impossible to implement. It goes like this. At the moment that a page fault occurs, some set of pages is in memory. One of these pages will be referenced on the very next instruction (the page containing that instruction). Other pages may not be referenced until 10, 100, or perhaps 1000 instructions later. Each page can be labeled with the number of instructions that will be executed before that page is first referenced.

The optimal page algorithm simply says that the page with the highest label should be removed. If one page will not be used for 8 million instructions and another page will not be used for 6 million instructions, removing the former pushes the page fault that will fetch it back as far into the future as possible. Computers, like people, try to put off unpleasant events for as long as they can.

The only problem with this algorithm is that it is unrealizable. At the time of the page fault, the operating system has no way of knowing when each of the pages will be referenced next. (We saw a similar situation earlier with the shortest job first scheduling algorithm—how can the system tell which job is shortest?) Still, by running a program on a simulator and keeping track of all page references, it is possible to implement optimal page replacement on the *second* run by using the page reference information collected on the *first* run.

In this way it is possible to compare the performance of realizable algorithms with the best possible one. If an operating system achieves a performance of, say, only 1 percent worse than the optimal algorithm, effort spent in looking for a better algorithm will yield at most a 1 percent improvement.

To avoid any possible confusion, it should be made clear that this log of page references refers only to the one program just measured. The page replacement algorithm derived from it is thus specific to that one program. Although this method is useful for evaluating page replacement algorithms, it is of no use in practical systems. Below we will study algorithms that *are* useful on real systems.

3.4.2. The Not-Recently-Used Page Replacement Algorithm

In order to allow the operating system to collect useful statistics about which pages are being used and which ones are not, most computers with virtual memory have two status bits associated with each page. R is set whenever the page is referenced (read or written). *M* is set when the page is written to (i.e., modified). The bits are contained in each page table entry, as shown in Fig. 3-14. It is important to realize that these bits must be updated on every memory reference, so it is essential that they be set by the hardware. Once a bit has been set to 1, it stays 1 until the operating system resets it to 0 in software.

If the hardware does not have these bits, they can be simulated as follows. When a process is started up, all of its page table entries are marked as not in memory. As soon as any page is referenced, a page fault will occur. The operating system then sets the *R* bit (in its internal tables), changes the page table entry to point to the correct page, with mode READ ONLY, and restarts the instruction. If the page is subsequently written on, another page fault will occur, allowing the operating system to set the *M* bit and change the page's mode to READ/WRITE.

The *R* and *M* bits can be used to build a simple paging algorithm as follows. When a process is started up, both page bits for all its pages are set to 0 by the operating system. Periodically (e.g., on each clock interrupt), the *R* bit is cleared, to distinguish pages that have not been referenced recently from those that have been.

When a page fault occurs, the operating system inspects all the pages and divides them into four categories based on the current values of their *R* and *M* bits:

Class 0: not referenced, not modified.
Class 1: not referenced, modified.
Class 2: referenced, not modified.
Class 3: referenced, modified.

Although class 1 pages seem, at first glance, impossible, they occur when a class 3 page has its *R* bit cleared by a clock interrupt. Clock interrupts do not clear the *M* bit because this information is needed to know whether the page has to be rewritten to disk or not.

The **NRU (Not Recently Used)** algorithm removes a page at random from the lowest numbered nonempty class. Implicit in this algorithm is that it is better to remove a modified page that has not been referenced in at least one clock tick (typically 20 msec) than a clean page that is in heavy use. The main attraction of NRU is that it is easy to understand, efficient to implement, and gives a performance that, while certainly not optimal, is often adequate.

3.4.3. The First-In, First-Out (FIFO) Page Replacement Algorithm

Another low-overhead paging algorithm is the **FIFO (First-In, First-Out)** algorithm. To illustrate how this works, consider a supermarket that has enough shelves to display exactly *k* different products. One day, some company introduces a new convenience food—instant, freeze-dried, organic yogurt that can be reconstituted in a microwave oven. It is an immediate success, so our finite supermarket has to get rid of one old product in order to stock it.

One possibility is to find the product that the supermarket has been stocking the longest (i.e., something it began selling 120 years ago), and get rid of it on the grounds that no one is interested any more. In effect, the supermarket maintains a linked list of all the products it currently sells in the order they were introduced. The new one goes on the back of the list, and the one at the front of the list is dropped.

As a page replacement algorithm, the same idea is applicable. The operating system maintains a list of all pages currently in memory, with the page at the head of the list the oldest one and the page at the tail the most recent arrival. On a page fault, the page at the head is removed and the new page added to the tail of the list. When applied to stores, FIFO might remove mustache wax, but it might also remove flour, salt, or butter. When applied to computers the same problem arises. For this reason, FIFO in its pure form is rarely used.

3.4.4. The Second Chance Page Replacement Algorithm

A simple modification to FIFO that avoids the problem of throwing out a heavily used page is to inspect the R bit of the oldest page. If it is 0, the page is both old and unused, so it is replaced immediately. If the R bit is 1, the bit is cleared, the page is put onto the end of the list of pages, and its load time is updated as though it had just arrived in memory. Then the search continues.

The operation of this algorithm, called **second chance**, is shown in Fig. 3-24. In Fig. 3-24(a) we see pages A through H, kept on a linked list and sorted by the time they arrived in memory.

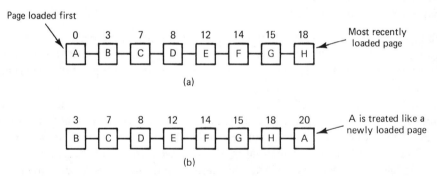

Fig. 3-24. Operation of second chance. (a) Pages sorted in FIFO order. (b) Page list if a page fault occurs at time 20 and A has its R bit set.

Suppose a page fault occurs at time 20. The oldest page is A, which arrived at time 0, when the process started. If A has the R bit cleared, it is evicted from memory, either by being written to the disk (if it is dirty), or just abandoned (if it is clean). On the other hand, if the R bit is set, A is put onto the end of the list and its "load time" is reset to the current time (20). The R bit is also cleared. The search for a suitable page continues with B.

What second chance is doing is looking for an old page that has not been referenced in the previous clock interval. If all the pages have been referenced, second chance degenerates into pure FIFO. Specifically, imagine that all the pages in Fig. 3-24(a) have their R bits set. One by one, the operating system moves the pages to the end of the list, clearing the R bit each time it appends a page to the end of the list. Eventually, it comes back to page A, which now has its R bit cleared. At this point A is evicted. Thus the algorithm always terminates.

3.4.5. The Clock Page Replacement Algorithm

Although second chance is a reasonable algorithm, it is unnecessarily inefficient because it is constantly moving pages around on its list. A better approach is to keep all the pages on a circular list in the form of a clock, as shown in Fig. 3-25. A hand points to the oldest page.

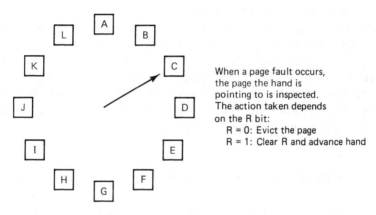

When a page fault occurs, the page the hand is pointing to is inspected. The action taken depends on the R bit:
R = 0: Evict the page
R = 1: Clear R and advance hand

Fig. 3-25. The clock page replacement algorithm.

When a page fault occurs, the page being pointed to by the hand is inspected. If its R bit is 0, the page is evicted, the new page is inserted into the clock in its place, and the hand is advanced one position. If R is 1, it is cleared and the hand is advanced to the next page. This process is repeated until a page is found with $R = 0$. Not surprisingly, this algorithm is called **clock**. It differs from second chance only in the implementation.

3.4.6. The Least Recently Used (LRU) Page Replacement Algorithm

A good approximation to the optimal algorithm is based on the observation that pages that have been heavily used in the last few instructions will probably be heavily used again in the next few. Conversely, pages that have not been used for ages will probably remain unused for a long time. This idea suggests a realizable algorithm: when a page fault occurs, throw out the page that has been unused for the longest time. This strategy is called **LRU** (**Least Recently Used**) paging.

Although LRU is theoretically realizable, it is not cheap. To fully implement LRU, it is necessary to maintain a linked list of all pages in memory, with the most recently used page at the front and the least recently used page at the rear. The difficulty is that the list must be updated on every memory reference. Finding a page in the list, deleting it, and then moving it to the front is a very time consuming operation. Either (expensive) special hardware is needed, or we will have to find a cheaper approximation in software.

Searching and manipulating a linked list on every instruction is prohibitively slow, even in hardware. However, there are other ways to implement LRU with special hardware. Let us consider the simplest way first. This method requires equipping the hardware with a 64-bit counter, C, that is automatically incremented after each instruction. Furthermore, each page table entry must also have a field large enough to contain the counter. After each memory reference, the current value of C is stored in the page table entry for the page just referenced. When a page fault occurs, the operating system examines all the counters in the page table to find the lowest one. That page is the least recently used.

Now let us look at a second hardware LRU algorithm. For a machine with n page frames, the LRU hardware can maintain a matrix of $n \times n$ bits, initially all zero. Whenever page frame k is referenced, the hardware first sets all the bits of row k to 1, then sets all the bits of column k to 0. At any instant, the row whose binary value is lowest is the least recently used, the row whose value is next lowest is next least recently used, and so forth. The workings of this algorithm are given in Fig. 3-26 for four page frames and page referenced in the order

0 1 2 3 2 1 0 3 2 3

After page 0 is referenced we have the situation of Fig. 3-26(a), and so on.

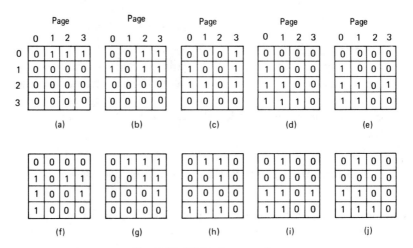

Fig. 3-26. LRU using a matrix.

3.4.7. Simulating LRU in Software

Although both of the previous LRU algorithms are realizable, they are dependent on special hardware, and are of little use to the operating system designer who is making a system for a machine that does not have this hardware. Instead, a solution that can be implemented in software is needed. One possibility is called the **not**

frequently used or **NFU** algorithm. It requires a software counter associated with each page, initially zero. At each clock interrupt, the operating system scans all the pages in memory. For each page, the R bit, which is 0 or 1, is added to the counter. In effect, the counters are an attempt to keep track of how often each page has been referenced. When a page fault occurs, the page with the lowest counter is chosen for replacement.

The main problem with NFU is that it never forgets anything. For example, in a multipass compiler, pages that were heavily used during pass 1 may still have a high count well into later passes. In fact, if pass 1 happens to have the longest execution time of all the passes, the pages containing the code for subsequent passes will always have lower counts than the pass 1 pages. Consequently, the operating system will remove useful pages instead of pages that are no longer in use.

Fortunately, a small modification to NFU makes it able to simulate LRU quite well. The modification has two parts. First, the counters are each shifted right 1 bit before the R bit is added in. Second, the R bit is added to the leftmost, rather than the rightmost bit.

Figure 3-27 illustrates how the modified algorithm, known as **aging**, works. Suppose that after the first clock tick the R bits for pages 0 to 5 have the values 1, 0, 1, 0, 1, and 1 respectively (page 0 is 1, page 1 is 0, page 2 is 1, etc.). In other words, between tick 0 and tick 1, pages 0, 2, 4, and 5 were referenced, setting their R bits to 1, while the other ones remain 0. After the six corresponding counters have been shifted and the R bit inserted at the left, they have the values shown in Fig. 3-27(a). The four remaining columns show the six counters after the next four clock ticks.

R bits for pages 0-5, clock tick 0	R bits for pages 0-5, clock tick 1	R bits for pages 0-5, clock tick 2	R bits for pages 0-5, clock tick 3	R bits for pages 0-5, clock tick 4
1 0 1 0 1 1	1 1 0 0 1 0	1 1 0 1 0 1	1 0 0 0 1 0	0 1 1 0 0 0

Page					
0	10000000	11000000	11100000	11110000	01111000
1	00000000	10000000	11000000	01100000	10110000
2	10000000	01000000	00100000	00010000	10001000
3	00000000	00000000	10000000	01000000	00100000
4	10000000	11000000	01100000	10110000	01011000
5	10000000	01000000	10100000	01010000	00101000
	(a)	(b)	(c)	(d)	(e)

Fig. 3-27. The aging algorithm simulates LRU in software. Shown are six pages for five clock ticks. The five clock ticks are represented by (a) to (e).

When a page fault occurs, the page whose counter is the lowest is removed. It is clear that a page that has not been referenced for, say, four clock ticks will have four leading zeros in its counter, and thus will have a lower value than a counter that has not been referenced for three clock ticks.

This algorithm differs from LRU in two ways. Consider pages 3 and 5 in Fig. 3-27(e). Neither has been referenced for two clock ticks; both were referenced in the tick prior to that. According to LRU, if a page must be replaced, we should choose one of these two. The trouble is, we do not know which of these two was referenced last in the interval between tick 1 and tick 2. By recording only one bit per time interval, we have lost the ability to distinguish references early in the clock interval from those occurring later. All we can do is remove page 3, because page 5 was also referenced two ticks earlier and page 3 was not.

The second difference between LRU and aging is that in aging the counters have a finite number of bits, 8 bits in this example. Suppose two pages each have a counter value of 0. All we can do is pick one of them at random. In reality, it may well be that one of the pages was last referenced 9 ticks ago and the other was last referenced 1000 ticks ago. We have no way of seeing that. In practice, however, 8 bits is generally enough if a clock tick is around 20 msec. If a page has not been referenced in 160 msec, it probably is not that important.

3.5. MODELING PAGING ALGORITHMS

Over the years, some work has been done on modeling page replacement algorithms from a theoretical perspective. In this section we will discuss some of these ideas.

3.5.1. Belady's Anomaly

Intuitively, it might seem that the more page frames the memory has, the fewer page faults a program will get. Surprisingly enough, this is not always the case. Belady et al. (1969) discovered a counterexample, in which FIFO caused more page faults with four page frames than with three. This strange situation has become known as **Belady's anomaly**. It is illustrated in Fig. 3-28 for a program with five virtual pages, numbered from 0 to 4. The pages are referenced in the order

0 1 2 3 0 1 4 0 1 2 3 4

In Fig. 3-28(a) we see how with three page frames a total of nine page faults are caused. In Fig. 3-28(b) we get ten page faults with four page frames.

3.5.2. Stack Algorithms

Many researchers in computer science were dumbfounded by Belady's anomaly and began investigating it. This work led to the development of a whole theory of paging algorithms and their properties. While most of this work is beyond the scope of this book, we will give a brief introduction below. For more details see (Maekawa et al., 1987).

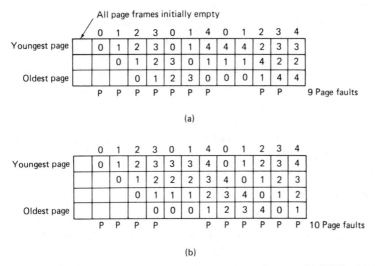

Fig. 3-28. Belady's anomaly. (a) FIFO with three page frames. (b) FIFO with four page frames. The *P*'s show which page references cause page faults.

All of this work begins with the observation that every process generates a sequence of memory references as it runs. Each memory reference corresponds to a specific virtual page. Thus conceptually, a process' memory access can be characterized by an (ordered) list of page numbers. This list is called the **reference string**, and plays a central role in the theory. For simplicity, in the rest of this section we will consider only the case of a machine with one process, so each machine has a single, deterministic reference string (with multiple processes, we would have to take into account the interleaving of their reference strings due to the multiprogramming).

A paging system can be characterized by three items:

1. The reference string of the executing process.

2. The page replacement algorithm.

3. The number of page frames available in memory, m.

Conceptually, we can imagine an abstract interpreter that works as follows. It maintains, in an internal array, M, that keeps track of the state of memory. It has as many elements as the process has virtual pages, which we will call n. The array M is divided into two parts. The top part, with m entries, contains all the pages that are currently in memory. The bottom part, with $n - m$ pages, contains all the pages that have been referenced once, but have been paged out and are not currently in memory. Initially, M is the empty set, since no pages have been referenced and no pages are in memory.

As execution begins, the process begins emitting the pages in the reference string, one at a time. As each one comes out, the interpreter checks to see if the page is in memory (i.e., in the top part of M). If it is not, a page fault occurs. If there is an empty slot in memory (i.e., the top part of M contains fewer than m entries), the page is loaded and entered in the top part of M. This situation arises only at the start of execution. If memory is full (i.e., the top part of M contains m entries), the page replacement algorithm is invoked to remove a page from memory. In the model, what happens is that one page is moved from the top part of M to the bottom part, and the needed page entered into the top part. In addition, the top part and the bottom part may be separately rearranged.

To make the operation of the interpreter clearer, let us look at a concrete example using LRU page replacement. The virtual address space has eight pages and the physical memory with four page frames. At the top of Fig. 3-29 we have a reference string consisting of the 24 pages:

0 2 1 3 5 4 6 3 7 4 7 3 3 5 5 3 1 1 1 7 2 3 4 1

Under the reference string, we have 25 columns of 8 items each. The first column, which is empty, reflects the state of M before execution begins. Each successive column shows M after one page has been emitted by the reference and processed by the paging algorithm. The heavy outline denotes the top of M, that is, the first four slots, which correspond to page frames in memory. Pages inside the heavy box are in memory, and pages below it have been paged out to disk.

Reference string		0	2	1	3	5	4	6	3	7	4	7	3	3	5	5	3	1	1	1	7	2	3	4	1
		0	2	1	3	5	4	6	3	7	4	7	3	3	5	5	3	1	1	1	7	2	3	4	1
			0	2	1	3	5	4	6	3	7	4	7	7	3	3	5	3	3	3	1	7	2	3	4
				0	2	1	3	5	4	6	3	3	4	4	7	7	7	5	5	5	3	1	7	2	3
					0	2	1	3	5	4	6	6	6	6	4	4	4	7	7	7	5	3	1	7	2
						0	2	1	1	5	5	5	5	5	6	6	6	4	4	4	4	5	5	1	7
							0	2	2	1	1	1	1	1	1	1	1	6	6	6	6	4	4	5	5
								0	0	2	2	2	2	2	2	2	2	2	2	2	2	6	6	6	6
									0	0	0	0	0	0	0	0	0	0	0	0	0	0	0	0	0
Page faults		P	P	P	P	P	P	P		P					P			P				P		P	P
Distance string		∞	∞	∞	∞	∞	∞	∞	4	∞	4	2	3	1	5	1	2	6	1	1	4	7	4	6	5

Fig. 3-29. The state of the memory array, M, after each item in the reference string is processed. The distance string will be discussed in the next section.

The first page in the reference string is 0, so it is entered in the top of memory, as shown in the second column. The second page is 2, so it is entered at the top of the third column. This action causes 0 to move down. In this example, a newly loaded page is always entered at the top, and everything else moved down, as needed.

Each of the first seven pages in the reference string causes a page fault. The first four can be handled without removing a page, but starting with the reference to page 5, loading a new page requires removing an old page.

The second reference to page 3 does not cause a page fault, because 3 is already in memory. Nevertheless, the interpreter removes it from where it was and puts it on the top, as shown. The process continues for a while, until page 5 is referenced. This page is moved from bottom part of M to the top part (i.e., it is loaded into memory from disk). Whenever a page is referenced that is not within the heavy box, a page fault occurs, as indicated by the p's below the matrix.

Let us now briefly summarize some of the properties of this model. First, when a page is referenced, it is always moved to the top entry in M. Second, if the page referenced was already in M, all pages above it move down one position. A transition from within the box to outside of it corresponds to a page being evicted from memory. Third, pages that were below the referenced page are not moved. In this manner, the contents of M exactly represent the contents of the LRU algorithm.

Although this example uses LRU, the model works equally well with other algorithms. In particular, there is one class of algorithms that is especially interesting: algorithms that have the property

$$M(m, r) \subseteq M(m + 1, r)$$

where m varies over the page frames and r is an index into the reference string. What this says is that the set of pages included in the top part of M for a memory with m page frames after r memory references are also included in M for a memory with $m + 1$ page frames. In other words, if we increase memory size by one page frame and re-execute the process, at every point during the execution, all the pages that were present in the first run are also present in the second run, along with one additional page.

From examination of Fig. 3-29 and a little thought about how it works, it should be clear that LRU has this property. Some other algorithms (e.g., optimal page replacement) also have it, but FIFO does not. Algorithms that have this property are called **stack algorithms**. These algorithms do not suffer from Belady's anomaly, and are thus much loved by virtual memory theorists.

3.5.3. The Distance String

For stack algorithms, it is often convenient to represent the reference string in a more abstract way than the actual page numbers. A page reference will be henceforth denoted by the distance from the top of the stack where the referenced page was located. For example, the reference to page 1 in the last column of Fig. 3-29 is a reference to a page at a distance 5 from the top of the stack (because page 1 was in fifth place *before* the reference). Pages that have not yet been referenced and thus are not yet on the stack (i.e., not yet in M) are said to be at a distance ∞. The distance string for Fig. 3-29 is given at the bottom of the figure.

Note that the distance string depends not only on the reference string, but also on the paging algorithm. With the same original reference string, a different paging algorithm would make different choices about which pages to evict. As a result, a different sequence of stacks arises.

The statistical properties of the distance string have a major impact on the performance of the algorithm. In Fig. 3-30(a) we see the probability density function for the entries in a (ficticious) distance string, d. Most of the entries in the string are between 1 and k. With a memory of k page frames, few page faults occur.

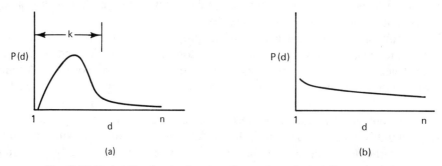

Fig. 3-30. Probability density functions for two hypothetical distance strings.

In contrast, in Fig. 3-30(b), the references are so spread out that the only way to avoid a large number of page faults is to give the program as many page frames as it has virtual pages.

3.5.4. Predicting Page Fault Rates

One of the nice properties of the distance string is that it can be used to predict the number of page faults that will occur with memories of different sizes. We will demonstrate how this computation can be made based on the example of Fig. 3-29. The goal is to make one pass over the distance string and, from the information collected, to be able to predict how many page faults the process would have in memories with 1, 2, 3, ..., n page frames, where n is the number of virtual pages in the process' address space.

The algorithm starts by scanning the distance string, page by page. It keeps track of the number of times 1 occurs, the number of times 2 occurs, and so on. Let C_i be the number of occurrences of i. For the distance string of Fig. 3-29, the C vector is listed in Fig. 3-31(a). In this example, it happens four times that the page referenced is already on top of the stack. Three times the reference is to the next-to-the-top page, and so forth. Let C_∞ be the number of times ∞ occurs in the distance string.

Now compute the F vector according to the formula

$$F_m = \sum_{k=m+1}^{n} C_k + C_\infty$$

The value of F_m is the number of page faults that will occur with the given distance string and m page frames. For the distance string of Fig. 3-29, Fig. 3-31(b) gives the F vector. For example, F_1 is 20, meaning that with a memory holding only 1 page frame, out of the 24 references in the string, all get page faults except the four that are the same as the previous page reference.

To see why this formula works, go back to the heavy box in Fig. 3-29. Let m be the number of page frames in the top part of M. A page fault occurs any time an element of the distance string is $m + 1$ or more. The summation in the formula above

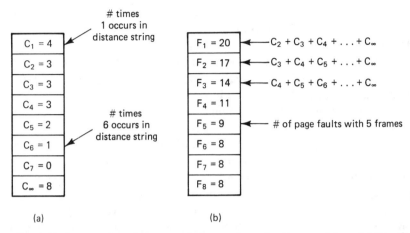

Fig. 3-31. Computation of the page fault rate from the distance string. (a) The C vector. (b) F vector.

adds up the number of times such elements occur. This model can be used to make other predictions as well (Maekawa et al., 1987).

3.6. DESIGN ISSUES FOR PAGING SYSTEMS

In the previous sections we have explained how paging works and have given a few of the basic page replacement algorithms. But knowing the bare mechanics is not enough. To design a system, you have to know a lot more to make it work well. It is like the difference between knowing how to move the rook, knight, bishop, and other pieces in chess, and being a good player. In the following sections, we will look at other issues that operating system designers must consider carefully in order to get good performance from a paging system.

3.6.1. The Working Set Model

In the purest form of paging, processes are started up with none of their pages in memory. As soon as the CPU tries to fetch the first instruction, it gets a page fault, causing the operating system to bring in the page containing the first instruction. Other page faults for global variables and the stack usually follow quickly. After a while, the process has most of the pages it needs and settles down to run with relatively few page faults. This strategy is called **demand paging** because pages are loaded only on demand, not in advance.

Of course, it is easy enough to write a test program that systematically reads all the pages in a large address space, causing so many page faults that there is not enough memory to hold them all. Fortunately, most processes do not work this way. They exhibit a **locality of reference**, meaning that during any phase of execution, the process references only a relatively small fraction of its pages. Each pass of a multipass compiler, for example, references only a fraction of all the pages, and a different fraction at that.

The set of pages that a process is currently using is called its **working set** (Denning, 1968a; Denning, 1980). If the entire working set is in memory, the process will run without causing many faults until it moves into another execution phase (e.g., the next pass of the compiler). If the available memory is too small to hold the entire working set, the process will cause many page faults and run very slowly since executing an instruction typically takes a fraction of a microsecond and reading in a page from the disk typically takes tens of milliseconds. At a rate of one or two instructions per 30 milliseconds, it will take a long time to finish. A program causing page faults every few instructions is said to be **thrashing** (Denning, 1968b).

In a timesharing system, processes are frequently moved to disk (i.e., all their pages are removed from memory) to let other processes have a turn at the CPU. The question arises of what to do when a process is brought back in again. Technically, nothing need be done. The process will just cause page faults until its working set has been loaded. The problem is that having 20, 50, or even 100 page faults every time a process is loaded is slow, and it also wastes considerable CPU time, since it takes the operating system a few milliseconds of CPU time to process a page fault.

Therefore, many paging systems try to keep track of each process' working set, and make sure that it is in memory before letting the process run. This approach is called the **working set model** (Denning, 1970). It is designed to greatly reduce the page fault rate. Loading the pages *before* letting processes run is also called **prepaging.**

To implement the working set model, it is necessary for the operating system to keep track of which pages are in the working set. One way to monitor this information is to use the aging algorithm discussed above. Any page containing a 1 bit among the high order n bits of the counter is considered to be a member of the working set. If a page has not been referenced in n consecutive clock ticks, it is dropped from the working set. The parameter n has to be determined experimentally for each system, but the system performance is usually not especially sensitive to the exact value.

Information about the working set can be used to improve the performance of the clock algorithm. Normally, when the hand points to a page whose R bit is 0, the page is evicted. The improvement is to check to see if that page is part of the working set of the current process. If it is, the page is spared. This algorithm is called **wsclock**.

3.6.2. Local versus Global Allocation Policies

In the preceding sections we have discussed several algorithms for choosing a page to replace when a fault occurs. A major issue associated with this choice (which we have carefully swept under the rug until now) is how memory should be allocated among the competing runnable processes.

Take a look at Fig. 3-32(a). In this figure, three processes, A, B, and C, make up the set of runnable processes. Suppose A gets a page fault. Should the page replacement algorithm try to find the least recently used page considering only the six pages currently allocated to A, or should it consider all the pages in memory? If it looks only at A's pages, the page with the lowest age value is $A5$, so we get the situation of Fig. 3-32(b).

(a)	Age	(b)	(c)
A0	10	A0	A0
A1	7	A1	A1
A2	5	A2	A2
A3	4	A3	A3
A4	6	A4	A4
A5	3	(A6)	A5
B0	9	B0	B0
B1	4	B1	B1
B2	6	B2	B2
B3	2	B3	(A6)
B4	5	B4	B4
B5	6	B5	B5
B6	12	B6	B6
C1	3	C1	C1
C2	5	C2	C2
C3	6	C3	C3

Fig. 3-32. Local versus global page replacement. (a) Original configuration. (b) Local page replacement. (c) Global page replacement.

On the other hand, if the page with the lowest age value is removed without regard to whose page it is, page $B3$ will be chosen and we will get the situation of Fig. 3-32(c). The algorithm of Fig. 3-32(b) is said to be a **local** page replacement algorithm, whereas Fig. 3-32(c) is said to be a **global** algorithm. Local algorithms correspond to assigning each process a fixed amount of memory. Global algorithms dynamically allocate page frames among the runnable processes. Thus the number of page frames assigned to each process varies in time.

In general, global algorithms work better, especially when the working set size can vary over the lifetime of a process. If a local algorithm is used and the working set grows, thrashing will result, even if there are plenty of free page frames. If the working set shrinks, local algorithms waste memory. If a global algorithm is used, the system must continually decide how many page frames to assign to each process. One way is to monitor the working set size as indicated by the aging bits, but this approach does not necessarily prevent thrashing. The working set may change size in microseconds, whereas the aging bits are a crude measure spread over a number of clock ticks.

Another approach is to have an algorithm for allocating page frames to processes. One way is to periodically determine the number of running processes and allocate each process an equal share. Thus with 475 available (i.e., non-operating system) page frames and 10 processes, each process gets 47 frames. The remaining five go into a pool to be used when page faults occur.

Although this method seems fair, it makes little sense to give equal shares of the memory to a 10K process and a 300K process. Instead, pages can be allocated in proportion to each process' total size, with a 300K process getting 30 times the allotment of a 10K process. It is probably wise to give process some minimum number, so it can run, no matter how small it is. On some machines, for example, a single instruction may need as many as six pages because the instruction, the source operand and the destination operand may all straddle page boundaries. With an allocation of only five pages, programs containing such instructions cannot run at all.

Neither the equal allocation nor the proportional allocation method directly deals with the thrashing problem. A more direct way to control it is to use the **page fault frequency** or **PFF** allocation algorithm. For a large class of page replacement algorithms, including LRU, it is known that the fault rate decreases as more pages are assigned, as we discussed above. (Belady's anomaly occurred with FIFO, which does not have this property.) This property is illustrated in Fig. 3-33.

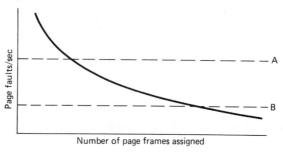

Fig. 3-33. Page fault rate as a function of the number of page frames assigned.

The dashed line marked *A* corresponds to a page fault rate that is unacceptably high, so the faulting process is given more page frames to reduce the fault rate. The dashed line marked *B* corresponds to a page fault rate so low that it can be concluded that the process has too much memory. In this case page frames may be taken away from it. Thus, PFF tries to keep the paging rate within acceptable bounds.

If it discovers that there are so many processes in memory that it is not possible to keep all of them below *A*, then some process is removed from memory, and its page frames are divided up among the remaining processes or put into a pool of available pages that can be used on subsequent page faults. The decision to remove a process from memory is a form of load control. It shows that even with paging, swapping is still needed, only now swapping is used to reduce potential demand for memory, rather than to reclaim blocks of it for immediate use.

3.6.3. Page Size

The page size is often a parameter that can be chosen by the operating system designers. Even if the hardware has been designed with, for example, 512-byte pages, the operating system can easily regard pages 0 and 1, 2 and 3, 4 and 5, and so on, as 1K pages by always allocating two consecutive 512-byte page frames for them.

Determining the optimum page size requires balancing several competing factors.

To start with, a randomly chosen text, data, or stack segment will not fill an integral number of pages. On the average, half of the final page will be empty. The extra space in that page is wasted (internal fragmentation). With n segments in memory and a page size of p bytes, $np/2$ bytes will be wasted on internal fragmentation. This reasoning argues for a small page size.

Another argument for a small page size becomes apparent if we think about a program consisting of eight sequential phases of 4K each. With a 32K page size, the program must be allocated 32K all the time. With a 16K page size, it needs only 16K. With a page size of 4K or smaller, it requires only 4K at any instant. In general, a large page size will cause more unused program to be in memory than a small page size.

On the other hand, small pages mean that programs will need many pages, hence a large page table. A 32K program needs only four 8K pages, but 64 512-byte pages. Transfers to and from the disk are generally a page at a time, with most of the time being for the seek and rotational delay, so that transferring a small page takes almost as much time as transferring a large page. It might take 64×15 msec to load 64 512-byte pages, but only 4×25 msec to load four 8K pages.

On some machines, the page table must be loaded into hardware registers every time the CPU switches from one process to another. On these machines having a small page size means that the time required to load the page registers gets longer as the page size gets smaller. Furthermore, the space occupied by the page table increases as the page size decreases.

This last point can be analyzed mathematically. Let the average process size be s bytes and the page size be p bytes. Furthermore, assume that each page entry requires e bytes. The approximate number of pages needed per process is then s/p, occupying se/p bytes of page table space. The wasted memory in the last page of the process due to internal fragmentation is $p/2$. Thus, the total overhead due to the page table and the internal fragmentation loss is given by

$$\text{overhead} = se/p + p/2$$

The first term (page table size) is large when the page size is small. The second term (internal fragmentation) is large when the page size is large. The optimum must lie somewhere in between. By taking the first derivative with respect to p and equating it to zero, we get the equation

$$-se/p^2 + 1/2 = 0$$

From this equation we can derive a formula that gives the optimum page size (considering only memory wasted in fragmentation and page table size). The result is:

$$p = \sqrt{2se}$$

For $s = 128K$ and $e = 8$ bytes per page table entry, the optimum page size is 1448 bytes. In practice 1K or 2K would be used, depending on the other factors (e.g., disk speed). Most commercially available computers use page sizes ranging from 512 bytes to 8K.

3.6.4. Implementation Issues

Implementers of virtual memory systems have to make choices among the major theoretical algorithms such as second chance versus aging, local versus global page allocation, and demand paging versus prepaging. But they also have to be aware of a number of practical implementation issues as well. In this section we will take a look at a few of the more common problems and some solutions.

Instruction Backup

When a program references a page that is not in memory, the instruction causing the fault is stopped part way through and a trap to the operating system occurs. After the operating system has fetched the page needed, it must restart the instruction causing the trap. This is easier said than done.

For one thing, most instructions consist of several bytes. The Motorola 68000 instruction

MOVE.L #6(A1),2(A0)

is 6 bytes, for example (see Fig. 3-34). In order to restart the instruction, the operating system must determine where the first byte of the instruction is. The value of the program counter at the time of the trap depends on which operand faulted and how the CPU's microcode has been implemented.

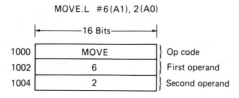

Fig. 3-34. An instruction causing a page fault.

In Fig. 3-34, we have an instruction starting at address 1000 that makes three memory references: the instruction word, and two offsets for the operands. Depending on which of these three memory references caused the page fault, the program counter might be 1000, 1002, or 1004 at the time of the fault. It is frequently impossible for the operating system to determine unambiguously where the instruction began. If the program counter is 1002 at the time of the fault, the operating system has no way of telling whether the word in 1002 is a memory address associated with an instruction at 1000, or an instruction opcode.

Bad as this problem may be, it could have been worse. Instructions that use autoincrement mode can also fault. Depending on the details of the microcode, the increment may be done before the memory reference, in which case the operating system must decrement the register in software before restarting the instruction. Or, the autoincrement may be done after the memory reference, in which case it will not have been done at the time of the trap and must not be undone by the operating system. Autodecrement causes the same problem.

The precise details of whether autoincrements and autodecrements have or have not been done before the corresponding memory references may differ from instruction to instruction and from CPU model to CPU model. As a result, paging on the 68000 is not possible, at least not without enormous contortions on the part of the operating system.

Fortunately, on some machines the CPU designers provide a solution, usually in the form of a register into which the program counter is copied just before each instruction is executed. These machines generally also have a second register telling which registers have already been autoincremented or autodecremented, and by how much. Given this information, the operating system can unambiguously undo all the effects of the faulting instruction so it can be started all over again. The PDP-11/45 works this way, for example.

On other machines, such as the Motorola 68010, the microcode dumps internal state information on the stack to allow restart. On still other machines, such as the VAX, the microcode rolls back the state of the machine to the point it had before the faulting instruction started, making restart easy. At the other extreme are many modern RISC machines that leave the machine in a horribly complex state after a fault. It is as though the hardware designers were unable to solve the problem, so they threw up their hands and told the operating system writers to deal with it.

Locking Pages in Memory

Although we have not discussed I/O much in this chapter, the fact that a computer has virtual memory does not mean that I/O (especially terminal I/O) is absent. Virtual memory and I/O interact in subtle ways. Consider a process that has just issued a system call to read from some file or device into a buffer within its address space. While waiting for the I/O to complete, the process is suspended and another process is allowed to run. This other process gets a page fault.

If the paging algorithm is global, there is a small, but nonzero, chance that the page containing the I/O buffer will be chosen to be removed from memory. If an I/O device is currently in the process of doing a DMA transfer to that page, removing it will cause part of the data to be written in the buffer where it belongs, and part of the data to be written over the newly loaded page. One solution to this problem is to lock pages engaged in I/O in memory so that they will not be removed. Another solution is to do all I/O to kernel buffers and then copy the data to user pages later.

Shared Pages

Another implementation issue is sharing. In a large timesharing system, it is common for several users to be running the same program (e.g., the editor, a compiler) at the same time. It is clearly more efficient to share the pages, to avoid having two copies of the same page in memory at the same time. One problem is that not all pages are sharable. In particular, pages that are read-only, such as program text, can be shared, but data pages cannot.

Even with this restriction, another problem occurs with shared pages. Suppose processes *A* and *B* are both running the editor and sharing its pages. If the scheduler decides to remove *A* from memory, evicting all its pages and filling the empty page frames with some other program will cause *B* to generate a large number of page faults to bring them back in again.

Similarly, when *A* terminates, it is essential to be able to discover that the pages are still in use so that their disk space will not be freed by accident. Searching all the page tables to see if a page is shared is usually too expensive, so special data structures are needed to keep track of shared pages.

Backing Store

In our discussion of page replacement algorithms, we saw how a page is selected for removal. We have not said much about where on the disk it is put when it is paged out. Let us now describe some of the issues related to disk management.

The simplest algorithm for allocating page space on the disk is to have a special swap area on the disk. When the system is booted, this area is empty, and is represented in memory as a single entry giving its origin and size. When the first process is started, a chunk of the swap area the size of the first process is reserved and the remaining area reduced by that amount. As new processes are started, they are assigned chunks of the swap area equal in size to their core images. As they finish, their disk space is freed. The swap area is managed as a list of free chunks.

Associated with each process is the disk address of its swap area, kept in the process table. Calculating the address to write a page to becomes simple: just add the offset of the page within the virtual address space to the start of the swap area. However, before a process can start, the swap area must be initialized. One way is to copy the entire process image to the swap area, so that it can be brought *in* as needed. The other is to load the entire process in memory, and let it be paged *out* as needed.

However, this simple model has a problem: processes can increase in size after starting. Although the program text is usually fixed, the data area can sometimes grow, and the stack can always grow. Consequently, it may be better to reserve separate swap areas for the text, data, and stack, and allow each of these areas to consist of more than one chunk on the disk.

The other extreme is to allocate nothing in advance, and allocate disk space for each page when it is swapped out and deallocate it when it is swapped back in. In this way, processes in memory do not tie up any swap space. The disadvantage is that a disk address is needed in memory to keep track of each page on disk.

Paging Daemons

Paging works best when there are plenty of free page frames that can be claimed as page faults occur. If every page frame is full, and furthermore modified, before a new page can be brought in, an old page must first be written to disk. To insure a plentiful supply of free page frames, many paging systems have a background process, called the **paging daemon**, that sleeps most of the time, but is awakened periodically to inspect the state of memory. If too few page frames are free, the paging daemon begins selecting pages to evict using the chosen page replacement algorithm. If these pages have been modified since being loaded, they are written to disk.

In any event, the previous contents of the page are remembered. In the event one of the evicted pages is needed again before its frame has been overwritten, it can be reclaimed by removing it from the pool of free page frames. Keeping a supply of page frames around yields better performance than using all of memory and then trying to find a frame at the moment it is needed. At the very least, the paging daemon ensures that all the free frames are clean, so they need not be written to disk in a big hurry when they are required.

Page Fault Handling

We are finally in a position to describe what happens on a page fault in some detail. The sequence of events is as follows:

1. The hardware traps to the kernel, saving the program counter on the stack. On most machines, some information about the state of the current instruction is saved in special CPU registers.

2. An assembly code routine is started to save the general registers and other volatile information, to keep the operating system from destroying it. This routine calls the operating system as a procedure.

3. The operating system discovers that a page fault has occurred, and tries to discover which virtual page is needed. Often one of the hardware registers contains this information. If not, the operating system must retrieve the program counter, fetch the instruction, and parse it in software to figure out what it was doing when the fault hit.

4. Once the virtual address that caused the fault is known, the operating system checks to see if this address is valid and the protection consistent with the access. If not, the process is sent a signal or killed. If the address is valid and no protection fault has occurred, the system attempts to acquire a page frame from the list of free frames. If no frames are free, the page replace algorithm is run to select a victim.

5. If the page frame selected is dirty, the page is scheduled for transfer to the disk, and a context switch takes place, suspending the faulting process and letting another one run until the disk transfer has completed. In any event, the frame is marked as busy to prevent it from being used for another purpose.

6. As soon as the page frame is clean (either immediately or after it is written to disk), the operating system looks up the disk address where the needed page is, and schedules a disk operation to bring it in. While the page is being loaded, the faulting process is still suspended and another user process is run, if one is available.

7. When the disk interrupt indicates that the page has arrived, the page tables are updated to reflect its position, and the frame is marked as being in normal state.

8. The faulting instruction is backed up to the state it had when it began and the program counter is reset to point to that instruction.

9. The faulting process is scheduled, and the operating system returns to the assembly language routine that called it.

10. This routine restores the registers and other volatile information, and returns to user space to continue execution, as if no fault had occurred.

3.7. SEGMENTATION

The virtual memory discussed so far is one-dimensional because the virtual addresses go from 0 to some maximum address, one address after another. For many problems, having two or more separate virtual address spaces may be much better than having only one. For example, a compiler has many tables that are built up as compilation proceeds, possibly including

1. The source text being saved for the printed listing (on batch systems).

2. The symbol table, containing the names and attributes of variables.

3. The table containing all the integer and floating-point constants used.

4. The parse tree, containing the syntactic analysis of the program.

5. The stack used for procedure calls within the compiler.

Each of the first four tables grows continuously as compilation proceeds. The last one grows and shrinks in unpredictable ways during compilation. In a one-dimensional memory, these five tables would have to be allocated contiguous chunks of virtual address space, as in Fig. 3-35.

Consider what happens if a program has an exceptionally large number of variables. The chunk of address space allocated for the symbol table may fill up, but there may be lots of room in the other tables. The compiler could, of course, simply issue a message saying that the compilation cannot continue due to too many variables, but doing so does not seem very sporting when unused space is left in the other tables.

Another possibility is to play Robin Hood, taking space from the tables with much room and giving it to the tables with little room. This shuffling can be done, but it is analogous to managing one's own overlays—a nuisance at best and a great deal of tedious, unrewarding work at worst.

What is really needed is a way of freeing the programmer from having to manage

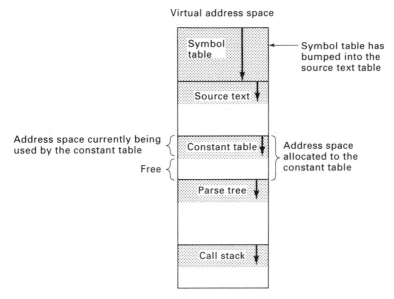

Fig. 3-35. In a one-dimensional address space with growing tables, one table may bump into another.

the expanding and contracting tables, in the same way that virtual memory eliminates the worry of organizing the program into overlays.

A straightforward and extremely general solution is to provide the machine with many completely independent address spaces, called **segments**. Each segment consists of a linear sequence of addresses, from 0 to some maximum. The length of each segment may be anything from 0 to the maximum allowed. Different segments may, and usually do, have different lengths. Moreover, segment lengths may change during execution. The length of a stack segment may be increased whenever something is pushed onto the stack and decreased whenever something is popped off the stack.

Because each segment constitutes a separate address space, different segments can grow or shrink independently, without affecting each other. If a stack in a certain segment needs more address space to grow, it can have it, because there is nothing else in its address space to bump into. Of course, a segment can fill up but segments are usually very large, so this occurrence is rare. To specify an address in this segmented or two-dimensional memory, the program must supply a two-part address, a segment number, and an address within the segment. Figure 3-36 illustrates a segmented memory being used for the compiler tables discussed earlier.

We emphasize that a segment is a logical entity, which the programmer is aware of and uses as a single logical entity. A segment might contain a procedure, or an array, or a stack, or a collection of scalar variables, but usually it does not contain a mixture of different types.

A segmented memory has other advantages besides simplifying the handling of data structures that are growing or shrinking. If each procedure occupies a separate segment, with address 0 as its starting address, the linking up of procedures compiled

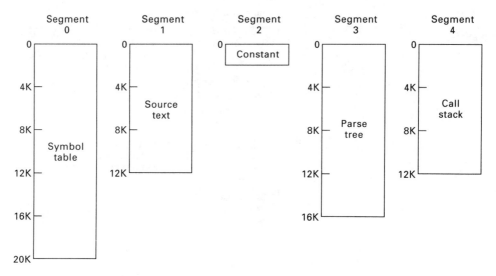

Fig. 3-36. A segmented memory allows each table to grow or shrink independently of the other tables.

separately is greatly simplified. After all the procedures that constitute a program have been compiled and linked up, a procedure call to the procedure in segment n will use the two-part address $(n, 0)$ to address word 0 (the entry point).

If the procedure in segment n is subsequently modified and recompiled, no other procedures need be changed (because no starting addresses have been modified), even if the new version is larger than the old one. With a one-dimensional memory, the procedures are packed tightly next to each other, with no address space between them. Consequently, changing one procedure's size can affect the starting address of other, unrelated procedures. This, in turn, requires modifying all procedures that call any of the moved procedures, in order to incorporate their new starting addresses. If a program contains hundreds of procedures, this process can be costly.

Segmentation also facilitates sharing procedures or data between several processes. A common example is the **shared library**. Modern workstations that run advanced window systems often have extremely large graphical libraries compiled into nearly every program. In a segmented system, the graphical library can be put in a segment and shared by multiple processes, eliminating the need for having it in every process' address space. While it is also possible to have shared libraries in pure paging systems, it is much more complicated. In effect, these systems do it by simulating segmentation.

Because each segment forms a logical entity of which the programmer is aware, such as a procedure, or an array, or a stack, different segments can have different kinds of protection. A procedure segment can be specified as execute only, prohibiting attempts to read from it or store into it. A floating-point array can be specified as read/write but not execute, and attempts to jump to it will be caught. Such protection is helpful in catching programming errors.

You should try to understand why protection makes sense in a segmented memory but not in a one-dimensional paged memory. In a segmented memory the user is aware of what is in each segment. Normally, a segment would not contain a procedure and a stack, for example, but one or the other. Since each segment contains only one type of object, the segment can have the protection appropriate for that particular type. Paging and segmentation are compared in Fig. 3-37.

Consideration	Paging	Segmentation
Need the programmer be aware that this technique is being used?	No	Yes
How many linear address spaces are there?	1	Many
Can the total address space exceed the size of physical memory?	Yes	Yes
Can procedures and data be distinguished and separately protected?	No	Yes
Can tables whose size fluctuates be accomodated easily?	No	Yes
Is sharing of procedures between users facilitated?	No	Yes
Why was this technique invented?	To get a large linear address space without having to buy more physical memory	To allow programs and data to be broken up into logically independent address spaces and to aid sharing and protection

Fig. 3-37. Comparison of paging and segmentation.

The contents of a page are, in a sense, accidental. The programmer is unaware of the fact that paging is even occurring. Although putting a few bits in each entry of the page table to specify the access allowed would be possible, to utilize this feature the programmer would have to keep track of where in his address space the page boundaries were, and that is precisely the sort of administration that paging was invented to eliminate. Because the user of a segmented memory has the illusion that all segments are in main memory all the time—that is, he can address them as though they were—he can protect each segment separately, without having to be concerned with the administration of overlaying them.

3.7.1. Implementation of Pure Segmentation

The implementation of segmentation differs from paging in an essential way: pages are fixed size and segments are not. Figure 3-38(a) shows an example of physical memory initially containing five segments. Now consider what happens if segment 1 is evicted and segment 7, which is smaller, is put in its place. We arrive at the memory configuration of Fig. 3-38(b). Between segment 7 and segment 2 is an unused area—that is, a hole. Then segment 4 is replaced by segment 5, as in Fig. 3-38(c), and segment 3 is replaced by segment 6, as in Fig. 3-38(d). After the system has been running for a while, memory will be divided up into a number of chunks, some containing segments and some containing holes. This phenomenon, checkerboarding, wastes memory in the holes. It can be dealt with by compaction, as shown in Fig. 3-38(e).

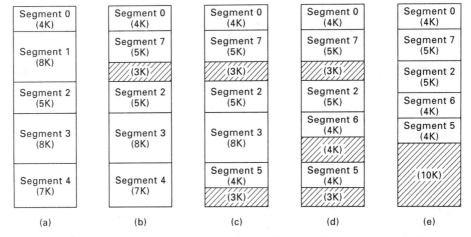

Fig. 3-38. (a)-(d) Development of checkerboarding. (e) Removal of the checkerboarding by compaction.

3.7.2. Segmentation with Paging: MULTICS

If the segments are large, it may be inconvenient, or even impossible, to keep them in main memory in their entirety. This leads to the idea of paging them, so that only those pages that are actually needed have to be around. Two significant systems have supported paged segments. In this section we will describe the first one, MULTICS. In the next one we will discuss the second one, the Intel 386.

MULTICS runs on the Honeywell 6000 machines and their descendants and provides each program with a virtual memory of up to 2^{18} segments (more than 250,000), each of which can be up to 65536 (36-bit) words long. To implement this, the MULTICS designers chose to treat each segment as a virtual memory and to page it, combining the advantages of paging (uniform page size and not having to keep the whole segment in memory if only part of it is being used) with the advantages of segmentation (ease of programming, modularity, protection, and sharing).

Each MULTICS program has a segment table, with one descriptor per segment. Since there are potentially more than a quarter of a million entries in the table, the segment table is itself a segment and is paged. A segment descriptor contains an indication of whether the segment is in main memory or not. If any part of the segment is in memory, the segment is considered to be in memory, and its page table will be in memory. If the segment is in memory, its descriptor contains an 18-bit pointer to its page table [see Fig. 3-39(a)]. Because physical addresses are 24 bits and all pages are aligned on 64-byte boundaries (implying that the low-order 6 bits of page addresses are 000000), only 18 bits are needed in the descriptor to store a page table address. The descriptor also contains the segment size, the protection bits, and a few other items. Figure 3-39(b) illustrates a MULTICS segment descriptor. The address of the segment in secondary memory is not in the segment descriptor but in another table used by the segment fault handler.

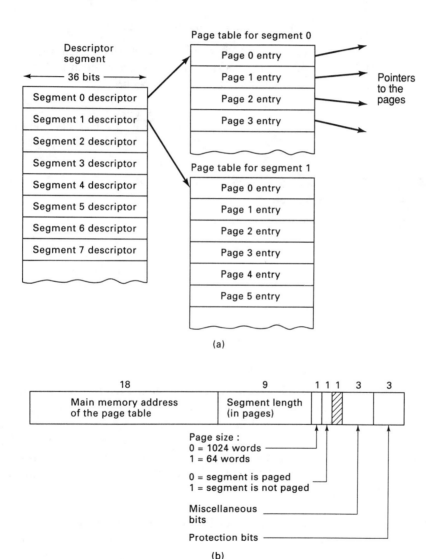

Fig. 3-39. The MULTICS virtual memory. (a) The descriptor segment points to the page tables. (b) A segment descriptor. The numbers are the field lengths.

Each segment is an ordinary virtual address space and is paged in the same way as the nonsegmented paged memory described earlier in this chapter. The normal page size is 1024 words (although a few small segments used by MULTICS itself are not paged or are paged in units of 64 words).

An address in MULTICS consists of two parts: the segment and the address within the segment. The address within the segment is further divided into a page number and a word within the page, as shown in Fig. 3-40. When a memory reference occurs, the following algorithm is carried out.

1. The segment number is used to find the segment descriptor.

2. A check is made to see if the segment's page table is in memory. If the page table is in memory, it is located. If it is not, a segment fault occurs. If there is a protection violation, a fault (trap) occurs.

3. The page table entry for the requested virtual page is examined. If the page is not in memory, a page fault occurs. If it is in memory, the main memory address of the start of the page is extracted from the page table entry.

4. The offset is added to the page origin to give the main memory address where the word is located.

5. The read or store finally takes place.

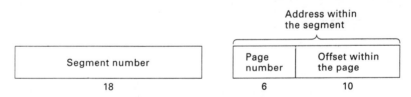

Fig. 3-40. A 34-bit MULTICS virtual address.

This process is illustrated in Fig. 3-41. For simplicity, the fact that the descriptor segment is itself paged has been omitted. What really happens is that a register (the descriptor base register), is used to locate the descriptor segment's page table, which, in turn, points to the pages of the descriptor segment. Once the descriptor for the needed segment has been found, the addressing proceeds as shown in Fig. 3-41.

As you have no doubt guessed by now, if the preceding algorithm were actually carried out by the operating system on every instruction, programs would not run very fast. In reality, the MULTICS hardware contains a 16-word high-speed associative memory that can search all its entries in parallel for a given key. It is illustrated in Fig. 3-42. When an address is presented to the computer, the addressing hardware first checks to see if the virtual address is in the associative memory. If so, it gets the page frame number directly from the associative memory and forms the actual address of the referenced word without having to look in the descriptor segment or page table.

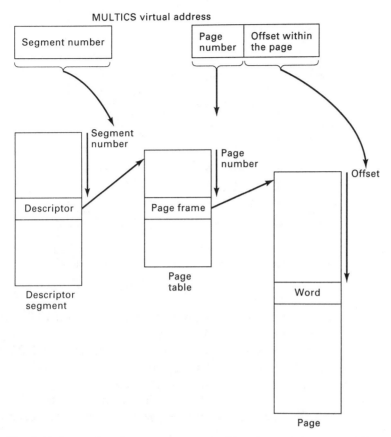

Fig. 3-41. Conversion of a two-part MULTICS address into a main memory address.

The addresses of the 16 most recently referenced pages are kept in the associative memory. Programs whose working set is smaller than the size of the associative memory will come to equilibrium with the addresses of the entire working set in the associative memory and therefore will run efficiently. If the page is not in the associative memory, the descriptor and page tables are actually referenced to find the page frame address, and the associative memory is updated to include this page, the least recently used page being thrown out. The age field keeps track of which entry has been least recently used. The reason that an associative memory is used is that segment and page number of all the entries can be compared simultaneously, for speed.

3.7.3. Segmentation with Paging: The Intel 386

In many ways, the virtual memory on the 386 resembles MULTICS, including the presence of both segmentation and paging. Whereas MULTICS has 256K independent segments, each up to 64K 36-bit words, the 386 has 16K independent segments, each holding up to 1 billion 32-bit words. Although there are fewer segments, the larger

	Comparison field				Is this entry used?
Segment number	Virtual Page	Page frame	Protection	Age	
4	1	7	Read / write	13	1
6	0	2	Read only	10	1
12	3	1	Read / write	2	1
					0
2	1	0	Execute only	7	1
2	2	12	Execute only	9	1

Fig. 3-42. A simplified version of the MULTICS associative memory. The existence of two page sizes makes the actual associative memory more complicated.

segment size is far more important, as few programs need more than 1000 segments, but many programs need segments holding megabytes.

The heart of the 386 virtual memory consists of two tables, the **LDT** (**Local Descriptor Table**) and the **GDT** (**Global Descriptor Table**). Each program has its own LDT, but there is a single GDT, shared by all the programs on the computer. The LDT describes segments local to each program, including its code, data, stack, and so on, whereas the GDT describes system segments, including the operating system itself.

To access a segment, a 386 program first loads a selector for that segment into one of the machine's six segment registers. During execution, the CS register holds the selector for the code segment and the DS register holds the selector for the data segment. The other segment registers are less important. Each selector is a 16-bit number, as shown in Fig. 3-43.

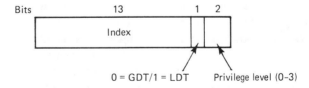

Fig. 3-43. A 386 selector.

One of the selector bits tells whether the segment is local or global (i.e., whether it is in the LDT or GDT). Thirteen other bits specify the LDT or GDT entry number, so these tables are each restricted to holding 8K segment descriptors. The other 2 bits relate to protection, and will be described later. Descriptor 0 is forbidden. It may be safely loaded into a segment register to indicate that the segment register is not currently available. It causes a trap if used.

At the time a selector is loaded into a segment register, the corresponding descriptor is fetched from the LDT or GDT and stored in microprogram registers, so it can be accessed quickly. A descriptor consists of 8 bytes, including the segment's base address, size, and other information, as depicted in Fig. 3-44.

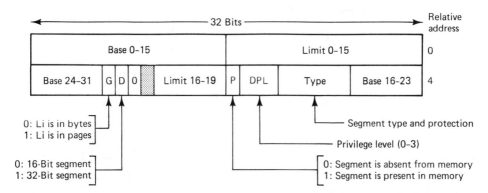

Fig. 3-44. 386 Code segment descriptor. Data segments differ slightly.

The format of the selector has been cleverly chosen to make locating the descriptor easy. First either the LDT or GDT is selected, based on selector bit 2. Then the selector is copied to a microprogram scratch register, and the 3 low-order bits set to 0. Finally, the address of either the LDT or GDT table is added to it, to give a direct pointer to the descriptor. For example, selector 72 refers to entry 9 in the GDT, which is located at address GDT + 72.

Let us trace the steps by which a (selector, offset) pair is converted to a physical address. As soon as the microprogram knows which segment register is being used, it can find the complete descriptor corresponding to that selector in its internal registers. If the segment does not exist (selector 0), or is currently paged out, a trap occurs.

It then checks to see if the offset is beyond the end of the segment, in which case a trap also occurs. Logically, there should simply be a 32-bit field in the descriptor giving the size of the segment, but there are only 20 bits available, so a different scheme is used. If the *Gbit* (Granularity) field is 0, the *Limit* field is the exact segment size, up to 1 MB. If it is 1, the *Limit* field gives the segment size in pages instead of bytes. The 386 page size is fixed at 4K bytes, so 20 bits is enough for segments up to 2^{32} bytes.

Assuming that the segment is in memory and the offset is in range, the 386 then adds the 32-bit *Base* field in the descriptor to the offset to form what is called a **linear address**, as shown in Fig. 3-45. The *Base* field is broken up into three pieces and spread all over the descriptor for compatibility with the 286, in which the *Base* is only 24 bits. In effect, the *Base* field allows each segment to start at an arbitrary place within the 32-bit linear address space.

If paging is disabled (by a bit in a global control register), the linear address is interpreted as the physical address and sent to the memory for the read or write. Thus with paging disabled, we have a pure segmentation scheme, with each

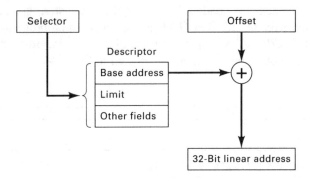

Fig. 3-45. Conversion of a (selector, offset) pair to a linear address.

segment's base address given in its descriptor. Segments are permitted to overlap, incidentally, probably because it would be too much trouble and take too much time to verify that they were all disjoint.

On the other hand, if paging is enabled, the linear address is interpreted as a virtual address and mapped onto the physical address using page tables, pretty much as in our earlier examples. The only complication is that with a 32-bit virtual address and a 4K page, a segment might contain 1 million pages, so a two-level mapping is used to reduce the page table size for small segments.

Each running program has a **page directory** consisting of 1024 32-bit entries. It is located at an address pointed to by a global register. Each entry in this directory points to a page table also containing 1024 32-bit entries. The page table entries point to page frames. The scheme is shown in Fig. 3-46.

In Fig. 3-46(a) we see a linear address broken up into three fields, *Dir*, *Page*, and *Off*. The *Dir* field is first used as an index into the page directory to locate a pointer to the proper page table. Then the *Page* field is used as an index into the page table to find the physical address of the page frame. Finally, *Off* is added to the address of the page frame to get the physical address of the byte or word addressed.

The page table entries are 32 bits each, 20 of which contain a page frame number. The remaining bits contain access and dirty bits, set by the hardware for the benefit of the operating system, protection bits, and other utility bits.

Each page table has entries for 1024 4K page frames, so a single page table handles 4 megabytes of memory. A segment shorter than 4M will have a page directory with a single entry, a pointer to its one and only page table. In this way, the overhead for short segments is only two pages, instead of the million pages that would be needed in a one-level page table.

To avoid making repeated references to memory, the 386, like MULTICS, has a small associative memory that directly maps the most recently used *Dir–Page* combinations onto the physical address of the page frame. Only when the current combination is not present in the associative memory is the mechanism of Fig. 3-46 actually carried out and the associative memory updated.

A little thought will reveal the fact that when paging is used, there is really no

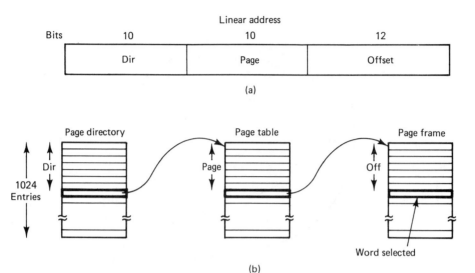

Fig. 3-46. Mapping of a linear address onto a physical address.

point in having the *Base* field in the descriptor be nonzero. All that *Base* does is cause a small offset to use an entry in the middle of the page directory, instead of at the beginning. The real reason for including *Base* at all is to allow pure (nonpaged) segmentation, and for compatibility with the 286, which always has paging disabled (i.e., the 286 has only pure segmentation, but not paging).

It is also worth mentioning that if a particular application does not need segmentation, but is content with a single, paged, 32-bit address space, that model is possible. All the segment registers can be set up with the same selector, whose descriptor has *Base* = 0 and *Limit* set to the maximum. The instruction offset will then be the linear address, with only a single address space used—in effect, normal paging.

All in all, one has to give credit to the 386 designers. Given the conflicting goals of implementing pure paging, pure segmentation, and paged segments, while at the same time being compatible with the 286, and doing all of this efficiently, the resulting design is surprisingly simple and clean.

Although we have covered the complete architecture of the 386 virtual memory, albeit briefly, it is worth saying a few words about protection, since this subject is intimately related to the virtual memory. Just as the virtual memory scheme is closely modeled on MULTICS, so is the protection system. The 386 supports four protection levels with level 0 being the most privileged and level 3 the least. These are shown in Fig. 3-47. At each instant, a running program is at a certain level, indicated by a 2-bit field in its PSW. Each segment in the system also has a level.

As long as a program restricts itself to using segments at its own level, everything works fine. Attempts to access data at a higher level are permitted. Attempts to access data at a lower level are illegal and cause traps. Attempts to call procedures at a different level (higher or lower) are allowed, but in a carefully controlled way. To

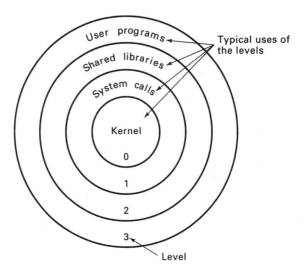

Fig. 3-47. Protection on the 386.

make an interlevel call, the CALL instruction must contain a selector instead of an address. This selector designates a descriptor called a **call gate**, which gives the address of the procedure to be called. Thus it is not possible to jump into the middle of an arbitrary code segment at a different level. Only official entry points may be used. The concepts of protection levels and call gates were pioneered in MULTICS, where they were viewed as **protection rings**.

A typical use for this mechanism is suggested in Fig. 3-47. At level 0, we find the kernel of the operating system, which handles I/O, memory management, and other critical matters. At level 1, the system call handler is present. User programs may call procedures here to have system calls carried out, but only a specific and protected list of procedures may be called. Level 2 contains library procedures, possibly shared among many running programs. User programs may call these procedures and read their data, but they may not modify them. Finally, user programs run at level 3, which has the least protection.

Traps and interrupts use a mechanism similar to the call gates. They, too, reference descriptors, rather than absolute addresses, and these descriptors point to specific procedures to be executed. The *Type* field in Fig. 3-44 distinguishes between code segments, data segments, and the various kinds of gates.

3.8. SUMMARY

In this chapter we have examined memory management. We saw that the simplest systems do not swap at all. Once a program is loaded into memory, it remains there until it finishes. Some operating systems allow only one process at a time in memory, while others support multiprogramming.

The next step up is swapping. When swapping is used, the system can handle more processes than it has room for in memory. Processes for which there is no room are swapped out to the disk. Free space in memory and on disk can be kept track of with a bit map, a hole list, or the buddy system.

More advanced computers often have some form of virtual memory. In the simplest form, each process' address space is divided up into uniform sized blocks called pages, which can be placed into any available page frame in memory. When the page tables are large, a multilevel paging scheme may be used to allow the page tables themselves to be paged out.

To improve performance, nearly all computers that support paging have an associative memory to do a rapid mapping of the virtual page number to the physical page frame number. Only on a miss is the page table consulted.

Many page replacement algorithms are known. Some are good but infeasible, such as optimal page replacement and LRU. Two of the better ones that are possible are clock and aging. Paging algorithms can be modeled theoretically using the distance string concept, which allows certain predictions to be made.

In practical paging systems, other aspects than the paging algorithm are important. These include the choice of the working set model versus demand paging, local versus global allocation, page size, and many implementation issues.

An alternative to pure paging is segmentation, with or without paged segments. MULTICS and the 386 both support segmentation with paging.

PROBLEMS

1. A computer system has enough room to hold four programs in its main memory. These programs are idle waiting for I/O half the time. What fraction of the CPU time is wasted?

2. Consider a swapping system in which memory consists of the following hole sizes in memory order: 10K, 4K, 20K, 18K, 7K, 9K, 12K, and 15K. Which hole is taken for successive segment requests of

   (a) 12K
   (b) 10K
   (c) 9K

   for first fit? Now repeat the question for best fit, worst fit, and next fit.

3. Using the model of Fig. 3-2, we can predict the increased throughput as a function of the degree of multiprogramming. Suppose that a computer has a 2M memory, of which the operating system takes 512K (one quarter of memory) and each user program also takes 512K. If all programs have 60 percent I/O wait, by what percentage will the throughput increase if another 1M is added?

4. Some swapping systems try to eliminate external fragmentation by compaction. Imagine that a computer with 1M user memory compacts once every second. If it takes 1/2 microsec to copy a byte, and the average hole is 0.4 as large as the average segment, what fraction of the total CPU time is used up on compaction?

5. A minicomputer uses the buddy system for memory management. Initially it has one block of 256K at address 0. After successive requests for 5K, 25K, 35K, and 20K come in, how many blocks are left and what are their sizes and addresses?

6. In a swapping system with variable partitions, the segments have the probability distribution $e^{-s/10}/10$, where s is the segment size in kilobytes. The holes have the probability distribution $e^{-h/5}/5$ where h is the hole size in kilobytes. What is the average fraction of wasted memory?

7. What is the difference between a physical address and a virtual address?

8. Using the page table of Fig. 3-11, give the physical address corresponding to each of the following virtual addresses:

    (a) 20
    (b) 4100
    (c) 8300

9. The Intel 8086 processor does not support virtual memory. Nevertheless, some companies have sold systems that contain an unmodified 8086 CPU and do paging. Make an educated guess as to how they did it. (Hint: think about the logical location of the MMU.)

10. If an instruction takes 1 microsec and a page fault takes an additional n microsec, give a formula for the effective instruction time if page faults occur every k instructions.

11. A machine has a 32-bit address space and an 8K page. The page table is entirely in hardware, with one 32-bit word per entry. When a process starts, the page table is copied to the hardware from memory, at one word every 100 nsec. If each process runs for 100 msec (including the time to load the page table), what fraction of the CPU time is devoted to loading the page tables?

12. A computer with a 32-bit address uses a two-level page table. Virtual addresses are split into a 9-bit top-level page table field, an 11-bit second-level page table field, and an offset. How large are the pages and how many are there in the virtual address space?

13. Below is the listing of a short assembly language program for a computer with 512-byte pages. The program is located at address 1020, and its stack pointer is at 8192 (the stack grows toward 0). Give the page reference string generated by this program. Each instruction occupies 4 bytes (1 word), and both instruction and data references count in the reference string.

    Load word 6144 into register 0
    Push register 0 onto the stack
    Call a procedure at 5120, stacking the return address
    Subtract the immediate constant 16 from the stack pointer
    Compare the actual parameter to the immediate constant 4
    Jump if equal to 5152

14. Suppose that a 32-bit virtual address is broken up into four fields, a, b, c, and d. The first three are used for a three-level page table system. The fourth field, d, is the offset. Does the number of pages depend on the sizes of all four fields? If not, which ones matter and which ones do not?

15. A computer whose processes have 1024 pages in their address spaces keeps its page tables in memory. The overhead required for reading a word from the page table is 500 nsec. To reduce this overhead, the computer has an associative memory, which holds 32 (virtual page, physical page frame) pairs, and can do a look up in 100 nsec. What hit rate is needed to reduce the mean overhead to 200 nsec?

16. The associative memory on the VAX does not contain an R bit. Why?

17. The R4000 is a RISC chip in the same line as the R2000, except that it is a full 64-bit machine, including 64-bit virtual addresses. Is the basic design of the MMU shown in Fig. 3-22 still applicable? If not, what can be done to fix it up?

18. A machine has 48-bit virtual addresses and 32-bit physical addresses. Pages are 8K. How many entries are needed for a conventional page table? For an inverted page table?

19. A computer has four page frames. The time of loading, time of last access, and the R and M bits for each page are as shown below (the times are in clock ticks):

Page	Loaded	Last ref.	R	M
0	126	279	0	0
1	230	260	1	0
2	120	272	1	1
3	160	280	1	1

   (a) Which page will NRU replace?
   (b) Which page will FIFO replace?
   (c) Which page will LRU replace?
   (d) Which page will second chance replace?

20. If FIFO page replacement is used with four page frames and eight pages, how many page faults will occur with the reference string 0172327103 if the four frames are initially empty? Now repeat this problem for LRU.

21. A small computer has four page frames. At the first clock tick, the R bits are 0111 (page 0 is 0, the rest are 1). At subsequent clock ticks, the values are 1011, 1010, 1101, 0010, 1010, 1100, and 0001. If the aging algorithm is used with an 8-bit counter, give the values of the four counters after the last tick.

22. How long does it take to load a 64K program from a disk whose average seek time is 30 msec, whose rotation time is 20 msec, and whose tracks hold 32K

   (a) for a 2K page size?
   (b) for a 4K page size?

The pages are spread randomly around the disk.

23. One of the first timesharing machines, the PDP-1, had a memory of 4K 18-bit words. It held one process at a time in memory. When the scheduler decided to run another

process, the process in memory was written to a paging drum, with 4K 18-bit words around the circumference of the drum. The drum could start writing (or reading) at any word, rather than only at word 0. Why do you suppose this drum was chosen?

24. A computer provides each process with 65,536 bytes of address space divided into pages of 4096 bytes. A particular program has a text size of 32,768 bytes, a data size of 16386 bytes, and a stack size of 15870 bytes. Will this program fit in the address space? If the page size were 512 bytes, would it fit? Remember that a page may not contain parts of two different segments.

25. It has been observed that the number of instructions executed between page faults is directly proportional to the number of page frames allocated to a program. If the available memory is doubled, the mean interval between page faults is also doubled. Suppose that a normal instruction takes 1 microsec, but if a page fault occurs, it takes 2001 microsec. If a program takes 60 sec to run, during which time it gets 15,000 page faults, how long would it take to run if twice as much memory were available?

26. A process generates the following distance string with a 5-frame memory and the LRU page replacement algorithm:

$\infty\ \infty\ \infty\ \infty\ \infty\ \infty\ \infty\ \infty$ 4 2 2 4 3 4 3 5 2 3 2 4 2 4 3 2 3 2 4 6 1 2 3 5

The process has 8 virtual pages in its address space. Compute the C and F vectors for this process.

27. The first three elements of the F vector for a certain process using a stack algorithm are F_1, F_2, and F_3. Can any general statements be made about the relationship among these three values?

28. A group of operating system designers for the Frugal Computer Company are thinking about ways of reducing the amount of backing store needed in their new operating system. The head guru has just suggested not bothering to save the program text in the swap area at all, but just page it in directly from the binary file whenever it is needed. Are there any problems with this approach?

29. Explain the difference between internal fragmentation and external fragmentation. Which one occurs in paging systems? Which one occurs in systems using pure segmentation?

30. When segmentation and paging are both being used, as in MULTICS, first the segment descriptor must be looked up, then the page descriptor. Does the associative memory also work this way, with two levels of lookup?

4

FILE SYSTEMS

All computer applications need to store and retrieve information. While a process is running, it can store a limited amount of information within its own address space. However, the storage capacity is restricted to the size of the virtual address space, at most. For some applications this size is adequate, but for others, such as airline reservations, banking, or record keeping in large companies, it is far too small.

A second problem with keeping information within a process' address space is that when the process terminates, the information is lost. For many applications, (e.g., for data bases), the information must be retained for weeks, months, or even forever. Having it vanish when a process using it terminates is unacceptable. Furthermore, it must not go away when the computer crashes and its processes die.

A third problem is that it is frequently necessary for multiple processes to access (parts of) the information at the same time. If we have an on-line telephone directory stored inside the address space of a single process, only that process can access it, so only one telephone number at a time can be looked up. The way to solve this problem is to make the information itself independent of any one process.

Thus we have three essential requirements for long-term information storage:

1. It must be possible to store a very large amount of information.

2. The information must survive the termination of the process using it.

3. Multiple processes must be able to access the information concurrently.

The solution to all these problems is to store information on disks and other external media in units called **files**. Processes can then read them and write new ones if need be. Information stored in files must be **persistent**, that is, not be affected by process creation and termination. A file should only disappear when its owner explicitly removes it.

Files are managed by the operating system. How they are structured, named, accessed, used, protected, and implemented are major topics in operating system design. As a whole, that part of the operating system dealing with files is known as the **file system**, and is the subject of this chapter.

From the users' standpoint, the most important aspect of a file system is how it appears to them, that is, what constitutes a file, how files are named and protected, what operations are allowed on files, and so on. The details of whether linked lists or bit maps are used to keep track of free storage and how many sectors there are in a logical block are of less interest, although they are of great importance to the designers of the file system. For this reason, we have structured the chapter as several sections. The first two are concerned with the user interface to files and directories, respectively. Then comes a detailed discussion of how the file system is implemented. After that we will look at security and protection mechanisms in file systems.

4.1. FILES

In this section we will look at files from the user's point of view, that is, how they are used and what properties they have.

4.1.1. File Naming

Files are an abstraction mechanism. They provide a way to store information on the disk and read it back later. This must be done in such a way as to shield the user from the details of how and where the information is stored, and how the disks actually work.

Probably the most important characteristic of any abstraction mechanism is the way the objects being managed are named, so we will start our examination of file systems with the subject of file naming. When a process creates a file, it gives the file a name. When the process terminates, the file continues to exist, and can be accessed by other processes using its name.

The exact rules for file naming vary somewhat from system to system, but all operating systems allow strings of one to eight letters as legal file names. Thus *andrea*, *bruce*, and *cathy* are possible file names. Frequently digits and special characters are also permitted, so names like *2*, *urgent!*, and *Fig.2-14* are often valid as well.

Some file systems distinguish between upper case letters and lower case letters, whereas others do not. UNIX falls in the first category; MS-DOS falls in the second. Thus a UNIX system can have all of the following as distinct files: *barbara*, *Barbara*,

BARBARA, *BARbara*, and *BarBaRa*. In MS-DOS they all designate the same file, just as the computer-generated bill sent to

C.L. Smith
123 Main St.
Hometown, NY 10000

and the engraved wedding invitation sent to

Dr. C.L. Smith
One hundred twenty three Main St.
Hometown, New York 10000

will arrive at the same house.

Many operating systems support two-part file names, with the two parts separated by a period, as in *prog.c*. The part following the period is called the **file extension**, and usually indicates something about the file. In MS-DOS, for example, file names are 1 to 8 characters, plus an optional extension of 1 to 3 characters. In UNIX, the size of the extension, if any, is up to the user, and a file may even have two or more extensions, as in *prog.c.Z*, where *.Z* is commonly used to indicate that the file (*prog.c*) has been compressed using the Ziv-Lempel compression algorithm. Some typical file extensions and their meanings are shown in Fig. 4-1.

Extension	Meaning
file.bak	Backup file
file.bas	BASIC source program
file.bin	Executable binary program
file.c	C source program
file.dat	Data file
file.doc	Documentation file
file.ftn	FORTRAN source program
file.hlp	Text for HELP command
file.lib	Library of .obj files used by the linker
file.man	Online manual page
file.obj	Object file (compiler output, not yet linked)
file.pas	Pascal source program
file.tex	Input text for the TEX formatting program
file.txt	General text file

Fig. 4-1. Some typical file extensions.

In some cases, the file extensions are just conventions, and are not enforced in any way. A file named *file.txt* is probably some kind of text file, but that name is more to remind the owner than to convey any specific information to the computer.

On the other hand, a C compiler may actually insist that the files it is to compile end in *.c*, and it may refuse to compile them if they do not.

Conventions like this are especially useful when the same program can handle several different kinds of files. The C compiler, for example, can be given a list of several files to compile and link together, some of them C files and some of them assembly language files. The extension then becomes essential for the compiler to tell which are which.

4.1.2. File Structure

Files can be structured in any of several ways. Three common possibilities are depicted in Fig. 4-2. The file in Fig. 4-2(a) is an unstructured sequence of bytes. In effect, the operating system does not know or care what is in the file. All it sees are bytes. Any meaning must be imposed by user-level programs. Both UNIX and MS-DOS use this approach.

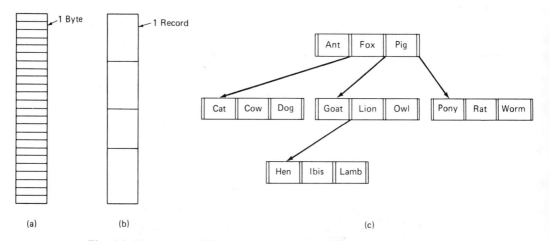

Fig. 4-2. Three kinds of files. (a) Byte sequence. (b) Record sequence. (c) Tree.

Having the operating system regard files as nothing more than byte sequences provides the maximum flexibility. User programs can put anything they want in files, and name them any way that is convenient. The operating system does not help, but it also does not get in the way. For users who want to do unusual things, the latter can be very important.

The first step up in structure is shown in Fig. 4-2(b). In this model, a file is a sequence of fixed-length records, each with some internal structure. Central to the idea of a file being a sequence of records is the idea that the read operation returns one record and the write operations overwrites or appends one record. In years gone by, when the 80-column punched card was king, many operating systems based their file systems on files consisting of 80-character records, in effect, card images. These systems also supported files of 132-character records, which were intended for the line printer (which in those days had 132 columns). Programs read input in units of

80 characters and wrote it in units of 132 characters, although the final 52 could be spaces, of course.

The most recent system that views files as sequences of fixed-length records is CP/M. It uses a 128-character record. With the advent of CRT terminals, which have variable length lines, the idea of a file as a sequence of fixed length records is losing popularity.

The third kind of file structure is shown in Fig. 4-2(c). In this organization, a file consists of a tree of records, not necessarily all the same length, each containing a **key** field in a fixed position in the record. The tree is sorted on the key field, to allow rapid searching for a particular key.

The basic operation here is not to get the "next" record, although that is also possible, but to get the record with a specific key. For the zoo file of Fig. 4-2(c), one could ask the system to get the record whose key is *pony*, for example, without worrying about its exact position in the file. Furthermore, new records can be added to the file, with the operating system, and not the user, deciding where to place them. This type of file is clearly quite different from the unstructured byte streams used in UNIX and MS-DOS. It is widely used on the large mainframe computers used in commercial data processing.

4.1.3. File Types

Many operating systems support several types of files. UNIX and MS-DOS, for example, have regular files, directories, character special files, and block special files. **Regular files** are the ones that contain user information. All the files of Fig. 4-2 are regular files. **Directories** are system files for maintaining the structure of the file system. We will study directories below. **Character special files** are related to input/output and used to model serial I/O devices such as terminals, printers, and networks. **Block special files** are used to model disks. In this chapter we will be primarily interested in regular files.

Regular files are generally either ASCII files or binary files. ASCII files consist of lines of text. In some systems each line is terminated by a carriage return character. In others, the line feed character is used. Occasionally, both are required. Lines need not all be of the same length.

The great advantage of ASCII files is that they can be displayed and printed as is, and they can be edited with an ordinary text editor. Furthermore, if large numbers of programs use ASCII files for input and output, it is easy to connect the output of one program to the input of another, as in shell pipelines. (The interprocess plumbing is not any easier, but interpreting the information certainly is if a standard convention, such as ASCII, is used for expressing it.)

Other files are binary files, which just means that they are not ASCII files. Listing them on the printer gives an incomprehensible listing full of what is apparently random junk. Usually they have some internal structure.

For example, in Fig. 4-3(a) we see a simple executable binary file taken from a version of UNIX. Although technically the file is just a sequence of bytes, the operating system will only execute a file if it has the proper format. It has five sections:

header, text, data, relocation bits, and symbol table. The header starts with a so-called **magic number**, identifying the file as an executable file (to prevent the accidental execution of a file not in this format). Then come 16-bit integers giving the sizes of the various pieces of the file, the address it starts execution at, and some flag bits. Following the header are the text and data of the program itself. These are loaded into memory, and relocated using the relocation bits. The symbol table is used for debugging.

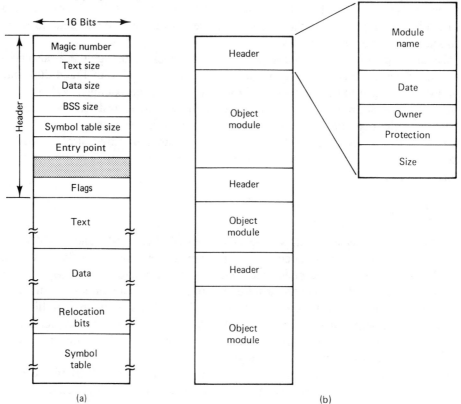

Fig. 4-3. (a) An executable file. (b) An archive.

Our second example of a binary file is an archive, also from UNIX. It consists of a collection of library procedures (modules) compiled but not linked. Each one is prefaced by a header telling its name, creation date, owner, protection code, and size. Just as with the executable file, the module headers are full of binary numbers. Copying them to the printer would produce complete gibberish.

All operating systems must recognize one file type, their own executable file, but some recognize more. The TOPS-20 system goes so far as to examine the creation time of any file to be executed. Then it locates the source file and sees if the source has been modified since the binary was made. If it has, it automatically recompiles the source. In UNIX terms, the *make* program has been built into the shell. The file extensions are mandatory so the operating system can tell which binary program was derived from which source.

Having strongly typed files like this causes problems whenever the user does anything that the system designers did not expect. Consider, as an example, a system in which program output files have type *dat* (data files). If a user writes a program formatter that reads a *.pas* file, transforms it (e.g., by converting it to a standard indentation layout), and then writes the transformed file as output, the output file will be of type *.dat*. If the user tries to offer this to the Pascal compiler to compile it, the system will refuse because it has the wrong extension. Attempts to copy *file.dat* to *file.pas* will be rejected by the system as invalid (to protect the user against mistakes).

While this kind of "protection" may help novices, it drives experienced users up the wall since they have to devote considerable effort to circumventing the operating system's idea of what is reasonable and what is not.

4.1.4. File Access

Early operating systems provided only one kind of file access: **sequential access**. In these systems, a process could read all the bytes or records in a file in order, starting at the beginning, but could not skip around and read them out of order. Sequential files can be rewound, however, so they can be read as often as needed. Sequential files are convenient when the storage medium is magnetic tape, rather than disk.

When disks came into use for storing files, it became possible to read the bytes or records of a file out of order, or to access records by key, rather than by position. Files whose bytes or records can be read in any order are called **random access files**.

Random access files are essential for many applications, for example, data base systems. If an airline customer calls up and wants to reserve a seat on a particular flight, the reservation program must be able to access the record for that flight without having to read the records for thousands of other flights first.

Two methods are used for specifying where to start reading. In the first one, every READ operation gives the position in the file to start reading at. In the second one, a special operation, SEEK, is provided to set the current position. After that has been done, the file can be read sequentially from the now-current position.

In some older mainframe operating systems, files are classified as either sequential or random access when they are created. This allows the operating system to use different storage techniques for the two classes. Modern operating systems do not make this distinction. All their files are automatically random access.

4.1.5. File Attributes

Every file has a name and its data. In addition, all operating systems associate other information with each file, for example, the date and time the file was created and the file's size. We will call these extra items the file's **attributes**. The list of attributes varies considerably from system to system. The table of Fig. 4-4 shows some of the possibilities, but other ones also exist. No existing system has all of these, but each one is present in some system.

The first four attributes relate to the file's protection and tell who may access it

Field	Meaning
Protection	Who can access the file and in what way
Password	Password needed to access the file
Creator	Id of person who created the file
Owner	Current owner
Read-only flag	0 for read/write, 1 for read only
Hidden flag	0 for normal, 1 for do not display in listings
System flag	0 for normal file, 1 for system file
Archive flag	0 has been backed up, 1 for needs to be backed up
ASCII/binary flag	0 for ASCII file, 1 for binary file
Random access flag	0 for sequential access only, 1 for random access
Temporary flag	0 for normal, 1 for delete on process exit
Lock flags	0 for unlocked, nonzero for locked
Record length	Number of bytes in a record
Key position	Offset of the key within each record
Key length	Number of bytes in the key field
Creation time	Date and time file was created
Time of last access	Date and time file was last accessed
Time of last change	Date and time file was last changed
Current size	Number of bytes in the file
Maximum size	Maximum size file may grow to

Fig. 4-4. Some possible file attributes.

and who may not. All kinds of schemes are possible, some of which we will study later. In some systems the user must present a password to access a file, in which case the password must be one of the attributes.

The flags are bits or short fields that control or enable some specific property. Hidden files, for example, do not appear in listings of all the files. The archive flag is a bit that keeps track of whether the file has been backed up. The backup program clears it, and the operating system sets it whenever a file is changed. In this way, the backup program can tell which files need backing up. The temporary flag allows a file to be marked for automatic deletion when the process that created it terminates.

The record length, key position, and key length fields are only present in files whose records can be looked up using a key. They provide the information required to find the keys.

The various times keep track of when the file was created, most recently accessed and most recently modified. These are useful for a variety of purposes. For example, a source file that has been modified after the creation of the corresponding object file needs to be recompiled. These fields provide the necessary information.

The current size tells how big the file is at present. Some mainframe operating systems require the maximum size to be specified when the file is created, to let the operating system reserve the maximum amount of storage in advance. Minicomputer and personal computer systems are clever enough to do without this item.

4.1.6. File Operations

Files exist to store information and allow it to be retrieved later. Different systems provide different operations to allow storage and retrieval. Below is a discussion of the most common system calls relating to files.

1. **CREATE**. The file is created with no data. The purpose of the call is to announce that the file is coming and to set some of the attributes.

2. **DELETE**. When the file is no longer needed, it has to be deleted to free up disk space. There is always a system call for this purpose. In addition, some operating systems automatically delete any file that has not been used in n days.

3. **OPEN**. Before using a file, a process must open it. The purpose of the OPEN call is to allow the system to fetch the attributes and list of disk addresses into main memory for rapid access on subsequent calls.

4. **CLOSE**. When all the accesses are finished, the attributes and disk addresses are no longer needed, so the file should be closed to free up internal table space. Many systems encourage this by imposing a maximum number of open files on processes.

5. **READ**. Data are read from file. Usually the bytes come from the current position. The caller must specify how much data is needed and must also provide a buffer to put it in.

6. **WRITE**. Data are written to the file, again, usually at the current position. If the current position is the end of the file, the file's size increases. If the current position is in the middle of the file, existing data are overwritten and lost forever.

7. **APPEND**. This call is a restricted form of WRITE. It can only add data to the end of the file. Systems that provide a minimal set of system calls do not generally have APPEND, but many systems provide multiple ways of doing the same thing, and these systems sometimes have APPEND.

8. **SEEK**. For random access files, a method is needed to specify from where to take the data. One common approach is a system call, SEEK, that repositions the pointer to the current position to a specific place in the file. After this call has completed, data can be read from, or written to, that position.

9. **GET ATTRIBUTES.** Processes often need to read file attributes to do their work. For example, the UNIX *make* program is commonly used to manage software development projects consisting of multiple source files. When *make* is called, it examines the modification times of all the source and object files, and arranges for the minimum number of compilations required to bring everything up to date. To do its job, it needs to look at the attributes, specifically, the modification times.

10. **SET ATTRIBUTES.** Some of the attributes are user-settable and can be changed after the file has been created. This system call makes that possible. The protection mode information is an obvious example. Most of the flags also fall in this category.

11. **RENAME.** It frequently happens that a user needs to change the name of an existing file. This system call makes that possible. It is not always strictly necessary, because the file can always be copied to a new file with the new name, and the old file then deleted. Usually this is good enough.

An Example Program Using File System Calls

In this section we will examine a simple UNIX program that copies one file from its source file to a destination file. It is listed in Fig. 4-5. The program has minimal functionality and even worse error reporting, but it gives a reasonable idea of how some of the system calls related to files work.

The program, *copyfile*, can be called, for example, by the command line

```
copyfile abc xyz
```

to copy the file *abc* to *xyz*. If *xyz* already exists, it will be overwritten. Otherwise, it will be created. The program must be called with exactly two arguments, both legal file names.

The four *#include* statements near the top of the program cause a large number of definitions and function prototypes to be included in the program. These are needed to make the program conformant to the relevant international standards, but will not concern us further. The next line is a function prototype for *main*, something required by ANSI C, but also not important for our purposes.

The *#define* statement is a macro definition that defines the string *BUF_SIZE* as a macro that expands into the number 4096. The program will read and write in chunks of 4096 bytes. It is considered good programming practice to give names to constants like this and to use the names instead of the constants. Not only does this convention make programs easier to read, but it also makes them easier to maintain.

The main program is called *main*, and it has two arguments, *argc*, and *argv*. These are supplied by the operating system when the program is called. The first one tells how many words were present on the command line that invoked the program. It should be 3. The second one is an array of pointers to the arguments. In the

```
/* cp src dest copies the file 'src' to 'dest'.  Error reporting is minimal. */

#include <sys/types.h>              /* contains certain type definitions */
#include <fcntl.h>                  /* defines O_RDONLY, etc. */
#include <stdlib.h>                 /* contains system call prototypes */
#include <unistd.h>                 /* contains system call prototypes */

void main(int argc, char *argv[]);  /* ANSI C prototype */

#define BUF_SIZE 4096               /* define unit to read/write in */
#define MODE 0666                   /* file mode (rw-rw-rw-) */

void main(int argc, char *argv[])   /* argc: # of args, argv: arg ptrs */
{
  int src, dst, in, out;
  char buf[BUF_SIZE];

  if (argc != 3) exit(1);           /* wrong number of arguments. */

  /* Open the source and create the destination. */
  src = open(argv[1], O_RDONLY);    /* open the source file read-only */
  if (src < 0) exit(2);             /* cannot open source file */
  dst = creat(argv[2], MODE);       /* try to create the destination */
  if (dst < 0) exit(3);             /* cannot create the destination */

  /* Everything worked.  Do the copy. */
  while (1) {                       /* repeat indefinitely */
        in = read(src, buf, BUF_SIZE);  /* read from the source file */
        if (in <= 0) break;         /* exit loop at end of file */
        out = write(dst, buf, in);  /* write the bytes to the dest file */
        if (out <= 0) break;        /* exit loop on error */
  }

  close(src);                       /* close the source file */
  close(dst);                       /* close the newly created file */
  exit(0);                          /* exit */
}
```

Fig. 4-5. A simple program to copy a file.

example call given above, the elements of this array would contain pointers to the
following values:

argv[0] = "copyfile"
argv[1] = "abc"
argv[2] = "xyz"

It is via this array that the program accesses its arguments.

Five variables are declared. The first two, *src* and *dst*, will hold the **file descriptors**, small integers returned when a file is opened. The next two, *in* and *out*, are the
byte counts returned by the READ and WRITE system calls, respectively. The last one,
buf, is the buffer used to hold the data read and supply the data to be written.

The first actual statement checks *argc* to see if it is 3. If not, it exits with status
code 1. Any status code other than 0 means that an error has occurred. The status

code is the only error reporting present in this program. A production version would normally print error messages as well.

Then we try to open the source file and create the destination file. If the source file is successfully opened, the system assigns a small integer to *src*, to identify the file. Subsequent calls must include this integer so the system knows which file it wants. Similarly, if the destination is successfully created, *dst* is given a value to identify it. The second argument to *creat* sets the protection mode. If either the open or the create fails, the corresponding file descriptor is set to −1, and the program exits with an error code.

Now comes the copy loop. It starts by trying to read in 4K of data to *buf*. It does this by calling the library procedure *read*, which actually invokes the READ system call. The first parameter identifies the file, the second gives the buffer, and the third tells how many bytes to read. The value assigned to *in* gives the number of bytes actually read. Normally this will be 4096, except if fewer bytes are remaining in the file. When end of file is reached, it will be 0. If *in* is ever zero or negative, the copying cannot continue, so the *break* statement is executed to terminate the (otherwise endless) loop.

The call to *write* outputs the buffer to the destination file. The first parameter identifies the file, the second gives the buffer, and the third tells how many bytes to write, analogous to *read*. Note that the byte count is the number of bytes actually read, not *BUF_SIZE*. This point is important because the last buffer will not be 4096, unless the file just happens to be a multiple of 4K bytes.

When the entire file has been processed, the first call beyond the end of file will return 0 to *in*, which will make it exit the loop. At this point the two files are closed and the program exits with a status indicating that it completed normally.

4.1.7. Memory-Mapped Files

Many people feel that accessing files as shown above is cumbersome and inconvenient, especially when compared to accessing ordinary memory. For this reason, some operating systems, starting with MULTICS, have provided a way to map files into the address space of a running process. Conceptually, we can imagine the existence of two new system calls, MAP and UNMAP. The former gives a file name and a virtual address, which causes the operating system to map the file into the address space at the virtual address.

For example, suppose that a file, *f*, of length 64K, is mapped onto virtual address 512K. Then any machine instruction that reads the contents of the byte at 512K gets byte 0 of the file, and so on. Similarly, a write to address 512K + 1100 modifies byte 1100 of the file. When the process terminates, the modified file is left on the disk, just as though it had been changed by a combination of SEEK and WRITE system calls.

What actually happens is that the system's internal tables are changed to make the file serve as the backing store for the file. Thus a read from 512K causes a page fault, bringing in page 0 of the file. Similarly, a write to 512K + 1100 causes a page fault, bringing in the page containing that address, after which the write to memory can take place. If that page is ever evicted by the page replacement algorithm, it is written back to the appropriate place in the file. When the process finishes, all mapped, modified pages are written back to their files.

File mapping works best in a system that supports segmentation. In such a system, each file can be mapped onto its own segment so that byte k in the file is also byte k in the segment. In Fig. 4-6(a) we see a process that has two segments, text and data. Suppose this process copies files, like the program of Fig. 4-5. First it maps the source file, say, *abc*, onto a segment. Then it creates an empty segment and maps it onto the destination file, *xyz* in our example. These operations give the situation shown in Fig. 4-6(b).

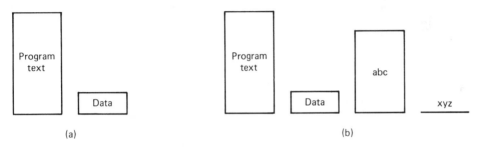

(a)   (b)

Fig. 4-6. (a) A segmented process before mapping files into its address space. (b) The process after mapping an existing file *abc* into one segment and creating a new segment for file *xyz*.

At this point the process can copy the source segment into the destination segment using an ordinary copy loop. No READ or WRITE system calls are needed. When it is all done, it can execute the UNMAP system call to remove the files from the address space, and then exit. The output file, *xyz*, will now exist, as though it had been created in the conventional way.

Although file mapping eliminates the need for I/O and thus makes programming easier, it introduces a few problems of its own. First, it is hard for the system to know the exact length of the output file, *xyz*, in our example. It can easily tell the number of the highest page written, but it has no way of knowing how many bytes in that page were written. Suppose the program only uses page 0, and after execution all the bytes are still 0 (their initial value). Maybe *xyz* is a file consisting of 10 zeros. Maybe it is a file consisting of 100 zeros. Who knows? The operating system cannot tell. All it can do is create a file whose length is equal to the page size.

A second problem can (potentially) occur if a file is mapped in by one process and opened for conventional reading by another. If the first process modifies a page, that change will not be reflected in the file on disk until the page is evicted. The system has to take great care to make sure the two processes do not see inconsistent versions of the file.

A third problem with mapping is that a file may be larger than a segment, or even larger than the entire virtual address space. The only way out is to arrange the MAP system call to be able to map a portion of a file, rather than the entire file. Although this works, it is clearly less satisfactory than mapping the entire file.

4.2. DIRECTORIES

To keep track of files, the file system normally provides **directories**, which, in many systems, are themselves files. In this section we will discuss directories, their organization, their properties, and the operations that can be performed on them.

4.2.1. Hierarchical Directory Systems

A directory typically contains a number of entries, one per file. One possibility is shown in Fig. 4-7(a), in which each entry contains the file name, the file attributes, and the disk addresses where the data are stored. Another possibility is shown in Fig. 4-7(b). Here a directory entry holds the file name and a pointer to another data structure where the attributes and disk addresses are found. Both of these systems are commonly used.

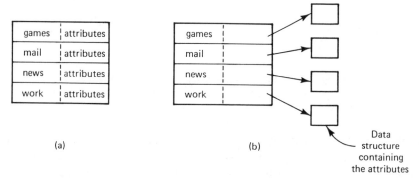

(a)   (b)

Data structure containing the attributes

Fig. 4-7. Directories. (a) Attributes in the directory entry. (b) Attributes elsewhere.

When a file is opened, the operating system searches its directory until it finds the name of the file to be opened. It then extracts the attributes and disk addresses, either directly from the directory entry or from the data structure pointed to, and puts them in a table in main memory. All subsequent references to the file use the information in main memory.

The number of directories varies from system to system. The simplest design is for the system to maintain a single directory containing all the files of all the users, as illustrated in Fig. 4-8(a). If there are many users, and they choose the same file names (e.g., *mail* and *games*), conflicts and confusion will quickly make the system unworkable. This system model is used only by the most primitive microcomputer operating systems.

An improvement on the idea of having a single directory for all files is to have one directory per user [see Fig. 4-8(b)]. This design eliminates name conflicts among users, but is not very satisfactory for users with many files. It is quite common for users to want to group their files together in logical ways. A professor, for example, might have a collection of files that together form a book that he is writing for one course, a second collection of files containing student programs submitted for

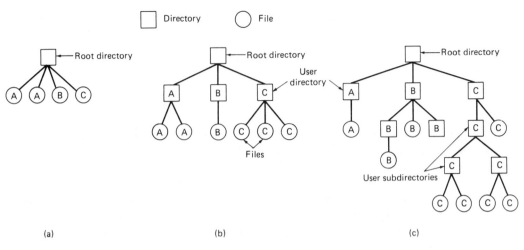

Fig. 4-8. Three file system designs. (a) Single directory shared by all users. (b) One directory per user. (c) Arbitrary tree per user. The letters indicate the directory or file's owner.

another course, a third group of files containing the code of an advanced compiler-writing system he is building, a fourth group of files containing grant proposals, as well as other files for electronic mail, minutes of meetings, papers he is writing, games, and so on. Some way is needed to group these files together reasonably.

What is needed is a general hierarchy (i.e., a tree of directories). With this approach, each user can have as many directories as are needed so that files can be grouped together in natural ways. This approach is shown in Fig. 4-8(c). Here, the directories *A*, *B*, and *C* contained in the root directory each belong to a different user, two of whom have created subdirectories for projects they are working on.

4.2.2. Path Names

When the file system is organized as a directory tree, some way is needed for specifying file names. Two different methods are commonly used. In the first method, each file is given an **absolute path name** consisting of the path from the root directory to the file. As an example, the path */usr/ast/mailbox* means that the root directory contains a subdirectory *usr*, which in turn contains a subdirectory *ast*, which contains the file *mailbox*. Absolute path names always start at the root directory and are unique. In UNIX the components of the path are separated by /. In MS-DOS the separator is \. In MULTICS it is >. No matter which character is used, if the first character of the path name is the separator, then the path is absolute.

The other kind of name is the **relative path name**. This is used in conjunction with the concept of the **working directory** (also called the **current directory**). A user can designate one directory as the current working directory, in which case all path names not beginning at the root directory are taken relative to the working directory. For example, if the current working directory is */usr/ast*, then the file whose absolute path is */usr/ast/mailbox* can be referenced simply as *mailbox*. In other words, the UNIX command

```
cp /usr/ast/mailbox /usr/ast/mailbox.bak
```

and the command

```
cp mailbox mailbox.bak
```

do exactly the same thing if the working directory is */usr/ast*. The relative form is often more convenient, but it does the same thing as the absolute form.

Some programs need to access a specific file without regard to what the working directory is. In that case, they should always use absolute path names. For example, a spelling checker might need to read */usr/lib/dictionary* to do its work. It should use the full, absolute path name in this case because it does not know what the working directory will be when it is called. The absolute path name will always work, no matter what the working directory is.

Of course, if the spelling checker needs a large number of files from */usr/lib*, an alternative approach is for it to issue a system call to change its working directory to */usr/lib*, and then use just *dictionary* as the first parameter to *open*. By explicitly changing the working directory, it knows for sure where it is in the directory tree, so it can then use relative paths.

In most systems, each process has its own working directory, so when a process changes its working directory and later exits, no other processes are affected and no traces of the change are left behind in the file system. In this way it is always perfectly safe for a process to change its working directory whenever that is convenient. On the other hand, if a library procedure changes the working directory and does not change back to where it was when it is finished, the rest of the program may not work since its assumption about where it is may now be invalid. For this reason, library procedures rarely change the working directory, and when they must, they always change it back again before returning.

Most operating systems that support a hierarchical directory system have two special entries in every directory, "." and "..", generally pronounced "dot" and "dotdot." Dot refers to the current directory; dotdot refers to its parent. To see how these are used, consider the UNIX file tree of Fig. 4-9. A certain process has */usr/ast* as its working directory. It can use .. to go up the tree. For example, it can copy the file */usr/lib/dictionary* to its own directory using the shell command

```
cp ../lib/dictionary .
```

The first path instructs the system to go upwards (to the *usr* directory), then to go down to the directory *lib* to find the file *dictionary*.

The second argument names the current directory. When the *cp* command gets a directory name (including dot) as its last argument, it copies all the files there. Of course, a more normal way to do the copy would be to type:

```
cp /usr/lib/dictionary .
```

Here the use of dot saves the user the trouble of typing *dictionary* a second time.

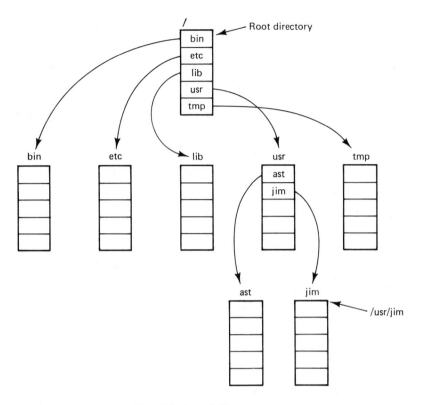

Fig. 4-9. A UNIX directory tree.

4.2.3. Directory Operations

The allowed system calls for managing directories exhibit more variation from system to system than those relating to files do. Nevertheless, to give an impression of what they are and how they work, we will give a sample (taken from UNIX).

1. **CREATE.** A directory is created. It is empty except for dot and dotdot, which are put there automatically by the system (or in a few cases, by the *mkdir* program).

2. **DELETE.** A directory is deleted. Only an empty directory can be deleted. A directory containing only dot and dotdot is considered empty as these usually cannot be deleted.

3. **OPENDIR.** Directories can be read. For example, to list all the files in a directory, a listing program opens the directory to read out the names of all the files it contains. Before a directory can be read, it must be opened.

4. **CLOSEDIR**. When a directory has been read, it should be closed to free up internal table space.

5. **READDIR**. This call returns the next entry in an open directory. Formerly, it was possible to read directories using the usual READ system call, but that approach has the disadvantage of forcing the programmer to know and deal with the internal structure of directories. In contrast, READDIR always returns one entry in a standard format, no matter which of the possible directory structures is being used.

6. **RENAME**. In many respects, directories are just like files, and can be renamed the same way files can be.

7. **LINK**. Linking is a technique that allows a file to appear in more than one directory. This system call specifies an existing file and a path name, and creates a link from the existing file to the name specified by the path. In this way, the same file may appear in multiple directories.

8. **UNLINK**. A directory entry is removed. If the file being unlinked is only present in one directory (the normal case), it is removed from the file system. If it is present in multiple directories, only the path name specified is removed. The others remain. In UNIX, the system call for deleting files (discussed earlier) is, in fact, UNLINK.

The above list gives the most important calls, but there are a few others as well, for example, for managing the protection information associated with a directory.

4.3. FILE SYSTEM IMPLEMENTATION

Now it is time to turn from the user's view of the file system to the implementer's view. Users are concerned with how files are named, what operations are allowed on them, what the directory tree looks like, and similar interface issues. Implementers are interested in how files and directories are stored, how disk space is managed, and how to make everything work efficiently and reliably. In the following sections we will examine a number of these areas to see what the issues and tradeoffs are.

4.3.1. Implementing Files

The key issue in implementing file storage is keeping track of which disk blocks go with which file. Various methods are used in different systems. In this section, we will examine a few of them.

Contiguous Allocation

The simplest allocation scheme is to store each file as a contiguous block of data on the disk. Thus on a disk with 1K blocks, a 50K file would be allocated 50 consecutive blocks. This scheme has two significant advantages. First, it is simple to implement because keeping track of where a file's blocks are is reduced to remembering one number, the disk address of the first block. Second, the performance is excellent because the entire file can be read from the disk in a single operation. No other allocation method even comes close.

Unfortunately, contiguous allocation also has two equally significant drawbacks. First, it is not feasible unless the maximum file size is known at the time the file is created. Without this information, the operating system does not know how much disk space to reserve. In systems where files must be written in a single blow, it can be used to great advantage, however.

The second disadvantage is the fragmentation of the disk that results from this allocation policy. Space is wasted that might otherwise have been used. Compaction of the disk is usually prohibitively expensive, although it can conceivably be done late at night when the system is otherwise idle.

Linked List Allocation

The second method for storing files is to keep each one as a linked list of disk blocks, as shown in Fig. 4-10. The first word of each block is used as a pointer to the next one. The rest of the block is for data.

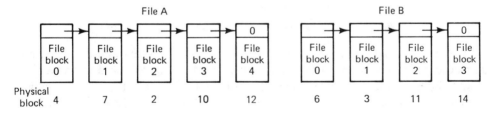

Fig. 4-10. Storing a file as a linked list of disk blocks.

Unlike contiguous allocation, every disk block can be used in this method. No space is lost to disk fragmentation. Also, it is sufficient for the directory entry to merely store the disk address of the first block. The rest can be found starting there.

On the other hand, although reading a file sequentially is straightforward, random access is extremely slow. Also, the amount of data storage in a block is no longer a power of two because the pointer takes up a few bytes. While not fatal, having a peculiar size is less efficient because many programs read and write in blocks whose size is a power of two (e.g., see *BUF_SIZE* in Fig. 4-5).

Linked List Allocation Using an Index

Both disadvantages of the linked list allocation can be eliminated by taking the pointer word from each disk block and putting it in a table or index in memory. Figure 4-11 shows what the table looks like for the example of Fig. 4-10. In both figures, we have two files. File A uses disk blocks 4, 7, 2, 10, and 12, in that order, and file B uses disk blocks 6, 3, 11, and 14, in that order. Using the table of Fig. 4-11, we can start with block 4 and follow the chain all the way to the end. The same can be done starting with block 6.

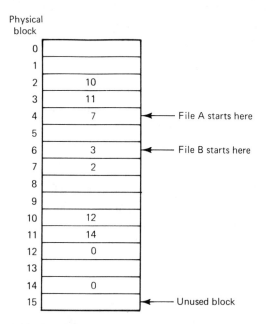

Fig. 4-11. Linked list allocation using a table in main memory.

Using this organization, the entire block is available for data. Furthermore, random access is much easier. Although the chain must still be followed to find a given offset within the file, the chain is entirely in memory, so it can be followed without making any disk references. Like the previous method, it is sufficient for the directory entry to keep a single integer (the starting block number) and still be able to locate all the blocks, no matter how large the file is. MS-DOS uses this method for disk allocation.

The primary disadvantage of this method is that the entire table must be in memory all the time to make it work. With a large disk, say, 500,000 1K blocks (500M), the table will have 500,000 entries, each of which will have to be a minimum of 3 bytes. For speed in lookup, they should be 4 bytes. Thus the table will take up 1.5 or 2 megabytes all the time depending on whether the system is optimized for space or time.

I-nodes

Our fourth and last method for keeping track of which blocks belong to which file is to associate with each file a little table called an **i-node** (**index-node**), which lists the attributes and disk addresses of the file's blocks, as shown in Fig. 4-12.

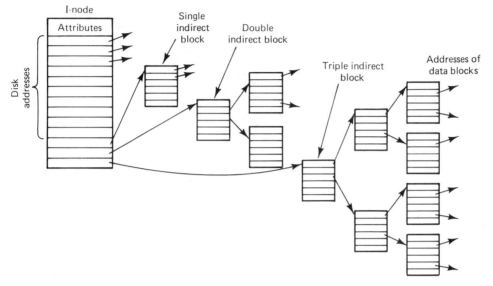

Fig. 4-12. An i-node.

The first few disk addresses are stored in the i-node itself, so for small files, all the necessary information is right in the i-node, which is fetched from disk to main memory when the file is opened. For somewhat larger files, one of the addresses in the i-node is the address of a disk block called a **single indirect block**. This block contains additional disk addresses. If this still is not enough, another address in the i-node, called a **double indirect block**, contains the address of a block that contains a list of single indirect blocks. Each of these single indirect blocks points to a few hundred data blocks. If even this is not enough, a **triple indirect block** can also be used. UNIX uses this scheme.

4.3.2. Implementing Directories

Before a file can be read, it must be opened. When a file is opened, the operating system uses the path name supplied by the user to locate the directory entry. The directory entry provides the information needed to find the disk blocks. Depending on the system, this information may be the disk address of the entire file (contiguous allocation), the number of the first block (both linked list schemes), or the number of the i-node. In all cases, the main function of the directory system is to map the ASCII name of the file onto the information needed to locate the data.

A closely related issue is where the attributes should be stored. One obvious possibility is to store them directly in the directory entry. Many systems do precisely that. For systems that use i-nodes, another possibility is to store the attributes in the i-node, rather than in the directory entry. As we shall see later, this method has certain advantages over putting them in the directory entry.

Directories in CP/M

Let us start our study of directories with a particularly simple example, that of CP/M (Golden and Pechura, 1986), illustrated in Fig. 4-13. In this system, there is only one directory, so all the file system has to do to look up a file name is search the one and only directory. When it finds the entry, it also has the disk block numbers, since they are stored right in the directory entry, as are all the attributes. If the file uses more disk blocks than fit in one entry, the file is allocated additional directory entries.

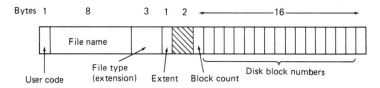

Fig. 4-13. A directory entry that contains the disk block numbers for each file.

The fields in Fig. 4-13 have the following meanings. The *User code* field keeps track of which user owns the file. During a search, only those entries belonging to the currently logged-in user are checked. The next two fields give the name and extension of the file. The *Extent* field is needed because a file larger than 16 blocks occupies multiple directory entries. This field is used to tell which entry comes first, second, and so on. The *Block count* field tells how many of the 16 potential disk block entries are in use. The final 16 fields contain the disk block numbers themselves. The last block may not be full, so the system has no way to determine the exact size of a file down to the last byte (i.e., it keeps track of file sizes in blocks, not bytes).

Directories in MS-DOS

Now let us consider some examples of systems with hierarchical directory trees. Figure 4-14 shows an MS-DOS directory entry. It is 32 bytes long and contains the file name, attributes, and the number of the first disk block. The first block number is used as an index into a table of the type of Fig. 4-11. By following the chain, all the blocks can be found.

In MS-DOS, directories may contain other directories, leading to a hierarchical file system. It is common in MS-DOS that different application programs each start out by creating a directory in the root directory, and putting all their files there, so that different applications do not conflict. We will study MS-DOS in considerable detail in Chap. 8.

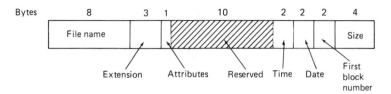

Fig. 4-14. The MS-DOS directory entry.

Directories in UNIX

The directory structure traditionally used in UNIX is extremely simple, as shown in Fig. 4-15. Each entry contains just a file name and its i-node number. All the information about the type, size, times, ownership, and disk blocks is contained in the i-node. Some UNIX systems have a different layout, but in all cases, a directory entry ultimately contains only an ASCII string and an i-node number.

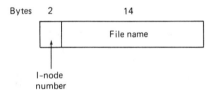

Fig. 4-15. A UNIX directory entry.

When a file is opened, the file system must take the file name supplied and locate its disk blocks. Let us consider how the path name */usr/ast/mbox* is looked up. We will use UNIX as an example, but the algorithm is basically the same for all hierarchical directory systems. First the file system locates the root directory. In UNIX its i-node is located at a fixed place on the disk.

Then it looks up the first component of the path, *usr*, in the root directory to find the i-node number of the file */usr*. Locating an i-node from its number is straightforward, since each one has a fixed location on the disk. From this i-node, the system locates the directory for */usr* and looks up the next component, *ast*, in it. When it has found the entry for *ast*, it has the i-node for the directory */usr/ast*. From this i-node it can find the directory itself and look up *mbox*. The i-node for this file is then read into memory and kept there until the file is closed. The lookup process is illustrated in Fig. 4-16.

Relative path names are looked up the same way as absolute ones, only starting from the working directory instead of starting from the root directory. Every directory has entries for . and .. which are put there when the directory is created. The entry . has the i-node number for the current directory, and the entry for .. has the i-node number for the parent directory. Thus, a procedure looking up *../dick/prog.c* simply looks up .. in the working directory, finds the i-node number for the parent directory, and searches that directory for *dick*. No special mechanism is needed to handle these names. As far as the directory system is concerned, they are just ordinary ASCII strings.

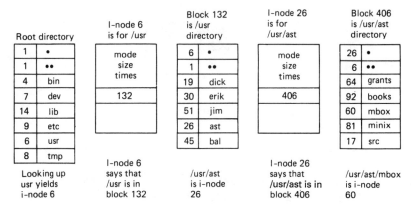

Fig. 4-16. The steps in looking up /usr/ast/mbox.

4.3.3. Shared Files

When several users are working together on a project, they often need to share files. As a result, it is often convenient for a shared file to appear simultaneously in different directories belonging to different users. Figure 4-17 shows the file system of Fig. 4-8(c) again, only with one of *C*'s files now present in one of *B*'s directories as well. The connection between *B*'s directory and the shared file is called a **link**. The file system itself is now a **directed acyclic graph**, or **DAG**, rather than a tree.

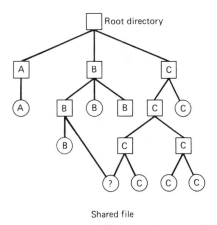

Fig. 4-17. File system containing a shared file.

Sharing files is convenient, but it also introduces some problems. To start with, if directories really do contain disk addresses, as in CP/M, then a copy of the disk addresses will have to be made in *B*'s directory when the file is linked. If either *B* or *C* subsequently appends to the file, the new blocks will be listed only in the directory of the user doing the append. The changes will not be visible to the other user, thus defeating the purpose of sharing.

This problem can be solved in two ways. In the first solution, disk blocks are not listed in directories, but in a little data structure associated with the file itself. The directories would then point just to the little data structure. This is the approach used in UNIX (where the little data structure is the i-node).

In the second solution, *B* links to one of *C*'s files by having the system create a new file, of type LINK, and entering that file in *B's* directory. The new file contains just the path name of the file to which it is linked. When *B* reads from the linked file, the operating system sees that the file being read from is of type LINK, looks up the name of the file, and reads that file. This approach is called **symbolic linking**.

Each of these methods has its drawbacks. In the first method, at the moment that *B* links to the shared file, the i-node records the file's owner as *C*. Creating a link does not change the ownership (see Fig. 4-18), but it does increase the link count in the i-node, so the system knows how many directory entries currently point to the file.

If *C* subsequently tries to remove the file, the system is faced with a problem. If it removes the file and clears the i-node, *B* will have a directory entry pointing to an invalid i-node. If the i-node is later reassigned to another file, *B*'s link will point to the wrong file. The system can see from the count in the i-node that the file is still in use, but there is no way for it to find all the directory entries for the file, in order to erase them. Pointers to the directories cannot be stored in the i-node because there can be an unlimited number of directories.

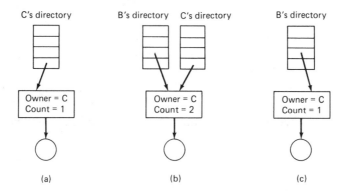

Fig. 4-18. (a) Situation prior to linking. (b) After the link is created. (c) After the original owner removes the file.

The only thing to do is remove *C*'s directory entry, but leave the i-node intact, with count set to 1, as shown in Fig. 4-18(c). We now have a situation in which *B* is the only user having a directory entry for a file owned by *C*. If the system does accounting or has quotas, *C* will continue to be billed for the file until *B* decides to remove it, at which time the count goes to 0 and the file is deleted.

With symbolic links this problem does not arise because only the true owner has a pointer to the i-node. Users who have linked to the file just have path names, not i-node pointers. When the *owner* removes the file, it is destroyed. Subsequent attempts to use the file via a symbolic link will fail when the system is unable to locate the file. Removing a symbolic link does not affect the file at all.

The problem with symbolic links is the extra overhead required. The file containing the path must be read, then the path must be parsed and followed, component by component, until the i-node is reached. All of this activity may require a considerable number of extra disk accesses. Furthermore, an extra i-node is needed for each symbolic link, as is an extra disk block to store the path, although if the path name is short, the system could store it in the i-node itself, as an optimization. Symbolic links have the advantage that they can be used to link to files on machines anywhere in the world, by simply providing the network address of the machine where the file resides in addition to its path on that machine.

There is also another problem introduced by links, symbolic or otherwise. When links are allowed, files can have two or more paths. Programs that start at a given directory and find all the files in that directory and its subdirectories will locate a linked file multiple times. For example, a program that dumps all the files in a directory and its subdirectories onto a tape may make multiple copies of a linked file. Furthermore, if the tape is then read into another machine, unless the dump program is clever, the linked file will be copied twice onto the disk, instead of being linked.

4.3.4. Disk Space Management

Files are normally stored on disk, so management of disk space is a major concern to file system designers. Two general strategies are possible for storing an n byte file: n consecutive bytes of disk space are allocated, or the file is split up into a number of (not necessarily) contiguous blocks. The same tradeoff is present in memory management systems between pure segmentation and paging.

Storing a file as a contiguous sequence of bytes has the obvious problem that if a file grows, it will probably have to be moved on the disk. The same problem holds for segments in memory, except that moving a segment in memory is a relatively fast operation compared to moving a file from one disk position to another. For this reason, nearly all file systems chop files up into fixed-size blocks that need not be adjacent.

Block Size

Once it has been decided to store files in fixed-size blocks, the question arises of how big the block should be. Given the way disks are organized, the sector, the track and the cylinder are obvious candidates for the unit of allocation. In a paging system, the page size is also a major contender.

Having a large allocation unit, such as a cylinder, means that every file, even a 1 byte file, ties up an entire cylinder. Studies (Mullender and Tanenbaum, 1984) have shown that the median file size in UNIX environments is about 1K, so allocating a 32K cylinder for each file would waste 31/32 or 97 percent of the total disk space. On the other hand, using a small allocation unit means that each file will consist of many blocks. Reading each block normally requires a seek and a rotational delay, so reading a file consisting of many small blocks will be slow.

As an example, consider a disk with 32768 bytes per track, a rotation time of

16.67 msec, and an average seek time of 30 msec. The time in milliseconds to read a block of k bytes is then the sum of the seek, rotational delay, and transfer times:

$$30 + 8.3 + (k/32768) \times 16.67$$

The solid curve of Fig. 4-19 shows the data rate for such a disk as a function of block size. If we make the gross assumption that all files are 1K (the measured median size), the dashed curve of Fig. 4-19 gives the disk space efficiency. The bad news is that good space utilization (block size < 2K) means low data rates and vice versa. Time efficiency and space efficiency are inherently in conflict.

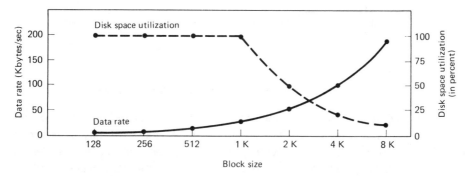

Fig. 4-19. The solid curve (left-hand scale) gives the data rate of a disk. The dashed curve (right-hand scale) gives the disk space efficiency. All files are 1K.

The usual compromise is to choose a block size of 512, 1K or 2K bytes. If a 1K block size is chosen on a disk with a 512-byte sector size, then the file system will always read or write two consecutive sectors, and treat them as a single, indivisible unit.

Keeping Track of Free Blocks

Once a block size has been chosen, the next issue is how to keep track of free blocks. Two methods are widely used, as shown in Fig. 4-20. The first one consists of using a linked list of disk blocks, with each block holding as many free disk block numbers as will fit. With a 1K block and a 16-bit disk block number, each block on the free list holds the numbers of 511 free blocks. A 20M disk needs a free list of maximum 40 blocks to hold all 20K disk block numbers. Often free blocks are used to hold the free list.

The other free space management technique is the bit map. A disk with n blocks requires a bit map with n bits. Free blocks are represented by 1s in the map, allocated blocks by 0s (or vice versa). A 20M disk requires 20K bits for the map, which requires only 3 blocks. It is not surprising that the bit map requires less space, since it uses 1 bit per block, versus 16 bits in the linked list model. Only if the disk is nearly full will the linked list scheme require fewer blocks than the bit map.

If there is enough main memory to hold the bit map, that method is generally

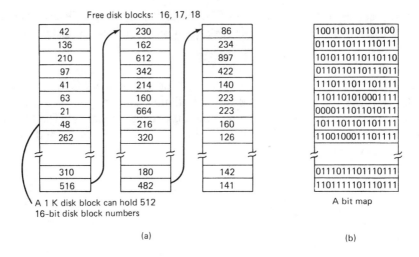

Free disk blocks: 16, 17, 18

A 1 K disk block can hold 512
16-bit disk block numbers

A bit map

(a)   (b)

Fig. 4-20. (a) Storing the free list on a linked list. (b) A bit map.

preferable. If, however, only 1 block of memory can be spared for keeping track of free disk blocks, and the disk is nearly full, then the linked list may be better. With only 1 block of the bit map in memory, it may turn out that no free blocks can be found on it, causing disk accesses to read the rest of the bit map. When a fresh block of the linked list is loaded into memory, 511 disk blocks can be allocated before having to go to the disk to fetch the next block from the list.

Disk Quotas

To prevent people from hogging too much disk space, multiuser operating systems, such as UNIX, often provide a mechanism for enforcing disk quotas. The idea is that the system administrator assigns each user a maximum allotment of files and blocks, and the operating system makes sure that the users do not exceed their quotas. A typical mechanism is described below.

When a user opens a file, the attributes and disk addresses are located and put into an open file table in main memory. Among the attributes is an entry telling who the owner is. Any increases in the file's size will be charged to the owner's quota.

A second table contains the quota record for every user with a currently open file, even if the file was opened by someone else. This table is shown in Fig. 4-21. It is an extract from a quota file on disk for the users whose files are currently open. When all the files are closed, the record is written back to the quota file.

When a new entry is made in the open file table, a pointer to the owner's quota record is entered into it, to make it easy to find the various limits. Every time a block is added to a file, the total number of blocks charged to the owner is incremented, and a check is made against both the hard and soft limits. The soft limit may be exceeded, but the hard limit may not. An attempt to append to a file when the hard block limit has been reached will result in an error. Analogous checks also exist for the number of files.

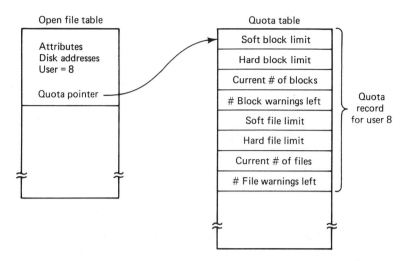

Fig. 4-21. Quotas are kept track of on a per-user basis in a quota table.

When a user attempts to log in, the system checks the quota file to see if the user has exceeded the soft limit for either number of files or number of disk blocks. If either limit has been violated, a warning is displayed, and the count of warnings remaining is reduced by one. If the count ever gets to zero, the user has ignored the warning one time too many, and is not permitted to log in. Getting permission to log in again will require some discussion with the system administrator.

This method has the property that users may go above their soft limits during a terminal session, provided they remove the excess before logging out. The hard limits may never be exceeded.

4.3.5. File System Reliability

Destruction of a file system is often a far greater disaster than destruction of a computer. If a computer is destroyed by fire, lightning surges, or a cup of coffee poured onto the keyboard, it is annoying and will cost money, but generally a replacement can be purchased with a minimum of fuss. Inexpensive personal computers can even be replaced within a few hours by just going to the dealer (except at universities, where issuing a purchase order takes three committees, five signatures, and 90 days).

If a computer's file system is irrevocably lost, whether due to hardware, software, or rats gnawing on the floppy disks, restoring all the information will be difficult, time consuming, and in many cases, impossible. For the people whose programs, documents, customer files, tax records, data bases, marketing plans, or other data are gone forever, the consequences can be catastrophic. While the file system cannot offer any protection against physical destruction of the equipment and media, it can help protect the information. In this section we will look at some of the issues involved in safeguarding the file system.

Bad Block Management

Disks often have bad blocks. Floppy disks are generally perfect when they leave the factory, but they can develop bad blocks during use. Winchester disks (hard disks) frequently have bad blocks right from the start: it is just too expensive to manufacture them completely free of all defects. In fact, most hard disk manufacturers supply with each drive a list of the bad blocks their tests have discovered.

Two solutions to the bad block problem are used, one hardware and one software. The hardware solution is to dedicate a sector on the disk to the bad block list. When the controller is first initialized, it reads the bad block list and picks a spare block (or track) to replace the defective ones, recording the mapping in the bad block list. Henceforth, all requests for the bad block will use the spare.

The software solution requires the user or file system to carefully construct a file containing all the bad blocks. This technique removes them from the free list, so they will never occur in data files. As long as the bad block file is never read or written, no problems will arise. Care has to be taken during disk backups to avoid reading this file.

Backups

Even with a clever strategy for dealing with bad blocks, it is important to back up the files frequently. After all, automatically switching to a spare track after a crucial data block has been ruined is somewhat akin to locking the barn door after the prize race horse has escaped.

File systems on floppy disk can be backed up by just copying the entire floppy disk to a blank one. File systems on small Winchester disks can be backed up by dumping the entire disk to magnetic tape, either industry standard 9-track tape (which holds about 50M per reel), streamer tape (which comes in several sizes), or 8mm video tape.

For large Winchesters (e.g., 500M), backing up the entire drive on tape is awkward and time consuming. One strategy that is easy to implement but wastes half the storage is to provide each computer with two drives instead of one. Both drives are divided into two halves: data and backup. Each night the data portion of drive 0 is copied to the backup portion of drive 1, and vice versa, as shown in Fig. 4-22. In this way, even if one drive is completely ruined, no information is lost.

An alternative to dumping the entire file system every day is to make **incremental dumps**. The simplest form of incremental dumping is to make a complete dump periodically, say weekly or monthly, and to make a daily dump of only those files that have been modified since the last full dump. A better scheme is to dump only those files that have changed since they were last dumped.

To implement this method, a list of the dump times for each file must be kept on disk. The dump program then checks each file on the disk. If it has been modified since it was last dumped, it is dumped again and its time-of-last-dump is changed to the current time. If done on a monthly cycle, this method requires 31 daily dump

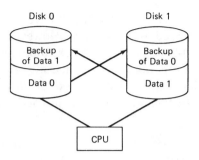

Fig. 4-22. Backing up each drive on the other one wastes half the storage.

tapes, one per day, plus enough tapes to hold a full dump, made once a month. Other more complex schemes that use fewer tapes are also in use.

MS-DOS provides some assistance in making backups. Associated with each file is an attribute bit called the **archive bit**. When the file system is backed up, the archive bits of all the files are cleared. Subsequently, whenever a file is modified, the operating system automatically sets its archive bit. When it is time for the next backup, the backup program checks all the archive bits and only backs up those files whose bit is set. It also clears all these bits to monitor further usage of the files.

File System Consistency

Another area where reliability is an issue is file system consistency. Many file systems read blocks, modify them, and write them out later. If the system crashes before all the modified blocks have been written out, the file system can be left in an inconsistent state. This problem is especially critical if some of the blocks that have not been written out are i-node blocks, directory blocks, or blocks containing the free list.

To deal with the problem of inconsistent file systems, most computers have a utility program that checks file system consistency. It can be run whenever the system is booted, particularly after a crash. The following description tells how such a utility works in UNIX but most other systems have something similar. These file system checkers verify each file system (disk) independently of the other ones.

Two kinds of consistency checks can be made: blocks and files. To check for block consistency, the program builds a table with two counters per block, both initially 0. The first counter keeps track of how many times the block is present in a file; the second records how often it is present in the free list (or bit map of free blocks).

The program then reads all the i-nodes. Starting from an i-node, it is possible to build a list of all the block numbers used in the corresponding file. As each block number is read, its counter in the first table is incremented. The program then examines the free list or bit map, to find all the blocks that are not in use. Each occurrence of a block in the free list results in its counter in the second table being incremented.

If the file system is consistent, each block will have a 1 either in the first table or in the second table, as illustrated in Fig. 4-23(a). However, as a result of a crash, the tables might look like Fig. 4-23(b), in which block 2 does not occur in either table. It will be reported as being a **missing block**. While missing blocks do no real harm, they do waste space and thus reduce the capacity of the disk. The solution to missing blocks is straightforward: the file system checker just adds them to the free list.

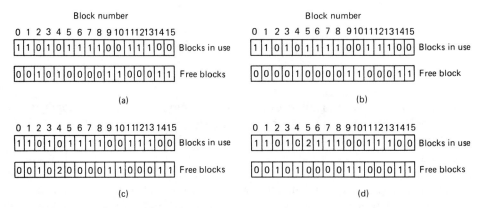

Fig. 4-23. File system states. (a) Consistent. (b) Missing block. (c) Duplicate block in free list. (d) Duplicate data block.

Another situation that might occur is that of Fig. 4-23(c). Here we see a block, number 4, that occurs twice in the free list. (Duplicates can occur only if the free list is really a list; with a bit map it is impossible.) The solution here is also simple: rebuild the free list.

The worst thing that can happen is that the same data block is present in two or more files, as shown in Fig. 4-23(d) with block 5. If either of these files is removed, block 5 will be put on the free list, leading to a situation in which the same block is both in use and free at the same time. If both files are removed, the block will be put onto the free list twice.

The appropriate action for the file system checker to take is to allocate a free block, copy the contents of block 5 into it, and insert the copy into one of the files. In this way, the information content of the files is unchanged (although almost assuredly garbled), but the file system structure is at least made consistent. The error should be reported, to allow the user to inspect the damage.

Finally, another possibility is that a block is present both in a file and in the free list. The solution here is simple: just remove it from the free list.

In addition to checking to see that each block is properly accounted for, the file system checker also checks the directory system. It too, uses a table of counters, but these are per file, rather than per block. It starts at the root directory and recursively descends the tree, inspecting each directory in the file system. For every file in every directory, it increments the counter for that file's i-node (see Fig. 4-15 for the layout of a directory entry).

When it is all done, it has a list, indexed by i-node number, telling how many directories point to that i-node. It then compares these numbers with the link counts stored in the i-nodes themselves. In a consistent file system, both counts will agree. However, two kinds of errors can occur: the link count in the i-node can be too high or it can be too low.

If the link count is higher than the number of directory entries, then even if all the files are removed from the directories, the count will still be nonzero and the i-node will not be removed. This error is not serious, but it wastes space on the disk with files that are not in any directory. It should be fixed by setting the link count in the i-node to the correct value. If the correct value is zero, the file should be deleted.

The other error is potentially catastrophic. If two directory entries are linked to a file, but the i-node says that there is only one, when either directory entry is removed, the i-node count will go to zero. When an i-node count goes to zero, the file system marks it as unused and releases all of its blocks. This action will result in one of the directories now pointing to an unused i-node, whose blocks may soon be assigned to other files. Again, the solution is just to force the link count in the i-node to the actual number of directory entries.

These two operations, checking blocks and checking directories, are often integrated for efficiency reasons (i.e., only one pass over the i-nodes is required). Other heuristic checks are also possible. For example, directories have a definite format, with i-node numbers and ASCII names. If an i-node number is larger than the number of i-nodes on the disk, the directory has been damaged.

Furthermore, each i-node has a mode, some of which are legal but strange, such as one that allows the owner and his group no access at all, but allows outsiders to read, write, and execute the file. It might be useful to at least report files that give outsiders more rights than the owner. Directories with more than, say, 1000 entries are also suspicious. Files located in user directories, but which are owned by the super-user and have the SETUID bit on, are potential security problems. With a little effort, one can put together a fairly long list of legal, but peculiar, situations that might be worth reporting.

The previous paragraphs have discussed the problem of protecting the user against crashes. Some file systems also worry about protecting the user against himself. If the user intends to type

```
rm *.o
```

to remove all the files ending with *.o* (compiler generated object files), but accidentally types

```
rm * .o
```

(note the space after the asterisk), *rm* will remove all the files in the current directory and then complain that it cannot find *.o*. In MS-DOS and some other systems, when a file is removed, all that happens is that a bit is set in the directory or i-node marking the file as removed. No disk blocks are returned to the free list until they are actually needed. Thus, if the user discovers the error immediately, it is possible to run a special utility program that "unremoves" (i.e., restores) the removed files.

4.3.6. File System Performance

Access to disk is much slower than access to memory. Reading a memory word typically takes a few hundred nanoseconds at most. Reading a disk block takes tens of milliseconds, a factor of 100,000 slower. As a result of this difference in access time, many file systems have been designed to reduce the number of disk accesses needed.

The most common technique used to reduce disk accesses is the **block cache** or **buffer cache**. (Cache is pronounced "cash," and is derived from the French *cacher*, meaning to hide.) In this context, a cache is a collection of blocks that logically belong on the disk, but are being kept in memory for performance reasons.

Various algorithms can be used to manage the cache, but a common one is to check all read requests to see if the needed block is in the cache. If it is, the read request can be satisfied without a disk access. If the block is not in the cache, it is first read into the cache, and then copied to wherever it is needed. Subsequent requests for the same block can be satisfied from the cache.

When a block has to be loaded into a full cache, some block has to be removed and rewritten to the disk if it has been modified since being brought in. This situation is very much like paging, and all the usual paging algorithms, such as FIFO, second chance, and LRU are applicable. One pleasant difference between paging and caching is that cache references are relatively infrequent, so that it is feasible to keep all the blocks in exact LRU order with linked lists.

Unfortunately, there is a catch. Now that we have a situation in which exact LRU is possible, it turns out that LRU is undesirable. The problem has to do with the crashes and file system consistency discussed in the previous section. If a critical block, such as an i-node block, is read into the cache and modified, but not rewritten to the disk, a crash will leave the file system in an inconsistent state. If the i-node block is put at the end of the LRU chain, it may be quite a while before it reaches the front and is rewritten to the disk.

Furthermore, some blocks, such as double indirect blocks, are rarely referenced two times within a short interval. These considerations lead to a modified LRU scheme, taking two factors into account:

1. Is the block likely to be needed again soon?

2. Is the block essential to the consistency of the file system?

For both questions, blocks can be divided into categories such as i-node blocks, indirect blocks, directory blocks, full data blocks, and partly-full data blocks. Blocks that will probably not be needed again soon go on the front, rather than the rear of the LRU list, so their buffers will be reused quickly. Blocks that might be needed again soon, such as a partly full block that is being written, go on the end of the list, so they will stay around for a long time.

The second question is independent of the first one. If the block is essential to the file system consistency (basically, everything except data blocks), and it has been modified, it should be written to disk immediately, regardless of which end of the LRU list it is put on. By writing critical blocks quickly, we greatly reduce the probability that a crash will wreck the file system. Careful choice of the order in which critical blocks are written can also help.

Even with this measure to keep the file system integrity intact, it is undesirable to keep data blocks in the cache too long before writing them out. Consider the plight of someone who is using a personal computer to write a book. Even if our writer periodically tells the editor to write the file being edited to the disk, there is a good chance that everything will still be in the cache and not on the disk. If the system crashes, the file system structure will not be corrupted, but a day's work will be lost.

This situation need not happen very often before we have a fairly unhappy user. Systems take two approaches to dealing with it. The UNIX way is to have a system call, SYNC, which forces all the modified blocks out onto the disk immediately. When the system is started up, a program, usually called *update*, is started up in the background to sit in an endless loop issuing SYNC calls, sleeping for 30 sec between calls. As a result, no more than 30 seconds of work is lost due to a crash.

The MS-DOS way is to write every modified block to disk as soon as it has been written. Caches in which all modified blocks are written back to the disk immediately are called **write-through caches**. They require much more disk I/O than nonwrite-through caches. The difference between these two approaches can be seen when a program writes a 1K block full, one character at a time. UNIX will collect all the characters in the cache, and write the block out once every 30 seconds, or whenever the block is removed from the cache. MS-DOS will make a disk access for every character written. Of course most programs do internal buffering, so they normally write not a character, but a line or a larger unit on each WRITE system call.

A consequence of this difference in caching strategy is that just removing a (floppy) disk from a UNIX system without doing a SYNC will almost always result in lost data, and frequently in a corrupted file system as well. With MS-DOS, no problem arises. These differing strategies were chosen because UNIX was developed in an environment in which all disks were hard disks and not removable, whereas MS-DOS started out in the floppy disk world. As hard disks become the norm, even on small microcomputers, the UNIX approach, with its better efficiency, will definitely be the way to go.

Caching is not the only way to increase the performance of a file system. Another important technique is to reduce the amount of disk arm motion by putting blocks that are likely to be accessed in sequence close to each other, preferably in the same cylinder. When an output file is written, the file system has to allocate the blocks one at a time, as they are needed. If the free blocks are recorded in a bit map, and the whole bit map is in main memory, it is easy enough to choose a free block as close as possible to the previous block. With a free list, part of which is on disk, it is much harder to allocate blocks close together.

However, even with a free list, some block clustering can be done. The trick is to keep track of disk storage not in blocks, but in groups of consecutive blocks. If a track consists of 64 sectors of 512 bytes, the system could use 1K blocks (2 sectors), but allocate disk storage in units of 2 blocks (4 sectors). This is not the same as having a 2K disk block, since the cache would still use 1K blocks and disk transfers would still be 1K but reading a file sequentially on an otherwise idle system would reduce the number of seeks by a factor of two, considerably improving performance.

A variation on the same theme is to take account of rotational positioning. When allocating blocks, the system attempts to place consecutive blocks in a file in the same cylinder, but interleaved for maximum throughput. Thus, if a disk has a rotation time of 16.67 msec and it takes about 4 msec for a user process to request and get a disk block, each block should be placed at least a quarter of the way around from its predecessor.

Another performance bottleneck in systems that use i-nodes or the equivalent is that reading even a short file requires two disk accesses: one for the i-node and one for the block. The usual i-node placement is shown in Fig. 4-24(a). Here all the i-nodes are near the beginning of the disk, so the average distance between an i-node and its blocks will be about half the number of cylinders, requiring long seeks.

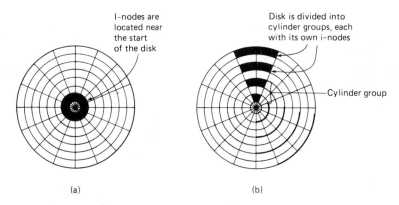

Fig. 4-24. (a) I-nodes placed at the start of the disk. (b) Disk divided into cylinder groups, each with its own blocks and i-nodes.

One easy performance improvement is to put the i-nodes in the middle of the disk, rather than at the start, thus reducing the average seek between the i-node and the first block by a factor of two. Another idea, shown in Fig. 4-24(b), is to divide the disk into cylinder groups, each with its own i-nodes, blocks, and free list (McKusick et al., 1984). When creating a new file, any i-node can be chosen, but having done this, an attempt is made to find a block in the same cylinder group as the i-node. If none is available, then a block in a cylinder group close by is used.

4.4. SECURITY

File systems often contain information that is highly valuable to their users. Protecting this information against unauthorized usage is therefore a major concern of all file systems. In the following sections we will look at a variety of issues concerned with security and protection.

4.4.1. The Security Environment

The terms "security" and "protection" are often used interchangeably. Nevertheless, it is frequently useful to make a distinction between the general problems involved in making sure that files are not read or modified by unauthorized persons, which include technical, managerial, legal, and political issues on the one hand, and the specific operating system mechanisms used to provide security, on the other. To avoid confusion, we will use the term **security** to refer to the overall problem, and the term **protection mechanisms** to refer to the specific operating system mechanisms used to safeguard information in the computer. The boundary between them is not well defined, however. First we will look at security; later on in the chapter we will look at protection.

Security has many facets. Two of the more important ones are data loss and intruders. Some of the common causes of data loss are:

1. Acts of God: fires, floods, earthquakes, wars, riots, or rats gnawing tapes or floppy disks.

2. Hardware or software errors: CPU malfunctions, unreadable disks or tapes, telecommunication errors, program bugs.

3. Human errors: incorrect data entry, wrong tape or disk mounted, wrong program run, lost disk or tape.

Most of these can be dealt with by maintaining adequate backups, preferably far away from the original data.

A more interesting problem is what to do about intruders. These come in two varieties. Passive intruders just want to read files they are not authorized to read. Active intruders are more malicious; they want to make unauthorized changes to data. When designing a system to be secure against intruders, it is important to keep in mind the kind of intruder one is trying to protect against. Some common categories are:

1. Casual prying by nontechnical users. Many people have terminals to timesharing systems on their desks, and human nature being what it is, some of them will read other people's electronic mail and other files if no barriers are placed in the way. Most UNIX systems, for example, have the default that all files are publicly readable.

2. Snooping by insiders. Students, system programmers, operators, and other technical personnel often consider it to be a personal challenge to break the security of the local computer system. They often are highly skilled and are willing to devote a substantial amount of time to the effort.

3. Determined attempt to make money. Some bank programmers have attempted to break into a banking system to steal from the bank.

Schemes have varied from changing the software to truncate rather than round interest, keeping the fraction of a cent for themselves, to siphoning off accounts not used in years, to blackmail ("Pay me or I will destroy all the bank's records.").

4. Commercial or military espionage. Espionage refers to a serious and well-funded attempt by a competitor or a foreign country to steal programs, trade secrets, patents, technology, circuit designs, marketing plans, and so forth. Often this attempt will involve wiretapping or even erecting antennas directed at the computer to pick up its electromagnetic radiation.

It should be clear that trying to keep the KGB from stealing military secrets is quite a different matter from trying to keep students from inserting a funny message-of-the-day into the system. The amount of effort that one puts into security and protection clearly depends on who the enemy is thought to be.

Another aspect of the security problem is **privacy**: protecting individuals from misuse of information about them. This quickly gets into many legal and moral issues. Should the government compile dossiers on everyone in order to catch X-cheaters, where X is "welfare" or "tax," depending on your politics? Should the police be able to look up anything on anyone in order to stop organized crime? Do employers and insurance companies have rights? What happens when these rights conflict with individual rights? All of these issues are extremely important, but are beyond the scope of this book.

4.4.2. Famous Security Flaws

Just as the transportation industry has the *Titanic* and the *Hindenburg*, computer security experts have a few things they would rather forget about. In this section we will look at some interesting security problems that have occurred in four different operating systems: UNIX, MULTICS, TENEX, and OS/360.

The UNIX utility *lpr*, which prints a file on the line printer, has an option to remove the file after it has been printed. In early versions of UNIX it was possible for anyone to use *lpr* to print, and then have the system remove, the password file.

Another way to break into UNIX was to link a file called *core* in the working directory to the password file. The intruder then forced a core dump of a SETUID program, which the system wrote on the *core* file, that is, on top of the password file. In this way, a user could replace the password file with one containing a few strings of his own choosing (e.g., command arguments).

Yet another subtle flaw in UNIX involved the command

```
mkdir foo
```

Mkdir, which was a SETUID program owned by the root, first created the i-node for the directory *foo* with the system call MKNOD, and then changed the owner of *foo* from its effective uid (i.e., root) to its real uid (the user's uid). When the system was slow, it was sometimes possible for the user to quickly remove the directory i-node and make a link to the password file under the name *foo* after the MKNOD but before the CHOWN. When *mkdir* did the CHOWN it made the user the owner of the password file. By putting the necessary commands in a shell script, they could be tried over and over until the trick worked.

The MULTICS security problem had to do with the fact that the system designers always perceived MULTICS as a timesharing system, with batch facilities thrown in as an afterthought to pacify some old batch diehards. The timesharing security was excellent; the batch security was nonexistent. It was possible for anyone to submit a batch job that read a deck of cards into an arbitrary user's directory.

To steal someone's files, all one had to do was get a copy of the editor source code, modify it to steal files (but still work perfectly as an editor), compile it, and put it into the victim's *bin* directory. The next time the victim called the editor, he got the intruder's version, which edited fine, but stole all his files as well. The idea of modifying a normal program to do nasty things in addition to its usual function and arranging for the victim to use the modified version is now known as the **Trojan horse attack**.

The TENEX operating system used to be very popular on the DEC-10 computers. It is no longer used much, but it will live on forever in the annals of computer security due to the following design error. TENEX supported paging. To allow users to monitor the behavior of their programs, it was possible to instruct the system to call a user function on each page fault.

TENEX also used passwords to protect files. To access a file, a program had to present the proper password. The operating system checked passwords one character at a time, stopping as soon as it saw that the password was wrong. To break into TENEX an intruder would carefully position a password as shown in Fig. 4-25(a), with the first character at the end of one page, and the rest at the start of the next page.

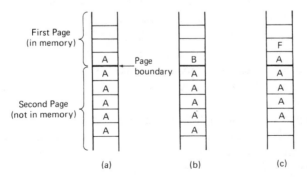

Fig. 4-25. The TENEX password problem.

The next step was to make sure that the second page was not in memory, for example, by referencing so many other pages that the second page would surely be evicted to make room for them. Now the program tried to open the victim's file, using the carefully aligned password. If the first character of the real password was anything but A, the system would stop checking at the first character and report back with ILLEGAL PASSWORD. If, however, the real password did begin with A, the system continued reading, and got a page fault, about which the intruder was informed.

If the password did not begin with A, the intruder changed the password to that of Fig. 4-25(b) and repeated the whole process to see if it began with B. It took at most 128 tries to go through the whole ASCII character set, and thus determine the first character.

Suppose the first character was an F. The memory layout of Fig. 4-25(c) allowed the intruder to test strings of the form FA, FB, and so on. Using this approach it took at most $128n$ tries to guess an n character ASCII password, instead of 128^n.

Our last flaw concerns OS/360. The description that follows is slightly simplified, but preserves the essence of the flaw. In this system it was possible to start up a tape read and then continue computing while the tape drive was transferring data to the user space. The trick here was to carefully start up a tape read, and then do a system call that required a user data structure, for example, a file to read and its password.

The operating system first verified that the password was indeed the correct one for the given file. Then it went back and read the file name again for the actual access (it could have saved the name internally, but it did not). Unfortunately, just before the system went to fetch the file name the second time, the file name was overwritten by the tape drive. The system then read the new file, for which no password had been presented. Getting the timing right took some practice, but it was not that hard. Besides, if there is one thing that computers are good at, it is repeating the same operation over and over *ad nauseam*.

4.4.3. The Internet Worm

The greatest computer security violation of all time began in the evening of Nov. 2, 1988 when a Cornell graduate student, Robert Tappan Morris, released a worm program into the Internet. This action brought down thousands of computers at universities, corporations, and government laboratories all over the world before it was tracked down and removed. It also started a controversy that has not yet died down. We will discuss the highlights of this event below. For more technical information see (Spafford, 1989). For the story viewed as a police thriller, see (Hafner and Markoff, 1991).

The story began sometime in 1988 when Morris discovered two bugs in Berkeley UNIX that made it possible to gain unauthorized access to machines all over the Internet, the vast research network connecting hundreds of thousands of machines in the U.S., Europe, and the Far East. Working alone, he wrote a self replicating program, called a **worm**, that would exploit these errors and replicate itself in seconds on every machine it could gain access to. He worked on the program for months, carefully tuning it and having it try to hide its tracks.

It is not known whether the release on Nov. 2, 1988 was intended as a test, or was the real thing. In any event, it did bring most of the Sun and VAX systems on the Internet to their knees within a few hours of its release. Morris' motivation is unknown, but it is possible that he intended the whole idea as a high-tech practical joke, but which due to a programming error got completely out of hand.

Technically, the worm consisted of two programs, the bootstrap and the worm proper. The bootstrap was 99 lines of C called *ll.c*. It was compiled and executed on the system under attack. Once running, it connected to the machine from which it came, uploaded the main worm, and executed it. After going to some trouble to hide its existence, the worm then looked through its new host's routing tables to see what machines that host was connected to, and attempted to spread the bootstrap to those machines.

Three methods were tried to infect new machines. Method 1 was to try to run a remote shell using the *rsh* command. Some machines trust other machines, and willingly run *rsh* without any further authentication. If this worked, the remote shell uploaded the worm program and continued infecting new machines from there.

Method 2 made use of a program present on all BSD systems called *finger*, that allows a user anywhere on the Internet to type

```
finger name@site
```

to display information about a person at a particular installation. This information usually includes the person's real name, login, home and work addresses and telephone numbers, secretary's name and telephone number, FAX number, and similar information. It is the electronic equivalent of the phone book.

Finger works as follows. At every BSD site a background process called the **finger daemon** runs all the time fielding and answering queries from all over the Internet. What the worm did was call *finger* with a specially handcrafted 536-byte string as parameter. This long string overflowed the daemon's buffer and overwrote its stack. The bug exploited here is the daemon's failure to check for overflow. When the daemon returned from the procedure it was in at the time it got the request, it returned not to *main*, but to a procedure inside the 536-byte string on the stack. This procedure tried to execute */bin/sh*. If it succeeded, the worm now had a shell running on the machine under attack.

Method 3 depended on a bug in the mail system, *sendmail*, which allowed the worm to mail a copy of the bootstrap and get it executed.

Once established, the worm tried to break user passwords. Morris did not have to do much research on how to accomplish this. All he had to do was ask his father, a security expert at the National Security Agency, the U.S. government's code breaking agency, for a reprint of a classic paper on the subject that Morris Sr. and Ken Thompson wrote a decade earlier at Bell Labs (Morris and Thompson, 1979). Each broken password allowed the worm to log in on any machines the password's owner had accounts on.

Every time the worm gained access to a new machine, it checked to see if any other copies of the worm were already active there. If so, the new copy exited, except one time in seven it kept going, possibly in an attempt to keep the worm propagating even if the system administration there started up their own version of the worm to fool the real worm. The use of 1 in 7 created far too many worms, and was the reason all the infected machines ground to a halt: they were infested with worms.

If Morris had left this out and just exited whenever another worm was sighted, the worm would probably have gone undetected.

Morris was caught when one of his friends spoke with the *New York Times* computer reporter, John Markoff, and tried to convince Markoff that the incident was an accident, the worm was harmless, and the author was sorry. The friend inadvertently let slip that the perpetrator's login was *rtm*. Converting *rtm* into the owner's name was easy—all that had to be done was to run *finger*. The next day the story was the lead on page one, even upstaging the presidential election three days later.

Morris was tried and convicted in federal court. He was sentenced to a 10,000 dollar fine, 3 years probation, and 400 hours of community service. His legal costs probably exceeded 150,000 dollars. This sentence generated a great deal of controversy. Many in the computer community felt that he was a bright graduate student whose harmless prank had gotten out of control. Nothing in the worm suggested that Morris was trying to steal or damage anything. Others felt he was a serious criminal and should have gone to jail.

4.4.4. Generic Security Attacks

The flaws described above have been fixed but the average operating system still leaks like a sieve. The usual way to test a system's security is to hire a group of experts, known as **tiger teams** or **penetration teams**, to see if they can break in. Hebbard et al. (1980) tried the same thing with graduate students. In the course of the years, these penetration teams have discovered a number of areas in which systems are likely to be weak. Below we have listed some of the more common attacks that are often successful. When designing a system, be sure it can withstand attacks like these.

1. Request memory pages, disk space, or tapes and just read them. Many systems do not erase them before allocating them, and they may be full of interesting information written by the previous owner.

2. Try illegal system calls, or legal system calls with illegal parameters, or even legal system calls with legal but unreasonable parameters. Many systems can easily be confused.

3. Start logging in and then hit DEL, RUBOUT or BREAK halfway through the login sequence. In some systems, the password checking program will be killed and the login considered successful.

4. Try modifying complex operating system structures kept in user space. In many systems, to open a file, the program builds a large data structure containing the file name and many other parameters and passes it to the system. As the file is read and written, the system sometimes updates the structure itself. Changing these fields can wreak havoc with the security.

5. Spoof the user by writing a program that types "login:" on the screen and go away. Many users will walk up to the terminal and willingly tell it their login name and password, which the program carefully records for its evil master.

6. Look for manuals that say "Do not do *X*." Try as many variations of *X* as possible.

7. Convince a system programmer to change the system to skip certain vital security checks for any user with your login name. This attack is known as a **trapdoor**.

8. All else failing, the penetrator might find the computer center director's secretary and trick or bribe her. The secretary probably has easy access to all kinds of wonderful information, and is usually poorly paid. Do not underestimate the problems caused by personnel.

These and other attacks are discussed by Linde (1975).

Viruses

A special category of attack is the computer virus, which has become a major problem for many computer users. A **virus** is a program fragment that is attached to a legitimate program with the intention of infecting other programs. It differs from a worm only in that a virus piggybacks on an existing program, whereas a worm is a complete program in itself. Viruses and worms both attempt to spread themselves and both can do severe damage.

A typical virus works as follows. The person writing the virus first produces a useful new program, often a game for MS-DOS. This program contains the virus code hidden away in it. The game is then uploaded to a public bulletin board system or offered for free or for a modest price on floppy disk. The program is then advertised, and people begin downloading and using it. Constructing a virus is not easy, so the people doing this are invariably quite bright, and the quality of the game or other program is often excellent.

When the program is started up, it immediately begins examining all the binary programs on the hard disk to see if they are already infected. When an uninfected program is found, it is infected by attaching the virus code to the end of the file, and replacing the first instruction with a jump to the virus. When the virus code is finished executing, it executes the instruction that had previously been first, and then jumps to the second instruction. In this way, every time an infected program runs, it tries to infect more programs.

In addition to just infecting other programs, a virus can do other things, such as erasing, modifying, or encrypting files. One virus even displayed an extortion note on the screen, telling the user to send 500 dollars in cash to a post office box in Panama or face the permanent loss of his data and damage to the hardware.

It is also possible for a virus to infect the hard disk's boot sector, making it impossible to boot the computer. Such a virus may ask for a password, which the virus' writer will supply in exchange for money.

Virus problems are easier to prevent than to cure. The safest course is only to buy shrink-wrapped software from respectable stores. Uploading free software from bulletin boards or getting pirated copies on floppy disk is asking for trouble. Commercial antivirus packages exist, but some of these work by just looking for specific known viruses.

A more general approach is to first reformat the hard disk completely, including the boot sector. Next, install all the trusted software and compute a checksum for each file. The algorithm does not matter, as long as it has enough bits (at least 16, preferably 32). Store the list of (file, checksum) pairs in a safe place, either offline on a floppy disk, or online but encrypted. Starting at that point, whenever the system is booted, all the checksums should be recomputed and compared to the secure list of original checksums. Any file whose current checksum differs from the original one is immediately suspect. While this approach does not prevent infection, it at least allows early detection.

Infection can be made more difficult if the directory where binary programs reside is made unwritable for ordinary users. This technique makes it difficult for the virus to modify other binaries. Although it can be used in UNIX, it is not applicable to MS-DOS because the latter's directories cannot be made unwritable at all.

4.4.5. Design Principles for Security

Viruses mostly occur on desktop systems. On larger systems other problems occur and other methods are needed for dealing with them. Saltzer and Schroeder (1975) have identified several general principles that can be used as a guide to designing secure systems. A brief summary of their ideas (based on experience with MULTICS) is given below.

First, the system design should be public. Assuming that the intruder will not know how the system works serves only to delude the designers.

Second, the default should be no access. Errors in which legitimate access is refused will be reported much faster than errors in which unauthorized access is allowed.

Third, check for current authority. The system should not check for permission, determine that access is permitted, and then squirrel away this information for subsequent use. Many systems check for permission when a file is opened, and not afterward. This means that a user who opens a file, and keeps it open for weeks, will continue to have access, even if the owner has long since changed the file protection.

Fourth, give each process the least privilege possible. If an editor has only the authority to access the file to be edited (specified when the editor is invoked), editors with Trojan horses will not be able to do much damage. This principle implies a fine-grained protection scheme. We will discuss such schemes later in this chapter.

Fifth, the protection mechanism should be simple, uniform, and built in to the lowest layers of the system. Trying to retrofit security to an existing insecure system is nearly impossible. Security, like correctness, is not an add-on feature.

Sixth, the scheme chosen must be psychologically acceptable. If users feel that protecting their files is too much work, they just will not do it. Nevertheless, they will complain loudly if something goes wrong. Replies of the form "It is your own fault" will generally not be well received.

4.4.6. User Authentication

Many protection schemes are based on the assumption that the system knows the identity of each user. The problem of identifying users when they log in is called **user authentication**. Most authentication methods are based on identifying something the user knows, something the user has, or something the user is.

Passwords

The most widely used form of authentication is to require the user to type a password. Password protection is easy to understand and easy to implement. In UNIX it works like this. The login program asks the user to type his name and password. The password is immediately encrypted. The login program then reads the password file, which is a series of ASCII lines, one per user, until it finds the line containing the user's login name. If the (encrypted) password contained in this line matches the encrypted password just computed, the login is permitted, otherwise it is refused.

Password authentication is easy to defeat. One frequently reads about groups of high school, or even junior high school students who, with the aid of their trusty home computers, have just broken into some top secret system owned by a giant corporation or government agency. Virtually all the time the break-in consists of guessing a user name and password combination.

Morris and Thompson (1979) made a study of passwords on UNIX systems. They compiled a list of likely passwords: first names, last names, street names, city names, words from a moderate-sized dictionary (also words spelled backward), valid license plate numbers, and short strings of random characters.

They then encrypted each of these using the known password encryption algorithm, and checked to see if any of the encrypted passwords matched entries in their list. Over 86 percent of all passwords turned up in their list.

If all passwords consisted of 7 characters chosen at random from the 95 printable ASCII characters, the search space becomes 95^7, which is about 7×10^{13}. At 1000 encryptions per second, it would take 2000 years to build the list to check the password file against. Furthermore, the list would fill 20 million magnetic tapes. Even requiring passwords to contain at least one lowercase character, one uppercase character, and one special character, and be at least seven characters long would be a big improvement on user-chosen passwords.

Even if it is considered politically impossible to require users to pick reasonable passwords, Morris and Thompson have described a technique that renders their own attack (encrypting a large number of passwords in advance) almost useless. Their idea is to associate an n-bit random number with each password. The random number is changed whenever the password is changed. The random number is stored in the password file in unencrypted form, so that everyone can read it. Instead of just storing the encrypted password in the password file, the password and the random number are first concatenated and then encrypted together. This encrypted result is stored in the password file.

Now consider the implications for an intruder who wants to build up a list of likely passwords, encrypt them, and save the results in a sorted file, f, so that any encrypted password can be looked up easily. If an intruder suspects that *Marilyn* might be a password, it is no longer sufficient just to encrypt *Marilyn* and put the result in f. He has to encrypt 2^n strings, such as *Marilyn0000, Marilyn0001, Marilyn0002*, and so forth and enter all of them in f. This technique increases the size of f by 2^n. UNIX uses this method with $n = 12$. It is known as **salting** the password file. Some versions of UNIX make the password file itself unreadable, but provide a program to look up entries upon request, adding just enough delay to greatly slow down any attacker.

Although this method offers protection against intruders who try to precompute a large list of encrypted passwords, it does little to protect a user *David* whose password is also *David*. One way to encourage people to pick better passwords is to have the computer offer advice. Some computers have a program that generates random easy-to-pronounce nonsense words, such as *fotally*, *garbungy*, or *bipitty* that can be used as passwords (preferably with some upper case and special characters thrown in).

Other computers require users to change their passwords regularly, to limit the damage done if a password leaks out. The most extreme form of this approach is the **one-time password**. When one-time passwords are used, the user gets a book containing a list of passwords. Each login uses the next password in the list. If an intruder ever discovers a password, it will not do him any good, since next time a different password must be used. It is suggested that the user try to avoid losing the password book.

It goes almost without saying that while a password is being typed in, the computer should not display the typed characters, to keep them from prying eyes near the terminal. What is less obvious is that passwords should never be stored in the computer in unencrypted form, and that not even the computer center management should have unencrypted copies. Keeping unencrypted passwords anywhere is looking for trouble.

A variation on the password idea is to have each new user provide a long list of questions and answers that are then stored in the computer in encrypted form. The questions should be chosen so that the user does not need to write them down. Typical questions are:

1. Who is Marjolein's sister?

2. On what street was your elementary school?

3. What did Mrs. Woroboff teach?

At login, the computer asks one of them at random and checks the answer.

Another variation is **challenge-response**. When this is used, the user picks an algorithm when signing up as a user, for example x^2. When the user logs in, the computer types an argument, say 7, in which case the user types 49. The algorithm can be different in the morning and afternoon, on different days of the week, from different terminals, and so on.

Physical Identification

A completely different approach to authorization is to check to see if the user has some item, normally a plastic card with a magnetic stripe on it. The card is inserted into the terminal, which then checks to see whose card it is. This method can be combined with a password, so a user can only log in if he (1) has the card and (2) knows the password. Automated cash-dispensing machines usually work this way.

Yet another approach is to measure physical characteristics that are hard to forge. For example, a fingerprint or a voiceprint reader in the terminal could verify the user's identity. (It makes the search go faster if the user tells the computer who he is, rather than making the computer compare the given fingerprint to the entire data base.) Direct visual recognition is not yet feasible, but may be one day.

Another technique is signature analysis. The user signs his name with a special pen connected to the terminal, and the computer compares it to a known specimen stored on line. Even better is not to compare the signature, but compare the pen motions made while writing it. A good forger may be able to copy the signature, but will not have a clue as to the exact order in which the strokes were made.

Finger length analysis is surprisingly practical. When this is used, each terminal has a device like the one of Fig. 4-26. The user inserts his hand into it, and the length of all his fingers is measured and checked against the data base.

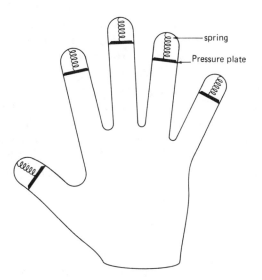

Fig. 4-26. A device for measuring finger length.

We could go on and on with more examples, but two more will help make an important point. Cats and other animals mark off their territory by urinating around its perimeter. Apparently cats can identify each other this way. Suppose someone comes up with a tiny device capable of doing an instant urinalysis, thereby providing a foolproof identification. Each terminal could be equipped with one of these devices, along with a discrete sign reading: "For login, please deposit sample here." This might be an absolutely unbreakable system, but it would probably have a fairly serious user acceptance problem.

The same could be said of a system consisting of a thumbtack and a small spectrograph. The user would be requested to press his thumb against the thumbtack, thus extracting a drop of blood for spectrographic analysis. The point is that any authentication scheme must be psychologically acceptable to the user community. Finger-length measurements probably will not cause any problem, but even something as nonintrusive as storing fingerprints on line may be unacceptable to many people.

Countermeasures

Computer installations that are really serious about security, something that frequently happens the day after an intruder has broken in and done major damage, often take steps to make unauthorized entry much harder. For example, each user could be allowed to log in only from a specific terminal, and only during certain days of the week and hours of the day.

Dialup telephone lines could be made to work as follows. Anyone can dial up and log in, but after a successful login, the system immediately breaks the connection and calls the user back at an agreed upon number. This measure means than an intruder cannot just try breaking in from any phone line; only the user's (home) phone will do. In any event, with or without call back, the system should take at least 10 seconds to check any password typed in on a dialup line, and should increase this time after several consecutive unsuccessful login attempts, in order to reduce the rate at which intruders can try. After three failed login attempts, the line should be disconnected for 10 minutes and security personnel notified.

All logins should be recorded. When a user logs in, the system should report the time and terminal of the previous login, so he can detect possible break ins.

The next step up is laying baited traps to catch intruders. A simple scheme is to have one special login name with an easy password (e.g., login name: guest, password: guest). Whenever anyone logs in using this name, the system security specialists are immediately notified. Other traps can be easy-to-find bugs in the operating system and similar things, designed for the purpose of catching intruders in the act.

4.5. PROTECTION MECHANISMS

In the previous sections we have looked at many potential problems, some of them technical and some of them not. In the following sections we will concentrate on some of the detailed technical ways that are used in operating systems to protect files and other things. All of these techniques make a clear distinction between policy (whose data are to be protected from whom) and mechanism (how the system enforces the policy). The separation of policy and mechanism is discussed in (Levin et al., 1975). Our emphasis will be on the mechanism, not the policy.

4.5.1. Protection Domains

A computer system contains many **objects** that need to be protected. These objects can be hardware, such as CPUs, memory segments, terminals, disk drives, or printers, or they can be software, such as processes, files, data bases, or semaphores.

Each object has a unique name by which it is referenced, and a set of operations that can be carried out on it. READ and WRITE are operations appropriate to a file; UP and DOWN make sense on a semaphore.

It is obvious that a way is needed to prohibit processes from accessing objects that they are not authorized to access. Furthermore, this mechanism must also make it possible to restrict processes to a subset of the legal operations when that is needed. For example, process A may be entitled to read, but not write, file F.

To provide a way to discuss different protection mechanisms, it is convenient to introduce the concept of a domain. A **domain** is a set of (object, rights) pairs. Each pair specifies an object and some subset of the operations that can be performed on it. A **right** in this context means permission to perform one of the operations.

Figure 4-27 depicts three domains, showing the objects in each domain and the rights [Read, Write, eXecute] available on each object. Note that *Printer1* is in two domains at the same time. Although not shown in this example, it is possible for the same object to be in multiple domains, with *different* rights in each domain.

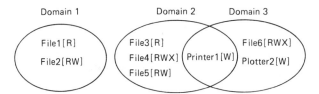

Fig. 4-27. Three protection domains.

At every instant of time, each process runs in some protection domain. In other words, there is some collection of objects it can access, and for each object it has some set of rights. Processes can also switch from domain to domain during execution. The rules for domain switching are highly system dependent.

To make the idea of a protection domain more concrete, let us look at UNIX. In UNIX, the domain of a process is defined by its uid and gid. Given any (uid, gid) combination, it is possible to make a complete list of all objects (files, including I/O devices represented by special files, etc.) that can be accessed, and whether they can be accessed for reading, writing, or executing. Two processes with the same (uid, gid) combination will have access to exactly the same set of objects. Processes with different (uid, gid) values will have access to a different set of files, although there will be considerable overlap in most cases.

Furthermore, each process in UNIX has two halves: the user part and the kernel part. When the process does a system call, it switches from the user part to the kernel part. The kernel part has access to a different set of objects from the user part. For example, the kernel can access all the pages in physical memory, the entire disk, and all the other protected resources. Thus, a system call causes a domain switch.

When a process does an EXEC on a file with the SETUID or SETGID bit on, it acquires a new effective uid or gid. With a different (uid, gid) combination, it has a different set of files and operations available. Running a program with SETUID or SETGID is also a domain switch.

The division of a UNIX process into a kernel part and a user part is a remnant of a much more powerful domain switching mechanism that was used in MULTICS. In that system, the hardware supported not two domains (kernel and user) per process, but up to 64. A MULTICS process could consist of a collection of procedures, each one running in some domain, which were called **rings** (Schroeder and Saltzer, 1972). Procedures could also be linked dynamically to a running process during execution.

Figure 4-28 shows four rings. The innermost ring, the operating system kernel, had the most power. Moving outward from the kernel, the rings became successively less powerful. Ring 1, for example, might contain the code for functions that in UNIX are handled by SETUID programs owned by the root, such as *mkdir*. Ring 2 might contain the grading program used to evaluate student programs, and ring 3 might contain the student programs.

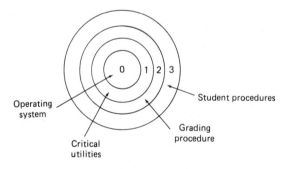

Fig. 4-28. A process in MULTICS occupying four rings. Each ring is a separate protection domain.

When a procedure in one ring called a procedure in another ring, a trap occurred, giving the system the opportunity to change the protection domain of the process. Thus, a MULTICS process could operate in as many as 64 different domains during its lifetime. (Actually, the situation was more complicated than we have sketched above; procedures could live in multiple consecutive rings, and parameter passing between rings was carefully controlled.) For a detailed description of MULTICS, see Organick (1972).

An important question is how the system keeps track of which object belongs to which domain. Conceptually, at least, one can envision a large matrix, with the rows being the domains and the columns being the objects. Each box lists the rights, if any, that the domain contains for the object. The matrix for Fig. 4-27 is shown in Fig. 4-29. Given this matrix and the current domain number, the system can tell if an access to a given object in a particular way from a specified domain is allowed.

Object

Domain	File1	File2	File3	File4	File5	File6	Printer1	Plotter2
1	Read	Read Write						
2			Read	Read Write Execute	Read Write		Write	
3						Read Write Execute	Write	Write

Fig. 4-29. A protection matrix.

Domain switching itself, as in MULTICS, can be easily included in the matrix model by realizing that a domain is itself an object, with the operation ENTER. Figure 4-30 shows the matrix of Fig. 4-29 again, only now with the three domains as objects themselves. Processes in domain 1 can switch to domain 2, but once there, they cannot go back. This situation models executing a SETUID program in UNIX. No other domain switches are permitted in this example.

Object

Domain	File1	File2	File3	File4	File5	File6	Printer1	Plotter2	Domain1	Domain2	Domain 3
1	Read	Read Write								Enter	
2			Read	Read Write Execute	Read Write		Write				
3						Read Write Execute	Write	Write			

Fig. 4-30. A protection matrix with domains as objects.

4.5.2. Access Control Lists

In practice, actually storing the matrix of Fig. 4-30 is rarely done because it is large and sparse. Most domains have no access at all to most objects, so storing a big, empty matrix is a waste of disk space. Two methods that are practical, however, are storing the matrix by rows or by columns, and then storing only the nonempty elements. The two approaches are surprisingly different. In this section we will look at storing it by column; in the next one we will study storing it by row.

The first technique consists of associating with each object an (ordered) list containing all the domains that may access the object, and how. This list is called the

access control list or **ACL**. If it were to be implemented in UNIX, the easiest way would be to put the ACL for each file in a separate disk block, and include the block number in the file's i-node. As only the nonempty entries of the matrix are stored, the total storage required for all the ACLs combined is much less than what would be needed for the whole matrix.

As an example of how ACLs work, let us continue to imagine that they were used in UNIX, where a domain is specified by a (uid, gid) pair. Actually, ACLs were used in UNIX's role model, MULTICS, more or less in the way we will describe, so the example is not so hypothetical.

Let us now assume that we have four users (i.e., uids) *Jan, Els, Jelle*, and *Maaike*, who belong to groups *system, staff, student*, and *student*, respectively. Suppose some files have the following ACLs:

File0: (Jan, *, RWX)
File1: (Jan, system, RWX)
File2: (Jan, *, RW–), (Els, staff, R– –), (Maaike, *, RW–)
File3: (*, student, R– –)
File4: (Jelle, *, – – –), (*, student, R– –)

Each ACL entry, in parentheses, specifies a uid, a gid, and the allowed accesses (Read, Write, eXecute). An asterisk means all uids or gids. *File0* can be read, written, or executed by any process with uid = *Jan*, and any gid. *File1* can be accessed only by processes with uid = *Jan* and gid = *system*. A process that has uid = *Jan* and gid = *staff* can access *File0* but not *File1*. *File2* can be read or written by processes with uid = *Jan* and any gid, read by processes with uid = *Els* and gid = *staff*, or by processes with uid = *Maaike* and any gid. *File3* can be read by any student. *File4* is especially interesting. It says that anyone with uid = *Jelle*, in any group, has no access at all, but all other students can read it. By using ACLs it is possible to prohibit specific uids or gids from accessing an object, while allowing everyone else in the same class.

So much for what UNIX does not do. Now let us look at what it *does* do. It provides three bits, *rwx*, per file for the owner, the owner's group, and others. This scheme is just the ACL again, but compressed to 9 bits. It is a list associated with the object saying who may access it and how. While the 9-bit UNIX scheme is clearly less general than a full-blown ACL system, in practice it is adequate, and its implementation is much simpler and cheaper.

The owner of an object can change its ACL at any time, thus making it easy to prohibit accesses that were previously allowed. The only problem is that changing the ACL will probably not affect any users who are currently using the object (e.g., have the file open).

4.5.3. Capabilities

The other way of slicing up the matrix of Fig. 4-30 is by rows. When this method is used, associated with each process is a list of objects that may be accessed, along with an indication of which operations are permitted on each, in other words, its domain. This list is called a **capability list**, and the individual items on it are called **capabilities** (Dennis and Van Horn, 1966; Fabry, 1974).

A typical capability list is shown in Fig. 4-31. Each capability has a *Type* field, which tells what kind of an object it is, a *Rights* field, which is a bit map indicating which of the legal operations on this type of object are permitted, and an *Object* field, which is a pointer to the object itself (e.g., its i-node number). Capability lists are themselves objects, and may be pointed to from other capability lists, thus facilitating sharing of subdomains. Capabilities are often referred to by their position in the capability list. A process might say: "Read 1K from the file pointed to by capability 2." This form of addressing is similar to using file descriptors in UNIX.

	Type	Rights	Object
0	File	R— —	Pointer to File3
1	File	RWX	Pointer to File4
2	File	RW—	Pointer to File5
3	Printer	—W—	Pointer to Printer1

Fig. 4-31. The capability list for domain 2 in Fig. 4-29.

It is fairly obvious that capability lists, or **C-lists** as they are often called, must be protected from user tampering. Three methods have been proposed to protect them. The first way requires a **tagged architecture**, a hardware design in which each memory word has an extra (or tag) bit that tells whether the word contains a capability or not. The tag bit is not used by arithmetic, comparison, or similar ordinary instructions, and it can be modified only by programs running in kernel mode (i.e., the operating system).

The second way is to keep the C-list inside the operating system, and just have processes refer to capabilities by their slot number, as mentioned above. Hydra (Wulf, 1974) worked this way.

The third way is to keep the C-list in user space, but encrypt each capability with a secret key unknown to the user. This approach is particularly suited to distributed systems, and is used extensively by Amoeba, which will be described in Chap. 14.

In addition to the specific object-dependent rights, such as read and execute, capabilities usually have **generic rights** which are applicable to all objects. Examples of generic rights are

1. Copy capability: create a new capability for the same object.

2. Copy object: create a duplicate object with a new capability.

3. Remove capability: delete an entry from the C-list; object unaffected.

4. Destroy object: permanently remove an object and a capability.

Many capability systems are organized as a collection of modules, with **type manager modules** for each type of object. Requests to perform operations on a file are sent to the file manager, whereas requests to do something with a mailbox go to the mailbox manager. These requests are accompanied by the relevant capability. A problem arises here, because the type manager module is just an ordinary program, after all. The owner of a file capability can perform only some of the operations on the file, but cannot get at its internal representation (e.g., its i-node). It is essential that the type manager module be able to do more with the capability than an ordinary process.

This problem was solved in Hydra by a technique called **rights amplification**, in which type managers were given a rights template that gave them more rights to an object than the capability itself allowed. Other capability systems that have strong typing of objects also need something like this.

A last remark worth making about capability systems is that revoking access to an object is quite difficult. It is hard for the system to find all the outstanding capabilities for any object to take them back, since they may be stored in C-lists all over the disk. One approach is to have each capability point to an indirect object, rather than to the object itself. By having the indirect object point to the real object, the system can always break that connection, thus invalidating the capabilities. (When a capability to the indirect object is later presented to the system, the user will discover that the indirect object is now pointing to a null object.)

Another way to achieve revocation is the scheme used in Amoeba. Each object contains a long random number, which is also present in the capability. When a capability is presented for use, the two are compared. Only if they agree is the operation allowed. The owner of an object can request that the random number in the object be changed, thus invalidating existing capabilities. Neither scheme allows selective revocation, that is, taking back, say, John's permission, but nobody else's.

4.5.4. Protection Models

Protection matrices, such as that of Fig. 4-29, are not static. They frequently change as new objects are created, old objects are destroyed, and owners decide to increase or restrict the set of users for their objects. A considerable amount of attention has been paid to modeling protection systems in which the protection matrix is constantly changing. In the remainder of this section, we will touch briefly upon some of this work.

Harrison et al. (1976) identified six primitive operations on the protection matrix that can be used as a base to model any protection system. These operations are: CREATE OBJECT, DELETE OBJECT, CREATE DOMAIN, DELETE DOMAIN, INSERT RIGHT, and REMOVE RIGHT. The two latter primitives insert and remove rights from specific matrix elements, such as granting domain 1 permission to read *File6*.

These six primitives can be combined into **protection commands**. It is these protection commands that user programs can execute to change the matrix. They may not execute the primitives directly. For example, the system might have a command to create a new file, which would test to see if the file already existed, and if not, create a new object and give the owner all rights to it. There might also be a command to allow the owner to grant permission to read the file to everyone in the system, in effect, inserting the "read" right in the new file's entry in every domain.

At any instant, the matrix determines what a process in any domain can do, not what it is authorized to do. The matrix is what is enforced by the system; authorization has to do with management policy. As an example of this distinction, let us consider the simple system of Fig. 4-32 in which domains correspond to users (similar to the UNIX model). In Fig. 4-32(a) we see the intended protection policy: *Henry* can read and write *mailbox7*, *Robert* can read and write *secret*, and all three users can read and execute *compiler*.

	Objects		
	compiler	mailbox7	secret
Eric	Read Execute		
Henry	Read Execute	Read Write	
Robert	Read Execute		Read Write

(a)

	Objects		
	compiler	mailbox7	secret
Eric	Read Execute		
Henry	Read Execute	Read Write	
Robert	Read Execute	Read	Read Write

(b)

Fig. 4-32. (a) An authorized state. (b) An unauthorized state.

Now imagine that *Robert* is very clever and has found a way to issue commands to have the matrix changed to Fig. 4-32(b). He has now gained access to *mailbox7*, something he is not authorized to have. If he tries to read it, the operating system will carry out his request because it does not know that the state of Fig. 4-32(b) is unauthorized.

It should now be clear that the set of all possible matrices can be partitioned into two disjoint sets: the set of all authorized states and the set of all unauthorized states. A question around which much theoretical research has revolved is this: "Given an initial authorized state and a set of commands, can it be proven that the system can never reach an unauthorized state?"

In effect, we are asking if the available mechanism (the protection commands) is adequate to enforce some protection policy. As a simple example of a policy, consider the security scheme used by the military. Each object is unclassified, confidential, secret, or top secret. Each domain (and thus each process) also belongs to one of these four security levels. The security policy has two rules:

1. No process may read any object whose level is higher than its own, but it may freely read objects at a lower level or at its own level. A secret process may read confidential objects, but not top secret ones.

2. No process may write information into any object whose level is lower than its own. A secret process may write in a top secret file but not in a confidential one.

In military terms, if we assume that privates operate at confidential level, lieutenants at secret level, and generals at top secret level, then a lieutenant may look at a private's papers, but not at a general's. A lieutenant may tell a general anything he knows, but he may not tell a private anything, because privates cannot be trusted.

Given this policy, some initial state of the matrix (including some way of telling which object is at which level), and the set of commands for modifying the matrix, what we would like is a way to prove that the system is secure. Such a proof turns out quite difficult to acquire; many general purpose systems are not theoretically secure. For more information, see Landwehr (1981) and Denning (1982).

4.5.5. Covert Channels

In the previous section we saw how it is possible to make formal models for protection systems. In this section we will see how futile it is to make such models. In particular, we will show that even in a system that has been rigorously proven to be absolutely secure, leaking information between processes that in theory cannot communicate at all is relatively straightforward. These ideas are due to Lampson (1973).

Lampson's model involves three processes, and is primarily applicable to large timesharing systems. The first process is the client, which wants some work performed by the second one, the server. The client and the server do not entirely trust each other. For example, the server's job is to help clients with filling out their tax forms. The clients are worried that the server will secretly record their financial data, for example, maintaining a secret list of who earns how much, and then selling the list. The server is worried that the clients will try to steal the valuable tax program.

The third process is the collaborator, which is conspiring with the server to indeed steal the client's confidential data. The collaborator and server are typically owned by the same person. These three processes are shown in Fig. 4-33. The object of this exercise is to design a system in which it is impossible for the server to leak to the collaborator the information that it has legitimately received from the client. Lampson called this the **confinement problem**.

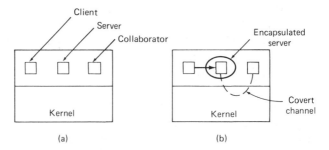

Fig. 4-33. (a) The client, server and collaborator processes. (b) The encapsulated server can still leak to the collaborator via covert channels.

From the system designer's point of view, the goal is to encapsulate or confine the server in such a way that it cannot pass information to the collaborator. Using a protection matrix scheme we can easily guarantee that the server cannot communicate with the collaborator by writing into a file to which the collaborator has read access. We can probably also ensure that the server cannot communicate with the collaborator by using the system's interprocess communication mechanism.

Unfortunately, more subtle communication channels may be available. For example, the server can try to communicate a binary bit stream as follows. To send a 1 bit, it computes as hard as it can for a fixed interval of time. To send a 0 bit, it goes to sleep for the same length of time.

The collaborator can try to detect the bit stream by carefully monitoring its response time. In general, it will get better response when the server is sending a 0 than when the server is sending a 1. This communication channel is known as a **covert channel**, and is illustrated in Fig. 4-33(b).

Of course the covert channel is a noisy channel, containing a lot of extraneous information, but information can be reliably sent over a noisy channel by using an error-correcting code (e.g., a Hamming code, or even something more sophisticated). The use of an error-correcting code reduces the already low bandwidth of the covert channel even more, but it still may be enough to leak substantial information. It is fairly obvious that no protection model based on a matrix of objects and domains is going to prevent this kind of leakage.

Modulating the CPU usage is not the only covert channel. The paging rate can also be modulated (many page faults for a 1, no page faults for a 0). In fact, almost any way of degrading system performance in a clocked way is a candidate. If the system provides a way of locking files, then the server can lock some file to indicate a 1, and unlock it to indicate a 0. It may be possible to detect the status of a lock even on a file that you cannot access.

Acquiring and releasing dedicated resources (tape drives, plotters, etc.) can also be used for signaling. The server acquires the resource to send a 1 and releases it to send a 0. In UNIX, the server could create a file to indicate a 1 and remove it to indicate a 0; the collaborator could use the ACCESS system call to see if the file exists. This call works even though the collaborator has no permission to use the file. Unfortunately, many other covert channels exist.

Lampson also mentions a way of leaking information to the (human) owner of the server process. Presumably the server process will be entitled to tell its owner how much work it did on behalf of the client, so the client can be billed. If the actual computing bill is, say, 100 dollars and the client's income is 53K dollars, the server could report the bill as 100.53 to its owner.

Just finding all the covert channels, let alone blocking them, is extremely difficult. In practice, there is little that can be done. Introducing a process that causes page faults at random, or otherwise spends its time degrading system performance in order to reduce the bandwidth of the covert channels is not an attractive proposition.

4.6. SUMMARY

When seen from the outside, a file system is a collection of files and directories, plus operations on them. Files can be read and written, directories can be created and destroyed, and files can be moved from directory to directory. File naming, structure, typing, access, and attributes are all important design issues. Most modern file systems support a hierarchical directory system, in which directories may have subdirectories *ad infinitum*.

When seen from the inside, a file system looks quite different. The file system implementers have to be concerned with keeping track of which disk blocks go with which file, how files can be shared, and how free disk space is managed. Directories can be arranged in various ways, ranging from putting the name, attributes, and disk addresses there to putting just the name and an i-node number there. Shared files, bad block management, backups, consistency, and caching are also important issues.

Security and protection are of vital concern to both the system users and implementers. We have discussed some security flaws in older systems, and generic problems that many systems have. We also looked at authentication, with and without passwords, access control lists, and capabilities.

PROBLEMS

1. Give 5 different path names for the file */etc/passwd*. (Hint: think about the directory entries "." and "..".)

2. Systems that support sequential files always have an operation to rewind files. Do systems that support random access files need this too?

3. In the list of file attributes in Fig. 4-4, one of the candidates is a bit that marks a file as temporary, and thus subject to automatic deletion when the process terminates. What is the point of having this? After all, the process can delete its own files when it is done, as is the case in Fig. 4-5.

4. Some operating systems provide a system call RENAME to give a file a new name. Is there any difference at all between using this call to rename a file, and just copying the file to a new file with the new name, followed by deleting the old one?

5. What happens if the program of Fig. 4-5 is called with a zero-length file as its first argument?

6. Consider the directory tree of Fig. 4-9. If */usr/jim* is the working directory, what is the absolute path name for the file whose relative path name is *../ast/x*?

7. Contiguous allocation of files leads to disk fragmentation, as mentioned in the text. Is this internal fragmentation or external fragmentation? Make an analogy with something discussed in the previous chapter.

8. An operating system only supports a single directory, but allows that directory to have arbitrarily many files with arbitrarily long file names. Can something approximating a hierarchical file system be simulated? How?

9. Free disk space can be kept track of using a free list or a bit map. Disk addresses require D bits. For a disk with B blocks, F of which are free, state the condition under which the free list uses less space than the bit map. For D having the value 16 bits, express your answer as a percentage of the disk space that must be free.

10. A file system checker has built up its counters as shown in Fig. 4-23. They are:

In use: 1 0 1 0 0 1 0 1 1 0 1 0 0 1 0
Free: 0 0 0 1 1 1 0 0 0 1 0 1 1 0 1

Are there any errors? If so, are they serious? Why?

11. It has been suggested that the first part of each UNIX file be kept in the same disk block as its i-node. What good would this do?

12. The performance of a file system depends critically upon the cache hit rate (fraction of blocks found in the cache). If it takes 1 msec to satisfy a request from the cache, but 40 msec to satisfy a request if a disk read is needed, give a formula for the mean time required to satisfy a request if the hit rate is h. Plot this function for values of h from 0 to 1.0.

13. A floppy disk has 40 cylinders. A seek takes 6 msec per cylinder moved. If no attempt is made to put the blocks of a file close to each other, two blocks that are logically consecutive (i.e., follow one another in the file) will be about 13 cylinders apart, on the average. If, however, the operating system makes an attempt to cluster related blocks, the mean interblock distance can be reduced to 2 cylinders (for example). How long does it take to read a 100 block file in both cases, if the rotational latency is 100 msec and the transfer time is 25 msec per block?

14. Would compacting disk storage periodically be of any conceivable value? Explain.

15. How could TENEX be modified not to have the password problem described in the text?

16. After getting your degree, you apply for a job as director of a large university computer center that has just put its ancient operating system out to pasture and switched over to UNIX. You get the job. Fifteen minutes after starting work, your assistant bursts into your office screaming: "Some students have discovered the algorithm we use for encrypting passwords and posted it on the bulletin board." What should you do?

17. The Morris-Thompson protection scheme with the n-bit random numbers was designed to make it difficult for an intruder to discover a large number of passwords by encrypting common strings in advance. Does the scheme also offer protection against a student user who is trying to guess the super-user password on his machine?

18. A computer science department has a large collection of UNIX machines on its local network. Users on any machine can issue a command of the form

```
machine4 who
```

and have it executed on *machine4*, without having the user login on the remote machine. This feature is implemented by having the user's kernel send the command and his uid to the remote machine. Is this scheme secure if the kernels are all trustworthy (e.g., large time-shared minicomputers with protection hardware)? What if some of the machines are students' personal computers, with no protection hardware?

19. When a file is removed, its blocks are generally put back on the free list, but they are not erased. Do you think it would be a good idea to have the operating system erase each block before releasing it? Consider both security and performance factors in your answer, and explain the effect of each.

20. Three different protection mechanisms that we have discussed are capabilities, access control lists, and the UNIX *rwx* bits. For each of the following protection problems, tell which of these mechanisms can be used.

   (a) Rick wants his files readable by everyone except Jennifer.
   (b) Helen and Anna want to share some secret files.
   (c) Cathy wants some of her files to be public.

   For UNIX, assume that groups are categories such as faculty, students, secretaries, and so on.

21. Consider the following protection mechanism. Each object and each process is assigned a number. A process can only access an object if the object has a higher number than the process. Which of the schemes discussed in the text does this resemble? In what essential way does it differ from the scheme in the text?

22. Can the Trojan Horse attack work in a system protected by capabilities?

23. Two computer science students, Carolyn and Elinor, are having a discussion about i-nodes. Carolyn maintains that memories have gotten so large and so cheap that when a file is opened, it is simpler and faster just to fetch a new copy of the i-node into the i-node table, rather than search the entire table to see if it is already there. Elinor disagrees. Who is right?

24. What is the difference between a virus and a worm? How do they each reproduce?

5

INPUT/OUTPUT

One of the main functions of an operating system is to control all the computer's input/output devices. It must issue commands to the devices, catch interrupts, and handle errors. It should also provide an interface between the devices and the rest of the system that is simple and easy to use. To the extent possible, the interface should be the same for all devices (device independence). The I/O code represents a significant fraction of the total operating system. How the operating system manages I/O is the subject of this chapter.

An outline of the chapter is as follows. First we will look briefly at some of the principles of I/O hardware, and then we will look at I/O software in general. I/O software can be structured in layers, with each layer having a well-defined task to perform. We will look at these layers to see what they do and how they fit together. Following that introduction, we will look at three common I/O devices in detail: disks, clocks, and terminals. For each device we will look at both its hardware and software aspects.

5.1. PRINCIPLES OF I/O HARDWARE

Different people look at I/O hardware in different ways. Electrical engineers look at it in terms of chips, wires, power supplies, motors and all the other physical components that make up the hardware. Programmers look at the interface presented to the software—the commands the hardware accepts, the functions it carries out, and the errors that can be reported back. In this book we are concerned with programming I/O devices, not designing, building, or maintaining them, so our interest will be restricted to how the hardware is programmed, not how it works inside. Nevertheless, the programming of many I/O devices is often intimately connected with their internal operation. In this section we will provide a little general background on I/O hardware as it relates to programming.

5.1.1. I/O Devices

I/O devices can be roughly divided into two categories: **block devices** and **character devices**. A block device is one that stores information in fixed-size blocks, each one with its own address. Common block sizes range from 128 bytes to 1024 bytes. The essential property of a block device is that it is possible to read or write each block independently of all the other ones. In other words, at any instant, the program can read or write any of the blocks. Disks are block devices.

If you look closely, the boundary between devices that are block addressable and those that are not is not well defined. Everyone agrees that a disk is a block addressable device because no matter where the arm currently is, it is always possible to seek to another cylinder and then wait for the required block to rotate under the head. Now consider a magnetic tape containing blocks of 1K bytes. If the tape drive is given a command to read block N, it can always rewind the tape and go forward until it comes to block N. This operation is analogous to a disk doing a seek, except that it takes much longer. Also, it may or may not be possible to rewrite one block in the middle of a tape. Even if it were possible to use magnetic tapes as block devices, that is stretching the point somewhat: they are normally not used that way.

The other type of I/O device is the character device. A character device delivers or accepts a stream of characters, without regard to any block structure. It is not addressable and does not have any seek operation. Terminals, line printers, paper tapes, punched cards, network interfaces, mice (for pointing), rats (for psychology lab experiments), and most other devices that are not disk-like can be seen as character devices.

This classification scheme is not perfect. Some devices just do not fit in. Clocks, for example, are not block addressable. Nor do they generate or accept character streams. All they do is cause interrupts at well-defined intervals. Memory-mapped screens also do not fit the model. Still, the model of block and character devices is general enough that it can be used as a basis for making some of the operating system software dealing with I/O device independent. The file system, for example, deals just with abstract block devices, and leaves the device-dependent part to lower-level software called **device drivers**.

5.1.2. Device Controllers

I/O units typically consist of a mechanical component and an electronic component. It is often possible to separate the two portions to provide a more modular and general design. The electronic component is called the **device controller** or

adapter. On mini- and microcomputers, it often takes the form of a printed circuit card that can be inserted into the computer. The mechanical component is the device itself.

The controller card usually has a connector on it, into which a cable leading to the device itself can be plugged. Many controllers can handle two, four, or even eight identical devices. If the interface between the controller and device is a standard interface, either an official standard such as ANSI, IEEE or ISO, or a de facto one, then companies can make controllers or devices that fit that interface. Many companies, for example, make disk drives that match the IBM disk controller interface.

We mention this distinction between controller and device because the operating system nearly always deals with the controller, not the device. Nearly all microcomputers and minicomputers use the single bus model of Fig. 5-1 for communication between the CPU and the controllers. Large mainframes often use a different model, with multiple buses and specialized I/O computers called **I/O channels** taking some of the load off the main CPU.

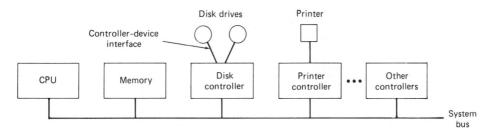

Fig. 5-1. A model for connecting the CPU, memory, controllers, and I/O devices.

The interface between the controller and the device is often a very low-level interface. A disk, for example, might be formatted with 8 sectors of 512 bytes per track. What actually comes off the drive, however, is a serial bit stream, starting with a **preamble**, then the 4096 bits in a sector, and finally a checksum or error-correcting code (ECC). The preamble is written when the disk is formatted, and contains the cylinder and sector number, the sector size, and similar data.

The controller's job is to convert the serial bit stream into a block of bytes and perform any error correction necessary. The block of bytes is typically first assembled, bit by bit, in a buffer inside the controller. After its checksum has been verified and the block declared to be error free, it can then be copied to main memory.

The controller for a CRT terminal also works as a bit serial device at an equally low level. It reads bytes containing the characters to be displayed from memory, and generates the signals used to modulate the CRT beam to cause it to write on the screen. The controller also generates the signals for making the CRT beam do a horizontal retrace after it has finished a scan line, as well as the signals for making it do a vertical retrace after the entire screen has been scanned. If it were not for the CRT controller, the operating system programmer would have to explicitly program the analog scanning of the tube. With the controller, the operating system initializes the controller with a few parameters, such as the number of characters per line and number of lines per screen, and lets the controller take care of actually driving the beam.

Each controller has a few registers that are used for communicating with the CPU. On some computers, these registers are part of the regular memory address space. This scheme is called **memory-mapped I/O**. The 680x0, for example, uses this method. Other computers use a special address space for I/O, with each controller allocated a certain portion of it. Figure 5-2 shows the I/O addresses and interrupt vectors allocated to some of the controllers on the IBM PC as an example. The assignment of I/O addresses to devices is made by bus decoding logic associated with the controller. Some manufacturers of so-called IBM PC compatibles use different I/O addresses from what IBM uses. Programs that actually use I/O addresses (including the operating system), must be modified to run on these machines.

I/O Controller	I/O Addresses	Interrupt vector
Clock	040 – 043	8
Keyboard	060 – 063	9
Secondary RS232	2F8 – 2FF	11
Hard disk	320 – 32F	13
Printer	378 – 37F	15
Monochrome display	380 – 3BF	–
Color display	3D0 – 3DF	–
Floppy disk	3F0 – 3F7	14
Primary RS232	3F8 – 3FF	12

Fig. 5-2. Some examples of controllers, their I/O addresses, and their interrupt vectors on the IBM PC.

The operating system performs I/O by writing commands into the controllers' registers. The IBM PC floppy disk controller, for example, accepts 15 different commands, such as READ, WRITE, SEEK, FORMAT, and RECALIBRATE. Many of the commands have parameters, which are also loaded into the controller's registers. When a command has been accepted, the CPU can leave the controller alone and go off to do other work. When the command has been completed, the controller causes an interrupt in order to allow the operating system to gain control of the CPU and test the results of the operation. The CPU gets the results and device status by reading one or more bytes of information from the controller's registers.

5.1.3. Direct Memory Access (DMA)

Many controllers, especially those for block devices, support **direct memory access** or **DMA**. To explain how DMA works, let us first look at how disk reads occur when DMA is not used. First the controller reads the block (one or more sectors) from the drive serially, bit by bit, until the entire block is in the controller's internal buffer. Next, it computes the checksum to verify that no read errors have occurred. Then the controller causes an interrupt. When the operating system starts running, it can read the disk block from the controller's buffer a byte or a word at a time by executing a loop, with each iteration reading one byte or word from a controller device register and storing it in memory.

Naturally, a programmed CPU loop to read the bytes one at a time from the controller wastes CPU time. DMA was invented to free the CPU from this low-level work. When it is used, the CPU gives the controller two items of information, in addition to the disk address of the block: the memory address where the block is to go, and the number of bytes to transfer, as shown in Fig. 5-3.

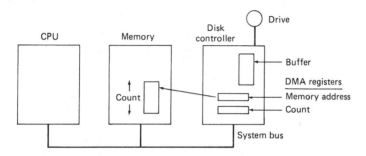

Fig. 5-3. A DMA transfer is done entirely by the controller.

After the controller has read the entire block from the device into its buffer and verified the checksum, it copies the first byte or word into the main memory at the address specified by the DMA memory address. Then it increments the DMA address and decrements the DMA count by the number of bytes just transferred. This process is repeated until the DMA count becomes zero, at which time the controller causes an interrupt. When the operating system starts up, it does not have to copy the block to memory: it is already there.

You may be wondering why the controller does not just store the bytes in main memory as soon as it gets them from the disk. In other words, why does it need an internal buffer? The reason is that once a disk transfer has started, the bits keep arriving from the disk at a constant rate, whether the controller is ready for them or not. If the controller tried to write data directly to memory, it would have to go over the system bus for each word transferred. If the bus were busy due to some other device using it, the controller would have to wait. If the next disk word arrived before the previous one had been stored, the controller would have to store it somewhere. If the bus were very busy, the controller might end up storing quite a few words and having a lot of administration to do as well. When the block is buffered internally, the bus is not needed until the DMA begins, so the design of the controller is much simpler because the DMA transfer to memory is not time critical. (Some controllers do, in fact, go directly to memory with only a small amount of internal buffering, but if the bus is very busy, a transfer may have to be terminated with an overrun error.)

The two-step buffering process described above has important implications for I/O performance. While the data are being transferred from the controller to the memory, either by the CPU or by the controller, the next sector will be passing under the disk head and the bits arriving in the controller. Simple controllers just cannot cope with doing input and output at the same time, so while a memory transfer is taking place, the sector passing under the disk head is lost.

As a result, the controller will be able to read only every other block. Reading a complete track will then require two full rotations, one for the even blocks and one for the odd blocks. If the time to transfer a block from the controller to memory over the bus is longer than the time to read a block from the disk, it may be necessary to read one block and then skip two (or more) blocks.

Skipping blocks to give the controller time to transfer data to memory is called **interleaving**. When the disk is formatted, the blocks are numbered to take account of the interleave factor. In Fig. 5-4(a) we see a disk with 8 blocks per track and no interleaving. In Fig. 5-4(b) we see the same disk with single interleaving. In Fig. 5-4(c) double interleaving is shown.

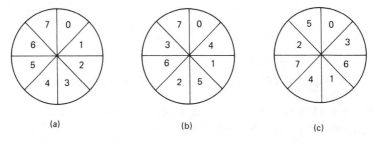

(a)   (b)   (c)

Fig. 5-4. (a) No interleaving. (b) Single interleaving. (c) Double interleaving.

The idea of numbering the blocks this way is to allow the operating system to read consecutively numbered blocks and still achieve the maximum speed of which the hardware is capable. If the blocks were numbered as in Fig. 5-4(a) but the controller could read only alternate blocks, an operating system that allocated an 8-block file in consecutive disk blocks would require eight disk rotations to read blocks 0 through 7 in order. (Of course, if the operating system knew about the problem and allocated its blocks differently, it could solve the problem in software, but it is better to have the controller worry about the interleaving.)

5.2. PRINCIPLES OF I/O SOFTWARE

Let's turn away from the hardware and now look at how the I/O software is structured. The general goals of the I/O software are easy to state. The basic idea is to organize the software as a series of layers, with the lower ones concerned with hiding the peculiarities of the hardware from the upper ones, and the upper ones concerned with presenting a nice, clean, regular interface to the users. In the following sections we will look at these goals and how they are achieved.

5.2.1. Goals of the I/O Software

A key concept in the design of I/O software is **device independence**. It should be possible to write programs that can be used with files on a floppy disk or a hard disk, without having to modify the programs for each device type. In fact, it should be possible to move the program without even recompiling it. One should be able to type the command

```
sort <input >output
```

and have it work with input and output on floppy disk or on hard disk or even coming from, or going to, the terminal. It is up to the operating system to take care of the problems caused by the fact that these devices really are different and require very different device drivers.

Closely related to device independence is the goal of **uniform naming**. The name of a file or a device should simply be a string or an integer and not depend on the device in any way. In UNIX, all disks can be integrated together in the file system hierarchy in arbitrary ways so the user need not be aware of which name corresponds to which device. For example, a floppy disk can be **mounted** on top of the directory /usr/ast/backup so that copying a file to /usr/ast/backup/monday copies the file to the floppy disk. In this way, all files and devices are addressed the same way: by a path name.

Another important issue for I/O software is error handling. In general, errors should be handled as close to the hardware as possible. If the controller discovers a read error, it should try to correct the error itself if it can. If it cannot, then the device driver should handle it, perhaps by just trying to read the block again. Many errors are transient, such as read errors caused by specks of dust on the read head, and will go away if the operation is repeated. Only if the lower layers are not able to deal with the problem should the upper layers be told about it. In many cases, error recovery can be done transparently at a low level.

Still another key issue is synchronous (blocking) versus asynchronous (interrupt-driven) transfers. Most physical I/O is asynchronous—the CPU starts the transfer and goes off to do something else until the interrupt arrives. User programs are much easier to write if the I/O operations are blocking—after a READ command the program is automatically suspended until the data are available in the buffer. It is up to the operating system to make operations that are actually interrupt-driven look blocking to the user programs.

The final concept that we will deal with here is sharable versus dedicated devices. Some I/O devices, such as disks, can be used by many users at the same time. No problems are caused by multiple users having open files on the same disk at the same time. Other devices, such as printers, have to be dedicated to a single user until that user is finished. Having five users printing lines intermixed at random on the printer just would not work. Introducing dedicated devices also introduces a variety of problems. Again, the operating system must handle both shared and dedicated devices in a way that avoids problems.

These goals can be achieved in a comprehensible and efficient way by structuring the I/O software in four layers:

1. Interrupt handlers.

2. Device drivers.

3. Device-independent operating system software.

4. User level software.

In the following sections we will look at each one in turn, starting at the bottom. The emphasis in this chapter is on the device drivers (layer 2), but we will summarize the rest of the I/O software to show how the various pieces of the I/O system fit together.

5.2.2. Interrupt Handlers

Interrupts are an unpleasant fact of life. They should be hidden away, deep in the bowels of the operating system, so that as little of the system as possible knows about them. The best way to hide them is to have every process starting an I/O operation block until the I/O has completed and the interrupt occurs. The process can block itself by doing a DOWN on a semaphore, a WAIT on a condition variable, or a RECEIVE on a message, for example.

When the interrupt happens, the interrupt procedure does whatever it has to in order to unblock the process that started it. In some systems it will do an UP on a semaphore. In others it will do a SIGNAL on a condition variable in a monitor. In still others, it will send a message to the blocked process. In all cases the net effect of the interrupt will be that a process that was previously blocked will now be able to run.

5.2.3. Device Drivers

All the device-dependent code goes in the device drivers. Each device driver handles one device type, or at most, one class of closely related devices. For example, it would probably be a good idea to have a single terminal driver, even if the system supported several different brands of terminals, all slightly different. On the other hand, a dumb, mechanical hardcopy terminal and an intelligent bit map graphics terminal with a mouse are so different that different drivers should be used.

Earlier in this chapter we looked at what device controllers do. We saw that each controller has one or more device registers used to give it commands. The device drivers issue these commands and check that they are carried out properly. Thus, the disk driver is the only part of the operating system that knows how many registers that disk controller has and what they are used for. It alone knows about sectors, tracks, cylinders, heads, arm motion, interleave factors, motor drives, head settling times, and all the other mechanics of making the disk work properly.

In general terms, the job of a device driver is to accept abstract requests from the device-independent software above it, and see to it that the request is executed. A typical request is to read block *n*. If the driver is idle at the time a request comes in, it starts carrying out the request immediately. If, however, it is already busy with a request, it will normally enter the new request into a queue of pending requests to be dealt with as soon as possible.

The first step in actually carrying out an I/O request, say, for a disk, is to translate it from abstract to concrete terms. For a disk driver, this means figuring out where on the disk the requested block actually is, checking to see if the drive's motor is running, determining if the arm is positioned on the proper cylinder, and so on. In short, it must decide which controller operations are required and in what sequence.

Once it has determined which commands to issue to the controller, it starts issuing them by writing into the controller's device registers. Some controllers can handle only one command at a time. Other controllers are willing to accept a linked list of commands, which they then carry out by themselves without further help from the operating system.

After the command or commands have been issued, one of two situations will apply. In many cases the device driver must wait until the controller does some work for it, so it blocks itself until the interrupt comes in to unblock it. In other cases, however, the operation finishes without delay, so the driver need not block. As an example of the latter situation, scrolling the screen on some terminals requires just writing a few bytes into the controller's registers. No mechanical motion is needed, so the entire operation can be completed in a few microseconds.

In the former case, the blocked driver will be awakened by the interrupt. In the latter case, it will never go to sleep. Either way, after the operation has been completed it must check for errors. If everything is all right, the driver may have data to pass to the device-independent software (e.g., a block just read). Finally it returns some status information for error reporting back to its caller. If any other requests are queued, one of them can now be selected and started. If nothing is queued, the driver blocks waiting for the next request.

5.2.4. Device-Independent I/O Software

Although some of the I/O software is device specific, a large fraction of it is device-independent. The exact boundary between the drivers and the device-independent software is system dependent, because some functions that could be done in a device-independent way may actually be done in the drivers, for efficiency or other reasons. The functions shown in Fig. 5-5 are typically done in the device-independent software.

The basic function of the device-independent software is to perform the I/O functions that are common to all devices, and to provide a uniform interface to the user-level software.

A major issue in an operating system is how objects such as files and I/O devices are named. The device independent software takes care of mapping symbolic device names onto the proper driver. In UNIX a device name, such as */dev/tty0*, uniquely

Uniform interfacing for the device drivers
Device naming
Device protection
Providing a device-independent block size
Buffering
Storage allocation on block devices
Allocating and releasing dedicated devices
Error reporting

Fig. 5-5. Functions of the device-independent I/O software.

specifies the i-node for a special file, and this i-node contains the **major device number**, which is used to locate the appropriate driver. The i-node also contains the **minor device number**, which is passed as a parameter to the driver to specify the unit to be read or written.

Closely related to naming is protection. How does the system prevent users from accessing devices that they are not entitled to access? In some microcomputer systems, such as MS-DOS, there is no protection at all. Any process can do anything it wants. In most mainframe systems, access to I/O devices by user processes is completely forbidden. In UNIX, a more flexible scheme is used. The special files corresponding to I/O devices are protected by the usual *rwx* bits. The system administrator can then set the proper permissions for each device.

Different disks may have different sector sizes. It is up to the device-independent software to hide this fact and provide a uniform block size to higher layers, for example, by treating several sectors as a single logical block. In this way, the higher layers only deal with abstract devices that all use the same logical block size, independent of the physical sector size. Similarly, some character devices deliver their data one byte at a time (e.g., paper tape readers), while others deliver theirs in larger units (e.g., card readers). These differences must also be hidden.

Buffering is also an issue, both for block and character devices. For block devices, the hardware generally insists upon reading and writing entire blocks at once, but user processes are free to read and write in arbitrary units. If a user process writes half a block, the operating system will normally keep the data around internally until the rest of the data are written, at which time the block can go out to the disk. For character devices, users can write data to the system faster than it can be output, necessitating buffering. Keyboard input can also arrive before it is needed, also requiring buffering.

When a file is created and filled with data, new disk blocks have to be allocated to the file. To perform this allocation, the operating system needs a list or bit map of free blocks per disk, but the algorithm for locating a free block is device independent and can be done above the level of the driver.

Some devices, such as magnetic tape drives, can be used only by a single process at any given moment. It is up to the operating system to examine requests for device usage and accept or reject them, depending on whether the requested device is available or not. A simple way to handle these requests is to require processes to perform

OPENs on the special files for devices directly. If the device is unavailable, the OPEN will fail. Closing such a dedicated device would then release it.

Error handling, by and large, is done by the drivers. Most errors are highly device-dependent, so only the driver knows what to do (e.g., retry, ignore it, panic). A typical error is caused by a disk block that has been damaged and cannot be read any more. After the driver has tried to read the block a certain number of times, it gives up and informs the device-independent software. How the error is treated from here on is device independent. If the error occurred while reading a user file, it may be sufficient to report the error back to the caller. However, if it occurred while reading a critical system data structure such as the block containing the bit map showing which blocks are free, the operating system may have no choice but to print an error message and terminate.

5.2.5. User-Space I/O Software

Although most of the I/O software is within the operating system, a small portion of it consists of libraries linked together with user programs, and even whole programs running outside the kernel. System calls, including the I/O system calls, are normally made by library procedures. When a C program contains the call

```
count = write(fd, buffer, nbytes);
```

the library procedure *write* will be linked with the program and contained in the binary program present in memory at run time. The collection of all these library procedures is clearly part of the I/O system.

While these procedures do little more than put their parameters in the appropriate place for the system call, there are other I/O procedures that actually do real work. In particular, formatting of input and output is done by library procedures. One example from C is *printf*, which takes a format string and possibly some variables as input, builds an ASCII string, and then calls WRITE to output the string. An example of a similar procedure for input is *gets* which reads in one line and returns it as a string. The standard I/O library contains a number of procedures that involve I/O and all run as part of user programs.

Not all user-level I/O software consists of library procedures. Another important category is the spooling system. **Spooling** is a way of dealing with dedicated I/O devices in a multiprogramming system. Consider a typical spooled device: the line printer. Although it would be technically easy to let any user process open the character special file for the printer, suppose a process opened it and then did nothing for hours. No other process could print anything.

Instead what is done is to create a special process, called a **daemon**, and a special directory, called a **spooling directory**. To print a file, a process first generates the entire file to be printed and puts it in the spooling directory. It is up to the daemon, which is the only process having permission to use the printer's special file, to print the files in the directory. By protecting the special file against direct use by users, the problem of having someone keeping it open unnecessarily long is eliminated.

Spooling is not only used for printers. It is also used in other situations. For example, file transfer over a network often uses a network daemon. To send a file somewhere, a user puts it in a network spooling directory. Later on, the network daemon takes it out and transmits it. One particular use of spooled file transmission is the USENET network, which is primarily used as an electronic mail system. This network consists of thousands of machines around the world communicating by dial-up telephone lines and many computer networks. To send mail to someone on USENET, you call a program such as *send*, which accepts the letter to be sent and then deposits it in a spooling directory for transmission later. The entire mail system runs outside the operating system.

Figure 5-6 summarizes the I/O system, showing all the layers and the principal functions of each layer.

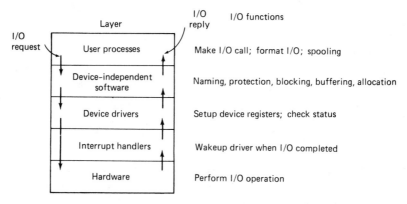

Fig. 5-6. Layers of the I/O system and the main functions of each layer.

The arrows in Fig. 5-6 show the flow of control. When a user program tries to read a block from a file, for example, the operating system is invoked to carry out the call. The device-independent software looks in the cache, for example. If the neeeded block is not there, it calls the device driver to issue the request to the hardware. The process is then blocked until the disk operation has been completed.

When the disk is finished, the hardware generates an interrupt. The interrupt handler is run to discover what has happened. It then extracts the status from the device, and wakes up the sleeping process to finish off the I/O request and let the user process continue.

5.3. DISKS

Nearly all computers have disks for storing information. Disks have three major advantages over using main memory for storage:

1. The storage capacity available is much larger.

2. The price per bit is much lower.

3. Information is not lost when the power is turned off.

In the following sections we will first say a few words about disk hardware, and then take a look at disk software.

5.3.1. Disk Hardware

All real disks are organized into cylinders, each one containing as many tracks as there are heads stacked vertically. The tracks are divided into sectors, with the number of sectors around the circumference typically being 8 to 32. All sectors contain the same number of bytes, although a little thought will make it clear that sectors close to the outer rim of the disk will be physically longer than those close to the hub. The extra space is not used.

A device feature that has important implications for the disk driver is the possibility of a controller doing seeks on two or more drives at the same time. These are known as **overlapped seeks**. While the controller and software are waiting for a seek to complete on one drive, the controller can initiate a seek on another drive. Many controllers can also read or write on one drive while seeking on one or more other drives, but none can read or write on two drives at the same time. (Reading or writing requires the controller to move bits on a microsecond time scale, so one transfer uses up most of its computing power.) The ability to perform two or more seeks at the same time can reduce the average access time considerably.

5.3.2. Disk Arm Scheduling Algorithms

In this section we will look at some of the issues related to disk driver performance. The time to read or write a disk block is determined by three factors: the seek time (the time to move the arm to the proper cylinder), the rotational delay (the time for the proper sector to rotate under the head), and the actual transfer time. For most disks, the seek time dominates, so reducing the mean seek time can improve system performance substantially.

If the disk driver accepts requests one at a time and carries them out in that order, that is, First-Come, First-Served (FCFS), little can be done to optimize seek time. However, another strategy is possible when the disk is heavily loaded. It is likely that while the arm is seeking on behalf of one request, other disk requests may be generated by other processes. Many disk drivers maintain a table, indexed by cylinder number, with all the pending requests for each cylinder chained together in a linked list headed by the table entries.

Given this kind of data structure, we can improve upon the First-Come, First-Served scheduling algorithm. To see how, consider a disk with 40 cylinders. A request comes in to read a block on cylinder 11. While the seek to cylinder 11 is in progress, new requests come in for cylinders 1, 36, 16, 34, 9, and 12, in that order. They are entered into the table of pending requests, with a separate linked list for each cylinder. The requests are shown in Fig. 5-7.

When the current request (for cylinder 11) is finished, the disk driver has a choice of which request to handle next. Using FCFS, it would go next to cylinder 1, then to

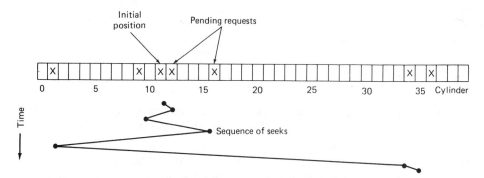

Fig. 5-7. Shortest seek first (SSF) disk scheduling algorithm.

36, and so on. This algorithm would require arm motions of 10, 35, 20, 18, 25, and 3, respectively, for a total of 111 cylinders.

Alternatively, it could always handle the closest request next, to minimize seek time. Given the requests of Fig. 5-7, the sequence is 12, 9, 16, 1, 34, and 36, as shown as the jagged line at the bottom of Fig. 5-7. With this sequence, the arm motions are 1, 3, 7, 15, 33, and 2, for a total of 61 cylinders. This algorithm, **shortest seek first** (SSF), cuts the total arm motion almost in half compared to FCFS.

Unfortunately, SSF has a problem. Suppose more requests keep coming in while the requests of Fig. 5-7 are being processed. For example, if, after going to cylinder 16, a new request for cylinder 8 is present, that request will have priority over cylinder 1. If a request for cylinder 13 then comes in, the arm will next go to 13, instead of 1. With a heavily loaded disk, the arm will tend to stay in the middle of the disk most of the time, so requests at either extreme will have to wait until a statistical fluctuation in the load causes there to be no requests near the middle. Requests far from the middle may get poor service. The goals of minimal response time and fairness are in conflict here.

Tall buildings also have to deal with this tradeoff. The problem of scheduling an elevator in a tall building is similar to that of scheduling a disk arm. Requests come in continuously calling the elevator to floors (cylinders) at random. The microprocessor running the elevator could easily keep track of the sequence in which customers pushed the call button, and service them using FCFS. It could also use SSF.

However, most elevators use a different algorithm to reconcile the conflicting goals of efficiency and fairness. They keep moving in the same direction until there are no more outstanding requests in that direction, then they switch directions. This algorithm, known both in the disk world and the elevator world as the **elevator algorithm**, requires the software to maintain 1 bit: the current direction bit, *UP* or *DOWN*. When a request finishes, the disk or elevator driver checks the bit. If it is *UP*, the arm or cabin is moved to the next highest pending request, if any. If no requests are pending at higher positions, the direction bit is reversed. When the bit is set to *DOWN*, the move is to the next lowest requested position, if any.

Figure 5-8 shows the elevator algorithm using the same seven requests as Fig. 5-

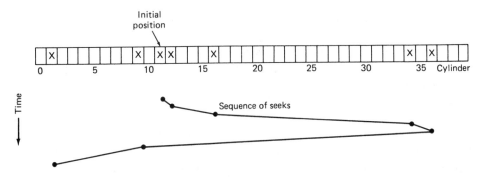

Fig. 5-8. The elevator algorithm for scheduling disk requests.

7, assuming the direction bit was initially *UP*. The order in which the cylinders are serviced is 12, 16, 34, 36, 9, and 1, which yields arm motions of 1, 4, 18, 2, 27, and 8, for a total of 60 cylinders. In this case the elevator algorithm is slightly better than SSF, although it is usually worse. One nice property that the elevator algorithm has is that given any collection of requests, the upper bound on the total motion is fixed: it is just twice the number of cylinders.

A slight modification of this algorithm that has a smaller variance in response times (Teory, 1972) is to always scan in the same direction. When the highest numbered cylinder with a pending request has been serviced, the arm goes to the lowest-numbered cylinder with a pending request and then continues moving in an upward direction. In effect, the lowest-numbered cylinder is thought of as being just above the highest-numbered cylinder.

Some disk controllers provide a way for the software to inspect the current sector number under the head. With one of these controllers, another optimization is possible. If two or more requests for the same cylinder are pending, the driver can issue a request for the sector that will pass under the head next. Note that when multiple tracks are present in a cylinder, consecutive requests can be for different tracks with no penalty. The controller can select any of its heads instantaneously, because head selection involves neither arm motion nor rotational delay.

When several drives are present a pending request table should be kept for each drive separately. Whenever any drive is idle, a seek should be issued to move its arm to the cylinder where it will be needed next (assuming the controller allows overlapped seeks). When the current transfer finishes, a check can be made to see if any drives are positioned on the correct cylinder. If one or more are, the next transfer can be started on a drive that is already on the right cylinder. If none of the arms is in the right place, the driver should issue a new seek on the drive that just completed a transfer, and wait until the next interrupt to see which arm gets to its destination first.

As disk technology improves, the seek times are getting shorter, but the rotational delay is not changing. On some disks, the average case seek time is already shorter than the rotational delay. If this trend continues, at a certain point the elevator algorithm will become obsolete because the rotational delay will be the dominant component. It will then be necessary to change the algorithm to take rotational position into account.

Another trend is having multiple disks working together, especially on high-end systems. An interesting configuration is to have 38 drives running in parallel. When a read operation is taking place, 38 bits at a time pour into the computer, one from each drive. These 38 bits form a 32-bit word along with six check bits. By using bits 1, 2, 4, 8, 16, and 32, as parity bits, the 38-bit word can be encoded as a Hamming code (error correcting code). In this way, if a drive stops working, one bit in each word is lost, but since Hamming codes can recover from a lost bit, the system can continue. Such a design is called a **RAID** (**Redundant Array of Inexpensive Disks**).

5.3.3. Error Handling

Disks are subject to a wide variety of errors. Some of the more common ones are:

1. Programming error (e.g., request for nonexistent sector).

2. Transient checksum error (e.g., caused by dust on the head).

3. Permanent checksum error (e.g., disk block physically damaged).

4. Seek error (e.g., the arm sent to cylinder 6 but it went to 7).

5. Controller error (e.g., controller refuses to accept commands).

It is up to the disk driver to handle each of these as best it can.

Programming errors occur when the driver tells the controller to seek to a nonexistent cylinder, read from a nonexistent sector, use a nonexistent head, or transfer to or from nonexistent memory. Most controllers check the parameters given to them and complain if they are invalid. In theory, these errors should never occur, but what should the driver do if the controller indicates that one has happened? For a home-grown system, the best thing to do is stop and print a message like "Call the programmer" so the error can be tracked down and fixed. For a commercial software product in use at thousands of sites around the world, this approach is less attractive. Probably the only thing to do is terminate the current disk request with an error and hope it will not recur too often.

Transient checksum errors are caused by specks of dust in the air that get between the head and the disk surface. Most of the time they can be eliminated by just repeating the operation a few times. If the error persists, the block can be marked as a **bad block** and avoided in software, as discussed in Chap. 4.

Alternatively some "intelligent" disk controllers reserve a few tracks not normally available to user programs. When a disk drive is formatted, the controller determines which blocks are bad and automatically substitutes one of the spare tracks for the bad one. The table that maps bad tracks to spare tracks is kept in the controller's internal memory and on the disk. This substitution is transparent (invisible) to the driver, except that its carefully worked out elevator algorithm may perform poorly if the controller is secretly using cylinder 800 whenever cylinder 3 is requested.

Seek errors are caused by mechanical problems in the arm. The controller keeps track of the arm position internally. To perform a seek, it issues a series of pulses to the arm motor, one pulse per cylinder, to move the arm to the new cylinder. When the arm gets to its destination, the controller reads the actual cylinder number (written when the drive was formatted). If the arm is in the wrong place, a seek error has occurred.

Some controllers correct seek errors automatically, but others just set an error bit and leave the rest to the driver. The driver handles this error by issuing a RECALIBRATE command, to move the arm as far out as it will go, and reset the controller's internal idea of the current cylinder to 0. Usually this solves the problem. If it does not, the drive must be repaired.

As we have seen, the controller is really a specialized little computer, complete with software, variables, buffers, and occasionally, bugs. Sometimes an unusual sequence of events such as an interrupt on one drive occurring simultaneously with a RECALIBRATE command for another drive will trigger a bug and cause the controller to go into a loop or lose track of what it was doing. Controller designers usually plan for the worst and provide a pin on the chip or board, which, when set high, forces the controller to forget whatever it was doing and reset itself. If all else fails, the disk driver can set a bit to invoke this signal and reset the controller. If that does not help, all the driver can do is print a message and give up.

5.3.4. Track-at-a-Time Caching

For current drives, the time required to seek to a new cylinder is still more than the rotation or transfer time (although that is changing, as mentioned above). Once the driver has gone to the trouble of moving the arm somewhere, it matters little whether it reads one sector or a whole track. This effect is especially true if the controller provides rotational sensing, so the driver can see which sector is currently under the head and issue a request for the next sector, thereby making it possible to read a track in one rotation time. (Normally it takes half a rotation plus one sector time just to read a single sector, on the average.)

Some disk drivers take advantage of this property by maintaining a secret track-at-a-time cache, unknown to the device-independent software. If a sector that is in the cache is needed, no disk transfer is required. A disadvantage of track-at-a-time caching (in addition to the software complexity and buffer space needed) is that transfers from the cache to the calling program will have to be done by the CPU using a programmed loop, rather than letting the DMA hardware do the job.

Some controllers take this process a step further, and do track-at-a-time caching in their own internal memory, transparent to the driver, so that transfer between the controller and memory can use DMA. If the controller works this way, there is little point in having the disk driver do it as well. Note that both the controller and the driver are in a good position to read and write entire tracks in one command, but that the device-independent software cannot, because it regards a disk as a linear sequence of blocks, without regard to how they are divided up into tracks and cylinders.

5.3.5. RAM Disks

The idea behind a RAM disk is simple. A block device is a storage medium with two commands: write a block and read a block. Normally these blocks are stored on rotating memories, such as floppy disks or hard disks. A RAM disk is simpler. It just uses a preallocated portion of the main memory for storing the blocks. A RAM disk has the advantage of having instant access (no seek or rotational delay), making it suitable for storing programs or data that are frequently accessed.

Figure 5-9 shows the idea behind a RAM disk. The RAM disk is split up into n blocks, depending on how much memory has been allocated for it. Each block is the same size as the block size used on the real disks. When the driver receives a message to read or write a block, it just computes where in the RAM disk memory the requested block lies, and reads or writes from it, instead of from a floppy or hard disk. Normally the transfer will be done by calling an assembly language procedure that copies to or from the user program at the maximum speed of which the hardware is capable.

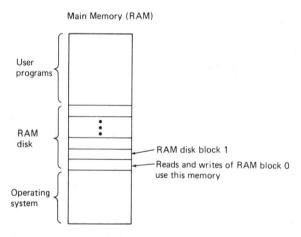

Fig. 5-9. A RAM disk.

5.4. CLOCKS

Clocks (also called **timers**) are essential to the operation of any timesharing system for a variety of reasons. They maintain the time of day and prevent one process from monopolizing the CPU, among other things. The clock software generally takes the form of a device driver, even though a clock is neither a block device, like a disk, nor a character device, like a terminal.

5.4.1. Clock Hardware

Two types of clocks are commonly used in computers, and both are quite different from the clocks and watches used by people. The simpler clocks are tied to the 110 or 220 volt power line, and cause an interrupt on every voltage cycle, at 50 or 60 Hz.

The other kind of clock is built out of three components: a crystal oscillator, a counter, and a holding register, as shown in Fig. 5-10. When a piece of quartz crystal is properly cut and mounted under tension, it can be made to generate a periodic signal of very high accuracy, typically in the range of 5 to 100 MHz, depending on the crystal chosen. This signal is fed into the counter to make it count down to zero. When the counter gets to zero, it causes a CPU interrupt. What happens next is up to the operating system.

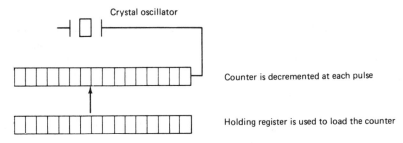

Crystal oscillator

Counter is decremented at each pulse

Holding register is used to load the counter

Fig. 5-10. A programmable clock.

Programmable clocks typically have several modes of operation. In **one-shot mode**, when the clock is started, it copies the value of the holding register into the counter, and then decrements the counter at each pulse from the crystal. When the counter gets to zero, it causes an interrupt and stops until it is explicitly started again by the software. In **square-wave mode**, after getting to zero and causing the interrupt, the holding register is automatically copied into the counter, and the whole process is repeated again indefinitely. These periodic interrupts are called **clock ticks**.

The advantage of the programmable clock is that its interrupt frequency can be controlled by software. If a 1 MHz crystal is used, then the counter will be pulsed every microsecond. With 16-bit registers, interrupts can be programmed to occur at rates from 1 microsec to 65.535 msec. Programmable clock chips usually contain two or three independently programmable clocks and have many other options as well (e.g., counting up instead of down, interrupts disabled, and more).

To implement a time-of-day clock, the software asks the user for the current time, which is then translated into the number of clock ticks since 12 A.M on Jan. 1, 1970, as UNIX does, or since some other benchmark. At every clock tick, the real time is incremented by one count. To prevent the current time from being lost when the computer's power is turned off, some computers store the real time in a special register powered by a battery (battery backup).

5.4.2. Clock Software

All the clock hardware does is generate interrupts at known intervals. Everything else involving time must be done by the software, the clock driver. The exact duties of the clock driver vary among operating systems, but usually include most of the following:

1. Maintaining the time of day.

2. Preventing processes from running longer than they are allowed to.

3. Accounting for CPU usage.

4. Handling the ALARM system call made by user processes.

5. Providing watchdog timers for parts of the system itself.

6. Doing profiling, monitoring, and statistics gathering.

The first clock function, maintaining the time of day (also called the **real time**) is not difficult. It just requires incrementing a counter at each clock tick, as mentioned before. The only thing to watch out for is the number of bits in the time-of-day counter. With a clock rate of 60 Hz, a 32-bit counter will overflow in just over 2 years. Clearly the system cannot store the real time as the number of ticks since Jan. 1, 1970 in 32 bits.

Three approaches can be taken to solve this problem. The first way is to use a 64-bit counter, although doing so makes adding one to the counter a more expensive operation since it will have to be done many times a second. The second way is to maintain the time of day in seconds, rather than in ticks, using a subsidiary counter to count ticks until a whole second has been accumulated. Because 2^{32} seconds is more than 136 years, this method will work until well into the twenty-second century. If the 32-bit integer is signed, as it usually is in UNIX, clock overflow will occur in 2038. Students now about 20 should expect their computer to go berserk just as it is time to retire.

The third approach is to count in ticks, but do that relative to the time the system was booted, rather than relative to a fixed external moment. When the user types in the real time, the system boot time is calculated from the current time-of-day value and stored in memory in any convenient form. Later, when the time of day is requested, the stored time of day is added to the counter to get the current time of day. All three approaches are shown in Fig. 5-11.

The second clock function is preventing processes from running too long. Whenever a process is started, the scheduler should initialize a counter to the value of that process' quantum in clock ticks. At every clock interrupt, the clock driver decrements the quantum counter by 1. When it gets to zero, the clock driver calls the scheduler to set up another process.

The third clock function is doing CPU accounting. The most accurate way to do it is to start a second timer, distinct from the main system timer, whenever a process

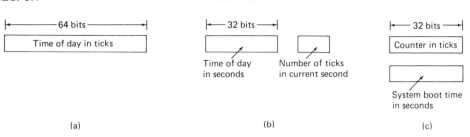

Fig. 5-11. Three ways to maintain the time of day.

is started. When that process is stopped, the timer can be read out to tell how long the process has run. To do things right, the second timer should be saved when an interrupt occurs and restored afterward.

A less accurate, but much simpler, way to do accounting is to maintain a pointer to the process table entry for the currently running process in a global variable. At every clock tick, a field in the current process' entry is incremented. In this way, every clock tick is "charged" to the process running at the time of the tick. A minor problem with this strategy is that if many interrupts occur during a process' run, it will still be charged for a full tick, even though it did not get much work done. Properly accounting for the CPU during interrupts is too expensive and is never done.

In UNIX and many other systems, a process can request the operating system to give it a warning after a certain interval. The warning is usually a signal, interrupt, message, or something similar. One application requiring such warnings is networking, in which a packet not acknowledged within a certain time interval is retransmitted. Another application is computer aided instruction, where a student not providing a response within a certain time is told the answer.

If the clock driver had enough clocks, it could set a separate clock for each request. This not being the case, it must simulate multiple virtual clocks with a single physical clock. One way is to maintain a table in which the signal time for all pending timers is kept, as well as a variable giving the time of the next one. Whenever the time of day is updated, the driver checks to see if the closest signal has occurred. If it has, the table is searched for the next one to occur.

If many signals are expected, it is more efficient to simulate multiple clocks by chaining all the pending clock requests together, sorted on time, in a linked list, as shown in Fig. 5-12. Each entry on the list tells how many clock ticks following the previous one to wait before causing a signal. In this example, signals are pending for 4203, 4207, 4213, 4215, and 4216.

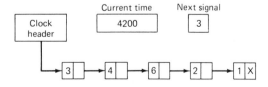

Fig. 5-12. Simulating multiple timers with a single clock.

In Fig. 5-12, the next interrupt occurs in 3 ticks. On each tick, *Next signal* is decremented. When it gets to 0, the signal corresponding to the first item on the list is caused, and that item is removed from the list. Then *Next signal* is reset to the value in the entry now at the head of the list, in this example, 4.

Note that during a clock interrupt, the clock driver has several things to do— increment the real time, decrement the quantum and check for 0, do CPU accounting, and decrement the alarm counter. However, each of these operations has been carefully arranged to be very fast because they have to be repeated many times a second.

Parts of the system also need to set timers. These are called **watchdog timers**. For example, to use a floppy disk, the system must turn on the motor and then wait about 500 msec for it to come up to speed. After the I/O is finished, it is a good idea to start a watchdog timer and only turn the motor off if no subsequent I/O operation is done within, say, 3 seconds, to avoid the 500 msec delay on every operation. (Leaving the motor on all the time wears it out.) Similarly, some hardcopy terminals can print at 200 characters/sec, but cannot return the print head to the left margin in 5 msec, so the terminal driver must delay after typing a carriage return.

The mechanism used by the clock driver to handle watchdog timers is the same as for user signals. The only difference is that when a timer goes off, instead of causing a signal, the clock driver calls a procedure supplied by the caller. The procedure is part of the caller's code, but since all the drivers are in the same address space, the clock driver can call it anyway. The called procedure can do whatever is necessary, even causing an interrupt, although within the kernel interrupts are often inconvenient and signals do not exist. That is why the watchdog mechanism is provided.

The last thing in our list is profiling. Some operating systems provide a mechanism by which a user program can have the system build up a histogram of its program counter, so it can see where it is spending its time. When profiling is a possibility, at every tick the driver checks to see if the current process is being profiled, and if so, computes the bin number (a range of addresses) corresponding to the current program counter. It then increments that bin by one. This mechanism can also be used to profile the system itself.

5.5. TERMINALS

Every computer has one or more terminals used to communicate with it. Terminals come in an extremely large number of different forms. It is up to the terminal driver to hide all these differences, so that the device-independent part of the operating system and the user programs do not have to be rewritten for each kind of terminal. We will first look at terminal hardware, then at the software.

5.5.1. Terminal Hardware

From the operating system's point of view, terminals can be divided into two broad categories based on how the operating system communicates with them. The first category consists of terminals that interface via the RS-232 standard; the second category consists of memory-mapped terminals. Each category can be further subdivided, as shown in Fig. 5-13.

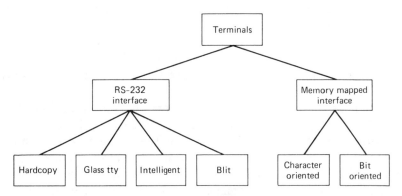

Fig. 5-13. Terminal types.

RS-232 terminals are devices containing a keyboard and a display that communicate using a serial interface, one bit at a time. These terminals use a 25-pin connector, of which one pin is used for transmitting data, one pin is for receiving data, and one pin is ground. The other 22 pins are for various control functions, most of which are generally not used. To send a character to an RS-232 terminal, the computer must transmit it 1 bit at a time, prefixed by a start bit, and followed by 1 or 2 stop bits to delimit the character. Common transmission rates are 1200, 2400, 4800, and 9600 bps.

Since both computers and terminals work internally with whole characters, but must communicate over a serial line a bit at a time, chips have been developed to do the character-to-serial and serial-to-character conversions. They are called **UART**s (Universal Asynchronous Receiver Transmitters). UARTs are attached to the computer by plugging RS-232 interface cards into the bus as illustrated in Fig. 5-14.

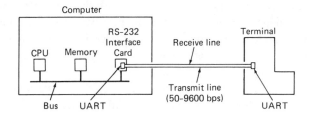

Fig. 5-14. An RS-232 terminal communicates with a computer over a communication line, one bit at a time. The computer and the terminal are completely independent.

To print a character, the terminal driver writes the character to the interface card, where it is buffered and then shifted out over the serial line one bit at a time by the UART. Even at 9600 bps, it takes just over 1 msec to send a character. As a result of this slow transmission rate, the driver will generally output a character to the RS-232 card and block, waiting for the interrupt generated by the interface when the character has been transmitted and the UART is able to accept another character. Some interface cards have a CPU and memory and can handle multiple lines, taking over much of the I/O load from the main CPU.

RS-232 terminals can be subdivided into several categories, as mentioned above. The simplest ones are hardcopy (printing) terminals. Characters typed on the keyboard are transmitted to the computer. Characters sent by the computer are typed on the paper. That's all there is.

Dumb CRT terminals work the same way, only with a screen instead of paper. These are often called "glass ttys" because they are functionally the same as hardcopy ttys. (The term "tty" is an abbreviation for Teletype, a company that pioneered in the computer terminal business; "tty" has come to mean any terminal.)

Intelligent CRT terminals are in fact miniature computers. They have a CPU and memory, and contain complex programs, usually in EPROM or ROM. From the operating system's viewpoint, the main difference between a glass tty and an intelligent terminal is that the latter understands certain escape sequences. For example, by sending the ASCII ESC character (033), followed by various other characters, it may be possible to move the cursor to any position on the screen, insert text in the middle of the screen, and so forth.

The ultimate in intelligent terminals is a terminal that contains a CPU as powerful as the main computer, along with a megabyte or so of memory that can be downloaded from the computer to contain any program at all. The Blit (Pike et al., 1985) is an example of a terminal with a powerful microprocessor and a screen containing 800 by 1024 points, but still communicating with the computer over an RS-232 line. The advantage of the RS-232 interface is that every computer in the world has one. The disadvantage is that downloading the Blit is slow, even at 19.2 kbps.

5.5.2. Memory-Mapped Terminals

The other broad category of terminals named in Fig. 5-13 consists of memory-mapped terminals. These do not communicate with the computer over a serial line. They are an integral part of the computers themselves. Memory-mapped terminals are interfaced via a special memory called a **video RAM**, which forms part of the computer's address space and is addressed by the CPU the same way as the rest of memory (see Fig. 5-15).

Also on the video RAM card is a chip called a **video controller**. This chip pulls bytes out of the video RAM and generates the video signal used to drive the display (monitor). The monitor generates a beam of electrons that scans horizontally across the screen, painting lines on it. Typically the screen has 200 to 1200 lines from top to bottom, with 200 to 1200 points per line. These points are called **pixels**. The video controller signal modulates the electron beam, determining whether a given pixel will be light or dark. Color monitors have three beams, for red, green and blue, which are independently modulated.

A typical monochrome display might fit each character in a box 9 pixels wide by 14 pixels high (including the space between characters), and have 25 lines of 80

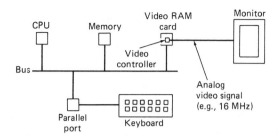

Fig. 5-15. Memory-mapped terminals write directly into video RAM.

characters. The display would then have 350 scan lines of 720 pixels each. Each of these frames is redrawn 45 to 70 times a second. The video controller could be set up to fetch the first 80 characters from the video RAM, generate 14 scan lines, fetch another 80 characters from the video RAM, generate the following 14 scan lines, and so on.

Alternatively, a cheaper chip could avoid buffering 80 characters by fetching the first character, mapping it onto the 9 by 14 bit map, extracting the 9 bits it needs, displaying them, and fetching the next character. This approach means that during the display of a single row of 80 characters, all 80 characters are fetched 14 times, once per scan line. The 9-by-14 bit patterns for the characters are kept in a 256-entry ROM used by the video controller. It is indexed by the character for rapid lookup.

As an example of a character-mapped display, consider the IBM PC. In Fig. 5-16(a) we see a portion of the video RAM, which starts at address 0xB0000 for the monochrome display and 0xB8000 for the color display. Each character on the screen of Fig. 5-16(b) occupies two characters in the RAM. The low-order character is the ASCII code for the character to be displayed. The high-order character is the attribute byte, which is used to specify color, reverse video, blinking, and so on. The full screen of 25 by 80 characters requires 4000 bytes of video RAM.

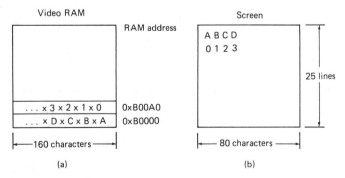

Fig. 5-16. (a) A video RAM image for the IBM monochrome display. (b) The corresponding screen. The *xs* are attribute bytes.

When a character is written into the video RAM by the CPU, it appears on the screen within one screen display time (1/50 sec for monochrome, 1/60 sec for color).

The CPU can load a 4K precomputed screen image to the video RAM in a few milliseconds. At 9600 bps, writing 2000 characters to an RS-232 terminal takes 2083 msec, which is hundreds of times slower. Thus memory-mapped terminals allow for extremely fast interaction, which is why they are used.

Bit-map terminals use the same principle, except that every bit in the video RAM directly controls a single pixel on the screen. A screen of 800 by 1024 pixels requires 100K bytes of RAM (more for color), but provides complete flexibility in character fonts and sizes, allows multiple windows, and makes arbitrary graphics possible.

With a memory-mapped display, the keyboard is completely decoupled from the screen. It is usually interfaced via a parallel port, although keyboards with RS-232 interfaces also exist. On every keystroke the CPU is interrupted, and the keyboard driver extracts the character typed by reading an I/O port. Sometimes, interrupts are generated when every key is struck and also when it is released.

Furthermore, some keyboards provide only the key number, not the ASCII code. On the IBM PC, for example, when the *A* key is struck, the key code (30) is put in an I/O register. It is up to the driver to determine whether it is lower case, upper case, CTRL-A, ALT-A, CTRL-ALT-A, or some other combination. Since the driver can tell which keys have been struck but not yet released (e.g., shift), it has enough information to do the job. Although this keyboard interface puts the full burden on the software, it is extremely flexible. For example, user programs may be interested in whether a digit just typed came from the top row of keys or the numeric key pad on the side. In principle, the driver can provide this information.

5.5.3. Input Software

The keyboard and display are almost independent devices, so we will treat them separately here. (They are not quite independent, since typed characters must be displayed on the screen.)

The basic job of the keyboard driver is to collect input from the keyboard and pass it to user programs when they read from the terminal. Two possible philosophies can be adopted for the driver. In the first one, the driver's job is just to accept input and pass it upward unmodified. A program reading from the terminal gets a raw sequence of ASCII codes. (Giving user programs the key numbers is too primitive, as well as being highly machine dependent.)

This philosophy is well suited to the needs of sophisticated screen editors such as Emacs, which allow the user to bind an arbitrary action to any character or sequence of characters. It does, however, mean that if the user types *dste* instead of *date*, and then corrects the error by typing three backspaces and *ate*, followed by a line feed, the user program will be given all 11 ASCII codes typed.

Most programs do not want this much detail. They just want the corrected input, not the exact sequence of how it was produced. This observation leads to the second philosophy: the driver handles all the intraline editing, and just delivers corrected lines to the user programs. The first philosophy is character-oriented; the second one is line-oriented. They are sometimes referred to as **raw mode** and **cooked mode**, respectively. Many systems provide both, with a system call available to select one or the other.

The first task of the keyboard driver is to collect characters. If every keystroke causes an interrupt, the driver can acquire the character during the interrupt. If interrupts are turned into messages by the low-level software, it is possible to put the newly acquired character in the message. Alternatively, it can be put in a small buffer in memory and the message used to tell the driver that something has arrived. The latter approach is actually safer if a message can be sent only to a waiting process and there is some chance that the keyboard driver might still be busy with the previous character.

Once the driver has received the character it must begin processing it. If the keyboard delivers key numbers rather than ASCII codes, as many do, then the driver must map the key numbers onto ASCII codes using some tables.

If the terminal is in cooked mode, characters must be stored until an entire line has been accumulated, because the user may subsequently decide to erase part of it. Even if the terminal is in raw mode, the program may not yet have requested input, so the characters must be buffered to allow type ahead. (System designers who do not allow users to type ahead ought to be tarred and feathered, or worse yet, be forced to use their own system.)

Two approaches to character buffering are common. In the first one, the driver contains a central pool of buffers, each buffer holding perhaps 16 characters. Associated with each terminal is a data structure, which contains, among other items, a pointer to the chain of buffers for input collected from that terminal. As more characters are typed, more buffers are acquired and hung on the chain. When the characters are passed to a user program, the buffers are removed and put back in the pool.

The other approach is to do the buffering directly in the terminal data structure itself, with no central pool of buffers. Since it is common for users to type a command that will take a little while (say, a compilation), and then type a few lines ahead, to be safe the driver should allocate something like 200 characters per terminal. In a large-scale timesharing system with 100 terminals, allocating 20K all the time for type ahead is probably overkill, so a central buffer pool with space for perhaps 5K is probably enough. On the other hand, a dedicated buffer per terminal makes the driver simpler (no linked list management), and is to be preferred on personal computers with only one or two terminals. Figure 5-17 shows the difference between these two methods.

Although the keyboard and display are logically separate devices, many users have grown accustomed to seeing the characters they have just typed appear on the screen. Some terminals oblige by automatically displaying (in hardware) whatever has just been typed, which is not only a nuisance when passwords are being entered, but greatly limits the flexibility of sophisticated editors and other programs. Fortunately, most terminals display nothing when keys are typed. It is therefore up to the software to display the input. This process is called **echoing.**

Echoing is complicated by the fact that a program may be writing to the screen while the user is typing. At the very least, the keyboard driver will have to figure out where to put the new input without it being overwritten by program output.

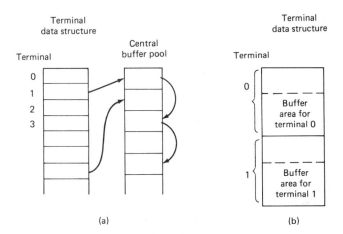

Fig. 5-17. (a) Central buffer pool. (b) Dedicated buffer for each terminal.

Echoing also gets complicated when more than 80 characters are typed on a terminal with 80 character lines. Depending on the application, wrapping around to the next line may be appropriate. Some drivers just truncate lines to 80 characters.

Another problem is tab handling. All terminals have a tab key, but few can handle tab on output. It is up to the driver to compute where the cursor is currently located, taking into account both output from programs and output from echoing, and compute the proper number of spaces to be echoed.

Now we come to the problem of device equivalence. Logically, at the end of a line of text one wants a carriage return, to move the cursor back to column 1, and a line feed, to advance to the next line. Requiring users to type both at the end of each line would not sell well (although some terminals have a key which generates both, with a 50 percent chance of doing so in the order that the software wants them). It is up to the driver to convert whatever comes in to the standard internal format used by the operating system.

If the standard form is just to store a line feed (the UNIX convention), then carriage returns should be turned into line feeds. If the internal format is to store both, then the driver should generate a line feed when it gets a carriage return and a carriage return when it gets a line feed. No matter what the internal convention, the terminal may require both a line feed and a carriage return to be echoed in order to get the screen updated properly. Since a large computer may well have a wide variety of different terminals connected to it, it is up to the keyboard driver to get all the different carriage return/line feed combinations converted to the internal system standard and arrange for all echoing to be done right.

A related problem is the timing of carriage return and line feeds. On some terminals, it takes longer to display a carriage return or line feed than a letter or number. If the microprocessor inside the terminal actually has to copy a large block of text to achieve scrolling, then line feeds may be slow. If a mechanical print head has to be returned to the left margin of the paper, carriage returns may be slow. In both cases it is up to the driver to insert **filler characters** (dummy null characters) into the output stream or just stop outputting long enough for the terminal to catch up. The amount of time to delay is often related to the terminal speed, for example, at 4800 bps or slower, no delays are needed, but at 9600 bps one filler character is required. Terminals with hardware tabs, especially hardcopy ones, may also require a delay after a tab.

When operating in cooked mode, a number of input characters have special meanings. Figure 5-18 shows typical values of these special characters for UNIX as an example. The **erase character** allows the user to rub out the character just typed. In UNIX it is usually the backspace (CTRL-H) or DEL. It is not added to the character queue, but instead removes the previous character from the queue. It should be echoed as a sequence of three characters, backspace, space, and backspace, in order to remove the previous character from the screen. If the previous character was a tab, erasing it requires keeping track of where the cursor was prior to the tab. In most systems, backspacing will only erase characters on the current line. It will not erase a carriage return and back up into the previous line.

Character	Comment
Backspace	Back up and erase 1 character
@	Erase current line
\	Escape – accept next character literally
tab	Possibly expand to spaces on output
CTRL-S	Stop output
CTRL-Q	Start output
DEL	Interrupt process (SIGINT)
CTRL-\	Force core dump (SIGQUIT)
CTRL-D	End of file

Fig. 5-18. Characters that are handled specially in cooked mode on some UNIX systems.

When the user notices an error at the start of the line being typed in, it is often convenient to erase the entire line and start again. The **kill character** erases the entire current line. As with the erase character, it is usually not possible to go further back than the current line. When a block of characters is killed, it may or may not be worth the trouble for the driver to return buffers to the pool, if one is used.

Sometimes the erase or kill characters must be entered as data. For example, the USENET mail system uses addresses of the form john@harvard. To make it possible to enter the local editing and other control characters, an escape character should be provided. In UNIX backslash is used. To enter an @ sign when @ is the erase character, one types \@. To enter a backslash, one types \\. After seeing a backslash, the driver sets a flag saying that the next character is exempt from special processing. The backslash itself is not entered in the character queue.

To allow users to stop a screen image from scrolling out of view, control codes are sometimes provided to freeze the screen and restart it later. In UNIX these are CTRL-S and CTRL-Q, respectively. They are not stored, but are used to set and clear a flag in the terminal data structure. Whenever output is attempted, the flag is inspected. If it is set, no output occurs. Whether echoing should also be suppressed along with program output is also a matter of the designer's taste and implementation convenience.

It is often necessary to kill a runaway program being debugged. The DEL, BREAK, or CTRL-C keys are often used for this purpose. In UNIX, DEL sends the SIGINT signal to all the processes started up from the terminal. Implementing DEL can be quite tricky. The hard part is getting the information from the driver to the part of the system that handles signals, which, after all, has not asked for this information. CTRL-\ is similar to DEL, except that it sends the SIGQUIT signal, which forces a core dump if not caught or ignored. When either of these keys is struck, the driver should echo a carriage return and line feed and discard all accumulated input to allow for a fresh start.

Another special character is CTRL-D, which in UNIX causes any pending read requests for the terminal to be satisfied with whatever is available in the buffer, even if the buffer is empty. Typing CTRL-D at the start of a line causes the program to get a read of 0 bytes, which is conventionally interpreted as end-of-file, and causes most programs to act the same way as they would upon seeing end-of-file on an input file.

Some terminal drivers allow much fancier intraline editing than we have sketched here. They have special control characters to erase a word, skip backward or forward characters or words, go to the beginning or end of the line being typed, and so forth. Adding all these functions to the terminal driver makes it much larger and, furthermore, is wasted when using fancy screen editors that work in raw mode anyway.

To allow programs to specify if they want raw mode or cooked mode input (and control other terminal parameters), UNIX provides a system call IOCTL called by

```
ioctl(file_descriptor, request, argp);
```

The variable *request* is used to specify whether the terminal parameters are to be read or changed, and which ones. The variable *argp* is a pointer to a structure containing the terminal parameters, including the erase and kill characters, and the terminal mode word, shown in Fig. 5-19.

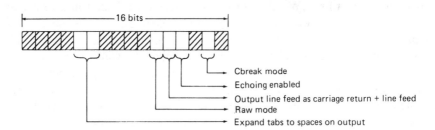

Fig. 5-19. The terminal mode word. The shaded bits are not used.

A few quick notes about the mode word are in order. Cbreak mode is a compromise between raw and cooked mode. Characters are passed to the program without waiting for a full line (as in raw mode), but DEL, CTRL-\, CTRL-S, and

CTRL-Q are processed as in cooked mode. If neither raw mode nor cbreak mode is enabled, then cooked mode is the default. Echoing, carriage return generation and tab expansion can all be turned on or off independently.

5.5.4. Output Software

Output is simpler than input, but drivers for RS-232 terminals are radically different from drivers for memory-mapped terminals. The method that is commonly used for RS-232 terminals is to have output buffers associated with each terminal. The buffers can come from the same pool as the input buffers, or be dedicated, as with input. When programs write to the terminal, the output is first copied to the buffers. Similarly, output from echoing is also copied to the buffers. After all the output has been copied to the buffers (or the buffers are full), the first character is output, and the driver goes to sleep. When the interrupt comes in, the next character is output, and so on.

With memory-mapped terminals, a simpler scheme is possible. Characters to be printed are extracted one at a time from user space and put directly in the video RAM. With RS-232 terminals, each character to be output is just sent across the line to the terminal. With memory mapping, some characters require special treatment, among them, backspace, carriage return, line feed, and the bell (CTRL-G). A driver for a memory-mapped terminal must keep track in software of the current position in the video RAM, so that printable characters can be put there and the current position advanced. Backspace, carriage return, and line feed all require this position to be updated appropriately.

In particular, when a line feed is output on the bottom line of the screen, the screen must be scrolled. Frequently, the hardware provides some help here. Most video controllers contain a register that determines where in the video RAM to begin fetching bytes for the top line on the screen. By adding the line length to this register, the line that was previously number two will move to the top, and the whole screen will scroll up one line. The only other thing the driver must do is copy whatever is needed to the new bottom line. When the video controller gets to the top of the RAM, it just wraps around and continues fetching bytes starting at the lowest address.

Another issue that the driver must deal with on a memory mapped terminal is cursor positioning. Again, the hardware usually provides some assistance in the form of a register that tells where the cursor is to go. Finally, there is the problem of the bell. It is sounded by outputting a sine or square wave to the loudspeaker, a part of the computer quite separate from the video RAM.

It is worth noting that many of the issues faced by the terminal driver for a memory-mapped display (scrolling, bell, and so on) are also faced by the microprocessor inside an RS-232 terminal. From the viewpoint of the microprocessor, it is the main processor in a system with a memory-mapped display.

Screen editors and many other sophisticated programs need to be able to update the screen in more complex ways than just scrolling text onto the bottom of the display. To accommodate them, many terminal drivers support a variety of escape sequences. Some of the more common ones are:

1. Move cursor up, down, left, or right one position.

2. Move cursor to (x, y).

3. Insert character or line at cursor.

4. Delete character or line at cursor.

5. Scroll screen up or down n lines.

6. Clear screen from cursor to end of line or end of screen.

7. Enter reverse video, underlining, blinking, or normal mode.

8. Create, destroy, move, or otherwise manage windows.

When the driver sees the character that starts the escape sequences, it sets a flag and waits until the rest of the escape sequence comes in. When everything has arrived, the driver must carry it out in software. Inserting and deleting text requires moving blocks of characters around the video RAM. The hardware is of no help with anything except scrolling and displaying the cursor.

5.6. SUMMARY

Input/Output is an often neglected, but important, topic. A substantial fraction of any operating system is concerned with I/O. A device driver for a fiber optic network may require more code than all of UNIX Version 7. Unfortunately, most of this code relates to getting around peculiarities of the hardware that should never have been there in the first place.

We started out by looking at I/O hardware, and the relation of I/O devices to I/O controllers, which are what the software has to deal with. Then we looked at the four levels of I/O software: the interrupt routines, the device drivers, the device-independent I/O software, and the I/O libraries and spoolers that run in user space. The interrupt routines save the machine's state, then service the device, checking for errors. In general, it is desirable to have them do as little as possible, consistent with the required performance. Device drivers manage all the device-specific details of one or more devices. Their job is to hide all the nasties from the higher levels. The device-independent software does things like buffer and allocation. These are common to many devices.

Next we looked at three major device types, disks, clocks, and terminals, and saw how the hardware and software work together. For disks, the major algorithm is how the arm is scheduled. For clocks, the issue is how to keep track of multiple requests for a single clock. For terminals, a distinction can be made between input and output. Input issues are raw vs. cooked mode, buffering, echoing, filler characters, line editing, and handling special characters. Output software deals with cursor motion and other escape sequences, among other issues.

PROBLEMS

1. Imagine that advances in chip technology make it possible to put an entire controller, including all the bus access logic, on an inexpensive chip. How will that affect the model of Fig. 5-1?

2. If a disk controller writes the bytes it receives from the disk to memory as fast as it receives them, with no internal buffering, is interleaving conceivably useful? Discuss.

3. A disk is double interleaved, as in Fig. 5-4(c). It has eight sectors of 512 bytes per track, and a rotation rate of 300 rpm. How long does it take to read all the sectors of a track in order, assuming the arm is already correctly positioned, and 1/2 rotation is needed to get sector 0 under the head? What is the data rate? Now repeat the problem for a noninterleaved disk with the same characteristics. How much does the data rate degrade due to interleaving?

4. The DM-11 terminal multiplexer, which was used on the PDP-11 many, many years ago, sampled each (half-duplex) terminal line at seven times the baud rate to see if the incoming bit was a 0 or a 1. Sampling the line took 5.7 microsec. How many 1200 baud lines could the DM-11 support?

5. A local network is used as follows. The user issues a system call to write to the network. The operating system then copies the data to a kernel buffer. Then it copies the data to the network controller board. When all the bytes are safely inside the controller, they are sent over the network at a rate of 10 megabits/sec. The receiving network controller stores each bit a microsecond after it is sent. When the last bit arrives, the destination CPU is interrupted, and the kernel copies the new data to a kernel buffer to inspect it. Once it has figured out which user they are for, the kernel copies the data to the user space. If we assume that each interrupt and its associated processing takes 1 msec, that packets are 1024 bytes (ignore the headers), and that copying a byte takes 1 microsec, what is the maximum rate at which one process can pump data to another?

6. What is "device independence"?

7. In which of the four I/O software layers is each of the following done.

   (a) Computing the track, sector, and head for a disk read.
   (b) Maintaining a cache of recently used blocks.
   (c) Writing commands to the device registers.
   (d) Checking to see if the user is permitted to use the device.
   (e) Converting binary integers to ASCII for printing.

8. Why are output files for the printer normally spooled on disk before being printed, instead of being directly from the application program?

9. Disk requests come in to the disk driver for cylinders 10, 22, 20, 2, 40, 6, and 38, in that order. A seek takes 6 msec per cylinder moved. How much seek time is needed for

   (a) First-come, first served.
   (b) Closest cylinder next.
   (c) Elevator algorithm (initially moving upwards).

   In all cases, the arm is initially at cylinder 20.

10. A personal computer salesman visiting a university in South-West Amsterdam remarked during his sales pitch that his company had devoted substantial effort to making their version of UNIX very fast. As an example, he noted that their disk driver used the elevator algorithm and also queued multiple requests within a cylinder in sector order. A student, Harry Hacker, was impressed and bought one. He took it home and wrote a program to randomly read 10,000 blocks spread across the disk. To his amazement, the performance that he measured was identical to what would be expected from first-come, first-served. Was the salesman lying?

11. A UNIX process has two parts—the user part and the kernel part. When the process makes a system call, the user part stops and the kernel part starts, and carries out the system call. Is the kernel part like a subroutine or a coroutine?

12. The clock interrupt handler on a certain computer requires 2 msec (including process switching overhead) per clock tick. The clock runs at 60 Hz. What fraction of the CPU is devoted to the clock?

13. Why are RS232 terminals interrupt driven, but memory mapped terminals not interrupt driven?

14. Consider how a terminal works. The driver outputs one character and then blocks. When the character has been printed, an interrupt occurs and a message is sent to the blocked driver, which outputs the next character and then blocks again. If the time to pass a message, output a character, and block is 4 msec, does this method work well on 110 baud lines? How about 4800 baud lines?

15. A bit map terminal contains 1200 by 800 pixels. To scroll a window, the CPU (or controller) must move all the lines of text upwards by copying their bits from one part of the video RAM to another. If a particular window is 66 lines high by 80 characters wide (5280 characters, total), and a character's box is 8 pixels wide by 12 pixels high, how long does it take to scroll the whole window at a copying rate of 500 nsec per byte? If all lines are 80 characters long, what is the equivalent baud rate of the terminal? Putting a character on the screen takes 50 microsec. Now compute the baud rate for the same terminal in color, with 4 bits/pixel. (Putting a character on the screen now takes 200 microsec.)

16. Why do operating systems provide escape characters, such as \ in MINIX?

17. Many RS232 terminals have escape sequences for deleting the current line and moving all the lines below it up one line. How do you think this feature is implemented inside the terminal?

18. On the IBM PC's color display, writing to the video RAM at any time other than during the CRT beam's vertical retrace causes ugly spots to appear all over the screen. A screen image is 25 by 80 characters, each of which fits in a box 8 pixels by 8 pixels. Each row of 640 pixels is drawn on a single horizontal scan of the beam, which takes 63.6 microsec, including the horizontal retrace. The screen is redrawn 60 times a second, each of which requires a vertical retrace period to get the beam back to the top. What fraction of the time is the video RAM available for writing?

6

DEADLOCKS

Computer systems are full of resources that can only be used by one process at a time. Common examples include printers, tape drives, and slots in the system's i-node table. Having two processes simultaneously writing to the printer leads to gibberish. Having two processes using the same slot in the i-node table will invariably lead to a corrupted file system. Consequently, all operating systems have the ability to (temporarily) grant a process exclusive access to certain resources.

For many applications, a process needs exclusive access to not one resource, but several. A process copying a file larger than the disk from a magnetic tape to the printer needs exclusive access to both the tape drive and the printer at the same time. In a system with only one process, the process can simply acquire access to all the resources it needs and do its work.

However, in a multiprogramming system, serious problems can arise. Suppose, for example, two processes each want to print a very large tape file. Process A requests permission to use the printer and is granted it. Process B then requests permission to use the tape drive, and is also granted it. Now A asks for the tape drive, but the request is denied until B releases it. Unfortunately, instead of releasing the tape drive, B asks for the printer. At this point both processes are blocked and will remain so forever. This situation is called a **deadlock**.

Deadlocks can occur in many situations besides requesting dedicated I/O devices. In a data base system, for example, a program may have to lock several records it is using, to avoid race conditions. If process A locks record $R1$ and process B locks record $R2$, and then each process tries to lock the other one's record, we also have a deadlock. Thus deadlocks can occur on hardware resources or on software resources.

In this chapter, we will look at deadlocks more closely, see how they arise, and study some ways of preventing or avoiding them. A great deal has been written about deadlocks. Two bibliographies on the subject have appeared in *Operating Systems Review* and should be consulted for references (Newton, 1979; Zobel, 1983).

6.1. RESOURCES

Deadlocks can occur when processes have been granted exclusive access to devices, files, and so forth. To make the discussion of deadlocks as general as possible, we will refer to the objects granted as **resources**. A resource can be a hardware device (e.g., a tape drive) or a piece of information (e.g., a locked record in a data base). A computer will normally have many different resources that can be acquired. For some resources, several identical instances may be available, such as three tape drives. When several copies of a resource are available, any one of them can be used to satisfy any request for the resource. In short, a resource is anything that can only be used by a single process at any instant of time.

Resources come in two types: preemptable and nonpreemptable. A **preemptable resource** is one that can be taken away from the process owning it with no ill effects. Memory is an example of a preemptable resource. Consider, for example, a system with 512K of user memory, one printer, and two 512K processes that each want to print something. Process *A* requests and gets the printer, then starts to compute the values to print. Before it has finished with the computation, it exceeds its time quantum and is swapped out.

Process *B* now runs and tries, unsuccessfully, to acquire the printer. Potentially, we now have a deadlock situation, because *A* has the printer and *B* has the memory, and neither can proceed without the resource held by the other. Fortunately, it is possible to preempt (take away) the memory from *B* by swapping it out and swapping *A* in. Now *A* can run, do its printing, and then release the printer. No deadlock occurs.

A **nonpreemptable resource**, in contrast, is one that cannot be taken away from its current owner without causing the computation to fail. If a process has begun to print output, taking the printer away from it and giving it to another process will result in garbled output. Printers are not preemptable.

In general, deadlocks involve nonpreemptable resources. Potential deadlocks that involve preemptable ones can usually be resolved by reallocating resources from one process to another. Thus our treatment will focus on nonpreemptable resources.

The sequence of events required to use a resource is:

1. Request the resource.

2. Use the resource.

3. Release the resource.

If the resource is not available when it is requested, the requesting process is forced to wait. In some operating systems, the process is automatically blocked when a resource request fails, and awakened when it becomes available. In other systems, the request fails with an error code, and it is up to the calling process to wait a little while and try again.

A process whose resource request has just been denied will normally sit in a tight loop requesting the resource, then sleeping, then trying again. Although this process is not blocked, for all intents and purposes, it is as good as blocked, because it cannot do any useful work. In our further treatment, we will assume that when a process is denied a resource request, it is put to sleep.

The exact nature of requesting a resource is highly system dependent. In some systems, a REQUEST system call is provided to allow processes to explicitly ask for resources. In others, the only resources that the operating system knows about are special files that only one process can have open at a time. These are opened by the usual OPEN call. If the file is already in use, the caller is blocked until its current owner closes it.

6.2. DEADLOCKS

Deadlock can be defined formally as follows:

A set of processes is deadlocked if each process in the set is waiting for an event that only another process in the set can cause.

Because all the processes are waiting, none of them will ever cause any of the events that could wake up any of the other members of the set, and all the processes continue to wait forever.

In most cases, the event that each process is waiting for is the release of some resource currently possessed by another member of the set. In other words, each member of the set of deadlocked processes is waiting for a resource that is owned by a deadlocked process. None of the processes can run, none of them can release any resources, and none of them can be awakened. The number of processes and the number and kind of resources possessed and requested are unimportant.

6.2.1. Conditions for Deadlock

Coffman et al. (1971) showed that four conditions must hold for there to be a deadlock:

1. Mutual exclusion condition. Each resource is either currently assigned to exactly one process or is available.

2. Hold and wait condition. Processes currently holding resources granted earlier can request new resources.

3. No preemption condition. Resources previously granted cannot be forcibly taken away from a process. They must be explicitly released by the process holding them.

4. Circular wait condition. There must be a circular chain of two or more processes, each of which is waiting for a resource held by the next member of the chain.

All four of these conditions must be present for a deadlock to occur. If one of them is absent, no deadlock is possible.

6.2.2. Deadlock Modeling

Holt (1972) showed how these four conditions can be modeled using directed graphs. The graphs have two kinds of nodes: processes, shown as circles, and resources, shown as squares. An arc from a resource node (square) to a process node (circle) means that the resource previously has been requested by, granted to, and is currently held by that process. In Fig. 6-1(a), resource R is currently assigned to process A.

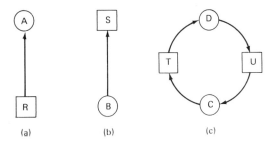

Fig. 6-1. Resource allocation graphs. (a) Holding a resource. (b) Requesting a resource. (c) Deadlock.

An arc from a process to a resource means that the process is currently blocked waiting for that resource. In Fig. 6-1(b), process B is waiting for resource S. In Fig. 6-1(c) we see a deadlock: process C is waiting for resource T, which is currently held by process D. Process D is not about to release resource T because it is waiting for resource U, held by C. Both processes will wait forever. A cycle in the graph means that there is a deadlock involving the processes and resources in the cycle. In this example, the cycle is $C-T-D-U-C$.

Now let us look at an example of how resource graphs can be used. Imagine that we have three processes, A, B, and C, and three resources, R, S, and T. The requests and releases of the three processes are given in Fig. 6-2(a)-(c). The operating system is free to run any unblocked process at any instant, so it could decide to run A until A finished all its work, then run B to completion, and finally run C.

This ordering does not lead to any deadlocks (because there is no competition for resources) but it also has no parallelism at all. In addition to requesting and releasing resources, processes compute and do I/O. When the processes are run sequentially, there is no possibility that while one process is waiting for I/O, another can use the CPU. Thus running the processes strictly sequentially may not be optimal. On the other hand, if none of the processes do any I/O at all, shortest job first is better than

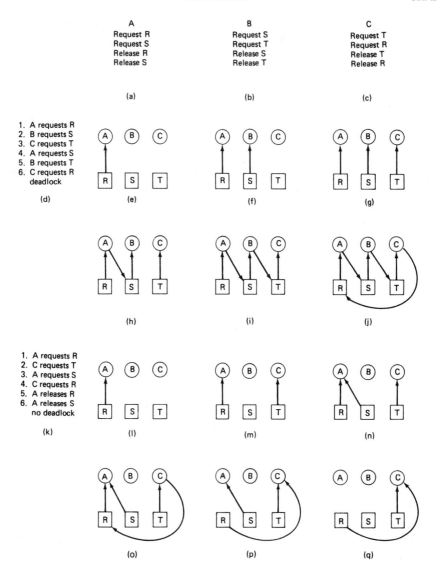

Fig. 6-2. An example of how deadlock occurs and how it can be avoided.

round robin, so under some circumstances running all processes sequentially may be the best way.

Let us now suppose that the processes do both I/O and computing, so that round robin is a reasonable scheduling algorithm. The resource requests might occur in the order of Fig. 6-2(d). If these six requests are carried out in that order, the six resulting resource graphs are shown in Fig. 6-2(e)-(j). After request 4 has been made, A blocks waiting for S, as shown in Fig. 6-2(h). In the next two steps B and C also block, ultimately leading to a cycle and the deadlock of Fig. 6-2(j).

However, as we have already mentioned, the operating system is not required to run the processes in any special order. In particular, if granting a particular request might lead to deadlock, the operating system can simply suspend the process without granting the request (i.e., just not schedule the process) until it is safe. In Fig. 6-2, if the operating system knew about the impending deadlock, it could suspend B instead of granting it S. By running only A and C, we would get the requests and releases of Fig. 6-2(k) instead of Fig. 6-2(d). This sequence leads to the resource graphs of Fig. 6-2(l)-(q), which do not lead to deadlock.

After step (q), process B can be granted S because A is finished and C has everything it needs. Even if B should eventually block when requesting T, no deadlock can occur. B will just wait until C is finished.

Later in this chapter we will study a detailed algorithm for making allocation decisions that do not lead to deadlock. The point to understand now is that resource graphs are a tool that let us see if a given request/release sequence leads to deadlock. We just carry out the requests and releases step by step, and after every step check the graph to see if it contains any cycles. If so, we have a deadlock; if not, there is no deadlock. Although our treatment of resource graphs has been for the case of a single resource of each type, resource graphs can also be generalized to handle multiple resources of the same type (Holt, 1972).

In general, four strategies are used for dealing with deadlocks.

1. Just ignore the problem altogether.

2. Detection and recovery.

3. Dynamic avoidance by careful resource allocation.

4. Prevention, by structurally negating one of the four necessary conditions.

We will examine each of these methods in turn in the next four sections.

6.3. THE OSTRICH ALGORITHM

The simplest approach is the ostrich algorithm: stick your head in the sand and pretend there is no problem at all. Different people react to this strategy in different ways. Mathematicians find it totally unacceptable and say that deadlocks must be prevented at all costs. Engineers ask how often the problem is expected, how often the system crashes for other reasons, and how serious a deadlock is. If deadlocks occur on the average once every five years, but system crashes due to hardware failures, compiler errors, and operating system bugs occur once a month, most engineers would not be willing to pay a large penalty in performance or convenience to eliminate deadlocks.

To make this contrast more specific, UNIX potentially suffers from deadlocks that are not even detected, let alone automatically broken. The total number of processes in the system is determined by the number of entries in the process table. Thus process table slots are finite resources. If a FORK fails because the table is full, a reasonable approach for the program doing the FORK is to wait a random time and try again.

Now suppose that a UNIX system has 100 process slots. Ten programs are running, each of which needs to create 12 (sub)processes. After each process has created 9 processes, the 10 original processes and the 90 new processes have exhausted the table. Each of the 10 original processes now sits in an endless loop forking and failing—a deadlock. The probability of this happening is minuscule, but it *could* happen. Should we abandon processes and the FORK call to eliminate the problem?

The maximum number of open files is similarly restricted by the size of the i-node table, so a similar problem occurs when it fills up. Swap space on the disk is another limited resource. In fact, almost every table in the operating system represents a finite resource. Should we abolish all of these because it might happen that a collection of n processes might each claim $1/n$ of the total, and then each try to claim another one?

The UNIX approach is just to ignore the problem on the assumption that most users would prefer an occasional deadlock to a rule restricting all users to one process, one open file, and one of everything. If deadlocks could be eliminated for free, there would not be much discussion. The problem is that the price is high, mostly in terms of putting inconvenient restrictions on processes, as we will see shortly. Thus we are faced with an unpleasant tradeoff between convenience and correctness, and a great deal of discussion about which is more important, and to whom. Under these conditions, general solutions are hard to find.

6.4. DEADLOCK DETECTION AND RECOVERY

A second technique is detection and recovery. When this technique is used, the system does not attempt to prevent deadlocks from occurring. Instead, it lets them occur, tries to detect when this happens, and then takes some action to recover after the fact. In this section we will look at some of the ways deadlocks can be detected and some of the ways recovery from them can be handled.

6.4.1. Deadlock Detection with One Resource of Each Type

Let us begin with the simplest case: only one resource of each type exists. Such a system might have one printer, one plotter, and one tape drive, but no more than one of each class of resource. In other words, we are excluding systems with two printers for the moment. We will treat them later, using a different method.

For such a system, we can construct a resource graph of the sort illustrated in Fig. 6-1. If this graph contains one or more cycles, a deadlock exists. Any process that is part of a cycle is deadlocked. If no cycles exist, the system is not deadlocked.

As an example of a more complex system than the ones we have looked at so far, consider a system with seven processes, *A* though *G*, and six resources, *R* through *W*. Resource ownership is as follows:

1. Process *A* holds *R* and wants *S*.

2. Process *B* holds nothing but wants *T*.

3. Process *C* holds nothing but wants *S*.

4. Process *D* holds *U* and wants *S* and *T*.

5. Process *E* holds *T* and wants *V*.

6. Process *F* holds *W* and wants *S*.

7. Process *G* holds *V* and wants *U*.

The question is: "Is this system deadlocked, and if so, which processes are involved?"

To answer this question, we can construct the resource graph of Fig. 6-3(a). This graph contains one cycle, which can be seen by visual inspection. The cycle is shown in Fig. 6-3(b). From this cycle, we can see that processes *D*, *E*, and *G* are all deadlocked. Processes *A*, *C*, and *F* are not deadlocked because *S* can be allocated to any one of them, which then finishes and returns it. Then the other two can take it in turn and also complete.

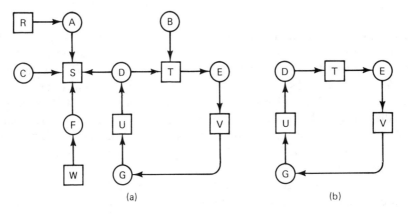

Fig. 6-3. (a) A resource graph. (b) A cycle extracted from (a).

Although it is relatively simple to pick out the deadlocked processes by eye from a simple graph, for use in actual systems we need a formal algorithm for detecting deadlocks. Many algorithms for detecting cycles in directed graphs are known. Below we will give a simple one that inspects a graph and terminates either when it has found a cycle or when it has shown that none exist. It uses one data structure, *L*, a list of nodes. During the algorithm, arcs will be marked to indicate that they have already been inspected.

1. For each node, N in the graph, perform the following 5 steps with N as the starting node.

2. Initialize L to the empty list, and designate all the arcs as unmarked.

3. Add the current node to the end of L and check to see if the node now appears in L two times. If it does, the graph contains a cycle (listed in L) and the algorithm terminates.

4. From the given node, see if there are any unmarked outgoing arcs. If so, go to step 5; if not, go to step 6.

5. Pick an umarked outgoing arc at random and mark it. Then follow it to the new current node and go to step 3.

6. We have now reached a dead end. Go back to the previous node, that is, the one that was current just before this one, make that one the current node, and go to step 3. If this node is the initial node, the graph does not contain any cycles and the algorithm terminates.

What this algorithm does is take each node, in turn, as the root of what it hopes will be a tree, and does a depth-first search on it. If it ever comes back to a node it has already encountered, then it has found a cycle. If it exhausts all the arcs from any given node, it backtracks to the previous node. If it backtracks to the root and cannot go further, the subgraph reachable from the current node does not contain any cycles. If this property holds for all nodes, the entire graph is cycle free, so the system is not deadlocked.

To see how the algorithm works in practice, let us use it on the graph of Fig. 6-3(a). The order of processing the nodes is arbitrary, so let us just inspect them from left to right, top to bottom, first running the algorithm starting at R, then successively, A, B, C, S, D, T, E, F, and so forth. If we hit a cycle, the algorithm stops.

We start at R and initialize L to the empty list. Then we add R to the list, and move to the only possibility, A, and add it to L, giving $L = [R, A]$. From A we go to S, giving $L = [R, A, S]$. S has no outgoing arcs, so it is a dead end, forcing us to backtrack to A. Since A has no unmarked outgoing arcs, we backtrack to R, completing our inspection of R.

Now we restart the algorithm starting at A, resetting L to the empty list. This search, too, quickly stops, so we start again at B. From B we continue to follow outgoing arcs until we get to D, at which time $L = [B, T, E, V, G, U, D]$. Now we must make a (random) choice. If we pick S we come to a dead end and backtrack to D. The second time we pick T and update L to be $[B, T, E, V, G, U, D, T]$, at which point we discover the cycle and stop the algorithm.

This algorithm is far from optimal. For a better one, see (Even, 1979). Nevertheless, it demonstrates that an algorithm for deadlock detection exists.

6.4.2. Deadlock Detection with Multiple Resource of Each Type

When multiple copies of some of the resources exist, a different approach is needed to detect deadlocks. We will now present a matrix-based algorithm for detecting deadlock among n processes, P_1 through P_n. Let the number of resource classes be m, with E_1 resources of class 1, E_2 resources of class 2, and generally, E_i resources of class i ($1 \leq i \leq m$). E is the **existing resource vector**. It gives the total number of instances of each resource in existence. For example, if class 1 is tape drives, then $E_1 = 2$ means the system has two tape drives.

At any instant, some of the resources are assigned and are not available. Let A be the **available resource vector**, with A_i giving the number of instances of resource i that are currently available (i.e., unassigned). If both of our two tape drives are assigned, A_1 will be 0.

Now we need two arrays, C, the **current allocation matrix**, and R, the **request matrix**. The i-th row of C tells how many instances of each resource class P_i currently holds. Thus C_{ij} is the number of instances of resource j that are held by process i. Similarly, R_{ij} is the number of instances of resource j that P_i wants. These four data structures are shown in Fig. 6-4.

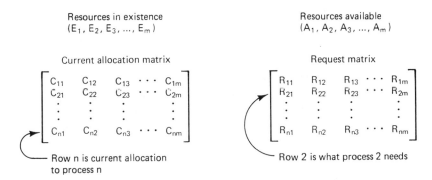

Fig. 6-4. The four data structures needed by the deadlock detection algorithm.

An important invariant holds for these four data structures. In particular, every resource is either allocated or is available. This observation means that

$$\sum_{i=1}^{m} C_{ij} + A_j = E_j$$

In other words, if we add up all the instances of resource j that have been allocated and to this add all the instances that are available, the result is the number of instances of that resource class that exist.

The deadlock detection algorithm is based on comparing vectors. Let us define the relation $A \leq B$ on two vectors A and B to mean that each element of A is less than or equal to the corresponding element of B. Mathematically, $A \leq B$ holds if and only if $A_i \leq B_i$ for $0 \leq i \leq m$.

Each process is initially said to be unmarked. As the algorithm progresses, processes will be marked, indicating that they are able to complete and are thus not deadlocked. When the algorithm terminates, any unmarked processes are known to be deadlocked.

The deadlock detection algorithm can now be given, as follows.

1. Look for an unmarked process, P_i for which the i-th row of R is less than A.

2. If such a process is found, add the i-th row of C to A, mark the process, and go back to step 1.

3. If no such process exists, the algorithm terminates.

When the algorithm finishes, all the unmarked processes, if any, are deadlocked.

What the algorithm is doing in step 1 is looking for a process that can be run to completion. Such a process is characterized as having resource demands that can be met by the currently available resources. The selected process is then run until it finishes, at which time it returns the resources it is holding to the pool of available resources. It is then marked as completed. If all the processes are ultimately able to run, none of them are deadlocked. If some of them can never run, they are deadlocked. Although the algorithm is nondeterministic (because it may run the processes in any feasible order), the result is always the same.

As an example of how the deadlock detection algorithm works, consider Fig. 6-5. Here we have three processes and four resource classes, which we have arbitrarily labeled tape drives, plotters, printers, and CD ROM drives (high capacity optical disks). Process 1 has one printer. Process 2 has two tape drives and a CD ROM drive. Process 3 has a plotter and two printers. Each process needs additional resources, as shown by the R matrix .

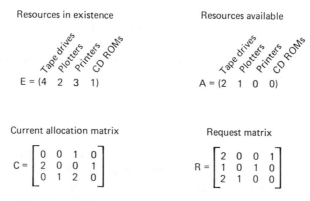

Fig. 6-5. An example for the deadlock detection algorithm.

To run the deadlock detection algorithm, we look for a process whose resource request can be satisfied. The first one cannot be satisfied because there is no CD ROM drive available. The second cannot be satisfied either, because there is no printer free. Fortunately, the third one can be satisfied, so process 3 runs and eventually returns all its resources, giving

$$A = (2\ 2\ 2\ 0)$$

At this point process 2 can run and return its resources, giving

$$A = (4\ 2\ 2\ 1)$$

Now the remaining process can run. There is no deadlock in the system.

Now consider a minor variation of the situation of Fig. 6-5. Suppose that process 2 needs a CD ROM drive as well as the two tape drives and the plotter. None of the requests can be satisfied, so the entire system is deadlocked.

Now that we know how to detect deadlocks, the question of when to look for them comes up. One possibility is to check every time a resource request is made. This is certain to detect them as early as possible, but it is potentially expensive in terms of CPU time. An alternative strategy is to check every k minutes, or perhaps only when the CPU utilization has dropped below some threshold. The reason for considering the CPU utilization is that if enough processes are deadlocked, there will be few runnable processes, and the CPU will often be idle.

6.4.3. Recovery from Deadlock

Suppose our deadlock detection algorithm has succeeded and detected a deadlock. What next? Some way is needed to recover and get the system going again. In this section we will discuss various ways of recovering from deadlock. None of them are especially attractive, however.

Recovery through Preemption

In some cases it may be possible to temporarily take a resource away from its current owner and give it to another process. In many cases, manual intervention may be required, especially in batch processing operating systems running on mainframes.

For example, to take a laser printer away from its owner, the operator can collect all the sheets already printed and put them in a pile. Then the process can be suspended (marked as not runnable). At this point the printer can be assigned to another process. When that process finishes, the pile of printed sheets can be put back in the printer's output tray and the original process restarted.

The ability to take a resource away from a process, have another process use it, and then give it back without the process noticing it is highly dependent on the nature of the resource. Recovering this way is frequently difficult or impossible. Choosing the process to suspend depends largely on which ones have resources that can be easily taken back.

Recovery through Rollback

If the system designers and machine operators know that deadlocks are likely, they can arrange to have processes **checkpointed** periodically. Checkpointing a process means that its state is written to a file so that it can be restarted later. The checkpoint contains not only the memory image, but also the resource state, that is, which resources are currently assigned to the process. To be most effective, new checkpoints should not overwrite old ones, but should be written to new files, so as the process executes, a whole sequence of checkpoint files are accumulated.

When a deadlock is detected, it is easy to see which resources are needed. To do the recovery, a process that owns a needed resource is rolled back to a point in time before it acquired some other resource by starting one of its earlier checkpoints. All the work done since the checkpoint is lost (e.g., output printed since the checkpoint must be discarded, since it will be printed again). In effect, the process is reset to an earlier moment when it did not have the resource, which is now assigned to one of the deadlocked processes. If the restarted process tries to acquire the resource again, it will have to wait until it becomes available.

Recovery through Killing Processes

The crudest, but simplest way to break a deadlock is to kill one or more processes. One possibility is to kill a process in the cycle. With a little luck, the other processes will be able to continue. If this does not help, it can be repeated until the cycle is broken.

Alternatively, a process not in the cycle can be chosen as the victim in order to release its resources. In this approach, the process to be killed is carefully chosen because it is holding resources that some process in the cycle needs. For example, one process might hold a printer and want a plotter, with another process holding a plotter and wanting a printer. These two are deadlocked. A third process may hold both and be happily running. Killing the third process will break the deadlock involving the first two.

Where possible, it is best to kill a process that can be rerun from the beginning with no ill effects. For example, a compilation can always be rerun because all it does is read a source file and produce an object file. If it is killed part way through, the first run has no influence on the second run.

On the other hand, a process that updates a data base cannot always be run a second time safely. If the process adds 1 to some record in the data base, running it once, killing it, and then running it again will add 2 to the record, which is incorrect.

6.5. DEADLOCK AVOIDANCE

In the discussion of deadlock detection, we tacitly assumed that when a process asks for resources, it asks for them all at once (the R matrix of Fig. 6-4). In most systems, however, resources are requested one at a time. The system must be able to decide whether granting a resource is safe or not, and only make the allocation when it is safe. Thus the question arises: Is there an algorithm that can always avoid deadlock by making the right choice all the time? The answer is a qualified yes—we can avoid deadlocks, but only if certain information is available in advance. In this section we examine ways to avoid deadlock by careful resource allocation.

6.5.1. Resource Trajectories

The main algorithms for doing deadlock avoidance are based on the concept of safe states. Before describing the algorithms, we will make a slight digression to look at the concept of safety in a graphic and easy-to-understand way. Although the graphical approach does not translate directly into a usable algorithm, it gives a good intuitive feel for the nature of the problem.

In Fig. 6-6 we see a model for dealing with two processes and two resources, for example, a printer and a plotter. The horizontal axis represents the number of instructions executed by process A. The vertical axis represents the number of instructions executed by process B. At I_1 A requests a printer; at I_2 it needs a plotter. The printer and plotter are released at I_3 and I_4, respectively. Process B needs the plotter from I_5 to I_7 and the printer from I_6 to I_8.

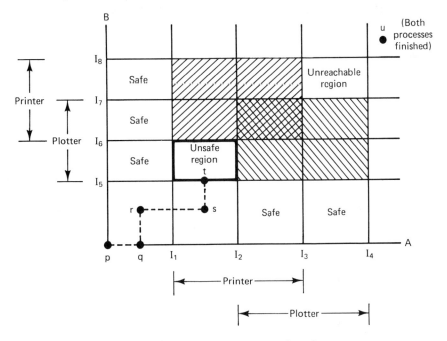

Fig. 6-6. Two process resource trajectories.

Every point in the diagram represents a joint state of the two processes. Initially, the state is at p, with neither process having executed any instructions. If the scheduler chooses to run A first, we get to the point q, in which A has executed some number of instructions, but B has executed none. At point q the trajectory becomes vertical, indicating that the scheduler has chosen to run B. With a single processor, all paths must be horizontal or vertical, never diagonal. Furthermore, motion is always to the north or east, never to the south or west (processes cannot run backwards).

When A crosses the I_1 line on the path from r to s, it requests and is granted the printer. When B reaches point t, it requests the plotter.

The regions that are shaded are especially interesting. The region with lines slanting from southwest to northeast represents both processes having the printer. The mutual exclusion rule makes it impossible to enter this region. Similarly, the region shaded the other way represents both processes having the plotter, and is equally impossible.

If the system ever enters the box bounded by I_1 and I_2 on the sides and I_5 and I_6 top and bottom, it will eventually deadlock when it gets to the intersection of I_2 and I_6. At this point, A is requesting the plotter and B is requesting the printer, and both are already assigned. The entire box is unsafe and must not be entered. At point t the only safe thing to do is run process A until it gets to I_4. Beyond that, any trajectory to u will do.

The important thing to see here is at point t B is requesting a resource. The system must decide whether to grant it or not. If the grant is made, the system will enter an unsafe region and eventually deadlock. To avoid the deadlock, B should be suspended until A has requested and released the plotter.

6.5.2. Safe and Unsafe States

The deadlock avoidance algorithms that we will study use the information of Fig. 6-4. At any instant of time, there is a current state consisting of E, A, C, and R. A state is said to be **safe** if it is not deadlocked and there is a way to satisfy all requests currently pending by running the processes in some order. It is easiest to illustrate this concept by an example using one resource. In Fig. 6-7(a) we have a state in which A has 3 instances of the resource, but may need as many as 9 eventually. B currently has 2 and may need 4 altogether, later. Similarly, C also has 2, but may need an additional 5. A total of 10 instances of the resource exist, so with 7 allocated, 3 are free.

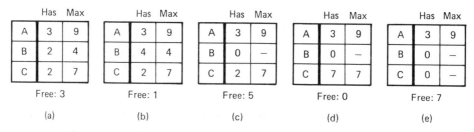

Fig. 6-7. Demonstration that the state in (a) is safe.

The state of Fig. 6-7(a) is safe because there exists a sequence of allocations that allows all processes to complete. Namely, the scheduler could simply run B exclusively, until it asked for and got two more instances of the resource, leading to the state of Fig. 6-7(b). When B completes, we get the state of Fig. 6-7(c). Then the scheduler can run C, leading eventually to Fig. 6-7(d). When C completes, we get Fig. 6-7(e). Now A can get the six instances of the resource it needs and also complete. Thus the state of Fig. 6-7(a) is safe because the system, by careful scheduling, can avoid deadlock.

Now suppose we have the initial state shown in Fig. 6-8(a), but this time A requests and gets another resource, giving Fig. 6-8(b). Can we find a sequence that is guaranteed to work? Let us try. The scheduler could run B until it asked for all its resources, as shown in Fig. 6-8(c).

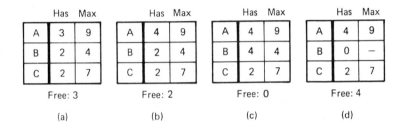

Fig. 6-8. Demonstration that the state in (b) is not safe.

At this point we are stuck. We only have four instances of the resource free, and each of the active processes needs five. There is no sequence that guarantees completion. Thus the allocation decision that moved the system from Fig. 6-8(a) to Fig. 6-8(b) went from a safe state to an unsafe state. In retrospect, A's request should not have been granted.

It is worth noting that an unsafe state is not a deadlocked state. Starting at Fig. 6-8(b), the system can run for a while. In fact, one process can even complete. Furthermore, it is possible that A might release a resource before asking for any more, allowing C to complete and avoiding deadlock altogether. Thus the difference between a safe state and an unsafe state is that from a safe state the system can guarantee that all processes will finish, whereas from an unsafe state, no such guarantee can be given.

6.5.3. The Banker's Algorithm for a Single Resource

A scheduling algorithm that can avoid deadlocks is due to Dijkstra (1965) and is known as the **banker's algorithm**. It is modeled on the way a small-town banker might deal with a group of customers to whom he has granted lines of credit. In Fig. 6-9(a) we see four customers, A, B, C, and D, each of whom has been granted a certain number of credit units (e.g., 1 unit is 1K dollars). The banker knows that not all customers will need their maximum credit immediately, so he has reserved only

10 units rather than 22 to service them. (In this analogy, customers are processes, units are, say, tape drives, and the banker is the operating system.)

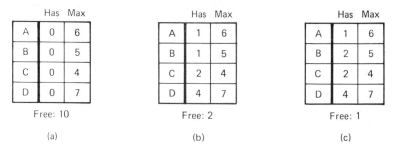

Fig. 6-9. Three resource allocation states: (a) Safe. (b) Safe. (c) Unsafe.

The customers go about their respective businesses, making loan requests from time to time (i.e., asking for resources). At a certain moment, the situation is as shown in Fig. 6-9(b). This state is safe because with two units left, the banker can delay any requests except C's, thus letting C finish and release all four of his resources. With four units in hand, the banker can let either D or B have the necessary units, and so on.

Consider what would happen if a request from B for one more unit were granted in Fig. 6-9(b). We would have situation Fig. 6-9(c), which is unsafe. If all the customers suddenly asked for their maximum loans, the banker could not satisfy any of them, and we would have a deadlock. An unsafe state does not *have* to lead to deadlock, since a customer might not need the entire credit line available, but the banker cannot count on this behavior.

The banker's algorithm is thus to consider each request as it occurs, and see if granting it leads to a safe state. If it does, the request is granted; otherwise, it is postponed until later. To see if a state is safe, the banker checks to see if he has enough resources to satisfy some customer. If so, those loans are assumed to be repaid, and the customer now closest to the limit is checked, and so on. If all loans can eventually be repaid, the state is safe and the initial request can be granted.

6.5.4. The Banker's Algorithm for Multiple Resources

The banker's algorithm can be generalized to handle multiple resources. Figure 6-10 shows how it works.

In Fig. 6-10 we see two matrices. The one on the left shows how many of each resource is currently assigned to each of the five processes. The matrix on the right shows how many resources each process still needs in order to complete. These matrices are just C and R from Fig. 6-4. As in the single resource case, processes must state their total resource needs before executing, so that the system can compute the right-hand matrix at each instant.

The three vectors at the right of the figure show the existing resources, E, the possessed resources, P, and the available resources, A, respectively. From E we see that

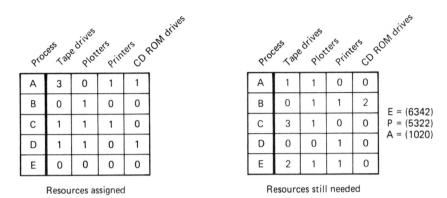

Fig. 6-10. The banker's algorithm with multiple resources.

the system has six tape drives, three plotters, four printers, and two CD ROM drives. Of these, five tape drives, three plotters, two printers, and two CD ROM drives are currently assigned. This fact can be seen by adding up the four resource columns in the left-hand matrix. The available resource vector is simply the difference between what the system has and what is currently in use.

The algorithm for checking to see if a state is safe can now be stated.

1. Look for a row, R, whose unmet resource needs are all smaller than or equal to A. If no such row exists, the system will eventually deadlock since no process can run to completion.

2. Assume the process of the row chosen requests all the resources it needs (which is guaranteed to be possible) and finishes. Mark that process as terminated and add all its resources to the A vector.

3. Repeat steps 1 and 2 until either all processes are marked terminated, in which case the initial state was safe, or until a deadlock occurs, in which case it was not.

If several processes are eligible to be chosen in step 1, it does not matter which one is selected: the pool of available resources either gets larger, or at worst, stays the same.

Now let us get back to the example of Fig. 6-10. The current state is safe. Suppose process B now requests a printer. This request can be granted because the resulting state is still safe (process D can finish, and then processes A or E, followed by the rest).

Now imagine that after giving B one of the two remaining printers, E wants the last printer. Granting that request would reduce the vector of available resources to (1 0 0 0), which leads to deadlock. Clearly E's request must be deferred for a while.

The banker's algorithm was first published by Dijkstra in 1965. Since that time, nearly every book on operating systems has described it in detail. Innumerable papers have been written about various aspects of it. Unfortunately, few authors have had the audacity to point out that although in theory the algorithm is wonderful, in practice it is essentially useless because processes rarely know in advance what their maximum resource needs will be. In addition, the number of processes is not fixed, but dynamically varying as new users log in and out. Furthermore, resources that were thought to be available can suddenly vanish (tape drives can break). Thus in practice, few, if any, existing systems use the banker's algorithm for avoiding deadlocks.

6.6. DEADLOCK PREVENTION

Having seen that deadlock avoidance is essentially impossible, because it requires information about future requests, which is not known, how do real systems avoid deadlock? The answer is to go back to the four conditions stated by Coffman et al. (1971) to see if they can provide a clue. If we can ensure that at least one of these conditions is never satisfied, then deadlocks will be structurally impossible (Havender, 1968).

6.6.1. Attacking the Mutual Exclusion Condition

First let us attack the mutual exclusion condition. If no resource was ever assigned exclusively to a single process, we would never have deadlocks. However, it is equally clear that allowing two processes to write on the printer at the same time will lead to chaos. By spooling printer output, several processes can generate output at the same time. In this model, the only process that actually requests the physical printer is the printer daemon. Since the daemon never requests any other resources, we can eliminate deadlock for the printer.

Unfortunately, not all devices can be spooled (the process table does not lend itself well to being spooled). Furthermore, competition for disk space for spooling can itself lead to deadlock. What would happen if two processes each filled up half of the available spooling space with output and neither was finished? If the daemon was programmed to begin printing even before all the output was spooled, the printer might lie idle if an output process decided to wait several hours after the first burst of output. For this reason, daemons are normally programmed to print only after the complete output file is available. Neither process will ever finish, so we have a deadlock on the disk.

Nevertheless, there is a germ of an idea here that is frequently applicable. Avoid assigning a resource when that is not absolutely necessary, and try to make sure that as few processes as possible may actually claim the resource.

6.6.2. Attacking the Hold and Wait Condition

The second of the conditions stated by Coffman et al. looks slightly more promising. If we can prevent processes that hold resources from waiting for more resources we can eliminate deadlocks. One way to achieve this goal is to require all processes to request all their resources before starting execution. If everything is available, the process will be allocated whatever it needs and can run to completion. If one or more resources are busy, nothing will be allocated and the process would just wait.

An immediate problem with this approach is that many processes do not know how many resources they will need until they have started running. In fact, if they knew, the banker's algorithm could be used. Another problem is that resources will not be used optimally with this approach. Take, as an example, a process that reads data from an input tape, analyzes it for an hour, and then writes an output tape as well as plotting the results. If all resources must be requested in advance, the process will tie up the output tape drive and the plotter for an hour.

Nevertheless, some mainframe batch systems require the user to list all the resources on the first line of each job. The system then acquires all resources immediately, and keeps them until the job finishes. While this method puts a burden on the programmer and wastes resources, it does prevent deadlocks.

A slightly different way to break the hold-and-wait condition is to require a process requesting a resource to first temporarily release all the resources it currently holds. Then it tries it get everything it needs all at once.

6.6.3. Attacking the No Preemption Condition

Attacking the third condition (no preemption) is even less promising than attacking the second one. If a process has been assigned the printer and is in the middle of printing its output, forcibly taking away the printer because a needed plotter is not available is tricky at best and impossible at worst.

6.6.4. Attacking the Circular Wait Condition

Only one condition is left. The circular wait can be eliminated in several ways. One way is simply to have a rule saying that a process is entitled only to a single resource at any moment. If it needs a second one, it must release the first one. For a process that needs to copy a huge file from a tape to a printer, this restriction is unacceptable.

Another way to avoid the circular wait is to provide a global numbering of all the resources, as shown in Fig. 6-11(a). Now the rule is this: processes can request resources whenever they want to, but all requests must be made in numerical order. A process may request first a printer and then a tape drive, but it may not request first a plotter and then a printer.

With this rule, the resource allocation graph can never have cycles. Let us see why this is true for the case of two processes, in Fig. 6-11(b). We can get a deadlock only if A requests resource j and B requests resource i. Assuming i and j are distinct resources, they will have different numbers. If $i > j$ then A is not allowed to request j. If $i < j$ then B is not allowed to request i. Either way, deadlock is impossible.

With multiple processes the same logic holds. At every instant, one of the assigned resources will be highest. The process holding that resource will never ask for a resource already assigned. It will either finish, or at worst, request even higher

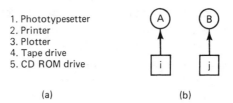

1. Phototypesetter
2. Printer
3. Plotter
4. Tape drive
5. CD ROM drive

(a)   (b)

Fig. 6-11. (a) Numerically ordered resources. (b) A resource graph.

numbered resources, all of which are available. Eventually it will finish and free its resources. At this point, some other process will hold the highest resource and can also finish. In short, there exists a scenario in which all processes finish, so no deadlock is present.

A minor variation of this algorithm is to drop the requirement that resources be acquired in strictly increasing sequence, and merely insist that no process request a resource lower than what it is already holding. If a process initially requests 9 and 10, and then releases both of them, it is effectively starting all over, so there is no reason to prohibit it from now requesting resource 1.

Although numerically ordering the resources eliminates the problem of deadlocks, it may be impossible to find an ordering that satisfies everyone. When the resources include process table slots, disk spooler space, locked data base records, and other abstract resources, the number of potential resources and different uses may be so large that no ordering could possibly work.

The various approaches to deadlock prevention are summarized in Fig. 6-12.

Condition	Approach
Mutual exclusion	Spool everything
Hold and wait	Request all resources initially
No preemption	Take resources away
Circular wait	Order resources numerically

Fig. 6-12. Summary of approaches to deadlock prevention.

6.7. OTHER ISSUES

In this section we will discuss a few miscellaneous issues related to deadlocks. These include two-phase locking, non-resource deadlocks, and starvation.

6.7.1. Two-Phase Locking

Although both avoidance and prevention are not terribly promising in the general case, for specific applications, many excellent special-purpose algorithms are known. As an example, in many data base systems, an operation that occurs frequently is requesting locks on several records and then updating all the locked records. When multiple processes are running at the same time, there is a real danger of deadlock.

The approach often used is called **two-phase locking**. In the first phase, the process tries to lock all the records it needs, one at a time. If it succeeds, it begins the second phase, performing its updates and releasing the locks. No real work is done in the first phase.

If during the first phase, some record is needed that is already locked, the process just releases all its locks and starts the first phase all over. In a certain sense, this approach is similar to requesting all the resources needed in advance, or at least before anything irreversible is done. In some versions of two-phase locking, there is no release and restart if a lock is encountered during the first phase. In these versions, deadlock can occur.

However, this strategy is not applicable in general. In real time systems and process control systems, for example, it is not acceptable to just terminate a process partway through because a resource is not available and start all over again. Neither is it acceptable to start over if the process has read or written messages to the network, updated files or anything else that cannot be safely repeated. The algorithm works only in those situations where the programmer has very carefully arranged things so that the program can be stopped at any point during the first phase and restarted. Many applications cannot be structured this way.

6.7.2. Non-resource Deadlocks

All of our work so far has concentrated on resource deadlocks. One process wants something that another process has, and must wait until the first one gives it up. Deadlocks can also occur in other situations, however, including those not involving resources at all.

For example, it can happen that two processes deadlock each waiting for the other one to do something. This often happens with semaphores. In Chap. 2 we saw examples in which a process had to do a DOWN on two semaphores, typically *mutex* and another one. If these are done in the wrong order, deadlock can result.

6.7.3. Starvation

A problem closely related to deadlock is **starvation**. In a dynamic system, requests for resources happen all the time. Some policy is needed to make a decision about who gets which resource when. This policy, although seemingly reasonable, may lead to some processes never getting service even though they are not deadlocked.

As an example, consider allocation of the printer. Imagine that the system uses some kind of algorithm to ensure that allocating the printer does not lead to deadlock. Now suppose that several processes all want it at once. Which one should get it?

One possible allocation algorithm is to give it to the process with the smallest file to print (assuming this information is available). This approach maximizes the number of happy customers and seems fair. Now consider what happens in a busy system when one process has a huge file to print. Every time the printer is free, the system will look around and choose the process with the shortest file. If there is a constant stream of processes with short files, the process with the huge file will never be allocated the printer. It will simply starve to death (be postponed indefinitely, even though it is not blocked).

Starvation can be avoided by using a first-come, first-serve resource allocation policy. With this approach, the process waiting the longest gets served next. In due course of time, any given process will eventually become the oldest, and thus get the needed resource.

6.8. SUMMARY

Deadlock is a potential problem in any operating system. It occurs when a group of processes each have been granted exclusive access to some resources, and each one wants yet another resource that belongs to another process in the group. All of them are blocked and none will ever run again.

Deadlock can be avoided by keeping track of which states are safe and which are unsafe. A safe state is one in which there exists a sequence of events that guarantee that all processes can finish. An unsafe state has no such guarantee. The banker's algorithm avoids deadlock by not granting a request if that request will put the system in an unsafe state.

Deadlock can be structurally prevented by building the system in such a way that it can never occur. For example, by allowing a process to hold only one resource at any instant the circular wait condition required for deadlock is broken. Deadlock can also be prevented by numbering all the resources, and making processes request them in strictly increasing order. Starvation can be avoided by a first-come, first-served allocation policy.

PROBLEMS

1. Fig. 6-1 shows the concept of a resource graph. Do illegal graphs exist, that is graphs that structurally violate the model we have used of resource usage? If so, give an example of one.

2. Suppose that in Fig. 6-4 $C_{ij} + R_{ij} > E_j$ for some i. What implications does this have for all the processes finishing without deadlock?

3. Consider Fig. 6-2. Suppose that in step (o) C requested S instead of requesting R. Would this lead to deadlock? Suppose it requested both S and R?

4. All the trajectories in Fig. 6-6 are horizontal or vertical. Can you envision any circumstances in which diagonal trajectories were also possible?

5. Can the resource trajectory scheme of Fig. 6-6 also be used to illustrate the problem of deadlocks with three processes and three resources? If so, how can this be done? If not, why not?

6. In theory resource trajectory graphs could be used to avoid deadlocks. By clever scheduling, the operating system could avoid unsafe regions. Suggest a practical problem with actually doing this.

7. Take a careful look at Fig. 6-9(b). If D asks for one more unit, does this lead to a safe state or an unsafe one? What if the request came from C instead of D?

8. Suppose that process A in Fig. 6-10 requests the last tape drive. Does this action lead to a deadlock?

9. A computer has six tape drives, with n processes competing for them. Each process may need two drives. For which values of n is the system deadlock free?

10. Can a system be in a state that is neither deadlocked nor safe? If so, give an example. If not, prove that all states are either deadlocked or safe.

11. A distributed system using mailboxes has two IPC primitives, SEND and RECEIVE. The latter primitive specifies a process to receive from, and blocks if no message from that process is available, even though messages may be waiting from other processes. There are no shared resources, but processes need to communicate frequently about other matters. Is deadlock possible? Discuss.

12. In an electronic funds transfer system, there are hundreds of identical processes that work as follows. Each process reads an input line specifying an amount of money, the account to be credited, and the account to be debited. Then it locks both accounts and transfers the money, releasing the locks when done. With many processes running in parallel, there is a very real danger that having locked account x it will be unable to lock y because y has been locked by a process now waiting for x. Devise a scheme that avoids deadlocks. Do not release an account record until you have completed the transactions. (In other words, solutions that lock one account and then release it immediately if the other is locked, are not allowed.)

13. The banker's algorithm is being run in a system with m resource classes and n processes. In the limit of large m and n, the number of operations that must be performed to check a state for safety is proportional to $m^a n^b$. What are the values of a and b?

14. Cinderella and the Prince are getting divorced. To divide their property, they have agreed on the following algorithm. Every morning, each one may send a letter to the other's lawyer requesting one item of property. Since it takes a day for letters to be delivered, they have agreed that if both discover that they have requested the same item on the same day, the next day they will send a letter canceling the request. Among their property is their dog, Woofer, Woofer's doghouse, their canary, Tweeter, and Tweeter's cage. The animals love their houses, so it has been agreed that any division of property separating an animal from its house is invalid, requiring the whole division to start over from scratch. Both Cinderella and the Prince desperately want Woofer. So they can go on (separate) vacations, each spouse has programmed a personal computer to handle the negotiation. When they come back from vacation, the computers are still negotiating. Why? Is deadlock possible? Is starvation possible? Discuss.

15. A student majoring in anthropology and minoring in computer science has embarked on a research project to see if African baboons can be taught about deadlocks. He locates a deep canyon and fastens a rope across it, so the baboons can cross hand-over-hand. Several baboons can cross at the same time, provided that they are all going in the same direction. If eastward moving and westward moving baboons ever get onto the rope at the same time, a deadlock will result (the baboons will get stuck in the middle) because it is impossible for one baboon to climb over another one while suspended over the canyon. If a baboon wants to cross the canyon, he must check to see that no other baboon is currently crossing in the opposite direction. Write a program using semaphores that avoids deadlock. Do not worry about a series of eastward moving baboons holding up the westward moving baboons indefinitely.

16. Repeat the previous problem, but now avoid starvation. When a baboon that wants to cross to the east arrives at the rope and finds baboons crossing to the west, he waits until the rope is empty, but no more westward moving baboons are allowed to start until at least one baboon has crossed the other way.

7

CASE STUDY 1: UNIX

In the previous chapters, we have examined many operating system principles, abstractions, algorithms, and techniques in general. In this one and the next, we will take a close look at two popular operating systems, UNIX and MS-DOS, to see how these ideas are applied in practice. These two systems have been chosen because they are both widely used and are representative of conventional, as opposed to distributed, operating systems. Later in the book, we will study some examples of distributed operating systems.

It is interesting to look at UNIX because it runs on a wider variety of computers than any other operating system. It is the dominant (almost the only) operating system on workstations and minicomputers, but it also is used on machines ranging from notebook computers to supercomputers. It was carefully designed, with a clear goal in mind, and despite its age, is still modern and elegant. Many important design principles are illustrated by UNIX.

Our discussion of both UNIX and MS-DOS will follow the same outline, to make it easier to compare the two. First, we will examine the history and evolution of the system under study, since both have changed enormously since they were introduced. Then we will provide an overview of the system, to give an idea of how they are used. After that, we will describe the fundamental concepts behind the system. Next we will examine some of the key system calls provided by each one. Since the system call interface determines what the operating system does and does not do, this material is especially important. Finally, we will look at how the system is implemented.

7.1. HISTORY OF UNIX

UNIX has a long and interesting history, so we will begin our study there. What started out as the pet project of one young researcher has become a multimillion dollar industry involving universities, multinational corporations, governments, and international standardization bodies. In the following pages we will tell how this story has unfolded.

7.1.1. UNICS

Back in the 1940s and 1950s, all computers were personal computers, at least in the sense that the normal way to use a computer was to sign up for an hour of time and take over the entire machine for that period. Of course these machines were physically immense, but only one person (the programmer) could use them at any given time. When batch systems took over, in the 1960s, the programmer submitted a job on punched cards by bringing it to the machine room. When enough jobs had been assembled, the operator read them all in as a single batch. It usually took an hour or more after submitting a job until the output was returned. Under these circumstances, debugging was a time-consuming process, because a single misplaced comma might result in wasting several hours of the programmer's time.

To get around what almost everyone viewed as an unsatisfactory and unproductive arrangement, timesharing was invented at Dartmouth College and M.I.T. The Dartmouth system ran only BASIC and enjoyed a short-term commercial success. The M.I.T. system, CTSS, was general purpose and was an enormous success among the scientific community. Within a short time, researchers at M.I.T. joined forces with Bell Labs and General Electric (then a computer vendor) and began designing a second generation system, **MULTICS** (MULTiplexed Information and Computing Service), as we discussed in Chap. 1.

MULTICS fizzled. It was designed to support hundreds of users on hardware only slightly more powerful than a modern PC/AT. (This is not quite as crazy as it sounds, since people knew how to write small programs in those days.) There were many reasons for MULTICS' failure, not the least of which is that it was written in PL/I, and the PL/I compiler was years late and barely worked at all when it finally arrived. In addition, it was enormously ambitious for its time, much like Charles Babbage's work in the Nineteenth Century.

Bell Labs eventually pulled out of the project altogether, which left one of the Bell Labs researchers, Ken Thompson, looking around for something interesting to do. He eventually decided to rewrite a stripped down MULTICS by himself (in assembler this time) on a discarded PDP-7 minicomputer. Despite the tiny size of the PDP-7, Thompson's system actually worked and could support Thompson's development effort. Consequently, one of the other researchers at Bell Labs, Brian Kernighan, somewhat jokingly called it **UNICS** (**UNiplexed Information and Computing Service**). Despite puns about "EUNUCHS" being a castrated MULTICS, the name stuck, although the spelling was later changed to **UNIX**.

7.1.2. PDP-11 UNIX

Thompson's work so impressed his colleagues at Bell Labs, that he was soon joined by Dennis Ritchie, and later by his entire department. Two major developments occurred around this time. First, UNIX was moved from the obsolete PDP-7 to the much more modern PDP-11/20 and then later to the PDP-11/45 and PDP-11/70. The latter two machines dominated the minicomputer world for much of the 1970s. The PDP-11/45 and PDP-11/70 both had reasonably large memories (for their era) as well as memory protection hardware, making it possible to support multiple users at the same time.

The second development concerned the language in which UNIX was written. By now it was becoming painfully obvious that having to rewrite the entire system for each new machine was no fun at all, so Thompson decided to rewrite UNIX in a high-level language of his own design, called **B**. B was a simplified form of BCPL (which itself was a simplified form of CPL, which, like PL/I, never worked). Due to weaknesses in B, primarily lack of structures, this attempt was not successful. Ritchie then designed a successor to B, called **C**, and wrote an excellent compiler for it. Together, Thompson and Ritchie rewrote UNIX in C. C was the right language at the right time, and has dominated system programming ever since. Many companies now sell commercial C compilers.

In 1974, Ritchie and Thompson published a landmark paper about UNIX (Ritchie and Thompson, 1974). For the work described in this paper they were later given the prestigious ACM Turing Award (Ritchie, 1984; Thompson, 1984). The publication of this paper stimulated many universities to ask Bell Labs for a copy of UNIX. Since Bell Labs' parent company, AT&T, was a regulated monopoly at the time and was not permitted to be in the computer business, it had no objection to licensing UNIX to universities for a modest fee.

In one of those coincidences that often shape history, the PDP-11 was the computer of choice at nearly all university computer science departments, and the operating systems that came with the PDP-11 were widely regarded as being dreadful by professors and students alike. UNIX quickly filled the void, not in the least because it was supplied with the complete source code, so people could, and did, tinker with it endlessly. Scientific meetings were organized around UNIX, with distinguished speakers getting up in front of the room to tell about some obscure kernel bug they had found and fixed. An Australian professor, John Lions, wrote a commentary on the UNIX source code of the type normally reserved for the works of Chaucer or Shakespeare. As a result of all this activity, new ideas and improvements to the system spread rapidly. The version that first became the de facto standard in the academic world was Version 6, so named because it was described in the sixth edition of the UNIX Programmer's Manual. Within a few years, Version 6 was replaced by Version 7. A whole generation of students was brought up on these systems, which contributed to its spread after they graduated and went to work in industry. By the mid 1980s, UNIX was in widespread use on minicomputers and engineering workstations from a variety of vendors.

7.1.3. Portable UNIX

Now that UNIX was written in C, moving it to a new machine, known as porting it, was much easier than in the early days. A port requires first writing a C compiler for the new machine. Then it requires writing device drivers for the new machine's I/O devices, such as terminals, printers, and disks. Although this code is in C, it cannot be transferred from one machine to another because no two disks work the same way. Finally, a small amount of machine-dependent code, such as the interrupt handlers and memory management routines, must be rewritten, usually in assembly language.

The first port beyond the PDP-11 was to the Interdata 8/32 minicomputer. This exercise revealed a large number of assumptions that UNIX implicitly made about the machine it was running on, such as the unspoken supposition that integers held 16 bits, pointers also held 16 bits (implying a maximum program size of 64K), and that the machine had exactly three registers available for holding important variables. None of these were true on the Interdata, so considerable work was needed to clean UNIX up .

Another problem was that although Ritchie's compiler was fast and produced good object code, it produced only PDP-11 object code. Rather than write a new compiler specifically for the Interdata, Steve Johnson of Bell Labs designed and implemented the **portable C compiler**, which could be retargeted to produce code for any reasonable machine with a only a moderate amount of effort. For years, nearly all C compilers were based on Johnson's compiler, which greatly aided the spread of UNIX to new computers.

The port to the Interdata initially went slowly because all the development work had to be done on the only working UNIX machine, a PDP-11, which happened to be on the fifth floor at Bell Labs. The Interdata was on the first floor. Generating a new version meant compiling it on the fifth floor and then physically carrying a magnetic tape down to the first floor to see if it worked. After several months, a great deal of interest arose in the possibility of connecting multiple machines together electronically. UNIX networking traces its roots to this period. After the Interdata port, UNIX was ported to the VAX and other computers.

After AT&T was broken up in 1984 by the U.S. government, the company was legally free to set up a computer subsidiary, and did. Shortly thereafter, AT&T released its first commercial UNIX product, System III. It was not well received, so it was replaced by an improved version, System V, a year later. Whatever happened to System IV is one of the great unsolved mysteries of computer science. The original System V has since been replaced by System V, releases 2, 3, and 4, each one bigger and more complicated than its predecessor. In the process, the original idea behind UNIX, of having a simple, elegant system has gradually vanished. Although Ritchie and Thompson's group later produced an 8th, 9th, and 10th edition of UNIX, these were never widely circulated, as AT&T put all its marketing muscle behind System V. However, some of the ideas from the 8th, 9th, and 10th editions were eventually incorporated into System V.

7.1.4. Berkeley UNIX

One of the many universities that acquired UNIX Version 6 early on was the University of California at Berkeley. Because the complete source code was available, Berkeley was able to modify the system substantially. Aided by grants from DARPA, the Defense Advanced Research Projects Agency, Berkeley produced and released an improved version for the PDP-11 called 1BSD (**First Berkeley Software Distribution**). This tape was followed quickly by 2BSD, also for the PDP-11.

More important were 3BSD and especially its successor, 4BSD, for the VAX. Although AT&T had a VAX version of UNIX, called **32V**, it was essentially Version 7. In contrast, 4BSD (including 4.1BSD, 4.2BSD, 4.3BSD, and 4.4BSD) contained a large number of improvements. Foremost among these was the use of virtual memory and paging, allowing programs to be larger than physical memory by paging parts of them in and out as needed. Another change allowed file names to be longer than 14 characters. The implementation of the file system was also changed, making it much faster. Signal handling was made more reliable. Networking was introduced, causing the BSD network protocol, **TCP/IP**, to become a de facto standard, far more widely used than any of the official standards, such as OSI.

Berkeley also added a substantial number of utility programs to UNIX, including a new editor (*vi*), a new shell (*csh*), Pascal and Lisp compilers, and many more. All these improvements caused Sun Microsystems, DEC, and other computer vendors to base their version of UNIX on Berkeley UNIX, rather than on AT&T's "official" version, System V. As a consequence, Berkeley UNIX became well established in the academic, research, and defense worlds. For more information about Berkeley UNIX, see Leffler et al. (1989).

7.1.5. Standard UNIX

By the late 1980s, two different, and quite incompatible, versions of UNIX were in widespread use: 4.3BSD and System V Release 3. In addition, virtually every vendor added its own nonstandard enhancements. This split in the UNIX world, together with the fact that there were no standards for binary program formats, greatly inhibited the commercial success of UNIX because it was impossible for software vendors to write and package UNIX programs with the expectation that they would run on any UNIX system (as was routinely done with MS-DOS). Various attempts at standardizing UNIX initially failed. AT&T, for example, issued the **SVID (System V Interface Definition)**, which defined all the system calls, file formats, and so on. This document was an attempt to keep all the System V vendors in line, but it had no effect on the enemy (BSD) camp, which just ignored it.

The first serious attempt to reconcile the two flavors of UNIX was initiated under the auspices of the IEEE Standards Board, a highly respected and, most important, neutral body. Hundreds of people from industry, academia, and government took part in this work. The collective name for this project is **POSIX**. The first three letters refer to Portable Operating System. The *IX* was added to make the name UNIXish.

After a great deal of argument and counterargument, the POSIX committee produced a standard known as **1003.1**. It defines a set of library procedures that every conformant UNIX system must supply. Most of these procedures invoke a system call, but a few can be implemented outside the kernel. Typical procedures are *open*, *read*, and *fork*. The idea of POSIX is that a software vendor who writes a program that uses only the procedures defined by 1003.1 knows that this program will run on every conformant UNIX system.

While it is true that most standards bodies tend to produce a horrible compromise with a few of everyone's pet features in it, 1003.1 is remarkably good considering the large number of parties involved and their respective vested interests. Rather than take the union of all features in System V and BSD as the starting point (the norm for most standards bodies), the IEEE committee took the intersection. Very roughly, if a feature was present in both System V and BSD, it was included in the standard; otherwise it was not. As a consequence of this algorithm, 1003.1 bears a strong resemblance to the direct ancestor of both System V and BSD, namely Version 7. The two areas in which it most strongly deviates from Version 7 are signals (which is largely taken from BSD) and terminal handling, which is new. The 1003.1 document is written in such a way that both operating system implementers and software writers can understand it, another novelty in the standards world, although work is already underway to remedy this.

Although the 1003.1 standard addresses only the system calls, related documents attempt to standardize the utility programs, networking, and many other features of UNIX. The various standards groups are listed in Fig. 7-1. In addition, the C language has also been standardized by ANSI and ISO.

Standard	Description
1003.0	Guide and overview
1003.1	Library functions (i.e., system calls)
1003.2	Shell and utilities
1003.3	Test methods and conformance
1003.4	Real time extension
1003.5	Ada language bindings
1003.6	Security extensions
1003.7	System administration
1003.8	Transparent file access
1003.9	Fortran 77 bindings
1003.10	Supercomputing

Fig. 7-1. The POSIX standards.

Unfortunately, a funny thing happened on the way back from the standards meeting. Now that the System V versus BSD split had been dealt with, another one appeared. A group of vendors led by IBM, DEC, Hewlett-Packard, and many others did not like the idea that AT&T had control of the rest of UNIX, so they set up a consortium known as **OSF (Open Software Foundation)** to produce a system that met all the IEEE and other standards, but also contained a large number of additional features, such as a windowing system (X11), a graphical user interface (MOTIF), distributed computing (DCE), distributed management (DME), and much more.

AT&T's reaction was to set up its own consortium, **UI (UNIX International)** to do precisely the same thing. UI's version of UNIX is based on System V. The net result is that we now have two powerful industry groups each offering their own version of UNIX, so the users are no closer to a standard than they were in the beginning. In addition, IBM has its own variant, **AIX**, as do other companies. Furthermore, all of these systems are continuing to evolve in different directions. Chaos still reigns supreme.

One property that all these systems have is that they are huge and complicated, in a sense, the exact antithesis of the original idea behind UNIX. Even if the source code were freely available, which it is not, it is out of the question that a single person could understand it all. This situation has given rise to systems like MINIX (Tanenbaum, 1987), which are attempts to produce new UNIX-like systems that are small enough to understand, are available with all the source code, and can be used for educational purposes. MINIX is available from Prentice-Hall and is widely used at universities worldwide for teaching operating systems. A user community of about 40,000 people keeps in contact via the USENET news group *comp.os.minix*.

7.2. OVERVIEW OF UNIX

In this section we will provide a general introduction to UNIX and how it is used, for the benefit of readers not already familiar with it. We will go into more detail in the following section. Although different versions of UNIX differ in subtle ways, the material presented here applies to all of them, except where stated otherwise. Later in the chapter we will focus more on POSIX.

7.2.1. UNIX Goals

UNIX is an interactive timesharing system. It was designed by programmers, for programmers, to use in an environment in which the majority of the users are relatively sophisticated and are engaged in (often quite complex) software development projects. In many cases, a large number of programmers are actively cooperating to produce a single system, so UNIX has extensive facilities to allow people to work together and share information in controlled ways. The model of a group of experienced programmers working together closely to produce advanced software is obviously very different from the personal computer model of a single beginner working alone with a word processor, and this difference is reflected throughout UNIX from start to finish.

What is it that good programmers want in a system? To start with, most like their systems to be simple, elegant, and consistent. For example, at the lowest level, a file should just be a collection of bytes. Having different classes of files for sequential access, random access, keyed access, remote access, and so on just gets in the way. Similarly, if the command

```
ls A*
```

means list all the files beginning with "A" then the command

```
rm A*
```

should mean remove all the files beginning with "A" and not remove the one file whose name consists of an "A" and an asterisk. This characteristic is sometimes called the *principle of least surprise*.

Another thing that experienced programmers generally want is power and flexibility. This means that a system should have a small number of basic elements that can be combined in an infinite variety of ways to suit the application. One of the basic guidelines behind UNIX is that every program should do just one thing, and do it well. Thus compilers do not produce listings, because other programs can do that better.

Finally, most programmers have a strong dislike for useless redundancy. Why type *copy* when *cp* is enough? To extract all the lines containing the string "ard" from the file *f*, the UNIX programmer types

```
grep ard f
```

The opposite approach is to have the programmer first select the *grep* program (with no arguments), and then have *grep* announce itself by saying: "Hi, I'm *grep*, I look for patterns in files. Please enter your pattern." After getting the pattern, *grep* prompts for a file name. Then it asks if there are any more file names. Finally it summarizes what it is going to do and ask if that is correct. While this kind of user interface may be suitable for novices, it tends to annoy skilled programmers. What they want is a servant, not a nanny.

7.2.2. Interfaces to UNIX

A UNIX system can be regarded as a kind of pyramid, as illustrated in Fig. 7-2. At the bottom is the hardware, consisting of the CPU, memory, disks, terminals, and other devices. Running on the bare hardware is the UNIX operating system. Its function is to control the hardware and provide a system call interface to all the programs. These system calls allow user programs to create and manage processes, files, and other resources.

Programs make system calls by putting the arguments in registers (or sometimes, on the stack), and issuing trap instructions to switch from user mode to kernel mode to start up UNIX. Since there is no way to write a trap instruction in C, a library is provided, with one procedure per system call. These procedures are written in assembly language, but can be called from C. Each one first puts its arguments in the proper place, then executes the trap instruction. Thus to execute the READ system call, a C program can call the *read* library procedure. As an aside, it is the library

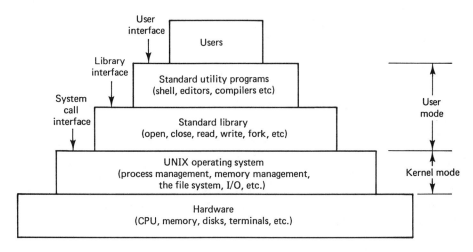

Fig. 7-2. The layers in a UNIX system.

interface, and not the system call interface that is specified by POSIX. In other words, POSIX tells which library procedures a conformant system must supply, what their parameters are, what they must do, and what results they must return. It does not even mention the actual system calls.

In addition to the operating system and system call library, all versions of UNIX supply a large number of standard programs, some of which are specified by the POSIX 1003.2 standard, and some of which differ between UNIX versions. These include the command processor (shell), compilers, editors, text processing programs, and file manipulation utilities. It is these programs that a user at a terminal invokes.

Thus we can speak of three different interfaces to UNIX: the true system call interface, the library interface, and the interface formed by the set of standard utility programs. While the latter is what the casual user thinks of as "UNIX," in fact, it has almost nothing to do with the operating system itself, and can be easily replaced.

Some versions of UNIX, for example, have replaced this keyboard-oriented user interface with a mouse-oriented graphical user interface, without changing the operating system itself at all. It is precisely this flexibility that makes UNIX so popular and has allowed it to survive numerous changes in the underlying technology so well.

7.2.3. Logging into UNIX

To use UNIX, you must first log in, by typing your name and password, which the *login* program reads and checks. This identification is necessary to provide security, as UNIX keeps track of who owns each file. A file may be accessed only by authorized users. Although this approach is standard for timesharing systems, it is in sharp contrast to personal computer systems like MS-DOS, which do not bother with protection at all. Any person running MS-DOS can access everything on the machine, no matter who created it.

However, unlike most timesharing systems, which keep all the user names and passwords in a secret file, UNIX uses a better scheme. The password file contains one line for each user, containing the user's login name, numerical user id, encrypted password, home directory, and other information. When a user logs in, the *login* program encrypts the password just read from the terminal and compares it to the (encrypted) one in the password file. If they agree, the login is permitted; if not, it is disallowed.

The beauty of this approach is that it eliminates a security loophole (the danger that the password file will somehow leak out) while at the same time increasing the generality of the system. A typical use of this feature is the ability of any program to ask the system for the owner of a file (returned as a numerical user id), and then look this up in the password file (which is not secret) to determine the user's login name. This kind of design simplicity is characteristic of UNIX in general.

7.2.4. The UNIX Shell

After a successful login, the *login* program starts up the command line interpreter specified by the user's password file entry and then exits. Although some users have special-purpose command line interpreters, most use one called the **shell**. The shell initializes itself, then types a **prompt** character, often a percent or dollar sign, on the screen and waits for the user to type a command line.

When the user types a command line, the shell extracts the first word from it, assumes it is the name of a program to be run, searches for this program, and if it finds it, runs the program. The shell then suspends itself until the program terminates, at which time it tries to read the next command. What is important here is simply the observation that the shell is an ordinary user program. All it needs is the ability to read from and write to the terminal, and the power to execute other programs.

Commands may take arguments, which are passed to the called program as character strings. For example, the command line

```
cp src dest
```

invokes the *cp* program with two arguments, *src* and *dest*. This program interprets the first one to be the name of an existing file. It makes a copy of this file and calls the copy *dest*.

Not all arguments are file names. In

```
head −20 file
```

the first argument, *−20*, tells *head* to print the first 20 lines of *file*, instead of the default number of lines, 10. Arguments that control the operation of a command or specify an optional value are called **flags**, and by convention are indicated with a dash. The dash is required to avoid ambiguity, because the command

```
head 20 file
```

is perfectly legal, and tells *head* to first print the initial 10 lines of a file called *20*, and then print the initial 10 lines of a second file called *file*. Most UNIX commands accept multiple flags and arguments.

To make it easy to specify multiple file names, the shell accepts **magic characters**, sometimes called **wildcards**. An asterisk, for example, matches all possible strings, so

```
ls *.c
```

tells *ls* to list all the files whose name ends in *.c* If files named *x.c*, *y.c*, and *z.c* all exist, the above command is equivalent to typing

```
ls x.c y.c z.c
```

Another wildcard is the question mark, which matches any one character.

A program like the shell does not have to open the terminal in order to read from it or write to it. Instead, when it (or any other program) starts up, it automatically has access to a file called **standard input** (for reading), a file called **standard output** (for writing normal output), and a file called **standard error** (for writing error messages). Normally all three default to the terminal, so that reads from standard input come from the keyboard and writes to standard output or standard error go to the screen. Many UNIX programs read from standard input and write to standard output as the default. For example,

```
sort
```

invokes the *sort* program, which reads lines from the terminal (until the user types a CTRL-D, to indicate end of file), sorts them alphabetically, and writes the result to the screen.

It is possible to **redirect** standard input and standard output, which often is useful. The syntax for redirecting standard input uses a less than sign (<) followed by the input file name. Similarly, standard output is redirected using a greater than sign (>). It is permitted to redirect both in the same command. For example, the command

```
sort <in >out
```

causes *sort* to take its input from the file *in* and write its output to the file *out*. Since standard error has not been redirected, any error messages go to the screen. A program that reads its input from standard input, does some processing on it, and writes its output to standard output is called a **filter**.

Consider the following command line:

```
sort <in >temp; head -30 <temp; rm temp
```

It first runs *sort*, taking the input from *in* and writing the output to *temp*. When that has been completed, the shell runs *head*, telling it to print the first 30 lines of *temp* and print them on standard output, which defaults to the terminal. Finally, the temporary file is removed.

It frequently occurs that the first program in a command line produces output that is used as the input on the next program. In the above example, we have used the file *temp* to hold this output. However, UNIX provides a simpler construction to do the same thing. In

```
sort <in | head −30
```

the vertical bar, called the **pipe symbol**, says to take the output from *sort* and use it as the input to *head*, eliminating the need for creating, using, and removing the temporary file. A collection of commands connected by pipe symbols, called a **pipeline**, may contain arbitrarily many commands. A four-component pipeline is shown by the following example:

```
grep ter *.t | sort | head −20 | tail −5 >foo
```

Here all the lines containing the string "ter" in all the files ending in *.t* are written to standard output, where they are sorted. The first 20 of these are selected out by *head* which passes then to *tail*, which writes the last five (i.e., lines 16 to 20 in the sorted list) to *foo*. This is an example of how UNIX provides basic building blocks (numerous filters), each of which does one job, along with a mechanism for them to be put together in almost limitless ways.

UNIX is not only a timesharing system; it is also a general-purpose multiprogramming system. A single user can run several programs at once, each as a separate process. The shell syntax for running a process in the background is to follow its command with an ampersand. Thus

```
wc −l <a >b &
```

runs the word count program, *wc*, to count the number of lines (−*l* flag) in its input, *a*, writing the result to *b*, but does it in the background. As soon as the command has been typed, the shell types the prompt and is ready to accept and handle the next command. Pipelines can also be put in the background, for example, by

```
sort <x | head &
```

Multiple pipelines can run in the background simultaneously.

It is possible to put a list of shell commands in a file and then start a shell with this file as standard input. The (second) shell just processes them in order, the same as it would with commands typed on the keyboard. Files containing shell commands are called **shell scripts**. Shell scripts may assign values to shell variables and then read them later. They may also have parameters, and use **if**, **for**, **while**, and **case** constructs. Thus a shell script is really a program written in shell language. The Berkeley C shell is an alternative shell that has been designed to make shell scripts (and the command language in general) look like C programs in many respects.

7.2.5. Files and Directories in UNIX

Above we have described processes and the shell in UNIX. Now let us say a little about the file system. A UNIX file is a sequence of 0 or more bytes containing arbitrary information. No distinction is made between ASCII files, binary files, or any other kinds of files. The meaning of the bits in a file is entirely up to the file's owner. The system does not care. File names were originally restricted to 14 arbitrary characters, but Berkeley UNIX increased the limit to 255 characters, and this has been adopted by some other versions as well. A file name consisting of three carriage returns is thus a legal file name (but not an especially convenient one).

By convention, many programs expect file names to consist of a base name and an extension, separated by a dot (which counts as a character). Thus *prog.c* is typically a C program, *prog.p* is usually a Pascal program, and *prog.f* is normally a FORTRAN program. These conventions are not enforced by the operating system.

Files can be protected by assigning each one a 9-bit mode, sometimes called the **rights bits**. The first 3 bits refer to the owner's access to the file. The next 3 bits apply to other members of the owner's group (e.g., department or project). The last 3 bits pertain to everyone else. The 3 bits control reading, writing, and executing the file, respectively. Thus a mode of 640 (octal) means that the owner can read and write the file, other members of the owner's group can read it, and outsiders have no access at all. A mode of 100 (octal) allows the owner to execute the file, but prohibits all other access. Not even the owner can read the file, although the owner can change the mode. On the screen, these two example modes are displayed as *rw-r-----* and *--x------* respectively. A mode allowing everyone to do everything (777 octal) is shown as *rwxrwxrwx*.

Files can be grouped together for convenience in directories. Directories are stored as files, and to a large extent can be treated like files. They are protected with the same 9 bits as files, except that the three execute bits grant or deny permission to search the directory rather than execute it.

Directories can contain subdirectories, leading to a hierarchical file system. The root directory is called / and usually contains several subdirectories. The / character is also used to separate directory names, so that the name */usr/ast/x* denotes the file *x* located in the directory *ast*, which itself is in the */usr* directory. Some of the major directories of the average UNIX file system are shown in Fig. 7-3.

7.2.6. UNIX Utility Programs

The user interface to UNIX consists not only of the shell, but also of a large number of standard utility programs. Roughly speaking, these programs can be divided into six categories, as follows:

1. File and directory manipulation commands.

2. Filters.

3. Compilers and program development tools.

4. Text processing.

5. System administration.

6. Miscellaneous.

The POSIX 1003.2 standard specifies the syntax and semantics of just under 100 of

Directory	Description
/bin	Frequently used system binaries
/dev	Special files for I/O devices
/etc	Miscellaneous system administration
/lib	Frequently used libraries
/tmp	Some utilities generate their temporary files here
/usr	All user files are in this part of the tree
/usr/adm	System accounting
/usr/ast	Home directory for the user whose login name is ast
/usr/bin	Other system binaries are kept here
/usr/include	System header files
/usr/lib	Libraries, compiler passes, miscellaneous
/usr/man	Online manuals
/usr/spool	Spooling directories for printer and other daemons
/usr/src	System source code
/usr/tmp	Other utilities put their temporary files here

Fig. 7-3. Some important directories found in most UNIX systems.

these, primarily in the first three categories. The idea of standardizing them is to make it possible for anyone to write shell scripts that use these programs and work on all UNIX systems.

Let us consider some examples of these programs, starting with file and directory manipulation.

```
cp a b
```

copies file *a* to *b*, leaving the original file intact. In contrast,

```
mv a b
```

copies *a* to *b* but removes the original. In effect, it moves the file rather than really making a copy in the usual sense. Several files can be concatenated using *cat*, which reads each of its input files and copies them all to standard output, one after another. Files can be removed by the *rm* command. The *chmod* command allows the owner to change the rights bits to modify access permissions. Directories can be created with *mkdir* and removed with *rmdir*. To see a list of the files in a directory, *ls* can be used. It has a vast number of flags, to control how much detail about each file is shown (e.g., size, owner, group, creation date), to determine the sort order (e.g., alphabetical, by time of last modification, reversed), to specify the layout on the screen, and much more.

We have already seen several filters: *grep* extracts lines containing a given pattern from standard input or one or more input files; *sort* sorts its input and writes it on standard output; *head* extracts the initial lines of its input; *tail* extracts the final lines of its input. Other filters defined by 1003.2 are *cut*, and *paste*, which allow columns of text to be cut and pasted into files; *od* which converts its (usually binary) input to ASCII text, in octal, decimal, or hexadecimal; *tr*, which does character translation (e.g., lower case to upper case), and *pr* which formats output for the printer, including options to include running heads, page numbers, and so on.

Compilers and programming tools include *cc*, which calls the C compiler, and *ar*, which collects library procedures into archive files.

Another important tool is *make*, which is used to maintain large programs whose source code consists of multiple files. Typically, some of these are **header files**, which contain type, variable, macro, and other declarations. Source files often include these using a special *include* directive. This way, two or more source files can share the same declarations. However, if a header file is modified, it is necessary to find all the source files that depend on it, and recompile them. The function of *make* is to keep track of which file depends on which header, and similar things, and arrange for all the necessary compilations to occur automatically. Nearly all UNIX programs, except the smallest ones, are set up to be compiled with *make*.

A selection of the POSIX utility programs is listed in Fig. 7-4, along with a short description of each one. All UNIX systems have these programs, and many more.

7.3. FUNDAMENTAL CONCEPTS IN UNIX

In the previous section, we have looked at UNIX as viewed from the keyboard, that is, what the user sees at the terminal. We gave examples of shell commands and utility programs that are frequently used. In this section we will look at the basic concepts UNIX supports, namely, processes, memory, the file system, and input/output. These notions are important because the system calls—the interface to the operating system itself—manipulate them. For example, system calls exist to create processes, allocate memory, open files, and do I/O.

7.3.1. Processes in UNIX

The only active entities in a UNIX system are the processes. UNIX processes are very similar to the classical sequential processes that we studied in Chap 2. Each process runs a single program and has a single thread of control. In other words, it has one program counter, which keeps track of the next instruction to be executed.

UNIX is a multiprogramming system, so multiple, independent processes may be running at the same time. Each user may have several active processes at once, so on a large system, there may be hundreds or even thousands of processes running. In fact, on most single-user workstations, even when the user is absent, dozens of background processes, called **daemons,** are running. These are started automatically when the system is booted.

A typical daemon is the *cron daemon*. It wakes up once a minute to check if

ar	Build and maintain multifile archives and libraries
awk	Pattern matching language
basename	Strip off prefixes and suffixes from a file name
bc	Programmable calculator
cat	Concatenate files and write them to standard output
cc	Compile a C program
chmod	Change protection mode for files
cmp	Compare two files to see if they are identical
comm	Print lines common to two sorted files
cp	Make a copy of a file
cut	Make each column in a document into a separate file
date	Print the date and time
dd	Copy all or part of file performing various conversions
diff	Print all the differences between two files
echo	Print the arguments (used mostly in shell scripts)
ed	Original line-oriented text editor
find	Find all the files meeting a given condition
grep	Search a file for lines containing a given pattern
head	Print the first few lines of one or more file
kill	Send a signal to a process
ln	Create a link to a file
lp	Print a file on the line printer
ls	List files and directories
make	Recompile those parts of a large program that have changed
mkdir	Make a directory
mv	Move or rename a file
od	Make a dump of a file in octal
paste	Combine multiple files as columns in a single file
pr	Format a file for printing
pwd	Print the working directory
rm	Remove a file
rmdir	Remove a directory
sed	Stream (i.e., noninteractive) editor
sh	Invoke the shell
sleep	Suspend execution for a given number of seconds
stty	Set terminal options such as the characters for line editing
sort	Sort a file consisting of ASCII lines
tail	Print the last few lines of a file
tee	Copy standard input to standard output and also to a file
tr	Translate character codes
uniq	Delete consecutive identical lines in a file
wc	Count characters, words, and lines in a file

Fig. 7-4. Some of the more common UNIX utility programs required by POSIX.

there is any work for it to do. If so, it does the work. Then it goes back to sleep until it is time for the next check.

This daemon is needed because it is possible in UNIX to schedule activities minutes, hours, days, or even months in the future. For example, suppose a user has a dentist appointment at 3 o'clock next Tuesday. He can make an entry in the cron daemon's data base telling the daemon to beep at him at, say, 2:30. When the appointed day and time arrives, the cron daemon sees that it has work to do, and starts up the beeping program as a new process.

The cron daemon is also used to start up periodic activities, such as making daily disk backups at 4 A.M., or reminding forgetful users every year on October 31 to stock up on trick-or-treat goodies for Halloween. Other daemons handle incoming and outgoing electronic mail, manage the line printer queue, check if there are enough free pages in memory, and so forth. Daemons are straightforward to implement in UNIX because each one is a separate process, independent of all other processes.

Processes are created in UNIX in an especially simple manner. The FORK system call creates an exact copy of the original process. The forking process is called the **parent process**. The new process is called the **child process**. The parent and child each have their own, private memory images. If the parent subsequently changes any of its variables, the changes are not visible to the child, and vice versa.

Open files are shared between parent and child. That is, if a certain file was open in the parent before the FORK, it will continue to be open in both the parent and the child afterwards. Changes made to the file by either one will be visible to the other. This behavior is only reasonable, because these changes are also visible to any unrelated process that opens the file as well.

The fact that the memory images, variables, registers, and everything else are identical in the parent and child leads to a small difficulty: How do the processes know which one should run the parent code and which one should run the child code? The secret is that the FORK system call returns a 0 to the child and a nonzero value, known as the **pid** (**process identifier**) to the parent. Both processes normally check the return value, and act accordingly, as shown in Fig. 7-5.

```
pid = fork();           /* if the fork succeeds, pid > 0 in the parent */

if (pid < 0) {
        /* Fork failed, usually because memory or some table is full. */
} else if (pid > 0) {
        /* Parent code goes here. */
} else {
        /* Child code goes here. */
}
```

Fig. 7-5. Process creation in UNIX.

Processes are named by their pids. As we have seen, when a process is created, the parent is given the child's pid. If the child wants to know its own pid, there is a system call, GETPID, that provides it. Pids are used in a variety of ways. For example, when a child terminates, the parent is given the pid of the child that just finished.

This can be important because a parent may have many children. Since children may also have children, an original process can build up an entire tree of children, grandchildren, and further descendants.

This ability to form a tree of process is the key to how timesharing works in UNIX. When the system is booted, a process called *init* is handcrafted by the kernel. This process then reads a file */etc/ttys* that tells how many terminals the system has, and provides certain information describing each one. *Init* then forks off a child process for each terminal and goes to sleep until some child terminates.

Each child runs the *login* program which prints

```
login:
```

on the terminal's screen and tries to read the user's name from the keyboard. When someone sits down at the terminal and provides a login name, *login* then asks for a password, encrypts it, and verifies it against the encrypted password stored in the password file, */etc/passwd*. If it is correct, *login* overlays itself with the user's shell, which then waits for the first command. If it is incorrect, *login* just asks for another user name.

This mechanism is illustrated in Fig. 7-6 for a system with three terminals. The *login* process running on behalf of terminal 0 is still waiting for input. The one running on behalf of terminal 1 has had a successful login, and is now running the shell, which is awaiting a command. A successful login has also occurred on terminal 2, only here the user has started the *cp* program, which is running as a child of the shell. The shell is blocked, waiting for the child to terminate, at which time the shell will type another prompt and read from the keyboard. If the user at terminal 2 had typed *cc* instead of *cp*, the main program of the C compiler would have been started, which in turn would have forked off more processes to run the various compiler passes.

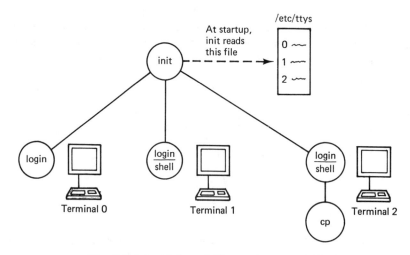

Fig. 7-6. *Init* with three children and one grandchild.

Processes in UNIX can communicate with each other using a form of message passing. It is possible to create a kind of channel between two processes into which one process can write a stream of bytes for the other to read. These channels are called **pipes**. Synchronization is possible because when a process tries to read from an empty pipe it is blocked until data are available.

Shell pipelines are implemented with pipes. When the shell sees a command such as

```
sort <f | head
```

it creates two processes, *sort* and *head*, and sets up a pipe between them in such a way that *sort*'s standard output is connected to *head*'s standard input. In this way, all the data that *sort* writes go directly to *head*, instead of going to a file. If the pipe fills up, the system stops running *sort* until *head* has removed some data from the pipe.

Processes can also communicate in another way: software interrupts. A process can send what is called a **signal** to another process. Processes can tell the system what they want to happen when a signal arrives. The choices are to ignore it, to catch it, or to let the signal kill the process (default). If a process elects to catch signals sent to it, it must specify a signal handling procedure. When a signal arrives, control will abruptly switch to the handler. When the handler is finished and returns, control goes back to where it came from, analogous to hardware I/O interrupts. A process can only send signals to members of its **process group**, which consists of its parent (and further ancestors), siblings, and children (and further descendants). A process may also send a signal to all members of its process group with a single system call.

Signals are also used for other purposes. For example, if a process is doing floating-point arithmetic, and inadvertently divides by 0, it gets a a SIGFPE (floating-point exception) signal. The signals that are required by POSIX are listed in Fig. 7-7. Many UNIX systems have additional signals as well, but programs using them may not be portable to other versions of UNIX.

Each user is identified by an integer called a **uid** (**user identification**) contained in the password file. They are assigned by the system administrator. Every process automatically acquires the uid of the person who created it.

The user with uid 0 is special and is called the **superuser** (or **root**). The superuser has the power to read and write all files in the system, no matter who owns them and no matter how they are protected. Processes with uid 0 also have the ability to make a small number of protected system calls denied to ordinary users. Normally only the system administrator knows the superuser's password, although many undergraduates consider it great sport to try to look for security flaws in the system so they can log in as the superuser without knowing the password.

The power of the superuser is exploited in a clever way to allow users to do certain potentially dangerous things in a controlled way. For example, many UNIX systems have programs that allow users to ask how much disk space is left. This information is stored on each disk in block 0, but normally the disks are protected in such a way as to prohibit ordinary users from just reading the raw bytes. The superuser can find out this information easily enough, but telling everyone the superuser's password would defeat the entire protection system.

Instead, UNIX has a bit associated with each executable program called the **setuid**

Signal	Cause
SIGABRT	Sent to abort a process and force a core dump
SIGALRM	The alarm clock has gone off
SIGFPE	A floating point error has occurred (e.g., division by 0)
SIGHUP	The phone line the process was using has been hung up
SIGILL	The process has executed an illegal machine instruction
SIGINT	The user has hit the DEL key to interrupt the process
SIGQUIT	The user has hit the key requesting a core dump
SIGKILL	Sent to kill a process (cannot be caught or ignored)
SIGPIPE	The process has written on a pipe with no readers
SIGSEGV	The process has referenced an invalid memory address
SIGTERM	Used to request that a process terminate gracefully
SIGUSR1	Available for application-defined purposes
SIGUSR2	Available for application-defined purposes

Fig. 7-7. The signals required by POSIX.

bit. The bit is actually part of the protection mode word (the protection part only uses 9 bits, so there are a few left over for other purposes). When a program with the setuid bit on is executed, the **effective uid** for that process becomes the uid of the executable file's owner instead of the uid of the user who invoked it. By making the program that reports on disk space be owned by the superuser but with the setuid bit on, any user can execute it, and get superuser privileges for that process only.

In this way it is possible for the superuser to make available to ordinary users a collection of programs that make use of superuser power, but in a limited and controlled way. Running the program that reports on disk space allows anyone to have a superuser process, but that does not allow the user to read protected files because that is not one of the options the disk space reporter offers. It just reports on disk space and then exits. The setuid mechanism is widely used throughout UNIX to avoid a mass of special purpose system calls such as one to allow users to read block 0 (and only block 0).

7.3.2. The UNIX Memory Model

The UNIX memory model is quite straightforward, to make programs portable and to make it possible to implement UNIX on machines with widely differing memory management units, ranging from essentially nothing (IBM PC) to sophisticated paging hardware. Every UNIX process has an address space consisting of three segments: text, data, and stack. An example process' address space is depicted in Fig. 7-8(a).

The **text segment** contains the machine instructions that form the program's executable code. It is produced by the compiler and assembler by translating the C, Pascal, or other program into machine code. The text segment is normally read-only.

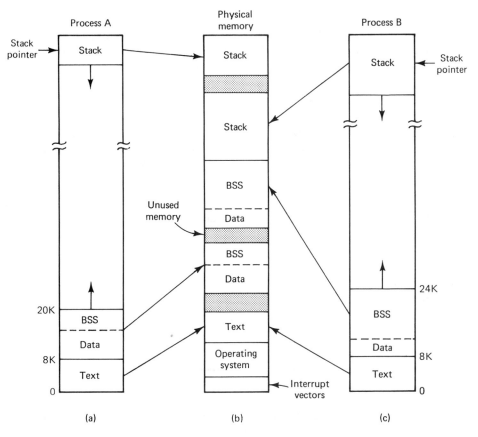

Fig. 7-8. (a) Process *A*'s virtual address space. (b) Physical memory. (c) Process *B*'s virtual address space.

Self modifying programs went out of style in about 1950 because they were too difficult to understand and debug. Thus the text segment neither grows nor shrinks or changes in any other way.

   The **data segment** contains storage for the program's variables, strings, arrays, and other data. It has two parts, the initialized data and the uninitialized data. For historical reasons, the latter is known as the **BSS**. The initialized part of the data segment contains variables and compiler constants that need an initial value when the program is started.

   For example, in C it is possible to declare a character string and initialize it at the same time. When the program starts up, it expects that the string has its initial value. To implement this construction, the compiler assigns the string a location in the address space, and ensures that when the program is started up, this location contains the proper string. From the operating system's point of view, initialized data are not all that different from program text—both contain bit patterns produced by the compiler that must be loaded into memory when the program starts.

The existence of uninitialized data is actually just an optimization. When a global variable is not explicitly initialized, the semantics of the C language say that its initial value is 0. In practice, most global variables are not initialized, and are thus 0. This could be implemented by simply having a section of the executable binary file exactly equal to the number of bytes of data, and initializing all of them, including the ones that have defaulted to 0.

However, to save space in the executable file, this is not done. Instead, the file contains all the explicitly initialized variables following the program text. The uninitialized variables are all gathered together after the initialized ones, so all the compiler has to do is put a word in the header telling how many bytes to allocate.

To make this point more explicit, consider Fig. 7-8(a) again. Here the program text is 8K and the initialized data is also 8K. The uninitialized data (BSS) is 4K. The executable file is only 16K (text + initialized data), plus a short header that tells the system to allocate another 4K after the initialized data and zero it before starting the program. This trick avoids storing 4K of zeros in the executable file.

Unlike the text segment, which cannot change, the data segment can change. Programs modify their variables all the time. Furthermore, many programs need to allocate space dynamically, during execution. UNIX handles this by permitting the data segment to grow and shrink as memory is allocated and deallocated. A system call is available to allow a program to set the size of its data segment. Thus to allocate more memory, a program can increase the size of its data segment. The C library procedure *malloc*, commonly used to allocate memory, makes heavy use of this system call.

The third segment is the stack segment. On most machines, it starts at the top of the virtual address space and grows down toward 0. If the stack grows below the bottom of the stack segment, a hardware fault normally occurs, and the operating system lowers the bottom of the stack segment by a few thousand bytes (e.g., one page). Programs do not explicitly manage the size of the stack segment.

When a program starts up, its stack is not empty. Instead, it contains all the environment (shell) variables as well as the command line typed to the shell to invoke it. In this way a program can discover its arguments. For example, when the command

```
cp src dest
```

is typed, the *cp* program is started up with the string "cp src dest" on the stack, so it can find out the names of the source and destination files. The string is represented as an array of pointers to the symbols in the string, to make it easier to parse.

When two users are running the same program, such as the editor, it would be possible, but inefficient to keep two copies of the editor's program text in memory at once. Instead, most UNIX systems support **shared text segments**. In Fig. 7-8(a) and Fig. 7-8(c) we see two processes that have the same text segment. In Fig. 7-8(b) we see a possible layout of physical memory, in which both processes share the same piece of text. The mapping is done by the virtual memory hardware.

Data and stack segments are never shared. If either one needs to grow and there is no room adjacent to it to grow into, it is moved elsewhere in memory.

On some computers, the hardware supports separate address spaces for instructions and data. When this feature is available, UNIX can use it. On the PDP-11/45, for example, addresses were 16 bits, so programs could only address 64K of memory. However, a program could have 64K of program text and an additional 64K for the combined data and stack segments. The text segment started at 0 and could go as far as 64K. The data segment also started at address 0 and grew upwards, and the stack segment started at 64K and grew downwards. A jump to 0 went to text space, whereas a move from 0 used data space. This feature effectively doubled the maximum program size that could be supported.

7.3.3. The UNIX File System

When a process wants to read or write a file, it must first open the file. A file is opened with the OPEN system call, whose first argument gives the path name of the file to be opened and whose second one specifies if the file is to be read, written, or both. The system checks to see if the file exists, and if so, then inspects the rights bits to see if the caller is entitled to access the file in the desired way. If the access is permitted, the system returns a small positive integer called a **file descriptor** to the caller. If the access is prohibited (or the file does not exist), −1 is returned to indicate an error. The calls for reading and writing the file use the file descriptor to identify the file.

When a process starts up, it always has three file descriptors available: 0 for standard input, 1 for standard output, and 2 for standard error. The first file opened is given file descriptor 3, the next one file descriptor 4, and so on. When a file is closed, its file descriptor is freed and can be allocated on a subsequent open.

There are two ways to specify file names in UNIX, both to the shell and to OPEN. The first way is using an **absolute path**, which means telling how to get to the file starting at the root directory. An example of an absolute path is */usr/ast/book/ch1*. This tells the system to look in the root directory for a directory called *usr*, then look there for another directory, *ast*. In turn, this directory contains a directory *book*, which contains the file *ch1*.

Absolute path names are often long and inconvenient. For this reason, UNIX allows users to designate the directory in which they are currently working as the **working directory**. Path names can also be specified relative to the working directory. Such a name is called a **relative path**. For example, if */usr/ast/book* is the working directory, then the shell command

```
cp ch1 backup
```

has exactly the same effect as the longer command

```
cp /usr/ast/book/ch1 /usr/ast/book/backup
```

It frequently occurs that a user needs to refer to a file that belongs to another user, or at least is located elsewhere in the file tree. For example, if two users are sharing a file, it will be located in a directory belonging to one of them, so the other will have to use an absolute path name to refer to it. If this is long enough, it may become irritating to have to keep typing it. UNIX provides a solution to this problem by allowing users to make a new directory entry that points to an existing file. Such an entry is called a **link**.

As an example, consider the situation of Fig. 7-9(a). Fred and Lisa are working together on a project, and each one needs frequent access to the other's files. If Fred has /usr/fred as his working directory, he can refer to the file x in Lisa's directory as /usr/lisa/x. Alternatively, Fred can create a new entry in his directory as shown in Fig. 7-9(b), after which he can use x to mean /usr/lisa/x.

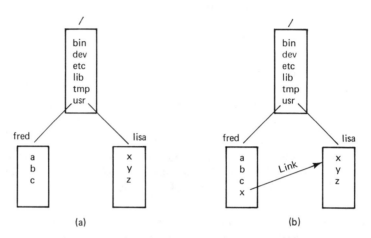

Fig. 7-9. (a) Before linking. (b) After linking.

In the example just discussed, we suggested that before linking, the only way for Fred to refer to Lisa's file x was using its absolute path. Actually, this is not really true. When a directory is created, two entries, . and .., are automatically made in it. The former refers to the working directory itself. The latter refers to the directory's parent. Thus from /usr/fred, another path to Lisa's file x is ../lisa/x.

Many computers have two or more disks. On mainframes at banks, for example, it is frequently necessary to have 100 or more disks on a single machine, in order to hold the huge data bases required. Even personal computers normally have a least two disks—a hard disk and a diskette drive. When there are multiple disk drives, the question arises of how to handle them.

One solution is to put a self-contained file system on each one and just keep them separate. Consider, for example, the situation depicted in Fig. 7-10(a). Here we have a hard disk, which we will call H: and a diskette, which we will call D:. Each has its own root directory and files. With this solution, the user has to specify both the device and the file when anything other than the default is needed. For example, to copy the file x to the directory d, (assuming H: is the default), one would type

```
cp D:/x /a/d/x
```

This is the approach taken by systems like MS-DOS and VMS.

The UNIX solution is to allow one disk to be mounted in another disk's file tree. In our example, we could mount the diskette on the directory /b, yielding the file

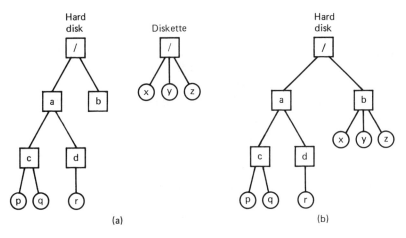

Fig. 7-10. (a) Separate file systems. (b) After mounting.

system of Fig. 7-10(b). The user now sees a single file tree, and no longer has to be aware of which file resides on which device. The above copy command now becomes

```
cp /b/x /a/d/x
```

exactly the same as it would have been if everything had been on the hard disk in the first place.

Another interesting property of the UNIX file system is **locking**. In some applications, two or more processes may be using the same file at the same time, which may lead to race conditions. One solution is to program the application with critical regions. However, if the processes belong to independent users who do not even know each other, this kind of coordination is generally inconvenient.

Consider, for example, a data base consisting of many files in one or more directories that are accessed by unrelated users. It is certainly possible to associate a semaphore with each directory or file and achieve mutual exclusion by having processes do a DOWN operation on the appropriate semaphore before accessing the data. The disadvantage, however, is that a whole directory or file is then made inaccessible, even though only one record may be needed.

For this reason, POSIX provides a flexible and fine-grained mechanism for processes to lock as little as a single byte and as much as an entire file in one indivisible operation. The locking mechanism requires the caller to specify the file to be locked, the starting byte, and the number of bytes. If the operation succeeds, the system makes a table entry noting that the bytes in question (e.g., a data base record) are locked.

Two kinds of locks are provided, **shared** and **exclusive**. If a portion of a file already contains a shared lock, a second attempt to place a shared lock on it is permitted, but an attempt to put an exclusive lock on it will fail. If a portion of a file contains an exclusive lock, all attempts to lock any part of that portion will fail until the lock has been released. In order to successfully place a lock, every byte in the region to be locked must be available.

When placing a lock, a process must specify whether it wants to block or not in the event that lock cannot be placed. If it chooses to block, when the existing lock has been removed, the process is unblocked and the lock is placed. If the process chooses not to block when it cannot place a lock, the system call returns immediately, with the status code telling whether the lock succeeded or not.

Locked regions may overlap. In Fig. 7-11(a) we see that process A has placed a shared lock on bytes 4 through 7 of some file. Later, process B places a shared lock on bytes 6 through 9, as shown in Fig. 7-11(b). Finally, C locks bytes 2 through 11. As long as all these locks are shared, they can co-exist.

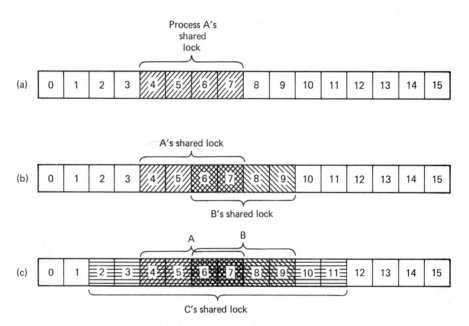

Fig. 7-11. (a) A file with one lock. (b) Addition of a second lock. (c) A third lock.

Now consider what happens if a process tries to acquire an exclusive lock to byte 9 of the file of Fig. 7-11(c), with a request to block if the lock fails. Since two previous locks cover this block, the caller will block and will remain blocked until both B and C release their locks.

7.3.4. Input/Output in UNIX

Like all computers, those running UNIX have I/O devices such as terminals, disks, printers, and networks connected to them. Some way is needed to allow programs to access these devices. Although various solutions are possible, the UNIX one is to integrate them into the file system as what are called **special files**. Each I/O device is assigned a path name, usually in */dev*. For example, the printer might be */dev/lp*, terminal 1 might be */dev/tty1*, and the network might be */dev/net*.

These special files can be accessed the same way as any other files. No special commands or system calls are needed. The usual READ and WRITE system calls will do just fine. For example, the command

```
cp file /dev/lp
```

copies the *file* to printer, causing it to be printed (assuming that this is permitted). Programs can open, read, and write special files the same way as they do regular files. In fact, *cp* in the above example is not even aware that it is printing. In this way, no special mechanism is needed for doing I/O.

An additional advantage is that the usual file protection rules apply automatically to I/O devices. If the protection bits for */dev* are set up to prohibit everyone except the superuser from directly accessing the files in it, then users are prohibited from doing direct I/O themselves. Restricted access to selected I/O devices can be given by installing setuid programs that have permission to read and write the files in */dev*, but do that in limited ways.

For example, a common way to manage access to the printer is to make */dev/lp* readable for no one and writable for only the superuser. A program called *lpr* is offered to allow users to print files. What *lpr* does is copy the files specified in its arguments to a spooling directory, where a daemon with access to */dev/lp* takes them out and prints them in order. It should be clear that */dev/lp* need not necessarily be owned by the superuser. All that matters is that the daemon has access to it. They could both be owned by *daemon* for example. By having the I/O devices integrated into the file system like this, great flexibility in access can be achieved.

Special files are divided into two categories, block and character. A **block special file** is one consisting of a sequence of numbered blocks. The key property of the block special file is that it each block can be individually addressed and accessed. In other words, a program can open a block special file and read, say, block 124 without first having to read blocks 0 to 123. Block special files are used for disks.

Character special files are normally used for devices that input or output a character stream. Terminals, printers, networks, mice, plotters, and most other I/O devices that accept or produce data for people use character special files. It is not possible (or even meaningful) to seek to block 124 on a mouse.

Although character special files cannot be randomly accessed, they often need to be controlled in ways that block special files do not. Consider, for example, a terminal. In addition to accepting read and write requests, a terminal has a number of special characteristics that must be managed. For example, when the user makes a typing error and wants to erase the last character typed, he presses some key. Some people prefer to use backspace, and others prefer DEL. Similarly, to erase the entire line just typed, many conventions abound. Some users prefer @, while others prefer CTRL-U, CTRL-C, or other character. Likewise, to interrupt the running program, some special key must be hit. Here too, different people have different preferences.

Rather than making a choice and forcing everyone to use it, UNIX allows all these special functions and many others to be customized by the user. A special system call is generally provided for setting these options. This system call also handles tab expansion, enabling and disabling of character echoing, conversion between carriage return and line feed, and similar items. The system call is not permitted on regular files or block special files.

Another example of I/O is networking, as pioneered by Berkeley UNIX, and summarized below. The central concept in the Berkeley design is the **socket**. Sockets are analogous to mailboxes and telephones in that they allow users to interface to the network, just as mailboxes allow people to interface to the postal system and telephones allow them to interface to the telephone system. The position of the sockets is shown in Fig. 7-12.

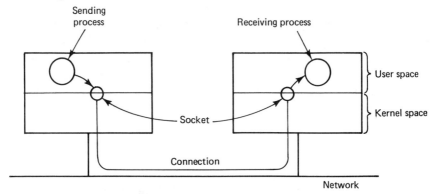

Fig. 7-12. The user of sockets for networking.

Sockets can be created and destroyed dynamically. Creating a socket returns a file descriptor, which is needed for establishing a connection, reading data, writing data, and releasing the connection.

Each socket supports a particular type of networking, specified when the socket is created. The most common types are:

1. Reliable connection-oriented byte stream.

2. Reliable, connection-oriented packet stream.

3. Unreliable packet transmission.

The first socket type effectively allows two processes on different machines to establish the equivalent of a pipe between them. Bytes are pumped in at one end and they come out in the same order at the other.

The second type is similar to the first one, except that it preserves packet boundaries. If the sender makes five separate calls to WRITE, each for 512 bytes, and the receiver asks for 2560 bytes, with a type 1 socket, all 2560 bytes will be returned at once. With a type 2 socket, only 512 bytes will be returned. Four more calls are needed to get the rest. The third type of socket is used to give the user access to the raw network. This type is especially useful for real-time applications, and for those situations in which the user wants to implement a specialized error handling scheme.

When a socket is created, one of the parameters specifies the protocol to be used for it. For reliable byte and packet streams, the most popular protocol is TCP/IP. For unreliable packet-oriented transmission, UDP is the usual choice. Both of these protocols originated with the U.S. Dept. of Defense's ARPANET, and are now widely used throughout the world.

Before a socket can be used for networking, it must have an address bound to it. This address can be in one of several naming domains. The most common domain is the Internet naming domain, which uses 32-bit integers for naming endpoints.

Once sockets have been created on both the source and destination computers, a connection can be established between them (for connection-oriented communication). One party makes a LISTEN system call on a local socket, which creates a buffer and blocks until data arrive. The other one makes a CONNECT system call, giving as parameters the file descriptor for a local socket and the address of a remote socket. If the remote party accepts the call, the system then establishes a connection between the sockets.

Once a connection has been established, it functions analogously to a pipe. A process can read and write from it using the file descriptor for its local socket. When the connection is no longer needed, it can be closed in the usual way.

7.4. UNIX SYSTEM CALLS

Armed with our general knowledge of how UNIX works, we can now look at the system calls. Rather than attempt to discuss every detail of every call, we will make a representative selection of the POSIX system calls (see Fig. 7-13) and study these.

To make the general system call mechanism clearer, let us take a quick look at CHDIR. It has one parameter, the name of the new working directory. A call to CHDIR from a C program might look like this:

```
status = chdir(dirname);
```

The system call (and the library procedure) return a status code telling whether the call was successful or not. A value of 0 is used for a successful call and a value of −1 is used if the call fails. In the event of failure, the error number is put in a global variable, *errno*. Programs should always check the results of a system call to see if an error occurred. For CHDIR, possible errors include an invalid directory name or a protection violation. Other system calls have other possible errors.

7.4.1. Process Management System Calls in UNIX

The first group of calls deals with process management. FORK is a good place to start the discussion. FORK is the only way to create a new process. It creates an exact duplicate of the original process, including all the file descriptors, registers and everything else. After the FORK, the original process and the copy (the parent and child) go their separate ways. All the variables have identical values at the time of the FORK, but since the entire parent core image is copied to create the child, subsequent changes in one of them do not affect the other one. The FORK call returns a value, which is zero in the child, and equal to the child's process identifier or **pid** in

Process management	Description
pid = fork ( )	Create a child process
s = waitpid (pid, &status, opts)	Wait for a child to terminate
s = execve (name, argv, envp)	Replace a process' core image
exit (status)	Terminate execution and return status
s = sigaction (sig, &act, &oact)	Specify action to take for a signal
s = kill (pid, sig)	Send a signal to a process
residual = alarm (seconds)	Schedule a SIGALRM signal later
pause ( )	Suspend the caller until the next signal

Memory management	Description
size = brk (addr)	Set the size of the data segment (not POSIX)

Files and directories	Description
fd = creat (name, mode)	Create a new file
fd = open (file, how)	Open a file for reading and/or writing
s = close (fd)	Close an open file
n = read (fd, buffer, nbytes)	Read data from a file into a buffer
n = write (fd, buffer nbytes)	Write data from a buffer into a file
pos = lseek (fd, offset, whence)	Move the file pointer somewhere in the file
s = stat (name, &buf)	Read and return information about a file
s = mkdir (name, mode)	Create a new directory
s = rmdir (name)	Delete an empty directory
s = link (name1, name2)	Create a new directory entry for an old file
s = unlink (name)	Remove a directory entry
s = chdir (dirname)	Change the working directory
s = chmod (name, mode)	Change a file's protection bits

Input/Output	Description
s = cfsetospeed (&termios, speed)	Set the output speed
s = cfsetispeed (&termios, speed)	Set the input speed
s = cfgetospeed (&termios, speed)	Get the output speed
s = cfgetispeed (&termios, speed)	Get the input speed
s = tcsetattr (fd, opt, &termios)	Set terminal attributes
s = tcgetattr (fd, &termios)	Get terminal attributes

Fig. 7-13. A selection of common UNIX system calls. The return code s is 0 for success, -1 if an error has occurred; fd is a file descriptor. The other names are suggestive of their functions.

the parent. Using the returned pid, the two processes can see which is the parent and which is the child.

In most cases, after a FORK, the child will need to execute different code from the parent. Consider the case of the shell. It reads a command from the terminal, forks off a child process, waits for the child to execute the command, and then reads the next command when the child terminates. To wait for the child to finish, the parent executes a WAITPID system call, which just waits until the child terminates (any child if more than one exists). WAITPID has three parameters. The first one allows the caller to wait for a specific child. If it is −1, the first child to terminate will do. The second parameter is the address of a variable that will be set to the child's exit status (normal or abnormal termination and exit value). The third one determines whether the caller blocks or returns if no child is already terminated.

In the case of the shell, the child process must execute the command typed by the user. It does this by using the EXEC system call, which causes its entire core image to be replaced by the file named in its first parameter. A highly simplified shell illustrating the use of FORK, WAIT, and EXEC is shown in Fig. 7-14.

```
while (1) {                          /* repeat forever */
    type_prompt();                   /* display prompt on the screen */
    read_command(command, params);   /* read input from terminal */

    pid = fork();
    if (pid < 0) {
        printf("Unable to fork.0);   /* error condition */
        continue;                    /* repeat the loop */
    }

    if (pid != 0) {                  /* fork off child process */
        waitpid(-1, &status, 0);     /* parent code */
    } else {
        execve(command, params, 0);  /* child  code */
    }
}
```

Fig. 7-14. A stripped-down shell.

In the most general case, EXEC has three parameters: the name of the file to be executed, a pointer to the argument array, and a pointer to the environment array. These will be described shortly. Various library procedures, including *execl*, *execv*, *execle*, and *execve* are provided to allow the parameters to be omitted or specified in various ways. All of procedures invoke the same underlying system call, EXEC.

Let us consider the case of a command such as

```
cp file1 file2
```

used to copy *file1* to *file2*. After the shell has forked, the child locates and executes the file *cp* and passes it information about the files to be copied.

The main program of *cp* (and many other programs) contains the declaration

```
main(argc, argv, envp)
```

where *argc* is a count of the number of items on the command line, including the program name. For the example above, *argc* is 3.

The second parameter, *argv*, is a pointer to an array. Element *i* of that array is a pointer to the *i*-th string on the command line. In our example, *argv*[0] would point to the string "cp". Similarly, *argv*[1] would point to the 5-character string "file1" and *argv*[2] would point to the 5-character string "file2".

The third parameter of *main*, *envp*, is a pointer to the environment, an array of strings containing assignments of the form *name* = *value* used to pass information such as the terminal type and home directory name to a program. In Fig. 7-14, no environment is passed to the child, so the third parameter of *execve* is a zero.

If EXEC seems complicated, do not despair; it is the most complex system call. All the rest are much simpler. As an example of a simple one, consider EXIT, which processes should use when they are finished executing. It has one parameter, the exit status (0 to 255), which is returned to the parent in the variable *status* of the WAITPID system call. The low-order byte of *status* contains the termination status, with 0 being normal termination and the other values being various error conditions. The high-order byte contains the child's exit status (0 to 255). For example, if a parent process executes the statement

```
n = waitpid(-1, &status, 0);
```

it will be suspended until some child process terminates. If the child exits with, say, 4 as the parameter to *exit*, the parent will be awakened with *n* set to the child's pid and *status* set to 0x0400 (0x as a prefix means hexadecimal in C).

Several system calls relate to signals, which are used in a variety of ways. For example, if a user accidently tells a text editor to display the entire contents of a very long file, and then realizes the error, some way is needed to interrupt the editor. The usual choice is for the user to hit some special key (e.g., DEL or CTRL-C), which sends a signal to the editor. The editor catches the signal and stops the print-out.

To announce its willingness to catch this (or any other) signal, the process can use the SIGACTION system call. The first parameter is the signal to be caught (see Fig. 7-7). The second is a pointer to a structure giving a pointer to the signal handling procedure, as well as some other bits and flags. The third one points to a structure where the system returns information about signal handling currently in effect, in case it must be restored later.

The signal handler may run for as long as it wants to. In practice, though, signal handlers are usually fairly short. When the signal handling procedure is done, it returns to the point from which it was interrupted.

The SIGACTION system call can also be used to cause a signal to be ignored, or to restore the default action, which is killing the process.

Hitting the DEL key is not the only way to send a signal. The KILL system call allows a process to signal another related process. The choice of the name "kill" for this system call is not an especially good one, since most processes send signals to other ones with the intention that they be caught.

For many real-time applications, a process needs to be interrupted after a specific time interval to do something, such as to retransmit a potentially lost packet over an unreliable communication line. To handle this situation, the ALARM system call has been provided. The parameter specifies an interval, in seconds, after which a SIGALRM signal is sent to the process. A process may have only one alarm outstanding at any instant. If an ALARM call is made with a parameter of 10 seconds, and then 3 seconds later another ALARM call is made with a parameter of 20 seconds, only one signal will be generated, 20 seconds after the second call. The first signal is canceled by the second call to ALARM. If the parameter to ALARM is zero, any pending alarm signal is canceled. If an alarm signal is not caught, the default action is taken and the signaled process is killed. Technically, alarm signals may be ignored, but that is a pointless thing to do.

It sometimes occurs that a process has nothing to do until a signal arrives. For example, consider a computer aided instruction program that is testing reading speed and comprehension. It displays some text on the screen and then calls ALARM to signal it after 30 seconds. While the student is reading the text, the program has nothing to do. It could sit in a tight loop doing nothing, but that would waste CPU time that a background process or other user might need. A better solution is to use the PAUSE system call, which tells UNIX to suspend the process until the next signal arrives.

7.4.2. Memory Management System Calls in UNIX

POSIX does not specify any system calls for memory management. This topic was considered too machine dependent for standardization. Instead, the problem was swept under the rug by saying that programs needing dynamic memory management can use the *malloc* library procedure (defined by the ANSI C standard). How *malloc* is implemented is thus moved outside the scope of the POSIX standard. In some circles this approach is known as passing the buck.

In practice, most UNIX systems have a system call BRK that specifies the size that the data segment is to be set to (see Fig. 7-8). If the new value is greater than the old one, the data segment becomes larger. If it is smaller, the data segment shrinks.

7.4.3. File and Directory System Calls in UNIX

Many system calls relate to files and the file system. First we will look at the system calls that operate on individual files. Later we will examine those that involve directories or the file system as a whole. To create a new file, the CREAT call is used. (When Ken Thompson was once asked what he would do differently if he had the chance to reinvent UNIX, he replied that he would spell CREAT as CREATE this time.) The parameters provide the name of the file and the protection mode. Thus

```
fd = creat("abc", mode);
```

creates a file called *abc* with the protection bits taken from *mode*.

CREAT not only creates a new file, but also opens it for writing, regardless of the file's mode. The file descriptor returned, *fd*, can be used to write the file. If a CREAT is done on an existing file, that file is truncated to length 0, provided, of course, that the permissions are all right.

To read or write an existing file, the file must first be opened using OPEN. This call specifies the file name to be opened and whether it is to be opened for reading, writing, or both. Various options can be specified as well. The file descriptor returned can then be used for reading or writing. Afterward, the file can be closed by CLOSE, which makes the file descriptor available for reuse on a subsequent CREAT or OPEN.

The most heavily used calls are undoubtedly READ and WRITE. We saw READ earlier. WRITE has the same parameters.

Although most programs read and write files sequentially, for some applications programs need to be able to access any part of a file at random. Associated with each file is a pointer that indicates the current position in the file. When reading (writing) sequentially, it normally points to the next byte to be read (written). The LSEEK call changes the value of the position pointer, so that subsequent calls to READ or WRITE can begin anywhere in the file, or even beyond the end of it.

LSEEK has three parameters: the first one is the file descriptor for the file; the second one is a file position; the third one tells whether the file position is relative to the beginning of the file, the current position, or the end of the file. The value returned by LSEEK is the absolute position in the file after the file pointer was changed.

For each file, UNIX keeps track of the file mode (regular, directory, special file), size, time of last modification, and other information. Programs can ask to see this information via the STAT system call. The first parameter is the file name. The second one is a pointer to a structure where the information requested is to be put. The fields in the structure are shown in Fig. 7-15.

Field	Description
st_mode	Mode word containing the protection bits
st_ino	I-node number, used to identify the file
st_dev	Device on which the file resides
st_nlink	Number of links to the file
st_uid	User id
st_gid	Group id
st_size	File size in bytes
st_atime	Time of last access
st_mtime	Time of last modification
st_ctime	Time this information was last changed

Fig. 7-15. The structure used to return information for the STAT system call.

Now let us look at some system calls that relate more to directories or the file system as a whole, rather than just to one specific file. Directories are created and destroyed using MKDIR and RMDIR, respectively. A directory can only be removed if it is empty.

As we saw in Fig. 7-9, linking to a file creates a new directory entry that points to an existing file. The LINK system call creates the link. The parameters specify the original and new names, respectively. Directory entries are removed with UNLINK. When the last link to a file is removed, the file is automatically deleted. For a file that has never been linked, the first UNLINK causes it to disappear.

The working directory is changed by the CHDIR system call. Doing so has the effect of changing the interpretation of relative path names.

The CHMOD system call makes it possible to change the mode of a file, that is, the protection bits.

7.4.4. Input/Output System Calls in UNIX

Prior to POSIX, most UNIX systems had a system call IOCTL that performed a large number of device-specific actions on special files. Over the course of the years, it had gotten to be quite a mess. POSIX cleaned it up by splitting its functions into separate system calls. The first four listed in the Input/Output section of Fig. 7-13 are used to set and get the terminal speed. Different calls are provided for input and output because some modems operate at split speed. For example, many videotex systems allow people with home computers to access public data bases, with (usually short) requests from the home to the computer going at 75 bits/sec, and (usually long) replies coming back at 1200 bits/sec. This standard was adopted at a time when 1200 bits/sec both ways was too expensive for home use.

The last two calls in the list are for setting and reading back all the special characters used for erasing characters and lines, interrupting processes, and so on. In addition, they enable and disable echoing, handle flow control, and other related functions. Additional I/O system calls also exist, but they are somewhat specialized so we will not discuss them further.

7.5. IMPLEMENTATION OF UNIX

So far we have described how to use UNIX, first at the terminal (shell commands) and then from within programs (system calls). Now we will take a peek under the hood to see how UNIX is implemented inside. Implementation details vary somewhat from version to version and from computer to computer, but the material presented here should give a good picture of how UNIX works, even if some of the details may be slightly different on some systems. For more information about UNIX internals, see (Bach, 1987) about System V or (Leffler et al., 1989) about 4.3BSD.

The UNIX kernel is not terribly well structured internally, but two parts are more-or-less distinguishable. At the very bottom is the **machine-dependent kernel**. This code consists of the interrupt handlers, the low-level I/O system device drivers, and part of the memory management software. Most of it is written in C, but since it directly drives the hardware, it has to be rewritten almost from scratch whenever UNIX is ported to a new machine.

In contrast, the **machine-independent kernel** is the same on all machines because it does not depend closely on the particular hardware it is running on. The machine-independent code includes system call handling, process management, scheduling, pipes, signals, paging and swapping, the file system, and the high-level part of the I/O system (disk strategy, etc.). Fortunately, the machine-independent part is much larger than the machine-dependent part, which is why it is relatively straightforward to port UNIX to new hardware. In the following sections we will look at the same items we have been considering throughout this chapter, namely, processes, memory management, the file system, and I/O.

7.5.1. Implementation of Processes in UNIX

A process in UNIX is like an iceberg: what you see is the part above the water, but there is also an important part underneath. Every process has a user part and a kernel part. The kernel part is normally idle, becoming active only when a system call is invoked. The kernel part has its own stack and its own program counter. These are important because a system call can block part way through, for example, waiting for a disk operation to complete.

The kernel maintains two key data structures related to processes, the **process table** and the **user structure**. The process table is resident all the time and contains information needed for all processes, even those that are currently not in memory. The user structure is swapped or paged out when its associated process is not in memory, in order not to waste memory on information that is not needed.

The information in the process table falls into the following broad categories:

1. **Scheduling parameters**. Process priority, amount of CPU time consumed recently, amount of time spent sleeping recently. Together, these are used to determined which process to run next.

2. **Memory image**. Pointers to the text, data, and stack segments, or, if paging is used, to their page tables. If the text segment is shared, the text pointer points to the shared text table. When the process is not in memory, information about how to find its parts on disk is here too.

3. **Signals**. Masks showing which signals are being ignored, which are being caught, which are being temporarily blocked, and which are in the process of being delivered.

4. **Miscellaneous**. Current process state, event being waited for, if any, time until alarm clock goes off, pid, pid of the parent process, and user and group identification.

The user structure contains information that is not needed when the process is not physically in memory and runnable. For example, although it is possible for a process to be sent a signal while it is swapped out, it is not possible for it to read a file. For this reason, information about signals must be in the process table, so they are in memory all the time, whereas information about file descriptors can be kept in the user structure and brought in only when the process is runnable.

The user structure includes the following items:

1. **Machine registers**. When a trap to the kernel occurs, the machine registers (including the floating point ones, if used) are saved here.

2. **System call state**. Information about the current system call, including the parameters, and results.

3. **File descriptor table**. When a system call involving a file descriptor is invoked, the file descriptor is used as an index into this table to locate the in-core data structure (i-node) corresponding to this file.

4. **Accounting**. Pointer to a table that keeps track of the user and system CPU time used by the process. Some systems also maintain limits here on the amount of CPU time a process may use, the maximum size of its stack, the number of page frames it may consume, and other items.

5. **Kernel stack**. A fixed stack for use by the kernel part of the process.

Bearing the use of these tables in mind, it is now easy to explain how processes are created in UNIX. When a FORK system call is executed, the calling process traps to the kernel and looks for a free slot in the process table for use by the child. If it finds one, it copies all the information from the parent's process table entry to the child's entry. It then allocates memory for the child's data and stack segments, and makes exact copies of the parent's segments there. The user structure is kept adjacent to the stack segment, and is copied along with it. At this point, the child is ready to run.

Let us now examine the UNIX scheduling algorithm. Because UNIX is a timesharing system, its scheduling algorithm has been designed to provide good response to interactive processes. It is a two-level algorithm. The low-level algorithm picks the process to run next from the set of processes in memory and ready to run. The high-level algorithm moves processes between memory and disk so that all processes get a chance to be in memory and run.

The low-level algorithm uses multiple queues. Each queue is associated with a priority value. Processes executing in user mode (the top of the iceberg) have positive values. Processes executing in kernel mode (doing system calls) have negative values. Negative values have the highest priority and large positive values have the lowest, as illustrated in Fig. 7-16. Only processes that are in memory and ready to run are located on the queues, since the choice must be made from this set.

When the (low-level) scheduler runs, it searches the queues starting at the highest priority until it finds a queue that is occupied. The first process on that queue is then chosen and started. It is allowed to run for a maximum of one quantum, typically 100 msec, or until it blocks. Clock ticks usually occur at the power line frequency, (60 Hz in North America, 50 Hz in Europe), so 1 quantum is usually 5 or 6 clock ticks. Every time the clock ticks, the CPU usage counter in the running process'

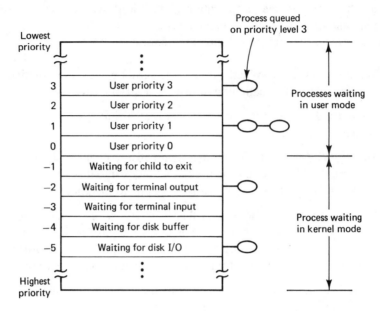

Fig. 7-16. The UNIX scheduler is based on a multilevel queue structure.

process table entry is incremented by 1. This counter will ultimately be added to the process' priority, moving it to a lower priority queue.

If a process uses up its quantum, it is put back on the end of its queue, and the scheduling algorithm run again. Thus processes with the same priority share the CPU using a round robin algorithm.

Once a second, all process priorities are recalculated. First, all the CPU usage counters are divided by 2, so that processes are not punished forever for past CPU use. Then each process' priority is calculated according to the formula

$$\text{New priority} = \text{base} + \text{CPU usage}$$

The base is normally 0, but a user wishing *worse* than normal service can change it to a positive value using the NICE system call. A user computing π to a billion places in the background might put this call in his program to be nice to the other users. Only the superuser may ask for *better* than normal service. Deducing the reason for this rule is left as an exercise for the reader.

When a process traps to the kernel to make a system call, it is entirely possible that the process has to block before completing the system call and returning to user mode. For example, it may have just done a WAITPID system call and have to wait for one of its children to exit. It may also have to wait for terminal input or for disk I/O to complete, to mention only two of the many possibilities. When it blocks, it is removed from the queue structure, since it is unable to run.

However, when the event it was waiting for occurs, it is put onto a queue with a negative value. The choice of queue is determined by the event it was waiting for. In Fig. 7-16, disk I/O is shown as having the highest priority, so a process that has just read or written a block from the disk will probably get the CPU within 100 msec. The relative priority of disk I/O, terminal I/O, etc. is hardwired into the operating system, and can only be modified by changing some constants in the source code and recompiling the system.

The idea behind this scheme is to get processes out of the kernel fast. If a process is trying to read a disk file, making it wait a second between READ calls will slow it down enormously. It is far better to let it run immediately after each request is completed, so it can make the next one quickly. Similarly, if a process was blocked waiting for terminal input, it is clearly an interactive process, and as such should be given a high priority as soon as it is ready in order to ensure that interactive processes get good service. In this light, CPU bound processes (i.e., those on the positive queues) basically get any service that is left over when all the I/O bound and interactive processes are blocked.

7.5.2. Implementation of Memory Management in UNIX

Prior to 3BSD, most UNIX systems were based on swapping, which worked as follows. When more processes existed than could be kept in memory, some of them were swapped out to disk. A swapped out process was always swapped out in its entirety (except possibly for shared text). A process was thus either in memory or on disk.

Swapping

Movement between memory and disk was handled by the upper level of the two level scheduler, known as the **swapper**. Swapping from memory to disk was initiated when the kernel ran out out free memory on account of one of the following events:

1. A FORK system call needed memory for a child process.

2. A BRK system call needed to expand a data segment.

3. A stack became larger and ran out of the space allocated to it.

In addition, when it was time to bring in a process that had been on disk too long, it was frequently necessary to remove another process to make room for it.

To choose a victim to evict, the swapper first looked at the processes that were blocked waiting for something (e.g., terminal input). Better to remove a process that could not run than one that could. If one or more were found, the one whose priority plus residence time was the highest was chosen. Thus a process that had consumed a large amount of CPU time recently was a good candidate, as was one that had been in memory for a long time, even if it was mostly doing I/O. If no blocked process was available, then a ready process was chosen based on the same criteria.

Every few seconds, the swapper examined the list of processes currently swapped out to see if any of them were ready to run. If any were, the one that had been on disk longest was selected. Next, the swapper checked to see if this was going to be an easy swap or a hard one. An easy swap was one for which enough free memory currently existed, so that no process had to be removed to make room for the new one. A hard swap required removing one or more processes. An easy swap was implemented by just bringing in the process. A hard one was implemented by first freeing up enough memory by swapping out one or more, then bringing in the desired process.

This algorithm was then repeated until one of two conditions was met: (1) no processes on disk were ready to run, or (2) memory was so full of processes that had just been brought in that there was no room left for any more. To prevent thrashing, no process was ever swapped out until it had been in memory for 2 sec.

Free storage in memory and on the swap device was kept track of by linked lists of holes. When storage was needed on either one, the first fit algorithm read the appropriate hole list and returned the first sufficiently large hole it could find, removing the portion of the hole actually needed from the free list.

Paging

All versions of UNIX for the PDP-11 and Interdata machines, as well as the initial VAX implementation, were based on swapping, as just described. Starting with 3BSD, however, Berkeley added paging in order to handle the ever-larger programs that were being written. Both 4BSD and System V now implement demand paging. Below we will describe the 4BSD design, but the System V one is almost the same.

The basic idea behind paging in 4BSD is simple: a process need not be entirely in memory in order to run. All that is actually required is the user structure and the page tables. If these are swapped in, the process is deemed "in memory" and can be scheduled to run. The pages of the text, data, and stack segments are brought in dynamically, one at a time, as they are referenced. If the user structure and page table are not in memory, the process cannot be run until the swapper brings them in, the same way as on the PDP-11.

Berkeley UNIX does not use the working set model or any other form of prepaging because doing so requires knowing which pages are in use and which are not. Because the VAX does not have page reference bits, this information is not easily available (although it can be obtained in software at the cost of substantial additional overhead).

Paging is implemented partly by the main kernel, and partly by a new process called the **page daemon**. The page daemon is process 2. Process 0 is still the swapper, and process 1 is still init (see Fig. 7-6). Like all daemons, the page daemon is started up periodically so it can look around to see if there is any work for it to do. If it discovers that the number of free pages in memory is too low, it initiates action to free up more pages.

Main memory in 4BSD is organized as shown in Fig. 7-17. It consists of three parts. The first two parts, the kernel and core map, are wired down (i.e., never paged out). The rest of memory is divided into page frames, each of which can contain a text, data, or stack page, a page table page, or be on the free list.

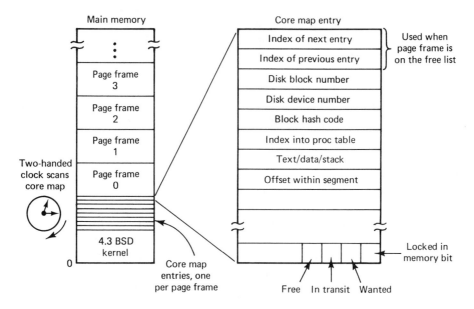

Fig. 7-17. The core map in 4BSD.

The **core map** contains information about the contents of the page frames. Core map entry 0 describes page frame 0, core map entry 1 describes page frame 1, and so forth. With 1K page frames and 16-byte core map entries, less than 2 percent of the memory is taken up by the core map. The first two items in the core map entry shown in Fig. 7-17 are used only when the corresponding page frame is on the free list. Then they are used to hold a doubly linked list stringing together all the free page frames. The next three entries are used when the page frame contains information. Each page in memory also has a location on some disk where it is put when it is paged out. These entries are used to find the disk location where the page is stored. The next three entries give the process table entry for the page's process, which segment it is in, and where it is located in that segment. The last one shows some of the flags needed by the paging algorithm.

When a process is started, it may get a page fault because one of its pages is not present in memory. If a page fault occurs, the operating system takes the first page frame on the free list, removes it from the list, and reads the needed page into it. If the free list is empty, the process is suspended until the page daemon has freed a page frame.

The Page Replacement Algorithm

The page replacement algorithm is executed by the page daemon. Every 250 msec it is awakened to see if the number of free page frames is at least equal to a system parameter called *lotsfree* (typically set to 1/4 of memory). If insufficient page frames are free, the page daemon starts transferring pages from memory to disk until *lotsfree* page frames are available. If the page daemon discovers that more than *lotsfree* page frames are on the free list, it just goes back to sleep. If the machine has plenty of memory and few active processes, it will sleep nearly all the time.

The page daemon uses a modified version of the clock algorithm. It is a global algorithm, meaning that when removing a page, it does not take into account whose page is being removed. Thus the number of pages each process has assigned to it varies in time.

The basic clock algorithm works by scanning the page frames circularly (as though they lay around the circumference of a clock). On the first pass, when the hand points to a page frame, the usage bit is cleared. On the second pass, any page frame that has not been accessed since the first pass will have its usage bit still cleared, and will be put on the free list (after writing it to disk, if it is dirty). A page frame on the free list retains its contents, which can be recovered if that page is needed before it is overwritten.

On a machine like the VAX that has no usage bits, when the clock hand points to a page frame on the first pass, the software usage bit is cleared and the page is marked as invalid in the page table. When the page is next accessed, a page fault occurs, which allows the operating system to set the software usage bit. The effect is the same as having a hardware usage bit, but the implementation is much more expensive.

Originally, Berkeley UNIX used the basic clock algorithm, but it was discovered that with large memories, the passes took too long. The algorithm was then modified to the **two-handed clock algorithm**, symbolized at the left of Fig. 7-17. With this algorithm, the page daemon maintains two pointers into the core map. When it runs, it first clears the usage bit at the front end, and then checks the usage bit at the back hand, after which it advances both hands. If the two hands are kept close together, then only very heavily used pages have much of a chance of being accessed between the time the front hand passes by and the time the back one does. If the two hands are 359 degrees apart (meaning the back hand is just ahead of the front hand), we are back to the original clock algorithm. Each time the page daemon runs, the hands rotate less than a full revolution, the amount depending on how far they have to go to get the number of pages on the free list up to *lotsfree*.

If the system notices that the paging rate is too high and the number of free pages is always way below *lotsfree*, the swapper is started to remove one or more processes from memory so that they will no longer compete for page frames The 4BSD swap out algorithm is as follows. First the swapper looks to see if any processes have been idle for 20 sec or more. If any exist, the one that has been idle the longest is swapped out. If none exist, the four largest processes are examined and the one that has been in memory the longest is swapped out. If need be, the algorithm is repeated until enough memory has been recovered.

Every few seconds the swapper checks to see if any ready processes on the disk should be brought in. Each process on disk is assigned a value that is a function of how long it has been swapped out, its size, the value it set using NICE (if any), and how long it was sleeping before being swapped out. The function is weighted to usually bring in the process that has been out the longest, unless it is extremely large. The theory is that bringing in large processes is expensive, so they should not be moved too often. Swap-in only occurs if there enough free pages, so that when the inevitable page faults start occurring, there will be page frames for them. Only the user structure and the page tables are actually brought in by the swapper. The text, data, and stack pages are paged in as they are used.

Each segment of each active process has a place on disk where it resides when it is paged or swapped out. Data and stack segments go to a scratch device, but program text is paged in from the executable binary file itself. No scratch copy is used.

Paging in System V is fundamentally similar to that in 4BSD, which is not entirely surprising since the Berkeley version had been running for years before paging was added to System V. Nevertheless, there are two interesting differences.

First, System V uses the original one-handed clock algorithm, instead of the two-handed one. Furthermore, instead of putting an unused page on the free list on the second pass, a page is only put there if it is unused for n consecutive passes. While this decision does not free pages as quickly as the Berkeley algorithm, it greatly increases the chance that a page once freed will not be needed again quickly.

Second, instead of a single variable *lotsfree*, System V has two variables, *min* and *max*. Whenever the number of free page frames falls below *min*, the page daemon is started to free up more pages. The daemon continues to run until there are *max* free page frames. This approach eliminates a potential instability in 4BSD. Consider a situation in which the number of free page frames is one less than *lotsfree*, so the page daemon runs to free one page and bring it up to *lotsfree*. Then another page fault occurs, using up one page frame, and reducing the number of available frames below *lotsfree* again, so the daemon has to run again. By setting *max* substantially above *min*, whenever the page daemon runs, it builds up a sufficient inventory that it does not have to run again for a substantial time.

7.5.3. Implementation of the UNIX File System

In this section we will describe the implementation of the traditional UNIX file system. Afterwards, we will discuss the Berkeley improvements. All disks that contain UNIX file systems have the layout illustrated in Fig. 7-18. Block 0 is not used by UNIX and often contains code to boot the computer. Block 1 is the **superblock**. It contains critical information about the layout of the file system, including the number of i-nodes, the number of disk blocks, and the start of the list of free disk blocks (typically a few hundred entries). Destruction of the superblock will render the file system unreadable.

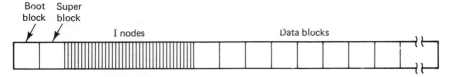

Fig. 7-18. Disk layout in traditional UNIX systems.

Following the superblock are the **i-nodes** (short for index-nodes, but never called that). They are numbered from 1 up to some maximum. Each i-node is 64 bytes long and describes exactly one file. An i-node contains accounting information (owner, protection bits, etc.) as well as enough information to locate all the disk blocks that hold the file's data.

Following the i-nodes are the data blocks. All the files and directories are stored here. If a file or directory consists of more than one block, the blocks need not be contiguous on the disk. In fact, the blocks of a large file are likely to be spread all over the disk. It is this scatter that the Berkeley improvements were designed to reduce.

A directory in the traditional file system consists of an unsorted collection of 16-byte entries. Each entry contains a file name (up to 14 arbitrary characters), and the number of the file's i-node. To open a file in the working directory, the system just reads the directory, comparing the name to be looked up to each entry until it either finds the name or concludes that it is not present. If the file is present, the system extracts the i-node number, and uses this as an index into the i-node table (on disk) to locate the corresponding i-node and bring it into memory. The i-node is put in the **i-node table**, a kernel data structure that holds all the i-nodes for currently open files and directories.

Looking up an absolute path name such as /usr/ast/file is slightly more complicated. First, the system locates the root directory, which always uses i-node 2 (i-node 1 is reserved for bad block handling). Then it looks up the string "usr" in the root directory, to get the i-node number of the /usr directory. This i-node is then fetched, and the disk blocks are extracted from it, so the /usr directory can be read and searched for the string "ast". Once this entry is found, the i-node number for the /usr/ast directory can be taken from it. Armed with the i-node number of the /usr/ast directory, this i-node can be read and the directory blocks located. Finally, "file" is looked up and its i-node number found. Thus the use of a relative path name is not only more convenient for the user, but it also saves a substantial amount of work for the system as well.

Let us now see how the system reads a file. Remember, a typical call to the library procedure for invoking the READ system call looks like this:

```
count = read(fd, buffer, nbytes);
```

When the kernel gets control, all it has to start with are these three parameters, and the information in the caller's user structure. One of the items in the user structure is the file descriptor table. It is indexed by a file descriptor and contains one entry for each open file (up to the maximum number, usually about 20).

The idea is to start with this file descriptor and end up with the corresponding i-node. Let us consider one possible design: just put a pointer to the i-node in the file descriptor table. Although simple, unfortunately, this method does not work. The problem is as follows. Associated with every file descriptor is a file position that tells at which byte the next read (or write) will start. Where should it go? One possibility is to put it in the i-node table. However, this approach fails if two or more unrelated processes happen to open the same file at the same time because each one has its own file position.

A second possibility is to put the file position in the file descriptor table. In that way, every process that opens a file gets its own private file position. Unfortunately, this scheme fails too, but the reasoning is more subtle and has to do with the nature of file sharing in UNIX. Consider a shell script, *s*, consisting of two commands, *p1* and *p2* to be run in order. If the shell script is called by the command line

```
s >x
```

it is expected that *p1* will write its output to *x*, and then *p2* will write its output to *x* also, starting at the place where *p1* stopped.

When the shell forks off *p1*, *x* is initially empty, so *p1* just starts writing at file position 0. However, when *p1* finishes, some mechanism is needed to make sure that the initial file position that *p2* sees is not 0 (which it would be if the file position were kept in the file descriptor table), but the value *p1* ended with.

The way this is achieved is shown in Fig. 7-19. The trick is to introduce a new table, the **open file description** table between the file descriptor table and the i-node table, and put the file position (and read/write bit) there. In this figure, the parent is the shell and the child is first *p1* and later *p2*. When the shell forks off *p1*, its user structure (including the file descriptor table) is an exact copy of the shell's, so both of them point to the same open file description table entry. When *p1* finishes, the shell's file descriptor is still pointing to the open file description containing *p1*'s file position. When the shell now forks off *p2*, the new child automatically inherits the file position, without either it or the shell even having to know what that position is.

However, if an unrelated process opens the file, it gets its own open file description entry, with its own file position, which is precisely what is needed. Thus the whole point of the open file description table is to allow a parent and child to share a file position, but to provide unrelated processes with their own values.

Getting back to the problem of doing the READ, we have now shown how the file position and i-node are located. The i-node contains the disk addresses of the first 10 blocks of the file. If the file position falls in the first 10 blocks, the block is read and the data are copied to the user. For files longer than 10 blocks, a field in the i-node contains the disk address of a **single indirect block**, as shown in Fig. 7-19. This block contains the disk addresses of more disk blocks. For example, if a block is 1K and disk address is 4 bytes, the single indirect block can hold 256 disk addresses. Thus this scheme works for files of up to 266K in total.

Beyond that, a **double indirect block** is used. It contains the addresses of 256 single indirect blocks, each of which holds the addresses of 256 data blocks. If even this is not enough, the i-node has space for a triple indirect block.

The Berkeley Fast File System

The description above explains how the classical UNIX file system works. Let us now take a look at the improvements Berkeley made to it. First, directories have been reorganized. Instead of limiting file names to 14 characters, the limit is now 255 characters. Of course, changing the structure of all the directories meant that programs that naively read directories expecting a sequence of 16-byte entries no

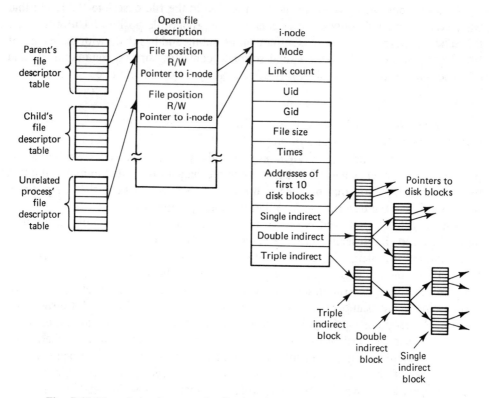

Fig. 7-19. The relation between the file descriptor table, the open file description table, and the i-node table.

longer worked. To provide portability across the two kinds of directories, POSIX provided system calls OPENDIR, READDIR, and CLOSEDIR, to allow programs to read directories without having to know their internal structure.

The second change is the division of the disk up into **cylinder groups**, each with its own superblock, i-nodes, and data blocks. The idea behind this change is to keep the i-node and data blocks of a file close together, to avoid long seeks. Whenever possible, blocks are allocated in the cylinder group containing the i-node.

The third change is the introduction of two block sizes instead of just one. For storing large files, it is more efficient to have a small number of large blocks rather than many small ones. On the other hand, many UNIX files are small, so having only 4K blocks would be wasteful of disk space. Having two sizes allows efficient transfers for large files and space efficiency for small ones. The price paid is considerable extra complexity in the code.

7.5.4. Implementation of Input/Output in UNIX

I/O in UNIX is implemented by a collection of device drivers, usually one driver per device. These drivers are linked with the operating system when the kernel is generated and cannot be added or deleted afterwards. Their function is to isolate the rest of the system from the idiosyncracies of the hardware. By providing standard interfaces between the drivers and the rest of the operating system, most of the I/O system can be put into the machine-independent part of the kernel.

The I/O system is split into two major components: the handling of block special files and the handling of character special files. We will now look at each of these components in turn.

The goal of that part of the system that does I/O on block special files (i.e., disks) is to minimize the number of actual transfers that must be done. To accomplish this goal, UNIX systems have a **buffer cache** between the disk drivers and the file system, as illustrated in Fig. 7-20. The buffer cache is a table in the kernel for holding dozens, or maybe even hundreds, of the most recently used blocks. When a block is needed from a disk for any purpose (i-node, directory, or data), a check is first made to see if it is in the buffer cache. If so, it is taken from there and a disk access is avoided.

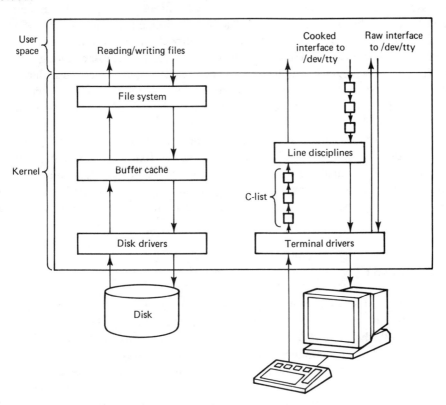

Fig. 7-20. The UNIX I/O system.

If the block is not in the buffer cache, it is read from the disk into the buffer cache and from there, copied to where it is needed. Since the buffer cache has room for only a fixed number of blocks, some algorithm is needed to manage it. Usually the blocks in the cache are linked together in a linked list. Whenever a block is accessed, it is moved to the head of the list. When a block must be removed from the cache to make room for a new block, the one at the rear of the chain is selected, since it is the least recently used block.

The buffer cache works for writes as well as for reads. When a program writes a block, it goes to the cache, not to the disk. Only when the cache fills up and the buffer must be reclaimed is the block forced out onto the disk. To avoid having blocks stay too long in the cache before being written to the disk, all the dirty blocks are written to the disk every 30 seconds.

Since character special files deal with character streams and do not move blocks of information between memory and disk, they do not use the buffer cache. Instead, they use data structures called **C-lists**, shown as small boxes in Fig. 7-20. Each one is a block of up to 64 characters, plus a count and a pointer to the next block. As characters arrive from terminals and other character devices, they are buffered in a chain of these blocks.

When a user process reads from */dev/tty* (e.g., standard input), the characters are not passed directly from the C-list to the process. Instead, they pass through a piece of kernel code called a **line discipline**. The line discipline acts like a filter, taking the raw character stream from the terminal driver, processing it, and producing what is called a **cooked character stream**. In the cooked stream, local line editing has been done (i.e., erased characters and lines have been removed), carriage returns have been mapped onto line feeds, and other special processing completed. The cooked stream is passed to the process. However, if the process wants to interact on every character, it can put the line in raw mode, in which case the line discipline will be bypassed.

Output works in a similar way, expanding tabs to spaces, converting line feeds to carriage returns + line feeds, adding filler characters following carriage returns on slow mechanical terminals, and so on. Like input, output can go through the line discipline (cooked mode) or bypass it (raw mode). Raw mode is especially useful when sending binary data to other computers over a serial line. Here, no conversions are desired.

7.6. SUMMARY

UNIX began life as a minicomputer timesharing system, but is now used on machines ranging from notebook computers to supercomputers. Three interfaces to it exist: the shell, the system call library, and the system calls themselves. The shell allows users to type commands for execution. These may be simple commands, pipelines, or more complex structures. Input and output may be redirected.

The key concepts in UNIX include the process, the memory model, the file system, and I/O. Processes may fork off subprocesses, leading to a tree of processes. The memory model consists of a text, data, and stack segment for each process. The file system supports regular files, directories, and two kinds of special files. Directories may contain subdirectories, leading to a hierarchical file system. I/O is done using character and block special files, which are integrated into the file system. Access to UNIX services is achieved via system calls.

Process management in UNIX uses two key data structures, the process table and the user structure. The former is always in memory, but the latter can be swapped or paged out. Process creation is done by duplicating the process table entry, and then the memory image. Scheduling is done using a priority-based algorithm that favors interactive users.

Memory management used to be done by swapping, but is now done by paging in most UNIX systems. The core map keeps track of the state of each page, and the page daemon uses a clock algorithm to keep enough free pages around.

The file system uses three main tables: the file descriptor table, the open file description table, and the i-node table. Each open file has entries in all three of them.

Block device I/O uses a buffer cache to reduce the number of disk accesses. An LRU algorithm is used to manage the cache. Character I/O can be done in raw or cooked mode, the latter of which is implemented by a line discipline.

PROBLEMS

1. What does the following UNIX pipeline do?

```
grep nd xyz | wc -l
```

2. Write a UNIX pipeline that prints the eighth line of file *z* on standard output.

3. Why does UNIX distinguish between standout output and standard error, when both default to the terminal?

4. If a UNIX file has protection mode 755 (octal), what can the owner, the owner's group, and everyone else do to the file?

5. When the UNIX shell starts up a process, it puts copies of its environment variables, such as *HOME*, on the process' stack, so the process can find out what its home directory is. If this process should later fork, will the child automatically get these variables too?

6. Why do you think the designers of UNIX made it impossible for a process to send a signal to a another process that is not in its process group?

7. To what hardware concept is a signal closely related? Give two examples of how signals are used.

8. Give two examples of the advantages of relative path names over absolute ones.

9. A certain editor has 100K of program text, 30K of initialized data, and 50K of BSS. The initial stack is 10K. Suppose three copies of this editor are started simultaneously. How much physical memory is needed (a) if shared text is used, and (b) if it is not?

10. The following locking calls are made by a collection of processes. For each call, tell what happens. If a process fails to get a lock, it blocks.

   (a) *A* wants a shared lock on bytes 0 through 10.
   (b) *B* wants an exclusive lock on bytes 20 through 30.
   (c) *C* wants a shared lock on bytes 8 through 40.
   (d) *A* wants a shared lock on bytes 25 through 35.
   (e) *B* wants an exclusive lock on byte 8.

11. Consider the locked file of Fig. 7-11(c). Suppose a process tries to lock bytes 10 and 11 and blocks. Then, before *C* releases its lock, yet another process tries to lock bytes 10 and 11, and also blocks. What kind of problems are introduced into the semantics by this situation. Propose and defend two solutions.

12. Suppose an LSEEK system call seeks to a negative offset in a file. Given two possible ways of dealing with it.

13. If a UNIX process runs for 1 sec without competition from other processes, how long does it take for its CPU usage counter to get back down to 0?

14. About how long does it take to fork off a child process under the following conditions: text size = 100K bytes, data size = 20K bytes, stack size = 10K bytes, process table size = 1K, user structure = 5K. The kernel trap and return takes 1 msec, and the machine can copy one 32-bit word every 500 nsec. Text segments are shared.

15. As megabyte programs became more common, the time spent executing the FORK system call grew proportionally. Worse yet, nearly all of this time was wasted, since most programs call EXEC shortly after forking. To improve performance, Berkeley invented a new system call, VFORK, in which the child shares the parent's address space, instead of getting its own copy of it. Describe a situation in which a poorly-behaved child can do something that makes the semantics of VFORK fundamentally different from those of FORK.

16. In 4BSD, each core map entry contains an index for the next entry on the free list, which is used when the current entry is on the free list. This field is 16 bits. Pages are 1K. Do these sizes have any implications for the total amount of memory 4BSD can support? Explain your answer.

17. In 4BSD, the data and stack segments are paged and swapped to a scratch copy kept on a special paging disk, but the text segment uses the executable binary file instead. Why?

18. As we have seen, absolute path names are looked up starting at the root directory and relative path names are looked up starting at the working directory. Suggest an efficient way to implement both kinds of searches.

19. When the file */usr/ast/work/f* is opened, several disk accesses are needed to read i-node and directory blocks. Calculate the number of disk accesses required under the assumption that the i-node for the root directory is always in memory, and all directories are one block long.

20. A UNIX i-node has 10 disk addresses for data blocks. as well as the addresses of single, double, and triple indirect blocks. If each of these holds 256 disk addresses, what is the size of the largest file that can be handled, assuming that a disk block is 1K?

21. Why does LRU work for managing the buffer cache, whereas it rarely works for keeping track of pages in a virtual memory system?

8

CASE STUDY 2: MS–DOS

For our second example of a single-processor operating system, we will now look at MS-DOS. Unlike UNIX, which runs on a wide variety of different machines, MS-DOS runs only on the Intel 8088 and its successors, the 286, 386, and 486. Nevertheless, with over 50 million of these in existence, MS-DOS is, without a doubt, the most widely used operating system of all time, and as such, is certainly worth studying.

The structure of this chapter closely parallels that of the previous one on UNIX. We will start with the history of MS-DOS and then give an overview of its use. After that we will look at the fundamental concepts underlying MS-DOS, examine some of its system calls, and finally say a few words about its implementation.

8.1. History of MS-DOS

The first personal computer was the Altair, produced in 1975 by a company called MITS of Albuquerque, New Mexico. It was powered by the 8-bit Intel 8080 CPU and had 256 bytes of memory. It did not have a keyboard, screen, tape, or disk, but for 400 dollars it was a true bargain and was popular with people who had become bored building radios and televisions. A young man named Bill Gates wrote a version of BASIC for the Altair that enjoyed a modest following among early microcomputer users. This program eventually made Gates a billionaire.

Within a few years, many companies started to make personal computers based on the 8080 chip. Nearly all of these ran an operating system called **CP/M** produced by Digital Research, a small California company. All of the personal computers (then called **microcomputers**) made from 1975 to about 1980 were essentially toys and were bought and used primarily by computer hobbyists.

8.1.1. The IBM PC

Around 1980, IBM, which then dominated the computer industry, decided that personal computers were an area it should be in. It knew that developing its own personal computer from scratch would take far too long, so it did something quite unusual for the normally bureaucratic and cautious IBM. It told one of its managers, Philip Estridge, to go to Boca Raton, Florida, 2000 km away from the prying eyes at Corporate Headquarters in Westchester County, New York, gave him a large bag of money, and told him not to come back until he had a personal computer.

Estridge soon decided that the only way he could produce a personal computer quickly was to use standard, off-the-shelf components, rather than designing his own as IBM had always done in the past. By this time, Intel had produced two successors to the 8080, the 16-bit 8086, and a version of the 8086 with an 8-bit bus, the 8088. Estridge chose the 8088 because its support chips were substantially cheaper, and the selling price of the machine was perceived as a major issue.

Although IBM had little interest in building its own chips for its personal computer, it had even less interest in writing the software. IBM knew that BASIC was popular among microcomputer users, so it went to Bill Gates, who had now formed a company called Microsoft, to license his BASIC interpreter for use on the IBM PC. It also asked Gates if he happened to have an operating system for them.

At that time, Microsoft was engaged in selling UNIX under license from AT&T Bell Labs, but UNIX, which originated in the minicomputer world, needed 100K just for the operating system alone and also needed a hard disk. The IBM machine had a total of 64K and no hard disk. Gates suggested that IBM use Digital Research's CP/M-86 operating system. IBM talked to Digital Research about this, but CP/M-86 was way behind schedule, and IBM could not wait.

Then IBM went back to Microsoft and asked them if they could write an operating system like CP/M. Gates knew there was no time for that, but he also knew of a nearby company, Seattle Computer Products, that had written a CP/M-like operating system called 86-DOS, primarily to test the memory boards it was manufacturing and selling. Microsoft then bought 86-DOS and in April 1981 hired its author, Tim Paterson, to fix it up a little. They renamed it MS-DOS (Micro Soft - Disk Operating System) and delivered it to IBM on schedule. When the IBM PC was announced in August 1981, MS-DOS was there with it.

In the eyes of IBM and many others, MS-DOS's chief virtue was that it could run most of the software then running on the 8080 under CP/M (the 8088 was backward compatible with the 8080 source code and could run most of its programs with only small changes). If anyone had realized that within 10 years this tiny system that was picked up almost by accident was going to be controlling 50 million computers, considerably more thought might have gone into it.

In all fairness, however, neither IBM nor anyone else had any idea of how successful the IBM PC would be. IBM originally thought it would be used mostly for playing games at home. The 4.77 MHz clock rate, for example, was chosen to be compatible with the colorburst frequency on U.S. color television sets, so people could use their home TVs instead of having to buy proper monitors. The PC also came equipped with hardware for controlling audio cassette tapes (as a storage medium), and joysticks (for playing games). Neither of these saw much use, at least in part because there was no software for them.

Probably the biggest thing IBM did right was to make the PC an open system. The complete design, right down to the ROM listings and electrical schematic diagrams, was described in great detail in a book available from all PC dealers. This meant that third party hardware and software vendors could make new hardware and software products to add onto the PC, which thousands of them did.

In fact, with the circuit diagrams available and the machine consisting entirely of off-the-shelf components one could buy in any electronics store, some companies began building and selling copies of the PC, sometimes referred to as **clones**, and selling them in direct competition to IBM itself. It was this enormous burst of energy and creativity that led to the success of the PC and along with it, the success of MS-DOS.

A few words about the PC's hardware are important. Although the 8088 has a 1 megabyte address space, IBM decided to allocate the first 640K of this to RAM, and the rest to ROMs, video boards, and other things. As a consequence, MS-DOS was set up to support programs whose maximum size was 640K. At first this was not a problem, since the machine had only 64K of RAM in it, but when later models came out with up to 16 megabytes, the inability to run programs larger than 640K became something of an embarrassment.

Another important feature of the IBM PC is the fact that it has no hardware protection at all. Programs were free to bypass the operating system and access the hardware directly, usually to obtain better performance. This style of programming has led to a vast number of poorly-written, nonportable programs that have frequently come back to haunt their creators later.

8.1.2. MS-DOS Version 1.0

The version of MS-DOS released along with the IBM PC in August 1981 was Version 1.0. It occupied 12K of the machine's 64K of memory, and was more-or-less compatible with CP/M. The source consisted of 4000 lines of assembly code. The only disk it supported was the 160K single-side 5¼ inch diskette. The 160K 5¼ inch diskette was something of a technological breakthrough, since most other microcomputers at the time were using 8-inch diskettes. In fact, the 5¼ inch diskettes were often called "mini-diskettes," to contrast them with the "normal" 8-inch diskettes.

The operating system consisted of three programs: *ibmbio.com*, the disk and character I/O system; *ibmdos.com*, the disk and file manager; and *command.com*, the command processor, a primitive shell. Unlike UNIX, which has always been totally self contained, MS-DOS has always made use of a hardware ROM built into the IBM PC called the **BIOS** (**Basic Input Output System**). The BIOS contains device drivers for the standard devices, so MS-DOS could just call them to do I/O. Whereas UNIX contains drivers for terminal I/O, disk I/O, etc., MS-DOS just used BIOS procedures to do this work. Since the BIOS was located near the top of the 8088's 1M address space in a ROM, it did not occupy any RAM, surely a plus on a machine with only 64K of it.

MS-DOS 1.0 supported only a single directory (like CP/M). When you logged in and typed *dir* to list the contents of the working directory, you saw all the files on the system, as there were no subdirectories at this point. In contrast, even the first version of UNIX had a full hierarchical file system.

Although MS-DOS Version 1.0 was compatible with CP/M, it also had some significant improvements over CP/M. It kept track of more information about each file (such as its exact size), had a superior disk allocation algorithm, was much faster, and had the ability to handle primitive shell scripts, called **batch files**.

Version 1.1 was released by Microsoft in October 1982 and supported 320K diskettes. Like many of the early versions, it was apparently released to provide support for yet another disk format, in this case the double-sided 320K diskette. Version 1.1 also fixed some bugs, but otherwise was similar to V1.0. By convention, releases such as 1.1, in which the number to the left of the decimal point is the same as the previous version represent relatively minor changes from the previous release. In contrast, 2.0 was largely a new system.

8.1.3. MS-DOS Version 2.0

In March 1983, IBM introduced the PC/XT, its first personal computer with a hard disk. It came with a new version of MS-DOS, Version 2.0. MS-DOS 2.0 was a major break with the past. Although it still supported the CP/M system calls, Microsoft essentially rewrote it from scratch and incorporated many ideas from their UNIX system in it. At this point, Microsoft was a major UNIX vendor, and clearly wanted to see MS-DOS and UNIX converge. The MS-DOS file system, for example, was taken largely from UNIX, with minor changes (e.g., the use of \ instead of / as the component separator). Also, since MS-DOS was a single-user system, not a timesharing system, none of UNIX' protection features were included. Nevertheless, the OPEN, READ, WRITE, and CLOSE system calls were now present in essentially the same form as in UNIX, using file descriptors (not present in Version 1.0). The shell was also improved, and could handle redirection of standard input and output, and supported pipelines and filters. All in all, it was a far cry from CP/M.

MS-DOS 2.0 also incorporated support for yet another diskette format, 360K, as well as user-installable device drivers, print spooling, system configuration, memory management, and customized shells.

In the process of adding all these features from UNIX, MS-DOS had grown to 20,000 lines of assembly language. It also killed off CP/M-86, which had finally appeared, and established MS-DOS as the dominant operating system for the PC. Because the hard disk made it possible to run reasonably large applications, the PC/XT quickly moved the entire focus of the personal computer from home use to business use. Small, medium, and large companies began to acquire PCs.

At this point MS-DOS was being maintained by only four people at Microsoft. With the emergence of a large worldwide demand for the PC/XT for business applications, Microsoft hired more programmers and produced Version 2.05, which supported the time, date, currency, and decimal symbols for many countries. It even supported 16-bit Japanese Kanji (Chinese characters) to some extent. IBM was not interested. What IBM was interested in was the PC jr, which came with MS-DOS 2.1 and was a total fiasco. Microsoft then combined 2.05 and 2.1 and sold millions of them under the name MS-DOS 2.11.

8.1.4. MS-DOS Version 3.0

In August 1984 IBM came out with the PC/AT, its first personal computer based on the 286 chip. The PC/AT supported memory up to 16 megabytes (versus 640K on the PC and PC/XT), had user and kernel modes, a ring-based protection mode similar to what MULTICS had, and the ability to run multiple programs at once. The version of MS-DOS shipped with the PC/AT was 3.0, which supported none of these. Instead, it ran the PC/AT in a mode that simulates an 8088, only faster. Subsequent versions of MS-DOS made some use of the extended memory (i.e., the memory above 1M).

Since the PC/AT came with a 1.2M diskette drive, battery backup clock, and configuration information in CMOS, support for these devices were added. Furthermore, hard disks larger than 10M were now supported, and RAM disks, in which a portion of memory was used as a fast disk, were introduced. In addition, the command processor (shell) was removed from the operating system and made into a separate program, so that users could replace it with their own version. By now the code was 40,000 lines and 30 people were working on it.

In November 1984 3.0 was replaced with 3.1, which provided the first support for networking. Unfortunately, only well-behaved programs worked with networking, and almost no programs were well behaved.

The next release was 3.2. It supported 3½ inch diskettes and the IBM token ring, but was notoriously full of bugs. Few users switched to it, and many of those who did went back to 3.1 later in disgust.

In 1987, IBM introduced the successor to the PC line, the PS/2 family. These came with 720K 3½ inch diskettes on the smaller versions and 1.44M 3½ inch diskettes on the larger ones. MS-DOS 3.3, which came with the PS/2, supported these new formats. It also had more international support and support for serial lines running at 19,200 bits/sec. Like all previous versions, this one too came with a few more utility programs, although still far fewer than UNIX.

Along with the PS/2 and MS-DOS 3.3 , IBM and Microsoft released a completely new operating system, called OS/2. In the vision of these companies, OS/2 was going to replace MS-DOS. It never happened. OS/2 was delivered late and incomplete. While it had many obvious advantages over MS-DOS, such as actually using all the memory, running in protected mode, and supporting multiprogramming in an elegant way, the users were not interested. In 1991, Microsoft announced they were dropping OS/2 altogether, which so angered IBM, that they dropped Microsoft and signed a contract with Apple Computer to provide their future software.

8.1.5. MS-DOS Version 4.0

When the great rush to OS/2 never happened, IBM surprised the industry by bringing out a new version of MS-DOS, Version 4.0, which Microsoft later reverse-engineered for distribution to PC clone makers. This event was widely perceived to be IBM's realization that MS-DOS was not going to disappear after all. Instead of killing off MS-DOS, they were enhancing it.

One of the big improvements in this release was support for disks larger than 32M, something whose absence in 3.3 was becoming a serious problem. MS-DOS 4.0 supports disks up to 2 gigabytes. Although programs were still restricted to 640K, up to 16M of extended memory could be used for RAM disk, to increase the performance of the file system. Another first with 4.0 was the DOS shell, a menu-driven shell rather than the previous keyboard-oriented ones. All in all, few people were impressed and like MS-DOS 3.2, this version was not widely used.

8.1.6. MS-DOS Version 5.0

MS-DOS 5.0 was a major new release announced in April 1991 (Microsoft, 1991a). It was the first version that made any serious use of the extended memory of which many 286 and 386 owners had several megabytes. Although it still had the restriction that programs could not exceed 640K, at least it had the ability to locate most of MS-DOS itself in extended memory, so about 600K of the lower 640K was now available for user programs. In addition, user-written device drivers could also be put into extended memory. MS-DOS 5.0 also had the ability to use the memory between 640K and 1M on 386 machines for device drivers and certain utilities, thus freeing up more of the lower 640K.

MS-DOS 5.0 also provided a new shell, which had the ability to have multiple programs in memory at once, with the user switching between them using the CTRL-ESC keys. Command line editing was also possible now. 5.0 also came with an extensive HELP facility, to aid new users. In addition, many commands and utility programs were upgraded. For example, the dreadful line editor, *edlin*, was finally replaced by a screen editor.

Finally, for the first time, MS-DOS 5.0 was sold in stores. (Previous versions were only sold to computer vendors, who delivered them with their machines.) This was seen as a serious commitment to end users on Microsoft's part. Another good sign was the extensive testing this release underwent before being shipped to customers, ensuring a higher quality product than some of its predecessors. In this chapter, we will discuss MS-DOS 5.0.

Figure 8-1 gives a summary of the various versions of MS-DOS, their dates of introduction, and some of their key features.

What does the future of MS-DOS hold? Technically it is completely obsolete. Programming it is a nightmare. To the user, it is idiosyncratic and unfriendly. IBM and Microsoft realized this years ago, and spent millions of dollars producing a modern, powerful, and easy-to-use replacement, OS/2, only to discover that the users were not interested. (They must have felt as if they were trying to sell the metric

Version	Date	Diskette	Comments
1.0	Aug. 1981	160K	CP/M compatible; supported only 1 directory
1.1	Oct. 1982	320K	Fixed some bugs in 1.0
2.0	Mar. 1983	360K	Supported HD; UNIX-like rather than CP/M-like
2.1	Nov. 1983		Came with the ill-fated PC jr.
2.11	Mar. 1984		Support for international users
3.0	Aug. 1984	1.2M	Supported the PC/AT
3.1	Nov. 1984		First release that supported networking
3.2	Jan. 1986	720K	3.5 inch disks and IBM token ring supported
3.3	Apr. 1987	1.44M	Came with the PS/2
4.0	Jul. 1988		Support for disks larger than 32M; DOS shell
5.0	Apr. 1991	2.88M	Major cleanup; better use of extended memory

Fig. 8-1. Summary of MS-DOS versions.

system as the successor to the inch-foot-yard-rod-furlong-mile system—arguments as to why the new one was better got the reply: "Yes, but we are used to the old one.")

When it became clear that OS/2 was going nowhere, Microsoft took a different tack, and developed *Windows* as a mouse-driven graphical interface on top of MS-DOS. The idea was, if we cannot get rid of it, at least we can hide it. While this is certainly true for the end user, for anyone trying to do programming on MS-DOS it remains the same old system, and is likely to remain so for years to come.

On the other hand, what MS-DOS has going for it is an immense collection of high-quality packaged software. Computer stores, book stores, and department stores frequently have hundreds or even thousands of programs, on every imaginable subject. UNIX has nothing like this at all. While the existence of this software base reflects neither positively nor negatively on the operating system itself, it certainly explains the popularity of MS-DOS and its resistance to change.

8.2. OVERVIEW OF MS-DOS

In this section we will give a brief overview of MS-DOS, mostly concerned with how it looks to the user at the terminal. In the following ones, we will look at how it appears to the programmer (system calls, etc.). Throughout, we will constantly compare and contrast it to UNIX, to gain more insight into both systems.

8.2.1. Using MS-DOS

Using MS-DOS can be best compared to using a stripped down early version of UNIX. There is a shell, called *command.com*, a file system, system calls, utility programs, and other features that are often similar to their UNIX counterparts, but more primitive. To the user of an integrated Lisp or Smalltalk system, MS-DOS and UNIX are essentially the same. No doubt to a Chinese person, English and Frisian are pretty much the same, too. Nevertheless, in both cases, to the expert, differences are discernable.

To use MS-DOS you just turn on the computer. A few seconds later, the shell prompt appears. There is no login procedure and no password because MS-DOS is really meant for a *personal* computer. The underlying assumption is that the machine is used by only one person. For the same reason, files and directories do not have owners, and there are no protection bits. There is also no concept of a superuser. The regular user can do everything.

To run a program, you type its name and arguments to the shell. The shell then forks off a child, passes the arguments to the child, and keeps quiet until the child has finished executing and exits. It is not possible to put an & at the end of the command line to start the command off in the background.

Some of the UNIX shell features are also present in MS-DOS, but others are not. The wildcard characters * and ? are present, and match all strings and one character, respectively, pretty much as in UNIX. Thus

```
copy *.c src
```

means copy all files in the current directory ending in *.c* to the *src* directory, and

```
del ???
```

means delete (remove) from the current directory all files whose name is precisely three characters.

Command.com, does not distinguish between upper and lower case. Thus typing

```
COPY A B
```

has exactly the same effect as typing

```
copy a b
```

Most people type commands in lower case, but when MS-DOS displays file names, it does so in upper case. We will generally use lower case in this book (and *italics* in running text), except where tradition strongly argues against it.

Redirection of standard input and output and filters work the same way as in UNIX and even use the same notation. Pipelines are also allowed, but they are implemented differently (using temporary files), which introduces some subtle changes in their behavior. Other features taken from UNIX are shell variables, user-settable prompts, and shell scripts, called **batch files** in MS-DOS.

On the other hand, only one command per line is permitted, there are no background jobs, the use of "[a-z]" for a range is not allowed, and the quoting of strings is not recognized.

Commands in MS-DOS are divided into two categories: internal and external. The internal ones are executed by the shell itself; the external ones are genuine programs, typically in the *\dos* or *\bin* directory. UNIX makes this distinction too, but nearly all of the internal commands in UNIX would make little sense as external commands.

For example, making *cd* a separate program would start up a new process, change that process' working directory, and then return to the shell–with the shell having precisely the same working directory it had before the command. Other UNIX internal commands include *eval, exec, exit, export, read, readonly, set, shift, times, trap,* and *wait,* few of which could profitably be made into separate programs.

In contrast, in MS-DOS, many of the most commonly executed utilities are internal to the shell. In all, about 40 internal commands exist. Some of the most common ones are listed in Fig. 8-2, along with their UNIX equivalent.

MS-DOS command	UNIX equivalent	Description
copy	cp	Copy one or more files
date	date	Display or change the current date
del	rm	Remove one or more files
dir	ls	List files and directories
mkdir	mkdir	Create a new directory
rename	mv	Give a file a new name
rmdir	rmdir	Remove an empty directory
type	cat	Display a file

Fig. 8-2. Some of the MS-DOS commands built into the shell.

Building so many commands into the shell represents a tradeoff. On the one hand, not having to fetch them from a slow diskette makes them much faster. Since the original IBM PC did not have a hard disk, this was no doubt the reason they were included in the shell in the first place. On the other hand, all that code makes the shell larger. To avoid this problem getting out of hand, all the internal commands have been kept minimal. For example, there is no way to delete several unrelated files at once. The command

```
del tom dick harry
```

does not work, as *del* only takes one argument. It is legal to say

```
del *.obj
```

however, to remove all files ending with *.obj*.

A related problem is the interpretation of the wildcard characters in general. Suppose a user types

```
dir *.c
```

and is told that the only file ending in *.c* is *hypertext.c*. He now types

```
edit *.c
```

expecting to call the editor with *hypertext.c*. Much to his surprise, the editor complains that **.c* is not a legal file and exits. The problem is that wildcard expansion only works for internal commands, but not for external ones (except for those that explicitly do wildcard expansion themselves). In MS-DOS the command line is literally passed as typed to the program, whereas in UNIX, it is the result of expanding the command line that is passed to the program. The net result of all this is that users must remember which commands handle wildcard expansion and which ones do not. What matters is not who does the expansion, but the fact that it is done inconsistently.

On the other hand, having the command see the wildcards sometimes is an advantage. For example, an external command like

```
replace *.c *.old
```

could systematically replace all the extensions of the files ending in *.c* with *.old*. Achieving the same effect in UNIX is nearly impossible.

Although shell scripts are allowed in MS-DOS they are much weaker than their UNIX counterparts. There are no **case** or **while** statements, and the **if** and **for** statements are very limited. Most batch files look like short BASIC programs.

MS-DOS has working directories, but they differ from those in UNIX in an important way. In UNIX each process has its own working directory. If a user types

```
cd /usr/ast/src
```

and then starts up a process, that process inherits */usr/ast/src* as its working directory. If the process then changes its working directory to */usr/ast/mail* and then exits, the shell will still have */usr/ast/src* as its working directory, and the next process started will also be located there. In contrast, the same events in MS-DOS will leave the second process in the *mail* directory because MS-DOS only has one working directory (per disk). It is kept track of by a global kernel variable, and when it is changed, not only the current process, but all future ones are affected as well.

MS-DOS 5.0 comes with a program *doskey* that can be installed to catch and buffer all keystrokes. Its function is to make it possible to repeat commands, with or without editing. For example, when the F7 function key is hit, *doskey* displays a list of the most recent commands that have been typed in. One of these can be selected using the F9 key. The command can either be re-executed directly, or edited first and then re-executed. Many other options exist to examine and re-execute previous commands. Some versions of UNIX also have a similar feature.

8.2.2. MS-DOS Shell

Many users, especially beginners, find the MS-DOS command line interface cryptic at best and downright hostile at worst, probably even worse than UNIX, whose shell has rarely been accused of being friendly to novices. To make life easier for these people, MS-DOS now comes with an alternative, screen-oriented interface called *dosshell*. It lists files and directories in windows, and allows users to do a considerable amount of work by pointing with the mouse and clicking. While it is by no means a full-blown graphical user interface such as *Windows*, it is a step in that direction. Since it has come free with all versions of MS-DOS since 4.0, many users have it and use it. We will give a brief description here.

When *dosshell* is started up, either manually or automatically when the system is booted, it displays several windows on the screen. Various displays are possible. One of them is shown in Fig. 8-3. This one contains eight windows.

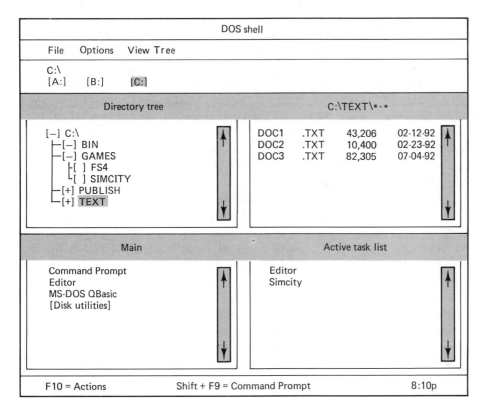

Fig. 8-3. A typical *dosshell* display.

The top window is the **title bar**, which identifies which program is running (useful because other shells exist, from third party vendors). Next comes the **menu bar**, which offers several choices. Clicking on *File* causes a menu to appear that allows users to move, copy, rename, and print files, create directories, and similar operations. Most of these use both the mouse and the keyboard. For example, to copy a file, the user first selects the file from one of the windows with the mouse, then clicks on *File*, to get the menu. He then clicks on *Copy* to get a **dialog box** that describes the *copy* command and asks the user to type in the name of the destination file.

The *Options* menu enables and disables various options, such as whether MS-DOS should ask for confirmation before doing anything. It also allows the user to select the screen colors and similar things.

The *View* menu controls which of the four types of windows are to be displayed, and how big each one should be. Unlike a true graphical user interface, only a limited number of choices are allowed.

The *Tree* menu controls choices for determining how subdirectories are displayed on the screen. These choices affect the [+] and [−] defaults.

Finally, the *Help* menu provides extensive on-line help about many aspects of *dosshell*.

The next section of the screen in Fig. 8-3 contains the **drive icons**. In MS-DOS, each disk drive is assigned a code. The first two diskettes are called A: and B:, and the (first) hard disk is called C:. By clicking on one of these, the user can select one of the diskettes or hard disks to work on. The string C:\ shown above the drives indicates that the working directory is the root directory of the hard disk.

Finally we come to the four most important windows. The *Directory Tree* window displays the root directory on the C drive. All the entries here are directories. An entry headed by [+] indicates that the directory in question, such as *PUBLISH* has subdirectories that are not shown. By clicking on the [+], the [+] becomes a [−] and the subdirectories are shown, as in the case of *GAMES*. In this way, the user can choose how much detail to show. Just [ ] with nothing inside means that the directory has no subdirectories. The **scroll bar** at the right of the window is needed if the information display exceeds the size of the window. By manipulating it, different portions of the directory list can be made visible.

When an entry in the *Directory Tree* is selected, its files appear in the *File List* window to the right of it. In Fig. 8-3, *TEXT* is selected, so its files are shown. These files can be selected copying, renaming, and so on, as discussed above. If the file is an executable program, double clicking on it causes it to be run. This is the usual way to execute a program from *dosshell*.

The *Main* window lists some commonly used programs. Clicking on these starts the corresponding program. The first three entries shown start the keyboard-oriented command line processor, the screen editor, and BASIC, respectively. The last produces another menu for formatting, dumping, and restoring disks.

The last window is in a way the most interesting. Originally, MS-DOS was strictly a single-process system. However, in version 5.0, it is possible to start up a command (by double clicking on its file name), and then suspend it by typing CTRL-ESC. The *dosshell* screen then reappears, with the name of the suspended program in the *Active Task List* window. At this point, the user is free to execute any commands he wishes, including starting up another program, which also may be suspended the same way. All the suspended programs are listed in this window. By double clicking on any of them, that program is restarted. While this is not the same thing as true multiprogramming (multiple independent processes that run in parallel), it is a weak second choice.

Finally, the one line window at the bottom of the screen in Fig. 8-3 is the *Status* window. It lists some shortcuts, displays messages, and shows the time of day.

8.2.3. Configuring MS-DOS

MS-DOS can be configured in an endless variety of ways. For example, users are free to install their own interrupt handlers, something that is unthinkable in UNIX. The reason for this disparity is clear, of course—UNIX is a timesharing system, with (potentially) multiple users. Allowing them to insert code into the kernel, in any way, is a monstrous security breach, as well as being an invitation to crashing the system. In a single-user system that has no security anyway, the danger is less.

The *doskey* program mentioned above is an example of how this feature can be used. By catching the keyboard interrupts, *doskey* can examine all typed characters before they are fed to the operating system. In this way, it can provide shortcuts and other tricks by passing old commands lines, with or without editing, to *command.com* as though they came directly from the terminal. In addition to recycling old commands, *doskey* allows users to define macros that give long key sequences short names.

Another form of user configurability is the ability to install custom device drivers. These drivers may handle nonstandard I/O devices, such as MIDI music synthesizers. They may also handle standard devices, such as extended memory, in nonstandard ways (e.g., simulating RAM disk). This ability provides a high degree of flexibility.

A completely different kind of configurability is the area of national language support. Microsoft has long been aware that not all its customers speak English and that they certainly do not agree about whether the Bastille was stormed on 07/14/1789 or 14/07/1789. Or maybe it was 14.07.1789. Or was it 1789-07-14? Traditional keyboard layouts also differ from country to country, even to the extent of Castillian Spanish being different from Mexican Spanish, not to mention the poor Swiss keyboard which has to handle four languages (French, German, Italian, and Romansch).

To handle different keyboards MS-DOS has the ability to map the key codes produced by the keyboard onto different characters, depending, for example, on whether the key to the right of the TAB is a "Q" (U.S.) or an "A" (France). It also has installable **code page files** that contain bit maps for the 255 displayable characters. Finally, a system call is provided to allow a program to ask for a structure containing information about the date and time formats, the currency symbol, the numeric separator (i.e., is 500 + 500 equal to 1,000 or 1.000?), and other items that vary from country to country. This information allows programs to accept input and produce output the way the user wants it, no matter what country he lives in.

Much of the configurability of MS-DOS is handled by a file called *config.sys* that is read when the system is booted. It can contain commands to install custom device drivers, set the national language support, determine where in memory to put the operating system, allocate memory for the buffer cache, specify the maximum number of open files, and select the shell. In addition, after this file is processed, a batch file called *autoexec.bat* is executed for additional initialization and configuration. The latter file has a counterpart in UNIX called */etc/rc*, but the former does not.

8.3. FUNDAMENTAL CONCEPTS IN MS-DOS

In UNIX, the concepts of processes and memory are cleanly separated and are machine-independent. A process has text, data, and stack segments, and a program counter that tells which instruction to execute next. Processes can run in parallel, without affecting one another. They can create child processes using the FORK system call, and can change the size of their data segment using the BRK system call. None of this depends in any way on the underlying machine architecture.

In MS-DOS, the model of a process and its memory usage are tightly intertwined and very closely related to the details (many would say, limitations) of the 8088 CPU architecture and IBM PC system architecture. Also, the programmer's model of processes and memory are inseparable from the implementation. For example, placing a process at addresses 400K and 800K are different, and the programmer must be aware of the exact properties of each one. In the next two sections we will examine process and memory models in MS-DOS and see how they are related to each other and the machine. In the two sections following that, we will look at the MS-DOS file system and I/O system.

8.3.1. Processes in MS-DOS

MS-DOS is not a multiprogramming system like UNIX, and cannot support multiple independent processes in the machine at once. On the other hand, it is not a monoprogramming system either. It is something in between. When the system is booted, one process, *command.com* (the keyboard-oriented shell) starts up and waits for input. When a line is typed, *command.com* starts up a new process and passes control to it, waiting until it is finished.

So far, this is no different from UNIX, where the shell also normally waits for a command to complete before typing the prompt. The difference is, in UNIX any user is free to write a shell that does not wait, but issues the prompt immediately. Furthermore, with the standard shell, if the user puts an & after the command, the shell does not wait. In any event, in UNIX after starting a child process, the parent does not *have* to wait for it. It can continue computing in parallel with the child.

In MS-DOS, the parent and child cannot run in parallel. When a process forks off a child, the parent is automatically suspended until the child exits. Nothing the parent can do can prevent this. Thus there may be arbitrarily many processes in memory at any moment, but only one of them is active. All the rest are suspended waiting for a child to finish. For this reason, even though MS-DOS allows multiple processes to exist at once, it is not a true multiprogramming system.

It is possible, however, to "cheat" and achieve a limited degree of multiprogramming by directly manipulating operating system data structures. This trick only works because MS-DOS runs in on machines that do not have or use memory protection. We will discuss this mechanism at the end of this section.

MS-DOS has two kinds of executable binary files, which result in two slightly different kinds of processes. A file with extension *.com*, as in *prog.com*, is a simple executable file. It has no header and only 1 segment. The executable file is an exact, byte-for-byte image of the executable code. The file is loaded into memory exactly as is and run. This model of a process comes directly from CP/M.

A process started from a *.com* file has one text + data + stack segment, of up to almost 64K. Even though the process cannot exceed 64K, it is nevertheless allocated all of available memory. The stack is at the top of the common 64K segment. If the process does not plan to fork off children, it can just run this way. If it does plan to create children, it must return the unused portion of memory to the operating system with a system call. If it neglects to free some memory, the attempt to fork off a child will fail due to lack of memory.

The other kind of executable file is the *.exe* file. A process created from one of these files can have a text segment, a data segment, a stack segment, and as many extra segments as it wants. Unlike *.com* files *.exe* files contain relocation information, so they can be relocated on-the-fly as they are being loaded. The operating system tells the difference between *.com* files and *exe* files by looking at the first two bytes, not by looking at the file name extension.

The first 256 bytes of every MS-DOS process is a special data block called the **PSP** (**Program Segment Prefix**). The concept comes directly from CP/M. The PSP is constructed by the operating system at the time the process is created. For *.com* files, it counts as part of the process' address space, and can be addressed using addresses 0 to 255. For this reason, all *.com* processes begin at address 256, not at address 0. In contrast, *.exe* files are relocated above the PSP, so their address 0 is the first byte above the PSP. This maneuver avoids wasting 256 bytes of address space.

The PSP contains the program's size, a pointer to the environment block, the address of the CTRL-C handler, the command string, a pointer to the parent's PSP, the file descriptor table, and other information. Some of this information is obsolete, and some is for MS-DOS's internal use only.

The environment block is a chunk of memory containing all the shell variables in the form *var=value*, with each string being terminated by a zero byte. With respect to the environment, MS-DOS is the same as UNIX, except that in UNIX, the environment pointer is not at a fixed address at the bottom of the process' address space, but is a parameter to *main*.

The address of the CTRL-C handler can be changed by the program. When the user types CTRL-C to interrupt the current process, this handler is invoked. This mechanism is analogous to a UNIX process catching SIGINT.

The command string is unparsed, except that the command name is skipped. If the user types

```
edit *.c
```

then the command string passed to *edit* is "*.c". It is up to the program itself to expand the asterisk, if it wants to. Some do and some do not, which is why wildcards can act differently with internal and external commands, as we saw earlier. In UNIX, children of the shell also get the command line, but the shell *always* expands wildcards first, so it is the fully expanded string that is passed to the child, not the string as typed.

A child in MS-DOS normally inherits its parent's open files and their file positions, unless the files were opened with a special mode to inhibit inheritance. If a child reads or writes an open file, when it exits, the parent sees the new file position, and can pass it to the next child. Any files that the child itself opened are automatically closed when it exits, and its memory is freed. A child can also return an exit status to its parent. All of these are exactly the same as the corresponding features of UNIX.

Unlike UNIX, MS-DOS does not support any form of swapping or paging. When a process forks off a child, there is a danger that there will not be enough memory for the child and further descendants. To reduce the chance of this happening, many processes that can have children are constructed in two parts. In Fig. 8-4(a) we see the machine just after it has been booted and *command.com* has started. In Fig. 8-4(b) we see what it looks like after a large editor has been started.

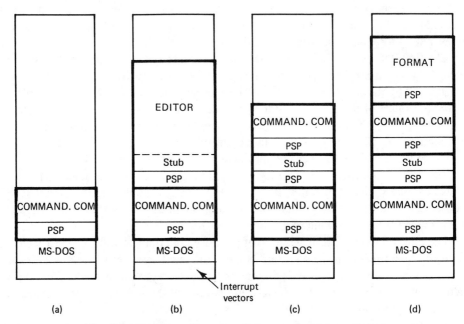

Fig. 8-4. MS-DOS may have several processes in memory at once.

Now suppose that this editor has the ability to let the user escape to *command.com* without losing the edit context. In UNIX, the editor would just fork off a shell and let the system swap the editor out. In MS-DOS this solution is impossible. Instead, the editor would probably have been constructed out of a small stub and the main editor. Before forking off *command.com*, the editor can copy its own core image to a file on disk, reduce its memory allocation to cover just the stub, and then do the fork, giving the situation of Fig. 8-4(c). If the user decides to format a diskette on which to save his file, we move to Fig. 8-4(d).

When the format program terminates, we come back to Fig. 8-4(c). When the user types

```
exit
```

to leave *command.com*, the editor stub gets control again, and reads in the rest of its process. Editing can now continue from where it left off.

Normally when a process exits, its memory is reclaimed and the process vanishes forever. However MS-DOS also has an alternative way for a process to exit that instructs the system *not* to take back its memory, but to otherwise treat it as exited.

This feature, which is obviously easy to implement, has spawned a small industry: the manufacture and sale of **TSR (Terminate and Stay Resident)** software.

At first glance, having a dead process around that cannot be activated does not sound terribly attractive. Remember, however, that processes in MS-DOS can install their own interrupt handlers. In particular, a process can install a new keyboard handler that is invoked on every keyboard interrupt (which on the PC occurs when any key is depressed or released, even CTRL, ALT or SHIFT). This handler can be located inside the unreachable TSR process.

The handler quickly examines the keystroke to see if it is the special key or combination of keys, called a **hot key**, that activates the TSR code. If not, the character is put into the operating system's character input queue, and the TSR program returns from the interrupt, back to the application program. If it is the hot key, the TSR program springs to life and does whatever it is supposed to do. This sequence of events is depicted in Fig. 8-5.

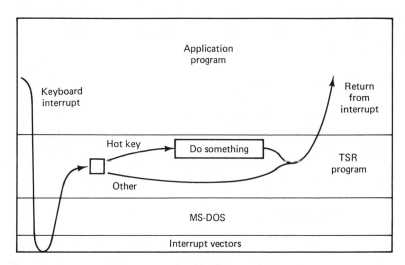

Fig. 8-5. Operation of a TSR program.

It is also possible to have an interrupt handler that searches for multiple hot keys, and dispatches to the appropriate procedure. For example, one could have a TSR program that pops up a calendar for ALT-F1, a calculator for ALT-F2, a memo pad for ALT-F3, a clock for ALT-F4, a phonebook for ALT-F5, a cardfile for ALT-F6, and so on.

Writing a TSR program is a bit tricky. Several problems must be solved. For one thing, the TSR program must copy the current screen image and save it away, so it can be restored when the TSR program finishes its little job. Far worse, however, it must do its work without calling MS-DOS, because MS-DOS might well have been active at the time of the interrupt. MS-DOS is not reentrant, meaning that it cannot handle a second call until it is finished with the first one. Among other things, the TSR program cannot use MS-DOS to read the keyboard for subsequent input and cannot use it to write on the screen. It certainly cannot use it to access files. It cannot even use the BIOS because it, too, might have been in the middle of a call at the time of the keystroke. Thus the TSR program must either do its own I/O, or engage in great deception to fool MS-DOS into thinking it is the currently running program by craftily manipulating MS-DOS' internal data structures. Writing a TSR program is not a suitable exercise for the Freshman Introduction to Computer Programming course. Nevertheless, a large number of TSR programs are on the market. The *doskey* program we discussed earlier in this chapter is a TSR program that comes standard with MS-DOS.

In actuality MS-DOS contains some hooks that make it possible for TSR programs to do system calls by tricking MS-DOS. None of these are documented in the official *Microsoft MS-DOS Programmer's Reference Manual* (Microsoft, 1991b), and while Microsoft does not deny that they exist, it strongly cautions programmers to avoid using undocumented system calls since it reserves the right to change or eliminate them in future versions. In contrast, official system calls are almost never removed, no matter how obsolete they are. Nevertheless, many, if not most, commercial TSR programs, of necessity, make heavy use of undocumented features of MS-DOS. Undocumented system calls and other "advanced" features of MS-DOS are described in Duncan (1988), Schulman (1991), and Schulman et al. (1990).

8.3.2. The MS-DOS Memory Model

MS-DOS has a fairly complicated memory model. The address space is divided into four separate regions, with different sizes and different properties. This complexity is entirely due to the peculiarities of the underlying machine architecture. Thus to understand the MS-DOS memory model, it is essential to understand the architecture of the IBM PC and its successors.

The 8088 Memory Architecture

The best place to start is the 8080, an 8-bit CPU that Intel sold in the early 1970s. This machine had several 8-bit registers, including an 8-bit accumulator and two 8-bit address registers, H and L, that could also be used as a 16-bit memory address registers. A program could load H and L separately, forming a 16-bit memory address in the combined HL register. Once HL was loaded, a program could issue an instruction to fetch the byte in memory whose address was given by HL and put that byte in the accumulator. Similarly, the accumulator could be stored in memory at the address held in HL. Thus although the 8080 had only 8-bit arithmetic, it had true 16-bit addressing and could address up to 64K bytes of memory, each byte being separately addressable.

The successors to the 8080, the 8086 and 8088, were designed to be better than the 8080, but also be backward compatible with their ancestor. In particular, it was deemed necessary that the 8088 be able to address up to 1 megabyte of memory, but it was deemed equally necessary to preserve the 16-bit addressing structure used by the 8080 so that old 8080 assembly language programs could be converted easily. Needless to say, these two constraints are in direct conflict.

The result was an awkward compromise. The 8088 has 12 registers, as shown in Fig. 8-6. The first block, AX, BX, CX, and DX, are 16-bit registers, each of which consists of a pair of 8-bit registers. Instructions exist for loading and storing both the 16-bit registers and the 8-bit registers.

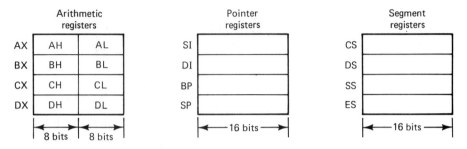

Fig. 8-6. The 8088 has 12 registers, all different.

The second block, SI, DI, BP, and SP, are all true 16-bit registers. SI and DI are index registers, BP is generally used to point to the base of the current stack frame (for accessing local variables), and SP is the stack pointer. All of these are for holding pointers.

The third block, CS, DS, SS, and ES, are called **segment registers**. They form the mechanism by which 1 megabyte memories and 16-bit addresses can co-exist in an uneasy truce. Each segment register holds the high-order 16 bits of a 20-bit address. The low-order 4 bits are always zero. Thus a value of 0 refers to address 0x00000, a value of 1 refers to address 0x00010 (16 decimal), a value of 2 refers to address 0x00020 (32 decimal), and so on (following the C convention, numbers beginning with 0x in this book are in hexadecimal).

In effect, the segment registers hold memory addresses measured not in bytes, but in units of 16 bytes, called **paragraphs**. For example, a segment register holding the value 3 points to paragraph 3, which is at address 0x00030 (48 decimal). A segment register holding the highest possible value 0xFFFF (65535 decimal) points to address 0xFFFF0, which is just 16 bytes less than the 1 megabyte mark. The highest byte in memory is 0xFFFFF, which is $2^{20} - 1$.

Each segment register has a separate use. CS is for the **code segment**, and is used to relocate the program counter. DS is for the **data segment**, and is used to relocate data addresses. SS is for the **stack segment**, and is used to relocate stack references. The stack segment is mainly of use to assembly-language programmers. Compilers often set SS to DS, and have a single segment for data and stack. Finally, ES is a spare segment register, for the **extra segment**. It is used for scratch purposes. Segments are 64K bytes long and can be located anywhere within the 1-megabyte (i.e., 20-bit) address space.

Figure 8-7(a) shows two segments within the 1M address space. The code segment occupies the region from 8K to 72K, and the data segment goes from 512K to 576K. The stack segment overlies the data segment, and the extra segment is not currently in use. To place the code segment at 8K, the CS register must hold the value 8192/16, which is 512. Similarly, DS is 524,288/16, which is 32768. Note that it is not possible to have the code segment begin at address 8190 or address 8194, because neither of these lies on a paragraph boundary, that is, neither can be expressed as a 20-bit number whose low-order 4 bits are all 0. Only addresses that are divisible by 16 have this property.

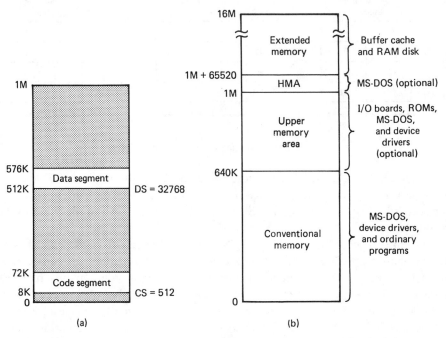

Fig. 8-7. Two 64K segments within the 8088's 1M address space. The shaded regions fall outside the segments and are not addressable without changing a segment register.

Machine instructions on the 8088 contain 16-bit addresses and 16-bit offsets. The program counter is also 16 bits. Thus memory references, both data and text, are always in the range 0 to 65535. This is where the segment registers come in. Before fetching an instruction from the memory address pointed to by the 16-bit program counter, the 8088 hardware automatically relocates the program counter into the code segment by adding the (implicit) 20-bit code segment address to the program counter, to get a full 20-bit physical memory address.

For example, if the program jumps to address 40, in Fig. 8-7(a) it really goes to address 8232. Similarly, data references are relocated into the data segment and stack references are relocated into the stack segment (normally the same as the data segment). In Fig. 8-7(a), a load with address 100 will actually fetch the data at address 524,388.

Consequently, the segment register scheme meets both design constraints. To run old 8080 programs, one merely sets all the segment registers to 0, and the 8088 functions as a machine with 64K of memory. Using the segment registers, programs and data can be placed in any portion of the 1M address space. The price paid is that only 128K is easily accessed. To get at anything outside the code or data segments, the program must either load one of these with a different value or load ES and use a special kind of addressing that tells the CPU to use ES instead of DS. Either way, it is more cumbersome than just having a traditional linear address space from 0 to the maximum address.

The 8088's segmented architecture means that writing a program that uses more than 64K of code or data is expensive. Instead of using 16-bit addresses for everything, a more complicated mechanism is needed. The hardware supports procedure calls to procedures located anywhere in the 1M address space, but these instructions are both larger and slower than the 16-bit ones because they use 32-bit addresses to address memory. Accessing data outside the current data segment requires setting up ES and then using it, also an expensive proposition. All pointers in this model must be 32 bits.

As a consequence, several different programming models have been developed for the 8088, depending on what the program actually needs. Sample models are shown in Fig. 8-8. The choice depends on whether the code and data segments are mapped onto the same memory or not (separate I and D space), how long code and data pointers are, and whether more than 64K of static data are required. In all cases, the smaller choice uses 16-bit addresses and pointers; the larger one uses 32-bit ones.

	Separate segments for code and data?	Bits in code pointers	Bits in data pointers	Static data size
Tiny	No	16	16	⩽ 64K
Small	Yes	16	16	⩽ 64K
Medium	Yes	32	16	⩽ 64K
Compact	Yes	16	32	⩽ 64K
Large	Yes	32	32	⩽ 64K
Huge	Yes	32	32	> 64K

Fig. 8-8. Some common MS-DOS programming models (from Turbo C)

The High Memory Area

The addressing scheme also introduces a strange quirk that is used by MS-DOS. Segment registers with values between 0xF001 and 0xFFFF have part of their segments lying above 1M. For example, with CS equal to 0xF001, a jump to 0xFFF4 goes to address 0x100004, four bytes above the top of memory. Similarly, with DS equal to 0xFFFF, an instruction that tries to load the byte at 0xFFFF will reference address 0x10FFEF, which is 1M + 65519. The 65520 bytes between 0x100000 and 0x10FFEF are called the **HMA** (**High Memory Area**). On the 8088, the hardware ignores the 21st bit, so the addresses are mapped to the 0 to 65519.

On the 286 and later processors, their behavior depends on how the A20 address pin on the CPU chip is wired. If it is wired to work like all the other pins, the HMA can be used for memory, and MS-DOS itself can be kept there. However, if it is grounded (forced to 0), then all addresses between 0x100000 and 0x10FFEF will be wrapped to the range 0x00000 to 0x0FFEF. To be fully 100 percent compatible with the 8088, the pin must be grounded because some perverted software may actually generate addresses above 1M with the expectation that they will wrap around to low addresses. Theoretically, on the 8088 address 0x100004 is a legal synonym for 4. Its being legal does not mean it is good programming practice, however. Thus the hardware vendor is faced with a choice of either enabling HMA and thereby allowing MS-DOS to run above 1M, freeing up 64K of conventional memory, or being 8088 compatible.

Extended Memory

The 286 and subsequent CPUs can have memory above the 1M mark. The 286 can have up to 16M; the 386 and 486 can have as much as 4 gigabytes. The memory above 1M is called **extended memory**. Unfortunately, the 286 and higher machines have two or more CPU modes, one of which is called **real mode**. Only real mode provides backward compatibility with the 8088.

MS-DOS only works in real mode, which makes it difficult to use extended memory. Initially, MS-DOS made no use of extended memory at all. With the exception of the first 65520 bytes (the HMA), extended memory is even now only used for RAM disks and the buffer cache. The structure of MS-DOS does not allow it to be used for programs. This is the main reason IBM and Microsoft wrote OS/2, which had no such limitation.

The Upper Memory Area

In addition to all these CPU idiosyncracies, IBM created some other ones by the way the original PC used its memory. In this machine, memory between 0 and 640K was reserved for the operating system, device drivers, and ordinary programs. This region is now called **conventional memory**. The remaining 384K, from 640K to 1M, called the **UMA (upper memory area)**, was reserved for video RAMs, BASIC ROMs, and other I/O-related functions. No ordinary RAM was present above the 640K mark, so the operating system, device drivers, and all user programs and data were restricted to the 640K conventional memory.

Initially, 640K was enough, but as time went on and programs got bigger, it began to become a major nuisance. In retrospect, the division of the 8088's address space into 640K conventional memory and 384K upper memory area was a mistake. The I/O devices do not need so much address space, and the programs need more, so a split of 832K for programs and 192K for I/O devices might have been better.

That cannot be rectified now because there currently exist thousands of I/O boards for the PC, many of which put ROMs and specialized RAMs at addresses scattered all over the upper memory area. Thus although most PCs have 200K to

300K of unused address space in the upper memory area, the exact addresses that are free vary from machine to machine. Furthermore, they are not in one contiguous block, but in a collection of holes between the I/O boards.

Despite all these complications, starting with MS-DOS 5.0, Microsoft decided to allow 386 and higher CPUs to use this address space by mapping pieces of the extended memory into the holes. Thus, for example, if a particular machine has no I/O devices, ROMs, or video RAMS at addresses 640K to 704K, 768K to 800K, and 896K to 960K, it can instruct MS-DOS to map 160K of its extended memory into these holes, making them usable as RAM. Remember, that as far as the *CPU* is concerned, all memory below 1M is the same. It was IBM's decision to allocate the upper 384K to I/O that created the 640K barrier. Mapping extended memory onto the holes in the upper memory area is just an attempt to undo some of the damage. The upper memory area is available only for user programs on the 386 and 486 because the smaller machines do not have paging hardware and cannot map physical extended memory onto virtual addresses in the 640K to 1M range.

When MS-DOS comes up, it reads the *config.sys* file, in which the user can specify that MS-DOS itself is to be placed in the HMA instead of in conventional memory. It is also possible to specify that device drivers and TSR programs are to be kept in the upper memory area. The effect of all this is to free up some additional memory below the 640K magic limit. For users who have many buffers, many device drivers, and many TSR programs, moving all of this to upper memory, and moving MS-DOS itself to HMA can free up a considerable chunk of conventional memory for user programs. The four memory zones and their potential usages are shown in Fig. 8-7(b).

Overlays

The need for more than 640K of address space predates the 286. At that time, a solution was needed that worked with the 8088. Two solutions were devised, one software and one hardware. The software solution that MS-DOS offers is a system call that allows a running program to load a *.com* or *.exe* file, called an **overlay**, into memory, and then get control back. The calling program then calls a procedure in the overlay. After the overlay has finished, it returns to the calling program, which can then deallocate the overlay's memory, and continue. It is free to load that or other overlays later. In this manner, it is possible to have an arbitrarily large program fit in a relatively small amount of memory.

Figure 8-9 shows how overlays work. In Fig. 8-9(a), we see the main program of a two-pass compiler in memory. The main program is also called the **root overlay**. It contains the code to control the overlay mechanism, and may also contain tables and data structures that are shared among the compiler passes.

Shortly after starting, the root overlay makes a system call that loads the pass 1 overlay. After the load completes, the root overlay can call the main procedure in pass 1 using a procedure call instruction. It can pass parameters if it wishes. Pass 1 runs and puts information in the tables located in the root overlay. When it is finished, the main procedure of pass 1 returns to its caller in the root overlay. At this point, the root overlay can ask for pass 2 to be loaded, and then call it. Pass 2 can

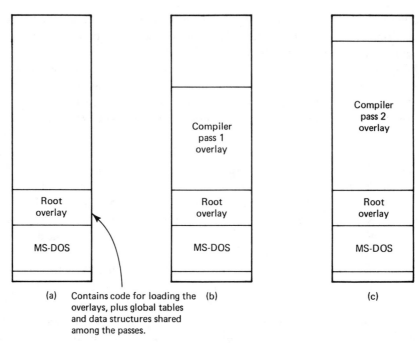

(a)   Contains code for loading the   (b)   (c)
       overlays, plus global tables
       and data structures shared
       among the passes.

Fig. 8-9. Overlays in MS-DOS

read information that pass 1 put in the root overlay's tables. Thus the overlay mechanism makes it easy to share information between different compiler passes. Many large MS-DOS programs use the overlay mechanism.

Expanded Memory

Overlays work adequately for programs consisting of large chunks of code that run sequentially, like compilers. They work less well when a program needs to operate on a large data structure that does not fit in the 640K address space. Some years ago, three companies, Lotus, Intel, and Microsoft got together and devised a hardware scheme they called **expanded memory** by which large amounts of memory could be attached to an 8088 and used. Lotus modified its popular 1-2-3 spread sheet to use it, Microsoft adapted MS-DOS to support it, and Intel built the special memory board required. Even though 286 and 386 CPUs no longer need expanded memory, since they have extended memory, MS-DOS supports it and many applications use it. In fact, because MS-DOS cannot properly use extended memory, on 386 and 486 machines part of the extended memory is normally used to fill in the holes in the upper memory area, and the rest is often used to simulate expanded memory. The expanded memory scheme developed by the three companies has been standardized and is known as **LIM EMS (Lotus/Intel/Microsoft Expanded Memory System)**.

The basic idea behind EMS is an old technique called **bank switching**. The PC's 1M address space is split up into 64 pages of 16K each. The memory, as much as

32M, is split up into as many as 2048 page frames, also of 16K each. Special hardware on the expanded memory board maps the 64 virtual pages onto any arbitrary set of the physical page frames, as illustrated in Fig. 8-10.

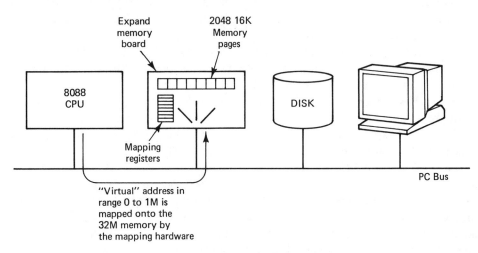

Fig. 8-10. LIM EMS expanded memory.

Although the setup of Fig. 8-10 looks a lot like ordinary paging, it is not. In fact, it is just the opposite. With paging, the problem is that there is not enough physical memory to hold a large virtual address space, so mapping is needed. For example, a program on the 386 might need 64M of memory, while the machine has a mere 16M. What paging does is assign a 64M piece of disk to hold the entire image, and then bring in individual pages as they are used.

The problem expanded memory is trying to solve is how to fit large programs and data structures into a 640K virtual address space. Suppose a program is doing a calculation on a matrix of 1000×1000 8-byte floating point numbers. Even if the machine has the necessary 8M of physical memory, there is no way to address it, because the 8088 cannot generate addresses above 1M, and those between 640K and 1M are reserved for I/O devices. What the EMS software does is allow the program to map a piece of the large physical memory into, say, the 512K to 640K region, and operate on it. When it is done, the program unmaps it, and maps in another piece.

In contrast to paging, which is transparent, expanded memory is totally visible to the programmer (or at least to the compiler and its runtime system). Nothing happens automatically. After all, to process the 8M array, the entire array will eventually have to be mapped into the 512K to 640K window, a chunk at a time. Only the program or the compiler knows which part it needs at each moment.

On a 386 or 486, which have paging hardware, pages from the extended memory can be mapped at any place in the address space. Thus on these machines, extended memory can be used to simulate expanded memory without special hardware.

To make it possible for programs to map and unmap memory in a way independent of whether extended or expanded memory is being used, the EMS standard defines system calls that programs can make and which the system must support, through a device driver for memory. While it probably would have been enough to provide four system calls, ALLOCATE PAGE, DEALLOCATE PAGE, MAP, and UNMAP, the EMS designers defined almost 40 calls for program use using the motto, "Small is beautiful, but big is better." In addition to the above four, there are calls for asking for all kinds of status information (how many pages are free?), map manipulation (save/restore page map), and context switching.

The latter is useful for programs like *dosshell* or *Windows*, in which many applications can run at once, each one with its own collection of pages. The operating system can, for example, allocate 0 to 128K for its own purposes, and then allocate a chunk of 512K for program 1, a second chunk of 512K for program 2, and so on. When program 1 is running, its chunk of expanded memory is mapped into the 128K to 640K address space, but when a context switch is done, program 1 is mapped out and another program is mapped in.

All in all, the MS-DOS memory model is very complicated. Six different techniques are used to break the 640K barrier and make some use of extended memory. These techniques are listed in Fig. 8-11. HMA and upper memory are areas for getting rid of MS-DOS, drivers, and TSR programs, thus freeing up more conventional memory. Overlays are primarily used when the problem is making the code fit into the 640K address space. Expanded memory, in contrast, is more useful in making the data fit. It also has much better performance, since it uses real memory, instead of the disk. Finally, if there is still extended memory left over, since MS-DOS does not allow running programs from it (except when simulating expanded memory), it can be used for a RAM disk or for a buffer cache, to at least improve disk performance.

Technique	Use
HMA	Move MS-DOS out of the bottom 640K
Upper memory	Get MS-DOS, drivers, and TSR programs out of the way
Overlays	Allow large programs to run by breaking them into pieces
Expanded memory	Allow large data sets to be used by mapping them in and out
RAM disk	Utilize extended memory by simulating a disk in memory
Caching	Utilize extended memory by putting a buffer cache there

Fig. 8-11. Memory management techniques in MS-DOS.

In addition to all these items, MS-DOS has system calls for allocating, freeing, and manipulating conventional memory. We will discuss these later in the chapter.

8.3.3. The MS-DOS File System

The original MS-DOS 1.0 file system was patterned after CP/M, including having only a single directory and the use of file control blocks for doing I/O. Starting with MS-DOS 2.0, a UNIX style hierarchical file system with file descriptors and system calls patterned after UNIX was added. The old CP/M style calls fell into disuse, and are now regarded as obsolete. Newly written programs should not use them.

Some points of comparison between the MS-DOS and UNIX file systems are listed in Fig. 8-12. Both systems allow the root directory to have subdirectories, and for these to have more subdirectories indefinitely deep. Both have a concept of a working directory, along with both relative path names and absolute path names. Both use the names . and .. for the current directory and the current directory's parent, respectively, and both support character special files for terminals, printers, and other serial devices, and block special files for disks.

Feature	UNIX	MS-DOS
Hierarchical directory system?	Yes	Yes
Current directory?	Yes	Yes
Absolute and relative paths?	Yes	Yes
Directories . and . . ?	Yes	Yes
Character special files?	Yes	Yes
Block special files?	Yes	Yes
Length of file names	14 or 255	8 + 3
Component separator in names	/	\
Is 'a' the same as 'A' ?	No	Yes
Owners, groups, protection?	Yes	No
Links	Yes	No
Mounted file systems?	Yes	No
File attributes?	No	Yes

Fig. 8-12. A comparison of the UNIX and MS-DOS file systems.

Despite these similarities, there are also differences. UNIX file names are either 14 characters or 255 characters, depending on the version. MS-DOS file names have a basic part of 8 characters, optionally followed by an extension. The extension always starts with a dot, and contains 1 to 3 characters. The most common ones are:

.bat   - Batch file
.com - CP/M-style single segment executable binary file
.doc   - Documentation file
.exe   - Modern multisegment executable binary file with header
.obj   - Object file produced by a compiler
.sys   - Device driver or other system file
.txt   - ASCII text file

In both cases, file names are made up of any legal character sequence. Since MS-DOS supports not only the full ASCII set, but also 128 additional characters, the following are all possible MS-DOS file names, none of which can even be expressed in UNIX: $3\frac{1}{2}$, αβγ , πr^2, *infinity.∞* , and even *déjà vu* (including the space).

Another difference that positively irritates everyone who has to use both systems is the use of / as the component separator in UNIX and the use of \ for the same function in MS-DOS. This means that the UNIX file */usr/ast/foobar* is *\usr\ast\foobar* in MS-DOS. The reason for this difference probably relates to MS-DOS' initial use of /x instead of –x in the shell to pass the *x* flag to a program (another fossil left over from CP/M). Since flags are parsed by the program itself, not the shell, some programs do it the UNIX way.

Another difference is that for the UNIX shell *ABC*, *Abc*, and *abc* are three unrelated files. For the MS-DOS shell they are the same file, as the UNIX file system regards "A" and "a" as being different characters and MS-DOS regards them as being the same. UNIX has owners, groups, protection, links, and mounted file systems, none of which MS-DOS has.

One feature that MS-DOS has that UNIX does not is the presence of file attributes. There are four of them, as follows:

1. Readonly - The file cannot be modified.

2. Archive - The file has been changed since the last archive.

3. System - System file that cannot be deleted by the *del* command.

4. Hidden - The file is not listed by the *dir* command.

Supporting multiple disks but not having mounting introduces a problem: How does the system know which disk a file is on? Suppose two diskettes are currently inserted, both containing a file *xyz* in the root directory. If the command

```
del \xyz
```

is given, how does MS-DOS know which file to remove? Answer: without additional information, it does not. It is necessary for the user to supply the device name, a: for the first diskette, b: for the second, and c: for the first hard disk. For example,

```
copy a:\abc c:\usr\ast\xyz
```

copies a file from diskette in the a: drive to the hard disk. If no device code is given, the current default is assumed. The default can be changed by just typing it, for example,

```
b:
```

makes the B: diskette the default.

8.3.4. Input/Output in MS-DOS

MS-DOS supports character special files for doing input and output to serial devices, much as UNIX does, except that the device names are not embedded in a directory like */dev*. To copy a file to the console (screen), the command

```
copy file con
```

can be used. The file *con* can also be opened by programs, much the same as */dev/tty* can be opened by UNIX programs. In fact, it can also be opened as \dev\con, even though there is no \dev directory. Opening a character special file returns a file descriptor, which can be used for reading and writing. Other character special files include *com1* (the first serial port), *lpt1* (the first parallel line printer port), and *nul*, the great bit bucket in the sky (like */dev/null* in UNIX). These names may not be used as the first part of any file names, no matter what the extension is.

The character special files support cooked and raw modes, much as UNIX character special files do. In cooked mode, intraline editing, such as erasing characters is done by the operating system, with only the final result being made available to the program. In raw mode, the characters are passed to the program exactly as received. Screen editors and other interactive programs often work this way.

Unlike UNIX in which a process starts with three special files already open, standard input, standard output, and standard error, all connected to the terminal, in MS-DOS when a process starts, it automatically has five open files: standard input, standard output, standard error, the serial line, and the printer, using file descriptors 0 through 4, respectively.

MS-DOS allows users to install their own custom device drivers just after the system is booted. This contrasts with the UNIX approach, in which device drivers are always compiled into the kernel, and are not installable afterwards. The difference is probably due to the fact that historically UNIX systems have been run and maintained at computing facilities, where a system administrator is always available for recompiling or relinking the system. For MS-DOS requiring users even to relink the system is impractical.

A device driver is installed by adding a simple statement to the *config.sys* file giving the path name of the file containing the driver. Some common device drivers are listed in Fig. 8-13.

Driver	Function
ANSI.SYS	Console driver with ANSI escape sequences
DISPLAY.SYS	Console driver with foreign language support
MOUSE.SYS	Mouse driver
PRINTER.SYS	Printer driver with foreign language support
RAMDRIVE.SYS	RAM disk driver for extended memory
SMARTDRV.SYS	Buffer cache driver for extended memory

Fig. 8-13. Some common MS-DOS device drivers.

8.4. MS-DOS SYSTEM CALLS

Some of the MS-DOS system calls are similar to their counterparts in UNIX, but others are completely different. In this section we will look at a small number of them, as examples. To make it easy to compare them to the UNIX calls, we will divide them into the same categories as we did in the previous chapter. The list of calls we will look at is given in Fig. 8-14. It is only a small sample. Many others exist as well.

System calls are made by trapping to the kernel. Most of them trap through vector 0x21 and put the system call number in a certain register, but a few trap through other vectors instead. A system call interface library is provided by C and other compilers to allow high-level language programmers to make system calls as well, just as in UNIX.

A substantial number of MS-DOS programs overwrite vector 0x21 with a pointer into their own code, allowing them to catch and inspect all system calls. Some of these calls are handled differently, typically to extend MS-DOS in some way. The rest just result in a jump to the address that vector 0x21 contained in the first place.

Although a system call is provided to read and write interrupt vectors, the technique is not portable to other systems or architectures, and will cause trouble if MS-DOS or its successors ever support multiple users. It is really an emergency measure to add functionality or hooks that should have been in the operating system in the first place. Networking, for example, is often implemented by adding network code as a TSR program that catches all system calls and inspects each one to see if it requires remote access. Those that do are handled by the TSR program, and those that do not are passed on to MS-DOS.

8.4.1. Process Management System Calls in MS-DOS

Unlike UNIX, MS-DOS does not have distinct FORK and EXEC system calls. The functions of both are combined in LOAD_AND_EXEC. The reason these are split in UNIX is to allow the shell to manipulate the file descriptors after the FORK but before the EXEC. In MS-DOS the shell first saves its own file descriptors, then sets up the child's, and then runs the child. When the child exits, the shell restores its own file descriptors. The first parameter names the binary file, and the second is a pointer to a structure that contains pointers to the command line and environment.

The LOAD_OVERLAY call is similar to the previous one, except that the overlay is not started. It is just loaded in memory. It is up to the parent to call some procedure in the overlay, with an ordinary procedure call.

The END_PROG call is the same as the UNIX EXIT call, but KEEP_PROG is unique to MS-DOS. It terminates a program, but does not destroy its memory image. All terminate and stay resident programs exit with this one.

Since there is no WAIT system call, another method is needed for the parent to pick up the status value returned by the child. The solution is a new system call, GET_CHILD_STATUS, which returns the status returned by the most recently run child.

8.4.2. Memory Management System Calls in MS-DOS

The memory management system calls are more complicated in MS-DOS than in UNIX, which is hardly surprising given the complexity of the underlying memory model. The first three system calls allow programs to allocate, free, and resize

Process management	Description
s = load_and_exec (name, args)	Create a child process and execute it
s = load_overlay (name, args)	Load an overlay into memory and return
end_prog (status)	Terminate execution and return status
keep_prog (mem_size, status)	Terminate and stay resident
code = get_child_status ( )	Get exit status returned by last child

Memory management	Description
addr = alloc_memory (nbytes)	Allocate a block of memory
s = free_allocated_mem (addr)	Free a block of previously allocated memory
s = set_mem_blk_siz (size, addr)	Change the size of an allocated block
s = set_alloc_strategy (type)	Select a memory allocation strategy
type = get_alloc_strategy ( )	Get the current memory allocation strategy
s = set_upper_mem_link (yesno)	Enables/disables usage of upper memory
yesno = get_upper_mem_link ( )	Specifies whether upper memory is allocatable

Files and directories	Description
fd = create (name, attributes)	Create a new file with the given attributes
fd = open (file, how)	Open a file for reading and/or writing
s = close (fd)	Close an open file
n = read (fd, buffer, nbytes)	Read data from a file into a buffer
n = write (fd, buffer, nbytes)	Write data from a buffer into a file
pos = mv_fil_ptr (fd, hi, lo, e)	Move the file pointer somewhere in the file
s = rename_file (old, new)	Rename a file
s = delete_file (name)	Remove a file
t = get_file_date (fd)	Get the date the file was last modified on
s = create_dir (dirname)	Create a new directory
s = remove_dir (dirname)	Delete an empty directory
s = change_cur_dir (dirname)	Change the working directory
s = get_cur_dir (drv, &dirname)	Get the current dir on the specified drive

Input/output	Description
s = ioctl (various)	Read and write device parameters

Fig. 8-14. A selection of common MS-DOS system calls. Some of the names have been abbreviated to get them to fit. The return code s is 0 for success, −1 if an error has occurred; *fd* is a file descriptor. The other names suggest their functions.

blocks of memory. In UNIX these functions are handled by the C library procedures *malloc*, *free*, and *realloc*, and not by the operating system itself.

The next two calls, SET_ALLOC_STRATEGY and GET_ALLOC_STRATEGY, are somewhat unusual. When allocating memory, MS-DOS uses an algorithm, of course, such as first fit or best fit. With these two system calls, a program can tell MS-DOS which allocation strategy to choose among first fit, best fit, and last fit. Furthermore, the argument specifies whether conventional memory, upper memory, or either one is desired. The search strategy is important because upper memory is always badly fragmented, even at boot time, because much of upper memory is full of ROMs, video RAMs, and blocks of memory reserved by various I/O devices. Putting the search strategy under program control provides more flexibility.

The last two system calls listed in this group, SET_UPPER_MEM_LINK and GET_UPPER_MEM_LINK, have to do with whether or not upper memory is included in the free list, and thus may be allocated. The SET_UPPER_MEM_LINK call enables or disables the use of upper memory, and the other one reports back on the current status of this enable/disable bit.

8.4.3. File and Directory System Calls in MS-DOS

The first five system calls in this group are the same as in UNIX. The only differences are (1) somebody decided to spell CREATE with the "E" here, and (2) instead of the protection mode, the four attribute bits are supplied. The next call is in fact LSEEK, but disguised slightly by splitting the file offset into two 16-bit words, instead of passing it as a long (although C interface libraries take a long and convert them into two shorts).

The operation of RENAME_FILE and DELETE_FILE are obvious, and correspond to the UNIX RENAME and UNLINK calls, respectively.

The GET_FILE_DATE call is not really a system call. The actual system call gets both the date and time and puts them in different registers. Since C functions cannot have two return values, most compiler libraries split this system call into two functions. The other one (not shown) gets the time the file was last modified. Note that these calls are needed because there is no STAT call.

The last four calls are also obvious and identical to their UNIX counterparts, except that GET_CUR_DIR specifies which drive it is interested in. In UNIX this is not necessary.

8.4.4. Input/Output System Calls in MS-DOS

The IOCTL call is actually a large number of different calls for manipulating special files. Some of the options allow programs to query a file descriptor to see if it is a character special file, to send it control data (e.g., terminal line speed), to check the device's input and output status, to select display or other modes, to set code pages for various national languages, to read and write device parameters, and more.

8.5. IMPLEMENTATION OF MS-DOS

In this section we will give a brief overview of how MS-DOS works inside. A good place to look for more information on this subject is (Schulman et al., 1990).

MS-DOS is structured in three layers, as follows:

1. The BIOS (Basic Input Output System).

2. The kernel.

3. The shell, *command.com.*

The BIOS is a collection of low-level device drivers that serve to isolate MS-DOS from the details of the hardware. For example, the BIOS contains calls to read and write from absolute disk addresses, and to read a character from the keyboard and write a character to the screen. The BIOS is usually supplied by the computer manufacturer, rather than by Microsoft, and is generally located, in part, in a ROM in the 64K block just under the 1M address space limit.

BIOS procedures are called by trapping to them via interrupt vectors, rather than via direct procedure calls. This makes it possible for the vendor to change the size and location of BIOS procedures in new models, without having to relink the operating system. The file *io.sys* (called *ibmbio.com* in the version that IBM itself ships) is a hidden file present on all MS-DOS systems. It is loaded immediately after the computer is booted, and provides a procedure call interface to the BIOS, so the kernel can access BIOS services by making procedure calls to *io.sys* instead of traps to the ROM. In addition, this file holds those BIOS procedures not in the ROM and a module called *sysinit* that is used to boot the system. The existence of *io.sys* further isolates the kernel from hardware details. For example, the kernel does not even have to know which vector goes with which BIOS service. These details are buried away in *io.sys.*

The kernel is contained in another hidden file, *msdos.sys* (which IBM calls *ibmdos.com*) and contains the machine-independent part of the operating system. It handles process management, memory management, and the file system, as well as the interpretation of all system calls.

The third part of what most people think of as the operating system is the shell, *command.com.* Of course, this program is not part of the operating system, and can be replaced by the user. The standard *command.com* consists of two pieces, a resident portion, that is always in memory, and a transient portion, that is only in memory when the shell is active. The transient portion is located at the high end of memory, and can be overwritten by user programs that need the space. When control passes back to *command.com*, it checks to see if the transient portion is still intact, and if not, reloads it.

MS-DOS computers are booted as follows. When the power is turned on, control is transferred to address 0xFFFF0 by hardware. This location is always in a ROM, and contains a jump to the bootstrap procedure in the BIOS ROM. The bootstrap procedure carries out some hardware tests, and if the machine passes, it tries to read in the boot sector from diskette A:. If no diskette is present in drive A:, the primary boot sector of the hard disk is read in. The partition table in the primary boot sector tells where the partitions are and which one is active. The active partition is then selected and its first sector, the secondary boot sector, is read in and executed. This two-step boot procedure is only used for hard disks. Its function is to allow automatic booting of both MS-DOS and other operating systems.

The boot sector reads its own root directory to see if *io.sys* and *msdos.sys* (or *ibmbio.com* and *ibmdos.com*) are present. If so, it reads them both into memory and transfers control to *io.sys*.

Once loaded, *io.sys* calls BIOS procedures to initialize the hardware. Then *sysinit* takes over and reads *config.sys* to configure the system. This job includes allocating the buffer cache, loading device drivers, and setting up code pages for the national language to be used. Finally *sysinit* uses MS-DOS itself to load and execute *command.com*. In this respect, *sysinit* does the work that *init* does in UNIX. After initializing itself, *command.com* reads and executes *autoexec.bat*, which is an ordinary shell script for doing whatever initialization the user wants. The layout of memory resulting from the boot procedure is shown in Fig. 8-15.

8.5.1. Implementation of Processes in MS-DOS

Process management is straightforward in MS-DOS because there is no multiprogramming. When a process invokes the LOAD_AND_EXEC system call, MS-DOS carries it out in the following steps:

1. Find a block of memory large enough to hold the child process. For an *.exe* file, the size can be deduced from information in the header. For a *.com* file, all of available memory is allocated, but the program can return unused memory if it so desires.

2. Build the PSP in the first 256 bytes of the allocated memory. Some of the information comes from the parent's PSP, and other information, such as the command line, is unique to this process. A pointer back to the parent's PSP is also included in the child's PSP. In a sense, the PSP is analogous to the user structure in UNIX.

3. Load the executable binary file into the allocated memory starting at the first byte above the PSP. For *.exe* files, a relocation constant must be added to all relocatable addresses. For *.com* files, nothing is changed.

4. Start the program. The starting address of an *.exe* file is contained in the header. The starting address of a *.com* file is address 0x100 (to skip over the PSP).

The PSPs play an important role in MS-DOS. A global variable inside the system points to the current process' PSP. The PSP contains all the state information needed

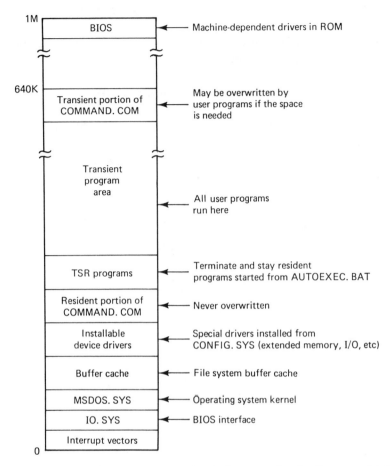

Fig. 8-15. Details of memory layout after the boot procedure has been completed.

to run the process. Since each PSP holds a pointer back to its parent's PSP, given a pointer to the current one, MS-DOS can follow the chain back all the way to *command.com* and locate all the (suspended) processes in the system. The address to return to after the exit is also contained in the PSP.

The pointer that MS-DOS maintains to the current process' PSP also plays a role in TSR programming. Undocumented system calls exist to read and write this pointer, thus allowing a TSR program to save the current PSP pointer and install its own. Once accomplished, the TSR program can call MS-DOS to do I/O for it. Actually, this trick only works if the user program, rather than the operating system, happens to be active at the time the TSR program gets control. However, another undocumented system call is available to find out who was active, allowing the TSR program to defer its work until the current system call, if any, is finished.

Alternatively, the TSR program can locate the pointer to MS-DOS's own internal data segment and switch it to another one, making the system temporarily "forget" whatever it was doing. While using undocumented system calls like this is an unclean and dangerous practice, virtually all TSR programs (including those written by Microsoft) work this way.

CPU scheduling is trivial. Since there is only one active process, that one runs all the time, except when a TSR program seizes control.

8.5.2. Implementation of Memory Management in MS-DOS

Just as MS-DOS avoids having a central process table by keeping track of processes via the chain of PSPs, it uses the same scheme for memory management. Memory is divided up into contiguous blocks called **arenas**, each arena starting on a paragraph boundary and containing a whole number of paragraphs, as depicted in Fig. 8-16.

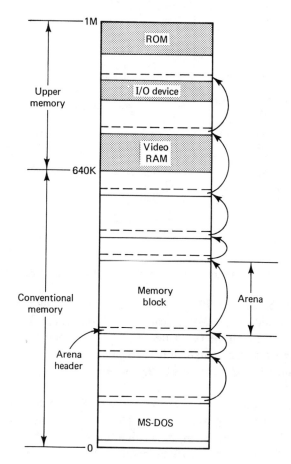

Fig. 8-16. MS-DOS keeps track of memory using arenas. The shaded areas are unavailable.

Each arena starts with a 16-byte arena header. The header begins with a magic number (for verifying that the word in question is, in fact, the start of an arena header). Then comes a pointer to the PSP of the process that allocated the arena, or 0 if it is free. Next is the arena's size in paragraphs. Finally is a field that can hold the name of the executable binary file that owns the arena, but only for the arena occupied by the program itself and not for memory acquired with the ALLOC_MEMORY system call.

Technically, the arenas do not form a linked list, because the headers contain sizes rather than pointers, but the effect is the same. If the use of upper memory has been enabled by the SET_UPPER_MEM_LINK system call, then memory blocks in upper memory are on the arena chain too. The memory block itself follows the arena header.

When MS-DOS has to allocate memory, either to load a child process or an overlay, or to satisfy a program's ALLOC_MEMORY system call, it searches the arena chain starting at the low end until it finds a block that is large enough. The algorithm used can be set by the program using the SET_ALLOC_STRATEGY system call. If the arena chosen is too large, a piece is broken off for use, and a new arena is created to represent the hole left over. When memory is freed, adjacent free arenas are not merged because the arena chain is not a doubly linked list. Merging occurs the next time the chain is searched starting at the beginning.

As a consequence of this memory management method, a program with dynamic tables for which it is constantly allocating and freeing memory is likely to own chunks of memory spread all over the 1M address space. Contrast this with the UNIX model of a single data segment that can grow or shrink as needed. Actually, the difference is less than it appears since few UNIX programs use the BRK system call directly. Most use the *malloc* and *free* library procedures that do the same as the MS-DOS system calls ALLOC_MEMORY and FREE_ALLOCATED_MEM. Thus the real difference is that in MS-DOS the operating system maintains the free list, and in UNIX it is maintained at two levels—the operating system keeps track of allocated and unallocated blocks of memory, and *malloc* manages the contents of the data segment.

Although the arena scheme works for upper memory, it does not work with extended memory because the sizes in the arena headers are only 16 bits. To use memory above the 1M mark, it is necessary to install one or more extended memory drivers. Figure 8-17 lists some of the more common ones and their functions.

Driver	Function
HIMEM.SYS	Coordinate extended memory usage
EMM386.EXE	Use extended memory to simulate expanded memory
SMARTDRV.SYS	Use extended memory for caching
RAMDRIVE.SYS	Use extended memory as a RAM disk

Fig. 8-17. MS-DOS extended memory drivers.

As we mentioned earlier, MS-DOS does not swap or page. If a process attempts to allocate memory and there is none left, or if a process attempts to fork and there is insufficient memory in which to construct the child, the system call simply returns an error code. Recovery is left entirely up to the caller.

8.5.3. Implementation of the MS-DOS File System

Let us start our tour through the MS-DOS file system by looking at the disk layout. The hard disk layout and floppy disk layouts are different. We will concentrate on the hard disk. All hard disks have the same layout, which is shown in Fig. 8-18. The **boot sector** contains critical information about the file system, as well as the code for starting the system. Then come tables that keep track of all disk space. These are followed by the root directory, and then everything else.

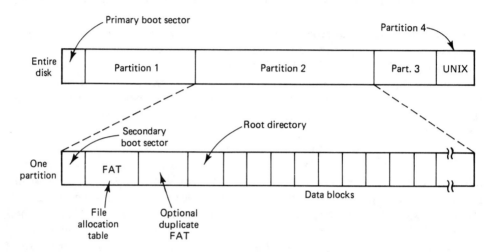

Fig. 8-18. The MS-DOS disk layout.

The boot sector always starts with a JUMP instruction that skips over the descriptive information in the sector and goes to the start of the code. In this way, the ROM bootstrap can read the boot sector into memory and just jump to the start of it, without having to worry about the internal layout. Then comes a list of key parameters, including the number of bytes per sector, the number of sectors per block, the number of file allocation tables, the size of the root directory, the device size, and similar data.

After these parameters comes the bootstrap code. Unlike the ROM bootstrap, which merely reads in sector 0 and transfers to it, this code knows it is booting MS-DOS. (The ROM code can equally well boot UNIX or any other operating system.) The boot sector code locates the root directory and searches it for *io.sys* and *msdos.sys* as discussed above. Then it uses the BIOS to load these and jump to the start of *io.sys*.

The boot sector contains the **partition table** at the end. This table contains entries for indicating the start and end of each partition, up to a maximum of four partitions. Each partition can contain a different file system. In this way, MS-DOS and UNIX can happily coexist on the same hard disk, each in its own partition, as shown in Fig. 8-18. One partition can be marked ACTIVE, to allow that one to start up when the system is booted from the hard disk. The MS-DOS utility program *fdisk* is provided to allow users to create, delete, and change the sizes of partitions. Once a disk has been partitioned and file systems have been put in each one, repartitioning the disk almost always requires scrapping all the file systems and building new ones from scratch.

Following the boot sector comes the **FAT** (**File Allocation Table**), which keeps track of all disk space on the device. This table performs the same functions in MS-DOS as the i-node table and free list do in UNIX. To provide extra reliability, sometimes the FAT is replicated, so the system will not be wiped out if the primary FAT becomes unreadable.

The FAT contains one entry for each block on the disk. The block size is given in the boot sector, and can be anything from 1 sector (e.g., for RAM disks) to 8 sectors (e.g., for large hard disks). The size of the FAT entry started at 12 bits in Version 1.0, but since this size can handle only disks up to 4096 blocks, when large hard disks were introduced, it was changed to 16 bits, allowing up to 64K blocks per partition. Partitions larger than 32M are handled by using block sizes larger than the standard 512 bytes (e.g., 2K blocks for 100M disks).

The conceptual layout of the FAT is shown in Fig. 8-19. (The actual layout is different, since the fields are encoded in a strange way, a throwback to MS-DOS's CP/M roots.) There is a one-to-one correspondence between FAT entries and disk blocks, except for the first two FAT entries, which encode the disk class. In this example, we show three files, A, B, and C. File A begins at block 6. The FAT entry for 6 is 8, meaning that the second block of the file is block 8. The FAT entry for 8 is 4, meaning that the next block is 4. The FAT entry for 4 is 2. Finally, the entry for 2 is a special code indicating end of file. Thus given the number of the first block of a file, it is possible to locate all the blocks by following the chain through the FAT. The directory entry for each file contains the starting block, and the FAT provides the rest of the chain.

Free blocks are marked by another special code in the FAT. When a file grows, MS-DOS looks for a free entry in the FAT and allocates that block to the file. Similarly, another code is used to mark unreadable blocks.

To see how the FAT is integrated into the file system, let us trace an OPEN system call from beginning to end. It starts when MS-DOS looks in the file descriptor table, kept in the PSP as an array of 20 bytes, looking for a free file descriptor. Each of the bytes in the file descriptor table holds either a 1-byte index into the master **system file table** (roughly analogous to the UNIX i-node table), or a code saying that the file descriptor is not in use. If a free file descriptor is located, the system file table is searched for a free slot.

If that also succeeds, then the path name of the file to be opened is examined to see if it is *con*, *lpt*, or the name of one of the other special files. The directory and extension are ignored in this comparison. If it is not a special file, the first character is checked to see if it is \. If it is, the path is absolute and the search begins in the root directory. Otherwise, the path is relative and the search begins in the working directory. In this respect, MS-DOS is essentially the same as UNIX.

A directory in MS-DOS has a 32-byte entry for each file or directory it contains, as illustrated in Fig. 8-20. The first 11 characters hold the file name and extension.

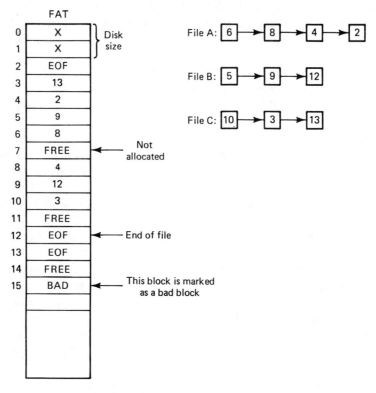

Fig. 8-19. The MS-DOS file allocation table.

Unlike UNIX, the dot separating the main part of the name from the extension is not stored in the directory explicitly. Next comes the attribute byte, containing the following bits:

A - Archive bit (set when file is modified, cleared when it is backed up)
D - Set to indicate that the entry is for a directory
V - Set to indicate that the entry is for the volume label
S - Set for system (i.e., undeletable) files
H - Set for hidden files (i.e., not listed by *dir*)
R - Read-only bit (file may not be written)

The attribute byte may be read and written using system calls.

The time and date of last modification are stored in the next two fields. The encoding uses 6 bits for the seconds, 6 bits for the minutes, 4 bits for the hour, 5 bits for the day, 4 bits for the month, and 7 bits for the year (starting at 1980). The last two fields hold the number of the first block and the file size. Using the block number, the start of the chain in the FAT can be located, thus making it possible to find all the blocks.

It is interesting to contrast the implementation of the MS-DOS file system with that of the UNIX file system. In UNIX, a directory entry contains the file name and the i-

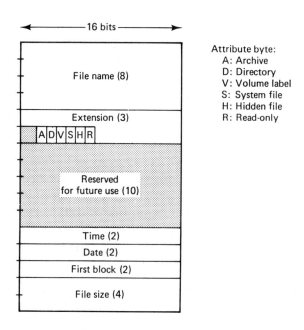

Fig. 8-20. An MS-DOS directory entry. The numbers in parentheses are the sizes in bytes. The shaded areas are not used.

node number, and nothing else. All the rest of the information, such as the file size, creation date and time, and block numbers are in the i-node. MS-DOS has no i-nodes, so everything is in the directory entry.

This design makes links impossible because having two directory entries holding the same initial block number cannot work. Each one would have its own time, date, and file size, leading to inconsistencies. It also means that randomly accessing a block near the end of a large file requires a considerable amount of searching through the FAT. On the other hand, in UNIX randomly accessing a block near the end of a large file requires one or more disk accesses.

Getting back to our OPEN system call, if the search is successful, the directory entry is copied into the system file table, which has one entry for each open file. The file position field is then set to 0. Having the file position field located here does not cause problems as it would in UNIX because there is no danger that an independent user might open the file. Finally, the file descriptor is returned to the caller and the OPEN completes.

Given this background, the implementation of READ and WRITE is straightforward. The system uses the file descriptor to index into the 20-byte array in the PSP to get the index of the system file table entry containing the information about the file. This information includes the start of the disk block chain, the current file position, and the current size, which together allow the operations to be performed. The size of the system file table is determined by a line in *config.sys*, but is limited to no more than 256 by the use of single byte entries in the PSP.

8.5.4. Implementation of Input/Output in MS-DOS

All input and output in MS-DOS is done through character special file and block special files. Character devices handle character-at-a-time devices, like terminals and printers, whereas block devices are for disks. Associated with each special file is a device driver, which contains the code that does the actual I/O. Some of the drivers, such as *com1*, *con*, and *lpt1*, are standard, and are contained in *io.sys*. Users may load additional device drivers when the system is booted by putting one or more

```
device=
```

lines in *config.sys*. Each such line specifies the name of a file containing an executable binary file holding one or more drivers.

The idea of having device drivers is to provide MS-DOS with a standard interface to all hardware devices. When a program reads or writes a special file (including all accesses to the file system), MS-DOS invokes the corresponding driver in a standardized way, telling it what it wants done, thus decoupling the operating system from the details of the hardware.

The idea of having *user-installable* drivers has to do with the fact that people can, and do, buy all kinds of special I/O devices for their PCs, including tape drives, speech synthesizers, plotters, and digital musical instruments. To use one of these, a new special file must be created, and a new driver must be installed to handle it. In UNIX, installing a new device driver requires recompiling the operating system, something acceptable in traditional minicomputer installations, but infeasible for a mass market product like MS-DOS.

A driver can be for a character special file or a block special file, but not both, since the interfaces to the two kinds are slightly different, and the functions they must support are also not quite the same (e.g., random access is permitted on block devices but not on character devices). Each driver is a separate program, written in assembly language, C, or some other language, and compiled into either a *.com* file or an *.exe* file. Drivers may also be given the extension *.sys*, as in *mouse.sys*, to distinguish them from other files.

All drivers have the structure shown in Fig. 8-21. First comes an 18-byte header that identifies the driver and describes some of its properties. Then comes the actual code, consisting of two parts, one for accepting requests for work from MS-DOS and one for actually doing the I/O.

When a driver is installed, it is put at the head of a linked list of drivers. MS-DOS keeps a pointer to the head of the list in an internal variable, and uses it to search the list. Since the list is searched starting at the head, a newly installed driver takes precedence over a previously installed driver. For example, the standard *con* driver does not support any escape sequences for screen output. A user who wants the ANSI escape sequences supported can put the line

```
device=c:\bin\ansi.sys
```

in *config.sys*, which loads a new driver for *con* from the file *\bin\ansi.sys* on the hard disk. From that point all, all screen I/O will be sent to *ansi.sys*.

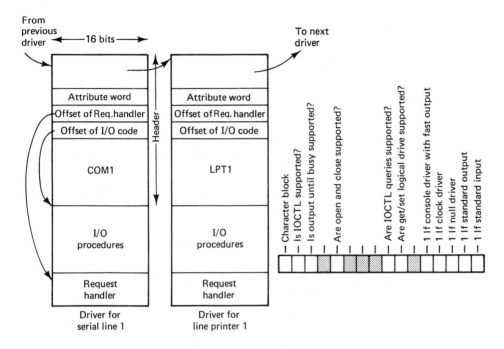

Fig. 8-21. Two MS-DOS character device drivers.

The next word in the header is a bit map used to distinguish character from block devices and tell whether certain optional driver functions are supported. The low-order 5 bits shown at the right of Fig. 8-21 are used to make it possible for MS-DOS to search the list rapidly to find the console driver, the clock driver, the null driver, standard input, and standard output without having to look at the driver's name.

The next two words give the offsets of the request handler and the I/O code, respectively. We will explain how these are used below.

Finally, we come to the name of the driver, up to 8 characters. Earlier, we described that when a file is opened, MS-DOS first checks to see if the name is a special file. The way that is done is to search the list of installed drivers to see if the name of the file to be opened matches the name in any of the drivers on the chain. If so, that driver is used for all reads and writes done on the file. The details shown in Fig. 8-21 are for character drivers. Block drivers differ from character drivers in minor ways.

Directly following the driver is the code. This code is typically invoked in the following steps.

1. A user program does a READ or WRITE system call. MS-DOS uses the file descriptor to locate the system file table entry (by looking in the PSP file descriptor table), and deduce which device must be read or written.

2. It then builds a request message consisting of a 13-byte header and, in some cases, extra parameters. The message contains the function code for the operation desired, the memory address to read to or write from, the device address (for block devices), and the byte count.

3. MS-DOS then looks up the offset of the device's request handler procedure, and calls it. This procedure examines the messages and saves the relevant fields. It then returns control, before even starting the work.

4. Next, MS-DOS looks up the offset of the I/O code in the device driver's header, and calls it to actually do the work. The reason for the split into two calls is not clear, but possibly might be helpful if multiprogramming is ever added to MS-DOS in the future.

5. When the driver has finished the work, it sets a status word indicating success or failure and returns control to its caller.

Device drivers can support a surprisingly large number of functions, although a particular driver can indicate that it does not support some of the more exotic ones by setting certain bits in the attribute word of Fig. 8-21 to 0. If a program does an IOCTL system call on a special file whose driver does not support IOCTL, for example, an error status is returned to the program.

Drivers cannot use MS-DOS system calls to do their work because MS-DOS is not reentrant, that is, it cannot accept a new system call while it is busy with an old one. Fortunately, most drivers do not call the operating system, and those that do, cheat.

8.6. SUMMARY

MS-DOS is a single-user operating system for the IBM PC and its successors. It was originally based on CP/M, but many elements from UNIX have been added over the years. Only one process at a time can be active, but a process can create and execute a child process. Doing so, however, suspends the parent until the child is finished. Terminate and stay resident programs continue to exist even after they exit.

Memory management in MS-DOS involves four separate regions: conventional memory (below 640K), upper memory (between 640K and 1M), high memory (the 64K just above 1M), and extended memory (above 1M). Each of these has different properties and is used in different ways. Ordinary programs are restricted to conventional memory, however, and thus cannot exceed 640K. Overlays and expanded memory are two of the techniques that are used to get around this limit to some extent.

The MS-DOS file system supports hierarchical directories, absolute and relative path names, and many of the same system calls as the UNIX file system, on which it was patterned. I/O is done using special files, both block and character.

The implementation of MS-DOS is closely tied to the underlying architecture. There are fewer central tables than in UNIX. Processes are kept track of via a list of

PSPs, for example, and memory is kept track of by a linked list of arenas. The file system is based on the use of a FAT for each disk. For each file, a chain of blocks is maintained in the FAT. Directory entries in MS-DOS contain some of the information which in UNIX is in the i-nodes.

I/O is handled using device drivers. Users are free to install their own drivers for special devices. The drivers are linked together on a chain, and each one contains its name and code.

PROBLEMS

1. Imagine that a floppy disk contains two large dictionaries, *dict1* and *dict2*, which together almost fill the disk. To find all the words containing "qu" the user types the following shell command:

```
cat dict1 dict2 | grep qu
```

UNIX implements pipelines with two processes connected by a pipe. MS-DOS implements it as though the user had typed:

```
cat dict1 dict2 >temp
grep qu <temp
del temp
```

It what way might the effect of the pipeline differ between UNIX and MS-DOS?

2. In UNIX, the working directory is kept track of separately for each process. In MS-DOS, the working directory is stored in a global variable inside the operating system, rather than separately for each process (actually, one working directory per disk). Give an example in which this difference can have visible effects. (*Hint:* think about processes that change their working directory.)

3. In UNIX, processes can form a tree. Is this also true for MS-DOS? If a tree is not the right data structure, what is?

4. Is it possible to program the producer-consumer problem in MS-DOS in the classical way, as we discussed in Chap. 2. Discuss your answer.

5. Is there any property of the way MS-DOS manages processes that makes swapping more difficult than in UNIX? Defend your answer.

6. Why are there no terminate and stay resident programs for UNIX?

7. Does an overlay mechanism fundamentally deal with running out of virtual address space or running out of physical memory? Suppose you had an immense amount of virtual address space, say 64 bits, but limited physical memory. Would you use overlays for large programs? What about the reverse situation? In all cases, assume that there is no swapping and no paging.

8. A TSR program called *eatmem* is invoked with an argument specifying a size in kilobytes. The program changes its own size to the size of the argument and then exits. It does not spy on the keyboard or catch any interrupts. Of what use could such a program possibly be? (Hint: think about its use to software developers rather than to end users.)

9. Suppose the segment registers have the following values: CS is 0x10, DS is 0x100, SS is 0x100, and ES is 0x1000. Which portions are memory are accessible for which purposes?

10. Why do compilers often set SS equal to DS? (Hint: think about a program that calls a procedure, *p*, several times in a program. On the first call it passes global variables as parameters. These are located in the data segment. On the second call, it passes local variables as parameter. These are located in the stack segment.)

11. Why can MS-DOS run in the HMA, but not in the 64K above it? What is so special about the HMA?

12. Suppose that while the 8086 and 8088 were being designed, Intel had deemed it necessary to give them a 16M address space, instead of a 1M address space, but had used the implementation technique using segment registers and so on. Would there still have been a high memory area, and if so, at what addresses?

13. List two differences between expanded memory and paging.

14. Why do arenas always begin on a paragraph boundary and have a size that is an integral number of paragraphs?

15. Why does MS-DOS not have a superblock like UNIX?

16. A FAT starts out with the following values:

x, x, 8, −1, −1, −1, 3, 2, 5, 0, 0

where *x* is not relevant for our purposes, 0 indicates a free slot, and −1 indicates end of file. If the directory entry for a certain file has 7 as the starting block, how many blocks does that file contain?

17. Propose a way to add file protection to MS-DOS and explain how it could be implemented.

18. MS-DOS stores the time and date in each directory entry. The time is stored as a 16-bit unsigned integer. How many combinations does this allow? How many seconds are there in a day? How do you think this problem is handled?

19. In Fig. 8-21, 4 bytes are needed for the link from one driver to the next. Since the total number of drivers is always less than 64K, why are 4 bytes used here instead of 2 bytes?

20. Why do most MS-DOS machines have the BIOS in ROM?

21. When a device driver is installed in MS-DOS it is put at the head of the device driver list. Why does it go at the head instead of at the tail?

22. Name 5 differences between MS-DOS and UNIX.

PART
2

DISTRIBUTED OPERATING SYSTEMS

9

INTRODUCTION
TO DISTRIBUTED SYSTEMS

The use of computers is in the process of undergoing a revolution. From 1945, when the modern computer era began, until about 1985, computers were large and expensive. Even minicomputers normally cost tens of thousands of dollars each. As a result, most organizations had only a handful of computers, and for lack of a way to connect them, these usually operated independently from one another.

Starting in the mid 1980s, however, two advances in technology began to change that situation. The first was the development of powerful microprocessors. Initially these were 8-bit machines, but soon 16, 32, and even 64-bit CPUs became common. Many of these had the computing power of a decent-sized mainframe (i.e., large) computer, but for a fraction of the price.

The second development was the invention of high-speed **local area networks** or **LANs**. These systems allowed dozens, or even hundreds, of machines to be connected in such a way that small amounts of information can be transferred between machines in a millisecond or so. Larger amounts of data can be moved between machines at rates of 10 million bits/sec and more.

The net result of these two technologies is that it is now not only feasible, but easy, to put together computing systems composed of large numbers of CPUs connected by a high-speed network. They are usually called **distributed systems,** in contrast to the previous **centralized systems** consisting of a single CPU, its memory, peripherals, and some terminals.

There is only one fly in the ointment: software. Distributed systems need radically different software than do centralized systems. In particular, the required operating systems for these distributed systems are only beginning to emerge. The first few steps have been taken, but there is still a long way to go. Nevertheless, enough is already known about these distributed operating systems that we can present the basic ideas. The rest of this book is devoted to studying concepts, implementation, and examples of distributed operating systems.

9.1. GOALS

Just because it is possible to build distributed systems does not necessarily mean that it is a good idea. After all, with current technology it is possible to put 4 floppy disk drives on a personal computer. It is just that doing so would be pointless. In this section we will discuss the motivation and goals of typical distributed systems, and look at their advantages and disadvantages compared to traditional centralized systems.

9.1.1. Advantages of Distributed Systems over Centralized Ones

The real driving force behind the trend towards decentralization is economics. A quarter of a century ago, computer pundit and gadfly Herb Grosch stated what later came to be known as Grosch's law: the computing power of a CPU is proportional to the square of its price. By paying twice as much, you could get four times the performance. This observation fit the mainframe technology of its time quite well, and led most organizations to buy the largest single machine they could afford.

With microprocessor technology, Grosch's law no longer holds. For a few hundred dollars you can get a CPU chip that can execute more instructions per second than one of the largest 1980s mainframes. If you are willing to pay twice as much, you get the same CPU, only running at a slightly higher clock speed. As a result, the most cost effective solution is frequently to harness a large number of cheap CPUs together in a system. Thus reason number one for the trend towards distributed systems is that these systems potentially have a much better price/performance ratio than a single large centralized system would. In effect, a distributed system gives more bang for the buck.

A slight variation on this theme is the observation that a collection of microprocessors can not only give a better price/performance ratio than a single mainframe, but may yield an absolute performance that no mainframe can achieve at any price. For example, with current technology it is possible to build a system from 1000 modern CPU chips, each of which runs at 20 MIPS (Millions of Instructions Per Second) for a total performance of 20,000 MIPS. For a single processor (i.e., CPU) to achieve this, it would have to execute an instruction in 0.05 nsec (50 picosec). No existing machine even comes close to this, and both theoretical and engineering considerations make it unlikely for some time. Theoretically, Einstein's theory of relativity dictates that nothing can travel faster than light, which can only cover 1.5 cm in 50 picosec. Practically, a computer of that speed fully contained in a 1.5 cm cube would generate so much heat that it would melt. Thus whether the goal is normal performance at low cost or extremely high performance at greater cost, distributed systems have much to offer.

As an aside, some authors make a distinction between *distributed systems*, which are designed to allow many users to work together, and *parallel systems*, whose only goal is to achieve maximum speedup on a single problem, as our 20,000 MIPS machine might. We believe that this distinction is difficult to maintain because the design spectrum is really a continuum. We prefer to use the term "distributed system" in the broadest sense to denote any system in which multiple interconnected CPUs work together.

A next reason for building a distributed system is that some applications are inherently distributed. In a factory automation system controlling robots and machines all along an assembly line, it often makes sense to give each robot and machine its own computer to manage it. When these are connected, we have an industrial distributed system. Similarly, when all the branches of a bank are connected, we have a commercial distributed system.

Another potential advantage of a distributed system over a centralized one is higher reliability. By distributing the workload over many machines, a single chip failure will bring down at most one machine, leaving the rest intact. Ideally, if 5 percent of the machines are down at any moment, the system should be able to continue to work with a 5 percent loss in performance. For critical applications, such as control of nuclear reactors or aircraft, using a distributed system to achieve high reliability may be the dominant consideration.

Finally, incremental growth is also potentially a big plus. Often a company will buy a mainframe with the intention of doing all its work on it. If the company prospers and the workload grows, at a certain point the mainframe will no longer be adequate. The only solutions are to either replace the mainframe with a larger one (if it exists), or add a second mainframe. Both of these can wreak major havoc with the company's operations. In contrast, with a distributed system, it may be possible to simply add more processors to the system, thus allowing it to expand gradually as the need arises. These advantages are summarized in Fig. 9-1.

Item	Description
Economics	Microprocessors offer a better price/performance than mainframes
Speed	A distributed system may have more total computing power than a mainframe
Inherent distribution	Some applications involve spatially separated machines
Reliability	If one machine crashes, the system as a whole can still survive
Incremental growth	Computing power can be added in small increments

Fig. 9-1. Advantages of distributed systems over centralized ones.

9.1.2. Advantages of Distributed Systems over Independent PCs

Given that microprocessors are a cost effective way to do business, why not just give everyone his own PC and let people work independently? For one thing, many users need to share data. For example, airline reservation clerks need access to the master data base of flights and existing reservations. Giving each clerk his own private copy of the entire data base would not work, since nobody would know which seats the other clerks had already sold. Shared data is absolutely essential to this and many other applications, so the machines must be interconnected. Interconnecting the machines leads to a distributed system. Data are not the only things that can be shared. Expensive peripherals, such as color laser printers, phototypesetters, and massive archival storage devices (e.g., optical juke boxes) are also candidates.

A third reason to connect a group of isolated computers into a distributed system is to achieve enhanced person-to-person communication. For many people, electronic mail has numerous attractions over paper mail, telephone, and FAX. It is much faster than paper mail, does not require both parties to be available at the same time as does the telephone, and unlike FAX, produces documents that can be edited, rearranged, stored in the computer, and manipulated with text processing programs.

Finally, a distributed system is potentially more flexible than giving each user an isolated personal computer. Although one model is to give each person a personal computer and connect them all with a LAN, this is not the only possibility. Another one is to have a mixture of personal and shared computers, perhaps of different sizes, and let jobs run on the most appropriate one, rather than always on the owner's machine. In this way, the workload can be spread over the computers more effectively, and the loss of a few machines may be compensated for by letting people run their jobs elsewhere. Figure 9-2 summarizes these points.

Item	Description
Data sharing	Allow many users access to a common data base
Device sharing	Allow many users to share expensive peripherals like color printers
Communication	Make human-to-human communication easier, for example, by electronic mail
Flexibility	Spread the workload over the available machines in the most cost effective way

Fig. 9-2. Advantages of distributed systems over isolated (personal) computers.

9.1.3. Disadvantages of Distributed Systems

Although distributed systems have their strengths, they also have their weaknesses. In this section, we will point out a few of them. We have already hinted at the worst problem: software. With the current state-of-the-art, we do not have much experience in designing, implementing, and using distributed software. What kinds of operating systems, programming languages, and applications are appropriate for these systems? How much should the users know about the distribution? How much should the system do and how much should the users do? The experts differ (not that this is unusual with experts, but when it comes to distributed systems, they are barely on speaking terms). As more research is done, this problem will diminish, but for the moment it should not be underestimated.

A second potential problem is due to the communication network. It can lose messages, which requires special software to handle, and it can become overloaded. When the network saturates, it must either be replaced or a second one must be added. In both cases, some portion of one or more buildings may have to be rewired at great expense, or network interface boards may have to be replaced (e.g., by fiber optics). Once the system comes to depend on the network, its loss or saturation can negate most of the advantages the distributed system was built to achieve.

Finally, the easy sharing of data, which we described above as an advantage, may turn out to be a two-edged sword. If people can conveniently access data all over the system, they may be equally able to conveniently access data that they have no business looking at. In other words, security is often a problem. For data that must be kept secret at all costs, it is often preferable to have a dedicated, isolated personal computer that has no network connections to any other machines, and is kept in a locked room with a secure safe in which all the floppy disks are stored. The disadvantages of distributed systems are summarized in Fig. 9-3.

Item	Description
Software	Little software exists at present for distributed systems
Networking	The network can saturate or cause other problems
Security.	Easy access also applies to secret data

Fig. 9-3. Disadvantages of distributed systems.

Despite these potential problems, many people feel that the advantages outweigh the disadvantages, and it is expected that distributed systems will become increasingly important in the coming years. In fact, it is likely that within a few years, most organizations will connect most of their computers into large distributed systems to provide better, cheaper, and more convenient service for the users.

9.2. HARDWARE CONCEPTS

Even though all distributed systems consist of multiple CPUs, there are several different ways the hardware can be organized, especially in terms of how they are interconnected and how they communicate. In this section we will take a brief look at distributed system hardware, in particular, how the machines are connected together. In the next section we will examine some of the software issues related to distributed systems.

Various classification schemes for multiple CPU computer systems have been proposed over the years, but none of them have really caught on and been widely adopted. Probably the most frequently cited taxonomy is Flynn's (1972), although it is fairly rudimentary. Flynn picked two characteristics that he considered essential: the number of instruction streams and the number of data streams. A computer with a single instruction stream and single data stream is called SISD. All traditional uniprocessor computers (i.e., those having only one CPU) fall in this category, from personal computers to large mainframes.

The next category is SIMD, single instruction stream, multiple data stream. This type refers to array processors with one instruction unit that fetches an instruction, and then commands many data units to carry it out in parallel, each with its own data. These machines are useful for computations that repeat the same calculation on many sets of data, for example, adding up all the elements of 64 independent vectors. Some supercomputers are SIMD.

The next category is MISD, multiple instruction stream, single data stream. No known computers fit this model. Finally comes MIMD, which essentially means a group of independent computers, each with its own program counter, program, and data. All distributed systems are MIMD, so this classification system is not tremendously useful for our purposes.

Although Flynn stopped here, we will go further. In Fig. 9-4, we divide all MIMD computers into two groups: those that have shared memory, usually called **multiprocessors**, and those that do not, sometimes called **multicomputers**. The essential difference is this: In a multiprocessor, there is a single virtual address space that is shared by all CPUs. If any CPU writes, for example, the value 44 to word 1000, any other CPU subsequently reading from *its* word 1000 will get the value 44. All the machines share the same memory.

In contrast, in a multicomputer, every machine has its own private memory. If one CPU writes the value 44 to word 1000, when another CPU reads word 1000 it will get whatever value was there before. The write of 44 does not affect *its* memory at all. A common example of a multicomputer is a collection of personal computers connected by a network.

Each of these categories can be further divided based on the architecture of the interconnection network. In Fig. 9-4 we describe these two categories as **bus** and **switched**. By bus we mean that there is a single network, backplane, bus, cable, or other medium that connects all the machines. Commercial cable television uses a scheme like this: the cable company runs a wire down the street, and all the subscribers have taps running from their televisions to it.

Switched systems do not have a single backbone like cable television. Instead there are individual wires from machine to machine, with many different wiring patterns in use. Messages move along the wires, with an explicit switching decision made at each step to route the message along one of the outgoing wires. The worldwide public telephone system is organized in this way.

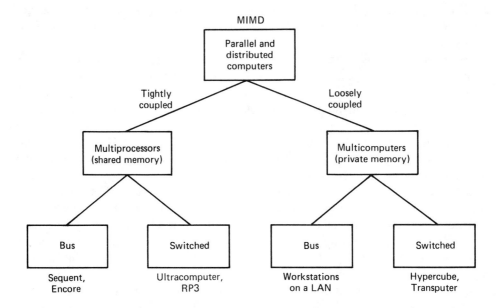

Fig. 9-4. A taxonomy of parallel and distributed computer systems.

Another dimension to our taxonomy is that in some systems the machines are **tightly coupled**, and in others they are **loosely coupled**. In a tightly-coupled system, the delay experienced when a message is sent from one computer to another is short, and the data rate is high, that is, the number of bits per second that can be transferred is large. In a loosely-coupled system, the opposite is true. The intermachine message delay is large, and the data rate is low. For example, two CPU chips on the same printed circuit board and connected by wires etched onto the board are likely to be tightly coupled, whereas two computers connected by a 1200 bit/sec modem over the telephone system are certain to be loosely-coupled.

Tightly-coupled systems tend to be used more as parallel systems (working on a single problem) and loosely-coupled ones tend to be used as distributed systems (working on many unrelated problems), although this is not always true. One famous counterexample is a project in which hundreds of computers all over the world worked together trying to factor a huge number (about 100 digits). Each computer was assigned a different range of divisors to try, and they all worked on the problem in their spare time, reporting the results back by electronic mail when they finished.

On the whole, multiprocessors tend to be more tightly coupled than multicomputers, because they can exchange data at memory speeds, but some fiber-optic based multicomputers can also work at memory speeds. Despite the vagueness of the terms "tightly coupled" and "loosely coupled," they are useful concepts, just as saying "Jack is fat and Jill is thin" conveys information even though one can get a fair amount of discussion about the concepts of fatness and thinness.

In the following four sections, we will look at the four categories of Fig. 9-4 in more detail, namely bus multiprocessors, switched multiprocessors, bus multicomputers, and switched multicomputers. Although these topics are not directly related to our main concern, distributed operating systems, they will shed some light on the subject because as we shall see, different categories of machines use different kinds of operating systems.

9.2.1. Bus-Based Multiprocessors

Bus-based multiprocessors consist of some number of CPUs all connected to a common bus, along with a memory module. A simple configuration is to have a high-speed backplane or motherboard, into which CPU and memory cards can be inserted. A typical bus has 32 address lines, 32 data lines, and perhaps 20 to 30 control lines, all of which operate in parallel. To read a word of memory, a CPU puts the address of the word it wants on the bus address lines, then puts a signal on the appropriate control lines to indicate that it wants to read. The memory responds by putting the value of the word on the data lines to allow the requesting CPU to read it in. Writes work in a similar way.

Since there is only one memory, if CPU A writes a word to memory and then CPU B reads that word back a microsecond later, B will get the value just written. A memory that has this property is said to be **coherent**. Coherence plays an important role in distributed operating systems in a variety of ways that we will study later.

The problem with this scheme is that with as few as 4 or 5 CPUs, the bus will usually be overloaded and performance will drop drastically. The solution is to add a high-speed **cache memory** between the CPU and the bus, as shown in Fig. 9-5. The cache holds the most recently accessed words. All memory requests go through the cache. If the requested word is in the cache, the cache itself responds to the CPU, and no bus request is made. If the cache is large enough, the probability of success, called the **hit rate**, will be high, and the amount of bus traffic per CPU will drop dramatically, allowing many more CPUs in the system. Cache sizes of 64K to 1M are common, which often gives a hit rate of 90 percent or more.

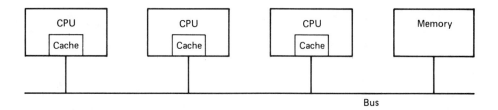

Fig. 9-5. A bus-based multiprocessor.

However, the introduction of caches also brings a serious problem with it. Suppose two CPUs, A and B, each read the same word into their respective caches. Then A overwrites the word. When B next reads that word, it gets its old value, not the value A just wrote. The memory is now incoherent, and the system hard to program.

Many researchers have studied this problem, and various solutions are known. Below we will sketch one of them. Suppose the cache memories are designed so that whenever a word is *written* to the cache, it also is written through to memory as well.

Such a cache is, not surprisingly, called a **write-through cache.** In this design, cache hits for reads do not cause bus traffic, but cache misses for reads, and all writes, hits and misses, cause bus traffic.

In addition, all caches constantly monitor the bus. Whenever a cache sees a write occurring to a memory address present in its cache, it either removes that entry from its cache, or updates the cache entry with the new value. Such a cache is called a **snoopy cache** (or sometimes, **snooping cache**) because it is always snooping (eavesdropping) on the bus. A design consisting of snoopy write-through caches is coherent and is invisible to the programmer. Nearly all bus-based multiprocessors use either this architecture or a closely-related one. Using it, it is possible to put about 32-64 CPUs on a single bus.

9.2.2. Switched Multiprocessors

To build a multiprocessor with more than 64 processors, a different method is needed to connect the CPUs with the memory. One possibility is to divide the memory up into modules, and connect them to the CPUs with a **crossbar switch**, as shown in Fig. 9-6(a). Each CPU and each memory has a connection coming out of it, as shown. At every intersection is a tiny electronic **crosspoint switch** that can be opened and closed in hardware. When a CPU wants to access a particular memory, the crosspoint switch connecting them is momentarily closed, to allow the access to take place. The virtue of the crossbar switch is that many CPUs can be accessing memory at the same time, although if two CPUs try to access the same memory simultaneously, one of them will have to wait.

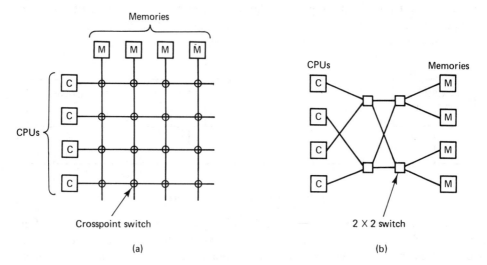

Fig. 9-6. (a) A crossbar switch. (b) An omega switching network.

The downside of the crossbar switch is that with n CPUs and n memories, n^2 crosspoint switches are needed. For large n, this number can be prohibitive. As a result, people have looked for, and found, alternative switching networks that require fewer switches. The **omega network** of Fig. 9-6(b) is one example. This network contains four 2×2 switches, each one having two inputs and two outputs. Each switch can route either input to either output. A careful look at the figure will show that with proper settings of the switches, every CPU can access every memory.

In the general case, with n CPUs and n memories, the omega network requires $\log_2 n$ switching stages, each containing $n/2$ switches, for a total of $(n\log_2 n)/2$ switches. Although for large n this is much better than n^2, it is still substantial.

Furthermore, there is another problem: delay. For example, for $n = 1024$, there are 10 switching stages from the CPU to the memory, and another 10 for the requested word to come back again. Suppose the CPU is a modern RISC chip running at 50 MHz, that is, the instruction execution time is 20 nsec. If a memory request is to traverse a total of 20 switching stages (10 outbound and 10 back) in 20 nsec, the switching time must be 1 nsec. The complete multiprocessor will need 5120 1-nsec switches. This is not going to be cheap.

People have attempted to reduce the cost by going to hierarchical systems. Some memory is associated with each CPU. Each CPU can access its own local memory quickly, but accessing anybody else's memory is slower. This design gives rise to what is known as a **NUMA (NonUniform Memory Access)** machine (LaRowe et al., 1991). Although NUMA machines have better average access times than machines based on omega networks, they have the new complication that the placement of the programs and data becomes critical in order to make most access go to the local memory.

To summarize, bus-based multiprocessors, even with snoopy caches, are limited by the amount of bus capacity to about 64 CPUs at most. To go beyond that requires a switching network, such as a crossbar switch, an omega switching network, or something similar. Large crossbar switches are very expensive, and large omega networks are both expensive and slow. NUMA machines require complex algorithms for good software placement. The conclusion is clear: building a large, tightly-coupled, shared memory multiprocessor is difficult and expensive.

9.2.3. Bus-Based Multicomputers

On the other hand, building a multicomputer (i.e., no shared memory) is easy. Each CPU has a direct connection to its own local memory. The only problem left is how the CPUs communicate with each other. Clearly some interconnection scheme is needed here too, but since it is only for CPU-to-CPU communication, the volume of traffic will be several orders of magnitude lower than when the interconnection network is also used for CPU-to-memory traffic.

In Fig. 9-7 we see a bus-based multicomputer. It looks topologically similar to the bus-based multiprocessor, but since there will be much less traffic over it, it need not be a high-speed backplane bus. In fact, it can be a much lower speed LAN (typically 10-100 Mbps, compared to 300 Mbps and up for a backplane bus). Thus Fig. 9-7 is more often a collection of workstations on a LAN than a collection of CPU cards inserted into a fast bus (although the latter is definitely possible).

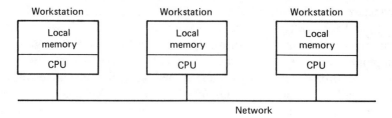

Fig. 9-7. A multicomputer consisting of workstations on a LAN.

9.2.4. Switched Multicomputers

Our last category consists of switched multicomputers. Various interconnection networks have been proposed and built, but all have the property that each CPU has direct and exclusive access to its own, private memory. Figure 9-8 shows two popular topologies, a grid and a hypercube. Grids are easy to understand and lay out on printed circuit boards. They are best suited to problems that have an inherent two-dimensional nature, such as graph theory or vision (e.g., robot eyes or analyzing photographs).

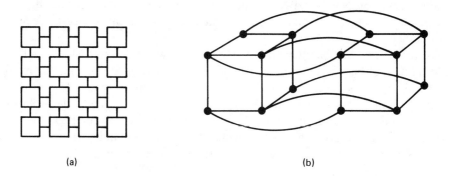

(a)   (b)

Fig. 9-8. (a) Grid. (b) Hypercube.

A **hypercube** is an n-dimensional cube. The hypercube of Fig. 9-8(b) is 4-dimensional. It can be thought of as two ordinary cubes, each with 8 vertices and 12 edges. Each vertex is a CPU. Each edge is a connection between two CPUs. The corresponding vertices in each of the two cubes are connected.

To expand the hypercube to five dimensions, we would add another set of two interconnected cubes to the figure, and connect the corresponding edges in the two halves, and so on. For an n-dimensional hypercube, each CPU has n connections to other CPUs. Thus the complexity of the wiring increases only logarithmically with the size. Since only nearest neighbors are connected, many messages have to make several hops to reach their destination. However, the longest possible path also grows logarithmically with the size, in contrast to the grid, where it grows as the square root of the number of CPUs. Hypercubes with 1024 CPUs have been commercially available for several years, and hypercubes with as many as 16,384 CPUs are starting to become available.

9.3. SOFTWARE CONCEPTS

Although the hardware is important, the software is even more important. The image that a system presents to its users, and how they think about the system, is largely determined by the operating system software, not the hardware. In this section we will give an introduction to the various types of operating systems for the multiprocessors and multicomputers we have just studied, and discuss which kind of software goes with which kind of hardware.

Operating systems cannot be put into nice, neat pigeonholes like hardware. By nature software is vague and amorphous. Still, it is more-or-less possible to distinguish two kinds of operating systems for multiple CPU systems: loosely coupled and tightly coupled. As we shall see, loosely and tightly-coupled software is roughly analogous to loosely and tightly-coupled hardware.

Loosely-coupled software allows machines and users of a distributed system to be fundamentally independent of one another, but still to interact to a limited degree where that is necessary. Consider a group of personal computers, each of which has its own CPU, its own memory, its own hard disk, and its own operating system, but which share some resources such as laser printers and data bases over a LAN. This system is loosely coupled, since the individual machines are clearly distinguishable, each with its own job to do. If the network should go down for some reason, the individual machines can still continue to run to a considerable degree, although some functionality may be lost (e.g., the ability to print files).

To show how difficult it is to make definitions in this area, now consider the same system as above, but without the network. To print a file, the user writes the file on a floppy disk, carries it to the machine with the printer, reads it in, and then prints it. Is this still a distributed system, only now even more loosely coupled? It's hard to say. From a fundamental point of view, there is not really any difference between communicating over a LAN and communicating by carrying floppy disks around. At most one can say that the delay and data rate are worse in the second example.

At the other extreme we might find a multiprocessor dedicated to running a single chess program in parallel. Each CPU is assigned a board to evaluate, and it spends its time examining that board and all the boards that can be generated from it. When the evaluation is finished, the CPU reports back the results, and is given a new board to work on. The software for this system, both the application program and the operating system required to support it, is clearly much more tightly coupled than in our previous example.

We have now seen four kinds of distributed hardware and two kinds of distributed software. In theory, there should be eight combinations of hardware and software. In fact, there are only four, because to the user, the interconnection technology is not visible. A multiprocessor is a multiprocessor, whether it uses a bus with snoopy caches or whether it uses an omega network. In the following sections we will look at some of the most common combinations of hardware and software.

9.3.1. Network Operating Systems and NFS

Let us start with loosely-coupled software on loosely-coupled hardware, since this is probably the most common combination at many organizations. A typical example is a network of engineering workstations connected by a LAN. In this model, each user has a workstation for his exclusive use. It may or may not have a hard disk. It definitely has its own operating system. All commands are normally run locally, right on the workstation.

However, it is sometimes possible for a user to remotely log into another workstation by using a command such as

```
rlogin machine
```

The effect of this command is to turn the user's own workstation into a remote terminal logged into the remote machine. Commands typed on the keyboard are sent to the remote machine, and output from the remote machine is displayed on the screen. To switch to a different remote machine, it is necessary to first log out, then to use the *rlogin* command to connect to another machine. At any instant, only one machine can be used, and the selection of the machine is entirely manual.

Networks of workstations often also have a remote copy command to copy files from one machine to another. For example, a command like

```
rcp machine1:file1 machine2:file2
```

might copy the file *file1* from *machine1* to *machine2* and give it the name *file2* there. Again here, the movement of files is explicit, and requires the user to be completely aware of where all files are located and where all commands are being executed.

While better than nothing, this form of communication is extremely primitive and has led system designers to search for more convenient forms of communication and information sharing. One approach is to provide a shared, global file system accessible from all the workstations. The file system is supported by one or more machines called **file servers**. The file servers accept requests from user programs running on the other (nonserver) machines, called **clients**, to read and write files. Each incoming request is examined and executed, and the reply is sent back, as illustrated in Fig. 9-9.

File servers generally maintain hierarchical file systems, each with a root directory containing subdirectories and files. Workstations can import or mount these file systems, augmenting their local file systems with those located on the servers. For example, in Fig. 9-10, two file servers are shown. One has a directory called *games*, while the other has a directory called *work*. These directories each contain several files. Both of the clients shown have mounted both of the servers, but they have mounted them in different places in their respective file systems. Client 1 has mounted them in its root directory, and can access them as /*games* and /*work*, respectively. Client 2, like client 1, has mounted *games* in its root directory, but regarding

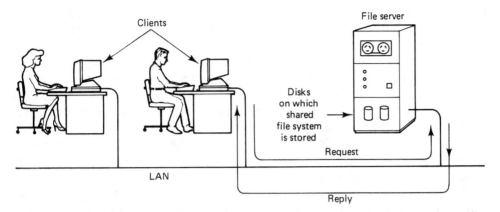

Fig. 9-9. Two clients and a server in a network operating system.

the reading of mail and news as a kind of game, has created a directory /games/work and mounted *work* there. Consequently, it can access *news* using the path /games/work/news rather than /work/news.

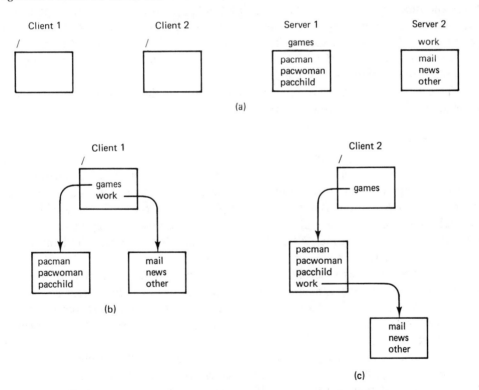

Fig. 9-10. Different clients may mount the servers in different places.

While it does not matter where a client mounts a server in its directory hierarchy, it is important to notice that different clients can have a different view of the file system. The name of a file depends on where it is being accessed from, and how that machine has set up its file system. Because each of the workstations operates relatively independently from the rest, there is no guarantee that they all present the same directory hierarchy to their programs.

The operating system that is used in this kind of environment must manage the individual workstations, file servers and also take care of the communication between them. It is possible that the machines all run the same operating system, but this is not required. If the clients and servers run on different systems, then as a bare minimum they must agree on the format and meaning of all the messages that they may potentially exchange. In a situation like this, where each machine has a high degree of autonomy and there are few system-wide requirements, people usually speak of a **network operating system**.

One of the best-known network operating systems is Sun Microsystem's **Network File System**, universally known as **NFS**. We will now examine this system, partly because it is widely used and partly to be able to contrast the true distributed systems we will look at later with a current commercial product.

NFS was originally designed and implemented by Sun Microsystems for use on its UNIX-based workstations. Other manufacturers now support it as well, for both UNIX and other operating systems (including MS-DOS). NFS supports heterogeneous systems, for example, MS-DOS clients making use of UNIX servers. It is not even required that all the machines use the same hardware. It is common to find MS-DOS clients running on Intel 386 CPUs getting service from UNIX file servers running on Motorola 68030 or Sun SPARC CPUs.

Three aspects of NFS are of interest: the architecture, the protocol, and the implementation. Let us look at these in turn.

NFS Architecture

The basic idea behind NFS is to allow an arbitrary collection of clients and servers to share a common file system. In most cases, all the clients and servers are on the same LAN, but this is not required. It is possible to run NFS over a wide-area network. For simplicity we will speak of clients and servers as though they were on distinct machines, but in fact, NFS allows every machine to be both a client and a server at the same time.

Each NFS server exports one or more of its directories for access by remote clients. When a directory is made available, so are all of its subdirectories, so in fact, entire directory trees are normally exported. The list of directories a server exports is maintained in the /etc/exports file, so these directories can be exported automatically when the server is booted.

Clients access exported directories by mounting them. When a client mounts a (remote) directory, it becomes part of its directory hierarchy, as shown in Fig. 9-10. Many Sun workstations are diskless. If it so desires, a diskless client can mount a remote file system on its root directory, resulting in a file system that is supported entirely on a remote server. Those workstations that do have local disks can mount remote directories anywhere they wish on top of their local directory hierarchy, resulting in a file system that is partly local and partly remote. To programs running on the client machine, there is (almost) no difference between a file located on a remote file server and a file located on the local disk.

Thus the basic architectural characteristic of NFS is that servers export directories and clients remotely mount them. If two or more clients mount the same directory at the same time, they can communicate by sharing files in their common directories. A program on one client can create a file, and a program on a different one can read the file. Once the mounts have been done, nothing special has to be done to achieve sharing. The shared files are just there in the directory hierarchy of multiple machines, and can be read and written the usual way. This simplicity is one of the great attractions of NFS.

NFS Protocols

Since one of the goals of NFS is to support a heterogeneous system, with clients and servers possibly running different operating systems on different hardware, it is essential that the interface between the clients and servers be well defined. Only then is it possible for anyone to be able to write a new client implementation and expect it to work correctly with existing servers, and vice versa.

NFS accomplishes this goal by defining two client-server protocols. A **protocol** is a set of requests sent by clients to servers, along with the corresponding replies sent by the servers back to the clients. (Protocols are an important topic in distributed systems; we will come back to them later in more detail.) As long as a server recognizes and can handle all the requests in the protocols, it need not know anything at all about its clients. Similarly, clients can treat servers as "black boxes" that accept and process a specific set of requests. How they do it is their own business.

The first NFS protocol handles mounting. A client can send a path name to a server and request permission to mount that directory somewhere in its directory hierarchy. The place where it is to be mounted is not contained in the message as the server does not care where it is to be mounted. If the path name is legal and the directory specified has been exported, the server returns a **file handle** to the client. The file handle contains fields uniquely identifying the file system type, the disk, the i-node number of the directory, and security information. Subsequent calls to read and write files in the mounted directory use the file handle.

Many clients are configured to mount certain remote directories without manual intervention. Typically, these clients contain a file called /etc/rc, which is a shell script containing the remote mount commands. This shell script is executed automatically when the client is booted.

Alternatively, Sun's version of UNIX also supports **automounting**. This feature allows a set of remote directories to be associated with a local directory. None of these remote directories are mounted (or their servers even contacted) when the client is booted. Instead, the first time a remote file is opened, the operating system sends a message to each of the servers. The first one to reply wins, and its directory is mounted.

Automounting has two principal advantages over static mounting via the /etc/rc file. First, if one of the NFS servers named in /etc/rc happens to be down, it is impossible to bring the client up, at least not without some difficulty, delay, and quite a few error messages. If the user does not even need that server at the moment, all that work is wasted. Second, by allowing the client to try a set of servers in parallel, a degree of fault tolerance can be achieved (because only one of them need to be up), and the performance can be improved (by choosing the first one to reply—presumably the least heavily loaded).

On the other hand, it is tacitly assumed that all the file systems specified as alternatives for the automount are identical. Since NFS provides no support for file or directory replication, it is up to the user to arrange for all the file systems to be the same. Consequently, automounting is most often used for read-only file systems containing system binaries and other files that rarely change.

The second NFS protocol is for directory and file access. Clients can send messages to servers to manipulate directories and to read and write files. In addition, they can also access file attributes, such as file mode, size, and time of last modification. Most UNIX system calls are supported by NFS, with the perhaps surprising exception of OPEN and CLOSE.

The omission of OPEN and CLOSE is not an accident. It is fully intentional. It is not necessary to open a file before reading it, nor to close it when done. Instead, to read a file, a client sends the server a message containing the file name, with a request to look it up and return a file handle, which is a structure that identifies the file. Unlike an OPEN call, this LOOKUP operation does not copy any information into internal system tables. The READ call contains the file handle of the file to read, the offset in the file to begin reading, and the number of bytes desired. Each such message is self contained. The advantage of this scheme is that the server does not have to remember anything about open connections in between calls to it. Thus if a server crashes and then recovers, no information about open files is lost, because there is none. A server like this that does not maintain state information about open files is said to be **stateless**.

In contrast, in UNIX System V, the **Remote File System, RFS**, requires a file to be opened before it can be read or written. The server then makes a table entry keeping track of the fact that the file is open, and where the reader currently is, so each request need not carry an offset. The disadvantage of this scheme is that if a server crashes and then quickly reboots, all open connections are lost, and client programs fail. NFS does not have this property.

Unfortunately, the NFS method makes it difficult to achieve the exact UNIX file semantics. For example, in UNIX a file can be opened and locked so that other processes cannot access it. When the file is closed, the locks are released. In a stateless server such as NFS, locks cannot be associated with open files, because the server does not know which files are open. NFS therefore needs a separate, additional mechanism to handle locking.

NFS uses the UNIX protection mechanism, with the rwx bits for the owner, group, and others. Originally, each request message simply contained the user and group ids of the caller, which the NFS server used to validate the access. In effect, it trusted the clients not to cheat. Several years' experience abundantly demonstrated that such an assumption was—how shall we put it?—naive. Currently, public key cryptography can be used to establish a secure key for validating the client and server on each request and reply. When this option is enabled, a malicious client cannot impersonate another client because it does not know that client's secret key. As an aside, cryptography is used only to authenticate the parties. The data themselves are never encrypted.

All the keys used for the authentication, as well as other information are maintained by the **NIS** (**Network Information Service**). The NIS was formerly known as the **yellow pages**. Its function is to store (key, value) pairs. When a key is provided, it returns the corresponding value. Not only does it handle encryption keys, but it also stores the mapping of user names to (encrypted) passwords, as well as the mapping of machine names to network addresses, and other items.

The network information servers are replicated using a master/slave arrangement. To read their data, a process can use either the master or any of the copies (slaves). However, all changes must be made only to the master, which then propagates them to the slaves. There is a short interval after an update in which the data base is inconsistent.

NFS Implementation

Although the implementation of the client and server code is independent of the NFS protocols, it is interesting to take a quick peek at Sun's implementation. It consists of three layers, as shown in Fig. 9-11. The top layer is the system call layer. This handles the calls like OPEN, READ, and CLOSE. After parsing the call and checking the parameters, it invokes the second layer, the virtual file system (VFS) layer.

The task of the VFS layer is to maintain a table with one entry for each open file, analogous to the table of i-nodes for open files in UNIX. In ordinary UNIX, an i-node is uniquely indicated by a (device, i-node number) pair. Instead, the VFS layer has an entry, called a **v-node** (**virtual i-node**), for every open file. V-nodes are used to tell whether the file is local or remote. For remote files, enough information is provided to be able to access them.

To see how v-nodes are used, let us trace a sequence of MOUNT, OPEN, and READ system calls. To mount a remote file system, the system administrator calls the *mount* program specifying the remote directory, the local directory on which it is to be mounted, and other information. The *mount* program parses the name of the remote directory to be mounted and discovers the name of the machine on which the remote directory is located. It then contacts that machine asking for a file handle for the remote directory. If the directory exists and is available for remote mounting, the server returns a file handle for the directory. Finally, it makes a MOUNT system call passing the handle to the kernel.

The kernel then constructs a v-node for the remote directory and asks the NFS client code in Fig. 9-11 to create an **r-node** (**remote i-node**) in its internal tables to hold the file handle. The v-node points to the r-node. Each v-node in the VFS layer will ultimately contain either a pointer to an r-node in the NFS client code, or a

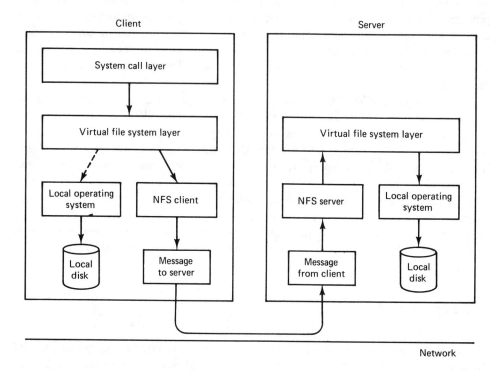

Fig. 9-11. NFS layer structure.

pointer to an i-node in the local operating system (see Fig. 9-11). Thus from the v-node it is possible to see if a file or directory is local or remote, and if it is remote, to find its file handle.

When a remote file is opened, at some point during the parsing of the path name, the kernel hits the directory on which the remote file system is mounted. It sees that this directory is remote and in the directory's v-node finds the pointer to the r-node. It then asks the NFS client code to open the file. The NFS client code looks up the remaining portion of the path name on the remote server associated with the mounted directory and gets back a file handle for it. It makes an r-node for the remote file in its tables and reports back to the VFS layer, which puts in its tables a v-node for the file that points to the r-node. Again here we see that every open file or directory has a v-node that points to either an r-node or an i-node.

The caller is given a file descriptor for the remote file. This file descriptor is mapped onto the v-node by tables in the VFS layer. Note that no table entries are made on the server side. Although the server is prepared to provide file handles upon request, it does not keep track of which files happen to have file handles outstanding and which do not. When a file handle is sent to it for file access, it checks the handle, and if it is valid, uses it. Validation can include verifying an authentication key contained in the RPC headers, if security is enabled.

When the file descriptor is used in a subsequent system call, for example, READ, the VFS layer locates the corresponding v-node, and from that determines whether it is local or remote and also which i-node or r-node describes it.

For efficiency reasons, transfers between client and server are done in large chunks, normally 8192 bytes, even if fewer bytes are requested. After the client's VFS layer has gotten the 8K chunk it needs, it automatically issues a request for the next chunk, so it will have it should it be needed shortly. This feature is known as **read ahead**, and improves performance considerably.

For writes an analogous policy is followed. If a WRITE system call supplies fewer than 8192 bytes of data, the data is just accumulated locally. Only when the entire 8K chunk is full is it sent to the server. However, when a file is closed, all of its data are sent to the server immediately.

Another technique used to improve performance is caching, as in ordinary UNIX. Servers cache data to avoid disk accesses, but this is invisible to the clients. Clients maintain two caches, one for file attributes (i-nodes) and one for file data. When either an i-node or a file block is needed, a check is first made to see if it can be satisfied out of the client's cache. If so, network traffic can be avoided.

While client caching helps performance enormously, it also introduces some nasty problems. Suppose two clients are both caching the same file block, and one of them modifies it. When the other one reads the block, it gets the old (stale) value. The cache is not coherent. We saw the same problem with multiprocessors earlier. However, there it was solved by having the caches snoop on the bus to detect all writes and invalidate or update cache entries accordingly. With a file cache that is not possible, because a write to a file that results in a cache hit on one client does not generate any network traffic. Even if it did, snooping on the network is nearly impossible with current hardware.

Given the potential severity of this problem, the NFS implementation does several things to mitigate it. For one, associated with each cache block is a timer. When the timer expires, the entry is discarded. Normally the timer is 3 sec for data blocks and 30 sec for directory blocks. Doing this reduces the risk somewhat. In addition, whenever a cached file is opened, a message is sent to the server to find out when the file was last modified. If the last modification occurred after the local copy was cached, the cache copy is discarded and the new copy fetched from the server. Finally, once every 30 sec a cache timer expires, and all the dirty (i.e., modified) blocks in the cache are sent to the server.

Still, NFS has been widely criticized for not implementing the proper UNIX semantics. A write to a file on one client may or may not be seen when another client reads the file, depending on the timing. Furthermore, when a file is created, it may not be visible to the outside world for as much as 30 sec. Other similar problems exist as well.

From this example we see that although NFS provides a shared file system, because the resulting system is kind of a patched up UNIX, the semantics of file access are not entirely well defined, and running a set of cooperating programs again may give different results, depending on the timing. Furthermore, the only issue NFS deals with is the file system. Other issues, such as process execution, are not addressed at all. Nevertheless, NFS is popular and widely used.

9.3.2. True Distributed Systems

NFS is an example of loosely-coupled software on loosely-coupled hardware. Other than the shared file system, it is quite apparent to the users that the system consists of numerous computers, each one having a specific task. Each one can run its own operating system, and do whatever its owner wants. There is essentially no coordination at all, except for the rule that client-server traffic must obey the NFS protocols.

The next evolutionary step beyond this is tightly-coupled software on the same loosely-coupled (i.e., multicomputer) hardware. The goal of such a system is to create the illusion in the minds of the users that the entire network of computers is a single timesharing system, rather than a collection of distinct machines. This brings us to our definition of a distributed system:

A distributed system is one that runs on a collection of machines that do not have shared memory, yet looks to its users like a single computer.

Some authors refer to this property as the **single system image**. Others put it slightly differently, saying that a distributed system is one that runs on a collection of networked machines but acts like a **virtual uniprocessor**. No matter how it is expressed, the essential idea is that the users should not have to be aware of the existence of multiple CPUs in the system. No current system fulfills this requirement entirely yet, but a number of promising candidates are on the horizon. Some of these will be discussed later in this book.

What are some characteristics of a distributed system? To start with, there must be a single, global interprocess communication mechanism so that any process can talk to any other process. It will not do to have different mechanisms on different machines or different mechanisms for local communication and remote communication. There must also be a global protection scheme. Mixing access control lists, the UNIX protection bits, and capabilities will not give a single system image. Process management must also be the same everywhere. How processes are created, destroyed, started, and stopped must not vary from machine to machine. In short, the idea behind NFS, that any machine can do whatever it wants to as long as it obeys the NFS protocols when engaging in client-server communication, is not enough. Not only must there be a single set of system calls available on all machines, but these calls must be designed so that they make sense in a distributed environment.

As a logical consequence of having the same system call interface everywhere, it is normal that identical kernels run on all the CPUs in the system. Doing so makes it easier to coordinate activities that must be global. For example, when a process has to be started up, all the kernels have to cooperate in finding the best place to execute it. In addition, a global file system is needed, preferably one whose semantics are better defined than those of NFS.

Nevertheless, each kernel can have considerable control over its own local resources. For example, since there is no shared memory, it is logical to allow each kernel to manage its own memory. For example, if swapping or paging is used, the kernel on each CPU is the logical place to determine what to swap or page. There is no reason to centralize this authority. Similarly, if multiple processes are running on some CPU, it makes sense to do the scheduling right there too.

A considerable body of knowledge is now available about designing distributed operating systems. Rather than going into it here, we will first finish off our survey of the different combinations of hardware and software, and come back to it in Sec. 9.4.

9.3.3. Multiprocessor Timesharing Systems

The last combination we wish to discuss is tightly-coupled software on tightly-coupled hardware. While various special-purpose machines exist in this category (such as dedicated data base machines), the most common general-purpose examples are multiprocessors such as those made by Sequent and Encore that are operated as a UNIX timesharing system, only with multiple CPUs instead of one CPU. To the outside world, a multiprocessor with 32 3 MIPS CPUs acts very much like a single 96 MIPS CPU. This is the single system image discussed above. Only implementing it on a multiprocessor makes life much easier, since the entire design can be centralized.

The key characteristic of this class of system is the existence of a single run queue: a list of all the processes in the system that are logically unblocked and ready to run. The run queue is a data structure kept in the shared memory. As an example, consider the system of Fig. 9-12, which has three CPUs and five processes that are ready to run. All five processes are located in the shared memory, and three of them are currently executing: process A on CPU 1, process B on CPU 2, and process C on CPU 3. The other two processes, D and E, are also in memory, waiting their turn.

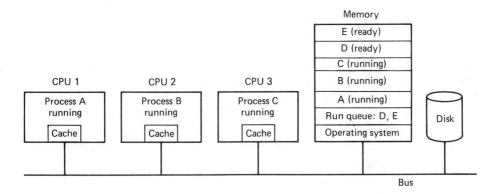

Fig. 9-12. A multiprocessor with a single run queue.

Now suppose that process B blocks waiting for I/O or its quantum runs out. Either way, CPU 2 must suspend it, and find another process to run. CPU 2 will normally begin executing operating system code (located in the shared memory). After having saved all of B's registers, it will enter a critical region to run the scheduler to look for another process to run. It is essential that the scheduler be run as a critical region to prevent two CPUs from choosing the same process to run next. The necessary mutual exclusion can be achieved by using monitors, semaphores, or any of the other standard constructions we studied in Chap. 2.

Once CPU 2 has gained exclusive access to the run queue, it can remove the first entry, D, exit from the critical region, and begin executing D. Initially, execution will be slow, since CPU 2's cache is full of words belonging to that part of the shared memory containing process B, but after a little while, these will have been purged and the cache will be full of D's code and data.

Because none of the CPUs have local memory and all programs are stored in the global shared memory, it does not matter on which CPU a process runs. If a long-running process is scheduled many times before it completes, on the average, it will spend about the same amount of time running on each CPU. The only factor that has any effect at all on CPU choice is the slight gain in performance when a process starts up on a CPU that is currently caching part of its address space. In other words, if all CPUs are idle, waiting for I/O, and one process becomes ready, it is slightly preferable to allocate it to the CPU it was last using, assuming that no other process has used that CPU since (Vaswani and Zahorjan, 1991).

As an aside, if a process blocks for I/O on a multiprocessor, the operating system has the choice of suspending it or just letting it do busy waiting. If most I/O is completed in less time than it takes to do a process switch, then busy waiting is preferable. Some systems let the process keep its processor for a few milliseconds, in the hope that the I/O will complete soon, but if that does not occur before the timer runs out, a process switch is done (Karlin et al., 1991).

An area in which this kind of multiprocessor differs appreciably from a network or distributed system is the organization of the file system. The operating system normally contains a traditional file system, including a single, unified block cache. When any process executes a system call, a trap is made to the operating system, which carries it out, using semaphores, monitors, or something equivalent to lock out other CPUs while critical sections are being executed or central tables are being accessed. In this way, when a WRITE system call is done, the central block cache is locked, the new data are entered into the cache, and the lock released. Any subsequent READ call will see the new data, just as on a single processor system. On the whole, the file system is hardly different from a single processor file system. In fact, on some multiprocessors, one of the CPUs is dedicated to running the operating system; the other ones run user programs. This situation is undesirable, however, as the operating system machine is often a bottleneck. This point is discussed in detail in (Boykin and Langerman, 1990).

It should be clear that the methods used on the multiprocessor to achieve the appearance of a virtual uniprocessor are not applicable to machines that do not have shared memory. Centralized run queues and block caches only work when all CPUs have access to them with very low delay. Although these data structures could be simulated on a network of machines, the communication costs make this approach prohibitively expensive.

Figure 9-13 shows some of the differences between the three kinds of systems we have examined above.

Item	Network operating system	Distributed operating system	Multiprocessor operating system
Does it look like a virtual uniprocessor?	No	Yes	Yes
Do all have to run the same operating system?	No	Yes	Yes
How many copies of the operating system are there?	N	N	1
How is communication achieved?	Shared files	Messages	Shared memory
Are agreed upon network protocols required?	Yes	Yes	No
Is there a single run queue?	No	No	Yes
Does file sharing have well-defined semantics?	Usually no	Yes	Yes

Fig. 9-13. Comparison of three different ways of organizing N CPUs.

9.4. DESIGN ISSUES

In the previous sections we have looked at distributed systems and related topics from both the hardware and the software point of view. In the remainder of this chapter we will briefly look at some of the key design issues that people contemplating building a distributed operating system must deal with. We will come back to them in more detail later in the book.

9.4.1. Transparency

Probably the single most important issue is how to achieve the single system image. In other words, how do the system designers fool everyone into thinking that the collection of machines is simply an old-fashioned single processor timesharing system? A system that realizes this goal is often said to be **transparent**.

Transparency can be achieved at two different levels. Easiest to do is to hide the distribution from the users. For example, when a UNIX user types *make* to recompile a large number of files in a directory, he need not be told that all the compilations are proceeding in parallel on different machines and are using a variety of file servers to do it. To him, the only thing that is unusual is that the performance of the system is half-way decent for a change. In terms of commands issued from the terminal and results displayed on the terminal, the distributed system can be made to look just like a single processor system.

At a lower level, it is also possible, but harder, to make the system look transparent to programs. In other words, the system call interface can be designed so that the existence of multiple processors is not visible. Pulling the wool over the programmer's eyes is harder than pulling the wool over the terminal user's eyes however. As we saw earlier, the semantics of file sharing are subtly different in NFS from UNIX. A programmer who is used to the UNIX semantics might well stumble over this problem. On the other hand, a distributed system could be designed to have well-defined, consistent semantics, even in the presence of file caching. It's just that these semantics might not be those of UNIX.

What does transparency really mean? It is one of those slippery concepts that sounds reasonable, but is hard to understand without looking at concrete examples. Let us look at a few to make the idea clearer. To start with, imagine a distributed system consisting of workstations each running some standard operating system. Normally system services (e.g., reading files) are obtained by issuing a system call that traps to the kernel. In such a system, remote files should be accessed the same way. A system in which remote files are accessed by explicitly setting up a network connection to a remote server and then sending messages to it is not transparent because remote services are then being accessed differently than local ones. The programmer can tell that multiple machines are involved, and this is not allowed.

The concept of transparency can be applied to several aspects of a distributed system, as shown in Fig. 9-14. **Location transparency** refers to the fact that in a true distributed system, users cannot tell where hardware and software resources such as CPUs, printers, files, and data bases are located. The name of the resource must not secretly encode the location of the resource, so names like *machine1:prog.c* or */machine1/prog.c* are not acceptable.

Kind	Meaning
Location transparency	The users cannot tell where resources are located
Migration transparency	Resources can move at will without changing their names
Replication transparency	The users cannot tell how many copies exist
Concurrency transparency	Multiple users can share resources automatically
Parallelism transparency	Activities can happen in parallel without users knowing

Fig. 9-14. Different kinds of transparency in a distributed system.

Migration transparency means that resources must be free to move from one location to another without having their names change. In the example of Fig. 9-10 we saw how server directories could be mounted in arbitrary places in the clients' directory hierarchy. Since a path like */work/news* does not reveal the location of the server, it is location transparent. However, now suppose that the folks running the servers decide that reading network news really falls in the category "games" rather than in the category "work." Accordingly, they move *news* from server 2 to server 1. The next time client 1 boots and mounts the servers in his customary way, he will notice that */work/news* no longer exists. Instead, there is a new entry */games/news*.

Thus the mere fact that a file or directory has migrated from one server to another has forced it to acquire a new name because the system of remote mounts is not migration transparent.

If a distributed system has **replication transparency**, then the operating system is free to make additional copies of files and other resources on its own without the users noticing. Clearly in the previous example, automatic replication is impossible because the names and locations are so closely tied together. To see how replication transparency might be achievable, consider a collection of n servers logically connected to form a ring. Each server maintains the entire directory tree structure, but holds only a subset of the files themselves. To read a file, a client sends a message containing the full path name to any of the servers. That server checks to see if it has the file. If so, it returns the data requested. If not, it forwards the request to the next server in the ring, which then repeats the algorithm. In this system, the servers can decide by themselves to replicate any file on any or all servers, without the users having to know about this at all. Such a scheme is replication transparent because it allows the system to transparently make copies of heavily used files without the users even being aware this is happening.

Distributed systems usually have multiple, independent users. What should the system do when two or more users try to access the same resource at the same time? For example, what happens if two users try to update the same file at the same time? If the system is **concurrency transparent**, the users will not notice the existence of other users. One mechanism for achieving this form of transparency would be for the system to automatically lock a resource once someone had started to use it, unlocking it only when the access was finished. In this manner, all resources would only be accessed sequentially, never concurrently.

Finally we come to the hardest one, **parallelism transparency**. In principle, a distributed system is supposed to appear to the users as a traditional, uniprocessor timesharing system. What happens if a programmer knows that his distributed system has 1000 CPUs and he wants to use a substantial fraction of them for a chess program that evaluates boards in parallel? The theoretical answer is that together the compiler, runtime system, and operating system should be able to figure out how to take advantage of this potential parallelism without the programmer even knowing it. Unfortunately, the current state-of-the-art is nowhere near allowing this to happen. Programmers who actually want to use multiple CPUs for a single problem will have to program this explicitly, at least for the foreseeable future. Parallelism transparency can be regarded as the holy grail for distributed systems designers. When that has been achieved, the work will have been completed, and it will be time to move on to new fields.

9.4.2. Flexibility

The second key design issue is flexibility. It is important that the system be flexible because we are just beginning to learn about how to build distributed systems. It is likely that this process will incur many false starts and considerable backtracking.

Design decisions that now seem reasonable may later prove to be wrong. The best way to avoid problems is thus to keep one's options open.

Flexibility, along with transparency, is like parenthood and apple pie: who could possibly be against them? It is hard to imagine anyone arguing in favor of an inflexible system. However, things are not as simple as they seem. There are two schools of thought concerning the structure of distributed systems. One school maintains that each machine should run a traditional kernel that provides most services itself. The other maintains that the kernel should provide as little as possible, with the bulk of the operating system services available from user-level servers. These two models, known as the monolithic kernel and microkernel, respectively, are illustrated in Fig. 9-15.

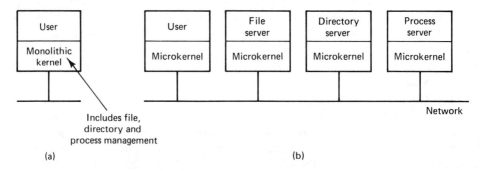

Fig. 9-15. (a) Monolithic kernel. (b) Microkernel.

The monolithic kernel is basically today's centralized operating system augmented with networking facilities and the integration of remote services. Most system calls are made by trapping to the kernel, having the work performed there, and having the kernel return the desired result to the user process. With this approach, most machines have disks and manage their own local file systems. Many distributed systems that are extensions or imitations of UNIX use this approach because UNIX itself has a large, monolithic kernel.

If the monolithic kernel is the reigning champion, the microkernel is the up-and-coming challenger. Most distributed systems that have been designed from scratch use this method. The microkernel is more flexible because it does almost nothing. It basically provides just four minimal services:

1. An interprocess communication mechanism.

2. Some memory management.

3. A limited amount of low-level process management and scheduling.

4. Low-level input/output.

In particular, unlike the monolithic kernel, it does not provide the file system, directory system, full process management, or much system call handling. The services that the microkernel does provide are included because they are difficult or expensive to provide anywhere else. The goal is to keep it small.

All the other operating system services are generally implemented as user-level servers. To look up a name, read a file, or obtain some other service, the user sends a message to the appropriate server, which then does the work and returns the result. The advantage of this method is that it is highly modular: there is a well-defined interface to each service (the set of messages the server understands), and every service is equally accessible to every client, independent of location. In addition, it is easy to implement, install, and debug new services, since adding or changing a service does not require stopping the system and booting a new kernel, as is the case with a monolithic kernel. It is precisely this ability to add, delete, and modify services that gives the microkernel its flexibility. Furthermore, users who are not satisfied with any of the official services are free to write their own.

As a simple example of this power, it is possible to have a distributed system with multiple file servers, one supporting MS-DOS file service and another supporting UNIX file service. Individual programs can use either or both, if they choose. In contrast, with a monolithic kernel, the file system is built into the kernel, and users have no choice but to use it.

The only potential advantage of the monolithic kernel is performance. Trapping to the kernel and doing everything there may well be faster than sending messages to remote servers. However, a detailed comparison of two distributed operating systems, one with a monolithic kernel (Sprite), and one with a microkernel (Amoeba), has shown that in practice this advantage is nonexistent (Douglis et al., 1991). Other factors tend to dominate, and the small amount of time required to send a message and get a reply (typically about 1 msec) is usually negligible. As a consequence, it is likely that microkernel systems will gradually come to dominate the distributed systems scheme, and monolithic kernels will eventually vanish or evolve into microkernels.

9.4.3. Reliability

One of the original goals of building distributed systems was to make them more reliable than single processor systems. The idea is that if some machine goes down, some other machine takes over the job. In other words, theoretically the overall system reliability could be the Boolean OR of the component reliabilities. For example, with four file servers, each with a 0.95 chance of being up at any instant, the probability of all four being down simultaneously is $0.05^4 = 0.000006$, so the probability of at least one being available is 0.999994, far better than any individual server.

That is the theory. The practice is that current distributed systems sometimes count on a number of specific servers being up in order to function at all. As a result, some of them have an availability more closely related to the Boolean AND of the components, than the Boolean OR. In a widely-quoted remark, Leslie Lamport once defined a distributed system as: "One on which I cannot get any work done because some machine I have never heard of has crashed." While this remark was (presumably) made somewhat tongue-in-cheek, there is clearly room for improvement here.

It is important to distinguish various aspects of reliability. **Availability**, as we have just seen, refers to the fraction of time that the system is usable. Lamport's system apparently did not score well in that regard. Availability can be enhanced by a design that does not require the simultaneous functioning of a substantial number of critical components. Another tool for improving availability is redundancy: key pieces of hardware and software should be replicated, so that if one of them fails the others will be able to take up the slack.

A highly reliable system must be highly available, but that is not enough. Data entrusted to the system must not be lost or garbled in any way, and if files are stored redundantly on multiple servers, all the copies must be kept consistent. In general, the more copies that are kept, the better the availability, but the greater the chance that they will be inconsistent, especially if updates are frequent. The designers of all distributed systems must keep this dilemma in mind at all times.

Another aspect of overall reliability is security. Files and other resources must be protected from unauthorized usage. Although the same issue occurs in single-processor systems, in distributed systems it is more severe. In a single-processor system, the user logs in and is authenticated. From then on, the system knows who the user is and can check whether each attempted access is legal. In a distributed system, when a message comes in to a server asking for something, the server has no simple way of determining who it is from. No name or identification field in the message can be trusted, since the sender may be lying. At the very least, considerable care is required here.

Still another issue relating to reliability is **fault tolerance**. Suppose a server crashes and then quickly reboots. What happens? Does the server crash bring down users with it? If the server has tables containing important information about ongoing activities, recovery will be difficult at best. We saw earlier than NFS was designed to be stateless, just to avoid this problem.

In general, distributed systems can be designed to mask failures, that is, to hide them from the users. If a file service or other service is actually constructed from a group of closely cooperating servers, then it should be possible to construct it in such a way that users do not notice the loss of one or two servers, other than some performance degradation. Of course, the trick is to arrange this cooperation so that it does not add substantial overhead to the system in the normal case, when everything is functioning correctly.

9.4.4. Performance

Lurking in the background all the time is the issue of performance. Building a transparent, flexible, reliable distributed system will not win you any prizes if it is as slow as molasses. In particular, when running a particular application on a distributed system, it should not be appreciably worse than running that same application on a single processor. Unfortunately, achieving this is easier said than done.

Various performance metrics can be used. Response time is one, but so are throughput (number of jobs per hour), system utilization, and amount of network capacity consumed. Furthermore, the results of any benchmark are often highly dependent on the nature of the benchmark. A benchmark that involves a large number of independent highly CPU-bound computations may give radically different results than a benchmark that consists of scanning a single large file for some pattern.

The performance problem is compounded by the fact that communication, which is essential in a distributed system (and absent in a single-processor system) is typically quite slow. Sending a message and getting a reply over a LAN takes about 1 msec. Most of this time is due to unavoidable protocol handling on both ends, rather than the time the bits spend on the wire. Thus to optimize performance, one often has to minimize the number of messages. The difficulty with this strategy is that the best way to gain performance is to have many activities running in parallel on different processors, but doing so requires sending many messages. (Another solution is to do all the work on one machine, but that is hardly appropriate in a distributed system.)

One possible way out is to pay considerable attention to the **grain size** of all computations. Starting up a small computation remotely, such as adding two integers, is rarely worth it, because the communication overhead dwarfs the extra CPU cycles gained. On the other hand, starting up a long compute-bound job remotely may be worth the trouble. In general, jobs that involve a large number of small computations, especially ones that interact highly with one another, may cause trouble on a distributed system with relatively slow communication. Such jobs are said to exhibit **fine-grained parallelism**. On the other hand, jobs that involve large computations, low interaction rates, and little data, that is, **coarse-grained parallelism**, may be a better fit.

Fault tolerance also exacts its price. Good reliability is often best achieved by having several servers closely cooperating on a single request. For example, when a request comes in to a server, it could immediately send a copy of the message to one of its colleagues so that if it crashes before finishing, the colleague can take over. Naturally when it is done, it must inform the colleague that the work has been completed, which takes another message. Thus we have at least two extra messages, which in the normal case cost time and network capacity and produce no tangible gain.

9.4.5. Scalability

Most current distributed systems are designed to work with a few hundred CPUs. It is possible that future systems will be orders of magnitude larger, and solutions that work well for 200 machines will fail miserably for 200,000,000. Consider the following. The French PTT (Post, Telephone and Telegraph administration) is in the process of installing a terminal in every household and business in France. The terminal, known as a **minitel**, will allow online access to a data base containing all the telephone numbers in France, thus eliminating the need for printing and distributing expensive telephone books. It will also vastly reduce the need for information operators who do nothing but give out telephone numbers all day. It has been calculated that the system will pay for itself within a few years. If the system works in France, other countries will inevitably adopt similar systems.

Once all the terminals are in place, the possibility of also using them for electronic mail (especially in conjunction with printers) is clearly present. Since postal services lose a huge amount of money in every country in the world, and telephone services are enormously profitable, there are great incentives to having electronic mail replace paper mail.

Next comes interactive access to all kinds of data bases and services, from electronic banking to reserving places in planes, trains, hotels, theaters, and restaurants, to name just a few. Before long, we have a distributed system with tens of millions of users. The question is: "Will the methods we are currently developing scale to such large systems?"

Although little is known about such huge distributed systems, one guiding principle is clear: avoid centralized components, tables, and algorithms (see Fig. 9-16). Having a single mail server for 50 million users would not be a good idea. Even if it had enough CPU and storage capacity, the network capacity into and out of it would surely be a problem. Furthermore, the system would not tolerate faults well. A single power outage could bring the entire system down. Lastly, most mail is local. Having a message sent by a user in Marseille to another user two blocks away pass through a machine in Paris is obviously inefficient.

Concept	Example
Centralized components	A single mail server for all users
Centralized tables	A single on-line telephone book
Centralized algorithms	Doing routing based on complete information

Fig. 9-16. Potential bottlenecks that designers should try to avoid in very large distributed systems.

Centralized tables are almost as bad as centralized components. How should one keep track of the telephone numbers and addresses of 50 million people? Suppose each data record could be fit into 50 characters. A single 2.5 gigabyte disk would provide enough storage. But here again, having a single data base would undoubtedly saturate all the communication lines into and out of it. It would also be vulnerable to failures (a single speck of dust could cause a head crash and bring down the entire directory service). Furthermore, here too, valuable network capacity would be wasted shipping queries far away for processing.

Finally, centralized algorithms are also a bad idea. In a large distributed system, an enormous number of messages have to be routed over many lines. From a theoretical point of view, the optimal way to do this is collect complete information about the load on all machines and lines, and then run a graph theory algorithm to compute all the optimal routes. This information can then be spread around the system to improve the routing.

The trouble is that collecting and transporting all the input and output information would again be a bad idea for the reasons discussed above. In fact, any algorithm that operates by collecting information from all sites, sends it to a single machine for processing, and then distributes the results must be avoided. Only decentralized algorithms should be used. These have the following characteristics:

1. No machine has complete information about the state of the system.

2. Machines make decisions based only on locally available information.

3. Failure of one machine does not ruin the algorithm.

4. There is no implicit assumption that a global clock exists.

The first three follow from what we have said so far. The last is perhaps less obvious, but also important. Any algorithm that starts out with: "At precisely 12:00:00 all machines shall note the size of their output queue" will fail because it is impossible to get all the clocks exactly synchronized. Algorithms should take into account the lack of exact clock synchronization. The larger the system, the larger the uncertainty. On a single LAN, with considerable effort it may be possible to get all clocks synchronized down to a few milliseconds, but doing this nationally is tricky. We will discuss distributed clock synchronization in Chap. 11.

9.5. SUMMARY

Distributed systems have a number of potential selling points. They can offer good price/performance ratios, are a good fit to distributed applications, can be made highly reliable, and can be gradually increased in size as the workload grows. They also have some disadvantages, such as having more complex software, potential communication bottlenecks, and weak security. Nevertheless, there is considerable interest worldwide in building and installing them.

Modern computer systems often have multiple CPUs. These can be organized as multiprocessors (with shared memory) or as multicomputers (without shared memory). Both types can be bus-based or switched. The former tend to be tightly coupled, while the latter tend to be loosely coupled.

The software for multiple CPU systems can be divided into three rough classes. Network operating systems allow users at independent workstations to communicate via a shared file system but otherwise leave each user as the master of his own workstation. Distributed operating systems turn the entire collection of hardware and software into a single integrated system, much like a traditional timesharing system. Shared-memory multiprocessors also offer a single system image, but do so by centralizing everything, so there really is only a single system. Shared-memory multiprocessors are not distributed systems.

Distributed systems have to be designed carefully, since there are many pitfalls for the unwary. A key issue is transparency—hiding all the distribution from the users and even from the application programs. Another issue is flexibility. Since the field is only now in its infancy, the design should be made with the idea of making future changes easy. In this respect, microkernels are superior to monolithic kernels. Other important issues are reliability, performance and scalability.

PROBLEMS

1. Name two advantages and two disadvantages of distributed systems over centralized ones.

2. A bus-based multiprocessor uses snoopy caches to achieve a coherent memory. Will semaphores work on this machine?

3. A multicomputer with 256 CPUs is organized as a 16×16 grid. What is the worst case delay (in hops) that a message might have to take?

4. Now consider a 256-CPU hypercube. What is the worst case delay here, again in hops?

5. Why are some servers designed to be stateless?

6. What is meant by a "Single system image"?

7. In UNIX, when an open file is deleted, it continues to be readable or writable by the processes (or processes) that have it open, although no other processes can open it. Can these semantics be maintained in NFS?

8. NFS allows machines to be both client and server at the same time. Is this a useful feature? Why?

9. What are the primary tasks of a microkernel?

10. Name two advantages of a microkernel over a monolithic kernel.

11. Concurrency transparency is a desirable goal for distributed systems. Do centralized systems have this property automatically?

12. An experimental file server is up 3/4 of the time and down 1/4 of the time due to bugs. How many times does this file server have to be replicated to give an availability of at least 99 percent?

13. Suppose you have a large source program consisting of m files to compile. The compilation is to take place on a system with n processors, where $n \gg m$. The best you can hope for is an m-fold speedup over a single processor. What factors might cause the speedup to be less than this maximum?

10

COMMUNICATION IN DISTRIBUTED SYSTEMS

The single most important difference between a distributed system and a uniprocessor system is the interprocess communication. In a uniprocessor system, most interprocess communication implicitly assumes the existence of shared memory. A typical example is the producer-consumer problem, in which one process writes into a shared buffer and another process reads from it. Even that most basic form of synchronization, the semaphore, requires that one word (the semaphore variable itself) is shared. In a distributed system there is no shared memory whatsoever, so the entire nature of interprocess communication must be completely rethought from scratch. In this chapter we will discuss numerous issues, examples, and problems associated with interprocess communication in distributed operating systems.

We will start out by discussing the rules that communicating processes must adhere to, known as protocols. For wide-area distributed systems these protocols often take the form of multiple layers, each with its own goals and rules. Then we will look at the client-server model introduced in Chap. 9 in more detail. After that, it is time to find out how messages are exchanged, and the many options available to system designers.

One particular option, remote procedure call, is important enough to warrant its own section. Remote procedure call is really a nicer way of packaging message passing, to make it more like conventional programming and thus easier to use. Nevertheless, it has its own peculiarities and problems, which we will also look at.

Finally, we will conclude the chapter by studying how groups of processes can communicate, instead of just two processes. A detailed example of group communication, ISIS, will be discussed.

10.1. LAYERED PROTOCOLS

Due to the absence of shared memory, all communication in distributed systems is based on message passing. When process A wants to communicate with process B, it first builds a message in its own address space. Then it executes a system call that causes the operating system to fetch the message and send it over the network to B. Although this basic idea sounds simple enough, in order to prevent chaos, A and B have to agree on the meaning of the bits being sent. If A sends a brilliant new novel written in French and encoded in IBM's EBCDIC character code, and B expects the inventory of a supermarket written in English and encoded in ASCII, communication will be less than optimal.

Many different agreements are needed. How many volts should be used to signal a 0-bit, and how many volts for a 1-bit? How does the receiver know which is the last bit of the message? How can it detect if a message has been damaged or lost, and what should it do if it finds out? How long are numbers, strings, and other data items, and how are they represented? In short, agreements are needed at a variety of levels, varying from the low-level details of bit transmission to the high-level details of how information is to be expressed.

To make it easier to deal with the numerous levels and issues involved in communication, the International Standards Organization, ISO, has developed a reference model that clearly identifies the various levels involved, gives them standard names, and points out which level should do which job. This model is called the **Open Systems Interconnection Reference Model** (Day and Zimmerman, 1983), usually abbreviated as **ISO OSI** or sometimes just the **OSI model**. Although we do not intend to give a full description of this model and all of its implications here, a short introduction will be helpful. For more details see (Tanenbaum, 1988).

To start with, the OSI model is designed to allow open systems to communicate. An **open system** is one that is prepared to communicate with any other open system by using standard rules that govern the format, contents, and meaning of the messages sent and received. These rules are formalized in what are called **protocols**. Basically, a protocol is an agreement on how communication is to proceed. When a woman is introduced to a man, she may choose to stick out her hand. He, in turn, may decide to either shake it or kiss it, depending, for example, whether she is an American lawyer at a business meeting or a European princess at a formal ball. Violating the protocol will make communication more difficult, if not impossible.

At a more technological level, many companies make memory boards for the IBM PC. When the CPU wants to read a word from memory, it puts the address and certain control signals on the bus. The memory board is expected to see these signals and respond by putting the word requested on the bus within a certain time interval. If the memory board observes the required bus protocol, it will work correctly, otherwise it will not.

Similarly, to allow a group of computers to communicate over a network, they must all agree on the protocols to be used. The OSI model distinguishes between two general types of protocols. With **connection-oriented** protocols, before exchanging data, the sender and receiver first explicitly establish a connection, and possibly negotiate the protocol they will use. When they are done, they must terminate the connection. The telephone is a connection-oriented communication system. With **connectionless** protocols, no setup in advance is needed. The sender just transmits the first message when it is ready. Dropping a letter in a mailbox is an example of connectionless communication. With computers, both connection-oriented and connectionless communication are common.

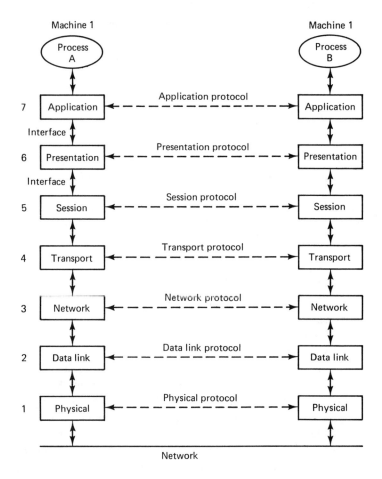

Fig. 10-1. Layers, interfaces, and protocols in the OSI model.

In the OSI model, communication is divided up into seven levels or layers, as shown in Fig. 10-1. Each layer deals with one specific aspect of the communication. In this way, the problem can be divided up into manageable pieces, each of which can be solved independently of the other ones. Each layer provides an **interface** to the one above it. The interface consists of a set of operations that together define the service the layer is prepared to offer to its users.

In the OSI model, when process *A* on machine 1 wants to communicate with process *B* on machine 2, it builds a message and passes the message to the application layer on its machine. This layer might be a library procedure, for example, but it could also be implemented some other way (e.g., inside the operating system, on an external coprocessor chip, etc.). The application layer software then adds a **header** to the front of the message and passes the resulting message across the layer 6/7 interface to the presentation layer. The presentation layer in turn adds its own header, and passes the result down to the session layer, and so on. Some layers add not only a header to the front, but also a trailer to the end. When it hits bottom, the physical layer actually transmits the message, which by now might look as shown in Fig. 10-2.

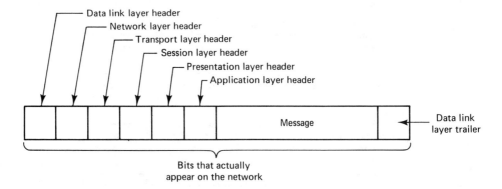

Fig. 10-2. A typical message as it appears on the network.

When the message arrives at machine 2, it is passed upwards, with each layer stripping off and examining its own header. Finally, the message arrives at the receiver, process B, which may reply to it using the reverse path. The information in the layer n header is used for the layer n protocol.

As an example of why layered protocols are important, consider communication between two companies, Zippy Airlines and its caterer, Mushy Meals, Inc. Every month, the head of passenger service at Zippy asks her secretary to contact the sales manager's secretary at Mushy to order 100,000 boxes of rubber chicken. Traditionally, the orders have gone via the post office. However, as the postal service deteriorates, at some point the two secretaries decide to abandon it and communicate by FAX. They can do this without bothering their bosses, since their protocol deals with the physical transmission of the orders, not their contents.

Similarly, the head of passenger service can decide to drop the rubber chicken and go for Mushy's new special, prime rib of goat, without that decision affecting the secretaries. The thing to notice is that we have two layers here, the bosses and the secretaries, and that each layer has its own protocol (subjects of discussion, technology, and so on) that can be changed independently of the other one. It is precisely this independence that makes layered protocols attractive. Each one can be changed as technology improves, without the other ones being affected.

In the OSI model, there are not two layers, but seven, as we saw in Fig. 10-1. The collection of protocols used in a particular system is called a **protocol suite** or

procotol stack. In the following sections, we will briefly examine each of the layers in turn, starting at the bottom. Where appropriate, we will also point out some of the protocols used in each layer.

10.1.1. The Physical Layer

The physical layer is concerned with transmitting the 0s and 1s. How many volts to use for 0 and 1, how many bits per second can be sent, and whether transmission can take place in both directions simultaneously are key issues in the physical layer. In addition, the size and shape of the network connector (plug), as well as the number of pins and meaning of each one are of concern here.

The physical layer protocol deals with standardizing the electrical, mechanical, and signaling interfaces so that when one machine sends a 0 bit it is actually received as a 0 bit and not a 1 bit. Many physical layer standards have been developed (for different media), for example, the RS-232-C standard for serial communication lines.

10.1.2. The Data Link Layer

The physical layer just sends bits. As long as no errors occur, all is well. However, real communication networks are subject to errors, so some mechanism is needed to detect and correct them. This mechanism is the main task of the data link layer. What it does is to group the bits into units, sometimes called **frames**, and see that each frame is correctly received.

The data link layer does its work by putting a special bit pattern on the start and end of each frame, to mark them, as well as computing a **checksum** by adding up all the bytes in the frame in a certain way. The data link layer appends the checksum to the frame. When the frame arrives, the receiver recomputes the checksum from the data and compares the result to the checksum following the frame. If they agree, the frame is considered correct and is accepted. It they disagree, the receiver asks the sender to retransmit it. Frames are assigned sequence numbers (in the header), so everyone can tell which is which.

In Fig. 10-3 we see a (slightly pathological) example of A trying to send two messages, 0 and 1, to B. At time 0, data message 0 is sent, but when it arrives, at time 1, noise on the transmission line has caused it to be damaged, so the checksum is wrong. B notices this, and at time 2 asks for a retransmission using a control message. Unfortunately, at the same time, A is sending data message 1. When A gets the request for retransmission, it resends 0. However, when B gets message 1, instead of the requested message 0, it sends control message 1 to A complaining that it wants 0, not 1. When A sees this, it shrugs its shoulders and sends message 0 for the third time.

The point here is not so much whether the protocol of Fig. 10-3 is a great one (it is not), but rather to illustrate that in each layer there is a need for discussion between the sender and the receiver. Typical messages are "Please retransmit message *n*," "I already retransmitted it," "No you did not," "Yes I did," "All right, have it your

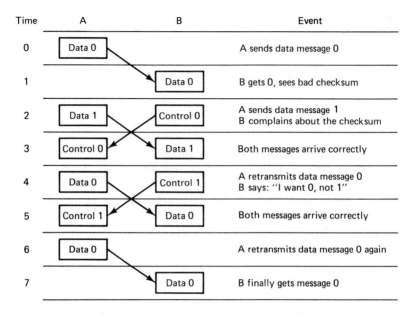

Time	A	B	Event
0	Data 0		A sends data message 0
1		Data 0	B gets 0, sees bad checksum
2	Data 1	Control 0	A sends data message 1 B complains about the checksum
3	Control 0	Data 1	Both messages arrive correctly
4	Data 0	Control 1	A retransmits data message 0 B says: "I want 0, not 1"
5	Control 1	Data 0	Both messages arrive correctly
6	Data 0		A retransmits data message 0 again
7		Data 0	B finally gets message 0

Fig. 10-3. Discussion between a receiver and a sender in the data link layer.

way, but send it again," and so forth. This discussion takes place in the header field, where various requests and responses are defined, and parameters (such as frame numbers) can be supplied.

10.1.3. The Network Layer

On a LAN, there is usually no need for the sender to locate the receiver. It just puts the message out on the network and the receiver takes it off. A wide-area network, however, consists of a large number of machines, each with some number of lines to other machines, rather like a large-scale map showing major cities and roads connecting them. For a message to get from the sender to the receiver it may have to make a number of hops, at each one, choosing an outgoing line to use. The question of how to choose the best path is called **routing**, and is the primary task of the network layer.

The problem is complicated by the fact that the shortest route is not always the best route. What really matters is the amount of delay on a given route, which, in turn, is related to the amount of traffic and the number of messages queued up for transmission over the various lines. The delay can thus change over the course of time. Some routing algorithms try to adapt to changing loads, whereas others are content to make decisions based on long term averages.

Two network-layer protocols are in widespread use, one connection-oriented and one connectionless. The connection-oriented one is called **X.25**, and is favored by the operators of public networks, such as telephone companies and the European PTTs. The X.25 user first sends a *Call Request* to the destination, which can either accept or reject the proposed connection. If the connection is accepted, the caller is given a connection identifier to use in subsequent requests. In many cases, the network chooses a route from the sender to the receiver during this setup, and uses it for subsequent traffic.

The connectionless one is called **IP** (for Internet Protocol), and is part of the DoD (U.S. Department of Defense) protocol suite. An IP **packet** (the technical term for a message in the network layer) can be sent without any setup. Each IP packet is routed to its destination independent of all other ones. No internal path is selected and remembered as is often the case with X.25.

10.1.4. The Transport Layer

Packets can be lost on the way from the sender to the receiver. Although some applications can handle their own error recovery, others prefer a reliable connection. The job of the transport layer is to provide this service. The idea is that the session layer should be able to deliver a message to the transport layer with the expectation that it will be delivered without loss.

Upon receiving a message from the session layer, the transport layer breaks it into pieces small enough for each to fit in a single packet, assigns each one a sequence number, and then sends them all. The discussion in the transport layer header concerns which packets have been sent, which have been received, how many more the receiver has room to accept, and similar topics.

Reliable transport connections (which by definition are connection-oriented) can be built on top of either X.25 or IP. In the former case all the packets will arrive in the correct sequence (if they arrive at all), but in the latter case it is possible for one packet to take a different route and arrive earlier than the packet sent before it. It is up to the transport layer software to put everything back in order to maintain the illusion that a transport connection is like a big tube—you put messages into it and they come out undamaged and in the same order they went in.

The official ISO transport protocol has five variants, known as **TP0** through **TP4**. The differences relate to error handling and the ability to send several transport connections over a single X.25 connection. The choice of which one to use depends on the properties of the underlying network layer.

The DoD transport protocol is called **TCP** (Transmission Control Protocol). It is similar to TP4. The combination TCP/IP is widely used at universities and on most UNIX systems. The DoD protocol suite also supports a connectionless transport protocol called **UDP** (Universal Datagram Protocol), which is essentially just IP with some minor additions. User programs that do not need a connection-oriented protocol normally use UDP.

10.1.5. The Session Layer

The session layer is essentially an enhanced version of the transport layer. It provides dialog control, to keep track of which party is currently talking, and it provides synchronization facilities. The latter are useful to allow users to insert checkpoints into long transfers, so that in the event of a crash it is only necessary to go back to the last checkpoint, rather than all the way back to the beginning. In practice, few applications are interested in the session layer and it is rarely supported. It is not even present in the DoD protocol suite.

10.1.6. Presentation Layer

Unlike the lower layers, which are concerned with getting the bits from the sender to the receiver reliably and efficiently, the presentation layer is concerned with the meaning of the bits. Most messages do not consist of random bit strings, but more structured information such as people's names, addresses, amounts of money, and so on. In the presentation layer it is possible to define records containing fields like these and then have the sender notify the receiver that a message contains a particular record in a certain format. This makes it easier for machines with different internal representations to communicate.

10.1.7. Application Layer

The application layer is really just a collection of miscellaneous protocols for common activities such as electronic mail, file transfer, and connecting remote terminals to computers over a network. The best known of these are the X.400 electronic mail protocol and the X.500 directory server. Neither this layer nor the two layers directly under it will be of any interest to us in this book.

10.2. THE CLIENT-SERVER MODEL

At first glance, layered protocols along the OSI lines look like a fine way to organize a distributed system. In effect, a sender sets up a connection (a bit pipe) with the receiver, and then pumps the bits in, which arrive without error, in order, at the receiver. What could be wrong with this?

Plenty. To start with, look at Fig. 10-2. The existence of all those headers generates a considerable amount of overhead. Every time a message is sent it must be processed by about half a dozen layers, each one generating and adding a header on the way down or removing and examining a header on the way up. All of this work takes time. On wide-area networks, where the number of bits/sec that can be sent is typically fairly low (often as little as 64K bits/sec), this overhead is not serious. The limiting factor is the capacity of the lines, and even with all the header manipulation, the CPUs are fast enough to keep the lines running at full speed. Thus a wide-area distributed system can probably use the OSI or TCP/IP protocols without any loss in (the already meager) performance.

However, for a LAN-based distributed system, the protocol overhead is often substantial. So much CPU time is wasted running protocols that the effective throughput over the LAN is often only a fraction of what the LAN can do. As a consequence, most LAN-based distributed systems do not use layered protocols at all, or if they do, they use only a subset of the entire protocol stack.

In addition, the OSI model only addresses a small aspect of the problem—getting the bits from the sender to the receiver (and in the upper layers, what they mean). It does not say anything about how the distributed system should be structured. Something more is needed.

10.2.1. Clients and Servers

This something is often the client-server model that we introduced in the previous chapter. The idea behind this model is to structure the operating system as a group of cooperating processes, called **servers**, that offer services to the users, called **clients**. The client and server machines normally all run the same microkernel, with both the clients and servers running as user processes, as we saw earlier. A machine may run a single process, or it may run multiple clients, multiple servers, or a mixture of the two.

To avoid the considerable overhead of the connection-oriented protocols such as OSI or TCP/IP, the client server model is usually based on a simple, connectionless **request/reply protocol**. The client sends a request message to the server asking for some service (e.g., read a block of a file). The server does the work and returns the data requested or an error code indicating why the work could not be performed, as depicted in Fig. 10-4(a).

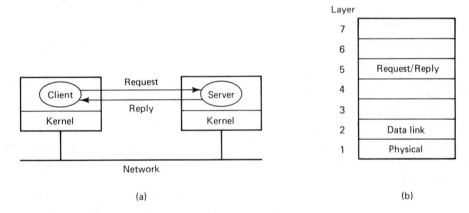

Fig. 10-4. The client-server model. Although all message passing is actually done by the kernels, this simplified form of drawing will be used when there is no ambiguity.

The primary advantage of Fig. 10-4(a) is the simplicity. The client sends a request and gets an answer. No connection has to be established before use or torn down afterwards. The reply message serves as the acknowledgement to the request.

From the simplicity comes another advantage: efficiency. The protocol stack is shorter and thus more efficient. Assuming all the machines are identical, only three levels of protocol are needed, as shown in Fig. 10-4(b). The physical and data link protocols take care of getting the packets from client to server and back. These are always handled by the hardware, for example, an Ethernet or token ring chip. No routing is needed and no connections are established, so layers 3 and 4 are not needed. Layer 5 is the request/reply protocol. It defines the set of legal requests and the set of legal replies to these requests. There is no session management because there are no sessions. The upper layers are not needed either.

Due to this simple structure, the communication services provided by the (micro)kernel can, for example, be reduced to two system calls, one for sending messages and one for receiving them. These system calls can be invoked through library procedures, say, *send(dest, &mptr)* and *receive(addr, &mptr)*. The former sends the message pointed to by *mptr* to a process identified by *dest* and causes the caller to be blocked until the message has been sent. The latter causes the caller to be blocked until a message arrives. When one does, the message is copied to the buffer pointed to by *mptr* and the caller is unblocked. The *addr* parameter specifies the address to which the receiver is listening. Many variants of these two procedures and their parameters are possible. We will discuss some of these later in this chapter.

10.2.2. An Example Client and Server

To provide more insight into how clients and servers work, in this section we will present an outline of a client and a file server in C. Both the client and the server need to share some definitions, so we will collect these into a file called *header.h* which is shown in Fig. 10-5. Both the client and server include these using the

```
#include <header.h>
```

statement. This statement has the effect of literally inserting the entire contents of *header.h* into the source program during compilation.

Let us first take a look at *header.h*. It starts out by defining two constants, *MAX_PATH* and *BUF_SIZE* that determine the size of two arrays needed in the message. The former tells how many characters a file name (i.e., a path name like */usr/ast/books/opsys/chapter1.t*) may contain. The latter fixes the amount of data that may be read or written in one operation by setting the buffer size. The next constant, *FILE_SERVER*, provides the network address of the file server, so clients can send messages to it.

The second group of constants defines the operation numbers. These are needed to ensure that the client and server agree on which code will represent a READ, which code will represent a WRITE, and so on. We have only shown four here, but in a real system there would normally be more.

Every reply contains a result code. If the operation succeeds, the result code often contains useful information (such as the number of bytes actually read). If there is no value to be returned (such as when a file is created), the value *OK* is used. If the operation is unsuccessful for some reason, the result code tells why, using codes such as *E_BAD_OPCODE*, *E_BAD_PARAM*, and so on.

Finally we come to the most important part of *header.h*, the definition of the message itself. In our example it is a structure with 10 fields. All requests from the

```
/* Definitions needed by clients and servers. */
#define MAX_PATH       255        /* maximum length of a file name */
#define BUF_SIZE       1024       /* how much data to transfer at once */
#define FILE_SERVER    243        /* file server's network address */

/* Definitions of the allowed operations. */
#define CREATE         1          /* create a new file */
#define READ           2          /* read a piece of a file and return it */
#define WRITE          3          /* write a piece of a file */
#define DELETE         4          /* delete an existing file */

/* Error codes. */
#define OK             0          /* operation performed correctly */
#define E_BAD_OPCODE   -1         /* unknown operation requested */
#define E_BAD_PARAM    -2         /* error in a parameter */
#define E_IO           -3         /* disk error or other I/O error */

/* Definition of the message format. */
struct message {
  long source;                    /* sender's identity */
  long dest;                      /* receiver's identity */
  long opcode;                    /* which operation: CREATE, READ, etc. */
  long count;                     /* how many bytes to transfer */
  long offset;                    /* where in file to start reading or writing */
  long extra1;                    /* extra field */
  long extra2;                    /* extra field */
  long result;                    /* result of the operation reported here */
  char name[MAX_PATH];            /* name of the file being operated on */
  char data[BUF_SIZE];            /* data to be read or written */
};
```

Fig. 10-5. The *header.h* file used by the client and server.

client to the server use this format, as do all replies. In a real system, one would probably not have a fixed format message (because not all the fields are needed in all cases), but it makes the explanation simpler here. The *source* and *dest* fields identify the sender and receiver respectively. The *opcode* field is one of the operations defined above, that is, *CREATE, READ, WRITE,* or *DELETE.* The *count* and *offset* fields are used for parameters, and two other fields, *extra1* and *extra2* are defined to provide space for additional parameters in case the server is expanded in the future. The *result* field is not used for client-to-server requests, but holds the result value for server-to-client replies. Finally we have two arrays. The first one, *name,* holds the name of the file being accessed. The second one, *data,* holds the data sent back on a reply to READ or the data sent to the server on a WRITE.

Let us now look at the code, as outlined in Fig. 10-6. In (a) we have the server; in (b) we have the client. The server is straightforward. The main loop starts out by calling *receive* to get a request message. The first parameter identifies the caller by giving its address, and the second parameter points to a message buffer where the incoming message can be stored. The library procedure *receive* traps to the kernel to suspend the server until a message arrives. When one comes in, the server continues and dispatches on the opcode type. For each opcode, a different procedure is called.

The incoming message and a buffer for the outgoing message are given as parameters. The procedure examines the incoming message, *m1*, and builds the reply in *m2*. It also returns a function value that is sent back in the *result* field. After the *send* has completed, the server goes back to the top of the loop to execute *receive* and wait for the next incoming message.

In Fig. 10-6(b) we have a procedure that copies a file using the server. Its body consists of a loop that reads one block from the source file and writes it to the destination file. The loop is repeated until the source file has been completely copied, as indicated by a zero or negative return code from the read.

The first part of the loop is concerned with building a message for the READ operation and sending it to the server. After the reply has been received, the second part of the loop is entered, which takes the data just received and sends it back to the server in the form of a WRITE to the destination file. The programs of Fig. 10-6 are just sketches of the code. Many details have been omitted. For example, the *do_xxx* procedures are not shown, and no error checking is done. Still, the general idea of how a client and a server interact should be clear. In the following sections we will look at some of the issues that relate to clients and servers in more detail.

10.2.3. Addressing

In order for a client to send a message to a server, it must know the server's address. In the example of the previous section, the server's address was simply hardwired into *header.h* as a constant. While this strategy might work in an especially simple system, usually a more sophisticated form of addressing is needed. In this section we will describe some of the issues concerning addressing.

In our example, the file server has been assigned a numerical address (243), but we have not really specified what this means. In particular, does it refer to a specific machine, or to a specific process? If it refers to a specific machine, the sending kernel can extract it from the message structure and use it as the hardware address for sending the packet to the server. All the sending kernel has to do then is build a frame using the 243 as the data link address and put the frame out on the LAN. The server's interface board will see the frame, recognize 243 as its own address, and accept it.

If there is only one process running on the destination machine, the kernel will know what to do with the incoming message—give it to the one and only process running there. However, what happens if there are several processes running on the destination machine? Which one gets the message? The kernel has no way of knowing. Consequently, a scheme that uses network addresses to identify processes means that only one process can run on each machine. While this limitation is not fatal, it is sometimes a serious restriction.

An alternative addressing system sends messages to processes rather than to machines. Although this method eliminates all ambiguity about who the real recipient is, it does introduce the problem of how processes are identified. One common scheme is to use two part names, specifying both a machine and a process number. Thus 243.4 or 4@243 or something similar designates process 4 on machine 243.

```
#include <header.h>
void main(void)
{
  struct message m1, m2;          /* incoming and outgoing messages */
  int r;                          /* result code */

  while (1) {                     /* server runs forever */
        receive(FILE_SERVER,&m1); /* block waiting for a message */
        switch(m1.opcode) {       /* dispatch on type of request */
                case CREATE:      r = do_create(&m1, &m2);       break;
                case READ:        r = do_read(&m1, &m2);         break;
                case WRITE:       r = do_write(&m1, &m2);        break;
                case DELETE:      r = do_delete(&m1, &m2);       break;
                default:          r = E_BAD_OPCODE;
        }
        m2.result = r;            /* return result to client */
        send(m1.source, &m2);     /* send reply */
  }
}
                                  (a)


#include <header.h>
int copy(char *src, char *dst)    /* procedure to copy file using the server */
{
  struct message m1;              /* message buffer */
  long position;                  /* current file position */
  long client = 110;              /* client's address */

  initialize();                   /* prepare for execution */
  position = 0;
  do {
        /* Get a block of data from the source file. */
        m1.opcode = READ;         /* operation is a read */
        m1.offset = position;     /* current position in the file */
        m1. count = BUF_SIZE;     /* how many bytes to read */
        strcpy(&m1.name, src);    /* copy name of file to be read to message */
        send(FILE_SERVER, &m1);   /* send the message to the file server */
        receive(client, &m1);     /* block waiting for the reply */

        /* Write the data just received to the destination file. */
        m1.opcode = WRITE;        /* operation is a write */
        m1.offset = position;     /* current position in the file */
        m1. count = m1.result;    /* how many bytes to write */
        strcpy(&m1.name, dst);    /* copy name of file to be written to buf */
        send(FILE_SERVER, &m1);   /* send the message to the file server */
        receive(client, &m1);     /* block waiting for the reply */
        position += m1.result;    /* m1.result is number of bytes written */
  } while (m1.result > 0);        /* iterate until done */
  return(m1.result >= 0 ? OK : m1.result);       /* return OK or error code */
}
                                  (b)
```

Fig. 10-6. (a) A sample server. (b) A client procedure using that server to copy a file.

The machine number is used by the kernel to get the message correctly delivered to the proper machine, and the process number is used by the kernel on that machine to determine which process the message is intended for. A nice feature of this approach is that every machine can number its processes starting at 0. No global coordination is needed because there is never any ambiguity between process 0 on machine 243 and process 0 on machine 199. The former is 243.0 and the latter is 199.0. This scheme is illustrated in Fig. 10-7(a).

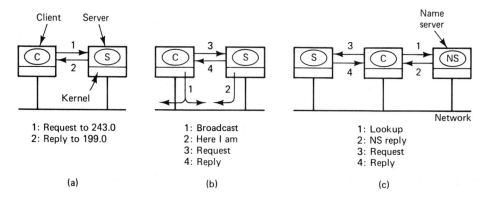

1: Request to 243.0
2: Reply to 199.0

1: Broadcast
2: Here I am
3: Request
4: Reply

1: Lookup
2: NS reply
3: Request
4: Reply

(a)   (b)   (c)

Fig. 10-7. (a) Machine.process addressing. (b) Process addressing with broadcasting. (c) Address lookup via a name server.

A slight variation on this addressing scheme uses *machine.local-id* instead of *machine.process*. The *local-id* field is normally a randomly chosen 16-bit or 32-bit integer. One process, typically, a server, starts up by making a system call to tell the kernel that it wants to listen to *local-id*. Later, when a message comes in addressed to *machine.local_id*, the kernel knows which process to give the message to. Most communication in Berkeley UNIX, for example, uses this method, with 32-bit Internet addresses used for specifying machines and 16-bit numbers for the *local-id* fields.

Nevertheless, *machine.process* addressing is far from ideal. Specifically, it is not transparent since the user is obviously aware of where the server is located, and transparency is one of the main goals of building a distributed system. To see why this matters, suppose the file server normally runs on machine 243, but one day that machine is down. Machine 176 is available, but programs previously compiled using *header.h* all have the number 243 built into them, so they will not work if the server is unavailable. Clearly this situation is undesirable.

An alternative approach is to assign each process a unique address that does not contain an embedded machine number. One way to achieve this goal is to have a centralized process address allocator that simply maintains a counter. Upon receiving a request for an address, it simply returns the current value of the counter and then increments it by one. The disadvantage of this scheme is that centralized components like this do not scale to large systems and thus should be avoided.

Yet another method for assigning process identifiers is to let each process pick its own identifier from a large, sparse address space, such as the space of 64-bit binary integers. The probability of two processes picking the same number is tiny, and the system scales well. However, here, too, there is a problem: "How does the sending kernel know what machine to send the message to?" On a LAN that supports broadcasting, the sender can broadcast a special **locate packet** containing the address of the destination process. Because it is a broadcast packet, it will be received by all machines on the network. All the kernels check to see if the address is theirs, and if so, send back a **here I am** message giving their network address (machine number). The sending kernel then uses this address, and furthermore caches it, to avoid broadcasting the next time the server is needed. This method is shown in Fig. 10-7(b).

Although this scheme is transparent, even with caching, the broadcasting puts extra load on the system. This extra load can be avoided by providing an extra machine to map high-level (i.e., ASCII) service names to machine addresses, as shown in Fig. 10-7(c). When this system is employed, processes such as servers are referred to by ASCII strings, and it is these strings that are embedded in programs, not binary machine or process numbers. Every time a client runs, on the first attempt to use a server, the client sends a query message to a special mapping server, often called a **name server**, asking it for the machine number where the server is currently located. Once this address has been obtained, the request can be sent directly. As in the previous case, addresses can be cached.

In summary, we have the following methods for addressing processes:

1. Hardwire *machine.number* into client code.

2. Let processes choose random addresses; locate them by broadcasting.

3. Put ASCII server names in clients; look them up at run time.

Each of these has problems. The first one is not transparent, the second one generates extra load on the system, and the third one requires a centralized component, the name server. Of course, the name server can be replicated, but doing so introduces the problems associated with keeping them consistent.

A completely different approach is to use special hardware. Let processes pick random addresses. However, instead of locating them by broadcasting, the network interface chips have to be designed to allow processes to store process addresses in them. Frames would then use process addresses instead of machine addresses. As each frame came by, the network interface chip would simply examine the frame to see if the destination process was on its machine. If so, the frame would be accepted, otherwise it would not be.

10.2.4. Blocking versus Nonblocking Primitives

The message passing primitives we have described so far are what are called **blocking primitives** (sometimes called **synchronous primitives**). When a process calls *send* it specifies a destination and a buffer to send to that destination. While the message is being sent, the sending process is blocked (i.e., suspended). The instruction following the call to *send* is not executed until the message has been completely sent, as shown in Fig. 10-8(a). Similarly, a call to *receive* does not return control until a message has actually been received and put in the message buffer pointed to by the parameter. The process remains suspended in *receive* until a message arrives, even if it takes hours. In some systems, the receiver can specify from whom it wishes to receive, in which case it remains blocked until a message from that sender arrives.

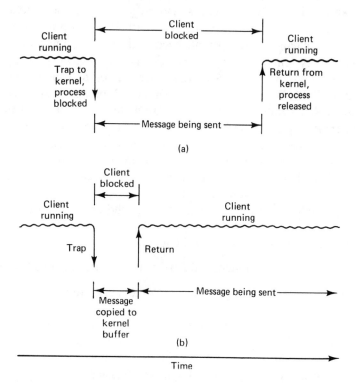

Fig. 10-8. (a) A blocking send primitive. (b) A nonblocking send primitive.

An alternative to blocking primitives are **nonblocking primitives** (sometimes called **asynchronous primitives**). If *send* is nonblocking, it returns control to the caller immediately, before the message is sent. The advantage of this scheme is that the sending process can continue computing in parallel with the message transmission, instead of having the CPU go idle (assuming no other process is runnable). The choice between blocking and nonblocking primitives is normally made by the system designers (i.e., either one primitive is available or the other), although in a few systems both are available and users can choose their favorite.

However, the performance advantage offered by nonblocking primitives is offset by a serious disadvantage: the sender cannot modify the message buffer until the message has been sent. The consequences of the process overwriting the message during transmission are too horrible to contemplate. Worse yet, the sending process has no idea of when the transmission has been completed, so it never knows when it is safe to reuse the buffer. It can hardly avoid touching it forever.

There are two possible ways out. The first solution is to have the kernel copy the message to an internal kernel buffer and then allow the process to continue, as shown in Fig. 10-8(b). From the sender's point of view, this scheme is the same as a blocking call: as soon as it gets control back, it is free to reuse the buffer. Of course the message will not yet have been sent, but the sender is not hindered by this fact. The disadvantage of this method is that every outgoing message has to be copied from user space to kernel space. With many network interfaces, the message will have to be copied to a hardware transmission buffer later anyway, so the first copy is essentially wasted. The extra copy can reduce the performance of the system considerably.

The second solution is to interrupt the sender when the message has been sent to inform it that the buffer is once again available. No copy is required here, which saves time, but user-level interrupts make programming tricky, difficult, and subject to race conditions, which makes them irreproducible. Most experts agree that although this method is highly efficient and allows the most parallelism, the disadvantages greatly outweigh the advantages: programs based on interrupts are difficult to write correctly and nearly impossible to debug when they are wrong.

Sometimes the interrupt can be disguised by starting up a new thread of control (discussed in Chap. 12) within the sender's address space. Although this is somewhat cleaner than a raw interrupt, it is still far more complicated than synchronous communication. If only a single thread of control is available, the choices come down to:

1. Blocking send (CPU idle during message transmission).

2. Nonblocking send with copy (CPU time wasted for the extra copy).

3. Nonblocking send with interrupt (makes programming difficult).

Under normal conditions, the first choice is the best one. It does not maximize the parallelism, but is simple to understand and simple to implement. It also does not require any kernel buffers to manage. Furthermore, as can be seen from comparing Fig. 10-8(a) to Fig. 10-8(b), the message will usually be out the door faster if no copy is required. On the other hand, if overlapping processing and transmission is essential for some application, a nonblocking send with copying is the best choice.

For the record, we would like to point out that some authors use a different criterion to distinguish synchronous from asynchronous primitives (Andrews, 1991). In our view, the essential difference between a synchronous primitive and an asynchronous one is whether the sender can reuse the message buffer immediately after getting control back without fear of messing up the *send*. When the message actually gets to the receiver is irrelevant.

In the alternative view, a synchronous primitive is one in which the sender is blocked until the receiver has accepted the message and the acknowledgement has gotten back to the sender. Everything else is asynchronous in this view. There is complete agreement that if the sender gets control back before the message has been copied or sent, the primitive is asynchronous. Similarly, everyone agrees that when the sender is blocked until the receiver has acknowledged the message, we have a synchronous primitive.

The disagreement comes on whether the intermediate cases (message copied or copied and sent, but not acknowledged) counts as one or the other. Operating systems designers tend to prefer our way, since their concern is with buffer management and message transmission. Programming language designers tend to prefer the alternative definition, because that is what counts at the language level.

Just as *send* can be blocking or nonblocking, so can *receive*. A nonblocking *receive* just tells the kernel where the buffer is, and returns control almost immediately. Again here, how does the caller know when the operation has completed? One way is to provide an explicit *wait* primitive that allows the receiver to block when it wants to. Alternatively (or in addition to *wait*), the designers may provide a *test* primitive to allow the receiver to poll the kernel to check on the status. A variant on this idea is a *conditional_receive*, which either gets a message or signals failure, but in any event returns immediately, or within some timeout interval. Finally, here too, interrupts can be used to signal completion. For the most part, a blocking version of *receive* is much simpler and greatly preferred.

If multiple threads of control are present within a single address space, the arrival of a message can cause a thread to be spontaneously created. We will come back to this issue after we have look at threads in Chap. 12.

An issue closely related to blocking versus nonblocking calls is that of timeouts. In a system in which *send* calls block, if there is no reply, the sender will block forever. To prevent this situation, in some systems the caller may specify a time interval within which it expects a reply. If none arrives in that interval, the *send* call terminates with an error status.

10.2.5. Buffered versus Unbuffered Primitives

Just as system designers have a choice between blocking and nonblocking primitives, they also have a choice between buffered and unbuffered primitives. The primitives we have described so far are essentially **unbuffered primitives**. What this means is that an address refers to a specific process, as in Fig. 10-6. A call *receive*(*addr*, &*m*) tells the kernel of the machine on which it is running that the calling process is listening to address *addr*, and is prepared to receive one message sent to that address. A single message buffer, pointed to by *m* is provided to hold the incoming message. When the message comes in, the receiving kernel copies it to the buffer and unblocks the receiving process. The use of an address to refer to a specific process is illustrated in Fig. 10-9(a).

This scheme works fine as long as the server calls *receive* before the client calls *send*. The call to *receive* is the mechanism that tells the server's kernel which address the server is using and where to put the incoming message. The problem arises when the *send* is done before the *receive*. How does the server's kernel know which of its processes (if any) is using the address in the newly arrived message, and how does it know where to copy the message? The answer is simple: it does not.

One implementation strategy is to just discard the message, let the client time out,

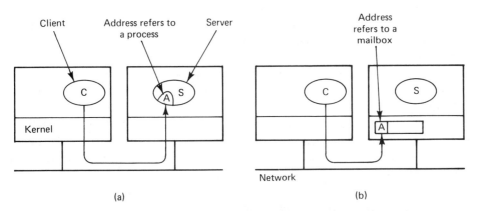

Fig. 10-9. (a) Unbuffered message passing. (b) Buffered message passing.

and hope the server has called *receive* before the client retransmits. This approach is easy to implement, but with bad luck, the client (or more likely, the client's kernel) may have to try several times before succeeding. Worse yet, if enough consecutive attempts fail, the client's kernel may give up, falsely concluding that the server has crashed or that the address is invalid.

In a similar vein, suppose two or more clients are using the server of Fig. 10-6(a). After the server has accepted a message from one of them, it is no longer listening to its address until it has finished its work and gone back to the top of the loop to call *receive* again. If it takes a while to do the work, the other clients may make multiple attempts to send to it, and some of them may give up, depending on the values of their retransmission timers and how impatient they are.

The second approach to dealing with this problem is to have the receiving kernel keep incoming messages around for a little while, just in case an appropriate *receive* is done shortly. Whenever an "unwanted" message arrives, a timer is started. If the timer expires before a suitable *receive* happens, the message is discarded.

Although this method reduces the chance that a message will have to be thrown away, it introduces the problem of storing and managing prematurely arriving messages. Buffers are needed and have to be allocated, freed, and generally managed. A conceptually simple way of dealing with this buffer management is to define a new data structure called a **mailbox**. A process that is interested in receiving messages tells the kernel to create a mailbox for it, and specifies an address to look for in network packets. Henceforth, all incoming messages with that address are put in the mailbox. The call to *receive* now just removes one message from the mailbox, or blocks (assuming blocking primitives) if none is present. In this way, the kernel knows what to do with incoming messages and has a place to put them. This technique is frequently referred to as a **buffered primitive**, and is illustrated in Fig. 10-9(b).

At first glance, mailboxes appear to eliminate the race conditions caused by messages being discarded and clients giving up. However, mailboxes are finite and can fill up. When a message arrives for a mailbox that is full, the kernel once again is confronted with the choice of either keeping it around for a while, hoping that at least one message will be extracted from the mailbox in time, or discarding it. These are precisely the same choices we had in the unbuffered case. Although we have perhaps reduced the probability of trouble, we have not eliminated it, and have not even managed to change its nature.

In some systems, another option is available: do not let a process send a message if there is no room to store it at the destination. To make this scheme work, the sender must block until an acknowledgement comes back saying that the message has been received. If the mailbox is full, the sender can be backed up and retroactively suspended as though the scheduler had decided to suspend it just *before* it tried to send the message. When space becomes available in the mailbox, the sender is allowed to try again.

10.2.6. Reliable versus Unreliable Primitives

So far we have tacitly assumed that when a client sends a message, the server will receive it. As usual, reality is more complicated than our abstract model. Messages can get lost, which affects the semantics of the message passing model. Suppose that blocking primitives are being used. When a client sends a message, it is suspended until the message has been sent. However, when it is restarted, there is no guarantee that the message has been delivered. The message might have been lost.

Three different approaches to this problem are possible. The first one is just to redefine the semantics of *send* to be unreliable. The system gives no guarantee about messages being delivered. Implementing reliable communication is entirely up to the users. The post office works this way. When you drop a letter in a letterbox, the post office does its best (more or less) to deliver it, but it promises nothing.

The second approach is to require the kernel on the receiving machine to send an acknowledgement back to the kernel on the sending machine. Only when this acknowledgement is received, will the sending kernel free the user (client) process. The acknowledgement goes from kernel to kernel; neither the client nor the server ever sees an acknowledgement. Just as the request from client to server is acknowledged by the server's kernel, the reply from the server back to the client is acknowledged by the client's kernel. Thus a request and reply now takes four messages, as shown in Fig. 10-10(a).

The third approach is to take advantage of the fact that client-server communication is structured as a request from the client to the server followed by a reply from the server to the client. In this method, the client is blocked after sending a message. The server's kernel does not send back an acknowledgement. Instead, the reply itself acts as the acknowledgement. Thus the sender remains blocked until the reply comes in. If it takes too long, the sending kernel can resend the request to guard against the possibility of a lost message. This approach is shown in Fig. 10-10(b).

Although the reply functions as an acknowledgement for the request, there is no acknowledgement for the reply. Whether this omission is serious or not depends on the nature of the request. If, for example, the client asks the server to read a block of a file and the reply is lost, the client will just repeat the request and the server will send the block again. No damage is done and little time is lost.

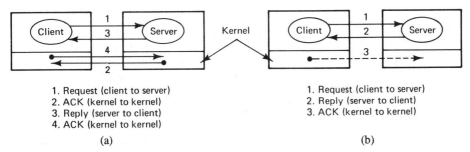

1. Request (client to server)
2. ACK (kernel to kernel)
3. Reply (server to client)
4. ACK (kernel to kernel)

(a)

1. Request (client to server)
2. Reply (server to client)
3. ACK (kernel to kernel)

(b)

Fig. 10-10. (a) Individually acknowledged messages. (b) Reply being used as the acknowledgement of the request. Note that the ACKs are handled entirely within the kernels.

On the other hand, if the request requires extensive computation on the part of the server, it would be a pity to discard the answer before the server is sure that the client has received the reply. For this reason, an acknowledgement from the client's kernel to the server's kernel is sometimes used. Until this packet is received, the server's *send* does not complete and the server remains blocked (assuming blocking primitives are used). In any event, if the reply is lost and the request is retransmitted, the server's kernel can see that the request is an old one, and just send the reply again without waking up the server. Thus in some systems the reply is acknowledged and in others it is not. Fig. 10-10(b).

A compromise between Fig. 10-10(a) and Fig. 10-10(b) that often works goes like this. When a request arrives at the server's kernel, a timer is started. If the server sends the reply quickly enough (i.e., before the timer expires), the reply functions as the acknowledgement. If the timer goes off, a separate acknowledgement is sent. Thus in most cases, only two messages are needed, but when a complicated request is being carried out, a third one is used.

10.2.7. Implementing the Client-Server Model

In the previous sections we have looked at four design issues, addressing, blocking, buffering, and reliability, each with several options. The major alternatives are summarized in Fig. 10-11. For each item we have listed three possibilities. Simple arithmetic shows that there are $3^4 = 81$ combinations. Not all of them are equally good. Nevertheless, just in this one area (message passing), the system designers have a considerable amount of leeway in choosing a set (or multiple sets) of communication primitives.

While the details of how message passing is implemented depend to some extent on which choices are made, it is still possible to make some general comments about the implementation, protocols, and software. To start with, virtually all networks have a maximum packet size, typically a few thousand bytes at most. Messages larger than this must be split up into multiple packets and sent separately. Some of these packets may be lost or garbled, and they may even arrive in the wrong order. To deal with this problem, it is usually sufficient to assign a message number to each

Item	Option 1	Option 2	Option 3
Addressing	Machine number	Sparse process addresses	ASCII names looked up via server
Blocking	Blocking primitives	Nonblocking with copy to kernel	Nonblocking with interrupt
Buffering	Unbuffered, discarding unexpected messages	Unbuffered, temporarily keeping unexpected messages	Mailboxes
Reliability	Unreliable	Request-Ack-Reply Ack	Request-Reply-Ack

Fig. 10-11. Four design issues for the communication primitives and some of the principal choices available.

message, and put it in each packet belonging to the message, along with a sequence number giving the order of the packets.

However, an issue that still must be resolved is the use of acknowledgements. One strategy is to acknowledge each individual packet. Another one is to acknowledge only entire messages. The former has the advantage that if a packet is lost, only that packet has to be retransmitted, but it has the disadvantage of requiring more packets on the network. The latter has the advantage of fewer packets, but the disadvantage of a more complicated recovery when a packet is lost (because a client timeout requires retransmitting the entire message). The choice largely depends on the loss rate of the network being used.

Another interesting issue is the underlying protocol used in client-server communication. Figure 10-12 shows six packet types that are commonly used to implement client-server protocols. The first one is the REQ packet, used to send a request message from a client to a server. (For simplicity, for the rest of this section we will assume that each message fits in a single packet.) The next one is the REP packet that carries results back from the server to the client. Then comes the ACK packet, which is used in reliable protocols to confirm the correct receipt of a previous packet.

The next four packet types are not essential, but often useful. Consider the situation in which a request has been successfully sent from the client to the server and the acknowledgement has been received. At this point the client's kernel knows that the server is working on the request. But what happens if no answer is forthcoming within a reasonable time? Is the request really that complicated, or has the server crashed? To be able to distinguish these two cases, the AYA packet is sometimes provided, so the client can ask the server what is going on. If the answer is IAA, the client's kernel knows that all is well and just continues to wait. Even better is a REP packet, of course. If the AYA does not generate any response, then the client's kernel waits a short interval and tries again. If this procedure fails more than some specified number of times, the client's kernel normally gives up and reports failure back to the user. The AYA and IAA packets can also be used even in a protocol in which REQ packets are not acknowledged. They allow the client to check on the server's status.

Code	Packet type	From	To	Description
REQ	Request	Client	Server	The client wants service
REP	Reply	Server	Client	Reply from the server to the client
ACK	Ack	Either	Other	The previous packet arrived
AYA	Are you alive?	Client	Server	Probe to see if the server has crashed
IAA	I am alive	Server	Client	The server has not crashed
TA	Try again	Server	Client	The server has no room
AU	Address unknown	Server	Client	No process is using this address

Fig. 10-12. Packet types used in client-server protocols.

Finally, we come to the last two packet types, which are useful in case a REQ packet cannot be accepted. There are two reasons why this might happen, and it is important for the client's kernel to be able to distinguish them. One reason is that the mailbox to which the request is addressed is full. By sending this packet back to the client's kernel, the server's kernel can indicate that the address is valid, and the request should be repeated later. The other reason is that the address does not belong to any process or mailbox. Repeating it later will not help.

This situation can also arise when buffering is not used, and the server is not currently blocked in a *receive* call. Since having the server's kernel forget that the address even exists in between calls to *receive* can lead to problems, in some systems a server can make a call whose only function is to register a certain address with the kernel. In that way, at least the kernel can tell the difference between an address to which no one is currently listening, and one which is simply wrong. It can then send TA in the former case and AU in the latter.

Many packet sequences are possible. A few common ones are shown in Fig. 10-13. In Fig. 10-13(a), we have the straight request/reply, with no acknowledgement. In Fig. 10-13(b), we have a protocol in which each message is individually acknowledged. In Fig. 10-13(c), we see the reply acting as the acknowledgement, reducing the sequence to three packets. Finally, in Fig. 10-13(d), we see a nervous client checking to see if the server is still there.

10.3. REMOTE PROCEDURE CALL

Although the client-server model provides a convenient way to structure a distributed operating system, it suffers from one incurable flaw: the basic paradigm around which all communication is built is input/output. The procedures *send* and *receive* are fundamentally engaged in doing I/O. Since I/O is not one of the key concepts of centralized systems, making it the basis for distributed computing has struck many workers in the field as a mistake. Their goal is to make distributed computing look like centralized computing. Building everything around I/O is not the way to do it.

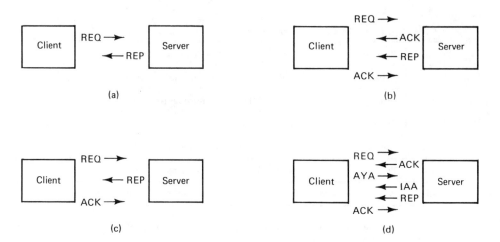

Fig. 10-13. Some examples of packet exchanges for client-server communication.

This problem has long been known but little was done about it until a paper by Birrell and Nelson (1984) introduced a completely different way of attacking the problem. Although the idea is refreshingly simple (once someone has thought of it), the implications are often subtle. In this section we will examine the concept, its implementation, its strengths and its weaknesses.

In a nutshell, what Birrell and Nelson suggested was allowing programs to call procedures located on other machines. When a process on machine *A* calls a procedure on machine *B*, the calling process on *A* is suspended, and the execution of the called procedure takes place on *B*. Information can be transported from the caller to the callee in the parameters, and can come back in the procedure result. No message passing or I/O at all is visible to the programmer. This method is known as **remote procedure call**, or often just **RPC**.

While the basic idea sounds simple and elegant, subtle problems exist. To start with, because the calling and called procedures run on different machines, they execute in different address spaces, which causes complications. Parameters and results also have to be passed, which can be complicated, especially if the machines are not identical. Finally, both machines can crash, and each of the possible failures causes different problems. Still, most of these can be dealt with, and RPC is a widely-used technique that underlies many distributed operating systems.

10.3.1. Basic RPC Operation

To understand how RPC works, it is important to first fully understand how a conventional (i.e., single machine) procedure call works. Consider a call like

```
count = read(fd, buf, nbytes);
```

where *fd* is an integer, *buf* is an array of characters, and *nbytes* is another integer. If the call is made from the main program, the stack will be as shown in Fig. 10-14(a) before the call. To make the call, the caller pushes the parameters onto the stack in order, last one first, as shown in Fig. 10-14(b). (The reason that C compilers push the parameters in reverse order has to do with *printf*—by doing so, *printf* can always locate its first parameter, the format string.) After *read* has finished running, it puts the return value in a register, removes the return address, and transfers control back to the caller. The caller then removes the parameters from the stack, returning it to the original state, as shown in Fig. 10-14(c).

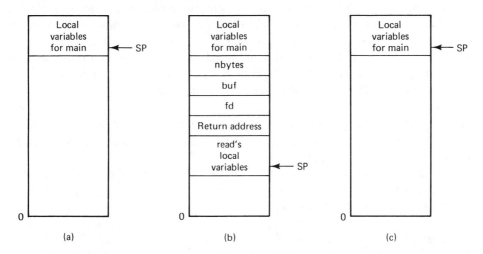

Fig. 10-14. (a) The stack before the call to *read*. (b) The stack while the called procedure is active. (c) The stack after the return to the caller.

Several things are worth noting. For one, in C, parameters can be **call-by-value** or **call-by-reference**. A value parameter, such as *fd* or *nbytes*, is simply copied to the stack as shown in Fig. 10-14(b). To the called procedure, a value parameter is just an initialized local variable. The called procedure may modify it, but such changes do not affect the value of the original variable in the calling procedure.

A reference parameter in C is a pointer to a variable (i.e., the address of the variable), rather than the value of the variable. In the call to *read*, the second parameter is a reference parameter because arrays are always passed by reference in C. What is actually pushed onto the stack is the address of the character array. If the called procedure uses this parameter to store something into the character array, it *does* modify the array in the calling procedure. The difference between call-by-value and call-by-reference is quite important for RPC, as we shall see.

One other parameter passing mechanism also exists, although it is not used in C. It is called **call-by-copy/restore**. It consists of having the variable copied to the stack by the caller, as in call-by-value, and then copied back after the call, overwriting the caller's original value. Under most conditions, this achieves the same effect as call-by-reference, but in some situations, such as the same parameter being present multiple times in the parameter list, the semantics are different.

The decision of which parameter passing mechanism to use is normally made by the language designers and is a fixed property of the language. Sometimes it depends on the data type being passed. In C, for example, integers and other scalar types are always passed by value, whereas arrays are always passed by reference, as we have seen. In contrast, Pascal programmers can choose which mechanism they want for each parameter. The default is call-by-value, but programmers can force call-by-reference by inserting the keyword **var** before specific parameters. Some Ada® compilers use copy/restore for **in out** parameters, but others use call-by-reference. The language definition permits either choice, which makes the semantics a bit fuzzy.

The idea behind RPC is to make a remote procedure call look as much as possible like a local one. In other words, we want RPC to be transparent—the calling procedure should not be aware that the called procedure is executing on a different machine, or vice versa. Suppose a program needs to read some data from a file. The programmer puts a call to *read* in the code to get the data. In a traditional (single-processor) system, the *read* routine is extracted from the library by the linker and inserted into the object program. It is a short procedure, usually written in assembly language, that puts the parameters in registers and then issues a READ system call by trapping to the kernel. In essence, the *read* procedure is a kind of interface between the user code and the operating system.

Even though *read* issues a kernel trap, it is called in the usual way, by pushing the parameters onto the stack, as shown in Fig. 10-14. Thus the programmer does not know that *read* is actually doing something fishy.

RPC achieves its transparency in an analogous way. When *read* is actually a remote procedure (e.g., one that will run on the file server's machine), a different version of *read,* called a **client stub**, is put into the library. Like the original one, it too, is called using the calling sequence of Fig. 10-14. Also like the original one, it too, traps to the kernel. Only unlike the original one, it does not put the parameters in registers and ask the kernel to give it data. Instead it packs the parameters into a message and asks the kernel to send the message to the server as illustrated in Fig. 10-15. Following the call to *send*, the client stub calls *receive*, blocking itself until the reply comes back.

When the message arrives at the server, the kernel passes it up to a **server stub** that is bound with the actual server. Typically the server stub will have called *receive* and be blocked waiting for incoming messages. The server stub unpacks the parameters from the message and then calls the server procedure in the usual way (i.e., as in Fig. 10-14). From the server's point of view, it is as though it is being called directly by the client—the parameters and return address are all on the stack where they belong and nothing seems unusual. The server performs its work and then returns the result to the caller in the usual way. For example, in the case of *read*, the server will fill the buffer, pointed to by the second parameter, with the data. This buffer will be internal to the server stub.

When the server stub gets control back after the call has completed, it packs the result (the buffer) in a message and calls *send* to return it to the client. Then it goes back to the top of its own loop to call *receive*, waiting for the next message.

When the message gets back to the client machine, the kernel sees that it is addressed to the client process (to the stub part of that process, but the kernel does not know that). The message is copied to the waiting buffer and the client process unblocked. The client stub inspects the message, unpacks the result, copies it to its

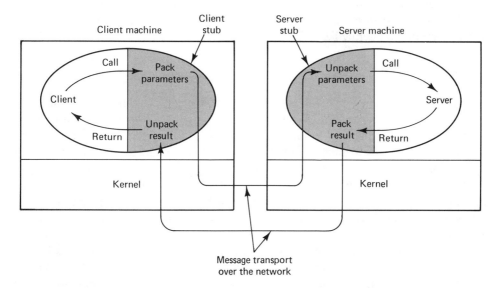

Fig. 10-15. Calls and messages in an RPC. Each ellipse represents a single process, with the shaded portion being the stub.

caller, and returns in the usual way. When the caller gets control following the call to *read*, all it knows is that its data are available. It has no idea that the work was done remotely instead of by the local kernel.

This blissful ignorance on the part of the client is the beauty of the whole scheme. As far as it is concerned, remote services are accessed by making ordinary (i.e., local) procedure calls, not by calling *send* and *receive* as in Fig. 10-6. All the details of the message passing are hidden away in the two library procedures, just as the details of actually making system call traps are hidden away in traditional libraries.

To summarize, a remote procedure call occurs in the following steps:

1. The client procedure calls the client stub in the normal way.

2. The client stub builds a message and traps to the kernel.

3. The kernel sends the message to the remote kernel.

4. The remote kernel gives the message to the server stub.

5. The server stub unpacks the parameters and calls the server.

6. The server does the work and returns the result to the stub.

7. The server stub packs it in a message and traps to the kernel.

8. The remote kernel sends the message to the client's kernel.

9. The client's kernel gives the message to the client stub.

10. The stub unpacks the result and returns to the client.

The net effect of all these steps is to convert the local call by the client procedure to the client stub to a local call to the server procedure without either client or server being aware of the intermediate steps.

10.3.2. Parameter Passing

The function of the client stub is to take its parameters, pack them into a message, and send it to the server stub. While this sounds straightforward, it is not quite as simple as it at first appears. In this section we will look at some of the issues concerned with parameter passing in RPC systems. Packing parameters into a message is called **parameter marshalling**.

As the simplest possible example, consider a remote procedure, *sum(i, j)*, that takes two integer parameters and returns their arithmetic sum. (As a practical matter, one would not normally make such a simple procedure remote due to the overhead, but as an example it will do.) The call to *sum*, with parameters 4 and 7, is shown in the left-hand portion of the client process in Fig. 10-16. The client stub takes its two parameters and puts them in a message as indicated. It also puts the name or number of the procedure to be called in the message because the server might support several different calls, and it has to be told which one is required.

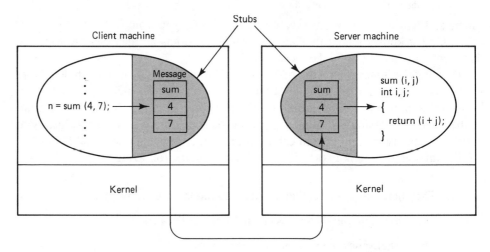

Fig. 10-16. Computing *sum*(4, 7) remotely.

When the message arrives at the server, the stub examines the message to see which procedure is needed, and then makes the appropriate call. If the server also supports the remote procedures *difference*, *product*, and *quotient*, the server stub might have a switch statement in it, to select the procedure to be called, depending on the first field of the message. The actual call from the stub to the server looks much like the original client call, except that the parameters are variables initialized from the incoming message, rather than constants.

When the server has finished, the server stub gains control again. It takes the result, provided by the server, and packs it into a message. This message is sent back to the client stub, which unpacks it and returns the value to the client procedure (not shown in the figure).

As long as the client and server machines are identical and all the parameters and results are scalar types, such as integers, characters, and Booleans, this model works fine. However, in a large distributed system, it is common that multiple machine types are present. Each machine often has its own representation for numbers, characters and other data items. For example, IBM mainframes use the EBCDIC character code, whereas IBM personal computers use ASCII. As a consequence, it is not possible to pass a character parameter from an IBM PC client to an IBM mainframe server using the simple scheme of Fig. 10-16: the server will interpret the character incorrectly.

Similar problems can occur with the representation of integers (1s complement versus 2s complement), and especially with floating point numbers. In addition, an even more annoying problem exists because some machines, such as the Intel 386, number their bytes from right to left, whereas others, such as the Sun SPARC, number them the other way. The Intel format is called **little endian** and the SPARC format is called **big endian**, after the politicians in *Gulliver's Travels* who went to war over which end of an egg to break (Cohen, 1981). As an example, consider a server with two parameters, an integer and a 4-character string. Each parameter requires one 32-bit word. Figure 10-17(a) shows what the parameter portion of a message built by a client stub on an Intel 386 might look like. The first word contains the integer parameter, 5 in this case, and the second contains the string, "JILL".

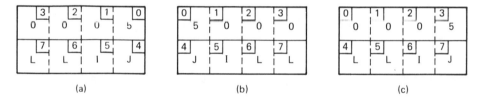

Fig. 10-17. (a) The original message on the 386. (b) The message after receipt on the SPARC. (c) The message after being inverted. The little numbers in boxes indicate the address of each byte.

Since messages are transferred byte for byte (actually, bit for bit) over the network, the first byte sent is the first byte to arrive. In Fig. 10-17(b) we show what the message of Fig. 10-17(a) would look like if received by a SPARC, which numbers its bytes with byte 0 at the left (high-order byte) instead of at the right (low-order byte) as do all the Intel chips. When the server stub reads the parameters at addresses 0 and 4, respectively, it will find an integer equal to 83,886,080 (5×2^{24}) and a string "JILL".

One obvious, but unfortunately incorrect, approach is to invert the bytes of each word after they are received, leading to Fig. 10-17(c). Now the integer is 5 and the string is "LLIJ". The problem here is that integers are reversed by the different byte ordering, but strings are not. Without additional information about what is a string and what is an integer there is no way to repair the damage.

Fortunately, this information is implicitly available. Remember that the items in the message correspond to the procedure identifier and parameters. Both the client and server know what the types of the parameters are. Thus a message corresponding to a remote procedure with n parameters will have $n + 1$ fields, one identifying the procedure and one for each of the n parameters. Once a standard has been agreed upon for representing each of the basic data types, given a parameter list and a message, it is possible to deduce which bytes belong to which parameter, and thus to solve the problem.

As a simple example, consider the procedure of Fig. 10-18(a). It has three parameters, a character, a floating-point number, and an array of 5 integers. We might decide to transmit a character in the rightmost byte of a word (leaving the next 3 bytes empty), a float as a whole word, and an array as a group of words equal to the array length, preceded by a word giving the length, as shown in Fig. 10-18(b). Thus given these rules, the client stub for *foobar* knows that it must use the format of Fig. 10-18(b), and the server stub knows that incoming messages for *foobar* will have the format of Fig. 10-18(b). Having the type information for the parameters makes it possible to make any necessary conversions.

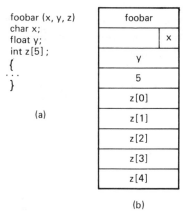

Fig. 10-18. (a) A procedure. (b) The corresponding message.

Even with this additional information, there are still some issues open. In particular, how should information be represented in the messages? One way is to devise a network standard or **canonical form** for integers, characters, Booleans, floating point numbers, and so on, and require all senders to convert their internal representation to this form while marshalling. For example, suppose it is decided to use two's complement for integers, ASCII for characters, 0 (false) and 1 (true) for Booleans, and IEEE format for floating point numbers, with everything stored in little endian. For any list of integers, characters, Booleans, and floating point numbers, the exact pattern required is now deterministic down to the last bit. As a result, the server stub no longer has to worry about which byte ordering the client has because the order of the bits in the message is now fixed, independent of the client's hardware.

The problem with this method is that it is sometimes inefficient. Suppose a big endian client is talking to a big endian server. According to the rules, the client must convert everything to little endian in the message, and the server must convert it back again when it arrives. While this is unambiguous, it requires two conversions when in fact none were necessary. This observation gives rise to a second approach: the client uses its own native format and indicates in the first byte of the message which format this is. Thus a little endian client builds a little endian message and a big endian client builds a big endian message. As soon as a message comes in, the server stub examines the first byte to see what the client is. If it is the same as the server, no conversion is needed. Otherwise, the server stub converts everything. Although we have only discussed converting from one endian to the other, conversions between one's and two's complement, EBCDIC to ASCII, and so on, can be handled the same way. The trick is knowing what the message layout is and what the client is. Once these are known, the rest is easy (provided that everyone can convert from everyone else's format).

Now we come to the question of where the stub procedures come from. In many RPC-based systems, they are automatically generated. As we have seen, given a specification of the server procedure and the encoding rules, the message format is uniquely determined. Thus it is possible to have a compiler read the server specification and generate a client stub that packs its parameters into the officially approved message format. Similarly, the compiler can also produce a server stub that unpacks them and calls the server. Having both stub procedures generated from a single formal specification of the server not only makes life easier for the programmers, but reduces the chance of error and makes the system transparent with respect to differences in internal representation of data items.

Finally we come to our last, and most difficult problem: "How are pointers passed?" The answer is: only with the greatest of difficulty, if at all. Remember that a pointer is only meaningful within the address space of the process in which it is being used. Getting back to our *read* example discussed earlier, if the second parameter (the address of the buffer), happens to be 1000 on the client, one cannot just pass the number 1000 to the server and expect it to work. Address 1000 on the server might be in the middle of the program text.

One solution is just to forbid pointers and reference parameters in general. However, these are so important, that this solution is highly undesirable. In fact, it is not necessary either. In the *read* example, the client stub knows that the second parameter points to an array of characters. Suppose, for the moment, that it also knows how big the array is. One strategy then becomes apparent: copy the array into the message and send it to the server. The server stub can then call the server with a pointer to this array, even though this pointer has a different numerical value than the second parameter of *read* has. Changes the server makes using the pointer (e.g., storing data into it) directly affect the message buffer inside the server stub. When the server finishes, the original message can be sent back to the client stub, which then copies it back to the client. In effect, call-by-reference has been replaced by copy/restore. While this is not always identical, it frequently is good enough.

One optimization makes this mechanism twice as efficient. If the stubs know whether the buffer is an input parameter or an output parameter to the server, one of the copies can be eliminated. If the array is input to the server (e.g., in a call to *write*) it need not be copied back. If it is output, it need not be sent over in the first place. The way to tell them is in the formal specification of the server procedure. Thus associated with every remote procedure is a formal specification of the procedure, written in some kind of specification language, telling what the parameters are, which are input and which are output (or both), and what their (maximum) sizes are. It is from this formal specification that the stubs are generated by a special stub compiler.

As a final comment, it is worth noting that although we can now handle pointers to simple arrays and structures, we still cannot handle the most general case of a pointer to an arbitrary data structure such as a complex graph. Some systems attempt to deal with this case by actually passing the pointer to the server stub and generating special code in the server procedure for using pointers.

Normally, a pointer is followed (dereferenced) by putting it in a register and indirecting through the register. When this special technique is used, a pointer is dereferenced by sending a message back to the client stub asking it to fetch and send the item being pointed to (reads) or store a value at the address pointed to (writes). While this method works, it is often highly inefficient. Imagine having the file server store the bytes in the buffer by sending back each one in a separate message. Still, it is better than nothing, and some systems use it.

10.3.3. Dynamic Binding

An issue that we have glossed over so far is how the client locates the server. One method is just to hardwire the network address of the server into the client. The trouble with this approach is that it is extremely inflexible. If the server moves or if the server is replicated or if the interface changes, numerous programs will have to be found and recompiled. To avoid all these problems, some distributed systems use what is called **dynamic binding** to match up clients and servers. In this section we will describe the ideas behind dynamic binding.

The starting point for dynamic binding is the server's formal specification. As an example, consider the server of Fig. 10-6(a), specified in Fig. 10-19. The specification tells the name of the server (*file_server*), the version number (3.1), and a list of procedures provided by the server (*read*, *write*, *create*, and *delete*).

For each procedure, the types of the parameters are given. Each parameter is specified as being an *in* parameter, an *out* parameter, or an *in out* parameter. The direction is relative to the server. An *in* parameter, such as the file name, *name*, is sent from the client to the server. This one is used to tell the server which file to read from, write to, create, or delete. Similarly, *bytes* tells the server how many bytes to transfer and *position* tells where in the file to begin reading or writing. An *out* parameter such as *buf* in *read*, is sent from the server to the client. *Buf* is the place where the file server puts the data that the client has requested. An *in out* parameter, of which there are none in this example, would be sent from the client to the server, modified there, and then sent back to the client (copy/restore). Copy/restore is

```
#include <header.h>

specification of file_server, version 3.1:

    long read(in char name[MAX_PATH], out char buf[BUF_SIZE],
             in long bytes, in long position);

    long write(in char name[MAX_PATH], in char buf[BUF_SIZE],
             in long bytes, in long position);

    int create(in char[MAX_PATH], in int mode);

    int delete(in char[MAX_PATH]);

end;
```

Fig. 10-19. A specification of the stateless server of Fig. 10-6.

typically used for pointer parameters in cases where the server both reads and modifies the data structure being pointed to. The directions are crucial, so the client stub knows which parameters to send to the server, and the server stub knows which ones to send back.

As we pointed out earlier, this particular example is a stateless server. For a UNIX-like server, one would have additional procedures *open* and *close*, and different parameters for *read* and *write*. The concept of RPC itself is neutral, permitting the system designers to build any kind of servers they desire.

The primary use of the formal specification of Fig. 10-19 is as input to the stub generator, which produces both the client stub and the server stub. Both are then put into the appropriate libraries. When a user (client) program calls any of the procedures defined by this specification, the corresponding client stub procedure is linked into its binary. Similarly, when the server is compiled, the server stubs are linked with it too.

When the server begins executing, the call to *initialize* outside the main loop [see Fig. 10-6(a)] **exports** the server interface. What this means is that the server sends a message to a program called a **binder**, to make its existence known. This process is referred to as **registering** the server. To register, the server gives the binder its name, its version number, a unique identifier, typically 32 bits long, and a **handle** used to locate it. The handle is system dependent, and might be an Ethernet address, an IP address, an X.500 address, a sparse process identifier, or something else. In addition, other information, for example, concerning authentication, might also be supplied. A server can also deregister with the binder when it is no longer prepared to offer service. The binder interface is shown in Fig. 10-20.

Given this background, now consider how the client locates the server. When the client calls one of the remote procedures for the first time, say, *read*, the client stub sees that it is not yet bound to a server, so it sends a message to the binder asking to **import** version 3.1 of the *file_server* interface. The binder checks to see if one or more servers have already exported an interface with this name and version number. If no currently running server is willing to support this interface, the *read* call fails.

Call	Input	Output
Register	Name, version, handle, unique id	
Deregister	Name, version, unique id	
Lookup	Name, version	Handle, unique id

Fig. 10-20. The binder interface.

By including the version number in the matching process, the binder can insure that clients using obsolete interfaces will fail to locate a server rather than locate one and get unpredictable results due to incorrect parameters.

On the other hand, if a suitable server exists, the binder gives its handle and unique identifier to the client stub. The client stub uses the handle as the address to send the request message to. The message contains the parameters and the unique identifier, which the server's kernel uses to direct the incoming message to the correct server in the event that several servers are running on that machine.

This method of exporting and importing interfaces is highly flexible. For example, it can handle multiple servers that support the same interface. The binder can spread the clients randomly over the servers to even the load if it wants to. It can also poll the servers periodically, automatically deregistering any server that fails to respond, to achieve a degree of fault tolerance. Furthermore, it can also assist in authentication. A server could specify, for example, that it only wished to be used by a specific list of users, in which case the binder would refuse to tell users not on the list about it. The binder can also verify that both client and server are using the same version of the interface.

However, this form of dynamic binding also has its disadvantages. The extra overhead of exporting and importing interfaces costs time. Since many client processes are short lived and each process has to start all over again, the effect may be significant. Also, in a large distributed system, the binder may become a bottleneck, so multiple binders are needed. Consequently, whenever an interface is registered or deregistered, a substantial number of messages will be needed to keep all the binders synchronized and up to date, creating even more overhead.

10.3.4. RPC Semantics in the Presence of Failures

The goal of RPC is to hide communication by making remote procedure calls look just like local ones. With a few exceptions, such as the inability to handle global variables and the subtle differences introduced by using copy/restore for pointer parameters instead of call-by-reference, so far we have come fairly close. Indeed, as long as both client and server are functioning perfectly, RPC does its job remarkably well. The problem comes in when errors occur. It is then that the differences between local and remote calls are not always easy to mask. In this section we will examine some of the possible errors and what can be done about them.

To structure our discussion, let us distinguish between five different classes of failures that can occur in RPC systems, as follows:

1. The client is unable to locate the server.

2. The request message from the client to the server is lost.

3. The reply message from the server to the client is lost.

4. The server crashes after receiving a request.

5. The client crashes after sending a request.

Each of these categories poses different problems and requires different solutions.

Client Cannot Locate the Server

To start with, it can happen that the client cannot locate a suitable server. The server might be down, for example. Alternatively, suppose that the client is compiled using a particular version of the client stub, and the binary is not used for a considerable period of time. In the meantime, the server evolves and a new version of the interface is installed and new stubs are generated and put into use. When the client is finally run, the binder will be unable to match it up with a server, and will report back failure. While this mechanism is used to protect the client from accidentally trying to talk to a server that may not agree with it in terms of what parameters are required or what it is supposed to do, the problem remains of how this failure should be dealt with.

With the server of Fig. 10-6(a), each of the procedures returns a value, with the code −1 conventionally used to indicate failure. For such procedures, just returning −1 will clearly tell the caller that something is amiss. In UNIX, a global variable, *errno*, is also assigned a value indicating the error type. In such a system, adding a new error type "Cannot locate server" is simple.

The trouble is, this solution is not general enough. Consider the *sum* procedure of Fig. 10-16. Here −1 is a perfectly legal value to be returned, for example, the result of adding 7 to −8. Another error reporting mechanism is needed.

One possible candidate is to have the error raise an **exception**. In some languages (e.g., Ada), programmers can write special procedures that are invoked upon specific errors, such as division by zero. In C, signal handlers can be used for this purpose. In other words, we could define a new signal type *SIGNOSERVER*, and allow it to be handled the same way as other exceptions and signals.

This approach, too, has drawbacks. To start with, not every language has exceptions or signals. To name one, Pascal does not. Another point is that having to write an exception or signal handler destroys the transparency we have been trying to achieve. Suppose you are a programmer and your boss tells you to write the *sum* procedure. You smile and tell her it will be written, tested, and documented in five minutes. Then she mentions that you also have to write an exception handler as well, just in case the procedure is not there today. At this point it is pretty hard to maintain the illusion that remote procedures are no different than local ones, since writing an exception handler for "Cannot locate server" would be a rather unusual request in a single processor system.

Lost Request Messages

The second item on the list is dealing with lost request messages. This is the easiest one to deal with: just have the kernel start a timer when sending the request. If the timer expires before a reply or acknowledgement comes back, the kernel sends the message again. If the message was truly lost, the server will not be able to tell the difference between the retransmission and the original, and everything will work fine. Unless, of course, so many request messages are lost that the kernel gives up and falsely concludes that the server is down, in which case we are back to "Cannot locate server."

Lost Reply Messages

Lost replies are considerably more difficult to deal with. The obvious solution is just to rely on the timer again. If no reply is forthcoming within a reasonable period, just send the request once more. The trouble with this solution is that the client's kernel is not really sure why there was no answer. Did the request get lost? Did the reply get lost? Or is the server merely slow? It may make a difference.

In particular, some operations can be safely repeated as often as necessary with no damage being done. A request like asking for the first 1024 bytes of a file has no side effects and can be executed as often as necessary without any harm being done. A request that has this property is said to be **idempotent**.

Now consider a request to a banking server asking to transfer a million dollars from one account to another. If the request arrives and is carried out, but the reply is lost, the client will not know this, and will retransmit the message. The bank server will interpret this request as a new one, and will carry it out too. Two million dollars will be transferred. Heaven forbid that the reply is lost 10 times. Transferring money is not idempotent.

One way of solving this problem is to try to somehow structure all requests in an idempotent way. In practice, however, many requests are inherently nonidempotent, like transferring money, so something else is needed. Another method is to have the client's kernel assign each request a sequence number. By having each server's kernel keep track of the most recently received sequence number from each client's kernel that is using it, the server's kernel can tell the difference between an original request and a retransmission, and can refuse to carry out any request a second time. An additional safeguard is to have a bit in the message header that is used to distinguish initial requests from retransmissions (the idea being that it is always safe to perform an original request; retransmissions may require more care).

Server Crashes

The next failure on the list is a server crash. It too relates to idempotency, but unfortunately it cannot be solved using sequence numbers. The normal sequence of events at a server is shown in Fig. 10-21(a). A request arrives, is carried out, and a reply is sent. Now consider Fig. 10-21(b). A request arrives and is carried out, just as before, but the server crashes before it can send the reply. Finally, look at Fig. 10-21(c). Again a request arrives, but this time the server crashes before it can even be carried out.

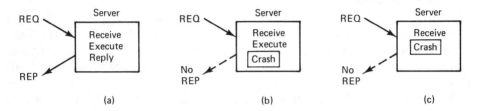

Fig. 10-21. (a) Normal case. (b) Crash after execution. (c) Crash before execution.

The annoying part of Fig. 10-21 is that the correct treatment differs for (b) and (c). In (b) the system has to report failure back to the client (e.g., raise an exception), whereas in (c) it can just retransmit the request. The problem is that the client's kernel cannot tell which is which. All it knows is that its timer has expired.

Three schools of thought exist on what to do here. One philosophy is to wait until the server reboots (or rebinds to a new server) and try the operation again. The idea is to keep trying until a reply has been received, then give it to the client. This technique is called **at least once semantics** and guarantees that the RPC has been carried out at least one time, but possibly more.

The second philosophy gives up immediately and reports back failure. This way is called **at most once semantics** and guarantees that the RPC has been carried out at most one time, but possibly none at all.

The third philosophy is to guarantee nothing. When a server crashes, the client gets no help and no promises. The RPC may have been carried out anywhere from 0 to a large number of times. The main virtue of this scheme is that it is easy to implement.

None of these are terribly attractive. What one would like is **exactly once semantics**, but as can be seen fairly easily, there is no way to arrange this in general. Imagine that the remote operation consists of printing some text, and is accomplished by loading the printer buffer and then setting a single bit in some control register to start the printer. The crash can occur a microsecond before setting the bit, or a microsecond afterwards. The recovery procedure depends entirely on which it is, but there is no way for the client to discover it.

In short, the possibility of server crashes radically changes the nature of RPC, and clearly distinguishes single processor systems from distributed ones. In the former case, a server crash also implies a client crash, so recovery is neither possible nor necessary. In the latter it is both possible and necessary to take some action.

Client Crashes

The final item on the list of failures is the client crash. What happens if a client sends a request to a server to do some work and crashes before the server replies? At this point a computation is active and no parent is waiting for the result. Such an unwanted computation is called an **orphan**.

Orphans can cause a variety of problems. As a bare minimum, they waste CPU cycles. They can also lock files or otherwise tie up valuable resources. Finally, if the client reboots and does the RPC again, but the reply from the orphan comes back immediately afterwards, confusion can result.

What can be done about orphans? Nelson (1981) proposed four solutions. In solution 1, before a client stub sends an RPC message, it makes a log entry telling what it is about to do. The log is kept on disk or some other medium that survives crashes. After a reboot, the log is checked and the orphan is explicitly killed off. This solution is called **extermination**.

The disadvantage of this scheme is the horrendous expense of writing a disk record for every RPC. Furthermore, it may not even work, since orphans themselves may do RPCs, thus creating **grandorphans** or further descendants that are impossible to locate. Finally, the network may be partitioned, due to a failed gateway, making it impossible to kill them, even if they can be located. All in all, this is not a promising approach.

In solution 2, called **reincarnation**, all these problems can be solved without the need to write disk records. The way it works is to divide time up into sequentially numbered epochs. When a client reboots, it broadcasts a message to all machines declaring the start of a new epoch. When such a broadcast comes in, all remote computations are killed. Of course, if the network is partitioned, some orphans may survive. However, when they report back, their replies will contain an obsolete epoch number, making them easy to detect.

Solution 3 is a variant on this idea, but less Draconian. It is called **gentle reincarnation**. When an epoch broadcast comes in, each machine checks to see if it has any remote computations, and if so, tries to locate their owner. Only if the owner cannot be found is the computation killed.

Finally, we have solution 4, **expiration**, in which each RPC is given a standard amount of time, T, to do the job. If it cannot finish, it must explicitly ask for another quantum, which is a nuisance. On the other hand, if after a crash the server waits a time T before rebooting, all orphans are sure to be gone. The problem to be solved here is choosing a reasonable value of T in the face of RPCs with wildly differing requirements.

In practice, none of these methods are desirable. Worse yet, killing an orphan may have unforeseen consequences. For example, suppose that an orphan has obtained locks on one or more files or data base records. If the orphan is suddenly killed, these locks may remain forever. Also, an orphan may have already made entries in various remote queues to start up other processes at some future time, so even killing the orphan may not remove all traces of it. Orphan elimination is discussed in more detail by Panzieri and Shrivastava (1988).

10.3.5. Implementation Issues

The success or failure of a distributed system often hinges on its performance. The system performance, in turn, is critically dependent on the speed of communication. The communication speed, more often than not, stands or falls with its implementation, rather than with its abstract principles. In this section we will look at some of the implementation issues for RPC systems, with a special emphasis on the performance.

RPC Protocols

The first issue is the choice of the RPC protocol. Theoretically, any old protocol will do as long as it gets the bits from the client's kernel to the server's kernel, but practically there are several major decisions to be made here, and the choices made can have a major impact on the performance. The first decision is between a connection-oriented protocol and a connectionless protocol. With a connection-oriented protocol, at the time the client is bound to the server, a connection is established between them. All traffic, in both directions, uses this connection.

The advantage of having a connection is that communication becomes much easier. When a kernel sends a message, it does not have to worry about it getting lost, nor does it have to deal with acknowledgements. All that is handled at a lower level, by the software that supports the connection. When operating over a wide-area network, this advantage is often too strong to resist.

The disadvantage, especially over a LAN, is the performance loss. All that extra software gets in the way. Besides, the main advantage (no lost packets) is hardly needed on a LAN, since LANs are so reliable. As a consequence, most distributed operating systems that are intended for use in a single building or campus use connectionless protocols.

The second major choice is whether to use a standard general-purpose protocol or one specifically designed for RPC. Since there are no standards in this area, using a custom RPC protocol often means designing your own (or borrowing a friend's). System designers are split about evenly on this one.

Some distributed systems use IP (or UDP, which is built on IP) as the basic protocol. This choice has several things going for it:

1. The protocol is already designed, saving considerable work.

2. Many implementations are available, again saving work.

3. These packets can be sent and received by nearly all UNIX systems.

4. IP and UDP packets can be directly carried over many existing networks.

In short, IP and UDP are easy to use and fit in well with existing UNIX systems and networks such as the Internet. This makes it straightforward to write clients and servers that run on UNIX systems, which certainly aids in getting code running quickly and in testing it.

As usual, the down side is the performance. IP was not designed as an end-user protocol. It was designed as a base upon which reliable TCP connections could be established over recalcitrant internetworks. For example, it can deal with gateways that fragment packets into little pieces so they can pass through networks with a tiny maximum packet size. Although this feature is never needed in a LAN-based distributed system, the IP packet header fields dealing with fragmentation have to be filled in by the sender and verified by the receiver to make them legal IP packets. IP packets have in total 13 header fields, of which three are useful: the source and destination addresses, and the packet length. The other 10 just come along for the ride, and one of them, the header checksum, is time consuming to compute. To make matters worse, UDP has another checksum, covering the data as well.

The alternative is to use a specialized RPC protocol that, unlike IP, does not attempt to deal with packets that have been bouncing around the network for a few minutes and then suddenly materialize out of thin air at an inconvenient moment. Of course, the protocol has to be invented, implemented, tested, and embedded in existing systems, so it is considerably more work. Furthermore, the rest of the world tends not to jump with joy at the birth of yet another new protocol. In the long run, the development and widespread acceptance of a high-performance RPC protocol is definitely the way to go, but we are not there yet.

One last protocol related issue is packet and message length. Doing an RPC has a large, fixed overhead, independent of the amount of data sent. Thus reading a 64K file in a single 64K RPC is vastly more efficient than reading it in 64 1K RPCs. It is therefore important that the protocol and network allow large transmissions. Some RPC systems are limited to small sizes (e.g., Sun Microsystem's limit is 8K). In addition, many networks cannot handle large packets (Ethernet's limit is 1536 bytes), so a single RPC will have to be split over multiple packets, causing extra overhead.

Acknowledgements

When large RPCs have to be broken up into many small packets as just described, a new issue arises: "Should individual packets be acknowledged or not?" Suppose, for example, a client wants to write a 4K block of data to a file server, but the system cannot handle packets larger than 1K. One strategy, known as a **stop-and-wait protocol**, is for the client to send packet 0 with the first 1K, then wait for an acknowledgement from the server, as shown in Fig. 10-22(b). Then the client sends the second 1K, waits for another acknowledgement, and so on.

The alternative, often called a **blast protocol**, is for the client to simply send all the packets as fast as it can. With this method, the server acknowledges the entire message when *all* the packets have been received, not one by one. The blast protocol is illustrated in Fig. 10-22(c).

These protocols have quite different properties. With stop-and-wait, if a packet is damaged or lost, the client fails to receive an acknowledgement on time, so it retransmits the one bad packet. With the blast protocol, the server is faced with a

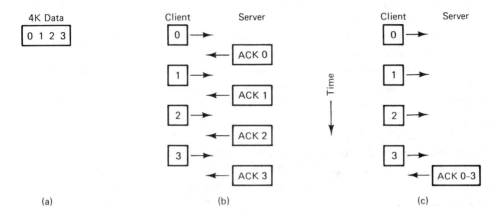

Fig. 10-22. (a) A 4K message. (b) A stop-and-wait protocol. (c) A blast protocol.

decision when, say, packet 1 is lost, but packet 2 subsequently arrives correctly. It can abandon everything and do nothing, waiting for the client to time out and retransmit the entire message. Or alternatively, it can buffer packet 2 (along with 0), hope that 3 comes in correctly, and then specifically ask the client to send it packet 1. This technique is called **selective repeat**.

Both stop-and-wait and abandoning everything when an error occurs are easy to implement. Selective repeat requires more administration, but uses less network bandwidth. On highly reliable LANs, lost packets are so rare that selective repeat is usually more trouble than it is worth, but on wide-area networks it is frequently a good idea.

However, error control aside, there is another consideration that is actually more important: **flow control**. Many network interface chips are able to send consecutive packets with almost no gap between them, but they are not always able to receive an unlimited number of back-to-back packets due to finite buffer capacity on chip. With some designs, a chip cannot even accept two back-to-back packets because after receiving the first one, the chip is temporarily disabled during the packet-arrived interrupt, so it misses the start of the second one. When a packet arrives and the receiver is unable to accept it, an **overrun error** occurs and the incoming packet is lost. In practice, overrun errors are a much more serious problem than packets lost due to noise or other forms of damage.

The two approaches of Fig. 10-22 are quite different with respect to overrun errors. With stop-and-wait, overrun errors are impossible, because the second packet is not sent until the receiver has explicitly indicated that it is ready for it. (Of course, with multiple senders, overrun errors are still possible.)

With the blast protocol, receiver overrun is a possibility, which is unfortunate, since the blast protocol is clearly much more efficient than stop-and-wait. However, there are also ways of dealing with overrun. If, on the one hand, the problem is caused by the chip being disabled temporarily while it is processing an interrupt, then a smart sender can insert a delay between packets to give the receiver just enough time to generate the packet-arrived interrupt and reset itself. If the required delay is

short, the sender can just loop (busy waiting); if it is long, it can set up a timer interrupt and go do something else while waiting. If it is in between (a few hundred
microseconds), which it often is, probably the best solution is busy waiting and just
accept the wasted time as a necessary evil.

If, on the other hand, the overrun is caused by the finite buffer capacity of the network chip, say n packets, then the sender can send n packets, followed by a substantial gap (or the protocol can be defined to require an acknowledgement after every n
packets).

It should be clear that minimizing acknowledgement packets and getting good
performance may be dependent on the timing properties of the network chip, so the
protocol may have to be tuned to the hardware being used. A custom-designed RPC
protocol can take issues like flow control into account more easily than a general-
purpose protocol, which is why specialized RPC protocols usually outperform systems based on IP or UDP by a wide margin.

Before leaving the subject of acknowledgements, there is one other sticky point
that is worth looking at. In Fig. 10-13(c) the protocol consists of a request, a reply,
and an acknowledgement. The last one is needed to tell the server that it can discard
the reply as it has arrived safely. Now suppose that the acknowledgement is lost in
transit (unlikely, but not impossible). The server will not discard the reply. Worse
yet, as far as the client is concerned, the protocol is finished. No timers are running
and no packets are expected.

We could change the protocol to have acknowledgements themselves acknowledged, but this adds extra complexity and overhead for very little potential gain.
In practice, the server can start a timer when sending the reply, and discard the reply
when either the acknowledgement arrives or the timer expires. Also, a new request
from the same client can be interpreted as a sign that the reply arrived, otherwise the
client would not be issuing the next request.

Critical Path

Since the RPC code is so crucial to the performance of the system, let us take a
closer look at what actually happens when a client performs an RPC with a remote
server. The sequence of instructions that is executed on every RPC is called the **critical path**, and is depicted in Fig. 10-23. It starts when the client calls the client stub,
proceeds through the trap to the kernel, the message transmission, the interrupt on the
server side, the server stub, and finally arrives at the server, which does the work and
sends the reply back along the reverse path.

Let us examine these steps a bit more carefully now. After the client stub has
been called, its first job is to acquire a buffer into which it can assemble the outgoing
message. In some systems, the client stub has a single fixed buffer that it fills in
from scratch on every call. In other systems, a pool of partially filled in buffers is
maintained, and an appropriate one for the server required is obtained. This method
is especially appropriate when the underlying packet format has a substantial number
of fields that must be filled in, but which do not change from call to call.

Next, the parameters are converted to the appropriate format and inserted into the

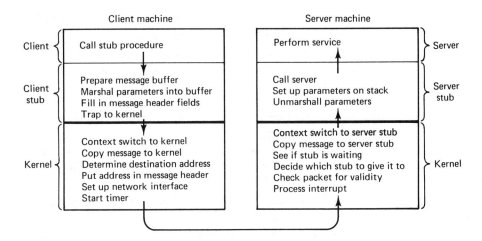

Fig. 10-23. Critical path from client to server.

message buffer, along with the rest of the header fields, if any. At this point the message is ready for transmission, so a trap to the kernel is issued.

When it gets control, the kernel switches context, saving the CPU registers and memory map, and setting up a new memory map that it will use while running in kernel mode. Since the kernel and user contexts are generally disjoint, the kernel must now explicitly copy the message into its address space so it can access it, fill in the destination address (and possibly other header fields), and have it copied to the network interface. At this point the client's critical path ends, as additional work done from here on does not add to the total RPC time: nothing the kernel does now affects how long it takes for the packet to arrive at the server. After starting the retransmission timer, the kernel can either enter a busy waiting loop to wait for the reply, or call the scheduler to look for another process to run. The former speeds up the processing of the reply, but effectively means that no multiprogramming can take place.

On the server side, the bits will come in and be put either in an on-board buffer or in memory by the receiving hardware. When all of them arrive, the receiver will generate an interrupt. The interrupt handler then examines the packet to see if it is valid, and determines which stub to give it to. If no stub is waiting for it, the handler must either buffer it or discard it. Assuming a stub is waiting, the message is copied to the stub. Finally, a context switch is done, restoring the registers and memory map to the values they had at the time the stub called *receive*.

The server can now be restarted. It unmarshals the parameters and sets up an environment in which the server call be called. When everything is ready, the call is made. After the server has run, the path back to the client is similar to the forward path, but the other way.

A question that all implementers are keenly interested in is: "Where is most of the time spent on the critical path?" Once that is known, work can begin on speeding it up. Schroeder and Burrows (1990) have provided us a glimpse by analyzing in detail the critical path of the RPC on the DEC Firefly multiprocessor workstation.

The results of their work are expressed in Fig. 10-24 as histograms with 14 bars, each bar corresponding to one of the steps from client to server (the reverse path is not shown, but is roughly analogous). Figure 10-24(a) gives results for a null RPC (no data), and Fig. 10-24(b) gives it for an array parameter with 1440 bytes. Although the fixed overhead is the same in both cases, considerably more time is needed for marshalling parameters and moving messages around in the second case.

For the null RPC, the dominant costs are the context switch to the server stub when a packet arrives, the interrupt service routine, and moving the packet to the network interface for transmission. For the 1440-byte RPC, the picture changes considerably, with the Ethernet transmission time now being the largest single component, with the time for moving the packet into and out of the interface coming in close behind.

Although Fig. 10-24 yields valuable insight into where the time is going, a few words of caution are necessary for interpreting these data. First, the Firefly is a multiprocessor, with five VAX CPUs. When the same measurements are run with only one CPU, the RPC time doubles, indicating that substantial parallel processing is taking place here, something that will not be true of most other machines.

Second, the Firefly uses UDP, and its operating system manages a pool of UDP buffers, which client stubs use to avoid having to fill in the entire UDP header every time.

Third, the kernel and user share the same address space, eliminating the need for context switches and for copying between kernel and user spaces, a great timesaver. Page table protection bits prevent the user from reading or writing parts of the kernel other than the shared buffers and certain other parts intended for user access. This design cleverly exploits particular features of the VAX architecture that facilitate sharing between kernel space and user space, but is not applicable to all computers.

Fourth and last, the entire RPC system has been carefully coded in assembly language and hand optimized. This last point is probably the reason that the various components in Fig. 10-24 are as uniform as they are. No doubt when the measurements were first made, they were more skewed, prompting the authors to attack the most time consuming parts until they no longer stuck out.

Schroeder and Burrows give some advice to future designers based on their experience. To start with, they recommend avoiding weird hardware (only one of the Firefly's five processors has access to the Ethernet, so packets have to be copied there before being sent, and getting them there is unpleasant). They also regret having based their system on UDP. The overhead, especially from the checksum, was not worth the cost. In retrospect, they believe a simple custom RPC protocol would have been better. Finally, using busy waiting instead of having the server stub go to sleep would have largely eliminated the single largest time sink in Fig. 10-24(a).

Copying

An issue that frequently dominates RPC execution times is copying. On the Firefly this effect does not show up because the buffers are mapped into both the kernel and user address spaces, but in most other systems the kernel and user address

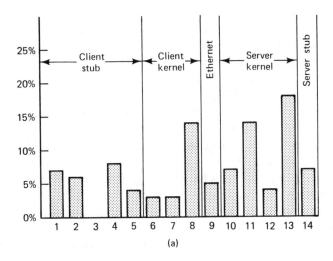

(a)

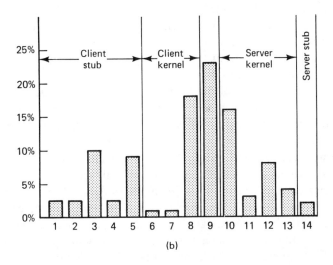

(b)

1. Call stub
2. Get message buffer
3. Marshal parameters
4. Fill in headers
5. Compute UDP checksum
6. Trap to kernel
7. Queue packet for transmission

8. Move packet to controller over the QBus
9. Ethernet transmission time
10. Get packet from controller
11. Interrupt service routine
12. Compute UDP checksum
13. Context switch to user space
14. Server stub code

(c)

Fig. 10-24. Breakdown of the RPC critical path. (a) For a null RPC. (b) For an RPC with a 1440-byte array parameter. (c) The 14 steps in the RPC from client to server.

spaces are disjoint. The number of times a message must be copied varies from one to about eight, depending on the hardware, software, and type of call. In the best case, the network chip can DMA the message directly out of the client stub's address space onto the network (copy 1), depositing it in the server kernel's memory in real time (i.e., the packet-arrived interrupt occurs within a few microseconds of the last bit being DMA'ed out of the client stub's memory). Then the kernel inspects the packet and maps the page containing it into the server's address space. If this type of mapping is not possible, the kernel copies the packet to the server stub (copy 2).

In the worst case, the kernel copies the message from the client stub into a kernel buffer for subsequent transmission, either because it is not convenient to transmit directly from user space or the network is currently busy (copy 1). Later, the kernel copies the message, in software, to a hardware buffer on the network interface board (copy 2). At this point, the hardware is started, causing the packet to be moved over the network to the interface board on the destination machine (copy 3). When the packet-arrived interrupt occurs on the server's machine, the kernel copies it to a kernel buffer, probably because it cannot tell where to put it until it has examined it, which is not possible until it has extracted it from the hardware buffer (copy 4). Finally, the message has to be copied to the server stub (copy 5). In addition, if the call has a large array passed as a value parameter, the array has to be copied onto the client's stack for the call stub, from the stack to the message buffer during marshaling within the client stub, and from the incoming message in the server stub to the server's stack preceding the call to the server, for three more copies or eight in all.

Suppose it takes an average of 500 nsec to copy a 32-bit word, then with eight copies, each word needs 4 microsec, giving a maximum data rate of about 1 Mbyte/sec, no matter how fast the network itself is. In practice, achieving even 1/10 of this would be pretty good.

One hardware feature that greatly helps eliminate unnecessary copying is **scatter-gather**. A network chip that can do scatter-gather can be set up to assemble a packet by concatenating two or more memory buffers. The advantage of this method is that the kernel can build the packet header in kernel space, leaving the user data in the client stub, with the hardware pulling them together as the packet goes out the door. Being able to gather up a packet from multiple sources eliminates copying. Similarly, being able to scatter the header and body of an incoming packet into different buffers also helps on the receiving end.

In general, eliminating copying is easier on the sending side than on the receiving side. With cooperative hardware, a reusable packet header inside the kernel and a data buffer in user space can be put out onto the network with no internal copying on the sending side. When it comes in at the receiver however, even a very intelligent network chip will not know which server it should be given to, so the best the hardware can do is dump it into a kernel buffer and let the kernel figure out what to do with it.

In operating systems using virtual memory, a trick is available to avoid the copy to the stub. If the kernel packet buffer happens to occupy an entire page, beginning on a page boundary, and the server stub's receive buffer also happens to be an entire page, also starting on a page boundary, the kernel can change the memory map to map the packet buffer into the server's address space, simultaneously giving the server stub's buffer to the kernel. When the server stub starts running, its buffer will contain the packet, and this will have been achieved without copying.

Whether going to all this trouble is a good idea is a close call. Again assuming that it takes 500 nsec to copy a 32-bit word, copying a 1K packet takes 128 microsec. If the memory map can be updated in less time, then mapping is faster than copying, otherwise it is not. This method also requires careful buffer control, making sure that all buffers are aligned properly with respect to page boundaries. If a buffer starts at a page boundary, the user process gets to see the entire packet, including the low-level headers, something that most systems try to hide in the name of portability.

Alternatively, if the buffers are aligned so that the header is at the end of one page and the data are at the start of the next one, the data can be mapped without the header. This approach is cleaner and more portable, but costs two pages per buffer: one mostly empty except for a few bytes of header at the end, and one for the data.

Finally, many packets are only a few hundred bytes, in which case it is doubtful that mapping will beat copying. Still, it is an interesting idea that is certainly worth thinking about.

Timer Management

All protocols consist of exchanging messages over some communication medium. In virtually all systems, messages can occasionally be lost, either due to noise or receiver overrun. Consequently, most protocols set a timer whenever a message is sent and an answer (reply or acknowledgement) is expected. If the reply is not forthcoming within the expected time, the timer expires and the original message is retransmitted. This process is repeated until the sender gets bored and gives up.

The amount of machine time that goes into managing the timers should not be underestimated. Setting a timer requires building a data structure specifying when the timer is to expire and what is to be done when that happens. The data structure is then inserted into a list consisting of the other pending timers. Usually the list is kept sorted on time, with the next timeout at the head of the list and the most distant one at the end, as shown in Fig. 10-25.

When an acknowledgement or reply arrives before the timer expires, the timeout entry must be located and removed from the list. In practice, very few timers actually expire, so most of the work of entering and removing a timer from the list is wasted effort. Furthermore, timers need not be especially accurate. The timeout value chosen is usually a wild guess in the first place ("a few seconds sounds about right"). Besides, using a poor value does not affect the correctness of the protocol, only the performance. Too low a value will cause timers to expire too often, resulting in unnecessary retransmissions. Too high a value will cause a needlessly long delay in the event that a packet is actually lost.

The combination of these factors suggests that a different way of handling the timers might be more efficient. Most systems maintain a process table, with one entry containing all the information about each process in the system. While an RPC is being carried out, the kernel has a pointer to the current process table entry in a

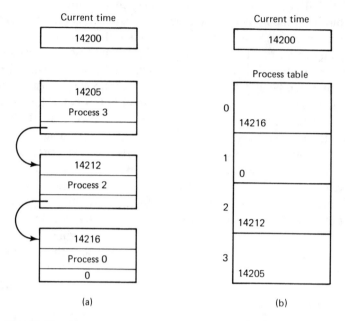

Fig. 10-25. (a) Timeouts in a sorted list. (b) Timeouts in the process table.

local variable. Instead of storing timeouts in a sorted linked list, each process table entry has a field for holding its timeout, if any, as shown in Fig. 10-25(b). Setting a timer for an RPC now consists of adding the length of the timeout to the current time and storing in the process table. Turning a timer off consists of merely storing a zero in the timer field. Thus the actions of setting and clearing timers are now reduced to a few machine instructions each.

To make this method work, periodically (say, once per second), the kernel scans the entire process table, checking each timer value against the current time. Any nonzero value that is less than or equal to the current time corresponds to an expired timer, which is then processed and reset. For a system that sends, for example, 100 packets/sec, the work of scanning the process table once per second is only a fraction of the work of searching and updating a linked list 200 times a second. Algorithms that operate by making a sequential pass through a table periodically like this are called **sweep algorithms**.

10.3.6. Problem Areas

Remote procedure call using the client-server model is widely used as the basis for distributed operating systems. It is a simple abstraction that makes dealing with the complexity inherent in a distributed system more manageable than pure message passing. Nevertheless, there are a few problem areas that still have to be resolved. In this section we will discuss some of them.

Ideally, RPC should be transparent. That is, the programmer should not have to know which library procedures are local and which are remote. He should also be able to write procedures without regard to whether they will be executed locally or remote. Even stricter, the introduction of RPC into a system that was previously run on a single CPU should not be accompanied by a set of new rules prohibiting constructions that were previously legal, or requiring constructions that were previously optional. Under this stringent criterion, few, if any, current distributed systems can be said to be transparent. Thus the holy grail of transparency remains a research topic for the foreseeable future.

As an example, consider the problem of global variables. In single CPU systems these are legal, even for library procedures. For example, in UNIX, there is a global variable *errno*. After an incorrect system call, *errno* contains a code telling what went wrong. The existence of *errno* is public information, since the official UNIX standard, POSIX, requires it to be visible in one of the mandatory header files, *errno.h*. Thus it is not permitted for an implementation to hide it from the programmers.

Now suppose a programmer writes two procedures that both directly access *errno*. One of these is run locally; the other is run remote. Since the compiler does not (and may not) know which variables and procedures are located where, no matter where *errno* is stored, one of the procedures will fail to access it correctly. The problem is that allowing local procedures unconstrained access to remote global variables, and vice versa, cannot be implemented, yet prohibiting this access violates the transparency principle (that programs should not have to act differently due to RPC).

A second problem is weakly-typed languages, like C. In a strongly-typed language, like Pascal, the compiler, and thus the stub procedure, knows everything there is to know about all the parameters. This knowledge allows the stub to marshal the parameters without difficulty. In C, however, it is perfectly legal to write a procedure that computes the inner product of two vectors (arrays), without specifying how large either one is. Each one could be terminated by a special value known only to the calling and called procedure. Under these circumstances, it is essentially impossible for the client stub to marshal the parameters: it has no way of determining how large they are.

The usual solution is to force the programmer to define the maximum size when writing the formal definition of the server, but suppose the programmer wants the procedure to work with any size input? He can put an arbitrary limit in the specification, say, 1 million, but that means the client stub will have to pass 1 million elements even when the actually array size is 100 elements. Furthermore, the call will fail when the actual array is 1,000,001 elements or the total memory can only hold 200,000 elements.

A similar problem occurs when passing a pointer to a complex graph as a parameter. On a single CPU system, doing so works fine, but with RPC, the client stub has no way to find the entire graph.

Still another problem occurs because it is not always possible to deduce the types of the parameters, not even from a formal specification or the code itself. An example is *printf*, which may have any number of parameters (at least one), and they can be an arbitrary mixture of integers, shorts, longs, characters, strings, floating point numbers of various lengths, and other types. Trying to call *printf* as a remote procedure would be practically impossible because C is so permissive. However, a rule saying that RPC can be used provided that you do not program in C would violate transparency.

The above problems deal with transparency, but there is another class of difficulties that is even more fundamental. Consider the implementation of the UNIX command

```
sort <f1 >f2
```

Since *sort* knows it is reading standard input and writing standard output, it can act as a client for both input and output, performing RPCs with the file server to read *f1* as well as performing RPCs with the file server to write *f2*. Similarly, in the command

```
grep rat <f3 >f4
```

the *grep* program acts as a client to read the file *f3*, extracting only those lines containing the string "rat" and writing them to *f4*.

Now consider the UNIX pipeline

```
grep rat < f5 | sort >f6
```

As we have just seen, both *grep* and *sort* act as a client for both standard input and standard output. This behavior has to be compiled into the code to make the first two examples work. But how do they interact? Does *grep* act as a client doing writes to the server *sort*, or does *sort* act as the client doing reads from the server *grep*? Either way, one of them has to act as a server (i.e., passive), but as we have just seen, both have been programmed as clients (active). The difficulty here is that the client-server model really is not suitable at all.

In general, there is a problem with all pipelines of the form

```
p1 <f1 | p2 | p3 > f2
```

One approach to avoiding the client-client interface we just saw is to make the entire pipeline **read driven**, as illustrated in Fig. 10-26(b). The program *p1* acts as the (active) client and issues a read request to the file server to get *f1*. The program *p2*, also acting as a client, issues a read request to *p1* and the program *p3* issues a read request to *p2*. So far, so good. The trouble is the file server does not act as a client issuing read requests to *p3* to collect the final output. Thus a read-driven pipeline does not work.

In Fig. 10-26(c) we see the write-driven approach. It has the mirror-image problem. Here *p1* acts as a client, doing writes to *p2*, which also acts as a client, doing writes to *p3*, which also acts as a client, writing to the file server. Only there is no client issuing calls to *p1* asking it to accept the input file.

While ad hoc solutions can be found, it should be clear that the client-server model inherent in RPC is not a good fit to this kind of communication pattern. As an aside, one possible ad hoc solution is to implement pipes as dual servers, responding to both write requests from the left and read requests from the right. Alternatively, pipes can be implemented with temporary files that are always read from, or written to, the file server. Doing so generates unnecessary overhead, however.

(a)   p1 < f1 | p2 | p3 > f2

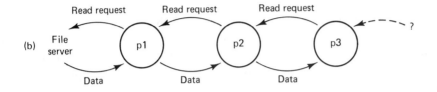

(b)

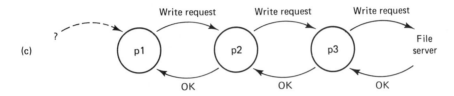

(c)

Fig. 10-26. (a) A pipeline. (b) The read-driven approach. (c) The write-driven approach.

A similar problem occurs when the shell wants to get input from the user. Normally, it sends read requests to the terminal server, which simply collects keystrokes and waits until the shell asks for them. But what happens when the user hits the interrupt key (DEL, CTRL-C, break, etc.)? If the terminal server just passively puts the interrupt character in the buffer waiting until the shell asks for it, it will be impossible for the user to break off the current program. On the other hand, how can the terminal server act as a client and make an RPC to the shell, which is not expecting to act as a server? Clearly this role reversal causes trouble, just as the role ambiguity does in the pipeline. In fact, any time an unexpected message has to be sent there is a potential problem. While the client-server model is frequently a good fit, it is not perfect.

10.4. GROUP COMMUNICATION

An underlying assumption intrinsic to RPC is that communication involves only *two* parties, the client and the server. Sometimes there are circumstances in which communication involves multiple processes, not just two. For example, consider a group of file servers cooperating together to offer a single, fault-tolerant file service. In such a system, it might be desirable for a client to send a message to all the servers, to make sure that the request could be carried out even if one of them crashed. RPC cannot handle communication from one sender to many receivers, other than by performing separate RPCs with each one. In this section we will discuss alternative communication mechanisms in which a message can be sent to multiple receivers in one operation.

10.4.1. Introduction to Group Communication

A group is a collection of processes that act together in some system or user-specified way. The key property that all groups have is that when a message is sent to the group itself, all members of the group receive it. It is a form of **one-to-many** communication (one sender, many receivers), and is contrasted with **point-to-point** communication in Fig. 10-27.

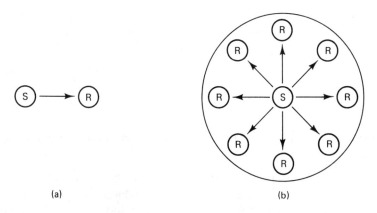

(a)   (b)

Fig. 10-27. (a) Point-to-point communication is from one sender to one receiver. (b) One-to-many communication is from one sender to multiple receivers.

Groups are dynamic. New groups can be created and old groups can be destroyed. A process can join a group or leave one. A process can be a member of several groups at the same time. Consequently, mechanisms are needed for managing groups and group membership.

Groups are roughly analogous to social organizations. A person might be a member of a book club, a tennis club, and an environmental organization. On a particular day, he might receive mailings (messages) announcing a new birthday cake cookbook, the annual Mother's Day tennis tournament, and the start of a campaign to save the Southern ground hog. At any moment, he is free to leave any or all of these groups, and possibly join other groups.

Although in this book we will study only operating system (i.e., process) groups, it is worth mentioning that other groups are also commonly encountered in computer systems. For example, on the USENET computer network, there are hundreds of news groups, each about a specific subject. When a person sends a message to a particular news group, all members of the group receive it, even if there are tens of thousands of them. These higher-level groups usually have looser rules about who is a member, what the exact semantics of message delivery are, and so on, than do operating system groups. In most cases, this looseness is not a problem.

The purpose of introducing groups is to allow processes to deal with collections of processes as a single abstraction. Thus a process can send a message to a group of servers without having to know how many there are or where they are, which may change from one call to the next.

How group communication is implemented depends to a large extent on the hardware. On some networks, it is possible to create a special network address (for example, indicated by setting one of the high-order bits to 1), to which multiple machines can listen. When a packet is sent to one of these addresses, it is automatically delivered to all machines listening to the address. This technique is called **multicasting**. Implementing groups using multicast is straightforward: just assign each group a different multicast address.

Networks that do not have multicasting sometimes still have **broadcasting**, which means that packets containing a certain address (e.g., 0) are delivered to all machines. Broadcasting can also be used to implement groups, but it is less efficient. Each machine receives each broadcast, so its software must check to see if the packet is intended for it. If not, the packet is discarded, but some time is wasted processing the interrupt. Nevertheless, it still takes only one packet to reach all the members of a group.

Finally, if neither multicasting nor broadcasting is available, group communication can still be implemented by having the sender transmit separate packets to each of the members of the group. For a group with n members, n packets are required, instead of one packet when either multicasting or broadcasting is used. Although less efficient, this implementation is still workable, especially if most groups are small. The sending of a message from a single sender to a single receiver is sometimes called **unicasting**, to distinguish it from multicasting and broadcasting.

10.4.2. Design Issues

Group communication has many of the same design possibilities as regular message passing, such as buffered versus unbuffered, blocking versus nonblocking, and so forth. However, there are also a large number of additional choices that must be made because sending to a group is inherently different from sending to a single process. Furthermore, groups can be organized in various ways internally. They can also be addressed in novel ways not relevant in point-to-point communication. In this section we will look at some of the most important design issues and point out the various alternatives.

Closed Groups versus Open Groups

Systems that support group communication can be divided into two categories depending on who can send to whom. Some systems support **closed groups**, in which only the members of the group can send to the group. Outsiders cannot send messages to the group as a whole, although they may be able to send messages to individual members. In contrast, other systems support **open groups**, which do not have this property. When open groups are used, any process in the system can send to any group. The difference between closed and open groups is shown in Fig. 10-28.

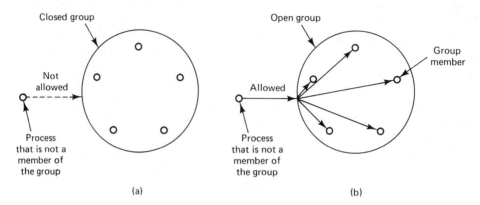

Fig. 10-28. (a) Outsiders may not send to a closed group. (b) Outsiders may send to an open group.

The decision as to whether a system supports closed or open groups usually relates to the reason groups are being supported in the first place. Closed groups are typically used for parallel processing. For example, a collection of processes working together to play a game of chess might form a closed group. They have their own goal, and do not interact with the outside world.

On the other hand, when the idea of groups is to support replicated servers, then it is important that processes that are not members (clients) can send to the group. In addition, the members of the group may also need to use group communication, for example to decide who should carry out a particular request. The distinction between closed and open groups is often made for implementation reasons.

Peer Groups versus Hierarchical Groups

The distinction between closed and open groups relates to who can communicate with the group. Another important distinction has to do with the internal structure of the group. In some groups, all the processes are equal. No one is boss and all decisions are made collectively. In other groups, some kind of hierarchy exists. For example, one process is the coordinator and all the others are workers. In this model, when a request for work is generated, either by an external client or by one of the workers, it is sent to the coordinator. The coordinator then decides which worker is best suited to carry it out, and forwards it there. More complex hierarchies are also possible, of course. These communication patterns are illustrated in Fig. 10-29.

Each of these organizations has its own advantages and disadvantages. The peer group is symmetric and has no single point of failure. If one of the processes crashes, the group simply becomes smaller, but can otherwise continue. A disadvantage is that decision making is more complicated. To decide anything, a vote has to be taken, incurring some delay and overhead.

The hierarchical group has the opposite properties. Loss of the coordinator brings

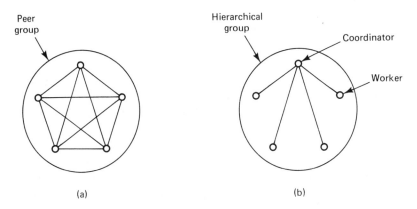

Fig. 10-29. (a) Communication in a peer group. (b) Communication in a simple hierarchical group.

the entire group to a grinding halt, but as long as it is running, it can make decisions without bothering everyone else. For example, a hierarchical group might be appropriate for a parallel chess program. The coordinator takes the current board, generates all the legal moves from it, and farms them out to the workers for evaluation. During this evaluation, new boards are generated and sent back to the coordinator to have them evaluated. When a worker is idle, it asks the coordinator for a new board to work on. In this manner, the coordinator controls the search strategy and prunes the game tree (e.g., using the alpha-beta search method), but leaves the actual evaluation to the workers.

Group Membership

When group communication is present, some method is needed for creating and deleting groups, as well as for allowing processes to join and leave groups. One possible approach is to have a **group server** to which all these requests can be sent. The group server can then maintain a complete data base of all the groups and their exact membership. This method is straightforward, efficient, and easy to implement. Unfortunately, it shares with all centralized techniques a major disadvantage: a single point of failure. If the group server crashes, group management ceases to exist. Probably most or all groups will have to be reconstructed from scratch, possibly terminating whatever work was going on.

The opposite approach is to manage group membership in a distributed way. In an open group, an outsider can send a message to all group members announcing its presence. In a closed group, something similar is needed (in effect, even closed groups have to be open with respect to joining). To leave a group, a member just sends a goodbye message to everyone.

So far, all of this is straightforward. However, there are two issues associated with group membership that are a bit trickier. First, if a member crashes, it effectively leaves the group. The trouble is, there is no polite announcement of this fact as there is when a process leaves voluntarily. The other members have to discover this experimentally by noticing that the crashed member no longer responds to anything. Once it is certain that the crashed member is really down, it can be removed from the group.

The other knotty issue is that leaving and joining have to be synchronous with messages being sent. In other words, starting at the instant that a process has joined a group, it must receive all messages sent to that group. Similarly, as soon as a process has left a group, it must not receive any more messages from the group, and the other members must not receive any more messages from it. One way of making sure that a join or leave is integrated into the message stream at the right place is to convert this operation into a message sent to the whole group.

One final issue relating to group membership is what to do if so many machines go down that the group can no longer function at all. Some protocol is needed to rebuild the group. Invariably, some process will have to take the initiative to start the ball rolling, but what happens if two or three try at the same time? The protocol will have to be able to withstand this.

Group Addressing

In order to send a message to a group, a process must have some way of specifying which group it means. In other words, groups need to be addressed, just as processes do. One way is to give each group a unique address, much like a process address. If the network supports multicast, the group address can be associated with a multicast address, so that every message sent to the group address can be multicast. In this way, the message will be sent to all those machines that need it, and no others.

If the hardware does not support multicast but does support broadcast, the message can be broadcast. Every kernel will then get it and extract from it the group address. If none of the processes on the machine is a member of the group, the broadcast is simply discarded. Otherwise, it is passed to all group members.

Finally, if neither multicast nor broadcast is supported, the kernel on the sending machine will have to have a list of machines that have processes belonging to the group. The kernel then sends each one a point-to-point message. These three implementation methods are shown in Fig. 10-30. The important thing to notice is that in all three cases, a process just sends a message to a group address and it is delivered to all the members. How that happens is up to the operating system. The sender is not aware of the size of the group or whether communication is implemented by multicasting, broadcasting, or unicasting.

A second method of group addressing is to require the sender to provide an explicit list of all destinations (e.g., IP addresses). When this method is used, the parameter in the call to *send* that specifies the destination is a pointer to a list of addresses. This method has the serious drawback that it forces user processes (i.e., the group members) to be aware of precisely who is a member of which group. In other words, it is not transparent. Furthermore, whenever group membership changes, the user processes must update their membership lists. In Fig. 10-30, this administration can easily be done by the kernels to hide it from the user processes.

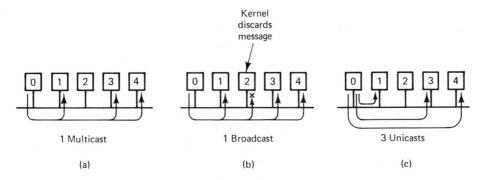

Fig. 10-30. Process 0 sending to a group consisting of processes 1, 3, and 4. (a) Multicast implementation. (b) Broadcast implementation. (c) Unicast implementation.

Group communication also allows a third, and quite novel method of addressing as well, which we will call **predicate addressing**. With this system, each message is sent to all members of the group (or possibly the entire system) using one of the methods described above, but with a new twist. Each message contains a predicate (Boolean expression) to be evaluated. The predicate can involve the receiver's machine number, its local variables, or other factors. If the predicate evaluates to TRUE, the message is accepted. If it evaluates to FALSE, the message is discarded. Using this scheme it is possible, for example, to send a message to only those machines that have at least 4M of free memory and which are willing to take on a new process.

Send and Receive Primitives

Ideally, point-to-point and group communication should be merged into a single set of primitives. However, if RPC is the usual user communication mechanism, rather than raw *send* and *receive*, then it is hard to merge RPC and group communication. Sending a message to a group cannot be modeled as a procedure call. The primary difficulty is that with RPC, the client sends one message to the server and gets back one answer. With group communication there are potentially n different replies. How can a procedure call deal with n replies? Consequently, a common approach is to abandon the (two-way) request/reply model underlying RPC, and go back to explicit calls for sending and receiving (one-way model).

The library procedures that processes call to invoke group communication may be the same as for point-to-point communication or they may be different. If the system is based on RPC, user processes never call *send* and *receive* directly anyway, so there is less incentive to merge the point-to-point and group primitives. If user programs directly call *send* and *receive* themselves, there is something to be said for doing group communication with these existing primitives instead of inventing a new set.

Suppose, for the moment, that we wish to merge the two forms of communication. To send a message, one of the parameters of *send* indicates the destination. If it is a process address, a single message is sent to that one process. If it is a group address (or a pointer to a list of destinations), a message is sent to all members of the group. A second parameter to *send* points to the message to be sent.

The call can be buffered or unbuffered, blocking or nonblocking, reliable or not reliable, for both the point-to-point and group cases. Generally these choices are made by the system designers and are fixed, rather than being selectable on a per message basis. Introducing group communication does not change this.

Similarly, *receive* indicates a willingness to accept a message, and possibly blocks until one is available. If the two forms of communication are merged, then *receive* completes when either a point-to-point message or a group message arrives. However, since these two forms of communication are frequently used for different purposes, some systems introduce new library procedures, say, *group_send* and *group_receive*, so a process can indicate whether it wants a point-to-point or a group message.

In the design just described, communication is one-way. Replies are independent messages in their own right, and are not associated with previous requests. Sometimes this association is desirable, to try to achieve more of the RPC flavor. In this case, after sending a message, a process is required to call *getreply* repeatedly to collect all the replies, one at a time.

Atomicity

A characteristic of group communication that we have alluded to several times is the all-or-nothing property. Most group communication systems are designed so that when a message is sent to a group, it will either arrive correctly at all members of the group, or at none of them. Situations in which some members receive a message and others do not are not permitted. The property of all-or-nothing delivery is called **atomicity** or **atomic broadcast**.

Atomicity is desirable because it makes programming distributed systems much easier. When any process sends a message to the group, it does not have to worry about what to do if some of them do not get it. For example, in a replicated distributed data base system, suppose a process sends a message to all the data base machines to create a new record in the data base, and then later sends a second message to update it. If some of the members miss the message creating the record, they will not be able to perform the update, and the data base will become inconsistent. Life is just a lot simpler if the system guarantees that every message is delivered to all the members of the group, or if that is not possible, that it is not delivered to any, and that failure is reported back to the sender so it can take appropriate action to recover.

Implementing atomic broadcast is not quite as simple as it looks. The method of Fig. 10-30 fails because receiver overrun is possible at one or more machines. The only way to be sure that every destination receives every message is to require them to send back an acknowledgement upon message receipt. As long as machines never crash, this method will do.

However, many distributed systems aim at fault tolerance, so for them it is essential that atomicity also holds even in the presence of machine failures. In this light, all the methods of Fig. 10-30 are inadequate because some of the initial messages might not arrive due to receiver overrun, followed by the sender's crashing. Under these circumstances, some members of the group will have received the message and others will not have, precisely the situation that is unacceptable. Worse yet, the group members that have not received the message do not even know they are missing anything, so they cannot ask for a retransmission. Finally, with the sender now down, even if they did know, there is no one to provide the message.

Nevertheless, there is hope. Here is a simple algorithm that demonstrates that atomic broadcast is at least possible (Joseph and Birman, 1989). The sender starts out by sending a message to all members of the group. Timers are set and retransmissions sent where necessary. When a process receives a message, if it has not yet seen this particular message, it, too, sends the message to all members of the group (again with timers and retransmissions if necessary). If it has already seen the message, this step is not necessary and the message is discarded. No matter how many machines crash or how many packets are lost, eventually all the surviving processes will get the message. Later we will describe more efficient algorithms for insuring atomicity.

Message Ordering

To make group communication easy to understand and use, two properties are required. The first one is atomic broadcast, as discussed above. It insures that a message sent to the group arrives at either all members or at none of them. The second property concerns message ordering. To see what the issue is here, consider Fig. 10-31, in which we have 5 machines, each with one process. Processes 0, 1, 3, and 4 belong to the same group. Processes 0 and 4 simultaneously want to send a message to the group. Assume multicasting and broadcasting are not available, so each process has to send three separate (unicast) messages. Process 0 sends to 1, 3, and 4; process 4 sends to 0, 1, and 3. These six messages are shown interleaved in time in Fig. 10-31(a).

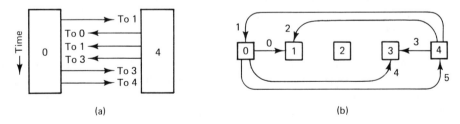

(a)   (b)

Fig. 10-31. (a) The three messages sent by processes 0 and 4 are interleaved in time. (b) Graphical representation of the six messages, showing the arrival order.

The trouble is that when two processes are contending for access to a LAN, the order in which the messages are sent is nondeterministic. In Fig. 10-31(a) we see that (by accident), process 0 has won the first round and sends to process 1. Then process 4 wins three rounds in a row and sends to processes 0, 1, and 3. Finally, process 0 gets to send to 3 and 4. The order of these six messages is shown in different ways in the two parts of Fig. 10-31.

Now consider the situation as viewed by processes 1 and 3 as shown in Fig. 10-31(b). Process 1 first receives a message from 0, then immediately afterwards it receives one from 4. Process 3 does not receive anything initially, then it receives messages from 4 and 0, in that order. Thus the two messages arrive in a different order. If processes 0 and 4 are both trying to update the same record in a data base, 1 and 3 end up with different final values. Needless to say, this situation is just as bad as one in which a (true hardware multicast) message sent to the group arrives at some members and not at others (atomicity failure). Thus to make programming reasonable, a system has to have well-defined semantics with respect to the order in which messages are delivered.

The best guarantee is to have all messages delivered instantaneously and in the order they were sent. If process 0 sends message A and then slightly later, process 4 sends message B, the system should first deliver A to all members of the group, and then deliver B to all members of the group. That way, all recipients get all messages in exactly the same order. This delivery pattern is something that programmers can understand and base their software on. We will call this **global time ordering**, since it delivers all messages in the exact order they were sent (conveniently ignoring the fact that according to Einstein's special theory of relativity there is no such thing as absolute global time).

Absolute time ordering is not always easy to implement, so some systems offer various watered-down variations. One of these is **consistent time ordering**, in which if two messages, say A and B are sent close together in time, the system picks one of them as being "first" and delivers it to all group members, followed by the other. It may happen that the one chosen as first was not really first, but since no one knows this, the argument goes, system behavior should not depend on it. In effect, messages are guaranteed to arrive at all group members in the same order, but that order may not be the real order in which they were sent.

Even weaker time orderings have been used. We will study one of these, based on the idea of causality, when we come to ISIS later in this chapter.

Overlapping Groups

As we mentioned earlier, a process can be a member of multiple groups at the same time. This fact can lead to a new kind of inconsistency. To see the problem, look at Fig. 10-32, which shows two groups, 1 and 2. Processes A, B, and C are members of group 1. Processes B, C, and D are members of group 2.

Now suppose that processes A and D each simultaneously decide to send a message to their respective groups, and that the system uses global time ordering within each group. As in our previous example, unicasting is used. The message order is shown in Fig. 10-32 by the numbers 1 through 4. Again we have the situation where two processes, in this case B and C, receive messages in a different order. B first gets a message from A followed by a message from D. C gets them in the opposite order.

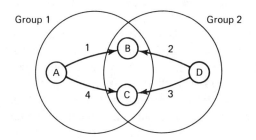

Fig. 10-32. Four processes, *A*, *B*, *C*, and *D*, and four messages. Processes *B* and *C* get the messages from *A* and *D* in a different order.

The culprit here is that although there is a global time ordering within each group, there is not necessarily any coordination among multiple groups. Some systems support well-defined time ordering among overlapping groups and others do not. (If the groups are disjoint, the issue does not arise.) Implementing time ordering among different groups is frequently difficult to do, so the question arises as to whether it is worth it.

Scalability

Our final design issue is scalability. Many algorithms work fine as long as all the groups only have a few members, but what happens when there are tens, hundreds, or even thousands of members per group? Or thousands of groups? Also, what happens when the system is so large that it no longer fits on a single LAN, so multiple LANs and gateways are required? And what happens when the groups are spread over several continents?

The presence of gateways can affect many properties of the implementation. To start with, multicasting becomes more complicated. Consider, for example, the internetwork shown in Fig. 10-33. It consists of four LANs and four gateways, to provide protection against the failure of any gateway.

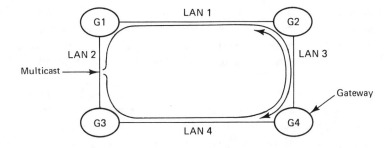

Fig. 10-33. Multicasting in an internetwork causes trouble.

Imagine that one of the machines on LAN 2 issues a multicast. When the multicast packet arrives at gateways *G1* and *G3*, what should they do? If they discard it, most of the machines will never see it, destroying its value as a multicast. If, however, the algorithm is just to have gateways forward all multicasts, then the packet will be copied to LAN 1 and LAN 4, and shortly thereafter to LAN 3 twice. Worse yet, gateway *G2* will see *G4*'s multicast, and copy it to LAN 2, and vice versa. Clearly a more sophisticated algorithm involving keeping track of previous packets is required to avoid exponential growth in the number of packets multicast.

Another problem with an internetwork is that some methods of group communication take advantage of the fact that only one packet can be on a LAN at any instant. In effect, the order of packet transmission defines an absolute global time order, which as we have seen, is frequently crucial. With gateways and multiple networks, it is possible for two packets to be "on the wire" simultaneously, thus destroying this useful property.

Finally, some algorithms may not scale well due to their computational complexity, their use of centralized components, or other factors.

10.4.3. Group Communication in ISIS

As an example of group communication, let us look at the ISIS system developed at Cornell (Birman and Joseph, 1987a; Birman and Joseph, 1987b; Birman and Joseph, 1989; Joseph and Birman, 1989). ISIS is a toolkit for building distributed applications, for example, coordinating stock trading among all the brokers at a Wall Street securities firm. ISIS is not a complete operating system, but rather a set of programs that can run on top of UNIX or other existing operating systems. It is interesting to study because it has been widely described in the literature and has been used for numerous real applications. In Chap. 14 we will study group communication in Amoeba, which takes a quite different approach.

The key idea in ISIS is **synchrony** and the key communication primitives are different forms of atomic broadcast. Before looking at how ISIS does atomic broadcast, it is necessary to first examine the various forms of synchrony it distinguishes. A **synchronous system** is one in which events happen strictly sequentially, with each event (e.g., a broadcast) taking essentially zero time to complete. For example, if process *A* sends a message to processes *B*, *C*, and *D*, as shown in Fig. 10-34(a), the message arrives instantaneously at all the destinations. Similarly, a subsequent message from *D* to the others also takes zero time to be delivered everywhere. As viewed by an outside observer, the system consists of discrete events, none of which ever overlap the other ones. This property makes it easy to understand system behavior.

Synchronous systems are impossible to build, so we need to investigate other types of systems, with weaker requirements on time. A **loosely synchronous system** is one like that of Fig. 10-34(b), in which events take a finite amount of time, but all events appear in the same order to all parties. In particular, all processes receive all messages in the same order. Earlier, we discussed essentially the same idea under the name consistent time ordering.

Such systems are possible to build, but for some applications even weaker semantics are acceptable, and the hope is to be able to capitalize on these weak semantics to

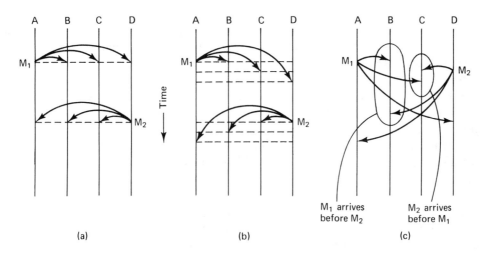

Fig. 10-34. (a) A synchronous system. (b) A loose synchrony. (c) Virtual synchrony.

gain performance. Fig. 10-34(c) shows a **virtually synchronous system**, one in which the ordering constraint has been relaxed, but in such a way that under carefully selected circumstances, it does not matter.

Let us look at these circumstances. In a distributed system, two events are said to be **causally related** if the nature or behavior of the second one might have been influenced in any way by the first one. Thus if A sends a message to B, which inspects it, and then sends a new message to C, the second message is causally related to the first one, since its contents might have been derived in part from the first one. Whether this actually happened is irrelevant. The relation holds if there *might* have been an influence.

Two events that are unrelated are said to be **concurrent**. If A sends a message to B, and about the same time, C sends a message to D, these events are concurrent because neither one can influence the other. What virtual synchrony really means is that if two messages are causally related, all processes *must* receive them in the same (correct) order. If, however, they are concurrent, no guarantees are made, and the system is free to deliver them in a different order to different processes if this is easier. Thus when it matters, messages are always delivered in the same order, but when it does not matter, they may or may not be.

Communication Primitives in ISIS

Now we come to the broadcast primitives used in ISIS. Three of them have been defined: ABCAST, CBCAST, and GBCAST, all with different semantics. ABCAST provides loosely synchronous communication and is used for transmitting data to the members of a group. CBCAST provides virtually synchronous communication and is also used for sending data. GBCAST is somewhat like ABCAST, except that it is used for managing group membership rather than for sending ordinary data.

Originally, ABCAST used a form of two-phase commit protocol that worked like this. The sender, A, assigned a timestamp (actually just a sequence number) to the message and sent it to all the group members (by explicitly naming them all). Each one picked its own timestamp, larger than any other timestamp number it had sent or received, and sent it back to A. When all of these arrived, A chose the largest one, and sent a *Commit* message to all the members again containing it. Committed messages were delivered to the application programs in order of the timestamps. It can be shown that this protocol guarantees that all messages will be delivered to all processes in the same order.

It can also be shown that this protocol is complex and expensive. For this reason, the ISIS designers invented the CBCAST primitive that only guarantees ordered delivery for messages that are causally related. (The ABCAST protocol just described has subsequently been replaced, but even the new one is much slower than CBCAST.) The CBCAST protocol works as follows. If a group has n members, each process maintains a vector with n components, one per group member. The i-th component of this vector is the number of the last message received in sequence from process i. The vectors are managed by the runtime system, not the user processes themselves, and are initialized to zero, as shown at the top of Fig. 10-35.

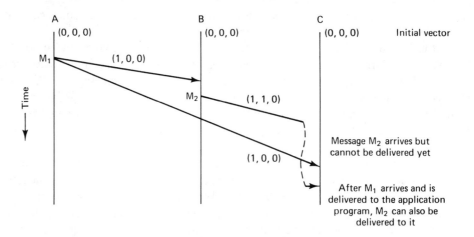

Fig. 10-35. Messages can only be delivered when all causally earlier messages have already been delivered.

When a process has a message to send, it increments its own slot in its vector, and sends the vector as part of the message. When M_1 in Fig. 10-35 gets to B, a check is made to see if it depends on anything that B has not yet seen. The first component of the vector is one higher than B's own first component, which is expected (and required) for a message from A, and the others are the same, so the message is accepted and passed to the group member running on B.

Now B sends a message of its own, M_2, to C, which arrives before M_1. From the vector, C sees that B had already received one message from A before M_2 was sent, and since it has not yet received anything from A, M_2 is buffered until a message from A arrives. Under no conditions may it be delivered before A's message.

The general algorithm for deciding whether to pass an incoming message to the user process or delay it can now be stated. Let V_i be the i-th component of the vector in the incoming message, and L_i be the i-th component of the vector stored in the receiver's memory. Suppose the message was sent by j. The first condition for acceptance is $V_j = L_j + 1$. This simply states that this is the next message in sequence from j, that is, no messages have been missed. (Messages from the same sender are always causally related.) The second condition for acceptance is $V_i \le L_i$ for all $i \ne j$. This condition simply states that the sender has not seen any message that the receiver has missed. If an incoming message passes both tests, the runtime system can pass it to the user process without delay. Otherwise, it must wait.

In Fig. 10-36 we show a more detailed example of the vector mechanism. Here process 0 has sent a message containing the vector (4, 6, 8, 2, 1, 5) to the other five members of its group. Process 1 has seen exactly the same messages as process 0, so the message passes the test, is accepted, and can be passed up to the user process. Process 2 has missed message 6 sent by process 1, so the incoming message must be delayed. Process 3 has seen everything the sender has seen, and in addition message 7 from process 1, which apparently has not yet gotten to process 0, so the message is accepted. Process 4 missed the previous message from 0 itself. This omission is serious, so the new message will have to wait. Finally, process 5 is also slightly ahead of 0, so the message can be accepted immediately.

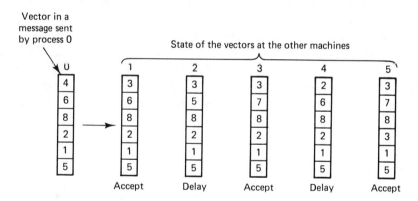

Fig. 10-36. Examples of the vectors used by CBCAST.

ISIS also provides fault tolerance and support for message ordering for overlapping groups using CBCAST. The algorithms used are somewhat complicated though. For details, see (Birman et al, 1991).

10.5. SUMMARY

The key difference between a centralized operating system and a distributed one is the importance of communication in the latter. Various approaches to communication in distributed systems have been proposed and implemented. For relatively slow, wide-area distributed systems, connection-oriented layered protocols such as

OSI and TCP/IP are sometimes used because the main problem to be overcome is how to transport the bits reliably over poor physical lines.

For LAN-based distributed systems, layered protocols are rarely used. Instead, a much simpler model is usually adopted, in which the client sends a message to the server and the server sends back a reply to the client. By eliminating most of the layers, much higher performance can be achieved. Many of the design issues in these message-passing systems concern the communication primitives: blocking versus nonblocking, buffered versus unbuffered, reliable versus unreliable, and so on.

The problem with the basic client-server model is that conceptually interprocess communication is handled as I/O. To prevent a better abstraction, remote procedure call is widely used. With RPC, a client running on one machine calls a procedure running on another machine. The runtime system, embodied in stub procedures, handles collecting parameters, building messages, and the interface with the kernel to actually move the bits.

Although RPC is a step forward above raw message passing, it has its own problems. The correct server has to be located. Pointers and complex data structures are hard to pass. Global variables are difficult to use. The exact semantics of RPC are tricky because clients and servers can fail independently of one another. Finally, implementing RPC efficiently is not straightforward and requires careful thought.

RPC is limited to those situations where a single client wants to talk to a single server. When a collection of processes, for example, replicated file servers, need to communicate with each other as a group, something else is needed. Systems such as ISIS provide a new abstraction for this purpose: group communication. ISIS offers a variety of primitives, the most important of which is CBCAST. CBCAST offers weakened communication semantics based on causality and implemented by including sequence number vectors in each message to allow the receiver to see whether the message should be delivered immediately or delayed until some prior messages have arrived.

PROBLEMS

1. In many layered protocols, each layer has its own header. Surely it would be more efficient to have a single header at the front of each message with all the control in it than all these separate headers. Why is this not done?

2. Suggest a simple modification to Fig. 10-6 that reduces network traffic.

3. If the communication primitives in a client-server system are nonblocking, a call to *send* will complete before the message has actually been sent. To reduce overhead, some systems do not copy the data to the kernel, but transmit it directly from user space. For such a system, devise two ways in which the sender can be told that the transmission has been completed and the buffer can be reused.

4. In many communication systems, calls to *send* set a timer to guard against hanging the client forever if the server crashes. Suppose a fault tolerant system is implemented using multiple processors for all clients and all servers, so the probability of a client or server crashing is effectively zero. Do you think it is it safe to get rid of timeouts in this system?

5. When buffered communication is used, a primitive is normally available for user processes to create mailboxes. In the text it was not specified whether this primitive must specify the size of the mailbox. Give an argument each way.

6. In all the examples in this chapter, a server can only listen to a single address. In practice, it is sometimes convenient for a server to listen to multiple addresses at the same time, for example, if the same process performs a set of closely related services that have been assigned separate addresses. Invent a scheme by which this goal can be accomplished.

7. Consider a procedure *incr* with two integer parameters. The procedure adds one to each parameter. Now suppose it is called with the same variable twice, for example, as *incr(i, i)*. If *i* is initially 0, what value will it have afterwards if call-by-reference is used? How about if copy/restore is used?

8. Pascal has a construction called a record variant, in which a field of a record can hold any one of several alternatives. At run time, there is no sure fire way to tell which one is in there. Does this feature of Pascal have any implications for remote procedure call? Explain your answer.

9. The usual sequence of steps in an RPC involves trapping to the kernel to have the message sent from the client to the server. Suppose a special co-processor chip for doing network I/O exists, and that this chip is directly addressable from user space. Would it be worth having? What steps would an RPC consist of in that case?

10. The SPARC chip uses a 32-bit word in big endian format. If a SPARC sends the integer 2 to an 386, which is little endian, what numerical value does the 386 see?

11. One way to handle parameter conversion in RPC systems is to have each machine send parameters in its native representation, with the other one doing the translation, if need be. In the text it was suggested that the native system could be indicated by a code in the first byte. However, since locating the first byte in the first word is precisely the problem, can this work, or is the book wrong?

12. In Fig. 10-20 the *deregister* call to the binder has the unique identifier as one of the parameters. Is this really necessary? After all, the name and version are also provided, which uniquely identifies the service.

13. Reading the first block of a file from a remote file server is an idempotent operation. What about writing the first block?

14. For each of the following applications, do you think at least once semantics or at most once semantics is best? Discuss.

    (a) Reading and writing files from a file server.
    (b) Compiling a program.
    (c) Remote banking.

15. Suppose that the time to do a null RPC (i.e., 0 data bytes) is 1.0 msec, with an additional 1.5 msec for every 1K of data. How long does it take to read 32K from the file server in a single 32K RPC? How about as 32 1K RPCs?

16. How can atomic broadcast be used to manage group membership?

17. When a computation runs for a long time, it is sometimes wise to make checkpoints periodically, that is, to save the state of the process on disk in case it crashes. In that way, the process can be restarted from the checkpoint instead of from the beginning. Try to devise a way of checkpointing a computation that consists of multiple processes running in parallel.

18. Imagine that in a particular distributed system all the machines are redundant multiprocessors, so that the possibility of a machine crashing is so low that it can be ignored. Devise a simple method for implementing global time ordered atomic broadcast using only unicasting. (Hint: arrange the machines in a logical ring.)

11

SYNCHRONIZATION
IN DISTRIBUTED SYSTEMS

In the previous chapter, we saw how processes in a distributed system communicate with one another. The methods used include layered protocols, request/reply message passing (including RPC), and group communication. While communication is important, it is not the entire story. Closely related is how processes cooperate and synchronize with one another. For example, how are critical regions implemented in a distributed system and how are resources allocated. In this chapter we will study these and other issues related to interprocess cooperation and synchronization in distributed systems.

In single CPU systems, critical regions, mutual exclusion, and other synchronization problems are generally solved using methods such as semaphores and monitors. These methods are not well-suited to use in distributed systems because they invariably rely (implicitly) on the existence of shared memory. For example, two processes that are interacting using a semaphore must both be able to access the semaphore. If they are running on the same machine, they can share the semaphore by having it stored in the kernel, and execute system calls to access it. If, however, they are running on different machines, this method no longer works, and other techniques are needed. Even seemingly simple matters, like determining whether event A happened before or after event B require careful thought.

In this chapter we will examine some of the problems that we looked at back in Chap. 2, but now in the context of distributed systems. In addition, we will look at some new problems that do not arise in single processor systems. We will start out by looking at time and how it can be measured because time plays a major role in some synchronization methods. Then we will come back to mutual exclusion, a topic we have studied before, but in the context of one machine. Next we come to election algorithms. After that we will study a high-level synchronization technique called atomic transactions. Finally, we will look at deadlock again, this time in distributed systems.

11.1. CLOCK SYNCHRONIZATION

Synchronization in distributed systems is more complicated than in centralized ones because the former have to use distributed algorithms. It is usually not possible (or desirable) to collect all the information about the system in one place, and then let some process examine it and make a decision as is done in the centralized case. In general, distributed algorithms have the following properties:

1. The relevant information is scattered among multiple machines.

2. Processes make decisions based only on locally available information.

3. A single point of failure in the system should be avoided.

4. No common clock or other precise global time source exists.

The first three points all say that it is unacceptable to collect all the information in a single place for processing. For example, to do resource allocation (assigning I/O devices in a deadlock-free way), it is generally not acceptable to send all the requests to a single manager process, which examines them all and grants or denies requests based on information in its tables. In a large system, such a solution puts a heavy burden on that one process.

Furthermore, having a single point of failure like this makes the system unreliable. Ideally, a distributed system should be more reliable than the individual machines. If one goes down, the rest should be able to continue to function. Having the failure of one machine (e.g., the resource allocator) bring a large number of other machines (its customers) to a grinding halt is the last thing we want. Achieving synchronization without centralization requires doing things in a different way from traditional operating systems.

The last point in the list is also crucial. In a centralized system, time is unambiguous. When a process wants to know the time, it makes a system call and the kernel tells it. If process A asks for the time, and then a little later process B asks for the time, the value that B gets will be higher than (or possibly equal to) the value A got. It will certainly not be lower. In a distributed system, achieving agreement on time is not trivial.

Just think, for a moment, about the implications of the lack of global time on the UNIX *make* program, as a single example. Normally in UNIX, large programs are split up into multiple source files, so that a change to one source file only requires one file to be recompiled, and not all the files. If a program consists of 100 files, not having to recompile everything because one file has been changed greatly increases the speed at which programmers can work.

The way *make* normally works is simple. When the programmer has finished changing all the source files, he starts *make*, which examines the times at which all the source and object files were last modified. If the source file *input.c* has time 2151 and the corresponding object file *input.o* has time 2150, *make* knows that *input.c* has been changed since *input.o* was created, and thus *input.c* must be recompiled. On the other hand, if *output.c* has time 2144 and *output.o* has time 2145, then no compilation is needed here. Thus *make* goes through all the source files to find out which ones need to be recompiled, and calls the compiler to recompile them.

Now imagine what could happen in a distributed system in which there is no global agreement on time. Suppose that *output.o* has time 2144 as above, and shortly thereafter *output.c* is modified, but is assigned time 2143 because the clock on its machine is a slightly slow, as shown in Fig. 11-1. *Make* will not call the compiler. The resulting executable binary program will then contain a mixture of object files from the old sources and the new sources. It will probably not work, and the programmer will go crazy trying to understand what is wrong with the code.

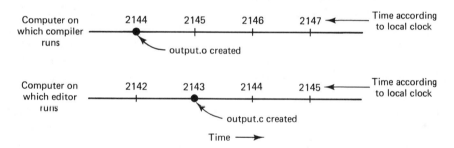

Fig. 11-1. When each machine has its own clock, an event that occurred after another event may nevertheless be assigned an earlier time.

Since time is so basic to the way people think, and the effect of not having all the clocks synchronized can be so dramatic, as we have just seen, it is fitting that we begin our study of synchronization with the simple question: "Is it possible to synchronize all the clocks in a distributed system?"

11.1.1. Logical Clocks

Nearly all computers have a circuit for keeping track of time. Despite the widespread use of the word "clock" to refer to these devices, they are not actually clocks in the usual sense. **Timer** is perhaps a better word. A computer timer is usually a precisely machined quartz crystal. When kept under tension, quartz crystals oscillate at a well-defined frequency that depends on the kind of crystal, how it is cut, and the amount of tension. Associated with each crystal are two registers, a **counter** and a **holding register**. Each oscillation of the crystal decrements the counter by one. When the counter gets to zero, an interrupt is generated and the counter is reloaded from the holding register. In this way, it is possible to program a timer to generate an interrupt 60 times a second, or at any other desired frequency. Each interrupt is called one **clock tick**.

When the system is booted initially, it usually asks the operator to enter the date and time, which is then converted to the number of ticks after some known starting date and stored in memory. At every clock tick, the interrupt service procedure adds one to the time stored in memory. In this way, the (software) clock is kept up to date.

With a single computer and a single clock, it does not matter much if this clock is off by a small amount. Since all processes on the machine use the same clock, they will still be internally consistent. For example, if the file *input.c* has time 2151 and file *input.o* has time 2150, *make* will recompile the source file, even if the clock is off by 2 and the true times are 2153 and 2152, respectively. All that really matters are the relative times.

As soon as multiple CPUs are introduced, each with its own clock, the situation changes. Although the frequency at which a crystal oscillator runs is usually fairly stable, it is impossible to guarantee that the crystals in different computers all run at exactly the same frequency. In practice, when a system has n computers all n crystals will run at slightly different rates, causing the (software) clocks to gradually get out of sync and give different values when read out. This difference in time values is called **clock skew**. As a consequence of this skew, programs that expect the time associated with a file, object, process, or message to be correct, and independent of where it was generated (i.e., which clock it used), can fail, as we saw in the *make* example above.

This brings us back to our original question, whether it is possible to synchronize all the clocks to produce a single, unambiguous time standard. In a classic paper, Lamport (1978) showed that clock synchronization is possible, and presented an algorithm for achieving it. He extended his work in (Lamport, 1990).

Lamport pointed out that clock synchronization need not be absolute. If two processes do not interact, it is not necessary that their clocks be synchronized because the lack of synchronization would not be observable and thus could not cause any problems. Furthermore, he pointed out that what usually matters is not that all processes agree on exactly what time it is, but rather that they agree on the order in which events occur. In the *make* example above, what counts is whether *input.c* is older or newer than *input.o*, not the exact times either was created.

For many purposes, it is sufficient that all machines agree on the same time. It is not essential that this time also agree with the real time as announced on the radio every hour. For running *make*, for example, it is adequate that all machines agree that it is 10:00, even if it is really 10:02. Thus for a certain class of algorithms, it is the internal consistency of the clocks that matters, not whether they are particularly close to the real time. For these algorithms, it is conventional to speak of the clocks as **logical clocks**.

When the additional constraint is present that the clocks must not only be the same, but also must not deviate from the real time by more than a certain amount, the clocks are called **physical clocks**. In this section we will discuss Lamport's algorithm, which synchronizes logical clocks. In the next ones we will introduce the concept of physical time and show how physical clocks can be synchronized.

To synchronize logical clocks, Lamport defined a relation called **happens-before**. The expression $a \rightarrow b$ is read: "a happens before b" and means that all processes agree that first event a occurs, then afterwards, event b occurs. The happens-before relation can be directly observed in two situations:

1. If a and b are events in the same process, and a occurs before b, then $a \rightarrow b$ is true.

2. If a is the event of a message being sent by one process, and b is the event of the message being received by another process, then $a \rightarrow b$ is also true. A message cannot be received before it is sent, or even at the same time it is sent, since it takes a finite amount of time to arrive.

Happens-before is a transitive relation, so if $a \rightarrow b$ and $b \rightarrow c$, then $a \rightarrow c$. If two events, x and y, happen in different processes that do not exchange messages (not even indirectly via third parties), then $x \rightarrow y$ is not true, but neither is $y \rightarrow x$. These events are said to be **concurrent**, which simply means that nothing can be said (or need be said) about when they happened or which is first.

What we need is a way of measuring time such that for every event, a, we can assign it a time value $C(a)$ on which all processes agree. These time values must have the property that if $a \rightarrow b$, then $C(a) < C(b)$. To rephrase the conditions we stated earlier, if a and b are two events within the same process and a occurs before b, then $C(a) < C(b)$. Similarly, if a is the sending of a message by one process and b is the reception of that message by another process, then $C(a)$ and $C(b)$ must be assigned in such a way that everyone agrees on the values of $C(a)$ and $C(b)$ with $C(a) < C(b)$. In addition, the clock time, C, must always go forward (increasing), never backwards (decreasing). Corrections to time can be made by adding a positive value to the clock, but never by subtracting one.

Now let us look at the algorithm Lamport proposed for assigning times to events. Consider the three processes depicted in Fig. 11-2(a). The processes run on different machines, each with its own clock, running at its own speed. As can be seen from the figure, when the clock has ticked 6 times in process 0, it has ticked 8 times in process 1 and 10 times in process 2. Each clock runs at a constant rate, only the rates are different due to differences in the crystals.

At time 6, process 0 sends message A to process 1. How long this message takes to arrive depends on whose clock you believe. In any event, the clock in process 1 reads 16 when it arrives. If the message carries the starting time, 6, in it, process 1 will conclude that it took 10 ticks to make the journey. This value is certainly possible. According to this reasoning, message B from 1 to 2 takes 16 ticks, again a plausible value.

Now comes the fun part. Message C from 2 to 1 leaves at 60 and arrives at 56. Similarly, message D from 1 to 0 leaves at 64 and arrives at 54. These values are clearly impossible. It is this situation that must be prevented.

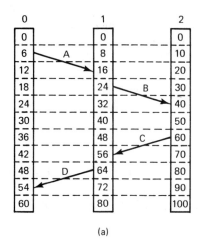
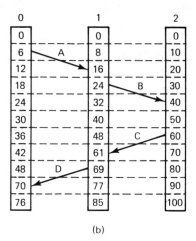

(a)   (b)

Fig. 11-2. (a) Three processes, each with its own clock. The clocks run at different rates. (b) Lamport's algorithm corrects the clocks.

Lamport's solution follows directly from the happened-before relation. Since C left at 60, it must arrive at 61 or later. Therefore each message carries the sending time, according to the sender's clock. When a message arrives and the receiver's clock shows a value prior to the time the message was sent, the receiver fast forwards its clock to be one more than the sending time. In Fig. 11-2(b) we see that C now arrives at 61. Similarly, D arrives at 70.

With one small addition, this algorithm meets our requirements for global time. The addition is that between every two events, the clock must tick at least once. If a process sends or receives two messages in quick succession, it must advance its clock by (at least) one tick in between them.

In some situations, an additional requirement is desirable: no two events ever occur at exactly the same time. To achieve this goal, we can attach the number of the process in which the event occurs to the low-order end of the time, separated by a decimal point. Thus if events happen in processes 1 and 2, both with time 40, then the former becomes 40.1 and the latter becomes 40.2.

Using this method, we now have a way to assign time to all events in a distributed system subject to the following conditions:

1. If a happens before b in the same process, $C(a) < C(b)$.

2. If a and b are the sending and receiving of a message, $C(a) < C(b)$.

3. For all events a and b, $C(a) \neq C(b)$.

This algorithm gives us a way to provide a total ordering of all events in the system. Many other distributed algorithms need such an ordering to avoid ambiguities. We will use it repeatedly in this book. The algorithm is widely cited in the literature.

11.1.2. Physical Clocks

Although Lamport's algorithm gives an unambiguous event ordering, the time values assigned to events are not necessarily close to the actual times at which they occur. In some systems (e.g., real-time systems), the actual clock time is important. For these systems external physical clocks are required. For reasons of efficiency and redundancy, multiple physical clocks are generally considered desirable, which yields two problems: (1) How do we synchronize them with real-world clocks, and (2) How do we synchronize the clocks with each other?

Before answering these questions, let us digress slightly to see how time is actually measured. It is not nearly as simple as one might think, especially when high accuracy is required. Since the invention of mechanical clocks in the Seventeenth century, time has been measured astronomically. Every day, the sun appears to rise on the eastern horizon, climbs to a maximum height in the sky, and sinks in the west. The event of the sun's reaching its highest apparent point in the sky is called the **transit of the sun**. This event occurs at about noon each day. The interval between two consecutive transits of the sun is called the **solar day**. Since there are 24 hours in a day, each containing 3600 seconds, the **solar second** is defined as exactly 1/86400th of a solar day. The geometry of the mean solar day calculation is shown in Fig. 11-3.

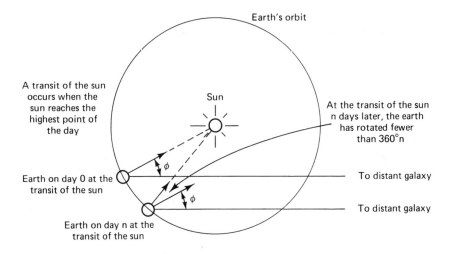

Fig. 11-3. Computation of the mean solar day.

In the 1940s, it was established that the period of the earth's rotation is not constant. The earth is slowing down due to tidal friction and atmospheric drag. Based on studies of growth patterns in ancient coral, geologists now believe that 300 million years ago there were about 400 days per year. The length of the year, that is, the time for one trip around the sun, is not thought to have changed; the day has simply become longer. In addition to this long term trend, short term variations in the length of the day also occur, probably caused by turbulence deep in the earth's core of molten iron. These revelations led astronomers to compute the length of the day by measuring a large number of days and taking the average before dividing by 86,400. The resulting quantity was called the **mean solar second**.

With the invention of the atomic clock in 1948, it became possible to measure time much more accurately, and independent of the wiggling and wobbling of the earth, by counting transitions of the cesium 133 atom. The physicists took over the job of timekeeping from the astronomers, and defined the second to be the time it takes the cesium 133 atom to make exactly 9,192,631,770 transitions. The choice of 9,192,631,770 was made to make the atomic second equal to the mean solar second in the year of its introduction. Currently, about 50 laboratories around the world have cesium 133 clocks. Periodically, each laboratory tells the Bureau International de l'Heure (BIH) in Paris how many times its clock has ticked. The BIH averages these to produce **International Atomic Time**, which is abbreviated **TAI**. Thus TAI is just the mean number of ticks of the cesium 133 clocks since midnight on Jan 1, 1958 (the beginning of time) divided by 9,192,631,770.

Although TAI is highly stable and available to anyone who wants to go to the trouble of buying a cesium clock, there is a serious problem with it; 86,400 TAI seconds is now about 3 msec less than a mean solar day (because the mean solar day is getting longer all the time). Using TAI for keeping time would mean that over the course of the years, noon would get earlier and earlier, until it would eventually occur in the wee hours of the morning. People might notice this and we could have the same kind of situation as occurred in 1582 when Pope Gregory XIII decreed that 10 days be omitted from the calendar. This event caused riots in the streets because landlords demanded a full month's rent and bankers a full month's interest, while employers refused to pay workers for the 10 days they did not work, to mention only a few of the conflicts. The Protestant countries, as a matter of principle, refused to have anything to do with papal decrees, and did not accept the Gregorian calendar for 170 years.

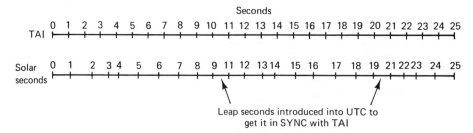

Fig. 11-4. TAI seconds are of constant length, unlike solar seconds. Leap seconds are introduced when necessary to keep in phase with the sun.

BIH solves the problem by introducing **leap seconds** whenever the discrepancy between TAI and solar time grows to 800 msec. The use of leap seconds is illustrated in Fig. 11-4. This correction gives rise to a time system based on constant TAI seconds but which stays in phase with the apparent motion of the sun. It is called **Universal Coordinated Time**, but is abbreviated as **UTC**. UTC is the basis of all modern civil time keeping. It has essentially replaced the old standard, Greenwich Mean Time, which is astronomical time.

Most electric power companies base the timing of their 60 Hz or 50 Hz clocks on UTC, so when BIH announces a leap second, the power companies raise their frequency to 61 Hz or 51 Hz for 60 or 50 sec, to advance all the clocks in their distribution area. Since 1 sec is a noticeable interval for a computer, an operating system that needs to keep accurate time over a period of years must have special software to account for leap seconds as they are announced (unless they use the power line for time, which is usually too crude). The total number of leap seconds introduced into UTC so far is about 30.

To provide UTC to people who need precise time, the National Institute of Standard Time (NIST) operates a short wave radio station with call letters WWV from Fort Collins, Colorado. WWV broadcasts a short pulse at the start of each UTC second. The accuracy of WWV itself is about ± 1 msec, but due to random atmospheric fluctuations that can affect the length of the signal path, in practice the accuracy is no better than ± 10 msec. In England, the station MSF operating from Rugby, Warwickshire, provides a similar service, as do stations in several other countries.

Several earth satellites also offer a UTC service. The Geostationary Environment Operational Satellite can provide UTC accurately to 0.5 msec, and some other satellites do even better.

Using either short wave radio or satellite services requires an accurate knowledge of the relative position of the sender and receiver, in order to compensate for the signal propagation delay. Radio receivers for WWV, GEOS, and the other UTC sources are commercially available. The cost varies from a few thousand dollars each to tens of thousands of dollars each, being more for the better sources. UTC can also be obtained more cheaply, but less accurately, by telephone from NIST in Fort Collins, but here too, a correction must be made for the signal path and modem speed. This correction introduces some uncertainty, making it difficult to obtain the time with extremely high accuracy.

11.1.3. Clock Synchronization Algorithms

If one machine has a WWV receiver, then the goal becomes keeping all the other machines synchronized to it. If no machines have WWV receivers, then each machine keeps track of its own time, and the goal is to keep all the machines together as well as possible. Many algorithms have been proposed for doing this synchronization. A survey is given in (Ramanathan et al., 1990b).

All the algorithms have the same underlying model of the system, which we will now describe. Each machine is assumed to have a timer that causes an interrupt H times a second. When this timer goes off, the interrupt handler adds 1 to a software clock that keeps track of the number of ticks (interrupts) since some agreed upon time in the past. Let us call the value of this clock C. More specifically, when the UTC time is t, the value of the clock on machine p is $C_p(t)$. In a perfect world, we would have $C_p(t) = t$ for all p and all t. In other words, dC/dt ideally should be 1.

Real timers do not interrupt exactly H times a second. Theoretically, a timer with

$H = 60$ should generate 216,000 ticks per hour. In practice, the relative error obtainable with modern timer chips is about 10^{-5}, meaning that a particular machine can get a value in the range 215,998 to 216,002 ticks per hour. More precisely, if there exists some constant ρ such that

$$1 - \rho \le \frac{dC}{dt} \le 1 + \rho$$

the timer can be said to be working within its specification. The constant ρ is specified by the manufacturer and is known as the **maximum drift rate**. Slow, perfect, and fast clocks are shown in Fig. 11-5.

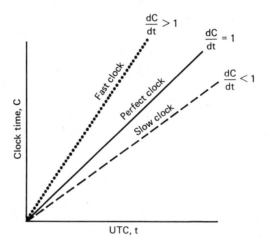

Fig. 11-5. Not all clocks tick precisely at the correct rate.

If two clocks are drifting from UTC in the opposite direction, at a time Δt after they were synchronized, they may be as much as $2\rho\Delta t$ apart. If the operating system designers want to guarantee that no two clocks ever differ by more than δ, then clocks must be resynchronized (in software) at least every $\delta/2\rho$ seconds. The various algorithms differ in precisely how this resynchronization is done.

Cristian's Algorithm

Let us start with an algorithm that is well suited to systems in which one machine has a WWV receiver, and the goal is to have all the other machines keep synchronized with it. Let us call the machine with the WWV receiver a **time server**. Our algorithm is based on the work of Cristian (1989) and prior work. Periodically, certainly no more than every $\delta/2\rho$ seconds, each machine sends a message to the time server asking it for the current time. That machine responds as fast as it can with a message containing its current time, C_{UTC}, as shown in Fig. 11-6.

As a first approximation, when the sender gets the reply, it can just set its clock to C_{UTC}. However, this algorithm has two problems, one major and one minor. The

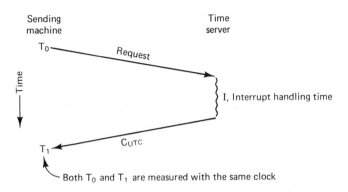

Fig. 11-6. Getting the current time from a time server.

major problem is that time must never run backwards. If the sender's clock is fast, C_{UTC} will be smaller than the sender's current value of C. Just taking over C_{UTC} could cause serious problems, such as an object file compiled just after the clock change having a time earlier than the source which was modified just before the clock change.

Such a change must be introduced gradually. One way is as follows. Suppose the timer is set to generate 100 interrupts per second. Normally, each interrupt would add 10 msec to the time. When slowing down, the interrupt routine only adds 9 msec each time, until the correction has been made. Similarly, the clock can be advanced gradually by adding 11 msec at each interrupt, instead of jumping it forward all at once.

The minor problem is that it takes a nonzero amount of time for the time server's reply to get back to the sender. Worse yet, this delay may be large and vary with the network load. Cristian's way of dealing with it is to attempt to measure it. It is simple enough for the sender to accurately record the interval between sending the request to the time server, and the arrival of the reply. Both the starting time, T_0 and the ending time, T_1, are measured using the same clock, so the interval will be relatively accurate, even if the sender's clock is off from UTC by a substantial amount.

In the absence of any other information, the best estimate of the message propagation time is $(T_1 - T_0)/2$. When the reply comes in, the value in the message can be increased by this amount to give an estimate of the server's current time. If the theoretical minimum propagation time is known, other properties of the time estimate can be calculated.

This estimate can be improved if it is known approximately how long it takes the time server to handle the interrupt and process the incoming message. Let us call the interrupt handling time I. Then the amount of the interval from T_0 to T_1 that was devoted to message propagation is $T_1 - T_0 - I$, so the best estimate of the one-way propagation time is half this.

To improve the accuracy, Cristian suggested making not one measurement, but a series of them. Any measurements in which $T_1 - T_0$ exceeds some threshold value are discarded as being victims of network congestion and thus unreliable. The estimates derived from the remaining probes can then be averaged to get a better value. Alternatively, the message that came back fastest can be taken to be the most accurate one.

The Berkeley Algorithm

In Cristian's algorithm, the time server is passive. Other machines ask it for the time periodically. All it does is respond to their queries. In Berkeley UNIX, exactly the opposite approach is taken (Gusella and Zatti, 1989). Here the time server (actually, a time daemon) is active, polling every machine periodically to ask what time it is there. Based on the answers, it computes an average time and tells all the other machines to advance their clocks to the new time or slow their clocks down until some specified reduction has been achieved. This method is suitable for a system in which no machine has a WWV receiver. The time daemon's time must be set manually by the operator periodically. The method is illustrated in Fig. 11-7.

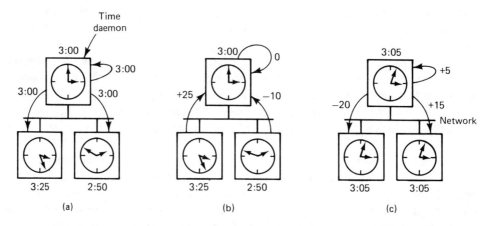

Fig. 11-7. (a) The time daemon asks all the other machines for their clock values. (b) The machines answer. (c) The time daemon tells everyone how to adjust their clock.

In Fig. 11-7(a), at 3:00, the time daemon tells the other machines its time, and asks for their times. In Fig. 11-7(b), they respond with how far ahead or behind the time daemon they are. Armed with these numbers, the time daemon computes the average time and tells each machine how to adjust its clock, in Fig. 11-7(c).

Averaging Algorithms

Both of the above methods are highly centralized, with the usual disadvantages. Decentralized algorithms are also known. One class of decentralized clock synchronization algorithms works by dividing time into fixed-length resynchronization intervals. The i-th interval starts at $T_0 + iR$ and runs until $T_0 + (i+1)R$, where T_0 is an agreed upon moment in the past, and R is a system parameter. At the beginning of each interval, every machine broadcasts the current time according to its clock. Because the clocks on different machines do not run exactly at the same speed, these broadcasts will not happen precisely simultaneously.

After a machine broadcasts its time, it starts a local timer to collect all other broadcasts that arrive during some interval S. When all the broadcasts arrive, an algorithm is run to compute a new time from them. The simplest algorithm is just to average the values from all the other machines. A slight variation on this theme is to first discard the m highest and m lowest values, and average the rest. Discarding the extreme values can be regarded as self defense against up to m faulty clocks sending out nonsense.

Another variation is to try to correct each message by adding to it an estimate of the propagation time from the source. This estimate can be made from the known topology of the network, or by timing how long it takes for probe messages to be echoed.

Additional clock synchronization algorithms are discussed in the literature (e.g., Lundelius-Welch and Lynch, 1988; Ramanathan et al., 1990a; and Srikanth and Toueg, 1987).

Multiple External Time Sources

For systems in which extremely accurate synchronization with UTC is required, it is possible to equip the system with multiple receivers for WWV, GEOS, or other UTC sources. However, due to inherent inaccuracy in the time source itself as well as fluctuations in the signal path, the best the operating system can do is establish a range (time interval) in which UTC falls. In general, the various time sources will produce different ranges, which requires the machines attached to them to come to agreement.

To reach this agreement, each processor with a UTC source can broadcast its range periodically, say, at the precise start of each UTC minute. None of the processors will get the time packets instantaneously. Worse yet, the delay between transmission and reception depends on the cable distance and number of gateways that the packets have to traverse, which is different for each (UTC source, processor) pair. Other factors can also play a role, such as delays due to collisions when multiple machines try to transmit on an Ethernet at the same instant. Furthermore, if a processor is busy handling a previous packet, it may not even look at the time packet for a considerable number of milliseconds, introducing additional uncertainty into the time.

Various methods of dealing with multiple, uncertain time sources are possible. Let us look at how the Open Software Foundation's Distributed Computing Environment does it as an example. When a processor gets all the UTC ranges, it first checks if any of them are disjoint from the others. If so, something is undoubtedly wrong, and these should be rejected, as shown in Fig. 11-8. Next, the intersection of the remaining ranges is computed, since everyone left agrees that UTC falls within it. Finally, the midpoint of this interval is taken as UTC and the internal clock set to it.

Even if great care is taken to compensate for all the potential delays between

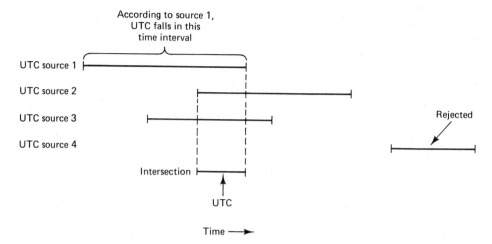

Fig. 11-8. Computing UTC from multiple time sources, each of which gives a time interval in which UTC falls.

WWV broadcasting the time and a processor setting its internal clock, there is still the problem that different clocks run at different speeds. Thus even if two processors manage to set their clocks to the correct UTC, after a few seconds, they may still drift apart due to clock skew. To some extent it can be dealt with by making accurate measurements of each crystal's frequency and attempting to compensate for individual variations. In addition, frequent updates from the UTC sources help, although care must be taken to make sure that clocks never go backwards when updates occur, lest *make* and other programs become confused.

Another technique that can be used to smooth out time differences is local averaging. Suppose that the machines in a distributed system can be arranged (at least conceptually, if not physically) in some kind of pattern, such as a ring or a grid. Periodically, at an interval small compared to UTC updates, each machine can exchange its idea of time with its neighbors in the ring, grid, or other structure, and then set its time value to the average of its value and its neighbors' values.

All in all, getting the clocks in a distributed system synchronized to within 5 or 10 msec of UTC is an expensive and nontrivial business.

11.2. MUTUAL EXCLUSION

Systems involving multiple processes are often most easily programmed using critical regions. When a process has to read or update certain shared data structures, it first enters a critical region to achieve mutual exclusion and insure that no other process will use the shared data structures at the same time. In single-processor systems, critical regions are protected using semaphores, monitors, and similar constructs. We will now look at a few examples of how critical regions and mutual exclusion can be implemented in distributed systems. For a taxonomy and bibliography of other methods see (Raynal, 1991). Other work is discussed in (Agrawal and El Abbadi, 1991; Chandy et al., 1983; and Sanders, B.A., 1987).

11.2.1. A Centralized Algorithm

The most straightforward way to achieve mutual exclusion in a distributed system is to simulate how it is done in a one-processor system. One process is elected as the coordinator (e.g., the one running on the machine with the highest network address). Whenever a process wants to enter a critical region, it sends a request message to the coordinator telling which critical region it wants to enter and asking for permission. If no other process is currently in that critical region, the coordinator sends back a reply granting permission, as shown in Fig. 11-9(a). When the reply arrives, the requesting process enters the critical region.

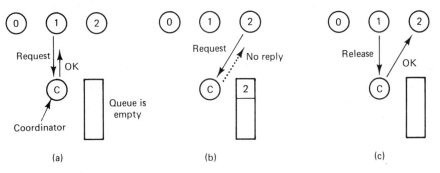

Fig. 11-9. (a) Process 1 asks the coordinator for permission to enter a critical region. Permission is granted. (b) Process 2 then asks permission to enter the same critical region. The coordinator does not reply. (c) When process 1 exits the critical region, it tells the coordinator, which then replies to 2.

Now suppose another process, 2 in Fig. 11-9(b), asks for permission to enter the same critical region. The coordinator knows that a different process is already in the critical region, so it cannot grant permission. The exact method used to deny permission is system dependent. In Fig. 11-9(b), the coordinator just refrains from replying, thus blocking process 2, which is waiting for a reply. Alternatively, it could send a reply saying "permission denied." Either way, it queues the request from 2 for the time being.

When process 1 exits the critical region, it sends a message to the coordinator releasing its exclusive access, as shown in Fig. 11-9(c). The coordinator takes the first item off the queue of deferred requests, and sends that process a grant message. If the process was still blocked (i.e., this is the first message to it), it unblocks and enters the critical region. If an explicit message has already been sent denying permission, then the process will have to poll for incoming traffic, or block later. Either way, when it sees the grant, it can enter the critical region.

It is easy to see that the algorithm guarantees mutual exclusion: the coordinator only lets one process at a time into each critical region. It is also fair, since requests are granted in the order they are received. No process ever waits forever (no starvation). The scheme is easy to implement too, and only requires three messages per use of a critical region (request, grant, release). It can also be used for more general resource allocation, rather than just managing critical regions.

The centralized approach also has shortcomings. The coordinator is a single point of failure, so if it crashes, the entire system may go down. If processes normally block after making a request, they cannot distinguish a dead coordinator from "permission denied" since in both cases no message comes back. In addition, in a large system, a single coordinator can become a performance bottleneck.

11.2.2. A Distributed Algorithm

Having a single point of failure is frequently unacceptable, so researchers have looked for distributed mutual exclusion algorithms. Lamport's 1978 paper on clock synchronization presented the first one. Ricart and Agrawala (1981) made it more efficient. In this section we will describe their method.

Ricart and Agrawala's algorithm requires that there be a total ordering of all events in the system. That is, for any pair of events, such as messages, it must be unambiguous which one happened first. Lamport's algorithm presented in Sec. 11.1.1 is one way to achieve this ordering and can be used to provide timestamps for distributed mutual exclusion.

The algorithm works as follows. When a process wants to enter a critical region, it builds a message containing the name of the critical region it wants to enter, its process number, and the current time. It then sends the message to all other processes, conceptually including itself. The sending of messages is assumed to be reliable, that is, every message is acknowledged. If reliable group communication is available, that can be used instead of sending individual messages.

When a process receives a request message from another process, the action it takes depends on its state with respect to the critical region named in the message. Three cases have to be distinguished:

1. If the receiver is not in the critical region and does not want to enter it, it sends back an *OK* message to the sender.

2. If the receiver is already in the critical region, it does not reply. Instead it queues the request.

3. If the receiver wants to enter the critical region, but has not yet done so, it compares the timestamp in the incoming message with the one contained in the message that it has sent everyone. The lowest one wins. If the incoming message is lower, the receiver sends back an *OK* message. If its own message has a lower timestamp, the receiver queues the incoming request and sends nothing.

After sending out requests asking permission to enter a critical region, a process sits back and waits until everyone else has given permission. As soon as all the permissions are in, it may enter the critical region. When it exits the critical region, it sends *OK* messages to all processes on its queue, and deletes them all from the queue.

Let us try to understand why the algorithm works. If there is no conflict, it clearly works. However, suppose two processes try to enter the same critical region simultaneously, as shown in Fig. 11-10(a).

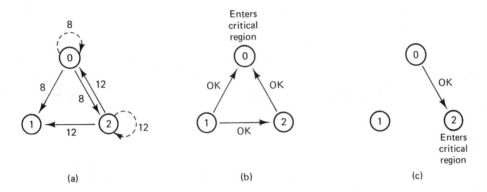

Fig. 11-10. (a) Two processes want to enter the same critical region at the same moment. (b) Process 0 has the lowest timestamp, so it wins. (c) When process 0 is done, it sends an *OK* also, so 2 can now enter the critical region.

Process 0 sends everyone a request with timestamp 8, while at the same time, process 2 sends everyone a request with timestamp 12. Process 1 is not interested in entering the critical region, so it sends *OK* to both senders. Processes 0 and 2 both see the conflict and compare timestamps. Process 2 sees that it has lost, so it grants permission to 0 by sending *OK*. Process 0 now queues the request from 2 for later processing and enters the critical region, as shown in Fig. 11-10(b). When it is finished, it removes the request from 2 from its queue and sends an *OK* message to process 2, allowing the latter to enter its critical region, as shown in Fig. 11-10(c). The algorithm works because in the case of a conflict, the lowest timestamp wins, and everyone agrees on the ordering of the timestamps.

Note that the situation in Fig. 11-10 would have been essentially different if process 2 had sent its message earlier in time so that process 0 had gotten it and granted permission before making its own request. In this case, 2 would have noticed that it itself was in a critical region at the time of the request, and queued it instead of sending a reply.

As with the centralized algorithm discussed above, mutual exclusion is guaranteed without deadlock or starvation. The number of messages required per entry is now $2(n - 1)$, where the total number of processes in the system is n. Best of all, no single point of failure exists.

Unfortunately, the single point of failure has been replaced by n points of failure. If any process crashes, it will fail to respond to requests. This silence will be (incorrectly) interpreted as denial of permission, thus blocking all subsequent attempts by all processes to enter all critical regions. Since the probability of one of the n processes failing is n times as large as a single coordinator failing, we have managed to replace a poor algorithm with one that is n times worse and requires much more network traffic to boot.

The algorithm can be patched up by the same trick that we proposed earlier. When a request comes in, the receiver always sends a reply, either granting or denying permission. Whenever either a request or a reply is lost, the sender times out and keeps trying until either a reply comes back, or the sender concludes that the destination is dead. After a request is denied, the sender should block waiting for a subsequent *OK* message.

Another problem with this algorithm is that either a group communication primitive must be used, or each process must maintain the group membership list itself, including processes entering the group, leaving the group, and crashing. The method works best with small groups of processes that never change their group memberships.

Finally, recall that one of the problems with the centralized algorithm is that making it handle all requests can lead to a bottleneck. In the distributed algorithm, *all* processes are involved in *all* decisions concerning entry into critical regions. If one process is unable to handle the load, it is unlikely that forcing everyone to do exactly the same thing in parallel is going to help much.

Various minor improvements are possible to this algorithm. For example, getting permission from everyone to enter a critical region is really overkill. All that is needed is a method to prevent two processes from entering the critical region at the same time. The algorithm can be modified to allow a process to enter a critical region when it has collected permission from a simple majority of the other processes, rather than from all of them. Of course in this variation, after a process has granted permission to one process to enter a critical region, it cannot grant the same permission to another process until the first one has released that permission. Other improvements are also possible (e.g., Maekawa et al., 1987).

Nevertheless, this algorithm is slower, more complicated, more expensive, and less robust that the original centralized one. Why bother studying it under these conditions? For one thing, it shows that a distributed algorithm is at least possible, something that was not obvious when we started. Also, by pointing out the shortcomings, we may stimulate future theoreticians to try to produce algorithms that are actually useful. Finally, like eating spinach and learning Latin in high school, some things are said to be good for you in some abstract way.

11.2.3. A Token Ring Algorithm

A completely different approach to achieving mutual exclusion in a distributed system is illustrated in Fig. 11-11. Here we have a bus network, as shown in Fig. 11-11(a), (e.g., Ethernet), with no inherent ordering of the processes. In software, a logical ring is constructed in which each process is assigned a position in the ring, as shown in Fig. 11-11(b). The ring positions may be allocated in numerical order of network addresses or some other means. It does not matter what the ordering is. All that matters is that each process knows who is next in line after itself.

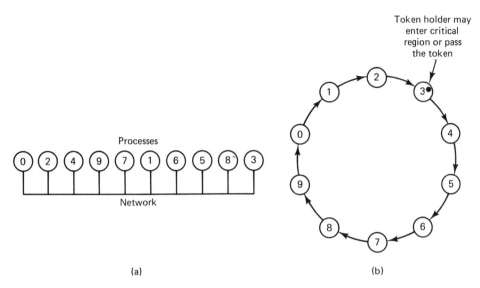

Fig. 11-11. (a) An unordered group of processes on a network. (b) A logical ring constructed in software.

When the ring is initialized, process 0 is given a **token**. The token circulates around the ring. It is passed from process k to process $k+1$ (modulo the ring size) in point-to-point messages. When a process acquires the token from its neighbor, it checks to see if it is attempting to enter a critical region. If so, the process enters the region, does all the work it needs to, and leaves the region. After it has exited, it passes the token along the ring. It is not permitted to enter a second critical region using the same token.

If a process is handed the token by its neighbor and is not interested in entering a critical region, it just passes it along. As a consequence, when no processes want to enter any critical regions, the token just circulates at high speed around the ring.

The correctness of this algorithm is evident. Only one process has the token at any instant, so only one process can be in a critical region. Since the token circulates among the processes in a well-defined order, starvation cannot occur. Once a process decides it wants to enter a critical region, at worst it will have to wait for every other process to enter and leave one critical region.

As usual, this algorithm has problems too. If the token is ever lost, it must be regenerated. In fact, detecting that it is lost is difficult, since the amount of time between successive appearances of the token on the network is unbounded. The fact that the token has not been spotted for an hour does not mean it has been lost; somebody may be still be using it.

The algorithm also runs into trouble if a process crashes, but recovery is easier than in the other cases. If we require a process receiving the token to acknowledge receipt, then a dead process will be detected when its neighbor tries to give it the token and fails. At that point the dead process can be removed from the group, and the token holder can throw the token over the head of the dead process to the next member down the line, or the one after that, if necessary. Of course, doing so requires that everyone maintains the current ring configuration.

11.2.4. A Comparison of the Three Algorithms

A brief comparison of the three mutual exclusion algorithms we have looked at is instructive. In Fig. 11-12 we have listed the algorithms and three key properties: the number of messages required for a process to enter and exit a critical region, the delay before entry can occur (assuming messages are passed sequentially over a LAN), and some problems associated with each algorithm.

Algorithm	Messages per entry/exit	Delay before entry (in message times)	Problems
Centralized	3	2	Coordinator crash
Distributed	$2(n-1)$	$2(n-1)$	Crash of any process
Token ring	1 to ∞	0 to $n-1$	Lost token, process crash

Fig. 11-12. A comparison of three mutual exclusion algorithms.

The centralized algorithm is simplest and also most efficient. It requires only three messages to enter and leave a critical region: a request and a grant to enter, and a release to exit. The distributed algorithm requires $n-1$ request messages, one to each of the other processes, and an additional $n-1$ grant messages, for a total of $2(n-1)$. With the token ring algorithm, the number is variable. If every process constantly wants to enter a critical region, then each token pass will result in one entry and exit, for an average of one message per critical region entered. At the other extreme, the token may sometimes circulate for hours without anyone being interested in it. In this case, the number of messages per entry into a critical region is unbounded.

The delay from the moment a process needs to enter a critical region until its actual entry also varies for the three algorithms. When critical regions are short and rarely used, the dominant factor in the delay is the actual mechanism for entering a critical region. When they are long and frequently used, the dominant factor is waiting for everyone else to take their turn. In Fig. 11-12 we show the former case. It takes only two message times to enter a critical region in the centralized case, but $2(n-1)$ message times in the distributed case, assuming that the network can only handle one message at a time. For the token ring, the time varies from 0 (token just arrived) to $n-1$ (token just departed).

Finally, all three algorithms suffer badly in the event of crashes. Special measures and additional complexity must be introduced to avoid having a crash bring down the entire system. It is slightly ironic that the distributed algorithms are even more sensitive to crashes than the centralized one. In a fault tolerant system, none of these would be suitable, but if crashes are very infrequent, they are all acceptable.

11.3. ELECTION ALGORITHMS

Many distributed algorithms require one process to act as coordinator, initiator, sequencer, or otherwise perform some special role. We have already seen several examples, such as the coordinator in the centralized mutual exclusion algorithm. In general, it does not matter which process takes on this special responsibility, but one of them has to do it. In this section we will look at algorithms for electing a coordinator (using this as a generic name for the special process).

If all processes are exactly the same, with no distinguishing characteristics, there is no way to select one of them to be special. Consequently, we will assume that each process has a unique number, for example its network address (for simplicity, we will assume one process per machine). In general, election algorithms attempt to locate the process with the highest process number and designate it as coordinator. The algorithms differ in the way they do this.

Furthermore, we also assume that every process knows the process number of every other process. What the processes do not know is which ones are currently up and which ones are currently down. The goal of an election algorithm is to insure that when an election starts, it concludes with all processes agreeing on who the new coordinator is to be.

11.3.1. The Bully Algorithm

As a first example, consider the **bully algorithm** devised by Garcia-Molina (1982). When a process notices that the coordinator is no longer responding to requests, it initiates an election. A process, P, holds an election as follows:

1. P sends an *ELECTION* message to every process with a higher number.

2. If no one responds, P wins the election and becomes coordinator.

3. If one of the higher-ups answers, it takes over. P's job is done.

At any moment, a process can get an *ELECTION* message from one of its lower-numbered colleagues. When such a message arrives, the receiver sends an *OK* message back to the sender to indicate that he is alive and will take over. The receiver then holds an election, unless it is already holding one. Eventually, all processes give up but one, and that one is the new coordinator. It announces its victory by sending all processes a message telling them that starting immediately it is the new coordinator.

If a process that was previously down comes back up, it holds an election. If it happens to be the highest numbered process currently running, it will win the election and take over the coordinator's job. Thus the biggest guy in town always wins, hence the name "bully algorithm."

In Fig. 11-13 we see an example of how the bully algorithm works. The group consists of eight processes, numbered from 0 to 7. Previously process 7 was the coordinator, but it has just crashed. Process 4 is the first one to notice this, so it sends *ELECTION* messages to all the processes higher than it, namely 5, 6, and 7, as shown in Fig. 11-13(a). Processes 5 and 6 both respond with *OK*, as shown in Fig. 11-13(b). Upon getting the first of these responses, 4 knows that its job is over. It knows that one of these bigwigs will take over and become coordinator. It just sits back and waits to see who the winner will be (although at this point it can make a pretty good guess).

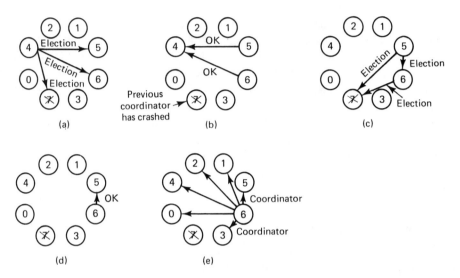

Fig. 11-13. The bully election algorithm. (a) Process 4 holds an election. (b) Processes 5 and 6 respond, telling 4 to stop. (c) Now 5 and 6 each hold an election. (d) Process 6 tells 5 to stop. (e) Process 6 wins and tells everyone.

In Fig. 11-14(c), both 5 and 6 hold elections, each one only sending messages to those processes higher than itself. In Fig. 11-14(d) process 6 tells 5 that it will take over. At this point 6 knows that 7 is dead and that it (6) is the winner. If there is state information to be collected from disk or elsewhere to pick up where the old coordinator left off, 6 must now do what is needed. When it is ready to take over, 6 announces this by sending a *COORDINATOR* message to all running processes. When 4 gets this message, it can now continue with the operation it was trying to do when it discovered that 7 was dead, only using 6 as the coordinator this time.

If process 7 is ever restarted, it will just send all the others a *COORDINATOR* message and bully them into submission.

11.3.2. A Ring Algorithm

Another election algorithm is based on the use of a ring, only unlike the previous ring, this one does not use a token. We assume the processes are physically or logically ordered, so that each process knows who its successor is. When any process notices that the coordinator is not functioning, it builds an *ELECTION* message containing its own process number and sends the message to its successor. If the successor is down, the sender skips over the successor and goes to the next member along the ring, or the one after that, until a running process is located. At each step, the sender adds its own process number to the list in the message.

Eventually, the message gets back to the process that started it all. That process recognizes this event when it receives an incoming message containing its own process number. At that point, the message type is changed to *COORDINATOR* and circulated once again, this time to inform everyone else who the coordinator is (the list member with the highest number) and who the members of the new ring are. When this message has circulated once, it is removed and everyone goes back to work.

In Fig. 11-14 we see what happens if two processes, 2 and 5, simultaneously discover that the previous coordinator, process 7, has crashed. Each of these builds an *ELECTION* message and starts circulating it. Eventually both messages will go all the way around, and both 2 and 5 will convert them into *COORDINATOR* messages, with exactly the same members and in the same order. When both have gone around again, both will be removed. It does no harm to have extra messages circulating; at most it wastes a little bandwidth.

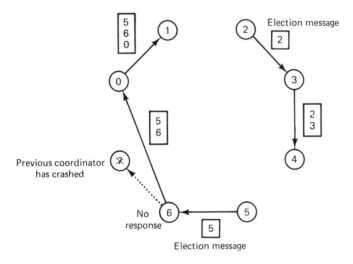

Fig. 11-14. Election algorithm using a ring.

11.4. ATOMIC TRANSACTIONS

All the synchronization techniques we have studied so far are essentially low level, like semaphores. They require the programmer to be intimately involved with all the details of mutual exclusion, critical region management, deadlock prevention, and crash recovery. What we would really like is a much higher level abstraction, one that hides these technical issues and allows the programmer to concentrate on the algorithms and how the processes work together in parallel. Such an abstraction exists, and is widely used in distributed systems. We will call it an **atomic transaction**, or just transaction for short. The term **atomic action** is also widely used. In this section we will examine the use, design, and implementation of atomic transactions.

11.4.1. Introduction to Atomic Transactions

The original model of the atomic transaction comes from the world of business. Suppose that the International Dingbat Corporation needs a batch of widgets. They approach a potential supplier, U.S. Widget, known far and wide for the quality of its widgets, for a quote on 100,000 10 cm purple widgets for June delivery. U.S. widget makes a bid on 100,000 4 inch, mauve widgets to be delivered in December. International Dingbat agrees to the price, but dislikes mauve, wants them by July, and insists on 10 cm for its international customers. U.S. Widget replies by offering 3 15/16 inch lavender widgets in October. After much further negotiation, they finally agree on 3 959/1024 inch violet widgets for delivery on August 15.

Up until this point, both parties are free to terminate the discussion, in which case the world returns to the state it was in before they started talking. However, once both companies have signed a contract, they are both legally bound to complete the sale, come what may. Thus until both parties have signed on the dotted line, either one can back out and it is as if nothing ever happened, but at the moment they both sign, they pass the point of no return, and the transaction must be carried out.

The computer model is similar. One process announces that it wants to begin a transaction with one or more other processes. They can negotiate various options, create and delete objects, and perform operations for a while. Then the initiator announces that it wants all the others to commit themselves to the work done so far. If all of them agree, the results are made permanent. If one or more processes refuse (or crash before agreement), then the situation reverts to exactly the state it had before the transaction began, with all side effects on objects, files, data bases, and so on magically wiped out. This all-or-nothing property eases the programmer's job.

The concept of transaction in computer systems is actually an outgrowth of the way computers worked in the 1960s. Before there were disks and online data bases, all files were kept on magnetic tape. Imagine a supermarket with an automated inventory system. Every day after closing, a computer run was made with two input tapes. The first one contained the complete inventory as of opening time that morning. The second one contained a list of the day's updates: products sold to customers and products delivered by suppliers. The computer read both input tapes and produced a new master inventory tape, as shown in Fig. 11-15.

The great beauty of this scheme (although the people who had to live with it did not realize that) is that if a run failed for any reason, all the tapes could be rewound and the job restarted with no harm done. Primitive as it was, the old magnetic tape system had the all-or-nothing property of an atomic transaction.

Now look at a modern banking application that updates an online data base in place. The customer calls up the bank using a PC with a modem with the intention of

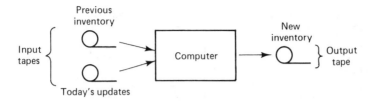

Fig. 11-15. Updating a master tape is fault tolerant.

withdrawing money from one account and depositing it in another. The operation is performed in two steps:

1. Withdraw(amount, account1).

2. Deposit(amount, account2).

If the telephone connection is broken after the first one but before the second one, the first account will have been debited but the second one will not have been credited. The money vanishes into thin air.

Being able to group these two operations in an atomic transaction would solve the problem. Either both would be completed, or neither would be completed. The key is rolling back to the initial state if the transaction fails to complete. What we really want is a way to rewind the data base as we could the magnetic tapes. This ability is what the atomic transaction has to offer.

11.4.2. The Transaction Model

We will now develop a more precise model of what a transaction is and what its properties are. The system is assumed to consist of some number of independent processes, each of which can fail at random. Communication is normally unreliable in that messages can be lost, but lower levels can use a timeout and retransmission protocol to recover from lost messages. Thus for this discussion we can assume that communication errors are handled transparently by underlying software.

Stable Storage

Storage comes in three categories. First we have ordinary RAM memory which is wiped out when the power fails or a machine crashes. Next we have disk storage, which survives CPU failures, but which can be lost in disk head crashes.

Finally, we have **stable storage**, which is designed to survive anything except major calamities like floods and earthquakes. Stable storage can be implemented with a pair of ordinary disks, as shown in Fig. 11-16(a). Each block on drive 2 is an exact copy of the corresponding block on drive 1. When a block is updated, first the block on drive 1 is updated and verified, then the same block on drive 2 is done.

Suppose the system crashes after drive 1 is updated, but before drive 2 is updated,

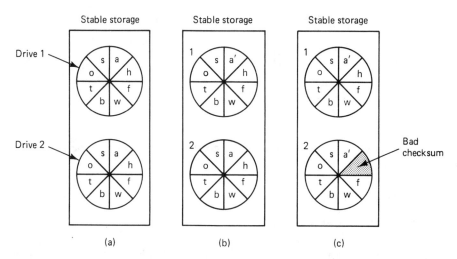

Fig. 11-16. (a) Stable storage. (b) Crash after drive 1 is updated. (c) Bad spot.

as shown in Fig. 11-16(b). Upon recovery, the disk can be compared block for block. Whenever two corresponding blocks differ, it can be assumed that drive 1 is the correct one (because drive 1 is always updated before drive 2), so the new block is copied from drive 1 to drive 2. When the recovery process is complete, both drives will again be identical.

Another potential problem is the spontaneous decay of a block. Dust particles or general wear and tear can give a previously valid block a sudden checksum error, without cause or warning, as shown in Fig. 11-16(c). When such an error is detected, the bad block can be regenerated from the corresponding block on the other drive.

As a consequence of its implementation, stable storage is well suited to applications that require a high degree of fault tolerance, such as atomic transactions. When data are written to stable storage and then read back to check that they have been written correctly, the chance of them subsequently being lost is extremely small.

Transaction Primitives

Programming using transactions requires special primitives that must either be supplied by the operating system or by the language runtime system. Examples are:

1. BEGIN_TRANSACTION- The commands that follow form a transaction.

2. END_TRANSACTION- Terminate the transaction and try to commit.

3. ABORT_TRANSACTION- Kill the transaction; restore the previous values.

4. READ- Read data from a file (or other object).

5. WRITE- Write data to a file (or other object).

The exact list of primitives depends on what kinds of objects are being used in the transaction. In a mail system, there might be primitives to send, receive, and forward mail. In an accounting system, they might be quite different. READ and WRITE are typical examples, however. Ordinary statements, procedure calls, and so on, are also allowed inside a transaction.

BEGIN_TRANSACTION and END_TRANSACTION are used to delimit the scope of a transaction. The operations between them form the body of the transaction. Either all of them are executed or none are executed. These may be system calls, library procedures, or bracketing statements in a language, depending on the implementation.

Consider, for example, the process of reserving a seat from White Plains, New York, to Malindi, Kenya, in an airline reservation system. One route is White Plains to JFK, JFK to Nairobi, and Nairobi to Malindi. In Fig. 11-17(a) we see reservations for these three separate flights being made as three actions. Now suppose that the first two flights have been reserved, but the third one is booked solid. The transaction is aborted and the results of the first two bookings are undone—the airline data base is restored to the value it had before the transaction started [see Fig. 11-17(b)].

```
BEGIN_TRANSACTION                     BEGIN_TRANSACTION
    reserve WP-JFK;                       reserve WP-JFK;
    reserve JFK-Nairobi;                  reserve JFK-Nairobi;
    reserve Nairobi-Malindi;              Nairobi-Malindi full ⇒ABORT_TRANSACTION;
END_TRANSACTION

            (a)                                       (b)
```

Fig. 11-17. (a) Transaction to reserve three flights commits. (b) Transaction aborts when third flight is unavailable.

Properties of Transactions

Transactions have three essential properties:

1. Serializability- Concurrent transactions do not interfere with each other.

2. Atomicity- To the outside world, the transaction happens indivisibly.

3. Permanence- Once a transaction commits, the changes are permanent.

The first property, **serializability,** insures that if two or more transactions are running at the same time, to each of them and to other processes, the final result looks as though all transactions ran sequentially in some (system dependent) order.

In Fig. 11-18(a)-(c) we have three transactions that are executed simultaneously by three separate processes. If they were to be run sequentially, the final value of x would be 1, 2, or 3, depending which one ran last (x could be a shared variable, a file, or some other kind of object). In Fig. 11-18(d) we see various orders, called **schedules,** in which they might be interleaved. Schedule 1 is actually serialized. In other words, the transactions run strictly sequentially, so it meets the serializability condition by definition. Schedule 2 is not serialized, but is still legal because it results in a value for x that could have been achieved by running the transactions strictly sequentially. The third one is illegal since it sets x to 5, something that no sequential order of the transactions could produce. It is up to the system to insure that individual operations are correctly interleaved. By allowing the system the freedom to choose any ordering of the operations it wants to—provided it gets the answer right—we eliminate the need for programmers to do their own mutual exclusion, thus simplifying the programming.

```
BEGIN_TRANSACTION          BEGIN_TRANSACTION          BEGIN_TRANSACTION
   x = 0;                     x = 0;                     x = 0;
   x = x + 1;                 x = x + 2;                 x = x + 3;
END_TRANSACTION            END_TRANSACTION            END_TRANSACTION

      (a)                        (b)                        (c)
```

Time ⟶

Schedule 1	x = 0;	x = x + 1;	x = 0;	x = x + 2;	x = 0;	x = x + 3;	Legal
Schedule 2	x = 0;	x = 0;	x = x + 1;	x = x + 2;	x = 0;	x = x + 3;	Legal
Schedule 3	x = 0;	x = 0;	x = x + 1;	x = 0;	x = x + 2;	x = x + 3;	Illegal

(d)

Fig. 11-18. (a) - (c) Three transactions. (d) Possible schedules.

The second key property exhibited by all transactions, **atomicity**, insures that each transaction either happens completely, or not at all, and if it happens, it happens in a single indivisible, instantaneous action. While a transaction is in progress, other processes (whether or not they are themselves involved in transactions) cannot see any of the intermediate states.

Suppose, for example, that some file is 10 bytes long when a transaction starts to append to it. If other processes read the file while the transaction is in progress, they see only the original 10 bytes, no matter how many bytes the transaction has appended. If the transactions successfully commits, the file instantaneously grows to its new size at the moment of commitment, with no intermediate states, no matter how many operations it took to get it there.

The third property, **permanence**, refers to the fact that once a transaction commits, no matter what happens, the transaction goes forward and the results become permanent. No failure after the commit can undo the results or cause them to be lost.

Nested Transactions

Transactions may contain subtransactions, often called **nested transactions**. The top-level transaction may fork off children that run in parallel with one another, on different processors, to gain performance or simplify programming. Each of these children may execute one or more subtransactions, or fork off its own children.

Subtransactions give rise to a subtle, but important, problem. Imagine that a transaction starts several subtransactions in parallel, and one of these commits, making its results visible to the parent transaction. After further computation, the parent aborts, restoring the entire system to the state it had before the top-level transaction started. Consequently, the results of the subtransaction that committed nevertheless must be undone. Thus the permanence referred to above only applies to top-level transactions.

Since transactions can be nested arbitrarily deeply, considerable administration is needed to get everything right. The semantics are clear, however. When any transaction or subtransaction starts, it is conceptually given a private copy of all objects in the entire system for it to manipulate as it wishes. If it aborts, its private universe just vanishes, as if it had never existed. If it commits, its private universe replaces the parent's one. Thus if a subtransaction commits and then later a new subtransaction is started, the second one sees the results produced by the first one.

11.4.3. Implementation

Transactions sound like a great idea, but how are they implemented? That is the question we will tackle in this section. It should be clear by now that if each process executing a transaction just updates the objects it uses (files, data base records, etc.) in place, then transactions will not be atomic, and changes will not magically vanish if the transaction aborts. Furthermore, the results of running multiple transactions will not be serializable either. Clearly some other implementation method is required. Two methods are commonly used. They will be discussed in turn below.

Private Workspace

Conceptually, when a process starts a transaction, it is given a private workspace containing all the files (and other objects) to which it has access. Until the transaction either commits or aborts, all of its reads and writes go to the private workspace, rather than the "real" one, by which we mean the normal file system. This observation leads directly to the first implementation method: actually giving a process a private workspace at the instant it begins a transaction.

The problem with this technique is that the cost of copying everything to a private workspace is prohibitive, but various optimizations make it feasible. The first optimization is based on the realization that when a process reads a file, but does not modify it, there is no need for a private copy. It can just use the real one (unless it has been changed since the transaction started). Consequently, when a process starts a transaction, it is sufficient to create a private workspace for it that is empty except for a pointer back to its parent's workspace. When the transaction is at the top level, the parent's workspace is the "real" file system. When the process opens a file for reading, the back pointers are followed until the file is located in the parent's (or further ancestor's) workspace.

When a file is opened for writing, it can be located in the same way as for reading, except that now it is first copied to the private workspace. However, a second optimization removes most of the copying, even here. Instead of copying the entire file, only the file's index is copied into the private workspace. The index is the block of data associated with each file telling where its disk blocks are. In UNIX, the index is the i-node. Using the private index, the file can be read in the usual way, since the disk addresses it contains are for the original disk blocks. However, when a file block is first modified, a copy of the block is made and the address of the copy inserted into the index, as shown in Fig. 11-19. The block can then be updated without affecting the original. Appended blocks are handled this way too. The new blocks are sometimes called **shadow blocks**.

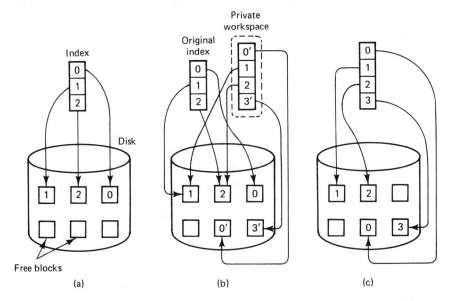

Fig. 11-19. (a) The file index and disk blocks for a three block file. (b) The situation after a transaction has modified block 0 and appended block 3. (c) After committing.

As can be seen from Fig. 11-19(b), the process running the transaction sees the modified file, but all other processes continue to see the original file. In a more complex transaction, the private workspace might contain a large number of files, instead of just one. If the transaction aborts, the private workspace is just deleted, and all the private blocks that it points to are put back on the free list. If the transaction commits, the private indices are moved into the parent's workspace atomically, as shown in Fig. 11-19(c). The blocks that are no longer reachable are put onto the free list.

Writeahead Log

The other common method of implementing transactions is the **writeahead log**, sometimes called an **intentions list**. With this method, files are actually modified in place, but before any block is changed, a record is written to the writeahead log on stable storage telling which transaction is making the change, which file and block is being changed, and what the old and new values are. Only after the log has been successfully written is the change made to the file.

Figure 11-20 gives an example of how the log works. In Fig. 11-20(a) we have a simple transaction that uses two shared variables (or other objects), x and y, both initialized to 0. For each of the three statements inside the transaction, a log record is written before executing the statement giving the old and new values, separated by a slash.

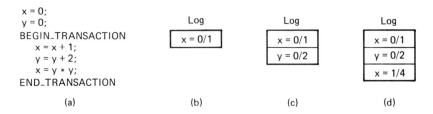

Fig. 11-20. (a) A transaction. (b) - (d) The log before each statement is executed.

If the transaction succeeds and is committed, a commit record is written to the log, but the data structures do not have to be changed as they have already been updated. If the transaction aborts, the log can be used to back up to the original state. Starting at the end and going backwards, each log record is read and the change described in it undone. This action is called a **rollback**.

The log can also be used for recovering from crashes. Suppose the process doing the transaction crashes just after having written the last log record of Fig. 11-20(d), but before changing x. After the failed machine is rebooted, the log is checked to see if any transactions were in progress at the time of the crash. When the last record is read and the current value of x is seen to be 1, it is clear that the crash occurred *before* the update was made, so x is set to 4. If, on the other hand, x is 4 at the time of recovery, it is equally clear that the crash occurred *after* the update, so nothing need be changed. Using the log, it is possible to go forward (do the transaction) or go backward (undo the transaction).

Two-Phase Commit Protocol

As we have pointed out repeatedly, the action of committing a transaction must be done atomically, that is, instantaneously and indivisibly. In a distributed system, the commit may require the cooperation of multiple processes on different machines, each of which holds some of the variables, files, and data bases, and other objects changed by the transaction. In this section we will study a protocol for achieving atomic commit in a distributed system.

The protocol we will look at is called the **two-phase commit protocol** (Gray, 1978). Although it is not the only such protocol, it is probably the most widely used one. The basic idea is illustrated in Fig. 11-21. One of the processes involved functions as the coordinator. Usually this is the one executing the transaction. The commit protocol begins when the coordinator writes a log entry saying that it is starting the commit protocol, followed by sending each of the other processes involved (the subordinates) a message telling them to prepare to commit.

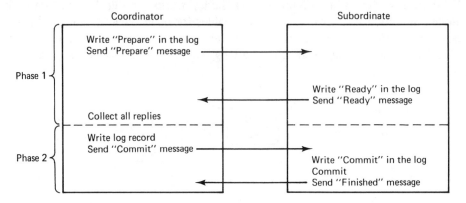

Fig. 11-21. The two-phase commit protocol when it succeeds.

When a subordinate gets the message it checks to see if it is ready to commit, makes a log entry, and sends back its decision. When the coordinator has received all the responses, it knows whether to commit or abort. If all the processes are prepared to commit, then the transaction is committed. If one or more are unable to commit (or do not respond), the transaction is aborted. Either way, the coordinator writes a log entry and then sends a message to each subordinate informing it of the decision. It is this write to the log that actually commits the transaction and makes it go forward no matter what else happens afterwards.

Due to the use of the log on stable storage, this protocol is highly resilient in the face of (multiple) crashes. If the coordinator crashes after having written the initial log record, upon recovery it can just continue where it left off, repeating the initial message if need be. If it crashes after having written the result of the vote to the log, upon recovery it can just reinform all the subordinates of the result. If a subordinate crashes before having replied to the first message, the coordinator will keep sending it messages, until it gives up. If it crashes later, it can see from the log where it was, and thus what it must do.

11.4.4. Concurrency Control

When multiple transactions are executing simultaneously in different processes (on different processors), some mechanism is needed to keep them out of each other's way. That mechanism is called a **concurrency control algorithm**. In this section we will study three different ones.

Locking

The oldest and most widely used concurrency control algorithm is **locking**. In the simplest form, when a process needs to read or write a file (or other object) as part of a transaction, it first locks the file. Locking can be done using a single centralized lock manager, or with a local lock manager on each machine for managing local files. In both cases the lock manager maintains a list of locked files, and rejects all attempts to lock files that are already locked by another process. Since well behaved processes do not attempt to access a file before it has been locked, setting a lock on a file keeps everyone else away from it and thus ensures that it will not change during the lifetime of the transaction. Locks are normally acquired and released by the transaction system, and do not require any action by the programmer.

This basic scheme is overly restrictive and can be improved by distinguishing read locks from write locks. If a read lock is set on a file, other read locks are permitted. Read locks are set to make sure that the file does not change (i.e., exclude all writers), but there is no reason to forbid other transactions from reading the file. In contrast, when a file is locked for writing, no other locks of any kind are permitted. Thus read locks are shared, but write locks must be exclusive.

For simplicity, we have assumed that the unit of locking is the entire file. In practice, it might be a smaller item, such as an individual record or page, or a larger item, such as an entire data base. The issue of how large an item to lock is called the **granularity of locking**. The finer the granularity, the more precise the lock can be, and the more parallelism can be achieved (e.g., by not blocking a process that wants to use the end of a file just because some other process is using the beginning). On the other hand, fine-grained locking requires more locks, is more expensive, and is more likely to lead to deadlocks.

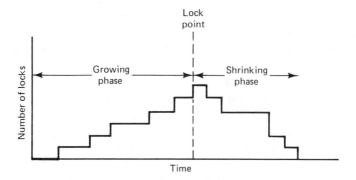

Fig. 11-22. Two-phase locking.

Acquiring and releasing locks precisely at the moment they are needed or no longer needed can lead to inconsistency and deadlocks. Instead, most transactions that are implemented by locking use what is called **two-phase locking**. In two-phase locking, which is illustrated in Fig. 11-22, the process first acquires all the locks it needs during the **growing phase**, then releases them during the **shrinking phase**. If the process refrains from updating any files until it reaches the shrinking phase, then failure to acquire some lock can be dealt with by simply releasing all locks, waiting a little while, and starting all over. Furthermore, it can be proven (Eswaran et al., 1976) that if all transactions use two-phase locking, then all schedules formed by interleaving them are serializable. This is why two-phase locking is widely used.

In many systems, the shrinking phase does not take place until the transaction has finished running, and has either committed or aborted. This policy is called **strict two-phase locking**, and has two main advantages. First, a transaction always reads a value written by a committed transaction; therefore one never has to abort a transaction because its calculations were based on a file it should not have seen. Second, all lock acquisitions and releases can be handled by the system without the transaction being aware of them: locks are acquired whenever a file is to be accessed and released when the transaction has finished. This policy eliminates **cascaded aborts**: having to undo a committed transaction because it saw a file it should not have seen.

Locking, even two phase-locking, can lead to deadlocks. If two processes each try to acquire the same pair of locks, but in the opposite order, a deadlock may result. The usual techniques apply here, such as acquiring all locks in some canonical order to prevent hold-and-wait cycles. Also possible is deadlock detection by maintaining an explicit graph of which process has which locks and wants which locks, and checking the graph for cycles. Finally, when it is known in advance that a lock will never be held longer than T sec, a timeout scheme can be used: if a lock remains continuously under the same ownership for longer than T sec, there must be a deadlock.

Optimistic Concurrency Control

A second approach to handling multiple transactions at the same time is **optimistic concurrency control** (Kung and Robinson, 1981). The idea behind this technique is surprisingly simple: just go ahead and do whatever you want to, without paying attention to what anybody else is doing. If there is a problem, worry about it later. (Many politicians use this algorithm too.) In practice, conflicts are relatively rare, so most of the time it works all right.

Although conflicts may be rare, they are not impossible, so some way is needed to handle them. What optimistic concurrency control does is keep track of which files have been read and written. At the point of committing, it checks all other transactions to see if any of its files have been changed since the transaction started. If so, the transaction is aborted. If not, it is committed.

Optimistic concurrency control fits best with the implementation based on private workspaces. That way, each transaction changes its files privately, without interference from the others. At the end, the new files are either committed or released.

The big advantages of optimistic concurrency control are that it is deadlock free and allows maximum parallelism because no process ever has to wait for a lock. The disadvantage is that sometimes it may fail, in which case the transaction has to be rerun. Under conditions of heavy load, the probability of failure may go up substantially, making optimistic concurrency control a poor choice.

Timestamps

A completely different approach to concurrency control is to assign each transaction a timestamp at the moment it does BEGIN_TRANSACTION (Reed, 1983). Using Lamport's algorithm, we can ensure that the timestamps are unique, which is important here. Every file in the system has a read timestamp and a write timestamp associated with it, telling which committed transaction last read and wrote it, respectively. If transactions are short and widely spaced in time, then it will normally occur that when a process tries to access a file, the file's read and write timestamps will be lower (older) than the current transaction's timestamp. This ordering means that the transactions are being processed in the proper order, so everything is all right.

When the ordering is incorrect, it means that a transaction that started later than the current one has managed to get in there, access the file, and commit. This situation means that the current transaction is too late, so it is aborted. In a sense, this mechanism is also optimistic, like that of Kung and Robinson, although the details are quite different. In Kung and Robinson's method, we are hoping that concurrent transactions do not use the same files. In the timestamp method, we do not mind if concurrent transactions use the same files, as long as the lower numbered transaction always goes first.

It is easiest to explain the timestamp method by means of an example. Imagine that there are three transactions, alpha, beta, and gamma. Alpha ran a long time ago, and used every file needed by beta and gamma, so all their files have read and write timestamps set to alpha's timestamp. Beta and gamma start concurrently, with beta having a lower timestamp than gamma (but higher than alpha, of course).

Let us first consider beta writing a file. Call its timestamp, T, and the read and write timestamps of the file to be written T_{RD} and T_{WR}, respectively. Unless gamma has snuck in already and committed, both T_{RD} and T_{WR} will be alpha's timestamp, and thus less than T. In Fig. 11-23(a) and (b) we see that T is larger than both T_{RD} and T_{WR} (gamma has not already committed), so the write is accepted and done tentatively. It will become permanent when beta commits. Beta's timestamp is now recorded in the file as a tentative write.

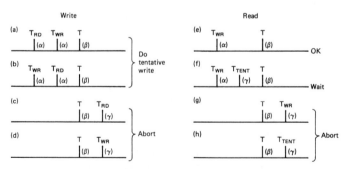

Fig. 11-23. Concurrency control using timestamps.

In Fig. 11-23(c) and (d) beta is out of luck. Gamma has either read (c) or written (d) the file and committed. Beta's transaction is aborted. However, it can apply for a new timestamp and start all over again.

Now look at reads. In Fig. 11-23(e), there is no conflict, so the read can happen immediately. In Fig. 11-23(f), some interloper has gotten in there and is trying to write the file. The interloper's timestamp is lower than beta's, so beta simply waits until the interloper commits, at which time it can read the new file and continue.

In Fig. 11-23(g), gamma has changed the file and already committed. Again beta must abort. In Fig. 11-23(h), gamma is in the process of changing the file, although it has not committed yet. Still, beta is too late and must abort.

Timestamping has different properties than locking. When a transaction encounters a larger (later) timestamp, it aborts, whereas under the same circumstances with locking it would either wait or be able to proceed immediately. On the other hand, it is deadlock free, which is a big plus.

All in all, transactions offer many advantages and thus are a promising technique for building reliable distributed systems. Their chief problem is their great implementation complexity, which yields low performance. These problems are being worked on, and perhaps in due course of time they will be solved.

11.5. DEADLOCKS IN DISTRIBUTED SYSTEMS

Deadlocks in distributed systems are similar to deadlocks in single processor systems, only worse. They are harder to avoid, prevent, or even detect, and harder to cure when tracked down because all the relevant information is scattered over many machines. In some systems, such as distributed data base systems, they can be extremely serious, so it is important to understand how they differ from ordinary deadlocks, and what can be done about them.

Some people make a distinction between two kinds of distributed deadlocks: communication deadlocks and resource deadlocks. A communication deadlock occurs, for example, when process A is trying to send a message to process B, which in turn is trying to send one to process C, which is trying to send one to A. There are various scenarios in which this situation leads to deadlock, such as no buffers being available. A resource deadlock occurs when processes are fighting over exclusive access to I/O devices, files, locks, or other resources.

We will not make that distinction here, since communication channels, buffers, and so on, are also resources and can be modeled as resource deadlocks. Furthermore, circular communication patterns of the type just described are quite rare in most systems. In client-server systems, for example, a client might send a message (or perform an RPC) with a file server, which might send a message to a disk server. However, it is unlikely that the disk server, acting as a client, would send a message to the original client, expecting it to act like a server. Thus the circular wait condition is unlikely to occur as a result of communication alone.

As we studied earlier, four strategies are commonly used to handle deadlocks:

1. The ostrich algorithm (ignore the problem).

2. Detection (allow deadlocks to occur, detect them, and try to recover).

3. Prevention (statically make deadlocks structurally impossible).

4. Avoidance (avoid deadlocks by allocating resources carefully).

All four are potentially applicable to distributed systems. The ostrich algorithm is as good and as popular in distributed systems as it is in single processor systems. In distributed systems used for programming, office automation, process control, and many other applications, no system-wide deadlock mechanism is present, although individual applications, such as distributed data bases, can implement their own if they need one.

Deadlock detection and recovery is also popular, primarily because prevention and avoidance are so difficult. We will discuss several algorithms for deadlock detection below.

Deadlock prevention is also possible, although more difficult than in single processor systems. However, in the presence of atomic transactions, some options become available that we have not previously considered. Two algorithms are discussed below.

Finally, deadlock avoidance is never used in distributed systems. It is not even used in single processor systems, so why should it be used in the more difficult case of distributed systems. The problem is that the banker's algorithm and similar algorithms need to know (in advance), how much of each resource every process will eventually need. This information is rarely, if ever, available.

Thus our discussion of deadlocks in distributed systems will focus on just two of the techniques: deadlock detection and deadlock prevention.

11.5.1. Distributed Deadlock Detection

Finding general methods for preventing or avoiding distributed deadlocks appears to be quite difficult, so many researchers have tried to deal with the simpler problem of just detecting deadlocks, rather than trying to inhibit their occurrence.

However, the presence of atomic transactions in some distributed systems makes a major conceptual difference. When a deadlock is detected in a conventional operating system, the way to resolve it is to kill off one or more processes. Doing so invariably leads to one or more unhappy users. When a deadlock is detected in a system based on atomic transactions, it is resolved by aborting one or more transactions. But as we have seen in detail above, transactions have been designed to withstand being aborted. When a transaction is aborted because it contributes to a deadlock, the system is first restored to the state it had before the transaction began, at which point the transaction can start again. With a little bit of luck, it will succeed the second time. Thus the difference is that the consequences of killing off a process are much less severe when transactions are used than when they are not used.

Centralized Deadlock Detection

As a first attempt, we can use a centralized deadlock detection algorithm and try to imitate the nondistributed algorithm. Although each machine maintains the resource graph for its own processes and resources, a central coordinator maintains the resource graph for the whole system (the union of all the individual graphs). When the coordinator detects a cycle, it kills off one process to break the deadlock.

Unlike the centralized case, where all the information is automatically available in the right place, in a distributed system it has to be sent there explicitly. Each machine maintains the graph for its own processes and resources. Several possibilities exist for getting it there. First, whenever an arc is added or deleted from the resource graph, a message can be sent to the coordinator providing the update. Second, periodically, every process can send a list of arcs added or deleted since the previous update. This method requires fewer messages than the first one. Third, the coordinator can ask for information when it needs it.

Unfortunately, none of these methods work well. Consider a system with processes A and B running on machine 0, and process C running on machine 1. Three resources exist: R, S, and T. Initially, the situation is as shown in Fig. 11-24(a) and (b), A holds S, but wants R, which it cannot have because B is using it. C has T and wants S too. The coordinator's view of the world is shown in Fig. 11-24(c). This configuration is safe. As soon as B finishes, A can get R and finish, releasing S for C.

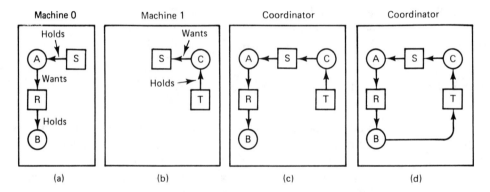

Fig. 11-24. (a) Initial resource graph for machine 0. (b) Initial resource graph for machine 1. (c) The coordinator's view of the world. (d) The situation after the delayed message.

After a while, B releases R and asks for T, a perfectly legal and safe swap. Machine 0 sends a message to the coordinator announcing the release of R, and machine 1 sends a message to the coordinator announcing the fact that B is now waiting for its resource, T. Unfortunately, the message from machine 1 arrives first, leading the coordinator to construct the graph of Fig. 11-24(d). The coordinator incorrectly concludes that a deadlock exists and kills some process. Such a situation is called a **false deadlock**. Many deadlock algorithms in distributed systems produce false deadlocks like this due to incomplete or delayed information.

One possible way out might be to use Lamport's algorithm to provide global time. Since the message from machine 1 to the coordinator is triggered by the request from machine 0, the message from machine 1 to the coordinator will indeed have a later timestamp than the message from machine 0 to the coordinator. When the coordinator gets the message from machine 1 that leads it to suspect deadlock, it could send a message to every machine in the system saying: "I just received a message with timestamp T which leads to deadlock. If anyone has a message for me with an earlier timestamp, please send it immediately." When every machine has replied, positively or negatively, the coordinator will see that the arc from R to B has vanished, so the system is still safe. Although this method eliminates the false deadlock, it requires global time and is expensive. Furthermore, other situations exist where eliminating false deadlock is much harder.

Distributed Deadlock Detection

Many distributed deadlock detection algorithms have been published. Surveys of the subject are given in Knapp (1987) and Singhal (1989). Let us examine a typical one here, the Chandy-Misra-Haas algorithm (Chandy et al., 1983). In this algorithm, processes are allowed to request multiple resources (e.g., locks) at once, instead of one at a time. By allowing multiple requests simultaneously, the growing phase of a transaction can be speeded up considerably. The consequence of this change to the model is that a process may now wait on two or more resources simultaneously.

In Fig. 11-25, we present a modified resource graph, where only the processes are shown. Each arc passes through a resource, as usual, only for simplicity the resources have been omitted from the figure. Notice that process 3 on machine 1 is waiting for two resources, one held by process 4 and one held by process 5.

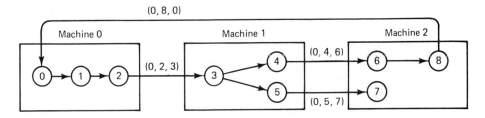

Fig. 11-25. The Chandy-Misra-Haas distributed deadlock detection algorithm.

Some of the processes are waiting for local resources, such as process 1, but others, such are process 2, are waiting for resources that are located on a different machine. It is precisely these cross-machine arcs that make looking for cycles difficult. The Chandy-Misra-Haas algorithm is invoked when a process has to wait for some resource, for example, process 0 blocking on process 1. At that point a special **probe** message is generated and sent to the process (or processes) holding the needed resources. The message consists of three numbers: the process that just blocked, the process sending the message, and the process to whom it is being sent. The initial message from 0 to 1 contains the triple (0, 0, 1).

When the message arrives, the recipient checks to see if it itself is waiting for any processes. If so, the message is updated, keeping the first field but replacing the second field by its own process number and the third one by the number of the process it is waiting for. The message is then sent to the process on which it is blocked. If it is blocked on multiple processes, all of them are sent (different) messages. This algorithm is followed whether the resource is local or remote. In Fig. 11-25 we see the remote messages labeled (0, 2, 3), (0, 4, 6), (0, 5, 7), and (0, 8, 0). If a message goes all the way around and comes back to the original sender, that is, the process listed in the first field, a cycle exists and the system is deadlocked.

There are various ways the deadlock can be broken. One way is to have the process that initiated the probe commit suicide. However, this method has problems if several processes simultaneously invoke the algorithm. In Fig. 11-25, for example, imagine that both 0 and 6 block at the same moment, and both initiate probes. Each would eventually discover the deadlock, and each would kill itself. This is overkill. Getting rid of one of them would have been sufficient.

An alternative algorithm is to have each process add its identity to the end of the probe message, so that when it returned to the initial sender, the complete cycle would be listed. The sender can then see which process has the highest number, and kill that one, or send it a message asking it to kill itself. Either way, if multiple processes discover the same cycle at the same time, they will all choose the same victim.

There are few areas of computer science in which theory and practice diverge as much as in distributed deadlock detection algorithms. Discovering yet another deadlock detection algorithm is the goal of many a researcher. Unfortunately, these models often have little relation to reality. For example, some of the algorithms require processes to send probes when they are blocked. However, sending a probe when you are blocked is not entirely trivial.

Many of the papers contain elaborate analyses of the performance of the new algorithm, pointing out for example, that while the new one requires two traversals of the cycle, it uses shorter messages, as if these factors balanced out somehow. The authors would no doubt be surprised to learn that a typical "short" message (20 bytes) on a LAN takes about 1 msec, and a typical "long" message (100 bytes) on the same LAN takes perhaps 1.1 msec. It would also no doubt come as a shock to these people to realize that experimental measurements have shown that 90 percent of all deadlock cycles involve exactly two processes (Gray, 1981).

Worst of all, a large fraction of all the published algorithms in this area are just plain wrong, including those proven to be correct (Knapp, 1987 and Singhal, 1989 point out some examples). It often occurs that shortly after an algorithm is invented, proven correct, and then published, somebody finds a counterexample. Thus we have an active research area in which the model of the problem does not correspond well to reality, the solutions found are generally impractical, the performance analyses given are meaningless, and the proven results are frequently incorrect. To end on a positive note, this is an area that offers great opportunities for improvement.

11.5.2. Distributed Deadlock Prevention

Deadlock prevention consists of carefully designing the system so that deadlocks are structurally impossible. Various techniques include allowing processes to hold only one resource at a time, requiring processes to request all their resources initially, and making processes release all resources when asking for a new one. All of these are cumbersome in practice. A method that sometimes works is to order all the resources and require processes to acquire them in strictly increasing order. This approach means that a process can never hold a high resource and ask for a low one, thus making cycles impossible.

However, in a distributed system with global time and atomic transactions, two other practical algorithms are possible. Both are based on the idea of assigning each transaction a global timestamp at the moment it starts. As in many timestamp-based algorithms, in these two it is essential that no two transactions are ever assigned exactly the same timestamp. As we have seen, Lamport's algorithm guarantees uniqueness (effectively by using process numbers to break ties).

The idea behind the algorithm is that when one process is about to block waiting for a resource that another process is using, a check is made to see which one has a larger timestamp (i.e., is younger). We can then allow the wait only if the waiting process has a lower timestamp (is older) than the process waited for. In this manner, following any chain of waiting processes, the timestamps always increase, so cycles are impossible. Alternatively, we can allow processes to wait only if the waiting process has a higher timestamp (is younger) than the process waited for, in which case the timestamps decrease along the chain.

Although both methods prevent deadlocks, it is wiser to give priority to older processes. They have run longer, so the system has a larger investment in them, and they are likely to hold more resources. Also, a young process that is killed off will eventually age to the point that it is the oldest one in the system, so this choice eliminates starvation. As we have pointed out before, killing a transaction is relatively harmless, since by definition it can be safely restarted later.

To make this algorithm clearer, consider the situation of Fig. 11-26. In (a), an old process wants a resource held by a young process. In (b), a young process wants a resource held by an old process. In one case we should allow the process to wait; in the other we should kill it. Suppose we label (a) *dies* and (b) *wait*. Then we are killing off an old process trying to use a resource held by a young process, which is inefficient. Thus we must label it the other way, as shown in the figure. Under these conditions, the arrows always point in the direction of increasing transaction numbers, making cycles impossible. This algorithm is called **wait-die**.

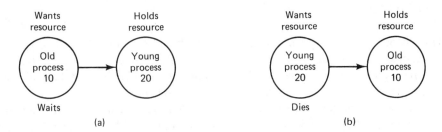

Fig. 11-26. The wait-die deadlock prevention algorithm.

Once we are assuming the existence of transactions, we can do something that had previously been forbidden: take resources away from running processes. In effect we are saying that when a conflict arises, instead of killing the process making the request, we can kill the resource owner instead. Without transactions, killing a process might have severe consequences, since the process might have modified files etc. With transactions, these effects will vanish magically when the transaction dies.

Now consider the situation of Fig. 11-27, where we are going to allow preemption. Given that our system believes in ancestor worship, as we discussed above, we do not want a young whippersnapper preempting an venerable old sage, so Fig. 11-27(a) and not Fig. 11-27(b) is labeled *preempt*. We can now safely label Fig. 11-27(b) *wait*. This algorithm is known as **wound-wait**, because one transaction is supposedly wounded (it is actually killed) and the other waits. It is unlikely that this algorithm will make it to the Nomenclature Hall of Fame.

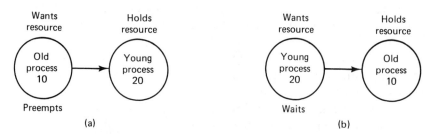

Fig. 11-27. The wound-wait deadlock prevention algorithm.

If an old process wants a resource held by a young one, the old process preempts the young one, whose transaction is then killed, as depicted in Fig. 11-27(a). The young one probably starts up again immediately, and tries to acquire the resource, leading to Fig. 11-27(b), forcing it to wait. Contrast this algorithm with wait-die. There, if an oldtimer wants a resource held by a young squirt, the oldtimer waits politely. However, if the young one wants a resource held by the old one, the young one is killed. It will undoubtedly start up again, and be killed again. This cycle may go on many times before the old one releases the resource. Wound-wait does not have this nasty property.

11.6. SUMMARY

This chapter is about synchronization in distributed systems. We started out by giving Lamport's algorithm for synchronizing clocks without reference to external time sources, and later saw how useful this algorithm is. We also saw how physical clocks can be used for synchronization when real time is important.

Next we looked at mutual exclusion in distributed systems and studied three algorithms. The centralized one kept all the information at a single site. The distributed one ran the computation at all sites in parallel. The token ring one passed control around the ring. Each one has its strengths and weaknesses.

Many distributed algorithms require a coordinator, so we looked at two ways of electing a coordinator, the bully algorithm and another ring algorithm.

Although all of the foregoing are interesting and important, they are all low level concepts. Transactions are a high level concept that makes it easier for the programmer to handle mutual exclusion, locking, fault tolerance, and deadlocks in a distributed system. We looked at the transaction model, how transactions are implemented, and three concurrency control schemes: locking, optimistic concurrency control, and timestamps.

Finally, we revisited the problem of deadlocks and saw some algorithms for detecting and preventing them in distributed systems.

PROBLEMS

1. Add a new message to Fig. 11-2(b) that is concurrent with message A, that is, it neither happens before A nor happens after A.

2. Name at least three sources of delay that can be introduced between WWV broadcasting the time and the processors in a distributed system setting their internal clocks.

3. Consider the behavior of two machines in a distributed system. Both have clocks that are supposed to tick 1000 times per millisec. One of them actually does, but the other only ticks 990 times per millisec. If UTC updates come in once a minute, what is the maximum clock skew that will occur?

4. In the centralized approach to mutual exclusion (Fig. 11-9), upon receiving a message from a processing releasing its exclusive access to the critical region it was using, the coordinator normally grants permission to the first process on the queue. Give another possible algorithm for the coordinator to use.

5. Consider Fig. 11-9 again. Suppose the coordinator crashes. Does this always bring the system down? If not, under what circumstances does this happen? Is there any way to avoid the problem and make the system able to tolerate coordinator crashes?

6. Ricart and Agrawala's algorithm has the problem that if a process has crashed and does not reply to a request from another process to enter a critical region, the lack of response will be interpreted as denial of permission. We suggested that all requests be answered immediately, to make it easy to detect crashed processes. Are there any circumstances where even this method is insufficient? Discuss.

7. A distributed system may have multiple, independent critical regions. Imagine that process 0 wants to enter critical region A and process 1 wants to enter critical region B. Can Ricart and Agrawala's algorithm lead to deadlocks? Explain your answer.

8. In Fig. 11-13 a small optimization is possible. What is it?

9. Suppose two processes detect the demise of the coordinator simultaneously and both decide to hold an election using the bully algorithm. What happens?

10. In Fig. 11-14 we have two *ELECTION* messages circulating simultaneously. While it does no harm to have two of them, it would be more elegant if one could be killed off. Devise an algorithm for doing this without affecting the operation of the basic election algorithm.

11. In Fig. 11-15 we saw a way to atomically update an inventory list using magnetic tape. Since a tape can easily be simulated on disk (as a file), why do you think this method is not used any more?

12. For some ultrasensitive applications it is conceivable that stable storage implemented with two disks is not reliable enough. Can the idea be extended to three disks? If so, how would it work? If not, why not?

13. In Fig. 11-18(d) three schedules are shown, two legal and one illegal. For the same transactions, give a complete list of all values that x might have at the end, and state which are legal and which are illegal.

14. When a private workspace is used to implement transactions, it may happen that a large number of file indices must be copied back to the parent's workspace. How can this be done without introducing race conditions?

15. In the writeahead log, both the old and new values are stored in the log entries. Is it not adequate to just store the new value? What good is the old one?

16. In Fig. 11-21, at what instant is the point-of-no-return reached? That is, when is the atomic commit actually performed?

17. Give the full algorithm for whether an attempt to lock a file should succeed or fail. Consider both read and write locks, and the possibility that the file was unlocked, read locked, or write locked.

18. Systems that use locking for concurrency control usually distinguish read locks from write locks. What should happen if a process has already acquired a read lock and now wants to change it into a write lock? What about changing a write lock into a read lock?

19. Is optimistic concurrency control more or less restrictive than using timestamps? Why?

20. Does using timestamping for concurrency control insure serializability? Discuss.

21. We have repeatedly said that when a transaction is aborted, the world is restored to its previous state, as though the transaction had never happened. We lied. Give an example where resetting the world is impossible.

22. The centralized deadlock detection algorithm described in the text initially gave a false deadlock, but was later patched up using global time. Suppose that it has been decided not to maintain global time (too expensive). Devise an alternative way to fix the bug in the algorithm.

23. A process with transaction timestamp 50 needs a resource held by a process with transaction timestamp 100. What happens in:

a. Wait-die?
b. Wound-wait?

12

PROCESSES AND PROCESSORS
IN DISTRIBUTED SYSTEMS

In the previous two chapters, we have looked at two related topics, communication and synchronization in distributed systems. In this chapter we will switch to a different subject: processes. Although processes are also an important concept in uniprocessor systems, in this chapter we will emphasize aspects of process management that are usually not studied in the context of classical operating systems. In particular, we will look at how the existence of multiple processors is dealt with.

In many distributed systems, it is possible to have multiple threads of control within a process. This ability provides some important advantages, but also introduces various problems. We will study these issues first. Then we come to the subject of how the processors and processes are organized, and see that several different models are possible. Finally we will look at processor allocation and scheduling in distributed systems.

12.1. THREADS

In most traditional operating systems, each process has an address space and a single thread of control. In fact, that is almost the definition of a process. Nevertheless, there are frequently situations in which it is desirable to have multiple threads of control that share a single address space, but run in quasi-parallel, as though they were in fact separate processes (except for the shared address space). In this section we will discuss these situations and how they can be best handled.

12.1.1. Introduction to Threads

Consider, for example, a file server that has to block occasionally waiting for the disk. If the server had multiple threads of control, a second thread could run while the first one was sleeping. The net result would be a higher throughput and better performance. It is not possible to achieve this goal by creating two independent server processes because they must share a common buffer cache, which requires them to be in the same address space. Thus a new mechanism is needed, one that is generally not found in single processor operating systems (although there is no reason why it could not be).

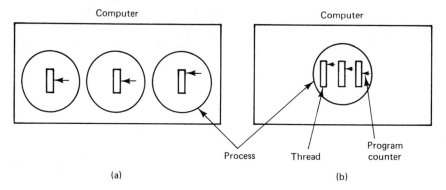

Fig. 12-1. (a) Three processes with one thread each. (b) One process with three threads.

In Fig. 12-1(a) we see a machine with three processes. Each process has its own program counter, its own stack, its own register set, and its own address space. The processes have nothing to do with each other, except that they may be able to communicate through the system's interprocess communication primitives, such as semaphores, monitors, or messages. In Fig. 12-1(b) we see another machine, with one process. Only this process contains multiple threads of control, usually just called **threads,** or sometimes **lightweight processes.** In many respects, threads are like little mini-processes. Each thread runs strictly sequentially, and has its own program counter and stack to keep track of where it is. Threads share the CPU, just as processes do: first one thread runs, then another does (timesharing). Only on a multiprocessor do they actually run in parallel. Threads can create child threads and can block waiting for system calls to complete, just like regular processes. While one thread is blocked, another thread in the same process can run, in exactly the same way that when one process blocks, another process in the same machine can run. The analogy, thread is to process as process is to machine, holds in many ways.

Different threads in a process are not quite as independent as different processes, however. All threads have exactly the same address space, which means they also share the same global variables. Since every thread can access every virtual address, one thread can read, write, or even completely wipe out another thread's stack. There is no protection between threads because (1) it is impossible, and (2) it should not be necessary. Unlike different processes, which may be from different users and which may be hostile to one another, a process is always owned by a single user, who has presumably created multiple threads so they can cooperate, not fight. In addition to sharing an address space, all the threads share the same set of open files, child processes, timers, and signals, etc. as shown in Fig. 12-2. Thus the organization of Fig. 12-1(a) would be used when the three processes are essentially unrelated, whereas Fig. 12-1(b) would be appropriate when the three threads are actually part of the same job and are actively and closely cooperating with each other.

Per thread items	Per process items
Program counter Stack Register set Child threads State	Address space Global variables Open files Child processes Timers Signals Semaphores Accounting information

Fig. 12-2. Per thread and per process concepts.

Like traditional processes (i.e., processes with only one thread), threads can be in any one of several states: running, blocked, ready, or terminated. A running thread currently has the CPU and is active. A blocked thread is waiting for another thread to unblock it (e.g., on a semaphore). A ready thread is scheduled to run, and will as soon as its turn comes up. Finally, a terminated thread is one that has exited, but which has not yet been collected by its parent (in UNIX terms, the parent thread has not yet done a WAIT).

12.1.2. Thread Usage

Threads were invented to allow parallelism to be combined with sequential execution and blocking system calls. Consider our file server example again. One possible organization is shown in Fig. 12-3(a). Here one thread, the **dispatcher**, reads incoming requests for work from the system mailbox. After examining the request, it chooses an idle (i.e., blocked) **worker thread** and hands it the request, most likely by writing a pointer to the message into a special word associated with each thread. The dispatcher then wakes up the sleeping worker (e.g., by doing an UP on the semaphore on which it is sleeping).

When the worker wakes up, it checks to see if the request can be satisfied from the shared block cache, to which all threads have access. If not, it sends a message to the disk to get the needed block (assuming it is a READ), and goes to sleep awaiting completion of the disk operation. The scheduler will now be invoked, and another thread will be started, possibly the dispatcher, in order to acquire more work, or possibly another worker that is now ready to run.

Consider how the file server could be written in the absence of threads. One

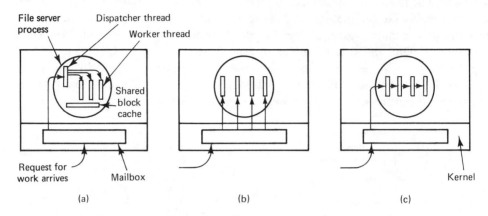

Fig. 12-3. Three organizations of threads in a process. (a) Dispatcher/worker model. (b) Team model. (c) Pipeline model.

possibility is to have it operate as a single thread. The main loop of the file server gets a request, examines it and carries it out to completion before getting the next one. While waiting for the disk, the server is idle and does not process any other requests. If the file server is running on a dedicated machine, as is commonly the case, the CPU is simply idle while the file server is waiting for the disk. The net result is that many fewer requests/sec can be processed. Thus threads gain considerable performance, but each thread is programmed sequentially, in the usual way.

So far we have seen two possible designs: a multithreaded file server and a single-threaded file server. Suppose that threads are not available, but the system designers find the performance loss due to single threading unacceptable. A third possibility is to run the server as a big finite-state machine. When a request comes in, the one and only thread examines it. If it can be satisfied from the cache, fine, but if not, send a message to the disk.

However, instead of blocking, it records the state of the current request in a table, and then goes and gets the next message. The next message may either be a request for new work, or a reply from the disk about a previous operation. If it is new work, that work is started. If it is a reply from the disk, the relevant information is fetched from the table, and the reply processed. Since it is not permitted to send a message and block waiting for a reply here, RPC cannot be used. The primitives must be non-blocking calls to *send* and *receive*.

In this design, the "sequential process" model that we had in the first two cases is lost. The state of the computation must be explicitly saved and restored in the table for every message sent and received. In effect, we are simulating the threads and their stacks the hard way. The process is being operated as a finite-state machine that gets an event and then reacts to it, depending on what is in it.

It should now be clear what threads have to offer. They make it possible to retain the idea of sequential processes that make blocking system calls (e.g., RPC to talk to the disk) and still achieve parallelism. Blocking system calls make programming easier and parallelism improves performance. The single-threaded server retains the ease of blocking system calls, but gives up performance. The finite-state machine approach achieves high performance through parallelism, but uses nonblocking calls and thus is hard to program. These models are summarized in Fig. 12-4.

Model	Characteristics
Threads	Parallelism, blocking system calls
Single-thread process	No parallelism, blocking system calls
Finite-state machine	Parallelism, nonblocking system calls

Fig. 12-4. Three ways to construct a server.

The dispatcher structure of Fig. 12-3(a) is not the only way to organize a multithreaded process. The **team** model of Fig. 12-3(b) is also a possibility. Here all the threads are equals, and each one gets and processes its own requests. There is no dispatcher. Sometimes work comes in that a thread cannot handle, especially if each thread is specialized to handle a particular kind of work. In this case, a job queue can be maintained, with pending work kept in the job queue. With this organization, a thread should first check the job queue before looking in the system mailbox.

Threads can also be organized in the **pipeline** model of Fig. 12-3(c). In this model, the first thread generates some data and passes them on to the next one for processing. The data continue from thread to thread, with processing going on at each step. Although this is not appropriate for file servers, for other problems, such as the producer-consumer, it may be a good choice. Pipelining is widely used in many areas of computer systems, from the internal structure of RISC CPUs to UNIX command lines.

Threads are frequently also useful for clients. For example, if a client wants a file to be replicated on multiple servers, it can have one thread talk to each server. Another use for client threads is to handle signals, such as interrupts from the keyboard (DEL or BREAK). Instead of letting the signal interrupt the process, one thread is dedicated full time to waiting for signals. Normally it is blocked, but when a signal comes in, it wakes up and processes the signal. Thus using threads can eliminate the need for user-level interrupts.

Another argument for threads has nothing to do with RPC or communication. Some applications are easier to program using parallel processes, the producer-consumer problem for example. Whether the producer and consumer actually run in parallel is secondary. They are programmed that way because it makes the software design simpler. Since they must share a common buffer, having them in separate processes will not do. Threads fit the bill exactly here.

Finally, although we are not explicitly discussing the subject here, in a multiprocessor system, it is possible for the threads in a single address space to actually run in parallel, on different CPUs. This is, in fact, one of the major ways sharing is done on such systems. On the other hand, a properly designed program that uses threads should work equally well on a single CPU that timeshares the threads or on a true multiprocessor, so the software issues are pretty much the same either way.

12.1.3. Design Issues for Threads Packages

A set of primitives (e.g., library calls) available to the user relating to threads is called a **threads package**. In this section we will consider some of the issues concerned with the architecture and functionality of threads packages. In the next one we will consider how threads packages can be implemented.

The first issue we will look at is thread management. Two alternatives are possible here, static threads and dynamic threads. With a static design, the choice of how many threads there will be is made when the program is written or when it is compiled. Each one is allocated a fixed stack. This approach is simple, but inflexible.

A more general approach is to allow threads to be created and destroyed on-the-fly during execution. The thread creation call usually specifies the thread's main program (as a pointer to a procedure) and a stack size, and may specify other parameters as well, for example, a scheduling priority. The call usually returns a thread identifier to be used in subsequent calls involving the thread. In this model, a process starts out with one (implicit) thread, but can create more threads as needed.

Threads can be terminated in one of two ways. A thread can exit of its own accord when it finishes its job, or it can be killed from outside. In this respect, threads are like processes. In many situations, such as the file servers of Fig. 12-3, the threads are created immediately after the process starts up and are never killed.

Since threads share a common memory, they can, and usually do, use it for holding data that are shared among multiple threads, such as the buffers in a producer-consumer system. Access to shared data is usually programmed using critical regions, to prevent multiple threads from trying to access the same data at the same time. Critical regions are most easily implemented using semaphores, monitors, and similar constructions. One technique that is commonly used in threads packages is the **mutex**, which is a kind of watered-down semaphore. A mutex is always in one of two states, unlocked or locked. Two operations are defined on mutexes. The first one, LOCK, attempts to lock the mutex. If the mutex is unlocked, the LOCK succeeds and the mutex becomes locked in a single atomic action. If two threads try to lock the same mutex at exactly the same instant, an event that is only possible on a multiprocessor, on which different threads run on different CPUs, one of them wins and the other loses. A thread that attempts to lock a mutex that is already locked, such as the loser above, is blocked.

The UNLOCK operation unlocks a mutex. If one or more threads are waiting on the mutex, exactly one of them is released. The rest continue to wait.

Another operation that is sometimes provided is TRYLOCK, which attempts to lock a mutex. If the mutex is unlocked, TRYLOCK returns a status code indicating success. If, however, the mutex is locked, TRYLOCK does not block the thread. Instead it returns a status code indicating failure.

Mutexes are like binary semaphores (i.e., semaphores that may only have the values 0 or 1). They are not like counting semaphores. Limiting them in this way makes them easier to implement.

Another synchronization feature that is sometimes available in threads packages is the **condition variable**, which is similar to the condition variable used for synchronization in monitors. Each condition variable is normally associated with a mutex at the time it is created. The difference between mutexes and condition variables is that mutexes are used for short-term locking, mostly for guarding the entry to critical regions. Condition variables are used for long-term waiting until a resource becomes available.

The following situation occurs all the time. A thread locks a mutex to gain entry to a critical region. Once inside the critical region, it examines system tables and discovers that some resource it needs is busy. If it simply locks a second mutex (associated with the resource), the outer mutex will remain locked and the thread holding the resource will not be able to enter the critical region to free it. Deadlock results. Unlocking the outer mutex lets other threads into the critical region, causing chaos.

One solution is to use condition variables to acquire the resource, as shown in Fig. 12-5(a). Here, waiting on the condition variable is defined to automatically perform the wait and unlock the mutex atomically. Later, when the thread holding the resource frees it, as shown in Fig. 12-5(b), it calls *wakeup*, which is defined to either wakeup exactly one thread, or all the threads waiting on the specified condition variable. The use of WHILE instead of IF in Fig. 12-5(a) guards against the case that the thread is awakened but that someone else seizes the resource before the thread runs.

```
lock mutex;                               lock mutex;
    check data structures;                    mark resource as free;
    while (resource busy)                 unlock mutex;
        wait (condition variable);        wakeup (condition variable);
    mark resource as busy;
unlock mutex;

        (a)                                       (b)
```

Fig. **12-5.** Use of mutexes and condition variables.

The need for the ability to wake up all the threads, rather than just one, is demonstrated in the reader-writer problem. When a writer finishes, it may choose to wake up pending writers or pending readers. If it chooses readers, it should wake them all up, not just one. Providing thread primitives for waking up exactly one thread and for waking up all the threads provides the needed flexibility.

The code of a thread normally consists of multiple procedures, just like a process. These may have local variables, global variables, and procedure parameters. Local variables and parameters do not cause any trouble, but variables that are global to a thread but not global to the entire program can cause difficulty.

As an example, consider the *errno* variable maintained by UNIX. When a process (or a thread) makes a system call that fails, the error code is put into *errno*. In Fig. 12-6, thread 1 executes the system call ACCESS to find out if it has permission to access a certain file. The operating system returns the answer in the global variable *errno*. After control has returned to thread 1, but before it has a chance to read *errno*, the scheduler decides that thread 1 has had enough CPU time for the moment and decides to switch to thread 2. Thread 2 executes an OPEN call that fails, which causes *errno* to be overwritten and thread 1's access code to be lost forever. When thread 1 starts up later, it will read the wrong value and behave incorrectly.

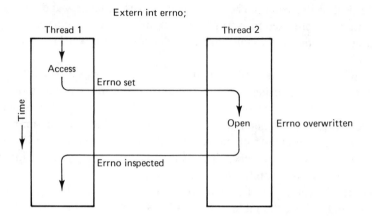

Fig. 12-6. Conflicts between threads over the use of a global variable.

Various solutions to this problem are possible. One is to prohibit global variables altogether. However worthy this ideal may be, it conflicts with much existing software, such as UNIX. Another is to assign each thread its own private global variables, as shown in Fig. 12-7. In this way, each thread has its own private copy of *errno* and other global variables, so conflicts are avoided. In effect, this decision creates a new scoping level, variables visible to all the procedures of a thread, in addition to the existing scoping levels of variables visible only in a specific procedure and variables visible everywhere in the program.

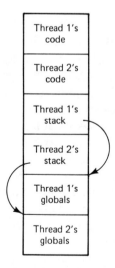

Fig. 12-7. Threads can have private global variables.

Accessing the private global variables is a bit tricky, however, since most programming languages have a way of expressing local variables and global variables, but not intermediate forms. It is possible to allocate a chunk of memory for the globals and pass it to each procedure in the thread, as an extra parameter. While hardly an elegant solution, it works.

Alternatively, new library procedures can be introduced to create, set, and read these thread-wide global variables. The first call might look like this:

```
create_global("bufptr");
```

It allocates storage for a pointer called *bufptr* on the heap or in a special storage area reserved for the calling thread. No matter where the storage is allocated, only the calling thread has access to the global variable. If another thread creates a global variable with the same name, it gets a different storage location that does not conflict with the existing one.

Two calls are needed to access global variables: one for writing them and the other for reading them. For writing, something like

```
set_global("bufptr", &buf);
```

will do. It stores the value of a pointer in the storage location previous created by the call to *create_global*. To read a global variable, the call might look like

```
bufptr = read_global("bufptr");
```

This call returns the address stored in the global variable, so the data value can be accessed.

Our last design issue relating to threads is scheduling. Threads can be scheduled using various scheduling algorithms, including priority, round robin, and others. Threads packages often provide calls to give the user the ability to specify the scheduling algorithm and set the priorities, if any.

12.1.4. Implementing a Threads Package

There are two ways to implement a threads package: in user space and in the kernel. The choice is moderately controversial. In this section we will describe both methods, along with their advantages and disadvantages.

The first method is to put the threads package entirely in user space. The kernel knows nothing about them. As far as the kernel is concerned, it is managing ordinary, single-threaded processes. The first, and most obvious, advantage is that a user-level threads package can be implemented on an operating system that does not support threads. For example, UNIX does not support threads, but various user-space threads packages exist for it.

All of these implementations have the same general structure, which is illustrated in Fig. 12-8(a). The threads run on top of a run-time system, which is a collection of procedures that manage threads. When a thread executes a system call, goes to sleep, performs an operation on a semaphore or mutex, or otherwise does something that may cause it to be suspended, it calls a run-time system procedure. This procedure checks to see if the thread must be suspended. If so, it stores the thread's registers (i.e., its own) in a table, looks for an unblocked thread to run, and reloads the machine registers with the new thread's saved values. As soon as the stack pointer and program counter have been switched, the new thread automatically comes to life again. If the machine has an instruction to store all the registers and another one to load them all, the entire thread switch can be done in a handful of instructions. Doing thread switching like this is at least an order of magnitude faster than trapping to the kernel, and is a strong argument in favor of user-level threads packages.

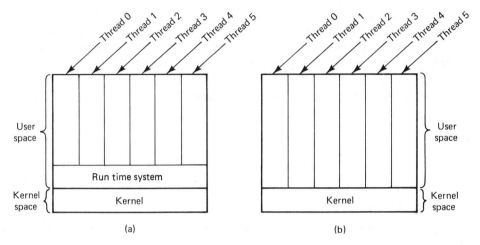

Fig. 12-8. (a) A user-level threads package. (b) A threads packaged managed by the kernel.

User-level threads also have other advantages. They allow each process to have its own customized scheduling algorithm. For some applications, for example, those with a garbage collector thread, not having to worry about a thread being stopped at an inconvenient moment is a plus. They also scale better, since kernel threads invariably require some table space and stack space in the kernel, which can be a problem if there are a very large number of threads.

Now let us consider having the kernel know about and manage the threads. No run-time system is needed, as shown in Fig. 12-8(b). For each process, the kernel has a table with one entry per thread, giving the thread's registers, state, priority, and other information. The information is the same as with user-level threads, only it is now in the kernel instead of in user space (inside the run-time system). All calls that might block a thread are implemented as system calls, at considerably greater cost than a call to a run-time system procedure. When a thread blocks, the kernel, at its option, can run either another thread from the same process (if one is ready), or a thread from a different process. With user-level threads, the run-time system keeps running threads from its own process until the kernel takes the CPU away from it (or there are no ready threads left to run).

Despite their better performance, user-level threads packages have some major problems. First among these is the problem of how blocking system calls are implemented. Suppose a thread reads from an empty pipe or does something else that will block. In the kernel implementation, the thread traps to the kernel, which blocks the thread and starts another one. In the user-space implementation, letting the thread actually make the system call is unacceptable, since this will stop all the threads. One of the main goals of having threads in the first place was to allow each one to use blocking calls, but to prevent one blocked thread from affecting the others. With blocking system calls, this goal cannot be achieved.

The system calls could all be changed to be nonblocking (e.g., a read on a empty pipe could just fail), but requiring changes to the operating system is unattractive. Besides, one of the arguments for user-level threads was precisely that they could run with *existing* operating systems. In addition, changing the semantics of READ will require changes to many user programs.

Another alternative is possible in the event that it is possible to tell in advance if a call will block. In some versions of UNIX, a call SELECT exists, which allows the caller to tell whether a pipe is empty, and so on. When this call is present, the library procedure *read* can be replaced with a new one that first does a SELECT call, and then only does the READ call if it is safe (i.e., will not block). If the READ call will block, the call is not made. Instead, another thread is run. The next time the run-time system gets control, it can check again to see if the READ is now safe. This approach requires rewriting parts of the system call library, is inefficient and inelegant, but there is little choice. The code placed around the system call to do the checking is called a **jacket**.

Another problem with user-level thread packages is that if a thread starts running, no other thread in that process will ever run unless the first thread voluntarily gives up the CPU. With kernel threads, clock interrupts occur periodically, forcing the scheduler to run. Within a single process, there are no clock interrupts, making round robin scheduling impossible. Unless a thread enters the run-time system of its own free will, the scheduler will never get a chance. One possible solution is to have the run-time system request a clock signal (interrupt) once a second to give it control, but this too is crude and messy to program. Furthermore, a thread might also need a clock interrupt, interfering with the run-time system.

A third, and probably most devastating argument against user-level threads, is that programmers generally want threads in applications where the threads block often, as, for example, in a multithreaded file server. These threads are constantly making system calls. Once a trap has occurred to the kernel to carry out the system call, it is hardly any more work for the kernel to switch threads if the old one has blocked, and having the kernel do this eliminates the need for constantly checking to see if system calls are safe. For applications that are essentially entirely CPU bound and rarely block, what is the point of having threads at all? No one would seriously propose to compute the first n prime numbers or play chess using threads because there is nothing to be gained by doing it that way.

In addition to all these problems, there are some other problems that occur both with user-level and with kernel managed threads. To start with, many library procedures are not re-entrant. For example, sending a message over the network may well be programmed to first assemble the message in a fixed buffer, then to trap to the kernel to send it. What happens if one thread has assembled its message in the buffer, then a clock interrupt forces a switch to a second thread that immediately overwrites the buffer with its own message? Similarly, after a system call completes, a thread switch may occur before the previous thread has had a chance to read out the error status (*errno*, as discussed above). Also, memory allocation procedures, like the UNIX *malloc*, fiddle with crucial tables without bothering to set up and use protected critical regions, because they were written for single-threaded environments where that was not necessary. Fixing all these problems properly effectively means rewriting the entire library.

A different solution is to provide each one with a jacket that locks a global semaphore or mutex when the procedure is started. In this way, only one thread may be active in the library at once. Effectively, the entire library becomes a big monitor.

Signals also present difficulties. Suppose one thread wants to catch a particular signal (say, the user hitting the DEL key), and another thread wants this signal to terminate the process. This situation can arise if one or more threads run standard library procedures and others are user-written. Clearly these wishes are incompatible. In general, signals are difficult enough to manage in a single-threaded environment. Going to a multithreaded one does not make them any easier to handle. Signals are typically a per-process concept, not a per-thread concept, especially if the kernel is not even aware of the existence of the threads.

12.1.5. Threads and RPC

It is common for distributed systems to use both RPC and threads. Since threads were invented as a cheap alternative to standard (heavyweight) processes, it is natural that researchers would take a closer look at RPC in this context, to see if it could be made more lightweight as well. In this section we will discuss some interesting work in this area.

Bershad et al. (1990) have observed that even in a distributed system, a substantial number of RPCs are to processes on the same machine as the caller (e.g., to the window manager). Obviously this result depends on the system, but it is common enough to be worth considering. They have proposed a new scheme that makes it possible for a thread in one process to call a thread in another process on the same machine much more efficiently than the usual way.

The idea works like this. When a server thread, *S*, starts up, it exports its interface by telling the kernel about it. The interface defines which procedures are callable, what their parameters are, and so on. When a client thread *C* starts up, it imports the interface from the kernel, and is given a special identifier to use for the call. The kernel now knows that *C* is going to call *S* later, and creates special data structures to prepare for the call.

One of these data structures is an argument stack that is shared by both *C* and *S* and is mapped read/write into both of their address spaces. To call the server, *C* pushes the arguments onto the shared stack, using the normal procedure passing conventions, and then traps to the kernel, putting the special identifier in a register. The kernel sees this and knows that the call is local. (If it had been remote, the kernel would have treated the call in the normal manner for remote calls.) It then changes the client's memory map to put the client in the server's address space, and starts the client thread executing the server's procedure. The call is made in such a way that the arguments are already in place, so no copying or marshalling is needed. The net result is that local RPCs can be done much faster this way.

Another technique is widely used to make remote RPCs faster as well. The idea is based on the observation that when a server thread blocks waiting for a new request, it really does not have any important context information. For example, it rarely has any local variables, and there is typically nothing important in its registers. Therefore, when a thread has finished carrying out a request, it simply vanishes.

When a new message comes in to the server's machine, the kernel creates a new thread on-the-fly to service the request. Furthermore, it maps the message into the server's address space, and sets up the new thread's stack to access the message. This scheme is sometimes called **implicit receive**. The thread that is spontaneously created to handle an incoming RPC is occasionally referred to as a **pop-up thread**. The idea is illustrated in Fig. 12-9.

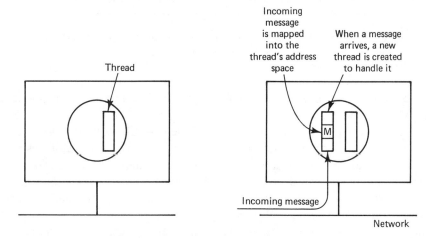

Fig. 12-9. Creating a thread when a message arrives.

The method has several major advantages over conventional RPC. First, threads do not have to block waiting for new work. Thus no context has to be saved. Second, creating a new thread is cheaper than restoring an existing one, since no context has to be restored. Finally, time is saved by not having to copy incoming messages to a buffer within a server thread. Other methods are also used to reduce overhead. All in all, a substantial gain in speed is possible.

Threads are an ongoing research topic. Some other results are presented in (Anderson et al., 1991; Marsh et al., 1991; and Draves et al., 1991).

12.1.6. An Example Threads Package

As an example threads package, in this section we will examine the Open Software Foundation's Distributed Computing Environment's threads package. Like most of OSF's software, this package is large and complicated. It has a total of 51 primitives (library procedures) relating to threads that user programs can call. Many of these are not strictly necessary, but are provided for convenience only. This approach is somewhat analogous to a four-function pocket calculator that not only has keys for +, −, ×, and /, but also has keys for +1, −1, × 2, × 10, × π, /2, and /10 on the grounds that these save the user time and effort. Due to the large number of calls, we will discuss only the most important ones (about half the total). Nevertheless, our treatment should give a reasonable impression of what the package can do.

Call	Description
Create	Create a new thread
Exit	Call by a thread when it is finished
Join	Like the WAIT system call in UNIX
Detach	Make it unnecessary for parent thread to wait when caller exits

Fig. 12-10. Selected DCE thread calls for managing threads. All the calls in this and subsequent tables are actually prefixed by *pthread_* (i.e., *pthread_create*, not *create*), which we have omitted to save space.

For our discussion, it is convenient to group the calls into seven categories, each dealing with a different aspect of threads and their use. The first category, listed in Fig. 12-10, deals with thread management. These calls allow threads to be created, and for them to exit when done. A parent thread can wait for a child using *join*, which is similar to the WAIT system call in UNIX. If a parent has no interest in a child and does plan to wait for it, the parent can disown the child by calling *detach*. In this case, when the child thread exits, its storage is reclaimed immediately, instead of having it wait for the parent to call *join*.

The DCE package allows the user to create, destroy, and manage templates for threads, mutexes, and condition variables. The templates can be set up to have appropriate initial values. When an object is created, one of the parameters to the create call is a pointer to a template. Thus, for example, a thread template can be created and given the attribute (property) that the stack size is 8K. Whenever a thread is created with that template as parameter, it will get an 8K stack. The point of having templates is to eliminate the need for specifying all the options as separate parameters. As the package evolves, the create calls can remain the same. Instead, new attributes can be added to the templates. Some of the template calls are listed in Fig. 12-11.

The *attr_create* and *attr_delete* calls create and delete thread templates, respectively. Other calls allow programs to read and write the template's attributes, such as the stack size and scheduling parameters to be used for threads created with the template. Similarly, calls are provided to create and delete templates for mutexes and condition variables. The need for the latter is not entirely obvious, since they have no attributes and no operations are defined on them. Clearly the designers were hoping that someone would one day think of an attribute.

Call	Description
Attr_create	Create template for setting thread parameters
Attr_delete	Delete template for threads
Attr_setprio	Set the default scheduling priority in the template
Attr_getprio	Read the default scheduling priority from the template
Attr_setstacksize	Set the default stack size in the template
Attr_getstacksize	Read the default stack size from the template
Attr_mutexattr_create	Create template for mutex parameters
Attr_mutexattr_delete	Delete template for mutexes
Attr_mutexattr_setkind_np	Set the default mutex type in the template
Attr_mutexattr_getkind_np	Read the default mutex type in the template
Attr_condattr_create	Create template for condition variable parameters
Attr_condattr_delete	Delete template for condition variables

Fig. 12-11. Selected template calls.

The third group deals with mutexes, which can be created and destroyed dynamically. Three operations are defined on mutexes, as shown in Fig. 12-12. The operations are for locking, unlocking mutexes, and for trying but accepting failure if locking cannot be done.

Call	Description
Mutex_init	Create a mutex
Mutex_destroy	Delete a mutex
Mutex_lock	Try to lock a mutex; if it is already locked
Mutex_trylock	Try to lock a mutex; fail if it is already locked
Mutex_unlock	Unlock a mutex

Fig. 12-12. Selected mutex calls.

An obvious question to ask about mutexes is: "What happens if you unlock a mutex that is not currently locked?" Does the unlock get saved, or is it lost? Unfortunately, the answer here is not defined, meaning that the programmer cannot count on any particular behavior. This choice is especially unfortunate because it was precisely the problem of lost wakeups that led Dijkstra to invent semaphores. With semaphores, if one process (or thread) is trying to increase a semaphore and another is trying to decrease it, the precise order in which the two actions is carried out does not matter. As a result, race conditions do not occur and programming is relatively straightforward. With DCE mutexes, the order may or may not matter, depending on the implementation, which certainly does not make it any easier to write correct and portable programs.

Two kinds of mutexes are available: **fast mutexes** and **friendly mutexes**. They differ in the way they deal with nested locks. A fast mutex is analogous to a lock in a data base system. If a process tries to lock an unlocked record, it will succeed. However, if it tries to acquire the same lock a second time, it will block, waiting for the lock to be released, something that will never happen.

A friendly mutex allows a thread to lock a mutex that it has already locked. The idea is this. Suppose the main program of a thread locks a mutex, then calls a procedure that also locks the mutex. To avoid deadlock, the second lock is accepted. As long as the mutex is ultimately unlocked as many times as it is locked, the nesting can be arbitrarily deep. The package designers probably could not agree on whether a second lock by the same thread should block or not, so they threw in both versions.

Call	Description
Cond_init	Create a condition variable
Cond_destroy	Delete a condition variable
Cond_wait	Wait on a condition variable until a signal or broadcast arrives
Cond_signal	Wake up at most one thread waiting on the condition variable
Cond_broadcast	Wake up all the threads waiting on the condition variable

Fig. 12-13. Selected condition variable calls.

Next come the calls relating to condition variables, listed in Fig. 12-13. These, too, can be created and destroyed dynamically. Threads can sleep on condition variables pending the availability of some needed resource. Two wakeup operations are provided: signaling, which wakes up exactly one waiting thread, and broadcasting, which wakes them all up.

Figure 12-14 lists the three calls for manipulating the per-thread global variables. These are variables that may be used by any procedure in the thread, but may not be used by procedures outside the thread. The concept of a per-thread global variable is not supported by any of the popular programming languages, so they have to be managed at run time. The first call allocates storage, the second one assigns a pointer to a global variable, and the third one allows the thread to read back a global variable value. Many computer scientists consider global variables to be in the same league as that all-time great pariah, the GOTO statement, so they would no doubt rejoice at the idea of making them cumbersome to use. (The author once tried to design a pro-gramming language with a

IKNOWTHISISASTUPIDTHINGTODOBUTNEVERTHELESSGOTO LABEL;

statement, but was forceably restrained from doing so by his colleagues.) On the other hand, it can be argued that having per-thread global variables use procedure calls instead of language scoping rules, like locals and globals, is an emergency measure introduced simply because most programming languages do not allow the concept to be expressed syntactically.

Call	Description
Keycreate	Create a global variable for this thread
Setspecific	Assign a pointer value to a per-thread global variable
Getspecific	Read a pointer value from a per-thread global variable

Fig. 12-14. Selected per-thread global variable calls.

The next group of calls (see Fig. 12-15) deals with killing threads, and the threads' ability to resist. The *cancel* call tries to kill a thread, but sometimes killing a thread can have devastating effects, for example, if the thread has a mutex locked at the time. For this reason, threads can arrange for attempts to kill them to be enabled or disabled in various ways, very roughly analogous for the ability of UNIX processes to catch signals instead of being terminated by them.

Call	Description
Cancel	Try to kill another thread
Setcancel	Enable or disable ability of other threads to kill this thread

Fig. 12-15. Selected calls relating to killing threads.

Finally, our last group (see Fig. 12-16) is concerned with scheduling. The pack-age allows the threads in a process to be scheduled according to FIFO, round robin, preemptive, nonpreemptive and other algorithms. By using these calls, the algorithm and priorities can be set. The system works best if threads do not elect to be scheduled with conflicting algorithms.

12.2. SYSTEM MODELS

Processes run on processors. In a traditional system, there is only one processor, so the question of how the processor should be used does not come up. In a distri-buted system, with multiple processors, it is a major design issue. The processors in a distributed system can be organized in several ways. In this section we will look at

Call	Description
Setscheduler	Set the scheduling algorithm
Getscheduler	Read the current scheduling algorithm
Setprio	Set the scheduling priority
Getprio	Read the current scheduling priority

Fig. 12-16. Selected scheduling calls.

two of the principal ones, the workstation model and the processor pool model, and a hybrid form encompassing features of each one. These models are rooted in fundamentally different philosophies of what a distributed system is all about.

12.2.1. The Workstation Model

The workstation model is straightforward: the system consists of workstations (high-end personal computers) scattered throughout a building or campus and connected by a high-speed LAN, as shown in Fig. 12-17. Some of the workstations may be in offices, and thus implicitly dedicated to a single user, whereas others may be in public areas and have several different users during the course of a day. In both cases, at any instant of time, a workstation either has a single user logged into it, and thus has an "owner" (however temporary) or it is idle.

Fig. 12-17. A network of personal workstations, each with a local file system.

In some systems the workstations have local disks and in others they do not. The latter are universally called **diskless workstations**, but the former are variously known as **diskful workstations**, or **disky workstations**, or even stranger names. If the workstations are diskless, then the file system must be implemented by one or more file servers somewhere in the network. Requests to read and write files are sent to a file server, which performs the work and sends back the replies.

Diskless workstations are popular at universities and companies for several reasons, not the least of which is price. Having a large number of workstations equipped with small, slow disks is typically much more expensive than having one or two file servers equipped with huge, fast disks and accessed over the LAN.

A second reason why diskless workstations are popular is their ease of maintenance. When a new release of some program, say a compiler, comes out, the system administrators can easily install it on a small number of file servers in the machine room. Installing it on dozens or hundreds of machines all over a building or campus is another matter entirely. Backup and hardware maintenance is also simpler with one centrally located 5-gigabyte disk than with fifty 100-megabyte disks scattered over the building.

Another point against disks is that they have fans and make noise. Many people find this noise objectionable and do not want it in their office.

Finally, diskless workstations provide symmetry and flexibility. A user can walk up to any workstation in the system and log in. Since all his files are on the file server, one diskless workstation is as good as another. In contrast, when all the files are stored on local disks, using someone else's workstation means that you have easy access to *his* files, but getting to your own requires extra effort, and is certainly different from using your own workstation.

When the workstations have private disks, these disks can be used in one of at least four ways:

1. Paging and temporary files.

2. Paging, temporary files, and system binaries.

3. Paging, temporary files, system binaries, and file caching.

4. Complete local file system.

The first design is based on the observation that while it may be convenient to keep all the user files on the central file servers (to simplify backup and maintenance, etc.) disks are also needed for paging (or swapping), and temporary files. In this model, the local disks are used only for paging and files that are temporary, unshared, and can be discarded at the end of the login session. For example, most compilers consist of multiple passes, each of which creates a temporary file read by the next pass. When the file has been read once, it is discarded. Local disks are ideal for storing such files.

The second model is a variant of the first one in which the local disks also hold the binary (executable) programs, such as the compilers, text editors, and electronic mail handlers. When one of these programs is invoked, it is fetched from the local disk instead of from a file server, further reducing the network load. Since these programs rarely change, they can be installed on all the local disks and kept there for long periods of time. When a new release of some system program is available, it is essentially broadcast to all machines. However, if that machine happens to be down when the program is sent, it will miss the program and continue to run the old version. Thus some administration is needed to keep track of who has which version of which program.

A third approach to using local disks is to use them as explicit caches (in addition to using them for paging, temporaries, and binaries). In this mode of operation, users can download files from the file servers to their own disks, read and write them locally, and then upload the modified ones at the end of the login session. The goal of this architecture is to keep long-term storage centralized, but reduce network load by keeping files local while they are being used. A disadvantage is keeping the caches consistent. What happens if two users download the same file and then each modifies it in different ways? This problem is not easy to solve, and we will discuss it in detail later in the book.

Fourth, each machine can have its own self-contained file system, with the possibility of mounting or otherwise accessing other machines' file systems. The idea here is that each machine is basically self-contained and that contact with the outside world is limited. This organization provides a uniform and guaranteed response time for the user and puts little load on the network. The disadvantage is that sharing is more difficult, and the resulting system is much closer to a network operating system than to a true transparent distributed operating system.

The one diskless and four diskful models we have discussed are summarized in Fig. 12-18. The progression from top to bottom in the figure is the progression from complete dependence on the file servers to complete independence from them.

The advantages of the workstation model are manifold and clear. The model is certainly easy to understand. Users have a fixed amount of dedicated computing power, and thus guaranteed response time. Sophisticated graphics programs can be very fast, since they can have direct access to the screen. Each user has a large degree of autonomy, and can allocate his workstation's resources as he sees fit. Local disks add to this independence, and make it possible to continue working to a lesser or greater degree even in the face of file server crashes.

Disk usage	Advantages	Disadvantages
(Diskless)	Low cost, easy hardware and software maintenance, symmetry and flexibility	Heavy network usage; file servers may become bottlenecks
Paging, scratch files	Reduces network load over diskless case	Higher cost due to large number of disks needed
Paging, scratch files, binaries	Reduces network load even more	Higher cost; additional complexity of updating the binaries
Paging, scratch files, binaries, file caching	Still lower network load; reduces load on file servers as well	Higher cost; cache consistency problems
Full local file system	Hardly any network load; eliminates need for file servers	Loss of transparency

(Dependence on file servers ↑)

Fig. 12-18. Disk usage on workstations.

However, the model also has two problems. First, as processor chips continue to get cheaper, it will soon become economically feasible to give each user first 10 and later 100 CPUs. Having 100 workstations in your office makes it hard to see out the window. Second, much of the time users are not using their workstations, which are idle, while other users may need extra computing capacity and cannot get it.

The first problem can be addressed by making each workstation a personal multiprocessor. For example, each window on the screen can have a dedicated CPU to run its programs. Preliminary evidence from some early personal multiprocessors such as the DEC Firefly, suggest, however, that the mean number of CPUs utilized is rarely more than one, since users rarely have more than one active process at once.

12.2.2. Using Idle Workstations

The second problem, idle workstations, has been the subject of considerable research, primarily because many universities have a substantial number of personal workstations, some of which are idle (an idle workstation is the devil's playground?). Measurements show that even at peak periods in the middle of the day, often as many as 30 percent of the workstations are idle at any given moment. In the evening, even more are idle. A variety of schemes have been proposed for using idle or otherwise underutilized workstations (Litzkow et al., 1988; Nichols, 1987; and Theimer et al., 1985). We will describe the general principles behind this work in this section.

The earliest attempt to allow idle workstations to be utilized was the *rsh* program that comes with Berkeley UNIX. This program is called by

```
rsh machine command
```

in which the first argument names a machine and the second names a command to run on it. What *rsh* does is run the specified command on the specified machine. Although widely used, this program has several serious flaws. First, the user must tell which machine to use, putting the full burden of keeping track of idle machines on the user. Second, the program executes in the environment of the remote machine, which is usually different from the local environment. Finally, if someone should log into an idle machine on which a remote process is running, the process continues to run and the newly logged in user has to either accept the lower performance or find another machine.

The research on idle workstations has centered on solving these problems. The key issues are:

1. How is an idle workstation found?

2. How can a remote process be run transparently?

3. What happens if the machine's owner comes back?

Let us consider these three issues, one at a time.

How is an idle workstation found? To start with, what is an idle workstation? At first glance, it might appear that a workstation with no one logged in at the console is an idle workstation, but with modern computer systems things are not always that simple. In many systems, even with no one logged in there may be dozens of processes running, such as clock daemons, mail daemons, news daemons, and all manner of other daemons. On the other hand, a user who logs in when arriving at his desk in the morning, but otherwise does not touch the computer for hours hardly puts any additional load on it. Different systems make different decisions as to what "idle" means, but typically if no one has touched the keyboard or mouse for several minutes and no user-initiated processes are running, the workstation can be said to be idle. Consequently, there may be substantial differences in load between one idle workstation and another, due, for example, to the volume of mail coming into the first one but not the second.

The algorithms used to locate idle workstations can be divided into two categories: server driven and client driven. In the former, when a workstation goes idle, and thus becomes a potential compute server, it announces its availability. It can do this by entering its name, network address, and properties in a registry file (or data base), for example. Later, when a user wants to execute a command on an idle workstation, he types something like:

```
remote command
```

and the *remote* program looks in the registry to find a suitable idle workstation. For reliability reasons, it is also possible to have multiple copies of the registry.

An alternative way for the newly idle workstation to announce the fact that it has become unemployed is to put a broadcast message onto the network. All other workstations then record this fact. In effect, each machine maintains its own private copy of the registry. The advantage of doing it this way is less overhead in finding an idle workstation and greater redundancy. The disadvantage is requiring all machines to do the work of maintaining the registry.

Whether there is one registry or many, there is a potential danger of race conditions occurring. If two users simultaneously invoke the *remote* command, and both of them discover that the same machine is idle, they may both try to start up processes there at the same time. To detect and avoid this situation, the *remote* program can check with the idle workstation, which, if still free, removes itself from the registry and gives the go-ahead sign. At this point, the caller can send over its environment and start the remote process, as shown in Fig. 12-19.

The other way to locate idle workstations is to use a client-driven approach. When *remote* is invoked, it broadcasts a request saying what program it wants to run, how much memory it needs, whether or not a floating point coprocessor chip is needed, and so on. These details are not needed if all the workstations are identical, but if the system is heterogeneous and not every program can run on every workstation, they are essential. When the replies come back, *remote* picks one and sets it up. One nice twist is to have "idle" workstations delay their responses slightly, with the delay being proportional to the current load. In this way, the reply from the least heavily loaded machine will come back first and be selected.

Finding a workstation is only the first step. Now the process has to be run there. Moving the code is easy. The trick is to set up the remote process so that it sees the same environment it would have locally, on the **home workstation**, and thus carries out the same computation it would have locally.

To start with, it needs the same view of the file system, the same working

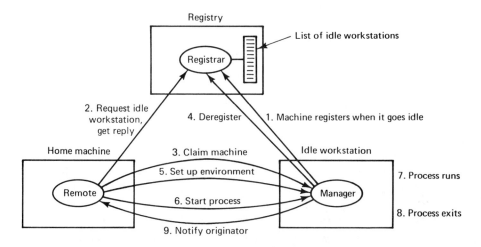

Fig. 12-19. A registry-based algorithm for finding and using idle workstations.

directory, and the same environment variables (shell variables), if any. After these have been set up, the program can begin running. The trouble starts when the first system call, say a READ, is executed. What should the kernel do? The answer depends very much on the system architecture. If the system is diskless, with all the files located on file servers, the kernel can just send the request to the appropriate file server, the same way the home machine would have done had the process been running there. On the other hand, if the system has local disks, each with a complete file system, then the request has to be forwarded back to the home machine for execution.

Some system calls must be forwarded back to the home machine no matter what, even if all the machines are diskless. For example, reads from the keyboard and writes to the screen can never be carried out on the remote machine. However, other system calls must be done remotely under all conditions. For example, the UNIX system calls SBRK (adjust the size of the data segment), NICE (set CPU scheduling priority), and PROFIL (enable profiling of the program counter), cannot be executed on the home machine. In addition, all system calls that query the state of the machine have to be done on the machine that the process is actually running on. These include asking for the machine's name and network address, asking how much free memory it has, and so on.

System calls involving time are a problem because the clocks on different machines may not be synchronized. In the previous chapter, we saw how hard it is to achieve synchronization. Using the time on the remote machine may cause programs that depend on time, like *make*, to give incorrect results. Forwarding all time-related calls back to the home machine, however, introduces delay, which also causes problems with time.

To further complicate matters, certain special cases of calls which normally might have to be forwarded back, such as creating and writing to a temporary file, can be done much more efficiently on the remote machine. In addition, mouse tracking and signal propagation have to be thought out carefully as well. Programs that directly write to hardware devices, such as the screen's frame buffer, diskette, or magnetic tape cannot be run remotely at all. All in all, making programs run on remote machines as though they were running on their home machines is possible, but it is a complex and tricky business.

The final question on our original list is what to do if the machine's owner comes back (i.e., somebody logs in or a previously inactive user touches the keyboard or mouse). The easiest thing is to do nothing, but this tends to defeat the idea of "personal" workstations. If other people can run programs on your workstation at the same time you are trying to use it, there goes your guaranteed response.

Another possibility is to kill off the intruding process. The simplest way is to do this abruptly and without warning. The disadvantage of this strategy is that all work will be lost and the file system may be left in a chaotic state. A better way is to give the process fair warning, by sending it a signal to allow it to detect impending doom, and shut down gracefully (write edit buffers to the disk, close files, and so on). If it has not exited within a few seconds, it is then terminated. Of course, the program must be written to expect and handle this signal, something most existing programs definitely are not.

A completely different approach is to migrate the process to another machine, either back to the home machine or to yet another idle workstation. Migration of running processes is important, but beyond the scope of this book. For more information on this subject, see (Artsy and Finkel, 1989; Douglis and Ousterhout, 1991; and Zayas, 1987).

In both cases, when the process is gone, it should leave the machine in the same state as it found it, to avoid disturbing the owner. Among other items, this requirement means that not only must the process go, but also all its children and their children. In addition, mailboxes, network connections, and other system-wide data structures must be deleted, and some provision must be made to ignore RPC replies and other messages that arrive for the process after it is gone. If there is a local disk, temporary files must be deleted, and if possible, any files that had to be removed from its cache restored.

12.2.3. The Processor Pool Model

Although using idle workstations adds a little computing power to the system, it does not address a more fundamental issue: "What happens when it is feasible to provide 10 or 100 times as many CPUs as there are active users?" One solution, as we saw, is to give everyone a personal multiprocessor. However this is a somewhat inefficient design.

An alternative approach is to construct a **processor pool**, a rack full of CPUs in the machine room, which can be dynamically allocated to users on demand. The processor pool approach is illustrated in Fig. 12-20. Instead of giving users personal workstations, in this model they are given high-performance graphics terminals, such as X terminals (although small workstations can also be used as terminals). This idea is based on the observation that what many users really want is a high-quality graphical interface and good performance. Conceptually, it is much closer to traditional timesharing than to the personal computer model, although it is built with modern technology (low-cost microprocessors).

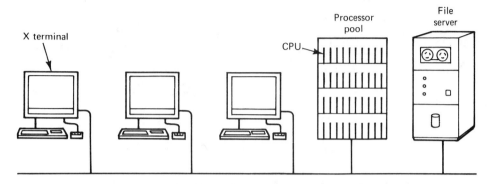

Fig. 12-20. A system based on the processor pool model.

The motivation for the processor pool idea comes from taking the diskless workstation idea a step further. If the file system can be centralized in a small number of file servers to gain economies of scale, it should be possible to do the same thing for compute servers. By putting all the CPUs in a big rack in the machine room, power supply and other packaging costs can be reduced, giving more computing power for a given amount of money. Furthermore, it permits the use of cheaper X terminals (or even ordinary ASCII terminals), and decouples the number of users from the number of workstations. The model also allows for easy incremental growth. If the computing load increases by 10 percent, just buy 10 percent more processors and put them in the pool.

In effect, we are converting all the computing power into "idle workstations" that can be accessed dynamically. Users can be assigned as many CPUs as they need for short periods, after which they are returned to the pool so other users can have them. There is no concept of ownership here: all the processors belong equally to everyone.

The biggest argument for centralizing the computing power in a processor pool comes from queueing theory. A queueing system is a situation in which users generate random requests for work from a server. When the server is busy, the users queue for service and are processed in turn. Common examples of queueing systems are bakeries, airport check-in counters, supermarket check-out counters, and numerous others. The bare basics are depicted in Fig. 12-21.

Queueing systems are useful because it is possible to model them analytically. Let us call the total input rate λ requests per second, from all the users combined. Let us call the rate at which the server can process requests μ. For stable operation, we must have $\mu > \lambda$. If the server can handle 100 requests/sec, but the users continuously generate 110 requests/sec, the queue will grow without bound. (Small intervals in which the input rate exceeds the service rate are acceptable, provided that the mean input rate is lower than the service rate and there is enough buffer space.)

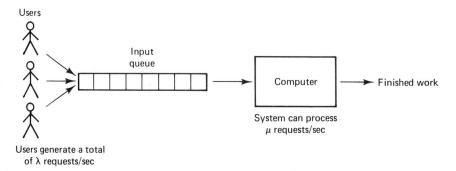

Fig. 12-21. A basic queueing system.

It can be proven (Kleinrock, 1974) that the mean time between issuing a request and getting a complete response, T is related to λ and μ by the formula:

$$T = \frac{1}{\mu - \lambda}$$

As an example, consider a file server that can handle 50 requests/sec and which gets 40 requests per second. The mean response time will be 1/10 sec or 100 msec. Note that when λ goes to 0 (no load), the response time of the file server does not go to 0, but to 1/50 sec or 20 msec. The reason is obvious once it is pointed out. If the file server can process only 50 requests/sec, it must take 20 msec to process a single request, even in the absence of any competition, so the response time, which includes the processing time, can never go below 20 msec.

Suppose we have n personal multiprocessors, each with some number of CPUs, and each one forms a separate queueing system with request arrival rate λ and CPU processing rate μ. The mean response time, T, will be as given above. Now consider what happens if we scoop up all the CPUs and place them in a single processor pool. Instead of having n small queueing systems running in parallel, we now have one large one, with an input rate $n\lambda$ and a service rate $n\mu$. Let us call the mean response time of this combined system T_1. From the above formula we find

$$T_1 = \frac{1}{n\mu - n\lambda} = T/n$$

This surprising result says that by replacing n small resources by one big one that is n times more powerful, we can reduce the average response time n-fold.

This result is extremely general and applies to a large variety of systems. It is one of the main reasons that airlines prefer to fly a 300-seat 747 once every 5 hours to a 10-seat business jet every 10 minutes. The effect arises because dividing the processing power into small servers (e.g., personal workstations) each with one user, is a poor match to a workload of randomly arriving requests. Much of the time, a few servers are busy, even overloaded, but most are idle. It is this wasted time that is eliminated in the processor pool model, and the reason why it gives better overall performance. The concept of using idle workstations is a weak attempt at recapturing the wasted cycles, but it is complicated and has many problems, as we have seen.

In fact, this queueing theory result is one of the main arguments against having distributed systems at all. Given a choice between one centralized 1000-MIPS CPU and 100 private, dedicated, 10-MIPS CPUs, the mean response time of the former will be 100 times better, because no cycles are ever wasted. The machine only goes idle when no user has any work to do. This fact argues in favor of concentrating the computing power as much as possible.

However, mean response time is not everything. There are also arguments in favor of distributed computing. Cost is one of them. If a single 1000-MIPS CPU is vastly more expensive than 100 10-MIPS workstations, the price/performance ratio of the latter may be much better. It may not even be possible to build such a large machine at any price. Reliability and fault tolerance are factors as well.

Also, personal workstations have a uniform response, independent of what other people are doing (except when the network or file servers are jammed). For some users, a low variance in response time may be perceived as more important than the mean response time itself. Consider, for example, editing on a private workstation on which asking for the next page to be displayed always takes 500 msec. Now consider editing on a large, centralized, shared computer on which asking for the next page takes 5 msec 95 percent of the time and 5 sec one time in 20. Even though the mean here is twice as good as on the workstation, the users may consider the performance intolerable. On the other hand, to the user with a large *make* or a huge simulation to run, the big computer may win hands down.

So far we have tacitly assumed that a pool of n processors is effectively the same thing as a single processor that is n times as fast as a single processor. In reality, this assumption is only justified if all requests can be split up in such a way as to allow them to run on all the processors in parallel. If a job can be split into, say, only 5 parts, then the processor pool model only has an effective service time 5 times better than a single processor, not n times better.

Still, the processor pool model is a much cleaner way of getting extra computing power than looking around for idle workstations and sneaking over there while nobody is looking. By starting out with the assumption that no processor belongs to anyone, we get a design based on the concept of requesting machines from the pool, using them, and putting them back when done. There is also no need to forward anything back to a "home" machine because there are none. There is also no danger of the owner coming back, because there are no owners.

In the end, it all comes down to the nature of the workload. If all people are doing is simple editing and occasionally sending an electronic mail message or two, having a personal workstation is probably enough. If, on the other hand, the users are engaged in a large software development project, frequently running *make* on large directories, or are trying to invert massive sparse matrices, or do major simulations or run big artificial intelligence or VLSI routing programs, constantly hunting for substantial numbers of idle workstations will be no fun at all. In all these situations, the processor pool idea is fundamentally much simpler and more attractive.

12.2.4. A Hybrid Model

A possible compromise is to provide each user with a personal workstation, and to have a processor pool in addition. Although this solution is more expensive than either a pure workstation model or a pure processor pool model, it combines the advantages of both of the others.

Interactive work can be done on workstations, giving guaranteed response. Idle workstations, however, are not utilized, making for a simpler system design. They are just left unused. Instead, all noninteractive processes run on the processor pool, as does all heavy computing in general. This model provides fast interactive response, an efficient use of resources, and simple design.

12.3. PROCESSOR ALLOCATION

By definition, a distributed system consists of multiple processors. These may be organized as a collection of personal workstations, a public processor pool, or some hybrid form. In all cases, some algorithm is needed for deciding which process should be run on which machine. For the workstation model, the question is when to run a process locally and when to look for an idle workstation. For the processor pool model, a decision must be made for every new process. In this section we will study the algorithms used to determine which process is assigned to which processor. We will follow tradition and refer to this subject as "processor allocation" rather than "process allocation," although a good case can be made for the latter.

12.3.1. Allocation Models

Before looking at specific algorithms, or even at design principles, it is worthwhile saying something about the underlying model, assumptions, and goals of the work on processor allocation. Nearly all work in this area assumes that all the machines are identical, or at least code-compatible, differing at most by speed. An occasional paper assumes that the system consists of several disjoint processor pools, each of which is homogeneous. These assumptions are usually valid, and make the problem much simpler, but leave unanswered for the time being questions like whether a command to start up the text formatter should be started up on a 486, SPARC, or MIPS CPU, assuming that binaries for all of them are available.

Almost all published models assume that the system is fully interconnected, that is, every processor can communicate with every other processor. We will assume this as well. This assumption does not mean that every machine has a wire to every other machine; just that transport connections can be established between every pair of machines. That messages may have to be routed hop by hop over a sequence of machines is only of interest to the lower layers. Some networks support broadcasting or multicasting, and some algorithms use these facilities.

New work is generated when a running process decides to fork or otherwise create a subprocess. In some cases the forking process is the command interpreter (shell) that is starting up a new job in response to a command from the user. In others, a user process itself creates one or more children, for example, in order to gain performance by having all the children run in parallel.

Processor allocation strategies can be divided into two broad classes. In the first one, which we shall call **nonmigratory**, when a process is created, a decision is made about where to put it. Once placed on a machine, the process stays there until it terminates. It may not move, no matter how badly overloaded its machine becomes and no matter how many other machines are idle. In contrast, with **migratory** allocation algorithms, a process can be moved even if it has already started execution. While migratory strategies allow better load balancing, they are substantially more complex, and have a major impact on system design.

Implicit in an algorithm that assigns processes to processors is that we are trying to optimize something. If this were not the case, we could just make the assignments at random or in numerical order. Precisely what it is that is being optimized, however, varies from one system to another. One possible goal is to maximize **CPU utilization**, that is, maximize the number of CPU cycles actually executed on behalf of user jobs per hour of real time. Maximizing CPU utilization is another way of saying that CPU idle time is to be avoided at all costs. When in doubt, make sure every CPU has something to do.

Another worthy objective is minimizing mean **response time**. Consider, for example, the two processors and two processes of Fig. 12-22. Processor 1 runs at 10 MIPS; processor 2 runs at 100 MIPS, but has a waiting list of backlogged processes that will take 5 sec to finish off. Process A has 100 million instructions and process B has 300 million. The response times for each process on each processor (including the wait time) are shown in the figure. If we assign A to processor 1 and B to processor 2, the mean response time will be $(10 + 8)/2$ or 9 sec. If we assign them the other way around, the mean response time will be $(30 + 6)/2$ or 18 sec. Clearly the former is a better assignment in terms of minimizing mean response time.

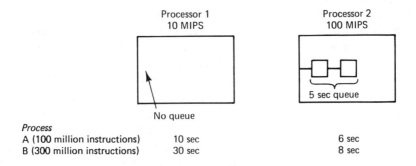

	Processor 1 10 MIPS	Processor 2 100 MIPS
	No queue	5 sec queue
Process		
A (100 million instructions)	10 sec	6 sec
B (300 million instructions)	30 sec	8 sec

Fig. 12-22. Response times of two processes on two processors.

A variation of minimizing the response time is minimizing the **response ratio**. The response ratio is defined as the amount of time it takes to run a process on some machine, divided by how long it would take on some unloaded benchmark processor. For many users, response ratio is a more useful metric than response time since it takes into account the fact that big jobs are supposed to take longer than small ones. To see this point, which is better, a 1 sec job that takes 5 sec or a 1 min job that takes 70 sec? Using response time, the former is better, but using response ratio, the latter is much better because $5/1 \gg 70/60$.

12.3.2. Design Issues for Processor Allocation Algorithms

A large number of processor allocation algorithms have been proposed over the years. In this section we will look at some of the key choices involved in these algorithms and point out the various tradeoffs. The major decisions the designers must make can be summed up in five issues:

1. Deterministic versus heuristic algorithms.

2. Centralized versus distributed algorithms.

3. Optimal versus suboptimal algorithms.

4. Local versus global algorithms.

5. Sender-initiated versus receiver-initiated algorithms.

Other decisions also come up, but these are the main ones. Let us look at each of these in turn.

Deterministic algorithms are appropriate when everything about process behavior is known in advance. Imagine that you have a complete list of all processes, their computing requirements, their file requirements, their communication requirements, and so on. Armed with this information, it is possible to make a perfect assignment. In theory, one could try all possible assignments and take the best one.

In few, if any, systems, is total knowledge available in advance, but sometimes a reasonable approximation is obtainable. For example, in banking, insurance, or airline reservations, today's work is just like yesterday's. The airlines have a pretty good idea of how many people want to fly from New York to Chicago on a Monday morning in early Spring, so the nature of the workload can be accurately characterized, at least statistically, making it possible to consider deterministic allocation algorithms.

At the other extreme are systems where the load is completely unpredictable. Requests for work depend on who's doing what, and can change dramatically from hour to hour, or even from minute to minute. Processor allocation in such systems cannot be done in a deterministic, mathematical way, but of necessity uses ad hoc techniques called **heuristics**.

The second design issue is centralized versus distributed. This theme has occurred repeatedly throughout the book. Collecting all the information in one place allows a better decision to be made, but is less robust and can put a heavy load on the central machine. Decentralized algorithms are usually preferable, but some centralized algorithms have been proposed for lack of suitable decentralized alternatives.

The third issue is related to the first two: "Are we trying to find the best alloca-tion, or merely an acceptable one?" Optimal solutions can be obtained in both cen-tralized and decentralized systems, but are invariably more expensive than subop-timal ones. They involve collecting more information and processing it more thoroughly. In practice, most actual distributed systems settle for heuristic, distri-buted, suboptimal solutions due to the difficulty of obtaining optimal ones.

The fourth issue relates to what is often called **transfer policy**. When a process is about to be created, a decision has to be made whether or not it can be run on the machine where it is being generated. If that machine is too busy, the new process must be transferred somewhere else. The choice here is whether to base the transfer decision entirely on local information or not. One school of thought advocates a sim-ple (local) algorithm: if the machine's load is below some threshold, keep the new process; otherwise try to get rid of it. Another school says that this heuristic is too crude. Better to collect (global) information about the load elsewhere before decid-ing whether the local machine is too busy for another process or not. Each one has its points. Local algorithms are simple, but may be far from optimal, whereas global ones may only give a slightly better result at much higher cost.

The last issue in our list deals with **location policy**. Once the transfer policy has decided to get rid of a process, the location policy has to figure out where to send it. Clearly the location policy cannot be local. It needs information about the load else-where to make an intelligent decision. This information can be disseminated in two ways, however. In one method, the senders start the information exchange. In another, it is the receivers that take the initiative.

As a simple example, look at Fig. 12-23(a). Here an overloaded machine sends out requests for help to other machines, in hopes of off-loading its new process on some other machine. The sender takes the initiative in locating more CPU cycles in this example. In contrast, in Fig. 12-23(b), a machine that is idle or underloaded announces to other machines that it has little to do and is prepared to take on extra work. Its goal is to locate a machine that is willing to give it some work to do.

For both the sender-initiated and receiver-initiated cases, various algorithms have different strategies for whom to probe, how long to continue probing, and what to do with the results. Nevertheless, the difference between the two approaches should be clear by now.

12.3.3. Implementation Issues for Processor Allocation Algorithms

The points raised in the previous section are all clear-cut theoretical issues about which one can have endless fine debates. In this section we will look at some other issues that are more related to the actual details of implementing processor allocation algorithms than to the great principles behind them.

To start with, virtually all the algorithms assume that machines know their own load, so they can tell if they are underloaded or overloaded, and can tell other machines about their state. Measuring load is not as simple as it first appears. One approach is simply to count the number of processes on each machine and use that

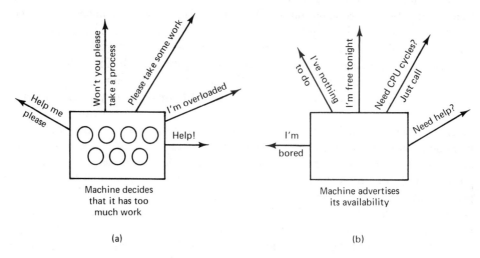

Fig. 12-23. (a) A sender looking for an idle machine. (b) A receiver looking for work to do.

number as the load. However, as we have pointed out before, even on an idle system there may be many processes running, including mail and news daemons, window managers, and other processes. Thus the process count says almost nothing about the current load.

The next step is to count only processes that are running or ready. After all, every running or runnable process puts some load on the machine, even if it is a background process. However, many of these daemons wake up periodically, check to see if anything interesting has happened, and if not, go back to sleep. Most put only a small load on the system.

A more direct measurement, although it is more work to capture, is the fraction of time the CPU is busy. Clearly a machine with a 20 percent CPU utilization is more heavily loaded than one with a 10 percent CPU utilization, no matter whether it is running user or daemon programs. One way to measure the CPU utilization is to set up a timer, and let it interrupt the machine periodically. At each interrupt, the state of the CPU is observed. In this way, the fraction of time spent in the idle loop can be observed.

A problem with timer interrupts is that when the kernel is executing critical code, it will often disable all interrupts, including the timer interrupt. Thus if the timer goes off while the kernel is active, the interrupt will be delayed until the kernel finishes. If the kernel was in the process of blocking the last active processes, the timer will not go off until the kernel has finished—and entered the idle loop. This effect will tend to underestimate the true CPU usage.

Another implementation issue is how overhead is dealt with. Many theoretical processor allocation algorithms ignore the overhead of collecting measurements and moving processes around. If an algorithm discovers that by moving a newly created process to a distant machine it can improve system performance by 10 percent, it may be better to do nothing, since the cost of moving the process may eat up all the gain. A proper algorithm should take into account the CPU time, memory usage, and network bandwidth consumed by the processor allocation algorithm itself. Few do, mostly because it is not easy.

Our next implementation consideration is complexity. Virtually all researchers measure the quality of their algorithms by looking at analytical, simulation, or experimental measures of CPU utilization, network usage, and response time. Seldom is the complexity of the software considered, despite the obvious implications for system performance, correctness, and robustness. It rarely happens that someone publishes a new algorithm, demonstrates how good its performance is, and then concludes that the algorithm is not worth using because its performance is only slightly better than existing algorithms but it is much more complicated to implement (or slower to run).

In this vein, a study by Eager et al. (1986) sheds some light on the subject of pursuing complex, optimal algorithms. They studied three algorithms. In all cases, each machine in the system measures its own load and decides for itself whether it is underloaded. Whenever a new process is created, the creating machine checks to see if it is overloaded. If so, it seeks out a remote machine to start the new process on. The three algorithms differ in how the candidate machine is located.

Algorithm 1 picks a machine at random and just sends the new process there. If the receiving machine itself is overloaded, it, too, picks a random machine and sends the process off. This process is repeated until either somebody is willing to take it, or a hop counter is exceeded, in which case no more forwarding is permitted.

Algorithm 2 picks a machine at random and sends it a probe asking if it is underloaded or overloaded. If the machine admits to being underloaded, it gets the new process; otherwise a new probe is tried. This loop is repeated until a suitable machine is found or the probe limit is exceeded, in which case it stays where it is created.

Algorithm 3 probes k machines to determine their exact loads. The process is then sent to the machine with the smallest load.

Intuitively, if we ignore all the overhead of the probes and process transfers, one would expect algorithm 3 to have the best performance, and indeed it does. But the gain in performance of algorithm 3 over algorithm 2 is small, even though the complexity and amount of additional work required are larger. Eager et al. concluded that if using a simple algorithm gives you most of the gain of a much more expensive and complicated one, it is better to use the simple one.

Our final point here is that stability is also an issue that crops up. Different machines run their algorithms asynchronously from one another, so the system is practically never in equilibrium. It is possible to get into situations where neither A nor B have quite up-to-date information, and each one thinks the other has a lighter load, resulting in some poor process being shuttled back and forth a large number of times. The problem is that most algorithms that exchange information can be shown to be correct after all the information has been exchanged and everything has settled down, but little can be said about their operation while tables are still being updated. It is in these nonequilibrium situations that unexpected problems often arise.

12.3.4. Example Processor Allocation Algorithms

To provide insight into how processor allocation can really be accomplished, in this section we will discuss several different algorithms. These have been selected to cover a broad range of possibilities, but they are by no means an exhaustive collection.

A Graph-Theoretic Deterministic Algorithm

A widely-studied class of algorithm is for systems consisting of processes with known CPU and memory requirements, and a known matrix giving the average amount of traffic between each pair of processes. If the number of CPUs, k, is smaller than the number of processes, several processes will have to be assigned to each CPU. The idea is to perform this assignment in such a way as to minimize network traffic.

The system can be represented as a weighted graph, with each node being a process and each arc representing the flow of messages between two processes. Mathematically, the problem then reduces to finding a way to partition (i.e., cut) the graph into k disjoint subgraphs, subject to certain constraints (e.g., total CPU and memory requirements below some limits for each subgraph). For each solution that meets the constraints, arcs that are entirely within a single subgraph represent intramachine communication, and can be ignored. Arcs that go from one subgraph to another represent network traffic. The goal is then to find the partitioning that minimizes the network traffic while meeting all the constraints. Figure 12-24 shows two ways of partitioning the same graph, yielding two different network loads.

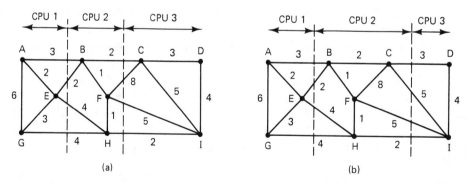

Fig. 12-24. Two ways of allocating 9 processes to 3 processors.

In Fig. 12-24(a), we have partitioned the graph with processes A, E, and G on one processor, processes B, F, and H on a second one, and processes C, D, and I on the third one. The total network traffic is the sum of the arcs intersected by the dotted cut lines, or 30 units. In Fig. 12-24(b) we have a different partitioning that has only 28 units of network traffic. Assuming that it meets all the memory and CPU constraints, this one is a better choice because it requires less communication.

Intuitively, what we are doing is looking for clusters that are tightly coupled (high intracluster traffic flow), but which interact little with other clusters (low intercluster traffic flow). Some of the many papers discussing the problem are (Chow and Abraham, 1982; Stone and Bokhari, 1978; and Lo, 1984).

A Centralized Algorithm

Graph-theoretic algorithms of the kind we have just discussed are of limited applicability since they require complete information in advance, so let us turn to a heuristic algorithm that does not require any advance information. This algorithm, called **up-down** (Mutka and Livny, 1987) is centralized in the sense that a coordinator maintains a **usage table** with one entry per personal workstation (i.e., per user), initially zero. When significant events happen, messages are sent to the coordinator to update the table. Allocation decisions are based on the table. These decisions are made when scheduling events happen: a processor is being requested, a processor has become free, or the clock has ticked.

The unusual thing about this algorithm, and the reason that it is centralized, is that instead of trying to maximize CPU utilization, it is concerned with giving each workstation owner a fair share of the computing power. Whereas other algorithms will happily let one user take over all the machines if he promises to keep them all busy (i.e., achieve a high CPU utilization), this algorithm is designed to prevent precisely that.

When a process is to be created, and the machine it is created on decides that the process should be run elsewhere, it asks the usage table coordinator to allocate it a processor. If there is one available and no one else wants it, the request is granted. If no processors are free, the request is temporarily denied, and a note is made of the request.

When a workstation owner is running processes on other people's machines, it accumulates penalty points, a fixed number per second, as shown in Fig. 12-25. These points are added to its usage table entry. When it has unsatisfied requests pending, penalty points are subtracted from its usage table entry. When no requests are pending and no processors are being used, the usage table entry is moved a certain number of points closer to zero, until it gets there. In this way, the score goes up and down, hence the name of the algorithm.

Usage table entries can be positive, zero, or negative. A positive score indicates that the workstation is a net user of system resources, whereas a negative one means that it needs resources. A zero score is neutral.

The heuristic used for processor allocation can now be given. When a processor becomes free, the pending request whose owner has the lowest score wins. As a consequence, a user who is occupying no processors and who has had a request pending for a long time will always beat someone who is using many processors. This property is the intention of the algorithm, to allocate capacity fairly.

In practice this means that if one user has a fairly continuous load on the system, and another user comes along and wants to start a process, the light user will be

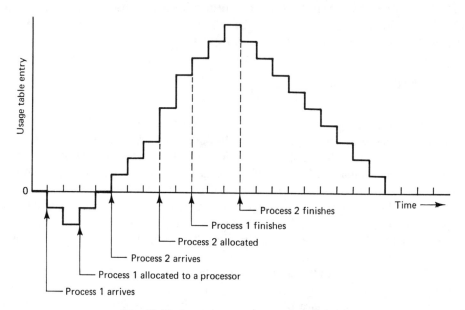

Fig. 12-25. Operation of the up-down algorithm.

favored over the heavy one. Simulation studies (Mutka and Livny, 1987) show that the algorithm works as expected under a variety of load conditions.

A Hierarchical Algorithm

Centralized algorithms, such as up-down, do not scale well to large systems. The central node soon becomes a bottleneck, not to mention a single point-of-failure. These problems can be attacked by using a hierarchical algorithm instead of a centralized one. Hierarchical algorithms retain much of the simplicity of centralized ones, but scale better.

One approach that has been proposed for keeping tabs on a collection of processors is to organize them in a logical hierarchy independent of the physical structure of the network, as in MICROS (Wittie and van Tilborg, 1980). This approach organizes the machines like people in corporate, military, academic, and other real-world hierarchies. Some of the machines are workers and others are managers.

For each group of k workers, one manager machine (the "department head") is assigned the task of keeping track of who is busy and who is idle. If the system is large, there will be an unwieldy number of department heads, so some machines will function as "deans," each riding herd on some number of department heads. If there are many deans, they too can be organized hierarchically, with a "big cheese" keeping tabs on a collection of deans. This hierarchy can be extended ad infinitum, with the number of levels needed growing logarithmically with the number of workers. Since each processor need only maintain communication with one superior and a few subordinates, the information stream is manageable.

An obvious question is: "What happens when a department head, or worse yet, a big cheese, stops functioning (crashes)?" One answer is to promote one of the direct subordinates of the faulty manager to fill in for the boss. The choice of which one can either be made by the subordinates themselves, by the deceased's peers, or in a more autocratic system, by the sick manager's boss.

To avoid having a single (vulnerable) manager at the top of the tree, one can truncate the tree at the top and have a committee as the ultimate authority, as shown in Fig. 12-26. When a member of the ruling committee malfunctions, the remaining members promote someone one level down as replacement.

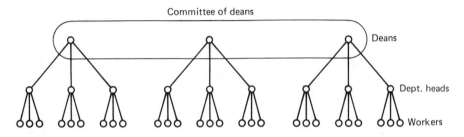

Fig. 12-26. A processor hierarchy can be modeled as an organizational hierarchy.

While this scheme is not really distributed, it is feasible, and in practice works well. In particular, the system is self-repairing, and can survive occasional crashes of both workers and managers without any long-term effects.

In MICROS, the processors are monoprogrammed, so if a job requiring S processes suddenly appears, the system must allocate S processors for it. Jobs can be created at any level of the hierarchy. The strategy used is for each manager to keep track of approximately how many workers below it are available (possibly several levels below it). If it thinks that a sufficient number are available, it reserves some number R of them, where $R \geq S$, because the estimate of available workers may not be exact and some machines may be down.

If the manager receiving the request thinks that it has too few processors available, it passes the request upwards in the tree to its boss. If the boss cannot handle it either, the request continues propagating upward until it reaches a level that has enough available workers at its disposal. At that point, the manager splits the request into parts, and parcels them out among the managers below it, which then do the same thing until the wave of allocation requests hits bottom. At the bottom level, the processors are marked as "busy" and the actual number of processors allocated is reported back up the tree.

To make this strategy work well, R must be large enough that the probability is high that enough workers will be found to handle the whole job. Otherwise the request will have to move up one level in the tree and start all over, wasting considerable time and computing power. On the other hand, if R is too large, too many processors will be allocated, wasting computing capacity until word gets back to the top and they can be released.

The whole situation is greatly complicated by the fact that requests for processors can be generated randomly anywhere in the system, so at any instant, multiple requests are likely to be in various stages of the allocation algorithm, potentially giving rise to out-of-date estimates of available workers, race conditions, deadlocks, and more. In Van Tilborg and Wittie (1981) a mathematical analysis of the problem is given and various other aspects not described here are covered in detail.

A Distributed Heuristic Algorithm

The above algorithms are all centralized or semicentralized. Distributed algorithms also exist. Typical of these are the ones described by Eager et al. (1986). As mentioned above, in the most cost effective algorithm they studied, when a process is created, the machine on which it originates sends probe messages to a randomly-chosen machine, asking if its load is below some threshold value. If so, the process is sent there. If not, another machine is chosen for probing. Probing does not go on forever. If no suitable host is found within N probes, the algorithm terminates and the process runs on the originating machine.

An analytical queueing model of this algorithm has been constructed and investigated. Using this model, it was established that the algorithm behaves well and is stable under a wide range of parameters, including different threshold values, transfer costs, and probe limits.

A Bidding Algorithm

Another class of algorithms tries to turn the computer system into a miniature economy, with buyers and sellers of services, and prices set by supply and demand (Ferguson et al., 1988). The key players in the economy are the processes, which must buy CPU time to get their work done, and processors, which auction their cycles off to the highest bidder.

Each processor advertises its approximate price by putting it in a publicly readable file. This price is not guaranteed, but gives an indication of what the service is worth (actually it is the price that the last customer paid). Different processors may have different prices depending on their speed, memory size, presence of floating-point hardware, and other features. An indication of the service provided, such as expected response time, can also be published.

When a process wants to start up a child process, it goes around and checks out who is currently offering the service that it needs. It then determines the set of processors whose services it can afford. From this set, it computes the best candidate, where "best" may mean cheapest, fastest, or best price/performance, depending on the application. It then generates a bid and sends the bid to its first choice. The bid may be higher or lower than the advertised price.

Processors collect all the bids sent to them, and make a choice, presumably by picking the highest one. The winners and losers are informed, and the winning process is executed. The published price of the server is then updated to reflect the new going rate.

Although Ferguson et al. do not go into the details, such an economic model raises all kinds of interesting questions, among them the following. Where do processes get money to bid? Do they get regular salaries? Does everyone get the same monthly salary, or do deans get more than professors, who in turn get more than students? If new users are introduced into the system without a corresponding increase in resources, do prices get bid up (inflation)? Can processors form cartels to gouge users? Are users' unions allowed? Is disk space also chargeable? How about laser printer output? The list goes on and on.

12.4. SCHEDULING IN DISTRIBUTED SYSTEMS

There is not really a lot to say about scheduling in a distributed system. Normally, each processor does its own local scheduling (assuming it has multiple processes running on it), without regard to what the other processors are doing. Usually this approach works fine. However, when a group of related, heavily interacting processes are all running on different processors, independent scheduling is not always the most efficient way.

The basic difficulty can be illustrated by an example in which processes A and B run on one processor and processes C and D run on another. Each processor is timeshared in, say, 100 msec time slices, with A and C running in the even slices, and B and D running in the odd ones, as shown in Fig. 12-27(a). Suppose that A sends many messages or makes many remote procedure calls to D. During time slice 0, A starts up and immediately calls D, which unfortunately is not running because it is now C's turn. After 100 msec, process switching takes place, and D gets A's message, carries out the work, and quickly replies. Because B is now running, it will be another 100 msec before A gets the reply and can proceed. The net result is one message exchange every 200 msec. What is needed is a way to ensure that processes that communicate frequently run simultaneously.

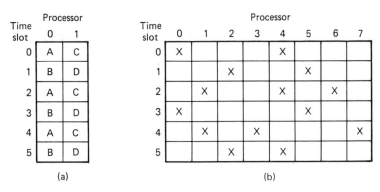

Fig. 12-27. (a) Two jobs running out of phase with each other. (b) Scheduling matrix for eight processors, each with six time slots. The Xs indicated allocated slots.

Although it is difficult to dynamically determine the interprocess communication patterns, in many cases, a group of related processes will be started off together. For example, it is usually a good bet that the filters in a UNIX pipeline will communicate with each other more than they will with other, previously started processes. Let us assume that processes are created in groups, and that intragroup communication is much more prevalent than intergroup communication. Let us further assume that a sufficiently large number of processors is available to handle the largest group, and that each processor is multiprogrammed with N process slots (N-way multiprogramming).

Ousterhout (1982) proposed several algorithms based on a concept he calls **coscheduling**, which takes interprocess communication patterns into account while scheduling to ensure that all members of a group run at the same time. The first algorithm uses a conceptual matrix in which each column is the process table for one processor, as shown in Fig. 12-27(b). Thus, column 4 consists of all the processes that run on processor 4. Row 3 is the collection of all processes that are in slot 3 of some processor, starting with the process in slot 3 of processor 0, then the process in slot 3 of processor 1, and so on. The gist of his idea is to have each processor use a round robin scheduling algorithm with all processors first running the process in slot 0 for a fixed period, then all processors running the process in slot 1 for a fixed period, etc. A broadcast message could be used to tell each processor when to do process switching, to keep the time slices synchronized.

By putting all the members of a process group in the same slot number, but on different processors, one has the advantage of N-fold parallelism, with a guarantee that all the processes will be run at the same time, to maximize communication throughput. Thus in Fig. 12-27(b), four processes that must communicate should be put into slot 3, on processors 1, 2, 3, and 4 for optimum performance. This scheduling technique can be combined with the hierarchical model of process management used in MICROS by having each department head maintain the matrix for its workers, assigning processes to slots in the matrix and broadcasting time signals.

Ousterhout also described several variations to this basic method to improve performance. One of these breaks the matrix into rows, and concatenates the rows to form one long row. With k processors, any k consecutive slots belong to different processors. To allocate a new process group to slots, one lays a window k slots wide over the long row such that the leftmost slot is empty but the slot just outside the left edge of the window is full. If sufficient empty slots are present in the window, the processes are assigned to the empty slots, otherwise the window is slid to the right and the algorithm repeated. Scheduling is done by starting the window at the left edge and moving rightward by about one window's worth per time slice, taking care not to split groups over windows. Ousterhout's paper discusses these and other methods in more detail and gives some performance results.

12.5. SUMMARY

Although threads are not an inherent feature of distributed operating systems, most of them have a threads package, so we have studied them in this chapter. A thread is a kind of lightweight process that shares an address space with one or more other threads. Each thread has its own program counter and stack, and is scheduled independently of the other threads. When a thread makes a blocking system call, the other threads in the same address space are not affected. Threads packages can be implemented in either user space or by the kernel, but there are problems to be solved either way. The use of lightweight threads has led to some interesting results in lightweight RPC as well.

Two models of organizing the processors are commonly used—the workstation model and the processor pool model. In the former, each user has his own workstation, sometimes with the ability to run processes on idle workstations. In the latter, the entire computing facility is a shared resource. Processors are then dynamically allocated to users as needed, and returned to the pool when the work is done. Hybrid models are also possible.

Given a collection of processors, some algorithm is needed for assigning processes to processors. Such algorithms can be deterministic or heuristic, centralized or distributed, optimal or suboptimal, local or global, and sender-initiated or receiver-initiated. Various examples were presented.

Finally, the chapter concluded with a discussion of co-scheduling.

PROBLEMS

1. In this problem you are to compare reading a file using a single threaded file server and multithreaded one. It takes 15 msec to get a request for work, dispatch it, and do the rest of the necessary processing, assuming that the data needed are in the block cache. If a disk operation is needed, as is the case 1/3 of the time, an additional 75 msec is required, during which time the thread sleeps. How many requests/sec can the server handle if it is single threaded? If it is multithreaded?

2. In Fig. 12-3 the register set is listed as a per-thread rather than a per process item. Why? After all, the machine only has one set of registers.

3. In the text, we described a multithreaded file server, showing why it is better than a single-threaded server and a finite-state machine server. Are there any circumstances in which a single-threaded server might be better? Give an example.

4. In the discussion on global variables in threads, we used a procedure *create_global* to allocate storage for a pointer to the variable, rather than the variable itself. Is this essential, or could the procedures work with the values themselves just as well?

5. Consider a system in which threads are implemented entirely in user space, with the run-time system getting a clock interrupt once a second. Suppose that a clock interrupt occurs while some thread is executing in the run-time system. What problem might occur? Can you suggest a way to solve it?

6. Suppose that an operating system does not have anything like the SELECT system call to see in advance if it is safe to read from a file, pipe, or device, but it does allow alarm clocks to be set that interrupt blocked system calls. Is it possible to implement a threads package in user space under these conditions? Discuss.

7. In a certain workstation-based system, the workstations have local disks that hold the system binaries. When a new binary is released, it is sent to each workstation. However, some workstations may be down (or switched off) when this happens. Devise an algorithm that allows the updating to be done automatically, even though workstations are occasionally down.

8. Can you think of any other kinds of files that can be safely stored on user workstations of the type described in the previous problem?

9. Would the scheme of Bershad et al. to make local RPCs go faster also work in a system with only one thread per process? How about the Peregrine method?

10. When two users examine the registry in Fig. 12-19 simultaneously, they may accidentally pick the same idle workstation. How can the algorithm be subtly changed to prevent this race?

11. Imagine that a process is running remotely on a previously idle workstation, which, like all the workstations, is diskless. For each of the following UNIX system calls, tell whether it has to be forwarded back to the home machine:

   a. READ (get data from a file).
   b. IOCTL (change the mode of the controlling terminal).
   c. GETPID (return the process id).

12. Compute the response ratios for Fig. 12-22 using processor 1 as the benchmark processor. Which assignment minimizes the average response ratio?

13. In the discussion of processor allocation algorithms, we pointed out that one choice is between centralized and distributed and another is between optimal and suboptimal. Devise two optimal location algorithms, one centralized and one decentralized.

14. In Fig. 12-24 we see two different allocation schemes, with different amounts of network traffic. Are there any other allocations that are better still? Assume that no machine may run more than four processes.

15. The up-down algorithm described in the text is a centralized algorithm design to allocate processors fairly. Invent a centralized algorithm whose goal is not fairness, but distributing the load uniformly.

16. Using the data of Fig. 12-27, what is the longest UNIX pipeline that can be co-scheduled?

13

DISTRIBUTED FILE SYSTEMS

A key component of any distributed system is the file system. As in single processor systems, in distributed systems the job of the file system is to store programs and data, and make them available as needed. Many aspects of distributed file systems are similar to the conventional file systems we studied in Chap. 4, so we will not repeat that material here. Instead we will concentrate on those aspects of distributed file systems that are different from centralized ones.

To start with, in a distributed system, it is important to distinguish between the concepts of the file service and the file server. The **file service** is the specification of what the file system offers to its clients. It describes the primitives available, what parameters they take, and what actions they perform. To the clients, the file service defines precisely what service they can count on, but says nothing about how it is implemented. In effect, the file service specifies the file system's interface to the clients.

A **file server**, in contrast, is a process that runs on some machine and helps implement the file service. A system may have one file server or several, but in a properly designed distributed system, the clients should not be aware of how the file system is implemented. In particular, they should not know how many file servers there are and what the location or function of each one is. All they know is that when they call the procedures specified in the file service, the required work is performed somehow, and the required results are returned. In fact, the clients should not even know that the file service is distributed. Ideally, it should look the same as a normal single processor file system.

Since a file server is normally just a user process (or sometimes a kernel process) running on some machine, a system may contain multiple file servers, each offering a different file service. For example, a distributed system may have two servers that offer UNIX file service and MS-DOS file service, respectively, with each user process using the one appropriate for it. In that way, it is possible to have a terminal with multiple windows, with UNIX programs running in some windows and MS-DOS programs running in other windows, with no conflicts. Whether the servers offer specific file services, such as UNIX or MS-DOS, or more general file services is up to the system designers. The type and number of file services available may even change as the system evolves.

13.1. DISTRIBUTED FILE SYSTEM DESIGN

A distributed file system typically has two reasonably distinct components: the true file service and the directory service. The former is concerned with the operations on individual files, such as reading, writing, and appending, whereas the latter is concerned with creating and managing directories, adding and deleting files from directories, and so on. In this section we will discuss the true file service interface; in the next one we will discuss the directory service interface.

13.1.1. The File Service Interface

For any file service, whether for a single processor or for a distributed system, the most fundamental issue is: "What is a file?" In many systems, such as UNIX and MS-DOS, a file is an uninterpreted sequence of bytes. The meaning and structure of the information in the files is entirely up to the application programs; the operating system is not interested.

On mainframes however, many types of files exist, each with different properties. A file can be structured as a sequence of records, for example, with operating system calls to read or write a particular record. The record can usually be specified by either giving its record number (i.e., position within the file), or the value of some field. In the latter case, the operating system either maintains the file as a B-tree or other suitable data structure, or uses hash tables to locate records quickly. Since most distributed systems are intended for UNIX or MS-DOS environments, most file servers support the notion of a file as a sequence of bytes, rather than as a sequence of keyed records.

A files can have **attributes**, which are pieces of information about the file but which are not part of the file itself. Typical attributes are the owner, size, creation date, and access permissions. The file service usually provides primitives to read and write some of the attributes. For example, it may be possible to change the access permissions but not the size (other than by appending data to the file). In a few advanced systems, it may be possible to create and manipulate user-defined attributes in addition to the standard ones.

Another important aspect of the file model is whether files can be modified after they have been created. Normally they can be, but in some distributed systems, the only file operations are CREATE and READ. Once a file has been created, it cannot be changed. Such a file is said to be **immutable**. Having files be immutable makes it much easier to support file caching and replication because it eliminates all the problems associated with having to update all copies of a file whenever it changes.

Protection in distributed systems uses essentially the same techniques as in single processor systems: capabilities and access control lists. With capabilities, each user has a kind of ticket, called a **capability**, for each object to which it has access. The capability specifies which kinds of accesses are permitted (e.g., reading is allowed but writing is not).

All **access control list** schemes associate with each file an implicit or explicit list of users who may access the file, and what kinds of access each one has. The UNIX scheme, with bits for controlling reading, writing, and executing each file separately for the owner, the owner's group, and everyone else is a simplified access control list.

File services can be split into two types, depending on whether they support an upload/download model or a remote access model. In the **upload/download model**, shown in Fig. 13-1(a), the file service provides only two major operations: read file and write file. The former operation transfers an entire file from one of the file servers to the requesting client. The latter operation transfers an entire file the other way, from client to server. Thus the conceptual model is moving whole files in either direction. The files can be stored in memory or on a local disk, as needed.

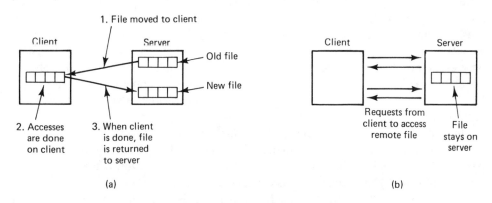

Fig. 13-1. (a) The upload/download model. (b) The remote access model.

The advantage of the upload/download model is its conceptual simplicity. Application programs fetch the files they need, then use them locally. Any modified files or newly created files are written back when the program finishes. No complicated file service interface has to be mastered to use this model. Furthermore, whole file transfer is highly efficient. The main disadvantage is that enough storage must be available on the client to store all the files required. Furthermore, if only a small fraction of a file is needed, moving the whole file is wasteful.

The other kind of file service is the **remote access model**, as illustrated in Fig. 13-1(b). In this model, the file service provides a large number of operations for opening and closing files, reading and writing parts of files, moving around within files (LSEEK), examining and changing file attributes, and so on. Whereas in the upload/download model, the file service merely provides physical storage and transfer, here the file system runs on the servers, not on the clients. It has the advantage of not requiring much space on the clients, as well as eliminating the need to pull in entire files when only small pieces are needed.

13.1.2. The Directory Server Interface

The other part of the file service is the directory service, which provides operations for creating and deleting directories, naming and renaming files, and moving them from one directory to another. The nature of the directory service does not depend on whether individual files are transferred in their entirety or accessed remotely.

The directory service defines some alphabet and syntax for composing file (and directory) names. File names can typically be from 1 to some maximum number of letters, numbers, and certain special characters. Some systems divide file names into two parts, usually separated by a period, such as *prog.c* for a C program or *man.txt* for a text file. The second part of the name, called the **file extension**, identifies the file type. Other systems use an explicit attribute for this purpose, instead of tacking an extension onto the name.

All distributed systems allow directories to contain subdirectories, to make it possible for users to group related files together. Accordingly, operations are provided for creating and deleting directories as well as entering, removing, and looking up files in them. Normally, each subdirectory contains all the files for one project, such as a large program or document (e.g., a book). When the (sub)directory is listed, only the relevant files are shown; unrelated files are in other (sub)directories and do not clutter the listing. Subdirectories can contain their own subdirectories, and so on, leading to a tree of directories, often called a **hierarchical file system**. Figure 13-2(a) illustrates a tree with five directories

In some systems, it is possible to create links or pointers to an arbitrary directory. These can be put in any directory, making it possible to build not only trees, but arbitrary directory graphs, which are more powerful. The distinction between trees and graphs is especially important in a distributed system.

The nature of the difficulty can be seen by looking at the directory graph of Fig. 13-2(b). In this figure, directory D has a link to directory B. The problem occurs when the link from A to B is removed. In a tree-structured hierarchy, a link to a directory can only be removed when the directory pointed to is empty. In a graph, it is allowed to remove a link to a directory as long as at least one other link exists. By keeping a reference count, shown in the upper right-hand corner of each directory in Fig. 13-2(b), it can be determined when the link being removed is the last one.

After the link from A to B is removed, B's reference count is reduced from 2 to 1, which on paper is fine. However, B is now unreachable from the root of the file system (A). The three directories, B, D, and E, and all their files are effectively orphans.

This problem exists in centralized systems as well, but it is more serious in distributed ones. If everything is on one machine, it is possible, albeit somewhat

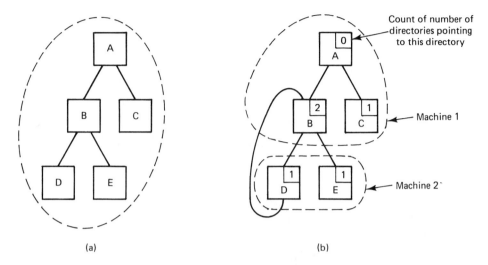

(a)   (b)

Fig. 13-2. (a) A directory tree contained on one machine. (b) A directory graph on two machines.

expensive, to discover orphaned directories, because all the information is in one place. All file activity can be stopped and the graph traversed starting at the root, marking all reachable directories. At the end of this process, all unmarked directories are known to be unreachable. In a distributed system, multiple machines are involved and all activity cannot be stopped so getting a "snapshot" is difficult, if not impossible.

A key issue in the design of any distributed file system is whether or not all machines (and processes) should have exactly the same view of the directory hierarchy. As an example of what we mean by this remark, consider Fig. 13-3. In Fig. 13-3(a) we show two file servers, each holding three directories and some files. In Fig. 13-3(b) we have a system in which all clients (and other machines) have the same view of the distributed file system. If the path /D/E/x is valid on one machine, then it is valid on all of them.

In contrast, in Fig. 13-3(c), different machines can have different views of the file system. To repeat the previous example, the path /D/E/x might well be valid on client 1 but not on client 2. In systems that manage multiple file servers by remote mounting, Fig. 13-3(c) is the norm. It is flexible and straightforward to implement, but it has the disadvantage of not making the entire system behave like a single old-fashioned timesharing system. In a timesharing system, the file system looks the same to any process [i.e., the model of Fig. 13-3(b)]. This property makes a system easier to program and understand.

A closely related question is whether or not there is a global root directory, which all machines recognize as the root. One way to have a global root directory is to have this root contain one entry for each server and nothing else. Under these circumstances, paths take the form /server/path, which has its own disadvantages, but at least is the same everywhere in the system.

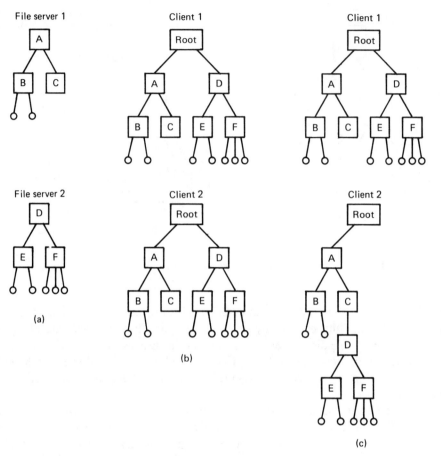

Fig. 13-3. (a) Two file servers. The squares are directories and the circles are files. (b) A system in which all clients have the same view of the file system. (c) A system in which different clients may have different views of the file system.

Naming Transparency

The principal problem with this form of naming is that it is not fully transparent. Two forms of transparency are relevant in this context, and are worth distinguishing. The first one, **location transparency**, means that the path name gives no hint as to where the file (or other object) is located. A path like */server1/dir1/dir2/x* tells everyone that *x* is located on server 1, but it does not tell where that server is located. The server is free to move anywhere it wants to in the network without the path name having to be changed. Thus this system has location transparency.

However, suppose file *x* is extremely large and space is tight on server 1. Furthermore, suppose that there is plenty of room on server 2. The system might well like to move *x* to server 2 automatically. Unfortunately, when the first component of all path names is the server, the system cannot move the file to the other server automatically, even if *dir1* and *dir2* exist on both servers. The problem is that moving the file automatically changes its path name from */server1/dir1/dir2/x* to */server2/dir1/dir2/x*. Programs that have the former string built into them will cease to work if the path changes. A system in which files can be moved without their names changing is said to have **location independence**. A distributed system that embeds machine or server names in path names clearly is not location independent. One based on remote mounting is not either, since it is not possible to move a file from one file group (the unit of mounting) to another and still be able to use the old path name. Location independence is not easy to achieve, but it is a desirable property to have in a distributed system.

To summarize what we have said earlier, there are three common approaches to file and directory naming in a distributed system:

1. Machine + path naming, such as */machine/path* or *machine:path*.

2. Mounting remote file systems onto the local file hierarchy.

3. A single name space that looks the same on all machines.

The first two are easy to implement, especially as a way to connect up existing systems that were not designed for distributed use. The latter is difficult, and requires careful design, but it is needed if the goal of making the distributed system act like a single computer is to be achieved.

Two-Level Naming

Most distributed systems use some form of two-level naming. Files (and other objects) have **symbolic names** such as *prog.c*, for use by people, but they can also have internal, **binary names** for use by the system itself. What directories in fact really do, is provide a mapping between these two naming levels. It is convenient for people and programs to use symbolic (ASCII) names, but for use within the system itself, these names are too long and cumbersome. Thus when a user opens a file or otherwise references a symbolic name, the system immediately looks up the symbolic name in the appropriate directory to get the binary name that will be used to actually locate the file. Sometimes the binary names are visible to the users and sometimes they are not.

The nature of the binary name varies considerably from system to system. In a system consisting of multiple file servers each of which is self contained (i.e., does not hold any references to directories or files on other file servers), the binary name can just be a local i-node number, as in UNIX.

A more general naming scheme is to have the binary name indicate both a server and a specific file on that server. This approach allows a directory on one server to hold a file on a different server. An alternative way to do the same thing that is sometimes preferred is to use a **symbolic link**. A symbolic link is a directory entry that maps onto a (server, file name) string, which can be looked up on the server named to find the binary name. The symbolic link itself is just a path name.

Yet another idea is to use capabilities as the binary names. In this method, looking up an ASCII name yields a capability, which can take one of many forms. For example, it can contain a physical or logical machine number or network address of the appropriate server, as well as a number indicating which specific file is required. A physical address can be used to send a message to the server without further interpretation. A logical address can be located either by broadcasting or looking it up on a name server.

One last twist that is sometimes present in a distributed system but rarely in a centralized one is the possibility of looking up an ASCII name and getting not *one*, but *several* binary names (i-nodes, capabilities, or something else). These would typically represent the original file and all its backups. Armed with multiple binary names, it is then possible to try to locate one of the corresponding files, and if that one is unavailable for any reason, to try one of the others. This method provides a degree of fault tolerance through redundancy.

13.1.3. Semantics of File Sharing

When two or more users share the same file, it is necessary to define the semantics of reading and writing precisely to avoid problems. In single-processor systems that permit processes to share files, such as UNIX, the semantics normally state that when a READ operation follows a WRITE operation, the READ returns the value just written, as shown in Fig. 13-4(a). Similarly, when two WRITEs happen in quick succession, followed by a READ, the value read is the value stored by the last write. In effect, the system enforces an absolute time ordering on all operations and always returns the most recent value. We will refer to this model as **UNIX semantics**. On a single-processor system (or even on a shared-memory multiprocessor) they are both easy to understand and straightforward to implement.

In a distributed system, UNIX semantics can be easily achieved as long as there is only one file server and clients do not cache files. All READs and WRITEs go directly to the file server, which processes them strictly sequentially. This approach gives UNIX semantics (except for the minor problem that network delays may cause a READ that occurred a microsecond after a WRITE to arrive at the server first and thus get the old value).

In practice, however, the performance of a distributed system in which all file requests must go to a single server is frequently poor. This problem is often solved by allowing clients to maintain local copies of heavily used files in their private caches. Although we will discuss the details of file caching below, for the moment it is sufficient to point out that if a client locally modifies a cached file and shortly thereafter another client reads the file from the server, the second client will get an obsolete file, as illustrated in Fig. 13-4(b).

One way out of this difficulty is to propagate all changes to cached files back to the server immediately. Although conceptually simple, this approach is inefficient. An alternative solution is to relax the semantics of file sharing. Instead of requiring a READ to see the effects of all previous WRITEs, one can have a new rule that says:

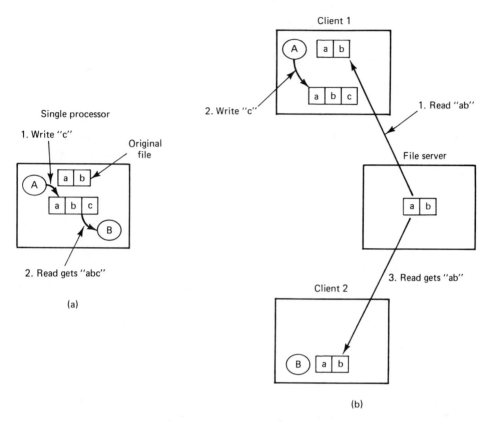

Fig. 13-4. (a) On a single processor, when a READ follows a WRITE, the value returned by the READ is the value just written. (b) In a distributed system with caching, obsolete values may be returned.

"Changes to an open file are initially visible only to the process (or possibly machine) that modified the file. Only when the file is closed are the changes made visible to other processes (or machines)." The adoption of such a rule does not change what happens in Fig. 13-4(b), but it does redefine the actual behavior (B getting the original value of the file) as being the correct one. When A closes the file, it sends a copy to the server, so that subsequent READs get the new value, as required. This rule is widely implemented and is known as **session semantics**.

Using session semantics raises the question of what happens if two or more clients are simultaneously caching and modifying the same file. One solution is to say that as each file is closed in turn, its value is sent back to the server, so the final result depends on who closes last. A less pleasant, but slightly easier to implement, alternative is to say that the final result is one of the candidates, but leave the choice of which one unspecified.

One final difficulty with using caching and session semantics is that it violates another aspect of the UNIX semantics in addition to not having all READs return the value most recently written. In UNIX, associated with each open file is a pointer that indicates the current position in the file. READs take data starting at this position and WRITEs deposit data there. This pointer is shared between the process that opened the file and all its children. With session semantics, when the children run on different machines, this sharing cannot be achieved.

To see what the consequences of having to abandon shared file pointers are, consider a command like:

```
run >out
```

where *run* is a shell script that executes two programs, *a* and *b*, one after another. If both programs produce output, it is expected that the output produced by *b* will directly follow the output from *a* within *out*. The way this is achieved is that when *b* starts up, it inherits the file pointer from *a*, which is shared by the shell and both processes. In this way, the first byte that *b* writes directly follows the last byte written by *a*. With session semantics and no shared file pointers, a completely different mechanism is needed to make shell scripts and similar constructions that use shared file pointers work. Since no general-purpose solution to this problem is known, each system must deal with it in an ad hoc way.

A completely different approach to the semantics of file sharing in a distributed system is to make all files immutable. There is thus no way to open a file for writing. In effect, the only operations on files are CREATE and READ.

What is possible is to create an entirely new file and enter it into the directory system under the name of a previous existing file, which now becomes inaccessible (at least under that name). Thus although it becomes impossible to modify the file *x*, it remains possible to (atomically) replace *x* by a new file. In other words, although *files* cannot be updated, *directories* can be. Once we have decided that files cannot be changed at all, the problem of how to deal with two processes, one of which is writing on a file and the other of which is reading it, simply disappears.

What does remain is the problem of what happens when two processes try to replace the same file at the same time. As with session semantics, the best solution here seems to be to allow one of the new files to replace the old one, either the last one or nondeterministically.

A somewhat stickier problem is what to do if a file is replaced while another process is busy reading it. One solution is to somehow arrange for the reader to continue using the old file, even if it is no longer in any directory, analogous to the way UNIX allows a process that has a file open to continue using it, even after it has been deleted from all directories. Another solution is to detect that the file has changed and make subsequent attempts to read from it fail.

A fourth way to deal with shared files in a distributed system is to use atomic transactions, as we discussed in detail in Chap. 11. To summarize briefly, to access a file or a group of files, a process first executes some type of BEGIN TRANSACTION primitive to signal that what follows must be executed indivisibly. Then come system calls to read and write one or more files. When the work has been completed, an END TRANSACTION primitive is executed. The key property of this method is that the system guarantees that all the calls contained within the transaction will be carried out in order, without any interference from other, concurrent transactions. If two or more transactions start up at the same time, the system ensures that the final result is the same as if they were all run in some (undefined) sequential order.

The classical example of where transactions make programming much easier is in a banking system. Imagine that a certain bank account contains 100 dollars, and that two processes are each trying to add 50 dollars to it. In an unconstrained system, each process might simultaneously read the file containing the current balance (100), individually compute the new balance (150), and successively overwrite the file with this new value. The final result could either be 150 or 200, depending on the precise timing of the reading and writing. By grouping all the operations into a transaction, interleaving cannot occur and the final result will always be 200.

In Fig. 13-5 we summarize the four approaches we have discussed for dealing with shared files in a distributed system.

Method	Comment
UNIX semantics	Every operation on a file is instantly visible to all processes
Session semantics	No changes are visible to other processes until the file is closed
Immutable files	No updates are possible; simplifies sharing and replication
Transactions	All changes have the all-or-nothing property

Fig. 13-5. Four ways of dealing with the shared files in a distributed system.

13.2. DISTRIBUTED FILE SYSTEM IMPLEMENTATION

In the previous section, we have described various aspects of distributed file systems from the user's perspective, that is, how they appear to the user. In this section we will see how these systems are implemented. We will start out by presenting some experimental information about file usage. Then we will go on to look at system structure, the implementation of caching, replication in distributed systems, and concurrency control. Finally, we will conclude with a short discussion of some lessons that have been learned from experience.

13.2.1. File Usage

Before implementing any system, distributed or otherwise, it is useful to have a good idea of how it will be used, in order to make sure that the most commonly executed operations will be efficient. To this end, Satyanarayanan (1981) made a comprehensive study of file usage patterns. We will present his major results below.

However, first, a few words of warning about these and similar measurements are in order. Some of the measurements are static, meaning they represent a snapshot of the system at a certain instant. Static measurements are made by examining the disk to see what is on it. These measurements include the distribution of file sizes, the distribution of file types, and the amount of storage occupied by files of various types and sizes. Other measurements are dynamic, made by modifying the file system to record all operations to a log for subsequent analysis. These data yield information about the relative frequency of various operations, the number of files open at any moment, and the amount of sharing that takes place. By combining the static and dynamic measurements, even though they are fundamentally different, we can get a better picture of how the file system is used.

One problem that always occurs with measurements of any existing system is knowing how typical the observed user population is. Satyanarayanan's measurements were made at a university. Do they also apply to industrial research labs? To office automation projects? To banking systems? No one really knows for sure until these systems, too, are instrumented and measured.

Another problem inherent in making measurements is watching out for artifacts of the system being measured. As a simple example, when looking at the distribution of file names in an MS-DOS system, one could quickly conclude that file names are never more than 8 characters (plus an optional three-character extension). However, it would be a mistake to draw the conclusion that eight characters are therefore enough, since nobody ever uses more than eight characters. Since MS-DOS does not allow more than eight characters in a file name, it is impossible to tell what users would do if they were not constrained to eight-character file names.

Finally, Satyanarayanan's measurements were made on more-or-less traditional UNIX systems. Whether or not they can be transferred or extrapolated to distributed systems is not really known.

This being said, the most important conclusions are listed in Fig. 13-6. From these observations, one can draw certain conclusions. To start with, most files are under 10K, which agrees with the results of Mullender and Tanenbaum (1984) made under different circumstances. This observation suggests that it may be feasible to transfer entire files rather than disk blocks between server and client. Since whole file transfer is typically simpler and more efficient, this idea is worth considering. Of course, some files are large, so provision has to be made for them too. Still, a good guideline is to optimize for the normal case and treat the abnormal case specially.

An interesting observation is that most files have short lifetimes. In other words, a common pattern is to create a file, read it (probably once) and then delete it. A typical usage might be a compiler that creates temporary files for transmitting information between its passes. The implication here is that it is probably a good idea to create the file on the client and keep it there until it is deleted. Doing so may eliminate a considerable amount of unnecessary client-server traffic.

The fact that few files are shared argues for client caching. As we have seen already, caching makes the semantics more complicated, but if files are rarely shared, it may well be best to do client caching and accept the consequences of session semantics in return for the better performance.

Finally, the clear existence of distinct file classes suggests that perhaps different mechanisms should be used to handle the different classes. System binaries need to

Most files are small (less than 10 K)
Reading is much more common than writing
Reads and writes are sequential; random access is rare
Most files have a short lifetime
File sharing is unusual
The average process uses only a few files
Distinct file classes with different properties exist

Fig. 13-6. Observed file system properties.

be widespread but hardly ever change, so they should probably be widely replicated, even if this means that an occasional update is complex. Compiler and other temporary files are short, unshared, and disappear quickly, so they should be kept locally wherever possible. Electronic mailboxes are frequently updated but rarely shared, so replication is not likely to gain anything. Ordinary data files may be shared, so they may need still other handling.

13.2.2. System Structure

In this section we will look at some of the ways that file servers and directory servers are organized internally, with special attention to alternative approaches. Let us start with a very simple question: "Are clients and servers different?" Surprisingly enough, there is no agreement on this matter.

In some systems (e.g., NFS), there is no distinction between a client and a server. All machines run the same basic software, so any machine that wants to offer file service to the public at large is free to do so. Offering file service is just a matter of exporting the names of selected directories so other machines can access them.

In other systems, the file server and directory server are just user programs, so a system can be configured to run client and server software on the same machines or not, as it wishes. Finally, at the other extreme, are systems in which clients and servers are fundamentally different machines, either in terms of hardware or software. The servers may even run a different version of the operating system from the clients. While separation of function may seem a bit cleaner, there is no fundamental reason to prefer one approach over the others.

A second implementation issue on which systems differ is how the file and directory service is structured. One organization is to combine the two into a single server that handles all the directory and file calls itself. Another possibility, however, is to keep them separate. In the latter case, opening a file requires going to the directory server to map its symbolic name onto its binary name (e.g., machine + i-node) and then going to the file server with the binary name to actually read or write the file.

Arguing in favor of the split is that the two functions are really unrelated, so keeping them separate is more flexible. For example, one could implement an MS-DOS directory server and a UNIX directory server, both of which use the same file server for physical storage. Separation of function is also likely to produce simpler software. Weighing against this is that having two servers requires more communication.

Let us consider the case of separate directory and file servers for the moment. In the normal case, the client sends a symbolic name to the directory server, which then returns the binary name that the file server understands. However, it is possible for a directory hierarchy to be partitioned among multiple servers, as illustrated in Fig. 13-7. Suppose, for example, we have a system in which the current directory, on server 1, contains an entry, *a*, for another directory on server 2. Similarly, this directory contains an entry, *b*, for a directory on server 3. This third directory contains an entry for a file *c*, along with its binary name.

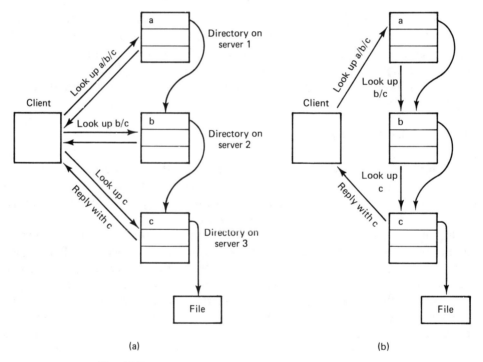

(a)   (b)

Fig. 13-7. (a) Iterative lookup of *a*/*b*/*c*. (b) Automatic lookup.

To look up *a*/*b*/*c*, the client sends a message to server 1, which manages its current directory. The server finds *a*, but sees that the binary name refers to another server. It now has a choice. It can either tell the client which server holds *b* and have the client look up *b*/*c* there itself, as shown in Fig. 13-7(a), or it can forward the remainder of the request to server 2 itself and not reply at all, as shown in Fig. 13-7(b). The former scheme requires the client to be aware of which server holds which directory, and requires more messages. The latter method is more efficient, but cannot be handled using normal RPC since the process to which the client sends the message is not the one that sends the reply.

Looking up path names all the time, especially if multiple directory servers are involved, can be expensive. Some systems attempt to improve their performance by maintaining a cache of hints, that is, recently looked up names and the results of these lookups. When a file is opened, the cache is checked to see if the path name is there. If so, the directory-by-directory lookup is skipped and the binary address is taken from the cache.

For name caching to work, it is essential that when an obsolete binary name is inadvertently used, the client is somehow informed so it can fall back on the directory-by-directory lookup to find the file and update the cache. Furthermore, to make hint caching worthwhile in the first place, the hints have to be right most of the time. When these conditions are fulfilled, caching hints can be a powerful technique that is applicable to many areas of distributed operating systems.

The final structural issue that we will consider here is whether or not file, directory, and other servers should maintain state information about clients. This issue is moderately controversial, with two competing schools of thought in existence.

One school thinks that servers should be **stateless**. In other words, when a client sends a request to a server, the server carries out the request, sends the reply, and then removes from its internal tables all information about the request. Between requests, no client-specific information is kept on the server. The other school of thought maintains that it is all right for servers to maintain state information about clients between requests. After all, centralized operating systems maintain state information about active processes, so why should this traditional behavior suddenly become unacceptable?

To better understand the difference, consider a file server that has commands to open, read, write, and close files. After a file has been opened, the server must maintain information about which client has which file open. Typically, when a file is opened, the client is given a file descriptor or other number which is used in subsequent calls to identify the file. When a request comes in, the server uses the file descriptor to determine which file is needed. The table mapping the file descriptors onto the files themselves is state information.

With a stateless server, each request must be self contained. It must contain the full file name and the offset within the file, in order to allow the server to do the work. This information increases message length.

Another way to look at state information is to consider what happens if a server crashes and all its tables are lost forever. When the server is rebooted, it no longer knows which clients have which files open. Subsequent attempts to read and write open files will then fail, and recovery, if possible at all, will be entirely up to the clients. As a consequence, stateless servers tend to be more fault tolerant than those that maintain state, which is one of the arguments in favor of the former.

The arguments both ways are summarized in Fig. 13-8. Stateless servers are inherently more fault tolerant, as we just mentioned. OPEN and CLOSE calls are not needed, which reduces the number of messages, especially for the common case in which the entire file is read in a single blow. No server space is wasted on tables.

When tables are used, if too many clients have too many files open at once, the tables can fill up and new files cannot be opened. Finally, with a stateful server, if a client crashes when a file is open, the server is in a bind. If it does nothing, its tables will eventually fill up with junk. If it times out inactive open files, then a client that happens to wait too long between requests will be refused service, and correct programs will fail to function correctly. Statelessness eliminates these problems.

Advantages of stateless servers	Advantages of stateful servers
Fault tolerance	Shorter request messages
No OPEN/CLOSE calls needed	Better performance
No server space wasted on tables	Readahead possible
No limits on number of open files	Idempotency easier
No problems if a client crashes	File locking possible

Fig. 13-8. A comparison of stateless and stateful servers.

Stateful servers also have things going for them. Since READ and WRITE messages do not have to contain file names, they can be shorter, thus using less network bandwidth. Better performance is frequently possible since information about open files (in UNIX terms, the i-nodes) can be kept in main memory until the files are closed. Blocks can be read in advance to reduce delay, since most files are read sequentially. If a client ever times out and sends the same request twice, for example, APPEND, it is much easier to detect this with state (by having a sequence number in each message). Achieving idempotency in the face of unreliable communication with stateless operation takes more thought and effort. Finally, file locking is impossible to do in a truly stateless system, since the only effect setting a lock has is to enter state into the system. In stateless systems, file locking has to be done by a special lock server.

13.2.3. Caching

In a client-server system, each with main memory and a disk, there are four potential places to store files, or parts of files: the server's disk, the server's main memory, the client's disk (if available), or the client's main memory, as illustrated in Fig. 13-9. These different storage locations all have different properties, as we shall see.

The most straightforward place to store all files is on the server's disk. There is generally plenty of space there and the files are then accessible to all clients. Furthermore, with only one copy of each file, no consistency problems arise.

The problem with using the server's disk is performance. Before a client can read a file, the file must first be transferred from the server's disk to the server's

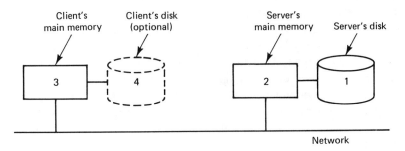

Fig. 13-9. Four places to store files or parts of files.

main memory, and then again over the network to the client's main memory. Both transfers take time.

A considerable performance gain can be achieved by **caching** (i.e., holding) the most recently used files in the server's main memory. A client reading a file that happens to be in the server's cache eliminates the disk transfer, although the network transfer still has to be done. Since main memory is invariably smaller than the disk, some algorithm is needed to determine which files or parts of files should be kept in the cache.

This algorithm has two problems to solve. First, what is the unit the cache manages? It can be either whole files or disk blocks. If entire files are cached, they can be stored contiguously on the disk (or at least in very large chunks), allowing high-speed transfers between memory and disk and generally good performance. Disk block caching, however, uses cache and disk space more efficiently.

Second, the algorithm must decide what to do when the cache fills up and something must be evicted. Any of the standard caching algorithms can be used here, but because cache references are so infrequent compared to memory references, an exact implementation of LRU using linked lists is generally feasible. When something has to be evicted, the oldest one is chosen. If an up-to-date copy exists on disk, the cache copy is just discarded. Otherwise, the disk is first updated.

Having a cache in the server's main memory is easy to do and totally transparent to the clients. Since the server can keep its memory and disk copies synchronized, from the clients' point-of-view, there is only one copy of each file, so no consistency problems arise.

Although server caching eliminates a disk transfer on each access, it still has a network access. The only way to get rid of the network access is to do caching on the client side, which is where all the problems come in. The tradeoff between using the client's main memory or its disk is one of space versus performance. The disk holds more, but is slower. When faced with a choice between having a cache in the server's main memory versus the client's disk, the former is usually somewhat faster, and it is always much simpler. Of course, if large amounts of data are being used, a client disk cache may be better. In any event, most systems that do client caching do it in the client's main memory, so we will concentrate on that.

If the designers decide to put the cache in the client's main memory, three options are open as to precisely where to put it. The simplest is to cache files directly inside each user process' own address space, as shown in Fig. 13-10(b). Typically, the cache is managed by the system call library. As files are opened, closed, read, and written, the library simply keeps the most heavily used ones around, so that when a file is reused, it may already be available. When the process exits, all modified files are written back to the server. Although this scheme has an extremely low overhead, it is only effective if individual processes open and close files repeatedly. A data base manager process might fit this description, but in the usual program development environment, most processes only read each file once, so caching within the library wins nothing.

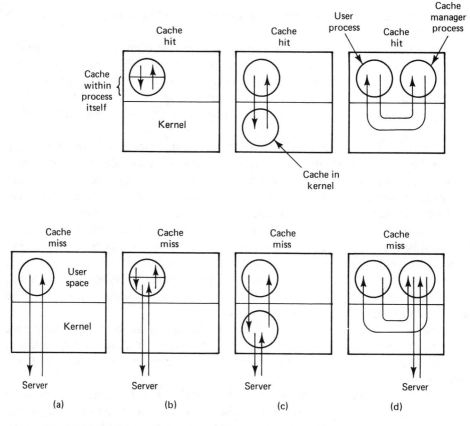

Fig. 13-10. Various ways of doing caching in client memory. (a) No caching. (b) Caching within each process. (c) Caching in the kernel. (d) The cache manager as a user process.

The second place to put the cache is in the kernel, as shown in Fig. 13-10(c). The disadvantage here is that a kernel call is needed in all cases, even on a cache hit, but the fact that the cache survives the process more than compensates. For example, suppose a two-pass compiler runs as two processes. Pass one writes an intermediate file read by pass two. In Fig. 13-10(c), after the pass one process terminates, the intermediate file will probably be in the cache, so no server calls will have to be made when the pass two process reads it in.

The third place for the cache is in a separate user-level cache manager process, as shown in Fig. 13-10(d). The advantage of a user-level cache manager is that it keeps the (micro)kernel free of file system code, is easier to program because it is completely isolated, and is more flexible.

On the other hand, when the kernel manages the cache, it can dynamically decide how much memory to reserve for programs and how much for the cache. With a user-level cache manager running on a machine with virtual memory, it is conceivable that the kernel could decide to page out some or all of the cache to a disk, so that a so-called "cache hit" requires one or more pages to be brought in. Needless to say, this defeats the idea of client caching completely. However, if it is possible for the cache manager to allocate and lock in memory some number of pages, this ironic situation can be avoided.

When evaluating whether caching is worth the trouble at all, it is important to note that in Fig. 13-10(a), it takes exactly one RPC to make a file request, no matter what. In both Fig. 13-10(c) and Fig. 13-10(d) it takes either one or two, depending on whether the request can be satisfied out of the cache or not. Thus the mean number of RPCs is always greater when caching is used. In a situation in which RPCs are fast and network transfers are slow (fast CPUs, slow networks) caching can give a big gain in performance. If, however, network transfers are very fast (e.g., with high-speed fiber optic networks), the network transfer time will matter less, so the extra RPCs may eat up a substantial fraction of the gain. Thus the performance gain provided by caching depends to some extent on the CPU and network technology available, and of course, on the applications.

Cache Consistency

As usual in computer science, you never get something for nothing. Client caching introduces inconsistency into the system. If two clients simultaneously read the same file and then both modify it, several problems occur. For one, when a third process reads the file from the server, it will get the original version, not one of the two new ones. This problem can be defined away by adopting session semantics (officially stating that the effects of modifying a file are not supposed to be visible globally until the file is closed). In other words, this "incorrect" behavior is simply declared to be the "correct" behavior. Of course, if the user expects UNIX semantics, the trick does not work.

Another problem, unfortunately, that cannot be defined away at all, is that when the two files are written back to the server, the one written last will overwrite the other one. The moral of the story is that client caching has to be thought out fairly carefully. Below we will discuss some of the problems and proposed solutions.

One way to solve the consistency problem is to use the **write through** algorithm. When a cache entry (file or block) is modified, the new value is kept in the cache, but is also immediately sent to the server. As a consequence, when another process reads the file, it gets the most recent value.

However, the following problem arises. Suppose a client process on machine A reads a file, f. The client terminates, but the machine keeps f in its cache. Later, a client on machine B reads the same file, modifies it, and writes it through to the server. Finally, a new client process is started up on machine A. The first thing it does is open and read f, which is taken from the cache. Unfortunately, the value there is now obsolete.

A possible way out is to require the cache manager to check with the server before providing any client with a file from the cache. This check could be done by comparing the time of last modification of the cached version with the server's version. If they are the same, the cache is up-to-date. If not, the current version must be fetched from the server. Instead of using dates, version numbers or checksums can also be used. Although going to the server to verify dates, version numbers, or checksums takes an RPC, the amount of data exchanged is small. Still, it takes some time.

Another trouble with the write through algorithm is that although it helps on reads, the network traffic for writes is the same as if there were no caching at all. Many system designers find this unacceptable, and cheat: instead of going to the server the instant the write is done, the client just makes a note that a file has been updated. Once every 30 seconds or so, all the file updates are gathered together and sent to the server all at once. A single bulk write is usually more efficient than many small ones.

Besides, many programs create scratch files, write them, read them back, and then delete them, all in quick succession. In the event that this entire sequence happens before it is time to send all modified files back to the server, the now-deleted file does not have to be written back at all. Not having to use the file server at all for temporary files can be a major performance gain.

Of course, delaying the writes muddies the semantics, because when another process reads the file, what it gets depends on the timing. Thus postponing the writes is a tradeoff between better performance and cleaner semantics (which translates into easier programming).

The next step in this direction is to adopt session semantics and only write a file back to the server after it has been closed. This algorithm is called **write-on-close**. Better yet, wait 30 seconds after the close to see if the file is going to be deleted. As we saw earlier, going this route means that if two cached files are written back in succession, the second one overwrites the first one. The only solution to this problem is to note that it is not nearly as bad as it first appears. In a single CPU system, it is possible for two processes to open and read a file, modify it within their respective address spaces, and then write it back. Consequently, write-on-close with session semantics is not that much worse than what can happen on a single CPU system.

A completely different approach to consistency is to use a centralized control algorithm. When a file is opened, the machine opening it sends a message to the file server to announce this fact. The file server keeps track of who has which file open, and whether it is open for reading, writing, or both. If a file is open for reading, there is no problem with letting other processes open it for reading, but opening it for writing must be avoided. Similarly, if some process has a file open for writing, all other accesses must be prevented. When a file is closed, this event must be reported, so the server can update its tables telling which client has which file open. The modified file can also be shipped back to the server at this point.

When a client tries to open a file and the file is already open elsewhere in the system, the new request can either be denied or queued. Alternatively, the server can send an **unsolicited message** to all clients having the file open, telling them to remove that file from their caches and disable caching just for that one file. In this way, multiple readers and writers can run simultaneously, with the results being no better and no worse than would be achieved on a single CPU system.

Although sending unsolicited messages is clearly possible, it is inelegant, since it reverses the client and server roles. Normally, servers do not spontaneously send messages to clients or initiate RPCs with them. If the clients are multithreaded, one thread can be permanently allocated to waiting for server requests, but if they are not, the unsolicited message must cause an interrupt.

Even with these precautions, one must be careful. In particular, if a machine opens, caches, and then closes a file, upon opening it again the cache manager must still check to see if the cache is valid. After all, some other process might have subsequently opened, modified, and closed the file. Many variations of this centralized control algorithm are possible, with differing semantics. For example, servers can keep track of cached files, rather than open files. All these methods have a single point of failure and none of them scale well to large systems.

The four cache management algorithms discussed above are summarized in Fig. 13-11. To summarize the subject of caching as a whole, server caching is easy to do and almost always worth the trouble, independent of whether client caching is present or not. Server caching has no effect on the file system semantics seen by the clients. Client caching, in contrast, offers better performance at the price of increased complexity and possibly fuzzier semantics. Whether it is worth doing or not depends on how the designers feel about performance, complexity, and ease of programming.

Method	Comments
Write through	Works, but does not affect write traffic
Delayed write	Better performance but possibly ambiguous semantics
Write on close	Matches session semantics
Centralized control	UNIX semantics, but not robust and scales poorly

Fig. 13-11. Four algorithms for managing a client file cache.

Earlier in this chapter, when we were discussing the semantics of distributed file systems, we pointed out that one of the design options is immutable files. One of the great attractions of an immutable file is the ability to cache it on machine A without having to worry about the possibility that machine *B* will change it. Changes are not permitted. Of course, a new file may have been created and bound to the same symbolic name as the cached file, but this can be checked for whenever a cached file is reopened. This model has the same RPC overhead discussed above, but the semantics are less fuzzy.

13.2.4. Replication

Distributed file systems often provide file replication as a service to their clients. In other words, multiple copies of selected files are maintained, with each copy on a separate file server. The reasons for offering such a service vary, but among the major reasons are:

1. To increase reliability by having independent backups of each file. If one server goes down, or is even lost permanently, no data are lost. For many applications, this property is extremely desirable.

2. To allow file access to occur even if one file server is down. The motto here is: "The show must go on." A server crash should not bring the entire system down until the server can be rebooted.

3. To split the workload over multiple servers. As the system grows in size, having all the files on one server can become a performance bottleneck. By having files replicated on two or more servers, the least heavily loaded one can be used.

The first two relate to improving reliability and availability; the third concerns performance. All are important.

A key issue relating to replication is transparency (as usual). To what extent are the users aware that some files are replicated? Do they play any role in the replication process, or is it handled entirely automatically? At one extreme, the users are fully aware of the replication process, and can even control it. At the other, the system does everything behind their backs. In the latter case, we say the system is **replication transparent**.

Figure 13-12 shows three ways replication can be done. The first way, shown in Fig. 13-12(a), is for the programmer to control the entire process. When a process makes a file, it does so on one specific server. Then, it can make additional copies on other servers, if desired. If the directory server permits multiple copies of a file, the network addresses of all copies can then be associated with the file name, as shown at the bottom of Fig. 13-12(a), so that when the name is looked up, all copies will be found. When the file is subsequently opened, the copies can be tried sequentially in some order, until an available one is found.

To make the concept of explicit replication more familiar, consider how it can be done in a system based on remote mounting in UNIX. Suppose that a programmer's home directory is */machine1/usr/ast*. After creating a file, for example the file, */machine1/usr/ast/xyz*, the programmer, process, or library can use the *cp* command

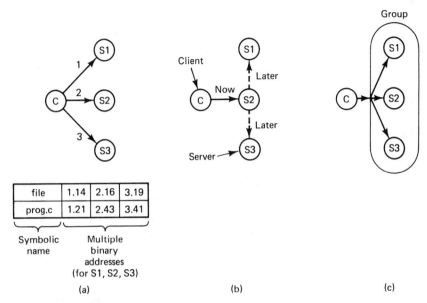

| file | 1.14 | 2.16 | 3.19 |
| prog.c | 1.21 | 2.43 | 3.41 |

Symbolic   Multiple
  name   binary
         addresses
     (for S1, S2, S3)

(a)   (b)   (c)

Fig. 13-12. (a) Explicit file replication. (b) Lazy file replication. (c) File replication using a group.

(or equivalent) to make copies in */machine2/usr/ast/xyz* and */machine3/usr/ast/xyz*. Programs can be written to accept strings like */usr/ast/xyz* as arguments, and successively try to open the copies until one succeeds. While this scheme can be made to work, it is a lot of trouble. For this reason, a distributed system should do better.

In Fig. 13-12(b) we see an alternative approach, **lazy replication**. Here, only one copy of each file is created, on some server. Later, the server itself makes replicas on other servers automatically, without the programmer's knowledge. The system must be smart enough to be able to retrieve any of these copies if need be. When making copies in the background like this, it is important to pay attention to the possibility that the file might change before the copies can be made.

Our final method is to use group communication, as shown in Fig. 13-13(c). In this scheme, all WRITE system calls are simultaneously transmitted to all the servers at once, so extra copies are made at the same time the original is made. There are two principal differences between lazy replication and using a group. First, with lazy replication, one server is addressed, rather than a group. Second, lazy replication happens in the background, when the server has some free time, whereas when group communication is used, all copies are made at the same time.

Update Protocols

Above we looked at the problem of how replicated files can be created. Now let us see how existing ones can be modified. Just sending an update message to each copy in sequence is not a good idea because if the process doing the update crashes part way through, some copies will be changed and others not. As a result, some future reads may get the old value and others may get the new value, hardly a desirable situation. We will look at two well-known algorithms that solve this problem.

The first one is called **primary copy replication**. When it is used, one server is designated as the primary. All the others are secondaries. When a replicated file is to be updated, the change is sent to the primary server, which makes the change locally, and then sends commands to the secondaries, ordering them to change too. Reads can be done from any copy, primary or secondary.

To guard against the situation that the primary crashes before it has had a chance to instruct all the secondaries, the update should be written to stable storage prior to changing the primary copy. In this way, when a server reboots after a crash, a check can be made to see if any updates were in progress at the time of the crash. If so, they can still be carried out. Sooner or later, all the secondaries will be updated.

Although the method is straightforward, it has the disadvantage that if the primary is down, no updates can be performed. To get around this asymmetry, Gifford (1979) proposed a more robust method, known as **voting**. The basic idea is to require clients to request and acquire the permission of multiple servers before either reading or writing a replicated file.

As a simple example of how the algorithm works, suppose that a file is replicated on N servers. We could make a rule stating that to update a file, a client must first contact at least half the servers plus 1 (a majority) and get them to agree to do the update. Once they have agreed, the file is changed and a new version number is associated with the new file. The version number is used to identify the version of the file, and is the same for all the newly updated files.

To read a replicated file, a client must also contact at least half the servers plus 1 and ask them to send the version numbers associated with the file. If all the version numbers agree, this must be the most recent version because an attempt to update only the remaining servers would fail because there are not enough of them.

For example, if there are five servers, and a client determines that three of them have version 8, it is impossible that the other two have version 9. After all, any successful update from version 8 to version 9 requires getting three servers to agree to it, not just two.

Gifford's scheme is actually somewhat more general than this. In it, to read a file of which N replicas exist, a client needs to assemble a **read quorum**, an arbitrary collection of any N_r servers, or more. Similarly, to modify a file, a **write quorum** of at least N_w servers is required. The values of N_r and N_w are subject to the constraint that $N_r + N_w > N$. Only after the appropriate number of servers has agreed to participate can a file be read or written.

To see how this algorithm works, consider Fig. 13-13(a), which has $N_r = 3$ and $N_w = 10$. Imagine that the most recent write quorum consisted of the 10 servers C through L. All of these get the new version and the new version number. Any subsequent read quorum of three servers will have to contain at least one member of this set. When the client looks at the version numbers, it will know which is most recent and take that one.

In Fig. 13-13(b) and Fig. 13-13(c) we see two more examples. The latter is especially interesting because it sets N_r to 1, making it possible to read a replicated file by

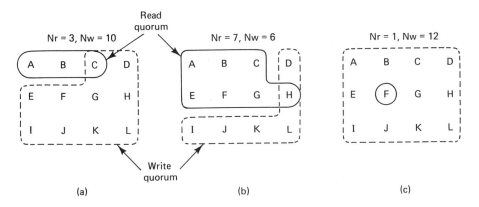

Fig. 13-13. Three examples of the voting algorithm.

finding any copy and using it. The price paid, however, is that write updates need to acquire all copies.

An interesting variation on voting is **voting with ghosts** (Van Renesse and Tanenbaum, 1988). In most applications, reads are much more common than writes, so N_r is typically a small number and N_w is nearly N. This choice means that if a few servers are down, it may be impossible to obtain a write quorum at all.

Voting with ghosts solves this problem by creating a dummy server, with no storage, for each real server that is down. A ghost is not permitted in a read quorum (it does not have any files, after all), but it may join a write quorum, in which case it just throws away the file written to it. A write only succeeds if at least one server is real.

When a failed server is rebooted, it must obtain a read quorum to locate the most recent version, which it then copies to itself before starting normal operation. The algorithm works because it has the same property as the basic voting scheme, namely, N_r and N_w are chosen so that acquiring a read quorum and a write quorum at the same time is impossible. The only difference here is that dead machines are allowed in a write quorum, subject to the condition that when they come back up they immediately obtain the current version before going into service.

Other replication algorithms are described in (Bernstein and Goodman, 1984; Brereton, 1986; Pu et al., 1986; and Purdin et al., 1987).

13.2.5. An Example: The Andrew File System

To illustrate some of the ideas discussed above, let us take a look at an example distributed file system in some detail. The example we have chosen is the **Andrew File System** (AFS) developed at Carnegie Mellon University (CMU) and named in honor of that university's original benefactors, Andrew Carnegie and Andrew Mellon. AFS grew out of a project started in the early 1980s to provide every student and faculty member at CMU with a powerful personal workstation running BSD UNIX. Normally, each person uses only his own private workstation (although there has been some experimenting with using idle workstations), so this is not really a transparent distributed system in which all resources are dynamically assigned to users as needed. Nevertheless, the file system has been designed to provide transparent access to all users, independent of which workstation they are using, so it is worth studying a little bit. For more information, see (Howard et al. 1988; Morris et al, 1986, and Satyanarayanan et al., 1985).

The characteristic that distinguishes AFS from other distributed file systems is its scale. It has been designed to handle 5000 to 10,000 connected workstations, a substantial fraction of which might be active at any instant. This requirement has had a major impact on the design, ruling out the use of virtually all centralized algorithms.

AFS Architecture

The system configuration is illustrated in Fig. 13-14. It consists of clusters, with a file server and several dozen client workstations per cluster. The idea is to arrange for most traffic to be local to a single cluster, to reduce the load on the backbone.

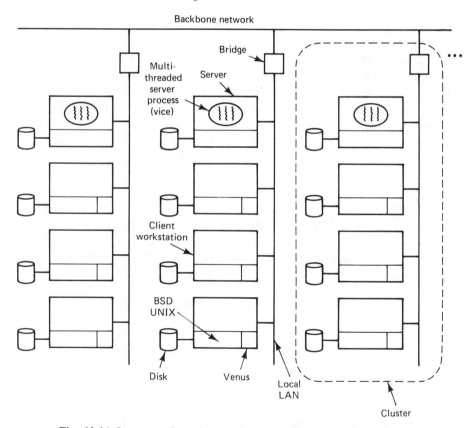

Fig. 13-14. System configuration used by AFS at Carnegie Mellon University.

However, since students may log into any workstation on campus, it is inevitable that some users will be far from the server holding their files. Nevertheless, a user

must be able to walk up to an arbitrary workstation and be able to use it as though it
was a personal computer.

Physically, there is no distinction between client and server machines, and all of
them run (slightly different) modified versions of the Berkeley UNIX operating system, with its large monolithic kernel. Above the kernel, clients and servers run completely different software, however. Client machines run window managers, editors,
and other standard UNIX software, whereas each server runs a single program, called
vice, which handles file requests for its clients. Each client also has a piece of code
called **venus**, which handles the interface between the client and *vice*. Originally
venus ran as a user program, but it was later moved to the kernel to improve the performance. *Venus* also functions as the cache manager.

The name space visible to user programs looks like a traditional UNIX tree, with
the addition of a directory */cmu*, as depicted in Fig. 13-15. The contents of */cmu* are
supported by AFS via the *vice* servers, and are identical on all workstations. The
other directories and files are strictly local and are not shared. They contain the temporary files, cache, workstation initialization files, and so on. In effect, the shared
file system is accessed by mounting it on */cmu*. Files that UNIX expects to find in the
upper part of the file system can be set up as symbolic links to the shared file system
(e.g., */bin/sh* can be a symbolic link to */cmu/bin/sh* if that is desired).

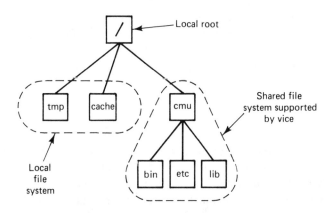

Fig. 13-15. A client workstation's view of the file system.

The basic idea behind AFS is for each user to do as much as possible on his
workstation and interact as little as possible with the rest of the system. When a file
is opened, the entire file (or if it is a huge file, a large chunk of it) is downloaded to
the workstation's disk and cached there, without the process that did the OPEN even
knowing about this. For this reason, every client workstation has a hard disk.

After a file has been downloaded, it is inserted into a local directory */cache*, so it
looks like a normal file to the operating system. The file descriptor returned by the
OPEN system call designates this file, so that READ and WRITE system calls work in
the usual way, without *venus* or *vice* being involved at all. In other words, although
the operating system code that handles the OPEN system call has been heavily modified to handle the interaction between the client, the cache, and the file server, the

code for READ and WRITE have not been touched. They just use the local file in /cache in blissful ignorance of the rest of the world.

Before getting into more details about the semantics and implementation of AFS, let us make a few other general comments. Security is a major issue in a system with 5000 to 10,000 users. Since users are able to reboot their workstations at will and can run specially doctored versions of the operating system on them, a basic design principle is for *vice* not to trust the client workstations. All traffic between the workstations and the servers is encrypted, supported by hardware. This measure should foil most peeping Toms.

Protection is done in a somewhat unusual way. Directories are protected by access control lists, but files have the usual 9 UNIX *rwx* bits for the owner, group and others. The designers really preferred the access control list scheme, but since many UNIX programs manipulate the *rwx* bits, they were left in for compatibility. The access control lists may contain **negative rights**, so it is possible to express the fact that everyone in the world except Joe Smith may read a certain directory.

Since the workstation disks are only used for temporary files, the file cache, and paging traffic, but no permanent information, system maintenance is greatly simplified. Only the servers need to be maintained and backed up. The client workstations do not, since they have nothing important on them. Conceptually, they can start out with a fresh disk each day.

AFS has been designed to scale to a national file system. The system shown in Fig. 13-14 is actually just the contents of a single **cell**. Each cell is an administrative entity, such as a department or a company. Multiple cells can be attached together using a form of mounting, to build a shared file tree that spans multiple sites.

AFS Semantics

In addition to the concepts of file, directory, and cell, AFS supports another important entity, the volume. A **volume** is a collection of directories that are managed together. Typically, each user's files form a volume. Thus the subtree under */usr/john* might be one volume and the subtree under */usr/mary* might be another. Each cell is, in fact, no more than a collection of volumes glued together in some appropriate way at mount points. While many volumes contain user files, others are used for executable binaries and other system information. Volumes can be read-only or read-write.

The semantics offered by AFS are close to session semantics. When a file is opened, it is fetched from the appropriate server and placed in /cache on the workstation's local disk. All reads and writes operate on the cached copy. When the file is closed, it is uploaded back to the server. As a consequence of this model, when a process opens an already open file, the version it sees depends on where it is.

A process on the same workstation sees the copy in /cache, no matter what state it is in (partly modified, etc.). On a single workstation, exact UNIX semantics apply, because nearly all of the operating system thinks of itself as a normal single CPU UNIX system. It knows next to nothing about all the other machines.

In contrast, a process on another workstation continues to see the original file on the server. Only when the file is closed and sent back to the server will subsequent attempts to open it acquire the new version.

After a file is closed, it is kept in the cache, in case it is opened again soon. As we saw earlier, reopening a file that is still cached creates a dilemma: "How does *venus* know if the cached file is still valid?" In the first version of AFS, the problem was solved by having *venus* contact the server to simply ask. Unfortunately, these requests contributed a substantial amount of traffic to the network, so the algorithm was later changed.

In the new algorithm, when *venus* downloads a file into its cache, it tells *vice* whether or not it cares about subsequent opens by processes on other workstations. If it does, *vice* makes a table entry noting the location of the cached file. If another process elsewhere in the system opens the file, *vice* sends a message to *venus* telling it to mark the cache entry as invalid. If the file is currently in use, the processes using it can continue to do so. If, however, another process tries to open it, *venus* is required to check with *vice* to see if the cache entry is still valid, and if not, to fetch a 0w copy. If a workstation crashes and then reboots, for safety's sake, all cache entries are marked as invalid.

File locking is supported using the UNIX FLOCK system call. If a lock is not released within 30 minutes, it times out and is released. Although read-only volumes, such as the system binaries, are replicated, user files are not.

AFS Implementation

As discussed above, each workstation runs a more-or-less standard single CPU copy of Berkeley UNIX. The major change made is the addition of the *venus* code to the kernel, and the redirection of the OPEN and CLOSE system calls to *venus* to do cache management. In addition, for OPEN, *venus* returns a file descriptor for an i-node belonging to a file in /*cache*, instead of one for the original file on *vice*.

Although application programs see a traditional UNIX name space, internally, *vice* and *venus* use a completely different naming scheme. They use a two-level naming system in which directory lookups of path names yield structures called **fids** (**file identifiers**) instead of the traditional i-node numbers. A fid is pictured in Fig. 13-16.

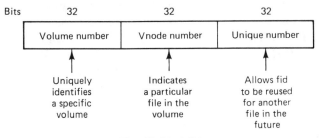

Fig. 13-16. A fid.

A fid has three 32-bit fields. The first field is the *Volume number*, which uniquely identifies a single volume in the system. This field tells which volume contains the file. The second field is the *Vnode number*, an index into the system tables for the specified volume. It is used to identify and locate a particular file within that volume. The third field is the *Unique number*, which is used to make it possible to reuse vnodes. If a file is deleted, its vnode can be reused, but with a different value for *Unique number*, in order to detect and reject any old fids still floating around.

The protocol between *venus* and *vice* uses fids to identify files. When a fid comes in to *vice*, the *volume number* field is looked up in a data base maintained by all the *vice* servers in order to locate the appropriate one. Volumes may migrate between servers (but not parts of volumes), so the data base needs to be updated from time to time, but volume migration is not a common event, so the update traffic is manageable.

Volume migration is atomic—first a copy of the volume is made at the destination site, then the original is deleted. This mechanism is also used for replicating read-only volumes, except that the original is not deleted after the copy is made. Furthermore, it is also used for making backups. When the copy is made, it is put into the file system as a read-only volume and the original left intact. During the course of the next 24 hours, a daemon process will copy the read-only backup copy to tape. An additional advantage of this method is that a user who accidentally deletes a file still has access to yesterday's copy.

We can now explain the full mechanism by which files are accessed in AFS. When an application program makes an OPEN system call, the call is caught by *venus*, which first checks the path name to see if it starts with /cmu. If not, the file is local and is processed in the usual way. If the name does start with /cmu, the file is shared. The name is parsed and looked up component by component until the fid is found. *Venus* then uses the fid to check the cache, yielding one of three possibilities:

1. The file is present and valid.
2. The file is present and invalid.
3. The file is not in the cache.

In the first case, the cached file is used. In the second case, *venus* asks *vice* if the file has changed since it was downloaded. The fact that it is invalid either means that the workstation has recently crashed and rebooted or that some other process has opened the file for writing, but neither imply that the file has already been modified and uploaded to the server. If the file is unchanged, the cached file is used. If it has changed, a new copy is downloaded. In the third case, the file is also downloaded. In all three cases, the final result is that a copy of the file is on the local disk in /cache and marked valid.

Application program calls to READ and WRITE are not caught by *venus*. They are handled in the usual way. Calls to CLOSE are trapped by *venus*, which then checks to see if the file has been modified, and if so, uploads it to the server that manages its volume.

In addition to caching files, *venus* also maintains a cache that maps path names to fids. Thus when a path name has to be parsed to get the fid, a quick check is made to see if the path name happens to be in the cache. If so, the whole lookup procedure is skipped and the cached fid is used. A problem exists if the file was removed after the fid was cached, and replaced by another file. However, this new file will have a different *Unique number* field, so the fid will be detected as invalid. *Venus* will handle this by deleting the (path, fid) entry and parsing the name from scratch. If the disk cache fills up, *venus* deletes files from it using the LRU algorithm.

Having looked at *venus*, let us say a few words about *vice*. *Vice* runs as a single multithreaded program on each of the server machines. Each thread handles one request. The protocol between *vice* and *venus* uses RPC and is built directly on IP. Commands are available for moving files in both directions, locking and unlocking files, managing directories, and other things. *Vice* keeps its tables in virtual memory, so it need not be concerned with how big they are. The underlying operating system pages them in and out as needed.

Vice is basically just an ordinary user program. Since *venus* identifies files it needs by giving their fids, *vice* has a potential problem: how can it access a UNIX file whose vnode number it knows, but whose path name it does not know? The solution chosen by AFS was to add new system calls to UNIX to allow *vice* to access files by vnode number.

13.2.6. Lessons Learned

Based on his experience with AFS and other distributed file systems, Satyanarayanan (1990b) has stated some general principles that he believes distributed file system designers should follow. We have summarized these in Fig. 13-17. The first principle says that workstations have enough CPU power that it is wise to use them wherever possible. In particular, given a choice of doing something on a workstation or on a server, choose the workstation because server cycles are precious and workstation cycles are not.

Workstations have cycles to burn
Cache whenever possible
Exploit the usage properties
Minimize systemwide knowledge and change
Trust the fewest possible entities
Batch work where possible

Fig. 13-17. Distributed file system design principles.

The second principle says to use caches. They can frequently save a large amount of computing time and network bandwidth.

The third principle says to exploit usage properties. For example, in a typical UNIX system, about a third of all file references are to temporary files, which have short lifetimes and are never shared. By treating these specially, as in AFS, considerable performance gains are possible. In all fairness, there is another school of thought that says: "Pick a single mechanism and stick to it. Do not have five ways of doing the same thing." Which view one takes depends on whether one prefers efficiency or simplicity.

Minimizing systemwide knowledge and change is important for making the system scale. Hierarchical designs help in this respect.

Trusting the fewest possible entities is a long established principle in the security world. If the correct functioning of the system depends on 10,000 workstations all doing what they are supposed to, the system has a big problem.

Finally, batching can lead to major performance gains. An example is the whole file transfers used in AFS. Transmitting a 50K file in one blast is much more efficient than sending it as 50 1K blocks.

13.3. TRENDS IN DISTRIBUTED FILE SYSTEMS

Although rapid change has been a part of the computer industry since its inception, new developments seem to be coming faster than ever in recent years. Many of these hardware changes are likely to have major impact on the distributed file systems of the future. Changing user expectations are also likely to have a major impact. In this section, we will survey some of the changes that can be expected in the foreseeable future, and discuss some of the implications these changes may have for file systems. This section will raise more questions than it will answer, but it will suggest some interesting directions for future research.

13.3.1. New Hardware

Before looking at new hardware, let us first look at old hardware with new prices. As memory continues to get cheaper and cheaper, we may see a revolution in the way file servers are organized. Currently, all file servers use magnetic disks for storage. Main memory is often used for server caching, but this is merely an optimization for better performance. It is not essential.

Within a few years, memory may become so cheap that even small organizations can afford to equip all their file servers with gigabytes of physical memory. As a consequence, the file system may permanently reside in memory, and no disks will be needed. Such a step will give a large gain in performance, and will greatly simplify file system structure.

Most current file systems organize files as a collection of blocks, either as a tree (e.g., UNIX) or as a linked list (e.g., MS-DOS). With an in-core file system, it may be much simpler to store each file contiguously in memory, rather than breaking it up into blocks. Contiguously stored files are easier to keep track of and can be shipped over the network faster. The reason that contiguous files are not used on disk is that if a file grows, moving it to an area of the disk with more room is too expensive. In contrast, moving a file to another area of memory is feasible.

Main memory file servers introduce a serious problem, however. If the power fails, all the files are lost. Unlike disks, which do not lose information in a power failure, main memory is erased when the electricity is removed. The solution may be to make continuous or at least incremental backups onto video tape. With current technology, it is possible to store about 5 gigabytes on a single 8mm video tape that costs less than 10 dollars. While access time is long, if access is needed only once or twice a year to recover from power failures, this scheme may prove irresistible.

A hardware development that may affect file systems is the optical disk. Originally these devices had the property that they could be written once (by burning holes in the surface with a laser), but not changed thereafter. They were sometimes referred to as **WORM (Write Once Read Many)** devices. Some current optical disks use lasers to affect the crystal structure of the disk, but do not damage them, so they can be erased.

Optical disks have three important properties:

1. They are slow.

2. They have huge storage capacities.

3. They have random access.

They are also relatively cheap, although more expensive than video tape. The first two properties are the same as video tape, but the third one opens the following possibility. Imagine a file server with an n gigabyte file system in main memory, and an n gigabyte optical disk as backup. When a file is created, it is stored in main memory and marked as not yet backed up. All accesses are done using main memory. When the work load is low, files that are not yet backed up are transferred to the optical disk in the background, with byte k in memory going to byte k on the disk. Like the first scheme, what we have here is a main memory file server, but with a more convenient backup device having a one-to-one mapping with the memory.

Another interesting hardware development is very fast fiber optic networks. As we discussed earlier, the reason for doing client caching, with all its inherent complications, is to avoid the slow transfer from the server to the client. But suppose that we could equip the system with a main memory file server and a fast fiber optic network. It might well become feasible to get rid of the client's cache and the server's disk and just operate out of the server's memory, backed up by optical disk. This would certainly simplify the software.

When studying client caching, we saw that a large fraction of the trouble is caused by the fact that if two clients are caching the same file and one of them modifies it, the other does not discover this, which leads to inconsistencies. A little thought will reveal that this situation is highly analogous to memory caches in a multiprocessor. Only there, when one processor modifies a shared word, a hardware signal is sent over the memory bus to the other caches to allow them to invalidate or update that word. With distributed file systems, this is not done.

Why not, actually? The reason is that current network interfaces do not support such signals. Nevertheless, it should be possible to build network interfaces that do. As a very simple example, consider the system of Fig. 13-18 in which each network interface has a bit map, one bit per cached file. To modify a file, a processor sets the corresponding bit in the interface, which is 0 if no processor is currently updating the file. Setting a bit causes the interface to create and send a packet around the ring that checks and sets the corresponding bit in all interfaces. If the packet makes it all the way around without finding any other machines trying to use the file, some other register in the interface is set to 1. Otherwise it is set to 0. In effect, this mechanism provides a way to globally lock the file on all machines in a few microseconds.

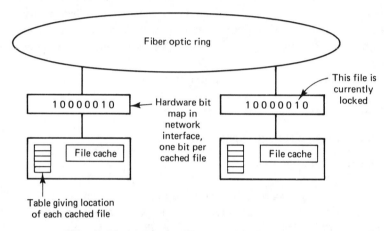

Fig. 13-18. A hardware scheme to updating shared files.

After the lock has been set, the processor updates the file. Each block of the file that is changed is noted (e.g., using bits in the page table). When the update is complete, the processor clears the bit in the bit map, which causes the network interface to locate the file using a table in memory and automatically deposit all the modified blocks in their proper locations on the other machines. When the file has been updated everywhere, the bit in the bit map is cleared on all machines.

Clearly this is a simple solution that can be improved in many ways, but it shows how a small amount of well designed hardware can solve problems that are difficult to handle in software. It is likely that future distributed systems will be assisted by specialized hardware of various kinds.

13.3.2. Scalability

A definite trend in distributed systems is toward larger and larger systems. This observation has implications for distributed file system design. Algorithms that work well for systems with 100 machines may work poorly for systems with 1000 machines and not at all for systems with 10,000 machines. For starters, centralized algorithms do not scale well. If opening a file requires contacting a single centralized server to record the fact that the file is open, that server will eventually become a bottleneck as the system grows.

A general way to deal with this problem is to partition the system into smaller units and try to make each one relatively independent of the others. The AFS approach of having one server per cluster scales much better than a single server. Even having the servers record all the opens may be acceptable under these circumstances.

Broadcasts are another problem area. If each machine issues one broadcast per second, with n machines, a total of n broadcasts per second appear on the network, generating a total of n^2 interrupts total. Obviously as n grows, this will eventually be a problem.

Resources and algorithms should not be linear in the number of users. For example, having any server maintain a linear list of users for protection or other purposes is not a good idea. In contrast, hash tables are usually acceptable, since the access time is more or less constant, almost independent of the number of entries.

In general, strict semantics, such as UNIX semantics, get harder to implement as systems get bigger. Weaker guarantees are much easier to implement. Clearly there is a tradeoff here, since programmers prefer easily well defined semantics, but these are precisely the ones that do not scale well.

In a very large system, the concept of a single UNIX-like file tree may have to be reexamined. It is inevitable that as the system grows, the length of path names will grow too, adding more overhead. At some point it may be necessary to partition the tree into smaller trees.

13.3.3. Wide Area Networking

Most current work on distributed systems focuses on LAN-based systems. In the future, many LAN-based distributed systems will be interconnected to form transparent distributed systems covering countries and continents. As an example, the French PTT is currently putting a small computer in every apartment and house in France. Although the initial goal is to eliminate the need for information operators and telephone books, at some point in time someone is going to ask if it is possible to connect ten million or more computers spread over all of France into a single transparent system, for applications as yet undreamed of. What kind of file system would be needed to serve all of France? All of Europe? The whole world? At present, no one knows.

Although the French machines are all identical, in most wide-area networks, a large variety of equipment is encountered. This diversity is inevitable when multiple buyers with different sized budgets and goals are involved, and the purchasing is spread over many years in an era of rapid technological change. Thus a wide-area distributed system must of necessity deal with heterogeneity. This raises issues such as how should you store a character file if not everyone uses ASCII, or what format should one use for files containing floating-point numbers if multiple representations are in use.

Also important is the expected change in applications. Most experimental distributed systems being built at universities focus on programming in a UNIX-like environment as the canonical application, because that is what the researchers themselves do all day (at least when they are not in committee meetings or writing grant proposals). Initial data suggest that not all 50 million French citizens are going to list C programming as their primary activity. As distributed systems become more widespread, we are likely to see a shift to electronic mail, electronic banking, accessing data bases, and recreational activities, which will change file usage, access patterns, and a great deal more in ways we as yet do not know.

An inherent problem with massive distributed systems is that the network bandwidth is extremely low. If the telephone line is the main connection, getting more than 64 kbps out of it seems unlikely. Bringing fiber optics into everyone's house will take decades and cost billions. On the other hand, vast amounts of data can be stored cheaply on compact disks and video tapes. Instead of logging into the telephone company's computer to look up a telephone number, it may be cheaper for them to send everyone a disk or tape containing the entire data base. We may have to develop file systems in which a distinction is made between static, read-only information (e.g., the phone book), and dynamic information (e.g., electronic mail). This distinction may have to become the basis of the entire file system.

13.3.4. Mobile Users

Portable computers are the fastest growing segment of the computer business. Laptop computers, notebook computers, and pocket computers can be found everywhere these days, and they are multiplying like rabbits. Although computing while driving is hard, computing while flying is not. Telephones are now common in airplanes, so can flying FAXes and mobile modems be far behind? Nevertheless, the total bandwidth available from an airplane to the ground is quite low, and many places users want to go have no online connection at all.

The inevitable conclusion is that a large fraction of the time, the user will be offline, disconnected from the file system. Few current systems were designed for such use, although Satyanarayanan et al. (1990) have reported some initial work in this direction.

Any solution is probably going to have to be based on caching. While connected, the user downloads to the portable those files expected to be needed later. These are used while disconnected. When reconnect occurs, the files in the cache will have to be merged with those in the file tree. Since disconnect can last for hours or days, the problems of maintaining cache consistency are much more severe than in online systems.

Another problem is that when reconnection does occur, the user may be in a city far away from his home base. Placing a phone call to the home machine is one way to get resynchronized, but the telephone bandwidth is low. Besides, in a truly distributed system contacting the local file server should be enough. The design of a worldwide, fully transparent distributed file system for simultaneous use by millions of mobile and frequently disconnected users is left as an exercise for the reader.

13.3.5. Fault Tolerance

Current computer systems, except for very specialized ones like air traffic control, are not fault tolerant (Cristian, 1991; Nelson, 1990). When the computer goes down, the users are expected to accept this as a fact of life. Unfortunately, the general population expects things to work. If a television channel, the phone system, or the electric power company goes down for half an hour, there are many unhappy people the next day. As distributed systems become more and more widespread, the demand for systems that essentially never fail will grow. Current systems cannot meet this need.

Obviously, such systems will need considerable redundancy in hardware and the communication infrastructure, but they will also need it in software and especially data. File replication, often an afterthought in current distributed systems, will become an essential requirement in future ones. Systems will also have to be designed that manage to function when only partial data are available, since insisting that all the data be available all the time does not lead to fault tolerance. Down times that are now considerable acceptable, will be increasingly unacceptable as computer use spreads to nonspecialists.

13.4. SUMMARY

The heart of any distributed system is the distributed file system. The design of such a file system begins with the interface: "What is the model of a file and what functionality is provided?" As a rule, the nature of a file is no different for the distributed case than for the single-processor case. As usual, an important part of the interface is file naming and the directory system. Naming quickly brings up the issue of transparency. To what extent is the name of a file related to its location? Can the system move a single file on its own without the file name being affected? Different systems have different answers to these questions.

File sharing in a distributed system is a complex but important topic. Various semantic models have been proposed, including UNIX semantics, session semantics, immutable files, and transaction semantics. Each has its own strengths and weaknesses. UNIX semantics is intuitive and familiar to most programmers (even non-UNIX programmers), but it is expensive to implement. Session semantics is less deterministic, but more efficient. Immutable files are unfamiliar to most people, and make updating files difficult. Transactions are frequently overkill.

Implementing a distributed file system involves making many decisions. These include whether the system should be stateless or stateful, if and how caching should be done, and how file replication can be managed. Each of these has far-ranging consequences for the designers and the users. As an example, we looked at AFS and saw that it works by caching whole files on client disks, uploading them when they are closed.

Finally, we briefly examined some issues that are likely to become more important in the design of future distributed file systems, including changes in hardware technology, scalability, wide-area systems, mobile users, and fault tolerance.

PROBLEMS

1. A file system allows links from one directory to another. In this way, a directory can "include" a subdirectory. In this context, what is the essential criterion that distinguishes a tree-structured directory system from a general graph-structured system?

2. When session semantics are used, it is always true that changes to a file are immediately visible to the process making the change and never visible to processes on other machines. However, it is an open question as to whether or not they should be immediately visible to other processes on the same machine. Give an argument each way.

3. In the text it was pointed out that shared file pointers cannot be implemented reasonably with session semantics. Can they be implemented when there is a single file server that provides UNIX semantics?

4. Name two useful properties that immutable files have.

5. Why do some distributed systems use two-level naming?

6. Why do stateless servers have to include a file offset in each request? Is this also needed for stateful servers?

7. One of the arguments given in the text in favor of stateful file servers is that i-nodes can be kept in memory for open files, thus reducing the number of disk operations. Propose an implementation for a stateless server that achieves almost the same performance gain. In what ways, if any, is your proposal better or worse than the stateful one?

8. Why can file caches use LRU whereas virtual memory paging algorithms cannot? Back up your arguments with approximate figures.

9. In the section on cache consistency, we discussed the problem of how a client cache manager knows if a file in its cache is still up-to-date. The method suggested was to contact the server and have the server compare the client and server times. Does this method fail if the client and server clocks are very different?

10. Consider a system that does client caching using the write through algorithm. Individual blocks, rather than entire files, are cached. Suppose that a client is about to read an entire file sequentially, and some of the blocks are in the cache and others are not. What problem may occur, and what can be done about it?

11. Imagine that a distributed file uses client caching with a delayed write back policy. One machine opens, modifies and closes a file. About half a minute later, another machine reads the file from the server. Which version does it get?

12. Some distributed file systems use client caching with delayed writes back to the server or write-on-close. In addition to the problems with the semantics, these systems introduce another problem. What is it? (Hint: think about reliability.)

13. Some distributed file systems use two-level names, ASCII and binary, as we have discussed throughout this chapter; others do not, and use ASCII names throughout. Similarly some file servers are stateless and some are stateful, giving four combinations of these two features. One of these combinations is somewhat less desirable than its alternatives. Which one, and why?

14. When file systems replicate files, they do not normally replicate all files. Give an example of a kind of file that is not worth replicating.

15. A file is replicated on 10 servers. List all the combinations of read quorum and write quorum that are permitted by the voting algorithm.

16. In AFS, cached files are sometimes marked as valid and sometimes as invalid. Is this entire mechanism essential for the correct functioning of the system, or is it merely a performance optimization?

17. With a main memory file server that stores files contiguously, when a file grows beyond its current allocation unit, it will have to be copied. Suppose the average file is 20K bytes, and it takes 200 nsec to copy a 32-bit word. How many files can be copied per second? Can you suggest a way to do this copying without tying up the file server's CPU the whole time?

18. In the bit map scheme of Fig. 13-18, is it necessary that all machines caching a given file use the same table entry for it? If so, how can this be arranged?

14

CASE STUDY 3: AMOEBA

In this chapter we will give our first example of a distributed operating system: Amoeba. In the following one we will look at a second example: Mach. Amoeba is a distributed operating system: it makes a collection of CPUs and I/O equipment act like a single computer. It also provides facilities for parallel programming where that is desired. This chapter describes the goals, design, and implementation of Amoeba. For more information about Amoeba see (Mullender et al., 1990; and Tanenbaum et al., 1990).

14.1. INTRODUCTION TO AMOEBA

In this section we will give an introduction to Amoeba, starting with a brief history and its current research goals. Then we will look at the architecture of a typical Amoeba system. Finally, we will begin our study of the Amoeba software, both the kernel and the servers.

14.1.1. History of Amoeba

Amoeba originated at the Vrije Universiteit, Amsterdam, The Netherlands in 1981 as a research project in distributed and parallel computing. It was primarily designed by Andrew S. Tanenbaum and three of his Ph.D. students, Frans Kaashoek,

Sape J. Mullender and Robbert van Renesse, although many other people also contributed to the design and implementation. By 1983, an initial prototype, Amoeba 1.0, was operational.

Starting in 1984, the Amoeba fissioned, and a second group was set up at the Centre for Mathematics and Computer Science, also in Amsterdam, under Mullender's leadership. In the succeeding years, this cooperation was extended to sites in England and Norway in a wide-area distributed system project sponsored by the European Community. This work used Amoeba 3.0, which unlike the earlier versions, was based on RPC. Using Amoeba 3.0, it was possible for clients in Tromso to transparently access servers in Amsterdam, and vice versa.

The system evolved for several years, acquiring such features as partial UNIX emulation, group communication and a new low-level protocol. The version described in this chapter is Amoeba 5.0.

14.1.2. Research Goals

Many research projects in distributed operating systems have started with an existing system (e.g., UNIX) and added new features such as networking and a shared file system to make it more distributed. The Amoeba project took a different approach. It started with a clean slate and developed a new system from scratch. The idea was to make a fresh start and experiment with new ideas without having to worry about backward compatibility with any existing system. To avoid the chore of having to rewrite a huge amount of application software from scratch as well, a UNIX emulation package was added later.

The primary goal of the project was to build a transparent distributed operating system. To the average user, using Amoeba is like using a traditional timesharing system like UNIX. One logs in, edits and compiles programs, moves files around, and so on. The difference is, each of these actions makes use of multiple machines spread over the network. These include process servers, file servers, directory servers, compute servers, and other machines, but the user is not aware of any of this. At the terminal, it just looks like an ordinary timesharing system.

An important distinction between Amoeba and most other distributed systems is that Amoeba has no concept of a "home machine." When a user logs in, it is to the system as a whole, not to a specific machine. Machines do not have owners. The initial shell, started upon login, runs on some arbitrary machine, but as commands are started up, in general they do not run on the same machine as the shell. Instead, the system automatically looks around for the most lightly loaded machine to run each new command on. During the course of a long terminal session, the processes that run on behalf of any one user will be more-or-less uniformly spread over all the machines in the system, depending on the load, of course.

In other words, all resources belong to the system as a whole, and are managed by it. They are not dedicated to specific users, except for short periods of time to run individual processes. This model attempts to provide the transparency that is the holy grail of all distributed systems designers.

A simple example is *amake*, the Amoeba replacement for the UNIX *make* program. When the user types *amake*, all the necessary compilations happen, as expected, only the system (and not the user) determines whether they happen sequentially or in parallel, and on which machine or machines this occurs. None of this is visible to the user.

A secondary goal of Amoeba is to provide a testbed for doing distributed and parallel programming. While many users just use Amoeba the same way they would use any other timesharing system, unaware of all the machines, other users are specifically interested in experimenting with distributed and parallel algorithms, languages, tools, and applications. Amoeba supports these users by making the underlying parallelism available to people who want to take advantage of it. In practice, most of Amoeba's current user base consists of people who are specifically interested in distributed and parallel computing in its various forms. A language, Orca , has been specifically designed and implemented on Amoeba for this purpose. Orca and its applications are described in (Bal, 1991; Bal et al., 1990; Tanenbaum et al., 1992). Amoeba itself, however, is written in C.

14.1.3. The Amoeba System Architecture

Before describing how Amoeba is structured, it is useful to first outline the kind of hardware configuration for which Amoeba was designed, since it differs somewhat from what most organizations presently have. Amoeba was designed with two assumptions about the hardware in mind:

1. Systems will have a very large number of CPUs.

2. Each CPU will have tens of megabytes of memory.

These assumptions are already true at some installations, and will probably become true at almost all corporate, academic, and governmental sites within a few years.

The driving force behind the system architecture is the need to incorporate large numbers of CPUs in a straightforward way. In other words, what do you do when you can afford 10 or 100 CPUs per user? One solution is to give each user a personal 10-node or 100-node multiprocessor.

Although giving everyone a personal multiprocessor is certainly a possibility, doing so is not an effective way to spend the available budget. Most of the time, nearly all the processors will be idle, but some users will want to run massively parallel programs and will not be able to easily harness all the idle CPU cycles because they are in other users' personal machines.

Instead of this personal multiprocessor approach, Amoeba is based on the model shown in Fig. 14-1. In this model, all the computing power is located in one or more **processor pools**. A processor pool consists of a substantial number of CPUs, each with its own local memory and network connection. Shared memory is not required, or even expected, but if it is present it can be used to optimize message passing by doing memory-to-memory copying instead of sending messages over the network.

The CPUs in a pool can be of different architectures, for example, a mixture of

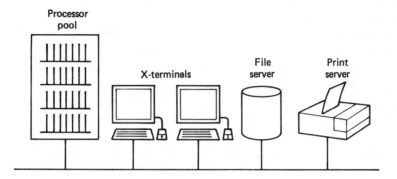

Fig. 14-1. The Amoeba system architecture.

68030, 386, VAX, and SPARC machines. Amoeba has been designed to deal with multiple architectures and heterogenous systems. It is even possible for the children of a single process to run on different architectures.

Pool processors are not "owned" by any one user. When a user types a command, the operating system dynamically allocates one or more processors to that command. When the command completes, the processors are released and go back into the pool, waiting for the next command, very likely from a different user. If there is a shortage of pool processors, individual processors are timeshared, with new processes being assigned to the most lightly loaded CPUs. The important point to note here is that this model is quite different from current systems in which each user has exactly one personal workstation for all his computing activities.

The expected presence of large memories in future systems has influenced the design in many ways. Many time-space tradeoffs have been made to provide high performance at the cost of using more memory. We will see examples of this later.

The second element of the Amoeba architecture is the terminal. It is through the terminal that the user accesses the system. A typical Amoeba terminal is an X terminal, with a large bit-mapped screen and a mouse. Alternatively, a personal computer or workstation running X windows can also be used as a terminal. Although Amoeba does not forbid running user programs on the terminal, the idea behind this model is to give the users relatively cheap terminals and concentrate the computing cycles in to a common pool so they can be used more efficiently.

Pool processors are inherently cheaper than workstations because they just consist of a single board with a network connection. There is no keyboard, monitor, or mouse, and the power supply can be shared by many boards. Thus, instead of buying 100 high-performance workstations for 100 users, one might buy 50 high-performance pool processors and 100 X terminals for the same price (depending on the economics, obviously). Since the pool processors are only allocated when needed, an idle user only ties up an inexpensive X terminal instead of an expensive workstation. The tradeoffs inherent in the pool processor model versus the workstation model were discussed in Chap. 12.

To avoid any confusion, the pool processors do not *have* to be single-board computers. If these are not available, a subset of the existing personal computers or workstations can be designated as pool processors. They also do not need to be located in one room. The physical location is actually irrelevant. The pool processors can even be in different countries, as we will discuss later.

Another important component of the Amoeba configuration consists of specialized servers, such as file servers, which for hardware or software reasons need to run on a separate processor. In some cases a server is able to run on a pool processor, being started up as needed, but for performance reasons it is better to have it running all the time.

An example is the directory server. There is nothing inherent about the directory server or the system design that would prevent a user from starting up a new directory server on a pool processor every time he wanted to look up a file name. However, doing so would be horrendously inefficient, so one or more directory servers are kept running all the time, generally on dedicated machines to enhance their performance. The decision to have some servers running all the time and others to be started explicitly when needed is up to the system administrator.

Servers provide services. A **service** is an abstract definition of what the server is prepared to do for its clients. This definition defines what the client can ask for and what the results will be, but it does not specify how many servers are working together to provide the service. In this way, the system has a mechanism for providing fault-tolerant services by having multiple servers doing the work.

14.1.4. The Amoeba Microkernel

Having looked at the Amoeba hardware model, let us now turn to the software model. Amoeba consists of two basic pieces: a microkernel, which runs on every processor, and a collection of servers that provide most of the traditional operating system functionality. The overall structure is shown in Fig. 14-2.

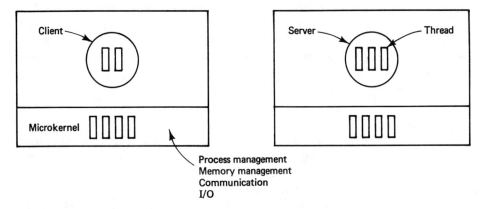

Fig. 14-2. Amoeba software structure.

The Amoeba microkernel runs on all machines in the system. The same kernel is used on the pool processors, the terminals (assuming that they are computers, rather than X terminals), and the specialized servers. The microkernel has four primary functions:

1. Manage processes and threads.

2. Provide low-level memory management support.

3. Support communication.

4. Handle low-level I/O.

Let us consider each of these in turn.

Like most operating systems, Amoeba supports the concept of a process. In addition, Amoeba also supports multiple threads of control within a single address space. A process with one thread is essentially the same as a process in UNIX. Such a process has a single address space, a set of registers, a program counter, and a stack.

In contrast, although a process with multiple threads still has a single address space shared by all threads, each thread logically has its own registers, its own program counter, and its own stack. In effect, a collection of threads in a process is similar to a collection of independent processes in UNIX, with the one exception that they all share a single common address space.

A typical use for multiple threads might be in a file server, in which every incoming request is assigned to a separate thread to work on. That thread might begin processing the request, then block waiting for the disk, then continue work. By splitting the server up into multiple threads, each thread can be purely sequential, even if it has to block waiting for I/O. Nevertheless, all the threads can, for example, have access to a single shared software cache. Threads can synchronize using semaphores or mutexes to prevent two threads from accessing the shared cache simultaneously.

The second task of the kernel is to provide low-level memory management. Threads can allocate and deallocate blocks of memory, called **segments**. These segments can be read and written, and can be mapped into and out of the address space of the process to which the calling thread belongs. A process must have at least one segment, but it may also have many more of them. Segments can be used for text, data, stack, or any other purpose the process desires. The operating system does not enforce any particular pattern on segment usage.

The third job of the kernel is to handle interprocess communication. Two forms of communication are provided: point-to-point communication and group communication. These are closely integrated to make them as similar as possible.

Point-to-point communication is based on the model of a client sending a message to a server, then blocking until the server has sent a reply back. This request/reply exchange is the basis on which almost everything else is built.

The other form of communication is group communication. It allows a message to be sent from one source to multiple destinations. Software protocols provide reliable, fault-tolerant group communication to user processes in the presence of lost messages and other errors.

The fourth function of the kernel is to manage low-level I/O. For each I/O device attached to a machine, there is a device driver in the kernel. The driver manages all I/O for the device. Drivers are linked with the kernel, and cannot be loaded dynamically.

Device drivers communicate with the rest of the system by the standard request and reply messages. A process, such as a file server, that needs to communicate with the disk driver, sends it request messages and gets replies back. In general, the client does not have to know that it is talking to a driver in the kernel. As far as it is concerned, it is just communicating with a thread somewhere.

Both the point-to-point message system and the group communication make use of a specialized protocol called FLIP. This protocol is a network layer protocol, and has been specifically designed to meet the needs of distributed computing. It deals with both unicasting and multicasting on complex internetworks. It will be discussed later.

14.1.5. The Amoeba Servers

Everything that is not done by the kernel is done by server processes. The idea behind this design is to minimize kernel size and enhance flexibility. By not building the file system and other standard services into the kernel, they can be changed easily, and multiple versions can run simultaneously for different user populations.

Amoeba is based on the client-server model. Clients are typically written by the users and servers are typically written by the systems programmers, but users are free to write their own servers if they wish. Central to the entire software design is the concept of an object, which is like an abstract data type. Each object consists of some encapsulated data with certain operations defined on it. File objects have a READ operation, for example, among others.

Objects are managed by servers. When a process creates an object, the server that manages the object returns to the client a cryptographically protected capability for the object. To use the object later, the proper capability must be presented. All objects in the system, both hardware and software, are named, protected, and managed by capabilities. Among the objects supported this way are files, directories, memory segments, screen windows, processors, disks, and tape drives. This uniform interface to all objects provides generality and simplicity.

All the standard servers have stub procedures in the library. To use a server, a client normally just calls the stub, which marshalls the parameters, sends the message, and blocks until the reply comes back. This mechanism hides all the details of the implementation from the user. A stub compiler is available for users who wish to produce stub procedures for their own servers.

Probably the most important server is the file server, known as the **bullet server**. It provides primitives to manage files, creating them, reading them, deleting them, and so on. Unlike most file servers, the files it creates are immutable. Once created, a file cannot be modified, but it can be deleted. Immutable files make automatic replication easier since they avoid many of the race conditions inherent in replicating files that are subject to being changed during the replication process.

Another important server is the **directory server**, for obscure historical reasons also known as the **soap server**. It is the directory server that manages directories and path names and maps them onto capabilities. To read a file, a process asks the directory server to look up the path name. On a successful lookup, the directory server returns the capability for the file (or other object). Subsequent operations on the file do not use the directory server, but go straight to the file server. Splitting the file system into these two components increases flexibility and makes each one simpler, since it only has to manage one type of object (directories or files), not two.

Other standard servers are present for handling object replication, starting processes, monitoring servers for failures, and communicating with the outside world. User servers perform a wide variety of application-specific tasks.

The rest of this chapter is structured as follows. First we will describe objects and capabilities, since these are the heart of the entire system. Then we will look at the kernel, focusing on process management, memory management, and communication. Finally, we will examine some of the main servers, including the bullet server, the directory server, the replication server, and the run server.

14.2. OBJECTS AND CAPABILITIES IN AMOEBA

The basic unifying concept underlying all the Amoeba servers and the services they provide is the **object**. An object is an encapsulated piece of data upon which certain well-defined operations may be performed. It is, in essence, an abstract data type. Objects are passive. They do not contain processes or methods or other active entities that "do" things. Instead, each object is managed by a server process.

To perform an operation on an object, a client does an RPC with the server, specifying the object, the operation to be performed, and optionally, any parameters needed. The server does the work and returns the answer. Operations are performed synchronously, that is, after initiating an RPC with a server to get some work done, the client thread is blocked until the server replies. Other threads in the same process are still runnable, however.

Clients are unaware of the locations of the objects they use and the servers that manage these objects. A server might be running on the same machine as the client, on a different machine on the same LAN, or even on a machine thousands of kilometers away. Furthermore, although most servers run as user processes, a few low-level ones, such as the memory server and process server, run as threads in the kernel. This distinction, too, is invisible to clients. The RPC protocol for talking to user servers or kernel servers, whether local or remote, is identical in all cases. Thus a client is entirely concerned with what it wants to do, not where objects are stored and where servers run, although in some cases where it matters, they can control where objects are stored. In addition, the system has a reasonable set of defaults built in, so, for example, files are normally stored on the local file server unless there is reason to use a different one. Usually the local one is adequate.

14.2.1. Capabilities

Objects are named and protected in a uniform way, by special tickets called **capabilities**. To create an object, a client does an RPC with the appropriate server specifying what it wants. The server then creates the object and returns a capability to the client. On subsequent operations, the client must present the capability to identify the object. A capability is just a long binary number. The Amoeba 5.0 format is shown in Fig. 14-3.

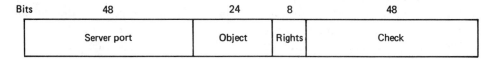

Fig. 14-3. A capability in Amoeba.

When a client wants to perform an operation on an object, it calls a stub procedure that builds a message containing the object's capability, and then traps to the kernel. The kernel extracts the *Server port* field from the capability and looks it up in its cache to locate the machine on which the server resides. If the port is not in the cache, it is located by broadcasting, as will be described later. The port is effectively a logical address at which the server can be reached. Server ports are thus associated with a particular server (or a set of servers), not with a specific machine. If a server moves to a new machine, it takes its server port with it. Many server ports, like that of the file server, are publicly known and stable for years. The only way a server can be addressed is via its port, which it initially chose itself.

The rest of the information in the capability is ignored by the kernels and passed to the server for its own use. The *Object* field is used by the server to identify the specific object in question. For example, a file server might manage thousands of files, with the object number being used to tell it which one is being operated on. In a sense, the *Object* field in a file capability is analogous to a UNIX i-node number.

The *Rights* field is a bit map telling which of the allowed operations the holder of a capability may perform. For example, although a particular object may support reading and writing, a specific capability may be constructed with all the rights bits except READ turned off.

The *Check* field is used for validating the capability. Capabilities are manipulated directly by user processes. Without some form of protection, there would be no way to prevent user processes from forging capabilities.

14.2.2. Object Protection

The basic algorithm used to protect objects is as follows. When an object is created, the server picks a random *Check* field and stores it both in the new capability and inside its own tables. All the rights bits in a new capability are initially on, and it is this **owner capability** that is returned to the client. When the capability is sent back to the server in a request to perform an operation, the *Check* field is verified.

To create a restricted capability, a client can pass a capability back to the server, along with a bit mask for the new rights. The server takes the original *Check* field from its tables, EXCLUSIVE ORs it with the new rights (which must be a subset of the rights in the capability), and then runs the result through a one-way function. Such a function, $y = f(x)$, has the property that given x it is easy to find y, but given only y, finding x requires an exhaustive search of all possible x values (Evans et al., 1974).

The server then creates a new capability, with the same value in the *Object* field, but the new rights bits in the *Rights* field and the output of the one-way function in the *Check* field. The new capability is then returned to the caller. The client may send this new capability to another process, if it wishes, as capabilities are managed entirely in user space.

The method of generating restricted capabilities is illustrated in Fig. 14-4. In this example, the owner has turned off all the rights except one. For example, the restricted capability might allow the object to be read, but nothing else. The meaning of the *Rights* field is different for each object type since the legal operations themselves also vary from object type to object type.

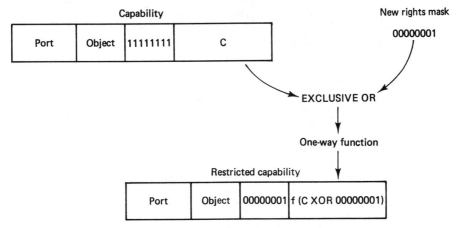

Fig. 14-4. Generation of a restricted capability from an owner capability.

When the restricted capability comes back to the server, the server sees from the *Rights* field that it is not an *owner capability* because at least one bit is turned off. The server then fetches the original random number from its tables, EXCLUSIVE ORs it with the *Rights* field from the capability, and runs the result through the one-way function. If the result agrees with the *Check* field, the capability is accepted as valid.

It should be obvious from this algorithm that a user who tries to add rights that he does not have will simply invalidate the capability. Inverting the *Check* field in a restricted capability to get the argument (C XOR 00000001 in Fig. 14-4) is impossible because the function f is a one-way function (that is what "one-way" means—no algorithm exists for inverting it). It is through this cryptographic technique that capabilities are protected from tampering.

Capabilities are used throughout Amoeba for both naming of all objects and for protecting them. This single mechanism leads to a uniform naming and protection scheme. It also is fully location transparent. To perform an operation on an object, it is not necessary to know where the object resides. In fact, even if this knowledge were available, there would be no way to use it.

Note that Amoeba does not use access control lists for authentication. The protection scheme used requires almost no administrative overhead. However, in an insecure environment, additional cryptography (e.g., link encryption) may be required to keep capabilities from being accidentally disclosed to wiretappers on the network.

14.2.3. Standard Operations

Although many operations on objects depend on the object type, there are some operations that apply to most objects. These are listed in Fig. 14-5. Some of these require certain rights bits to be set, but others can be done by anyone who can present a server with a valid capability for one of its objects.

Call	Description
Age	Perform a garbage collection cycle
Copy	Duplicate the object and return a capability for the copy
Destroy	Destroy the object and reclaim its storage
Getparams	Get parameters associated with the server
Info	Get an ASCII string briefly describing the object
Restrict	Produce a new, restricted capability for the object
Setparams	Set parameters associated with the server
Status	Get current status information from the server
Touch	Pretend the object was just used

Fig. 14-5. The standard operations valid on most objects.

It is possible to create an object in Amoeba and then lose the capability, so some mechanism is needed to get rid of old objects that are no longer accessible. The way that has been chosen is to have servers run a garbage collector periodically, removing all objects that have not been used in n garbage collection cycles. The AGE call starts a new garbage collection cycle. The TOUCH call tells the server that the object touched is still in use. When objects are entered into the directory server, they are touched periodically, to keep the garbage collector at bay.

The COPY operation is a shortcut that makes it possible to duplicate an object without actually transferring it. Without this operation, copying a file would require sending it over the network twice: from the server to the client and then back again. COPY can also fetch remote objects or send objects to remote machines.

The DESTROY operation deletes the object. It always needs the appropriate right, for obvious reasons.

The GETPARAMS and SETPARAMS calls normally deal with the server as a whole rather than with a particular object. They allow the system administrator to read and write parameters that control server operation. For example, the size of the file server's cache could be set using this mechanism.

The INFO and STATUS calls return status information. The former returns a short ASCII string briefly describing the object. The information in the string is server dependent, but in general, it tells something useful about the object (e.g., for files, it tells the size). The latter gets information about the server as a whole, for example, how much free memory it has. This information helps the system administrator monitor the system better.

The RESTRICT call generates a new capability for the object, with a subset of the current rights, as described above.

14.3. PROCESS MANAGEMENT IN AMOEBA

A process in Amoeba is basically an address space and a collection of threads that run in it. A process with one thread is roughly analogous to a UNIX or MS-DOS process in terms of how it behaves and what it can do. In this section we will explain how processes and threads work, and how they are implemented.

14.3.1. Processes

A process is an object in Amoeba. When a process is created, the parent process is given a capability for the child process, just as with any other newly created object. Using this capability, the child can be suspended, restarted, or destroyed.

Process creation in Amoeba is different from UNIX. The UNIX model of creating a child process by cloning the parent is inappropriate in a distributed system due to the considerable overhead of first creating a copy somewhere (FORK) and almost immediately afterwards replacing the copy with a new program (EXEC). Instead, in Amoeba it is possible to create a new process on a specific processor with the intended memory image starting right at the beginning. In this one respect, process creation in Amoeba is similar to MS-DOS. However, in contrast to MS-DOS, a process can continue executing in parallel with its child, and thus can create an arbitrary number of additional children. The children, can, in turn, create their own children, leading to a tree of processes.

Process management is handled at three different levels in Amoeba. At the lowest level are the process servers, which are kernel threads running on every machine. To create a process on a given machine, another process does an RPC with that machine's process server, providing it with the necessary information.

At the next level up we have a set of library procedures that provide a more convenient interface for user programs. Several flavors are provided. They do their job by calling the low-level interface procedures.

Finally, the simplest way to create a process is to use the run server, which does most of the work of determining where to run the new process. We will discuss the run server later in this chapter.

Some of the process management calls use a data structure called a **process descriptor** to provide information about a process to be run. One field in the process descriptor (see Fig. 14-6) tells which CPU architecture the process can run on. In heterogeneous systems, this field is essential to make sure 386 binaries are not run on SPARCs, and so on.

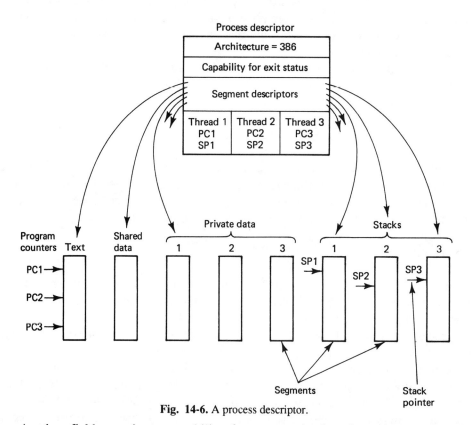

Fig. 14-6. A process descriptor.

Another field contains a capability for communicating the exit status to the owner. When the process terminates or is stunned (see below), RPCs will be done using this capability to report the event. It also contains descriptors for all the process' segments, which collectively define its address space, as well as descriptors for all its threads.

Finally, the process descriptor also contains a descriptor for each thread in the process. The content of a thread descriptor is architecture dependent, but as a bare minimum, it contains the thread's program counter and stack pointer. It may also contain additional information necessary to run the thread, including other registers, the thread's state, and various flags.

The low-level process interface consists of about a half-dozen library procedures.

Only three of these will concern us here. The first one, *exec*, is the most important. It has two input parameters, the capability for a process server and a process descriptor. Its function is to do an RPC with the specified process server asking it to run the process. If the call is successful, a capability for the new process is returned to the caller.

A second important library procedure is *getload*. It returns information about the CPU speed, current load, and amount of memory free at the moment. It is used by the run server to determine the best place to execute a new process.

A third major library procedure is *stun*. A process' parent can suspend it by **stunning** it. More commonly, the parent can give the process' capability to a debugger, which can stun it and later restart it for interactive debugging purposes. Two kinds of stuns are supported: normal and emergency. They differ with respect to what happens if the process is blocked on one or more RPCs at the time it is stunned. With a normal stun, the process sends a message to the server it is currently waiting for saying, in effect: "I have been stunned. Finish your work instantly and send me a reply." If the server is also blocked, waiting for another server, the message is propagated further, all the way down the line to the end. The server at the end of the line replies immediately with a special error message. In this way, all the pending RPCs are terminated almost immediately in a clean way, with all of the servers finishing properly. The nesting structure is not violated, and no "long jumps" are needed.

An emergency stun stops the process instantly and does not send any messages to servers that are currently working for the stunned process. The computations being done by the servers become orphans. When the servers finally finish and send replies, these replies are ultimately discarded.

The high-level process interface does not require a fully formed process descriptor. One of the calls, *newproc*, takes as its first three parameters, the name of the binary file and pointers to the argument and environment arrays, similar to UNIX. Additional parameters provide more detailed control of the initial state.

14.3.2. Threads

Amoeba supports a simple threads model. When a process starts up, it has at least one thread and possibly more. During execution, the process can create additional threads, and existing threads can terminate. The number of threads is therefore completely dynamic. When a new thread is created, the parameters to the call specify the procedure to run and the size of the initial stack.

Although all threads in a process share the same program text and global data, each thread has its own stack, its own stack pointer, and its own copy of the machine registers. In addition, if a thread wants to create and use variables that are global to all its procedures but invisible to other threads, library procedures are provided for that purpose. Such variables are called **glocal**. One library procedure allocates a block of glocal memory of whatever size is requested, and returns a pointer to it. Blocks of glocal memory are referred to by integers, rather than by strings as is done in the OSF/1 thread scheme described in Chap. 12.

Three methods are provided for threads to synchronize: signals, mutexes, and semaphores. Signals are asynchronous interrupts sent from one thread to another thread in the same process. They are conceptually similar to UNIX signals, except that they are between threads rather than between processes. Signals can be raised, caught, or ignored. Asynchronous interrupts between processes use the stun mechanism.

The second form of interthread communication is the mutex. A **mutex** is like a binary semaphore. It can be in one of two states, locked or unlocked. Trying to lock an unlocked mutex causes it to become locked. The calling thread continues. Trying to lock a mutex that is already locked causes the calling thread to block until another thread unlocks the mutex. If more than one thread is waiting on a mutex, when the mutex is unlocked, exactly one thread is released. In addition to the calls to lock and unlock mutexes, there is also one that tries to lock a mutex, but if it is unable to do so within a specified interval, times out and returns an error code.

The third way threads can communicate is by counting semaphores. These are slower than mutexes, but there are times when they are needed. They work in the usual way, except that here too an additional call is provided to allow a DOWN operation to time out if it is unable to succeed within a specified interval.

All threads are managed by the kernel. The advantage of this design is that when a thread does an RPC, the kernel can block that thread and schedule another one in the same process if one is ready. Thread scheduling is done using priorities, with kernel threads getting higher priority than user threads.

14.4. MEMORY MANAGEMENT IN AMOEBA

Amoeba has an extremely simple memory model. A process can have any number of segments it wants to, and they can be located wherever it wants in the process' virtual address space. Segments are not swapped or paged, so a process must be entirely memory resident to run. Furthermore, although the hardware MMU is used, each segment is stored contiguously in memory.

Although this design is perhaps somewhat unusual these days, it was done for three reasons: performance, simplicity, and economics. Having a process entirely in memory all the time makes RPC go faster. When a large block of data must be sent, the system knows that all of the data is contiguous not only in virtual memory, but also in physical memory. This knowledge saves having to check if all the pages containing the buffer happen to be around at the moment, and eliminates having to wait for them if they are not. Similarly, on input, the buffer is always in memory, so the incoming data can be placed there simply and without page faults. This design has allowed Amoeba to achieve extremely high transfer rates for large RPCs.

The second reason for the design is simplicity. Not having paging or swapping makes the system considerably simpler and makes the kernel smaller and more manageable. However, it is the third reason that makes the first two feasible. Memory is becoming so cheap that within a few years, all Amoeba machines will probably have tens of megabytes of it. Such large memories will substantially reduce the need for paging and swapping, namely, to fit large programs into small machines.

14.4.1. Segments

Processes have several calls available to them for managing segments. Most important among these is the ability to create, destroy, read, and write segments. When a segment is created, the caller gets back a capability for it. This capability is used for all the other calls involving the segment.

When a segment is created it is given an initial size. This size may change during process execution. The segment may also be given an initial value, either from another segment or from a file.

Because segments can be read and written, it is possible to use them to construct a main memory file server. To start, the server creates a segment as large as it can. It can determine the maximum size by asking the kernel. This segment will be used as a simulated disk. The server then formats the segment as a file system, putting in whatever data structures it needs to keep track of files. After that, it is open for business, accepting and processing requests from clients.

14.4.2. Mapped Segments

Virtual address spaces in Amoeba are constructed from segments. When a process is started, it must have at least one segment. However, once it is running, a process can create additional segments and map them into its address space at any unused virtual address. Figure 14-7 shows a process with three memory segments currently mapped in.

A process can also unmap segments. Furthermore, a process can specify a range of virtual addresses and request that the range be unmapped, after which those addresses are no longer legal. When a segment or a range of addresses is unmapped, a capability is returned, so the segment may still be accessed, or even mapped back in again later, possibly at a different virtual address.

A segment may be mapped into the address space of two or more processes at the same time. This allows processes to operate on shared memory. However, usually it is better to create a single process with multiple threads when shared memory is needed. The main reason for having distinct processes is better protection, but if the two processes are sharing memory, protection is generally not desired.

14.5. COMMUNICATION IN AMOEBA

Amoeba supports two forms of communication: RPC, using point-to-point message passing, and group communication. At the lowest level, an RPC consists of a request message followed by a reply message. Group communication uses hardware broadcasting or multicasting if it is available; otherwise it transparently simulates it with individual messages. In this section we will describe both of them, and then discuss the underlying FLIP protocol that is used to support them.

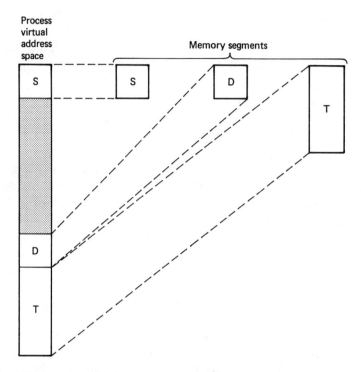

Fig. 14-7. A process with three segments mapped into its virtual address space.

14.5.1. Remote Procedure Call

All point-to-point communication in Amoeba consists of a client sending a message to a server followed by the server sending a reply back to the client. It is not possible for a client to just send a message and then go do something else. The primitive that sends the request automatically blocks the caller until the reply comes back, thus forcing a certain amount of structure on programs. Separate *send* and *receive* primitives can be thought of as the distributed system's answer to the *goto* statement: parallel spaghetti programming.

Each standard server defines a procedural interface that clients can call. These library routines are stubs that pack the parameters into messages and invoke the kernel primitives to actually send the message. During message transmission, the stub, and hence the calling thread, is blocked. When the reply comes back, the stub returns the status and results to the client. Although the kernel-level primitives are actually related to the message passing, the use of stubs makes this mechanism look like RPC to the programmer, so we will refer to the basic communication primitives as RPC, rather than the slightly more precise "request/reply message exchange."

In order for a client thread to do an RPC with a server thread, the client must know the server's address. Addressing is done by allowing any thread to choose a random 48-bit number, called a **port**, to be used as the address for messages sent to it. Different threads in a process may use different ports if they so desire. All messages are addressed from a sender to a destination port. A port is nothing more than a kind of logical thread address. There is no data structure and no storage associated with a port. It is similar to an IP address or an Ethernet address in that respect, except that it is not tied to any particular physical location. The first field in each capability gives the port of the server that manages the object (see Fig. 14-3).

RPC Primitives

The RPC mechanism makes use of three principal kernel primitives:

1. get_request - indicates a server's willingness to listen on a port

2. put_reply - done by a server when it has a reply to send

3. trans - send a message from client to server and wait for the reply

The first two are used by servers. The third is used by clients to *transmit* a message and wait for a reply. All three are true system calls, that is, they do not work by sending a message to a communication server thread. (If processes are able to send messages, why should they have to contact a server for the purpose of sending a message?) Users access the calls through library procedures, as usual, however.

When a server wants to go to sleep waiting for an incoming request, it calls *get_request*. This procedure has three parameters, as follows:

```
get_request(&header, buffer, bytes)
```

The first parameter points to a message header, the second points to a data buffer, and the third tells how big the data buffer is. This call is analogous to

```
read(fd, buffer, bytes)
```

in UNIX or MS-DOS in that the first parameter identifies what is being read, the second provides a buffer to put the data, and the third tells how big the buffer is.

When a message is transmitted over the network, it contains a header and (optionally) a data buffer. The header is a fixed 32-byte structure and is shown in Fig. 14-8. What the first parameter of the *get_request* call does is tell the kernel where to put the incoming header. In addition, prior to making the *get_request* call, the server must initialize the header's *Port* field to contain the port it is listening to. This is how the kernel knows which server is listening to which port. The incoming header overwrites the one initialized by the server.

When a message arrives, the server is unblocked. It normally first inspects the header to find out more about the request. The *Signature* field has been reserved for authentication purposes, but is not currently used.

The remaining fields are not specified by the RPC protocol, so a server and client can agree to use them any way they want. The normal conventions are as follows. Most requests to servers contain a capability, to specify the object being operated on. Many replies also have a capability as a return value. The *Private part* is normally used to hold the rightmost three fields of the capability.

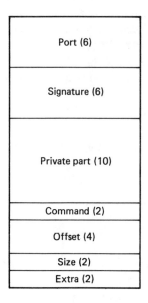

Fig. 14-8. The header used on all Amoeba request and reply messages. The numbers in parentheses give the field sizes in bytes.

Most servers support multiple operations on their objects, such as reading, writing, and destroying. The *Command* field is conventionally used on requests to indicate which operation is needed. On replies it tells whether the operation was successful or not, and if not, it gives the reason for failure.

The last three fields hold parameters, if any. For example, when reading a segment or file, they can be used to indicate the offset within the object to begin reading at, and the number of bytes to read.

Note that for many operations, no buffer is needed or used. In the case of reading again, the object capability, the offset, and the size all fit in the header. When writing, the buffer contains the data to be written. On the other hand, the reply to a READ contains a buffer, whereas the reply to a WRITE does not.

After the server has completed its work, it makes a call

```
put_reply(&header, buffer, bytes)
```

to send back the reply. The first parameter provides the header and the second provides the buffer. The third tells how big the buffer is. If a server does a *put_reply* without having previously done an unmatched *get_request*, the *put_reply* fails with an error. Similarly, two consecutive *get_request* calls fail. The two calls must be paired in the correct way.

Now let us turn from the server to the client. To do an RPC, the client calls a stub which makes the following call:

```
trans(&header1, buffer1, bytes1, &header2, buffer2, bytes2)
```

The first three parameters provide information about the header and buffer of the outgoing request. The last three provide the same information for the incoming reply.

The *trans* call sends the request and blocks the client until the reply has come in. This design forces processes to stick closely to the client-server RPC communication paradigm, analogous to the way structured programming techniques prevent programmers from doing things that generally lead to poorly structured programs (such as using unconstrained GOTO statements).

If Amoeba actually worked as described above, it would be possible for an intruder to impersonate a server just by doing a *get_request* on the server's port. These ports are public after all, since clients must know them to contact the servers. Amoeba solves this problem cryptographically. Each port is actually a pair of ports: the **get-port**, which is private, only known to the server, and the **put-port**, which is known to the whole world. The two are related through a one-way function, F, according to the relation:

$$\text{put--port} = F\,(\text{get--port})$$

The one-way function need not be the same one as used for protecting capabilities since the two concepts are unrelated.

When a server does a *get_request*, the corresponding put-port is computed by the kernel and stored in a table of ports being listened to. All *trans* requests use put-ports, so when a packet arrives at a machine, the kernel compares the put-port in the header to the put-ports in its table to see if any match. Since get-ports never appear on the network and cannot be derived from the publicly known put-ports, the scheme is secure. It is illustrated in Fig. 14-9 and described in more detail in (Tanenbaum et al., 1986).

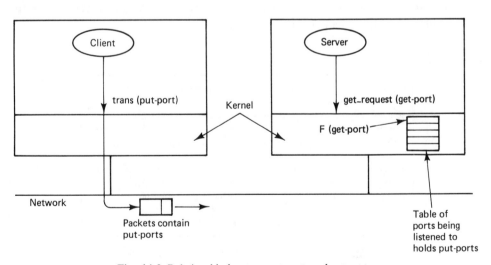

Fig. 14-9. Relationship between get-ports and put-ports.

Amoeba RPC supports at-most-once semantics. In other words, when an RPC is done, the system guarantees that an RPC will never be carried out more than one time, even in the face of server crashes and rapid reboots.

14.5.2. Group Communication in Amoeba

RPC is not the only form of communication supported by Amoeba. It also supports group communication. A group in Amoeba consists of one or more processes that are cooperating to carry out some task or provide some service. Processes can be members of several groups at the same time. Groups are closed. The usual way for a client to access a service provided by a group is to do an RPC with one of its members. That member then uses group communication within the group, if necessary, to determine who will do what.

This design was chosen to provide a greater degree of transparency than an open group structure would have. The idea behind it is that clients normally use RPC to talk to individual servers, so they should use RPC to talk to groups as well. The alternative—open groups and using RPC to talk to single servers but group communication to talk to group servers—is much less transparent. (Using group communication for everything would eliminate the many advantages of RPC that we have discussed earlier.) Once it has been determined that clients outside a group will use RPC to talk to the group (actually, to talk to one process in the group), the need for open groups vanishes, so closed groups, which are easier to implement, are adequate.

Group Communication Primitives

The operations available for group communication in Amoeba are listed in Fig. 14-10. *CreateGroup* creates a new group and returns a group identifier used in the other calls to identify which group is meant. The parameters specify various sizes and how much fault tolerance is required (how many dead members the group must be able to withstand and continue to function correctly).

Call	Description
CreateGroup	Create a new group and set its parameters
JoinGroup	Make the caller a member of a group
LeaveGroup	Remove the caller from a group
SendToGroup	Reliably send a message to all members of a group
ReceiveFromGroup	Block until a message arrives from a group
ResetGroup	Initiate recovery after a process crash

Fig. 14-10. Amoeba group communication primitives.

JoinGroup and *LeaveGroup* allow processes to enter and exit from existing groups. One of the parameters of *JoinGroup* is a small message that is sent to all group members to announce the presence of a newcomer. Similarly, one of the parameters of *LeaveGroup* is another small message sent to all members to say goodbye and wish them good luck in their future activities. The point of the little messages is to make it possible for all members to know who their comrades are, in case they are interested. It is not necessary for them to keep track, however. When the last member of a group calls *LeaveGroup*, the group is destroyed.

SendToGroup atomically broadcasts a message to all members of a specified group, in spite of lost messages, finite buffers, and processor crashes. Amoeba supports global time ordering, so if two processes call *SendToGroup* nearly simultaneously, the system ensures that all group members will receive the messages in the same order. This is guaranteed; programmers can count on it. If the two calls are exactly simultaneous, the first one to get its packet successfully onto the LAN is declared to be first.

ReceiveFromGroup tries to get a message from a specified group. If no message is available (buffered by the kernel) the caller blocks until one is available. If a message has already arrived, the caller gets the message with no delay. The protocol insures that under no conditions are messages irretrievably lost.

The final call, *ResetGroup* is used to recover from crashes. It specifies how many members the new group must have as a minimum. If the kernel is able to establish contact with the requisite number of processes and rebuild the group, it returns the size of the new group. Otherwise, it fails.

The Amoeba Reliable Broadcast Protocol

Let us now look at how Amoeba implements group communication. Amoeba works best on LANs that support either multicasting or broadcasting (or like Ethernet, both). For simplicity, we will just refer to broadcasting, although in fact the implementation uses multicasting when it can to avoid disturbing machines that are not interested in the message being sent. It is assumed that the hardware broadcast is good, but not perfect. In practice, lost packets are rare, but receiver overruns do happen occasionally. Since these errors can occur, the protocol has been designed to deal with them.

The key idea that forms the basis of the implementation of group communication is **reliable broadcasting**. By this we mean that when a user process broadcasts a message (e.g., with *SendToGroup*) the user-supplied message is correctly delivered to all members of the group, even though the hardware may lose packets. For simplicity, we will assume that each message fits into a single packet. For the moment, we will assume that processors do not crash. We will consider the case of unreliable processors afterwards. The description given below is just an outline. For more details, see (Kaashoek and Tanenbaum, 1991; and Kaashoek et al., 1989). Other reliable broadcast protocols are discussed in (Birman and Joseph, 1987a; Chang and Maxemchuk, 1984; Garcia-Molina and Spauster, 1991; Luan and Gligor, 1990; Melliar-Smith et al., 1990; and Tseung, 1989).

The hardware/software configuration required for reliable broadcasting in Amoeba is shown in Fig. 14-11. The hardware of all the machines is normally identical, and they all run exactly the same kernel. However, when the application starts up, one of the machines is elected as sequencer (like a committee electing a chairman). If the sequencer machine subsequently crashes, the remaining members elect a new one. Many election algorithms are known, such as choosing the process with the highest network address. We will discuss fault tolerance later in this chapter.

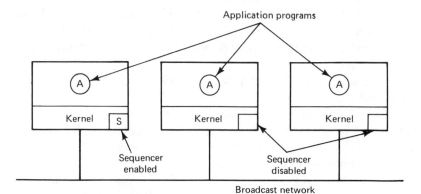

Fig. 14-11. System structure for group communication in Amoeba.

One sequence of events that can be used to achieve reliable broadcasting can be summarized as follows.

1. The user process traps to the kernel, passing it the message.

2. The kernel accepts the message and blocks the user process.

3. The kernel sends the message to the sequencer using an ordinary point-to-point message.

4. When the sequencer gets the message, it allocates the next available sequence number, puts the sequence number in a header field reserved for it, and broadcasts the message (and sequence number).

5. When the sending kernel sees the broadcast message, it unblocks the calling process to let it continue execution.

Let us now consider these steps in more detail. When an application process executes a broadcasting primitive, such as *SendToGroup*, a trap to its kernel occurs. The kernel then blocks the caller and builds a message containing a kernel-supplied header and the application-supplied data. The header contains the message type (*Request for Broadcast* in this case), a unique message identifier (used to detect duplicates), the number of the last broadcast received by the kernel (usually called a **piggybacked acknowledgement**), and some other information.

The kernel sends the message to the sequencer using a normal point-to-point message, and simultaneously starts a timer. If the broadcast comes back before the timer runs out (normal case), the sending kernel stops the timer and returns control to the caller. In practice, this case happens well over 99% of the time, because LANs are highly reliable.

On the other hand, if the broadcast has not come back before the timer expires, the kernel assumes that either the message or the broadcast has been lost. Either way, it retransmits the message. If the original message was lost, no harm has been done, and the second (or subsequent) attempt will trigger the broadcast in the usual way. If the message got to the sequencer and was broadcast, but the sender missed the broadcast, the sequencer will detect the retransmission as a duplicate (from the message identifier) and just tell the sender that everything is all right. The message is not broadcast a second time.

A third possibility is that a broadcast comes back before the timer runs out, but it is the wrong broadcast. This situation arises when two processes attempt to broadcast simultaneously. One of them, A, gets to the sequencer first, and its message is broadcast. A sees the broadcast and unblocks its application program. However its competitor, B, sees A's broadcast and realizes that it has failed to go first. Nevertheless, B knows that its message probably got to the sequencer (since lost messages are rare) where it will be queued, and broadcast next. Thus B accepts A's broadcast and continues to wait for its own broadcast to come back or its timer to expire.

Now consider what happens at the sequencer when a *Request for Broadcast* arrives there. First a check is made to see if the message is a retransmission, and if so, the sender is informed that the broadcast has already been done, as mentioned above. If the message is new (normal case), the next sequence number is assigned to it, and the sequencer counter incremented by 1 for next time. The message and its identifier are then stored in a **history buffer**, and the message is then broadcast. The message is also passed to the application running on the sequencer's machine (because the broadcast does not cause an interrupt on the machine that issued the broadcast).

Finally, let us consider what happens when a kernel receives a broadcast. First, the sequence number is compared to the sequence number of the most recently received broadcast. If the new one is 1 higher (normal case), no broadcasts have been missed so the message is passed up to the application program, assuming that it is waiting. If it is not waiting, it is buffered until the program calls *ReceiveFrom-Group*.

Suppose that the newly received broadcast has sequence number 25, while the previous one had number 23. The kernel is immediately alerted to the fact that it has missed number 24, so it sends a point-to-point message to the sequencer asking for a private retransmission of the missing message. The sequencer fetches the missing message from its history buffer and sends it. When it arrives, the receiving kernel processes 24 and 25, passing them to the application program in numerical order. Thus the only effect of a lost message is a minor time delay. All application programs see all broadcasts in the same order, even if some messages are lost.

The reliable broadcast protocol is illustrated in Fig. 14-12. Here the application program running on machine A passes a message, M, to its kernel for broadcasting. The kernel sends the message to the sequencer, where it is assigned sequence number 25. The message (containing the sequence number 25) is now broadcast to all machines and also passed to the application program running on the sequencer itself. This broadcast message is denoted by M25 in the figure.

The M25 message arrives at machines B and C. At machine B the kernel sees

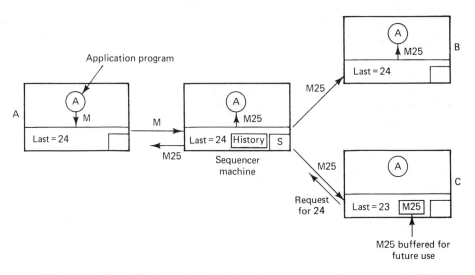

Fig. 14-12. The application of machine *A* sends a message to the sequencer, which then adds a sequence number (25) and broadcasts it. At *B* it is accepted, but at *C* it is buffered until 24, which was missed, can be retrieved from the sequencer.

that it has already processed all broadcasts up to and including 24, so it immediately passes *M25* up to the application program. At *C*, however, the last message to arrive was 23 (24 must have been lost), so *M25* is buffered in the kernel, and a point-to-point message requesting 24 is sent to the sequencer. Only after the reply has come back and been given to the application program will *M25* be passed upwards as well.

Now let us look at the management of the history buffer. Unless something is done to prevent it, the history buffer will quickly fill up. However, if the sequencer knows that all machines have correctly received broadcasts, say, 0 through 23, it can delete these from its history buffer.

Several mechanisms are provided to allow the sequencer to discover this information. The basic one is that each *Request for Broadcast* message sent to the sequencer carries a piggybacked acknowledgement, *k*, meaning that all broadcasts up to and including *k* have been correctly received. This way, the sequencer can maintain a piggyback table, indexed by machine number, telling for each machine which broadcast was the last one received. Whenever the history buffer begins to fill up, the sequencer can make a pass through this table to find the smallest value. It can then safely discard all messages up to and including this value.

If one machine happens to be silent for an unusually long period of time, the sequencer will not know what its status is. To inform the sequencer, it is required to send a short acknowledgement message when it has sent no broadcast messages for a certain period of time. Furthermore, the sequencer can broadcast a *Request for Status* message, which directs all other machines to send it a message giving the number of the highest broadcast received in sequence. In this way, the sequencer can update its piggyback table and then truncate its history buffer.

Although in practice *Request for Status* messages are rare, they do occur, and thus raise the mean number of messages required for a reliable broadcast slightly above 2, even when there are no lost messages. The effect increases slightly as the number of machines grows.

There is a subtle design point concerning this protocol that should be clarified. There are two ways to do the broadcast. In method 1 (described above), the user sends a point-to-point message to the sequencer, which then broadcasts it. In method 2, the user broadcasts the message, including a unique identifier. When the sequencer sees this, it broadcasts a special *Accept* message containing the unique identifier and its newly assigned sequence number. A broadcast is only ''official'' when the *Accept* message has been sent. The two methods are compared in Fig. 14-13.

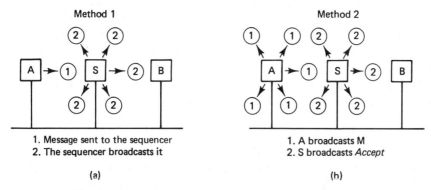

Fig. 14-13. Two methods for doing reliable broadcasting.

These protocols are logically equivalent, but they have different performance characteristics. In method 1, each message appears in full on the network twice: once to the sequencer and once from the sequencer. Thus a message of length m bytes consumes $2m$ bytes worth of network bandwidth. However, only the second of these is broadcast, so each user machine is only interrupted once (for the second message).

In method 2, the full message only appears once on the network, plus a very short *Accept* message from the sequencer, so only half the bandwidth is consumed. On the other hand, every machine is interrupted twice, once for the message and once for the *Accept*. Thus method 1 wastes bandwidth to reduce interrupts compared to method 2. Depending on the average message size, one may be preferable to the other.

In summary, this protocol allows reliable broadcasting to be done on an unreliable network in just over two messages per reliable broadcast. Each broadcast is indivisible, and all applications receive all messages in the same order, no matter how many are lost. The worst that can happen is that a short delay is introduced when a message is lost, which rarely happens. If two processes attempt to broadcast at the same time, one of them will get to the sequencer first and win. The other will see a broadcast from its competitor coming back from the sequencer, and will realize that its request has been queued and will appear shortly, so it simply waits.

Fault Tolerant Group Communication

So far we have assumed that no processors crash. In fact, this protocol has been designed to withstand the loss of an arbitrary collection of k processors (including the sequencer), where k (the resilience degree) is selected when the group is created. The larger k is, the more redundancy is required, and the slower the operation is in the normal case, so the user must choose k with care. We will sketch the recovery algorithm below. For more details, see (Kaashoek and Tanenbaum, 1991).

When a processor crashes, initially no one detects this event. Sooner or later, however, some kernel notices that messages sent to the crashed machine are not being acknowledged, so the kernel marks the crashed processor as dead and the group as unusable. All subsequent group communication primitives on that machine fail (return an error status).

Shortly thereafter, one of the user processes that has gotten an error return calls *ResetGroup* to initiate recovery. The recovery is done is two phases (Garcia-Molina, 1982). In phase one, one process is elected as coordinator. In phase two, the coordinator rebuilds the group and brings all the other processes up to date. At that point, normal operation continues.

In Fig. 14-14(a) we see a group of six machines, of which machine 5, the sequencer, has just crashed. The numbers in the boxes indicate the last message correctly received by each machine. Two machines, 0 and 1, simultaneously detect the sequencer failure, and both call *ResetGroup* to start recovery. This call results in the kernel sending a message to all other members inviting them to participate in the recovery and asking them to report back the sequence number of the highest message they have seen. At this point it is discovered that two processes have declared themselves coordinator. The one that has seen the message with the highest sequence number wins. In case of a tie, the one with the highest network address wins. This leads to a single coordinator, as shown in Fig. 14-14(b).

Once the coordinator has been voted into office, it collects from the other members any messages it may have missed. Now it is up to date, and is able to become the new sequencer. It builds a *Results* message announcing itself as sequencer and telling the others what the highest sequence number is. Each member can now ask for any messages that it missed. When a member is up to date, it sends an acknowledgement back to the new sequencer. When the new sequencer has an acknowledgement from all the surviving members, it knows that all messages have been correctly delivered to the application programs in order, so it discards its history buffer, and normal operation can resume.

Another problem remains: "How does the coordinator get any messages it has missed if the sequencer has crashed?" The solution lies in the value of k, the resilience degree, chosen at group creation time. When k is 0 (non-fault tolerant case), only the sequencer maintains a history buffer. However, when k is greater than 0, $k + 1$ machines continuously maintain an up-to-date history buffer. Thus if an arbitrary collection of k machines fail, it is guaranteed that at least one history buffer survives, and it is this one that supplies the coordinator with any messages it needs. The extra machines can maintain their history buffers simply by watching the network.

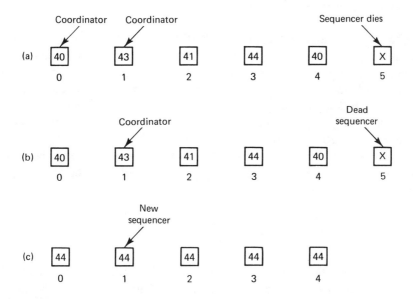

Fig. 14-14. (a) The sequencer crashes. (b) A coordinator is selected. (c) Recovery.

There is one additional problem that must be solved. Normally a *SendToGroup* terminates successfully when the sequencer has received and broadcast or approved the message. If $k > 0$, this protocol is insufficient to survive k arbitrary crashes. Instead, a slightly modified version of method 2 is used. When the sequencer sees a message, M, that was just broadcast, it does not immediately broadcast an *Accept* message, as it does when $k = 0$. Instead, it waits until the k lowest-numbered kernels have acknowledged that they have seen and stored it. Only then does the sequencer broadcast the *Accept* message. Since $k + 1$ machines (including the sequencer) now are known to have stored M in their history buffers, even if k machines crash, M will not be lost.

As in the usual case, no kernel may pass M up to its application program until it has seen the *Accept* message. Because the *Accept* message is not generated until it is certain that $k + 1$ machines have stored M, it is guaranteed that if one machine gets M, they all will eventually. In this way, recovery from the loss of any k machines is always possible. As an aside, to speed up operation for $k > 0$, whenever an entry is made in a history buffer, a short control packet is broadcast to announce this event to the world.

To summarize, the Amoeba group communication scheme guarantees atomic broadcasting with global time ordering even in the face of k arbitrary crashes, where k is chosen by the user when the group is created. This mechanism provides an easy to understand basis for doing distributed programming. It is used in Amoeba to support object-based distributed shared memory for the Orca programming language and for other facilities. It can also be implemented efficiently. Measurements with 68030 CPUs on a 10 Mbps Ethernet show that it is possible to continuously handle 800 reliable broadcasts per second (Tanenbaum et al., 1992).

14.5.3. The Fast Local Internet Protocol

Amoeba uses a custom protocol called **FLIP (Fast Local Internet Protocol)** for actual message transmission. This protocol handles both RPC and group communication and is below them in the protocol hierarchy. In OSI terms, FLIP is a network layer protocol, whereas RPC is more of a connectionless transport or session protocol (the exact location is arguable, since OSI was designed for connection-oriented networks). Conceptually, FLIP can be replaced by another network layer protocol, such as IP, although doing so would cause some of Amoeba's transparency to be lost. Although FLIP was designed in the context of Amoeba, it is intended to be useful in other operating systems as well. In this section we will describe its design and implementation.

Protocol Requirements for Distributed Systems

Before getting into the details of FLIP, it is useful to understand something about why it was designed. After all, there are plenty of existing protocols, so the invention of a new one clearly has to be justified. In Fig. 14-15 we list the principal requirements that a protocol for a distributed system should meet. First, the protocol must support both RPC and group communication efficiently. If the underlying network has hardware multicast or broadcast, as Ethernet does, for example, the protocol should use it for group communication. On the other hand, if the network does not have either of these features, group communication must still work exactly the same way, even though the implementation will have to be different.

Item	Description
RPC	The protocol should support RPC
Group communication	The protocol should support group communication
Process migration	Processes should be able to take their addresses with them
Security	Processes should not be able to impersonate other processes
Network management	Support is needed for automatic reconfiguration
Wide-area networks	The protocol should also work on wide area networks

Fig. 14-15. Desirable characteristics for a distributed system protocol.

A characteristic that is increasingly important is support for process migration. A process should be able to move from one machine to another, even to one in a different network, with nobody noticing. Protocols such as OSI, X.25, and TCP/IP that use machine addresses to identify processes make migration difficult, because a process cannot take its address with it when it moves.

Security is also an issue. Although the get-ports and put-ports provide security for Amoeba, a security mechanism should also be present in the packet protocol so it can be used with operating systems that do not have Amoeba-type cryptographically secure addresses.

Another point on which most existing protocols score badly is network management. It should not be necessary to have elaborate configuration tables telling which network is connected to which other network. Furthermore, if the configuration changes, due to gateways going down or coming back up, the protocol should adapt to the new configuration automatically.

Finally, the protocol should work on both local and wide-area networks. In particular, the same protocol should be usable on both.

The FLIP Interface

The FLIP protocol and its associated architecture was designed to meet all these requirements. A typical FLIP configuration is shown in Fig. 14-16. Here we see five machines, two on an Ethernet and four on a token ring. Each machine has one user process, *A* through *E*. One of the machines is connected to both networks, and as such automatically functions as a gateway. Gateways may also run clients and servers, just like other nodes.

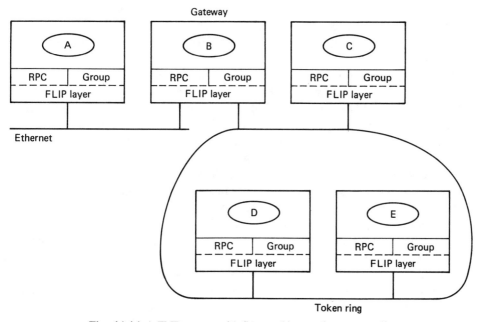

Fig. 14-16. A FLIP system with five machines and two networks.

The software is structured as shown in Fig. 14-16. The kernel contains two layers. The top layer handles calls from user processes for RPC or group communication services. The bottom layer handles the FLIP protocol. For example, when a client calls *trans*, it traps to the kernel. The RPC layer examines the header and buffer, builds a message from them, and passes the message down to the FLIP layer for transmission.

All low-level communication in Amoeba is based on **FLIP addresses**. Each process has exactly one FLIP address: a 64-bit random number chosen by the system when the process is created. If the process ever migrates, it takes its FLIP address with it. If the network is ever reconfigured, so that all machines are assigned new (hardware) network numbers or network addresses, the FLIP addresses still remain unchanged. It is the fact that a FLIP address uniquely identifies a process, not a machine, that makes communication in Amoeba insensitive to changes in network topology and network addressing.

A FLIP address is really two addresses, a public-address and a private-address, related by

$$\text{Public-address} = \text{DES}(\text{private-address})$$

where DES is the Data Encryption Standard. To compute the public-address from the private one, the private-address is used as a DES key to encrypt a 64-bit block of 0s. Given a public-address, finding the corresponding private address is computationally infeasible. Servers listen to private-addresses, but clients send to public-addresses, analogous to the way put-ports and get-ports work, but at a lower level.

FLIP has been designed to work not only with Amoeba, but also with other operating systems. A version for UNIX also exists, and there is no reason one could not be made for MS-DOS. The security provided by the private-address, public-address scheme also works for UNIX to UNIX communication using FLIP, independent of Amoeba.

Furthermore, FLIP has been designed so that it can be built in hardware, for example, as part of the network interface chip. For this reason, a precise interface with the layer above it has been specified. The interface between the FLIP layer and the layer above it (which we will call the RPC layer) has nine primitives, seven for outgoing traffic and two for incoming traffic. Each one has a library procedure that invokes it. The nine calls are listed in Fig. 14-17.

The first one, *init*, allows the RPC layer to allocate a table slot and initialize it with pointers to two procedures (or in a hardware implementation, two interrupt vectors). These procedures are the ones called when normal and undeliverable packets arrive, respectively. *End* deallocates the slot when the machine is being shut down.

Register is invoked to announce a process' FLIP address to the FLIP layer. It is called when the process starts up (or at least, on the first attempt at getting or sending a message). The FLIP layer immediately runs the private-address offered to it through the DES function, and stores the public-address in its tables. If an incoming packet is addressed to the public FLIP address, it will be passed to the RPC layer for delivery. The *unregister* call removes an entry from the FLIP layer's tables.

The next three calls are for sending point-to-point messages, multicast messages, and broadcast messages, respectively. None of these guarantee delivery. To make RPC reliable, acknowledgements are used. To make group communication reliable, even in the face of lost packets, the sequencer protocol discussed above is used.

Call	Description	Direction
Init	Allocate a table slot	↓
End	Return a table slot	↓
Register	Listen to a FLIP address	↓
Unregister	Stop listening	↓
Unicast	Send a point-to-point message	↓
Multiccast	Send a multicast message	↓
Broadcast	Send a broadcast message	↓
Receive	Packet received	↑
Notdeliver	Undeliverable packet received	↑

Fig. 14-17. The calls supported by the FLIP layer.

The last two calls are for incoming traffic. The first is for messages originating elsewhere and directed to this machine. The second is for messages sent by this machine but sent back as undeliverable.

Operation of the FLIP Layer

Packets passed by the RPC layer or group communication layer (see Fig. 14-16) to the FLIP layer are addressed by FLIP addresses, so the FLIP layer must be able to convert these addresses to network addresses for actual transmission. In order to perform this function, the FLIP layer maintains the routing table shown in Fig. 14-18. Currently this table is maintained in software, but future chip designers could implement it in hardware.

FLIP address	Network address	Hop count	Trusted bit	Age

Fig. 14-18. The FLIP routing table.

Whenever an incoming packet arrives at any machine, it is first handled by the FLIP layer, which extracts from it the FLIP address and network address of the sender. The number of hops the packet has made is also recorded. Since the hop count is only incremented when a packet is forwarded by a gateway, the hop count tells how many gateways the packet has passed through. The hop count is therefore a crude measure of how far away the source is. (Actually, things are slightly better than this, as slow networks count for multiple hops.) If the FLIP address is not presently in the routing table, it is entered. This entry can later be used to send packets *to* that FLIP address, since its network number and address are now known.

An additional bit present in each packet tells whether the path the packet has followed so far is entirely over trusted networks. It is managed by the gateways. If the packet has gone through one or more untrusted networks, packets to the source address should be encrypted if absolute security is desired. With trusted networks, encryption is not needed.

The last field of each routing table entry gives the age of the routing table entry. It is reset to 0 whenever a packet is received from the corresponding FLIP address. Periodically, all the ages are incremented. This field allows the FLIP layer to find a suitable table entry to purge if the table fills up (large numbers indicate that there has been no traffic for a long time).

Locating Put-Ports

To see how FLIP works in the context of Amoeba, let us consider a simple example using the configuration of Fig. 14-16. *A* is a client and *B* is a server. With FLIP, any machine having connections to two or more networks is automatically a gateway, so the fact that *B* happens to be running on a gateway machine is irrelevant.

When *B* is created, the kernel picks a new random FLIP address for it and registers it with the FLIP layer. After starting, *B* initializes itself and then does a *get_request* on its get-port, which causes a trap to the kernel. The RPC layer looks up the put-port in its get-port to put-port cache (or computes it if no entry is found) and makes a note that a process is listening to that port. It then blocks until a request comes in.

Later, *A* does a *trans* on the put-port. Its RPC layer looks in its tables to see if it knows the FLIP address of the server process that listens to the put-port. Since it does not, the RPC layer sends a special broadcast packet to find it. This packet has a maximum hop count of 1 to make sure that the broadcast is confined to its own network. (When a gateway sees a packet whose current hop count is already equal to its maximum hop count, the packet is discarded instead of being forwarded.) If the broadcast fails, the sending RPC layer times out and tries again with a maximum hop count of 2, and so on, until it locates the server.

When the broadcast packet arrives at *B*'s machine, the RPC layer there sends back a reply announcing its FLIP address. This packet, like all incoming packets, causes *A*'s FLIP layer to make an entry for that FLIP address before passing the reply packet up to the RPC layer. The RPC layer now makes an entry in its own tables mapping the put-port onto the FLIP address. Then it sends the request to the server. Since the FLIP layer now has an entry for the server's FLIP address, it can build a packet containing the proper network address and send it without further ado. Subsequent requests to the server's put-port use the RPC layer's cache to find the FLIP address and the FLIP layer's routing table to find the network address. Thus broadcasting is only used the very first time a server is contacted. After that, the kernel tables provide the necessary information.

To summarize, locating a put-port requires two mappings:

1. From the put-port to the FLIP address (done by the RPC layer).

2. From the FLIP address to the network address (done by the FLIP layer).

The reason for this two-stage process is twofold. First, FLIP has been designed as a general-purpose protocol for use in distributed systems, including non-Amoeba systems. Since these systems generally do not use Amoeba-style ports, the mapping of put-ports to FLIP addresses has not been built into the FLIP layer. Other users of FLIP may just use FLIP addresses directly.

Second, a put-port really identifies a *service* rather than a *server*. A service may be provided by multiple servers to enhance performance and reliability. Although all the servers listen to the same put-port, each one has its own private FLIP address. When a client's RPC layer issues a broadcast to find the FLIP address corresponding to a put-port, any or all of the servers may respond. Since each server has a different FLIP address, each response creates a different routing table entry. All the responses are passed to the RPC layer, which chooses one to use.

The advantage of this scheme over having just a single (port, network address) cache is that it permits servers to migrate to new machines or have their machines be wheeled over to new networks and plugged in without requiring any manual reconfiguration, as, say, TCP/IP does. There is a strong analogy here with a person moving and being assigned the same telephone number at the new residence as he had at the old one. (For the record, Amoeba does not currently support process migration, but this feature is envisioned for future releases.)

The advantage over having clients and servers use FLIP addresses directly is the protection offered by the one-way function used to derive put-ports from get-ports. In addition, if a server crashes, it will pick a new FLIP address when it reboots. Attempts to use the old FLIP address will time out, allowing the RPC layer to indicate failure to the client. This mechanism is how at-most-once semantics are guaranteed. The client, however, can just try again with the same put-port if it wishes, since that is not necessarily invalidated by server crashes.

FLIP over Wide-Area Networks

FLIP also works transparently over wide-area networks. In Fig. 14-19 we have three local-area networks connected by a wide-area network. Suppose the client A wants to do an RPC with the server E. A's RPC layer first tries to locate the put-port using a maximum hop count of 1. When that fails, it tries again with a maximum hop count of 2. This time, C forwards the broadcast packet to all the gateways that are connected to the wide-area network, namely, D and G. Effectively, C simulates broadcast over the wide-area network by sending individual messages to all the other gateways. When this broadcast fails to turn up the server, a third broadcast is sent, this time with a maximum hop count of 3. This one succeeds. The reply contains E's network address and FLIP address, which are then entered into A's routing table. From this point on, communication between A and E happens using normal point-to-point communication. No more broadcasts are needed.

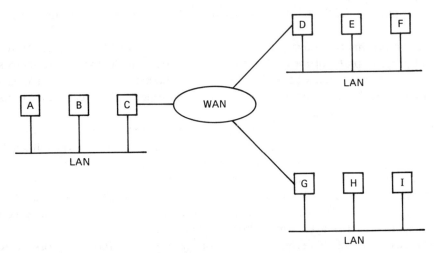

Fig. 14-19. Three LANs connected by a WAN.

Communication over the wide-area network is encapsulated in whatever protocol the wide-area network requires. For example, on a TCP/IP network, C might have open connections to D and G all the time. Alternatively, the implementation might decide to close any connection not used for a certain length of time.

Although this method does not scale well to thousands of LANs, for modest numbers it works quite well. In practice, few servers move, so that once a server has been located by broadcasting, subsequent requests will use the cached entries. Using this method, a substantial number of machines all over the world can work together in a totally transparent way. An RPC to a thread in the caller's address space and an RPC to a thread half-way around the world are done in exactly the same way.

Group communication also uses FLIP. When a message is sent to multiple destinations, FLIP uses the hardware multicast or broadcast on those networks where it is available. On those that do not have it, broadcast is simulated by sending individual messages, just as we saw on the wide-area network. The choice of mechanism is done by the FLIP layer, with the same user semantics in all cases.

14.6. THE AMOEBA SERVERS

Most of the traditional operating system services (such as the file server) are implemented in Amoeba as server processes. Although it would have been possible to put together a random collection of servers, each with its own model of the world, it was decided early on to provide a single model of what a server does to achieve uniformity and simplicity. Although voluntary, most servers follow it. The model, and some examples of key Amoeba servers, are described in this section.

All standard servers in Amoeba are defined by a set of stub procedures. The newer stubs are defined in **AIL**, the **Amoeba Interface Language**, although the older ones are hand written in C. The stub procedures are generated by the AIL compiler from the stub definitions and then placed in the library so clients can use them. In effect, the stubs define precisely what services the server provides, and what their parameters are. In our discussion below, we will refer to the stubs frequently.

14.6.1. The Bullet Server

Like all operating systems, Amoeba has a file system. However, unlike most other ones, the choice of file system is not dictated by the operating system. The file system runs as a collection of server processes. Users who do not like the standard ones are free to write their own. The kernel does not know, or care, which one is the "real" file system. In fact, different users may use different and incompatible file systems at the same time, if they so desire.

The standard file system consists of three servers, the **bullet server**, which handles file storage, the **directory server**, which takes care of file naming and directory management, and the **replication server**, which handles file replication. The file system has been split into these separate components to achieve increased flexibility and make each of the servers straightforward to implement. We will discuss the bullet server in this section and the other two in the following ones.

Very briefly, a client process can create a file using the *create* call. The bullet server responds by sending back a capability that can be used in subsequent calls to *read* to retrieve all or part of the file. In most cases, the user will then give the file an ASCII name, and the (ASCII name, capability) pair will be given to the directory server for storage in a directory, but this operation has nothing to do with the bullet server.

The bullet server was designed to be very fast (hence the name). It was also designed to run on machines having large primary memories and huge disks, rather than low-end machines where memory is always scarce. The organization is quite different from most conventional file servers. In particular, files are **immutable**. Once a file has been created, it cannot subsequently be changed. It can be deleted, and a new file created in its place, but the new file has a different capability from the old one. This fact simplifies automatic replication, as will be seen. It is also well suited for use on large-capacity, write-once optical disks.

Because files cannot be modified after their creation, the size of a file is always known at creation time. This property allows files to be stored contiguously on the disk, and also in the main memory cache. By storing files contiguously, they can be read into memory in a single disk operation, and they can be sent to users in a single RPC reply message. These simplifications lead to the high performance.

The conceptual model behind the file system is thus that a client creates an entire file in its own memory, and then transmits it in a single RPC to the bullet server, which stores it and returns a capability for accessing it later. To modify this file (e.g., to edit a program or document), the client sends back the capability and asks for the file, which is then (ideally) sent in one RPC to the client's memory. The client can then modify the file locally any way it wants to. When it is done, it sends the file to the server (ideally) in one RPC, thus causing a new file to be created and a new capability to be returned. At this point the client can ask the server to destroy the original file, or it can keep the old file as a backup.

As a concession to reality, the bullet server also supports clients that have too little memory to receive or send entire files in a single RPC. When reading, it is possible to ask for a section of a file, specified by an offset and a byte count. This feature allows clients to read files in whatever size unit they find convenient.

Writing a file in several operations is complicated by the fact that bullet server files are guaranteed to be immutable. This problem is dealt with by introducing two kinds of files, **uncommitted files**, which are in the process of being created, and **committed files**, which are permanent. Uncommitted files can be changed; committed files cannot be. An RPC doing a *create* must specify whether the file is to be committed immediately or not.

In both cases, a copy of the file is made at the server and a capability for the file is returned. If the file is not committed, it can be modified by subsequent RPCs; in particular, it can be appended to. When all the appends and other changes have been completed, the file can be committed, at which point it becomes immutable. To emphasize the transient nature of uncommitted files, they cannot be read. Only committed files can be read.

The Bullet Server Interface

The bullet server supports the six operations listed in Fig. 14-20, plus an additional three that are reserved for the system administrator. In addition, all the standard operations listed in Fig. 14-5 are also valid. All these operations are accessed by calling stub procedures from the library.

Call	Description
Create	Create a new file; optionally commit it as well
Read	Read all or part of a specified file
Size	Return the size of a specified file
Modify	Overwrite n bytes of an uncommitted file
Insert	Insert or append n bytes to an uncommitted file
Delete	Delete n bytes from an uncommitted file

Fig. 14-20. Bullet server calls.

The *create* procedure supplies some data, which is put into a new file whose capability is returned in the reply. If the file is committed (determined by a parameter), it can be read but not changed. If it is not committed, it cannot be read until it is committed, but it can be changed or appended to.

The *read* call can read all or part of any committed file. It specifies the file to be read by providing a capability for it. Presentation of the capability is proof that the operation is allowed. The bullet server does not make any checks based on the client's identity. In fact, it does not even know the client's identity. The *size* call takes a capability as parameter and tells how big the corresponding file is.

The last three calls all work on uncommitted files. They allow the file to be changed by overwriting, inserting, or deleting bytes. Multiple calls can be made in succession. The last call can indicate via a parameter that it wants to commit the file.

The bullet server also supports three special calls for the system administrator, who must present a special super-capability. These calls flush the main memory cache to disk, allow the disk to be compacted, and repair damaged file systems.

The capabilities generated and used by the bullet server use the *Rights* field to protect the operations. In this way, a capability can be made that allows a file to be read but not to be destroyed, for example.

Implementation of the Bullet Server

The bullet server maintains a file table with one entry per file, analogous to the UNIX i-node table, and shown in Fig. 14-21. The entire table is read into memory when the bullet server is booted, and kept there as long as the bullet server is running.

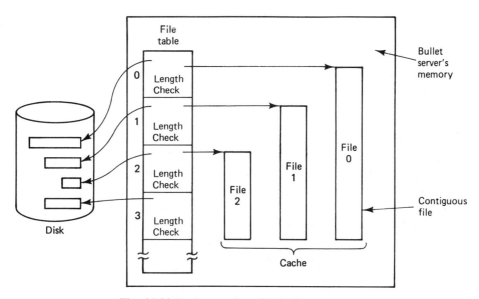

Fig. 14-21. Implementation of the bullet server.

Roughly speaking, each table entry contains two pointers and a length, plus some additional information. One pointer gives the disk address of the file and the other gives the main memory address, if the file happens to be in the main memory cache at the moment. All files are stored contiguously, both on disk and in the cache, so a pointer and a length is enough. Unlike UNIX, no direct or indirect blocks are needed.

Although this strategy wastes space due to external fragmentation, both in memory and on disk, it has the advantage of extreme simplicity and high performance. A file on disk can be read into memory in a single operation, at the maximum speed of the disk, and it can be transmitted over the network at the maximum speed of the network. As memories and disks get larger and cheaper, it is likely that the cost of the wasted memory will be acceptable in return for the speed provided.

When a client process wants to read a file, it sends the capability for the file to the bullet server. The server extracts the object number from the capability and uses it as an index into the file table to locate the entry for the file. The entry contains the random number used in the capability's *Check* field, which is then used to verify that the capability is valid. If it is invalid, the operation is terminated with an error code. If it is valid, the entire file is fetched from the disk into the cache, unless it is already there. Cache space is managed using LRU, but the implicit assumption is that the cache is usually large enough to hold the set of files currently in use.

If a file is created and the capability lost, the file can never be accessed but will remain forever. To prevent this situation, timeouts are used. An uncommitted file that has not been accessed in 10 minutes is simply deleted and its table entry freed. If the entry is subsequently reused for another file, but the old capability is presented 15 minutes later, the *Check* field will detect the fact that the file has changed, and the operation on the old file will be rejected. This approach is acceptable because files normally exist in the uncommitted state for only a few seconds.

For committed files, a less draconian method is used. Associated with every file (in the file table entry) is a counter, initialized to *MAX_LIFETIME*. Periodically, a daemon does an RPC with the bullet server, asking it to perform the standard *age* operation (see Fig. 14-5). This operation causes the bullet server to run through the file table, decrementing each counter by 1. Any file whose counter goes to 0 is destroyed and its disk, table, and cache space reclaimed.

To prevent this mechanism from removing files that are in use, another operation, *touch*, is provided. Unlike *age*, which applies to all files, *touch* is for a specific file. Its function is to reset the counter to *MAX_LIFETIME*. *Touch* is called periodically for all files listed in any directory, to keep them from timing out. Typically, every file is touched once an hour, and a file is deleted if it has not been touched in 24 hours. This mechanism removes lost files (i.e., files not in any directory).

The bullet server can run in user space as an ordinary process. However, if it is running on a dedicated machine, with no other processes on that machine, a small performance gain can be achieved by putting it in the kernel. The semantics are unchanged by this move. Clients cannot even tell where it is located.

14.6.2. The Directory Server

The bullet server, as we have seen, just handles file storage. The naming of files and other objects is handled by the **directory server**. Its primary function is to provide a mapping from human-readable (ASCII) names to capabilities. Processes can create one or more directories, each of which can contain multiple rows. Each row describes one object and contains both the object's name and its capability. Operations are provided to create and delete directories, add and delete rows, and look up names in directories. Unlike bullet files, directories are *not* immutable. Entries can be added to existing directories and entries can be deleted from existing directories.

Directories themselves are objects, and are protected by capabilities, just as other objects. The operations on a directory, such as looking up names and adding new entries, are protected by bits in the *Rights* field, in the usual way. Directory capabilities may be stored in other directories, permitting hierarchical directory trees and more general structures.

Although the directory server can be used to simply store (file-name, capability) pairs, it can also support a more general model. First, a directory entry can name any kind of object that is described by a capability, not just a bullet file or directory. The directory server neither knows nor cares what kind of objects its capabilities control. The entries in a single directory may be for a variety of different kinds of objects, and these objects may be scattered randomly all over the world. There is no requirement that objects in a directory all be the same kind or all be managed by the same server. When a capability is fetched and used, its server is located by broadcasting, as described in the section on FLIP above.

Second, a row may contain not just one capability, but a whole set of capabilities, as shown in Fig. 14-22. Generally, these capabilities are for identical copies of the object, and are managed by different servers. When a process looks up a name, it is given the entire set of capabilities. To see how this feature might be of use, consider the library procedure *open* for opening a file. It looks up a file and gets a capability set in return. It then tries each of the capabilities in turn, until it finds one whose server is alive. In this way, if one object is unavailable, another one can be used in its place, without the main program even knowing. It should be clear that this mechanism works best when the files are immutable, so there is no danger that any of them will have changed since they were created.

ASCII string	Capability set	Owner	Group	Others
Mail	▢ ▢ ▢	1111	0000	0000
Games	▢ ▢ ▢	1111	1110	1110
Exams	▢ ▢ ▢	1111	0000	0000
Papers	▢ ▢ ▢	1111	1100	1000
Committees	▢ ▢ ▢	1111	1010	0010

Fig. 14-22. A typical directory managed by the directory server.

Third, a row may contain multiple columns, each forming a different protection domain and having different rights. For example, a directory may have one column for the owner, one for the owner's group, and one for everyone else, to simulate the UNIX protection scheme. A capability for a directory is really a capability for a specific column in a directory, making it possible for the owner, group, and others to have different permissions. Since the underlying capability set is the same for all columns of a row, it is only necessary to store the rights bits for each column. The actual capabilities can be computed as needed.

The layout of an example directory with five entries is shown in Fig. 14-22. This directory has one row for each of the five file names stored in it. The directory also has three columns, each one representing a different protection domain, in this case for the owner, the owner's group, and everyone else. When the owner of a directory gives away a capability for, say, the last column, the recipient has no access to the more powerful capabilities in the first two columns.

As we mentioned above, directories may contain capabilities for other directories. This ability allows us to build not only trees, but also directory graphs in their full generality. One obvious use of this power is to place the capability for a file in two or more directories, thus creating multiple links to it. These capabilities may also have different rights, making it possible for people sharing a file to have different access permissions, something impossible in UNIX.

In any distributed system, especially one intended for use on wide-area networks, it is difficult to have any concept of a single, global root directory. In Amoeba, every user has his own root directory, as shown in Fig. 14-23. This directory contains capabilities for not only the user's private subdirectories, but also for various public directories containing system programs and other shared files.

Some of the directories in each user's root are similar to those in UNIX such as *bin*, *dev*, and *etc*. However, others are fundamentally different. One of these is *home*, which is the user's home directory.

Another is *public*, which contains the start of the shared public tree. Here we find *cap*, *hosts*, and *pool*, among others. When a process wants to contact the bullet server, the directory server, or any other server, for example, to create a new object, it must have a generic capability for talking to that server. These capabilities are kept in */public/cap*.

Another directory in *public* is *hosts*, which contains a directory for each machine in the system. This directory contains capabilities for various servers that can be found on a host, such as a disk server, a terminal server, a process server, a random number server, and so on.

Finally, *pool* contains capabilities for the pool processors, grouped by CPU architecture. A mechanism is present to restrict each user to a specific set of pool processors.

The Directory Server Interface

The principal directory server calls are listed in Fig. 14-24. The first two, *create* and *delete*, are used to make and remove directories, respectively. When a directory is created, its capability is returned, just as with making a file. This capability can subsequently be inserted into another directory to build a hierarchy. This low-level interface gives maximum control over the shape of the naming graph. Since many

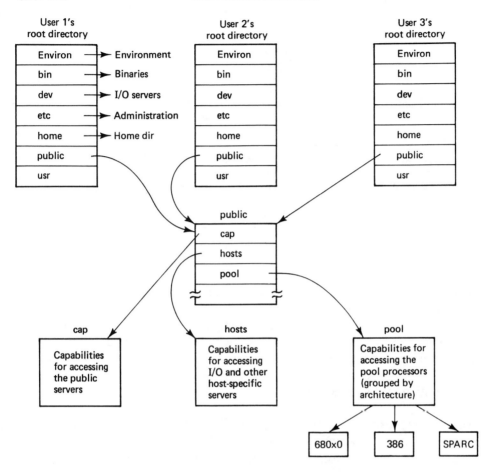

Fig. 14-23. A simplified version of the Amoeba directory hierarchy.

programs are content to work with conventional directory trees, a library package is available to make this easier.

It is worth noting that deleting a directory entry is not the same as destroying the object itself. If a capability is removed from a directory, the object itself continues to exist. The capability can be put into another directory, for example. To get rid of the object, it must be explicitly destroyed.

To add a new entry to a directory, be it a file, a directory, or another kind of object, the *append* call is used. Like most of the directory server calls, it specifies the capability of the directory to be used (added to), as well as the capability to put in the directory and the rights bits for all the columns. An existing entry can be overwritten with *replace*, for example, when a file has been edited and the new version is to be used instead of the old one.

The most common directory operation is *lookup*, which takes as parameters a capability for a directory (column) and an ASCII string and returns the corresponding capability set. Opening a file for reading requires first looking up its capabilities.

Call	Description
Create	Create a new directory
Delete	Delete a directory or an entry in a directory
Append	Add a new directory entry to a specified directory
Replace	Replace a single directory entry
Lookup	Return the capability set corresponding to a specified name
Getmasks	Return the rights masks for the specified entry
Chmod	Change the rights bits in an existing directory entry

Fig. 14-24. The principal directory server calls.

The last two operations listed are for reading and writing the rights masks for all the columns in a row specified by its string.

A few other directory operations also exist. These are mostly concerned with looking up or replacing multiple files at the same time. They can be useful for implementing atomic transactions involving multiple files.

Implementation of the Directory Server

The directory server is a critical component in the Amoeba system, so it has been implemented in a fault tolerant way. The basic data structure is an array of capability pairs stored on a raw disk partition. This array does not use the bullet server because it must be updated frequently.

When a directory is created, the object number put into its capability is an index into this array. When a directory capability is presented, the server inspects the object number contained in it, and uses it to fetch the corresponding capability pair from the array. These capabilities are for identical files, stored on different bullet servers, each of which contains the directory and the *Check* field used to verify the authenticity of the directory capability.

When a directory is changed, a new bullet file is created for it, and the arrays on the raw disk partition are overwritten. The second copy is created later by a background thread. The old directories are then destroyed. Although this mechanism has some extra overhead, it provides a much higher degree of reliability than traditional file systems. In addition, normally directory servers come in pairs, each with its own array of capability pairs (on different disks), to prevent disaster if one of the raw disk partitions is damaged. The two servers communicate to keep synchronized. It is also possible to run with only one. The two-server mode is shown in Fig. 14-25.

In Fig. 14-22 the capability set is shown as being stored only once per row, even though there are multiple columns. This organization is actually used. In most cases, the *owner* column contains rights bits that are all 1s, so the capabilities in the set are

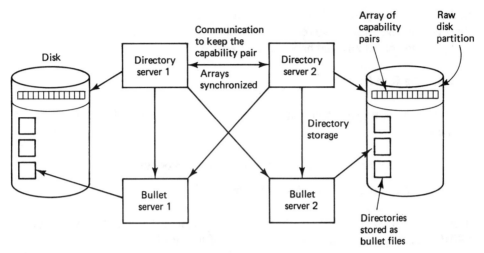

Fig. 14-25. A pair of directory servers. All data are stored twice, on different bullet servers.

true owner capabilities (i.e., the *Check* field has not been run through the one-way function). When a name in another column is looked up, the directory server itself computes the restricted capability by XORing the *rights* field taken from the directory entry with the *Check* field taken from the owner capability. This result is then run through the one-way function and returned to the caller.

This method eliminates the need to store large numbers of capabilities. Furthermore, the directory server caches heavily used capabilities to avoid unnecessary use of the one-way function. If the capability set does not contain owner capabilities, then the server has to be invoked to compute the restricted capabilities because the directory server then does not have access to the original *Check* field.

14.6.3. The Replication Server

Objects managed by the directory server can be replicated automatically by using the replication server. It practices what is called **lazy replication**. What this means is that when a file or other object is created, initially only one copy is made. Then the replication server can be invoked to produce identical replicas, when it has time. Instead of making direct calls to it, the replication server is kept running in the background all the time, scanning specified parts of the directory system periodically. Whenever it finds a directory entry that is supposed to contain *n* capabilities but contains fewer, it contacts the relevant servers and arranges for additional copies to be made. Although the replication server can be used to replicate any kind of object, it works best for immutable objects, such as bullet files.

In addition, the replication server runs the aging and garbage collection mechanism used by the bullet server and other servers. Periodically it touches every object under the directory server's control, to prevent them from timing out. It also sends the *age* messages to the servers to cause them to decrement all the object counters and garbage collect any that have reached zero.

14.6.4. The Run Server

When the user types a command (e.g., *grep*) at the terminal, two decisions must be made:

1. On what architecture type should the process be run?

2. Which processor should be chosen?

The first question relates to whether the process should run on a 386, VAX, SPARC, 680x0, etc. The second relates to the choice of the specific CPU, and depends on the load and memory availability of the candidate processors. The **run server** helps make these decisions.

Each run server manages one or more processor pools. A processor pool is represented by a directory called a **pooldir**, which contains subdirectories for each of the CPU architectures supported. The subdirectories contain capabilities for accessing the process servers on each of the machines in the pool. An example arrangement is shown in Fig. 14-26. Other arrangements are also possible, including mixed and overlapping pools, and dividing pools into subpools.

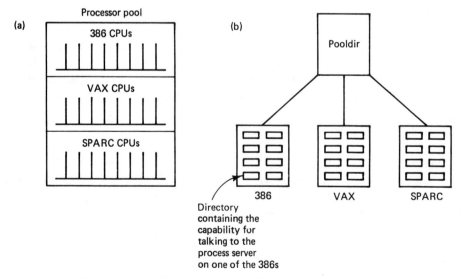

Fig. 14-26. (a) A processor pool. (b) The corresponding pooldir.

When the shell wants to run a program, it looks in */bin* to find, say, *sort*. If *sort* is available for multiple architectures, *sort* will not be a single file, but a directory containing executable programs for each available architecture. The shell then does an RPC with the run server sending it all the available process descriptors and asking it to pick both an architecture and a specific CPU.

The run server then looks in its pooldir to see what it has to offer. The selection is made approximately as follows. First, the intersection of the process descriptors and pool processors is computed. If there are process descriptors (i.e., binary programs) for the 386, SPARC, and 68030, and this run server manages 386, SPARC, and VAX pool processors, only the 386 and SPARC are possibilities, so the other machines are eliminated as candidates.

Second, the run server checks to see which of the candidate machines have enough memory to run the program. Those that do not are also eliminated. The run server keeps track of the memory and CPU usage of each of its pool processors by making *getload* calls to each one regularly to request these values, so the numbers in the run server's tables are continuously refreshed.

Third, and last, for each of the remaining machines, an estimate is made of the computing power that can be devoted to the new program. The heuristic uses as input the known total computing power of the CPU and the number of currently active threads running on it. For example, if a 20 MIPS machine currently has four active threads, then the addition of a fifth one means that each one, including the new one, will get 4 MIPS on the average. If another processor has 10 MIPS and one thread, then on this machine the new program can expect 5 MIPS. The run server chooses the processor that can deliver the most MIPS and returns the capability for talking to its process server to the caller. The caller then uses this capability to create the process, as described in Sec. 14.3.

14.6.5. The Boot Server

As another example of an Amoeba server, let us consider the *boot server*. The boot server is used to provide a degree of fault tolerance to Amoeba by checking that all servers that are supposed to be running are in tact running, and taking corrective action when they are not. A server that is interested in surviving crashes can be included in the boot server's configuration file. Each entry tells how often the boot server should poll and how it should poll. As long as the server responds correctly, the boot server takes no further action.

However, if the server should fail to respond after a specified number of attempts, the boot server declares it dead, and arranges to allocate a new pool processor on which a new copy is started. In this manner, critical services are automatically rebooted if they should ever fail. The boot server can itself be replicated, to guard against its own failure.

14.6.6. The TCP/IP Server

Although Amoeba uses the FLIP protocol internally to achieve high performance, sometimes it is necessary to speak TCP/IP, for example, to communicate with X terminals, to send and receive mail to non-Amoeba machines, and to interact with other

Amoeba systems via the Internet. To permit Amoeba to do these things, a TCP/IP server has been provided.

To establish a connection, an Amoeba process does an RPC with the TCP/IP server giving it a TCP/IP address. The caller is then blocked until the connection has been established or refused. In the reply, the TCP/IP server provides a capability for using the connection. Subsequent RPCs can send and receive packets from the remote machine without the Amoeba process having to know that TCP/IP is being used. This mechanism is less efficient than FLIP, so it is only used when it is not possible to use FLIP.

14.6.7. Other Servers

Amoeba supports various other servers. These include a disk server (used by the directory server for storing its arrays of capability pairs), various other I/O servers, a time-of-day server, and a random number server (useful for generating ports, capabilities, and FLIP addresses). The so-called Swiss Army Knife server deals with many activities that have to be done later by starting up processes at a specified time in the future. Mail servers deal with incoming and outgoing electronic mail.

14.7. SUMMARY

Amoeba is a new operating system designed to make a collection of independent computers appear to its users as a single timesharing system. In general, the users are not aware of where their processes are running (or even on what type of CPU), and are not aware of where their files are stored or how many copies are being maintained for reasons of availability and performance. However, users who are explicitly interested in parallel programming can exploit the existence of multiple CPUs for splitting a single job over many machines.

Amoeba is based on a microkernel that handles low-level process and memory management, communication, and I/O. The file system and the rest of the operating system can run as user processes. This division of labor keeps the kernel small and simple.

Amoeba has a single mechanism for naming and protecting all objects— capabilities. Each capability contains rights telling which operations may be performed using it. Capabilities are protected cryptographically using one-way functions. Each one contains a checksum field that assures the security of the capability.

Two communication mechanisms are supported: RPC for point-to-point communication and reliable group communication. The RPC guarantees at-most-once semantics. The group communication is based on reliable broadcasting as provided by the sequencer algorithm. Both mechanisms are supported on top of the FLIP protocol and are closely integrated.

The Amoeba file system consists of three servers: the bullet server for file storage, the directory server for file naming, and the replication server for file replication. The bullet server maintains immutable files that are stored contiguously on disk and in the cache. The directory server is a fault tolerant server that maps ASCII strings to capabilities. The replication server handles lazy replication.

PROBLEMS

1. The Amoeba designers assumed that memory would soon be available in large amounts for low prices. What impact did this assumption have on the design?

2. Give an advantage and a disadvantage of the processor pool model compared to the personal multiprocessor model.

3. List three functions of the Amoeba microkernel.

4. Some Amoeba servers can be run in the kernel as well as in user space. Their clients cannot tell the difference (except by timing them). What is it about Amoeba that makes it impossible for clients to tell the difference?

5. A malicious user is trying to guess the bullet server's get-port by picking a random 48-bit number, running it through the well-known one-way function, and seeing if the put-port comes out. It takes 1 msec per trial. How long will it take to guess the get-port, on the average?

6. How does a server tell that a capability is an owner capability, as opposed to a restricted capability? How are owner capabilities verified?

7. If a capability is not an owner capability, how do servers check it for validity?

8. Explain what a glocal variable is.

9. Why does the *trans* call have parameters for both sending and receiving? Would it not have been better and simpler to have two calls, *send_request* and *get_reply*, one for sending and one for receiving?

10. Amoeba claims to guarantee at-most-once semantics on RPCs. Suppose three file servers offer the same service. A client does an RPC with one of them, which carries out the request and then crashes. Then the RPC is repeated with another server, resulting in the work being done twice. Is this possible? If so, what does the guarantee mean? If not, how is it prevented?

11. Why does the sequencer need a history buffer?

12. Two algorithms for broadcasting in Amoeba were presented in the text. In method 1, the sender sends a point-to-point message to the sequencer, which then broadcasts it. In method 2, the sender does the broadcast, with the sequencer then broadcasting a small acknowledgement packet. Consider a 10 Mbps network on which processing a packet-arrived interrupt takes 500 microsec, independent of the packet size. If all data packets are 1K bytes, and acknowledgement packets are 100 bytes, how much bandwidth and how much CPU time are consumed per 1000 broadcasts by the two methods?

13. What property of FLIP addressing makes it possible to handle process migration and automatic network reconfiguration in a straightforward way?

14. The bullet server supports immutable files for its users. Are the bullet server's own tables also immutable?

15. Why does the bullet server have uncommitted and committed files?

16. In Amoeba, links to a file can be created by putting capabilities with different rights in different directories. These give different users different permissions. This feature is not present in UNIX. Why?

15

CASE STUDY 4: MACH

Our second example of a modern, microkernel-based operating system is Mach. We will start out by looking at its history and how it has evolved from earlier systems. Then we will examine in some detail the microkernel itself, focusing on processes and threads, memory management, and communication. Next comes a section on UNIX emulation. Finally, we will conclude with a short comparison of Amoeba and Mach. More information about Mach can be found in (Accetta et al., 1986; Baron et al., 1985; Draves et al., 1991; Rashid, 1986a; Rashid, 1986b; and Sansom et al., 1986).

15.1. INTRODUCTION TO MACH

In this section we will give a brief introduction to Mach. We will start with the history and goals. Then we will describe the main concepts of the Mach microkernel and the principal server that runs on the microkernel.

15.1.1. History of Mach

Mach earliest roots go back to a system called **RIG (Rochester Intelligent Gateway)** which began at the University of Rochester in 1975 (Ball et al., 1976). RIG was written for a 16-bit Data General minicomputer called the Eclipse. Its main research goal was to demonstrate that operating systems could be structured in a modular way, as a collection of processes that communicated by message passing, including over a network. The system was designed and built, and indeed showed that such an operating system could be constructed.

When one of its designers, Richard Rashid, left the University of Rochester and moved to Carnegie-Mellon University in 1979, he wanted to continue developing message passing operating systems, but on more modern hardware. Various machines were considered. The machine selected was the PERQ, an early engineering workstation, with a bitmapped screen, mouse, and network connection. It was also microprogrammable. The new operating system for the PERQ was called **Accent**. It improved on RIG by adding protection, the ability to operate transparently over the network, 32-bit virtual memory, and other features. An initial version was up and running in 1981.

By 1984 Accent was being used on 150 PERQs but it was clearly losing out to UNIX. This observation led Rashid to begin a third generation operating systems project called **Mach**. By making Mach compatible with UNIX, he hoped to be able to use the large volume of UNIX software becoming available. In addition, Mach had many other improvements over Accent, including threads, a better interprocess communication mechanism, multiprocessor support, and a highly imaginative virtual memory system.

Around this time, DARPA, the U.S. Department of Defense's Advanced Research Projects Agency was hunting around for an operating system that supported multiprocessors as part of its Strategic Computing Initiative. CMU was selected, and with DARPA funding, Mach was developed further. It was decided to make the system compatible with 4.2BSD by combining Mach and 4.2BSD into a single kernel. Although this approach led to a large kernel, it did guarantee absolute compatibility with 4.2BSD.

The first version of Mach was released in 1986 for the VAX 11/784, a four-CPU multiprocessor. Shortly thereafter, ports to the IBM PC/RT and Sun 3 were done. By 1987, Mach was also running on the Encore and Sequent multiprocessors. Although Mach had networking facilities, at this time it was primarily conceived of as a single machine or multiprocessor system rather than as a transparent distributed operating system for a collection of machines on a LAN.

Shortly thereafter, the Open Software Foundation, a consortium of computer vendors led by IBM, DEC, and Hewlett Packard was formed in an attempt to wrest control of UNIX from its owner, AT&T. It chose Mach 2.5 as the basis for its first operating system, OSF/1. Although Mach 2.5 and OSF/1 contained large amounts of Berkeley and AT&T code, the hope was that OSF would be able to at least control the direction in which UNIX was going.

As of 1988, the Mach 2.5 kernel was large and monolithic due to the presence of a large amount of Berkeley UNIX code in the kernel. In 1989, CMU removed all the Berkeley code from the kernel and put it in user space. What remained was a microkernel consisting of pure Mach. This version, 3.0, will be the basis of future OSF releases. In this chapter, we will focus on the Mach 3.0 microkernel and one user-level operating system emulator, for BSD UNIX.

15.1.2. Goals of Mach

Mach has evolved considerably since its first incarnation as RIG. The goals of the project have also changed as time has gone on. The current primary goals can be summarized as follows:

1. Providing a base for building other operating systems (e.g., UNIX).

2. Supporting large sparse address spaces.

3. Allowing transparent access to network resources.

4. Exploiting parallelism in both the system and the applications.

5. Making Mach portable to a larger collection of machines.

These goals encompass both research and development. The idea is to explore multiprocessor and distributed systems while at the same time being able to emulate existing systems such as UNIX, MS-DOS, and the Macintosh operating system.

Much of the initial work on Mach concentrated on single processor and multiprocessor systems. At the time Mach was designed, few systems had support for multiprocessors. Even now, few multiprocessor systems other than Mach are machine independent.

15.1.3. The Mach Microkernel

The Mach microkernel has been built as a base upon which UNIX and other operating systems can be emulated. This emulation is done by a software layer that runs outside the kernel, in user space, as shown in Fig. 15-1. It should be noted that multiple emulators can be running simultaneously, so it is possible to run 4.3BSD, System V, and MS-DOS programs on the same machine at the same time.

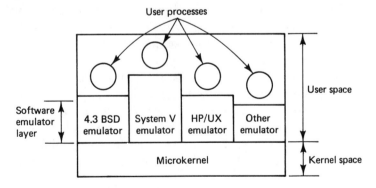

Fig. 15-1. The abstract model for UNIX emulation using Mach.

The Mach kernel, like other microkernels, provides process management, memory management, communication, and I/O services. Files, directories, and other traditional operating system functions are handled in user space. The idea behind the Mach kernel is to provide the necessary mechanisms for making the system work, but leaving the policy to user-level processes.

The kernel manages five principal abstractions:

1. Processes.

2. Threads.

3. Memory objects.

4. Ports.

5. Messages.

In addition, the kernel manages several other abstractions either related to these or less central to the model.

A process is basically an environment in which execution can take place. It has an address space holding the program text and data, and usually one or more stacks. The process is the basic unit for resource allocation. For example, a communication channel is always "owned" by a single process.

As an aside, for the most part we will stick with the traditional nomenclature throughout this chapter, as we have throughout the entire book. Adopting each system's own terminology would mean, for example, using the word "task" to mean "program" in Chap. 8 (MS-DOS), to mean "thread" in Chap. 14 (Amoeba) and to mean "process" in Chap. 15 (Mach).

A thread in Mach is an executable entity. It has a program counter and a set of registers associated with it. Each thread is part of exactly one process. A process with one thread is similar to a traditional (e.g., UNIX) process.

A concept that is unique to Mach is the **memory object**, a data structure that can be mapped into a process' address space. Memory objects occupy one or more pages, and form the basis of the Mach virtual memory system. When a process attempts to reference a memory object that is not presently in physical main memory, it gets a page fault. As in all operating systems, the kernel catches the page fault. However, unlike other systems, the Mach kernel can send a message to a user-level server to fetch the missing page.

Interprocess communication in Mach is based on message passing. To receive messages, a user process asks the kernel to create a kind of protected mailbox, called a **port**, for it. The port is stored inside the kernel, and has the ability to queue an ordered list of messages. Queues are not fixed in size, but for flow control reasons, if more than n messages are queued on a port, a process attempting to send to it is suspended to give the port a chance to be emptied. The parameter n is settable per port.

A process can give the ability to send to (or receive from) one of its ports to another process. This permission takes the form of a **capability**, and includes not only a pointer to the port, but also a list of rights that the other process has with respect to the port (e.g., SEND right). Once this permission has been granted, the other process can send messages to the port, which the first process can then read. All communication in Mach uses this mechanism.

15.1.4. The Mach BSD UNIX Server

As we described above, the Mach designers have modified Berkeley UNIX to run in user space, as an application program. This structure has a number of significant advantages over a monolithic kernel. First, by breaking the system up into a part that handles the resource management (the kernel) and a part that handles the system calls (the UNIX server), both pieces become simpler and easier to maintain. In a way, this split is somewhat reminiscent of the division of labor in IBM's mainframe operating system VM/370, in which the kernel simulates a collection of bare 370s, each of which runs a single-user operating system.

Second, by putting UNIX in user space, it can be made extremely machine independent, enhancing its portability to a wide variety of computers. All the machine dependencies can be removed from UNIX and hidden away inside the Mach kernel.

Third, as we mentioned earlier, multiple operating systems can run simultaneously. On a 386, for example, Mach can run a UNIX program and an MS-DOS program at the same time. Similarly, it is possible to test a new experimental operating system and run a production operating system at the same time.

Fourth, real-time operation can be added to the system because all the traditional obstacles that UNIX presents to real-time work, such as disabling interrupts in order to update critical tables are either eliminated altogether or moved into user space. The kernel can be carefully structured not to have this type of hindrance to real-time applications.

Finally, this arrangement can be used to provide better security between processes, if need be. If each process has its own version of UNIX, it is very difficult for one process to snoop on the other one's files.

15.2. PROCESS MANAGEMENT IN MACH

Process management in Mach deals with processes, threads, and scheduling. In this section we will look at each of these in turn.

15.2.1. Processes

A process in Mach consists primarily of an address space and a collection of threads that execute in that address space. Processes are passive. Execution is associated with the threads. Processes are used for collecting all the resources related to a group of cooperating threads into convenient containers.

Figure 15-2 illustrates a Mach process. In addition to an address space and threads, it has some ports and other properties. The ports shown in the figure all have special functions. The **process port** is used to communicate with the kernel. Many of the kernel services that a process can request are done by sending a message to the process port, rather than making a system call. This mechanism is used throughout Mach to reduce the actual system calls to a bare minimum. A small number of them will be discussed in this chapter, to give an idea of what they are like.

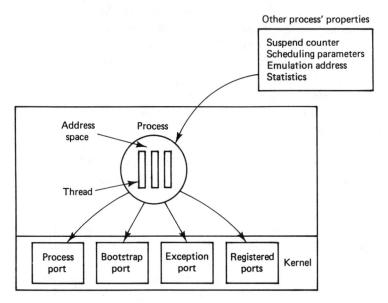

Fig. 15-2. A Mach process.

In general, the programmer is not even aware of whether a service requires a system call or not. All services, including both those accessed by system calls and those accessed by message passing, have stub procedures in the library. It is these procedures that are described in the manuals and called by application programs. The procedures are generated from a service definition by the **MIG** (**Mach Interface Generator**) compiler.

The **bootstrap port** is used for initialization when a process starts up. The very first process reads the bootstrap port to learn the names of kernel ports that provide essential services. UNIX processes also use it to communicate with the UNIX emulator.

The **exception port** is used by the system to report errors to the process. Typical exceptions are division by zero and illegal instruction executed. Debuggers also use the exception port.

The **registered ports** are normally used to provide a way for the process to communicate with standard system servers. For example, the name server makes it possible to present a string and get back the corresponding port for certain basic servers.

Processes also have other properties. A process can be runnable or blocked, independent of the state of its threads. If a process is runnable, then those threads that are also runnable can be scheduled and run. If a process is blocked, its threads may not run, no matter what state they are in.

The per-process items also include scheduling parameters. These include the ability to specify which processors the process' threads can run on. This feature is most useful on a multiprocessor system. For example, the process can use this power to force each thread to run on a different processor, or to force them all to run on the same processor, or anything in between. In addition, each process has a default priority that is settable. When a thread is created, the new thread is given this priority. It is also possible to change the priority of all the existing threads.

An emulation address can be set to tell the kernel where in the process' address space the emulation package is located. The kernel needs to know this address to handle UNIX system calls that need to be emulated. It is set once when the UNIX emulator is started up, and inherited by all of the emulator's children (i.e., all the UNIX processes).

Finally, every process has statistics associated with it, including the amount of memory consumed, the run times of the threads, and so on. A process that is interested in this information can acquire it by sending a message to the process port.

It is also worth mentioning what a Mach process does not have. A process does not have a uid, gid, signal mask, root directory, working directory, or file descriptor array, all of which UNIX processes do have. All of this information is managed by the emulation package, so the kernel knows nothing at all about it.

Process Management Primitives

Mach provides a small number of primitives for managing processes. Most of these are done by sending messages to the kernel via the process port, rather than actual system calls. The most important of these calls are shown in Fig. 15-3. These, like all calls in Mach, have prefixes indicating the group they belong to, but we have omitted these here (and in subsequent tables) for the sake of brevity.

Call	Description
Create	Create a new process, inheriting certain properties
Terminate	Kill a specified process
Suspend	Increment suspend counter
Resume	Decrement suspend counter. If it is 0, unblock the process
Priority	Set the priority for current or future threads
Assign	Tell which processor new threads should run on
Info	Return information about execution time, memory usage, etc.
Threads	Return a list of the process' threads

Fig. 15-3. Selected process management calls in Mach.

The first two calls in Fig. 15-3 are for creating and destroying processes, respectively. The process creation call specifies a prototype process, not necessarily the caller. The child is a copy of the prototype, except that the call has a parameter that tells whether or not the child is to inherit the parent's address space. If it does not inherit the parent's address space, objects (e.g., text, initialized data, and a stack) can be mapped in later. Initially the child has no threads. It does, however, automatically get a process port, a bootstrap port, and an exception port. Other ports are not automatically inherited since each port may have only one reader.

Processes can be suspended and resumed under program control. Each process has a counter, incremented by the *suspend* call and decremented by the *resume* call, that can block or unblock it. When the counter is 0, the process is able to run. When it is positive, it is suspended. Having a counter is more general than just having a bit, and helps avoid race conditions.

The *priority* and *assign* calls give the programmer control over how and where its threads run on multiprocessor systems. CPU scheduling is done using priorities, so the programmer has fine-grain control over which threads are most important and which are least important. The *assign* call makes it possible to control which thread runs on which CPU or group of CPUs.

The last two calls of Fig. 15-3 return information about the process. The former gives statistical information and the latter returns a list of all the threads.

15.2.2. Threads

The active entities in Mach are the threads. They execute instructions and manipulate their registers and address spaces. Each thread belongs to exactly one process. A process cannot do anything unless it has one or more threads.

All the threads in a process share the address space and all the process-wide resources shown in Fig. 15-2. Nevertheless, threads also have private per-thread resources. One of these is the **thread port**, which is analogous to the process port. Each thread has its own thread port, which it uses to invoke thread-specific kernel services, such as exiting when the thread is finished. Since ports are process-wide resources, each thread has access to its siblings' ports, so each thread can control the others if need be.

Mach threads are managed by the kernel, that is, they are what are sometimes called heavyweight threads rather than lightweight threads (pure user space threads). Thread creation and destruction are done by the kernel, and involve updating kernel data structures. They provide the basic mechanisms for handling multiple activities within a single address space. What the user does with these mechanisms is up to the user.

On a single CPU system, threads are timeshared, first one running, then another. On a multiprocessor, several threads can be active at the same time. This parallelism makes mutual exclusion, synchronization, and scheduling more important than they normally are, because performance now becomes a major issue, along with correctness. Since Mach is intended to run on multiprocessors, these issues have received special attention.

Like a process, a thread can be runnable or blocked. The mechanism is similar too: a counter per thread that can be incremented and decremented. When it is zero, the thread is runnable. When it is positive, the thread must wait until another thread lowers it to zero. This mechanism allows threads to control each other's behavior.

A variety of primitives is provided. The basic kernel interface provides about two dozen thread primitives, many of them concerned with controlling scheduling in detail. On top of these primitives one can build various thread packages.

We have already seen one thread package in Chap. 12, namely that provided by OSF's DCE package. A much more modest approach is the **C threads** package provided by Mach (on which the OSF package was based). This package is intended to make the kernel thread primitives available to users in a simple and convenient form. It does not have the full power that the kernel interface offers, but it is enough for the average garden-variety programmer. It has also been designed to be portable to a wide variety of operating systems and architectures.

The C threads package provides six calls for direct thread manipulation. They are listed in Fig. 15-4. The first one, *fork*, creates a new thread in the same address space as the calling thread. It runs the procedure specified by a parameter rather than the parent's code. After the call, the parent thread continues to run in parallel with the child. The thread is started with a priority and on a processor determined by the process' scheduling parameters, as discussed above.

Call	Description
Fork	Create a new thread running the same code as the parent thread
Exit	Terminate the calling thread
Join	Suspend the caller until a specified thread exits
Detach	Announce that the thread will never be joined (waited for)
Yield	Give up the CPU voluntarily
Self	Return the calling thread's identity to it

Fig. 15-4. The C threads calls for direct thread management.

When a thread has done its work, it calls *exit*. If the parent is interested in waiting for the thread to finish, it can call *join* to block itself until a specific child thread terminates. If the thread has already terminated, the parent continues immediately. These three calls are roughly analogous to the FORK, EXIT, and WAITPID system calls in UNIX.

The fourth call, *detach*, does not exist in UNIX. It provides a way to announce that a particular thread will never be waited for. If that thread ever exits, its stack and other state information will be deleted immediately. Normally this cleanup only happens after the parent has done a successful *join*. In a server, it might be desirable to start up a new thread to service each incoming request. When it has finished, the thread exits. Since there is no need for the initial thread to wait for it, the server thread should be detached.

The *yield* call is a hint to the scheduler that the thread has nothing useful to do at the moment, and is waiting for some event to happen before it can continue. An intelligent scheduler will take the hint and run another thread. In Mach, which normally schedules its threads preemptively, *yield* is only optimization. In systems that have nonpreemptive scheduling, it is essential that a thread that has no work to do release the CPU, to give other threads a chance to run.

Finally, *self* returns the callers identity, analogous to GETPID in UNIX.

Synchronization is done using mutexes and condition variables. The mutex primitives are *lock*, *trylock*, and *unlock*. Primitives are also provided to allocate and free mutexes. Since we have already studied the DCE mutex primitives in Chap. 12, which are the same as the C threads primitives, we will not repeat that material here.

Similarly, the operations on condition variables are *signal*, *wait*, and *broadcast*, also as in Chap. 12.

Implementation of C Threads in Mach

Various implementations of C threads are available on Mach. The original one did everything in user space inside a single process. This approach timeshared all the C threads over one kernel thread, as shown in Fig. 15-5(a). This approach can also be used on UNIX or any other system that provides no kernel support. The threads were run as coroutines, which means that they were scheduled nonpreemptively. A thread could keep the CPU as long as it wanted or was able to. For the producer-consumer problem, the producer would eventually fill the buffer and then block, giving the consumer a chance to run. For other applications, however, threads had to call *yield* from time to time to give other threads a chance.

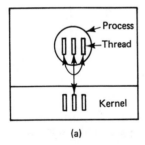 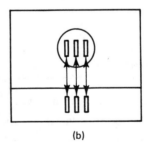 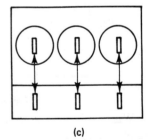

(a)   (b)   (c)

Fig. 15-5. (a) All C threads use one kernel thread. (b) Each C thread has its own kernel thread. (c) Each C thread has its own single-threaded process.

The original implementation package suffers from a problem inherent to most user-space threads packages that have no kernel support. If one thread makes a blocking system call, such as reading from the terminal, the whole process is blocked. To avoid this situation, the programmer must avoid blocking system calls. In Berkeley UNIX, there is a call SELECT that can be used to tell whether any characters are pending, but the whole situation is quite messy.

A second, and far better, implementation is to use one Mach thread per C thread, as shown in Fig. 15-5(b). These threads are scheduled preemptively. Furthermore, on a multiprocessor, they may actually run in parallel, on different CPUs. In fact, it is also possible to multiplex m user threads on n kernel threads, although the most common case is $m = n$.

A third implementation package has one thread per process, as shown in Fig. 15-5(c). The processes are set up so that their address spaces all map onto the same physical memory, allowing sharing in the same way as in the previous implementations. This implementation is only used when specialized virtual memory usage is required. The method has the drawback that ports, UNIX files, and other per-process resources cannot be shared, limiting its value appreciably.

The main practical value of the first approach is that because there is no true parallelism, successive runs give reproducible results, allowing easier debugging. For production systems, the second approach is the normal one to use. The third one is not normally used.

15.2.3. Scheduling

Mach scheduling has been heavily influenced by its goal of running on multiprocessors. Since a single processor system is effectively a special case of a multiprocessor (with only one CPU), our discussion will focus on scheduling in multiprocessor systems. For more information, see (Black, 1990).

The CPUs in a multiprocessor can be assigned to **processor sets** by software. Each CPU belongs to exactly one processor set. Threads can also be assigned to processor sets by software. Thus each processor set has a collection of CPUs at its disposal and a collection of threads that need computing power. The job of the scheduling algorithm is to assign threads to CPUs in a fair and efficient way. For purposes of scheduling, each processor set is a closed world, with its own resources and its own customers, independent of all the other processor sets.

This mechanism gives processes a large amount of control over their threads. A process can assign an important thread to a processor set with one CPU and no other threads, thus insuring that the thread runs all the time. It can also dynamically reassign threads to processor sets as the work proceeds, keeping the load balanced. While the average compiler is not likely to use this facility, a data base management system or a real-time system might well use it.

Thread scheduling in Mach is based on priorities. Priorities are integers from 0 to 31, with 0 being the highest priority and 31 being the lowest priority. This priority reversal comes from UNIX. Each thread has three priorities assigned to it. The first priority is a base priority, which the thread can set itself, within certain limits. The second priority is the lowest numerical value that the thread may set its base priority to. Since using a higher value gives worse service, a thread will normally set its value to the lowest value it is permitted, unless it is intentionally trying to defer to other threads. The third priority is the current priority, used for scheduling purposes. It is computed by the kernel by adding to the base priority a function based on the thread's recent CPU usage.

Mach threads are visible to the kernel, at least when the model of Fig. 15-5(b) is used. Each thread competes for CPU cycles with all other threads, without regard to which thread is in which process. The kernel does not take into account which thread belongs to which process when making scheduling decisions.

Associated with each processor set is an array of run queues, as shown in Fig. 15-6. The array has 32 queues, corresponding to threads currently at priorities 0 through 31. When a thread at priority *n* becomes runnable, it is put at the end of queue *n*. A thread that is not runnable is not present on any run queue.

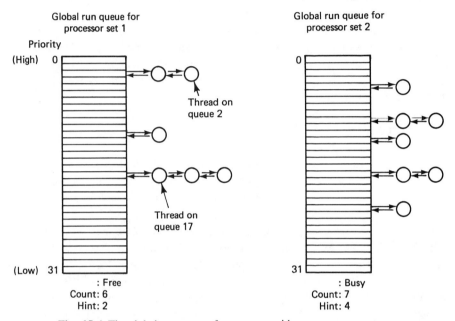

Fig. 15-6. The global run queues for a system with two processor sets.

Each run queue has three variables attached to it. The first one is a mutex that is used to lock the data structure. It is used to make sure that only one CPU at a time is manipulating the queues. The second one is the count of the number of threads on all the queues combined. If this count becomes 0, there is no work to do. The third variable is a hint as to where to find the highest priority thread. It is guaranteed that no thread is at a higher priority, but the highest one may be at a lower priority. This hint allows the search for the highest priority thread to avoid the empty queues at the top.

In addition to the global run queues shown in Fig. 15-6, each CPU has its own local run queue. Each local run queue holds those threads that are permanently bound to that CPU, for example, because they are device drivers for I/O devices attached to that CPU. These threads can only run on one CPU, so putting them on the global run queue is incorrect (because the "wrong" CPU might choose them).

We can now describe the basic scheduling algorithm. When a thread blocks, exits, or uses up its quantum, the CPU it is running on first looks on its local run queue to see if there are any active threads. This check merely requires inspecting the count variable associated with the local run queue. If it is nonzero, the CPU begins searching the queue for the highest priority thread, starting at the queue specified by the hint. If the local run queue is empty, the same algorithm is applied to the global run queue, the only difference being that the global run queue must be locked before it can be searched. If there are no threads to run on either queue, a special idle thread is run until some thread becomes ready.

If a runnable thread is found, it is scheduled and run for one quantum. At the end of the quantum, both the local and global run queues are checked to see if any other threads at its priority or higher are runnable, with the understanding that all threads on the local run queue have higher priority than all threads on the global run queue. If a suitable candidate is found, a thread switch occurs. If not, the thread is run for another quantum. Threads may also be preempted. On multiprocessors, the length of the quantum is variable, depending on the number of threads that are runnable. The more runnable threads and the fewer CPUs there are, the shorter the quantum. This algorithm gives good response time to short requests, even on heavily loaded systems, but provides high efficiency (i.e., long quanta) on lightly loaded systems.

On every clock tick, the CPU increments the priority counter of the currently running thread by a small amount. As the value goes up, the priority goes down and the thread will eventually move to a higher-numbered (i.e., lower-priority) queue. The priority counters are lowered by the passage of time.

For some applications, a large number of threads may be working together to solve a single problem, and it may be important to control the scheduling in detail. Mach provides a hook to give threads some additional control over their scheduling (in addition to the processor sets and priorities). The hook is a system call that allows a thread to lower its priority to the absolute minimum for a specified number of seconds. Doing so gives other threads a chance to run. When the time interval is over, the priority is restored to its previous value.

This system call has another interesting property: it can name its successor if it wants to. For example, after sending a message to another thread, the sending thread can give up the CPU and request that the receiving thread be allowed to run next. This mechanism, called **handoff scheduling**, bypasses the run queues entirely. If used wisely, it can enhance performance. The kernel also uses it in some circumstances, as an optimization.

Mach can be configured to do affinity scheduling, but generally this option is off. When it is on, the kernel schedules a thread on the CPU it last ran on, in hopes that part of its address space is still in that CPU's cache. Affinity scheduling is only applicable to multiprocessors.

15.3. MEMORY MANAGEMENT IN MACH

Mach has a powerful, elaborate, and highly flexible memory management system based on paging, including features found in few other operating systems. In particular, it separates the machine independent parts of the memory management system from the machine dependent parts in an extremely clear and unusual way. This separation makes the memory management far more portable than in other systems. In addition, the memory management system interacts closely with the communication system, which we will discuss in the following section.

The aspect of Mach's memory management that sets it apart from all others is that the code is split into three parts. The first part is the *pmap* module, which runs in the kernel, and is concerned with managing the MMU. It sets up the MMU registers and hardware page tables, and catches all page faults. This code depends on the MMU architecture, and must be rewritten for each new machine Mach is ported to. The second part is the machine-independent kernel code, and is concerned with processing page faults, managing address maps, and replacing pages.

The third part of the memory management code runs as a user process called a **memory manager** or sometimes an **external pager**. It handles the logical (as opposed to physical) part of the memory management system, primarily the management of the backing store (disk). For example, keeping track of which virtual pages are in use, which are in main memory, and where pages are kept on disk when they are not in main memory are all done by the memory manager.

The kernel and the memory manager communicate through a well-defined protocol, making it possible for users to write their own memory managers. This division of labor gives users the ability to implement special-purpose paging systems in order to write systems with special requirements. It also has the potential for making the kernel smaller and simpler by moving a large section of the code out into user space. On the other hand, it also has the potential for making it more complicated, since the kernel must protect itself from buggy or malicious memory managers and with two active entities involved in handling memory, there is now the danger of race conditions.

15.3.1. Virtual Memory

The conceptual model of memory that Mach user processes see is a large, linear virtual address space. For most 32-bit CPU chips, the address space runs from address 0 to address $2^{32} - 1$. The address space is supported by paging. Since paging was designed to give the illusion of ordinary memory, only more of it than there really is, in principle there should be nothing else to say about how Mach manages virtual address space.

In reality, there is a great deal more to say. Mach provides a great deal of fine-grain control over how the virtual pages are used (for processes that are interested in that). To start with, the address space can be used in a sparse way. For example, a process might have dozens of sections of the virtual address space in use, each one many megabytes from its nearest neighbor, with large holes of unused addresses between the sections.

Theoretically, any virtual address space can be used this way, so the ability to use a number of widely scattered sections is not really a property of the virtual address space architecture. In other words, any 32-bit machine should allow a process to have a 50K section of data spaced every 100 megabytes, from 0 to the 4 gigabyte limit. However, in many implementations, a linear page table from 0 to the highest used page is kept in kernel memory. On a machine with a 1K page size, this configuration requires 4 million page table entries, making it expensive, if not impossible.

Even with a multilevel page table, such sparse usage is inconvenient at best. With Mach, the intention is to fully support sparse address spaces.

In order to determine which virtual addresses are in use and which are not, Mach provides a way to allocate and deallocate sections of virtual address space, called **regions**. The allocation call can specify a base address and a size, in which case the indicated region is allocated, or it can just specify a size, in which case the system finds a suitable address range and returns its base address. A virtual address is only valid if it falls in an allocated region. An attempt to use an address between allocated regions results in a trap, which, however, can be caught by the process if it so desires.

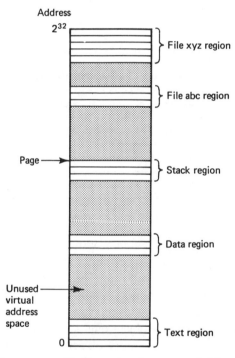

Fig. 15-7. An address space with allocated regions, mapped objects, and unused addresses.

A key concept relating to the use of virtual address space is the **memory object**. A memory object can be a page or a set of pages, but it can also be a file or other, more specialized data structure. A memory object can be mapped into an unused portion of the virtual address space, forming a new region, as shown in Fig. 15-7. When a file is mapped into the virtual address space, it can be read and written by normal machine instructions. Mapped files are paged in the usual way. When a process terminates, its mapped files automatically appear back in the file system, complete with all the changes that were made to them when they were mapped in. It is also possible to unmap files or other memory objects explicitly, freeing their virtual addresses and making them available for subsequent allocation or mapping.

As an aside, file mapping is not the only way to access files. They can also be read the conventional way. However, even then, the library may map the files behind the user's back rather than reading them using the I/O system. Doing so allows the file pages to use the virtual memory system, rather than using dedicated buffers elsewhere in the system.

Mach supports a number of calls for manipulating virtual address spaces. The main ones are listed in Fig. 15-8. None are true system calls. Instead, they all write messages to the caller's process port.

Call	Description
Allocate	Make a region of virtual address space usable
Deallocate	Invalidate a region of virtual address space
Map	Map a memory object into the virtual address space
Copy	Make a copy of a region at another virtual address
Inherit	Set the inheritance attribute for a region
Read	Read data from another process' virtual address space
Write	Write data to another process' virtual address space

Fig. 15-8. Selected Mach calls for managing virtual memory.

The first call, *allocate*, makes a region of virtual address space usable. A process may inherit allocated virtual address space and it may allocate more, but any attempt to reference an unallocated address will fail. The second call, *deallocate*, invalidates a region (i.e., removes it from the memory map) thus making it possible to allocate it again or map something into it, using the *map* call.

The *copy* call copies a memory object onto a new region. The original remains unchanged. In this way, a single memory object can appear multiple times in the address space. Conceptually, calling *copy* is no different than having the object copied by a programmed loop. However *copy* is implemented in an optimized way, using shared pages, to avoid physical copying.

The *inherit* call affects the way regions are inherited when new processes are created. The address space can be set up so that some regions are inherited and others are not. It will be discussed in the next section.

The *read* and *write* calls allow a thread to access virtual memory belonging to another process. These calls require the caller to have possession of the process port belonging to the remote process, something that process can pass to its friends if it wants to.

In addition to the calls listed in Fig. 15-8, a few other calls also exist. These calls are primarily concerned with getting and setting attributes, protection modes, and various kinds of statistical information.

15.3.2. Memory Sharing

Sharing plays an important role in Mach. No special mechanism is needed for the threads in a process to share objects: they all see the same address space automatically. If one of them has access to a piece of data, they all do. More interesting is the possibility of two or more processes sharing the same memory objects, or just sharing data pages for that matter. Sometimes sharing is important on single CPU systems. For example, in the classical producer-consumer problem, it may be desirable to have the producer and consumer be different processes, and yet share a common buffer so the producer can put data into the buffer and the consumer can take data out of it.

On multiprocessor systems, sharing of objects between two or more processes is frequently even more important. In many cases, a single problem is being solved by a collection of cooperating processes running in parallel on different CPUs (as opposed to being timeshared on a single CPU). These processes may need access to buffers, tables, or other data structures continuously, in order to do their work. It is essential that the operating system allow this sharing to take place. Early versions of UNIX did not have this ability, for example, although it was added later.

Consider, for example, a system that analyzes digitized satellite images of the earth in real time, as they are transmitted to the ground. Such analysis is time consuming, and the same picture has to be examined for use in weather forecasting, predicting crop harvests, and tracking pollution. As each picture is received, it is stored as a file.

A multiprocessor is available to do the analysis. Since the meteorological, agricultural, and environmental programs are all quite different, and were written by different people, it is not reasonable to make them threads of the same process. Instead, each one is a separate process, and each one maps the current photograph into its address space, as shown in Fig. 15-9. Note that the file containing the photograph may be mapped in at a different virtual address in each process. Although each page is only present once in memory, it may appear in each process' page map at a different place. In this manner, all three processes can work on the same file at the same time in a convenient way.

Another important use of sharing is process creation. As in UNIX, in Mach the basic way for a new process to be created is as a copy of an existing process. In UNIX, a copy is always a clone of the process executing the FORK system call, whereas in Mach the child can be a clone of a different process (the prototype). Either way, the child is a copy of some other process.

One way to create the child is to copy all the pages needed and map the copies into the child's address space. While this method is valid, it is unnecessarily expensive. The program text is normally read-only, so it cannot change, and parts of the data may also be read-only. There is no reason to copy read-only pages, since mapping them into both processes will do the job. Writable pages cannot always be shared because the semantics of process creation (at least in UNIX) say that although at the moment of creation the parent and child are identical, subsequent changes to either one are not visible in the other's address space.

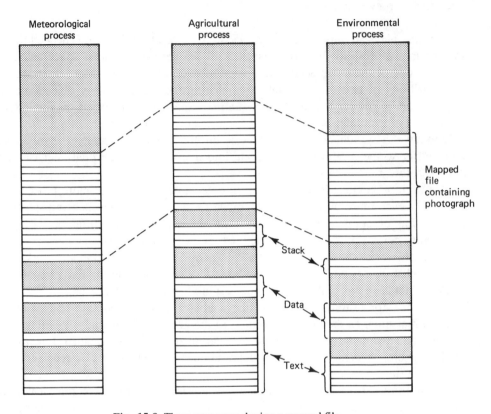

Fig. 15-9. Three processes sharing a mapped file.

In addition, some regions (e.g., certain mapped files) may not be needed in the child. Why go to a lot of trouble to arrange for them to be present in the child if they are not needed?

To achieve these various goals, Mach allows processes to assign an **inheritance attribute** to each region in its address space. Different regions may have different attributes. Three values are provided:

1. The region is unused in the child process.

2. The region is shared between the prototype process and the child.

3. The region in the child process is a copy of the prototype.

If a region has the first value, the corresponding region in the child is unallocated. References to it are treated as references to any other unallocated memory—they generate traps. The child is free to allocate the region for its own purposes, or to map a memory object there.

The second option is true sharing. The pages of the region are present in both the prototype's address space and the child's. Changes made by either one are visible to

the other one. This choice is not used for implementing the FORK system call in
UNIX, but is frequently useful for other purposes.

The third possibility is to copy all the pages in the region, and map the copies into
the child's address space. FORK uses this option. Actually, Mach does not really
copy the pages but uses a clever trick called **copy-on-write** instead. It places all the
necessary pages in the child's virtual memory map, but marks them all read-only, as
illustrated in Fig. 15-10. As long as the child makes only read references to these
pages, everything works fine.

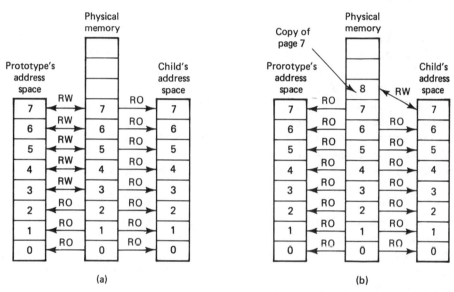

Fig. 15-10. Operation of copy-on-write. (a) After the FORK, all the child's pages are
marked read-only. (b) When the child writes page 7, a copy is made.

However, if the child attempts to write on any page, a protection fault occurs.
The operating system then makes a copy of the page, and maps the copy into the
child's address space, replacing the read-only page that was there. The new page is
marked read-write. In Fig. 15-10(b), the child has attempted to write to page 7. This
action has resulted in page 7 being copied to page 8, and page 8 being mapped into
the address space in place of page 7. Page 8 is marked read-write, so subsequent
writes do not trap.

Copy-on-write has several advantages over doing all the copying at the time the
new process is created. First, some pages are read-only, so there is no need to copy
them. Second, other pages may never be referenced, so even if they are potentially
writable, they do not have to be copied. Third, still other pages may be writable, but
the child may deallocate them rather than using them. Here too, avoiding a copy is
worthwhile. In this manner, only those pages that the child actually writes on have to
be copied.

Copy-on-write also has some disadvantages. For one thing, the administration is
more complicated, since the system must keep track of the fact that some pages are

genuinely read-only, with a write being a programming error, whereas other pages are to be copied if written. For another, copy-on-write requires multiple kernel traps, one for each page that is ultimately written. Depending on the hardware, one kernel trap followed by a multipage copy may not be that much more expensive than multiple kernel traps, each followed by a one-page copy. Finally, copy-on-write does not work well over a network because physical transport is always needed, so the advantage of copy-on-write, namely, not having to copy read-only data, is lost.

15.3.3. External Memory Managers

At the start of our discussion on memory management in Mach we briefly mentioned the existence of user-level memory managers. Let us now take a deeper look at them. Each memory object that is mapped in a process' address space must have an external memory manager that controls it. Different classes of memory objects are handled by different memory managers. Each of these can implement its own semantics, can determine where to store pages that are not in memory, and can provide its own rules about what becomes of objects after they are mapped out.

To map an object into a process' address space, the process sends a message to a memory manager asking it to do the mapping. Three ports are needed to do the job. The first one, the **object port**, is created by the memory manager and will later be used by the kernel to inform the memory manager about page faults and other events relating to the object. The second one, the **control port**, is created by the kernel itself so the memory manager can respond to these events (many require some action on the memory manager's part). The use of distinct ports is due to the fact that ports are unidirectional. The object port is written by the kernel and read by the memory manager; the control port works the other way around.

The third port, the **name port**, is used as a kind of name to identify the object. For example, a thread can give the kernel a virtual address and ask which region it belongs to. The answer is a pointer to the name port. If addresses belong to the same region, they will be identified by the same name port.

When the memory manager maps in an object, it provides the capability for the object port as one of the parameters. The kernel then creates the other two ports and sends an initial message to the object port telling it about the control, and name ports. The memory manager then sends back a reply telling the kernel what the object's attributes are, and also informing it whether or not to keep the object in its cache after it is unmapped. Initially, all the object's pages are marked as unreadable/unwritable, to force a trap on the first use.

At this point the memory manager does a read on the object port and blocks. The memory manager remains idle until the kernel requests it to do something by writing a message to the object port. The thread that mapped the object in is now unblocked and allowed to execute.

Sooner or later, the thread will undoubtedly attempt to read or write a page belonging to the memory object. This operation will cause a page fault and a trap to the kernel. The kernel will then send a message to the memory manager via the object port telling it which page has been referenced and asking it to please provide the page. This message is asynchronous because the kernel does not dare to block any of its threads waiting for a user process that may not reply. While waiting for a reply, the kernel suspends the faulting thread and looks for another thread to run.

When the memory manager hears about the page fault, it checks to see if the reference is legal. If not, it sends the kernel an error message. If it is legal, the memory manager gets the page by whatever method is appropriate for the object in question. If the object is a file, the memory manager seeks to the correct address and reads the page into its own address space. It then sends a reply back to the kernel providing a pointer to the page.

The kernel maps the page into the faulting thread's address space, The thread can now be unblocked. This process is repeated as often as necessary to load all the pages needed.

To make sure there is a steady supply of free page frames, a paging daemon thread in the kernel wakes up from time to time and checks the state of memory. If there are not enough free page frames, it picks an old dirty page and sends it to the memory manager in charge of the page's object. The memory manager is expected to write the page to disk and tell when it is done. If the page belongs to a file, the memory manager will first seek to the page's offset in the file, then write it there. The replacement algorithm used is second chance.

It is worth noting that the paging daemon is part of the kernel. Although the page replacement algorithm is completely machine independent, with a memory full of pages owned by different memory managers, there is no suitable way to let one of them decide which page to evict. The only method that might be possible is to statically partition the page frames among the various managers, and let each one do page replacement on its set. However, since global algorithms are generally more efficient than local ones, this approach was not taken.

In addition to the memory managers for mapped files and other specialized objects, there is also a default memory manager for "ordinary" paged memory. When a process allocates a region of virtual address space using the *allocate* call, it is in fact mapping an object managed by the default manager. This manager provides zero-filled pages as needed. It uses a temporary file for swap space, rather than a separate swap area as UNIX does.

To make the idea of an external memory manager work, a strict protocol must be used for communication between the kernel and the memory managers. This protocol consists of a small number of messages that the kernel can send to a memory manager, and a small number of replies the memory manager can send back to the kernel. All communication is initiated by the kernel in the form of an asynchronous message on an object port for some memory object. Later on, the memory manager sends an asynchronous reply on the control port.

Figure 15-11 lists the principal message types that the kernel sends to memory managers. When an object is mapped in using the *map* call of Fig. 15-8, the kernel sends an *init* message to the appropriate memory manager to let it initialize itself. The message specifies the ports to be used for discussing the object later on. Requests from the kernel to ask for a page and deliver a page use *data_request* and *data_write* respectively. These handle the page traffic in both directions, and as such are the most important calls.

Call	Description
Init	Initialize a newly mapped-in memory object
Data_request	Give kernel a specific page to handle a page fault
Data_write	Take a page from memory and write it out
Data_unlock	Unlock a page so kernel can use it
Lock_completed	Previous Lock_request has been completed
Terminate	Be informed that this object is no longer in use

Fig. 15-11. Selected message types from the kernel to the external memory managers.

Data_unlock is a request from the kernel for the memory manager to unlock a locked page so the kernel can use it for another process. *Lock_completed* signals the end of a *lock_request* sequence, and will be described below. Finally, *terminate* tells the memory manager that the object named in the message is no longer in use, and can be removed from memory. Some calls that are specific to the default memory manager also exist, as well as a few managing attributes and error handling.

The messages in Fig. 15-11 go from the kernel to the memory manager. The replies listed in Fig. 15-12 go the other way, from the memory manager back to the kernel. They are replies that the memory manager can use to respond to the above requests.

Call	Description
Set_attributes	Reply to Init
Data_provided	Here is the requested page (Reply to Data_request)
Data_unavailable	No page is available (Reply to Data_request)
Lock_request	Ask kernel to clean, flush, or lock pages
Destroy	Destroy an object that is no longer needed

Fig. 15-12. Selected message types from the external memory managers to the kernel.

The first one, *set_attributes*, is a reply to *init*. It tells the kernel that it is ready to handle a newly mapped-in object. The reply also provides mode bits for the object and tells the kernel whether or not to cache the object, even if no process currently has it mapped in. The next two are replies to *data_request*. That call asks the memory manager to provide a page. Which reply it gives depends on whether it can provide the page or it cannot. The former supplies the page; the latter does not.

Lock_request allows the memory manager to ask the kernel to make certain pages clean, that is, send it the pages so they can be written to disk. This call also can be used to change the protection mode on pages (read, write, execute). Finally, *destroy* is used to tell the kernel that a certain object is no longer needed.

It is worth noting that when the kernel sends a message to a memory manager, it is effectively making an upcall. Although flexibility is gained this way, some system designers consider it inelegant for the kernel to call user programs to perform services for it. These people usually believe in hierarchical systems, with the lower layers providing services to the upper layers, not vice versa.

15.3.4. Distributed Shared Memory in Mach

The Mach external memory manager concept lends itself well to implementing a page-based distributed shared memory. In this section we will briefly describe some of the work done in this area. For more details, see (Forin et al., 1989). To review the basic concept, the idea is to have a single, linear, virtual address space that is shared among processes running on computers that do not have any physical shared memory. When a thread references a page that it does not have, it causes a page fault. Eventually the page is located and shipped to the faulting machine where it is installed so the thread can continue executing.

Since Mach already has memory managers for different classes of objects, it is natural to introduce a new memory object, the shared page. Shared pages are managed by one or more special memory managers. One possibility is to have a single memory manager that handles all shared pages. Another is to have a different one for each shared page or collection of shared pages, to spread the load around.

Still another possibility is to have different memory managers for pages with different semantics. For example, one memory manager could guarantee complete memory coherence, meaning that any read following a write always sees the most recent data. Another memory manager could offer weaker semantics, for example, that a read never returns data that is more than 30 seconds out of date.

Let us consider the most basic case: one shared page, centralized control, and complete memory coherence. All other pages are local to a single machine. To implement this model, we need one memory manager that serves all the machines in the system. Let us call it the DSM (Distributed Shared Memory) server. The DSM server handles references to the shared page. Conventional memory managers handle the other pages. Up until now we have tacitly assumed that the memory manager or managers that service a machine must be local to that machine. In fact, because communication is transparent in Mach, a memory manager need not reside on the machine whose memory it is managing.

The shared page is always either readable or writable. If it is readable, it may be replicated on multiple machines. If it is writable, there is only one copy. The DSM server always knows the state of the shared page as well as which machine or machines it is currently on. If the page is readable, DSM has a valid copy itself.

Suppose the page is readable and a thread somewhere tries to read it. The DSM server just sends that machine a copy, updates its tables to indicate one more reader, and is finished. The page will be mapped in on the new machine for reading.

Now suppose that one of the readers tries to write the page. The DSM server sends a message to the kernel or kernels that have the page asking for it back. The page itself need not be transferred, because the DSM server has a valid copy itself. All that is needed is an acknowledgment that the page is no longer in use. When all the kernels have released the page, the writer is given a copy along with exclusive permission to use it (for writing).

If somebody else now wants the page (when it is writable), the DSM server tells the current owner to stop using it and send it back. When the page arrives, it can be given to one or more readers or one writer. Many variations on this centralized algorithm are possible, such as not asking for a page back until the machine currently using it has had it for some minimum time. A distributed solution is also possible.

15.4. COMMUNICATION IN MACH

The goal of communication in Mach is to support a variety of styles of communication in a reliable and flexible way (Draves, 1990). It can handle asynchronous message passing, RPC, byte streams, and other forms as well. Mach's interprocess communication mechanism is based on that of its ancestors, RIG and Accent. Due to this evolution, the mechanism used has been optimized for the local case (one node) rather than the remote case (distributed system).

We will first explain the single node case in considerable detail, and then come back to how it has been extended for networking. It should be noted that in these terms, a multiprocessor is a single node, so communication between processes on different CPUs within the same multiprocessor uses the local case.

15.4.1. Ports

The basis of all communication in Mach is a kernel data structure called a **port**. A port is essentially a protected mailbox. When a thread in one process wants to communicate with a thread in another process, the sending thread writes the message to the port and the receiving thread takes it out. Each port is protected to ensure that only authorized processes can send to it and receive from it.

Ports support unidirectional communication, like pipes in UNIX. A port that can be used to send a request from a client to a server cannot also be used to send the reply back from the server to the client. A second port is needed for the reply.

Ports support reliable, sequenced, message streams. If a thread sends a message to a port, the system guarantees that it will be delivered. Messages are never lost due to errors, overflow, or other causes (at least if there are no crashes). Messages sent by a single thread are also guaranteed to be delivered in the order sent. If two threads write to the same port in an interleaved fashion, taking turns, the system does not provide any guarantee about message sequencing, since some buffering may take place in the kernel due to locking and other factors.

Unlike pipes, ports support message streams, not byte streams. Messages are never concatenated. If a thread writes five 100-byte messages to a port, the receiver will always see them as five distinct messages, never as a single 500-byte message. Of course, higher level software can ignore the message boundaries if they are not important to it.

A port is shown in Fig. 15-13. When a port is created, 64 bytes of kernel storage space are allocated and maintained until the port is destroyed, either explicitly, or implicitly under certain conditions, for example, when all the processes that are using it have exited. The port contains the fields shown in Fig. 15-13 and a few others.

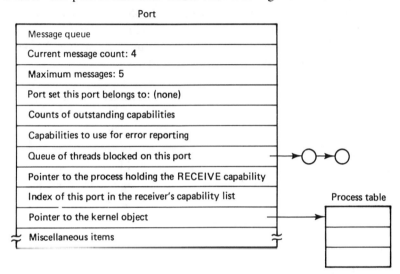

Fig. 15-13. A Mach port.

Messages are not actually stored in the port itself, but in another kernel data structure, the **message queue**. The port contains a count of the number of messages currently present in the message queue and the maximum permitted. If the port belongs to a port set, a pointer to the port set data structure is present in the port. As we mentioned briefly above, a process can give other processes capabilities to use its ports. For various reasons, the kernel has to know how many capabilities of each type are outstanding, so the port stores the counts.

If errors occur when using the port, they are reported by sending messages to other ports whose capabilities are stored there. Threads can block when reading from a port, so a pointer to the list of blocked threads is included. It is also important to be able to find the capability for reading from the port (there can only be one), so that information is present too. If the port is a process port, then the next field holds a pointer to the process it belongs to. If it is a thread port, then the field holds a pointer to the kernel's data structure for the thread, and so on. A few miscellaneous fields not described here are also needed.

When a thread creates a port, it gets back an integer identifying the port, analogous to a file descriptor in UNIX. This integer is used in subsequent calls that send messages to the port or receive messages from it in order to identify which port is to be used. Ports are kept track of per process, not per thread, so if one thread creates a port and gets back the integer 3 to identify it, another thread in the same process will never get 3 to identify its new port. The kernel, in fact, does not even maintain a record of which thread created which port.

A thread can pass port access to another thread in a different process. Clearly it cannot do so by merely putting the appropriate integer in a message, any more than a UNIX process can pass a file descriptor for standard output through a pipe by writing the integer 1 to the pipe. The exact mechanism used is protected by the kernel, and will be discussed later. For the moment, it is sufficient to know that it can be done.

In Fig. 15-14 we see a situation in which two processes, A and B, each have access to the same port. A has just sent a message to the port, and B has just read the message. The header and body of the message are physically copied from A to the port and later from the port to B.

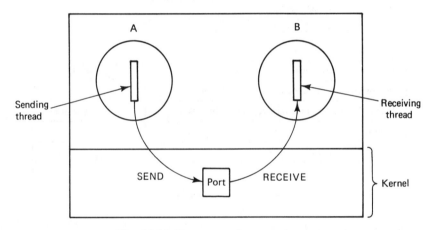

Fig. 15-14. Message passing goes via a port.

Ports may be grouped into **port sets** for convenience. A port may belong to at most one port set. It is possible to read from a port set (but not write to one). A server, for example, can use this mechanism to read from a large number of ports at the same time. The kernel returns one message from one of the ports in the set. No promises are made about which port will be selected. If all the ports are empty, the server is blocked. In this way a server can maintain a different port for each of the many objects that it supports, and get messages for any of them without having to dedicate a thread to each one. The current implementation queues all the messages for the port set onto a single chain, so in practice there is little difference between receiving from a port and receiving from a port set.

Some ports are used in special ways. Every process has a special **process port** that it needs to communicate with the kernel. Most of the "system calls" associated with processes (see Fig. 15-3) are done by writing messages to this port. Similarly, each thread also has its own port for doing the "system calls" related to threads. Communication with I/O drivers also uses the port mechanism.

Capabilities

To a first approximation, for each process, the kernel maintains a table of all ports to which the process has access. This table is kept safely inside the kernel, where user processes cannot get at it. Processes refer to ports by their position in this table, that is, entry 1, entry 2, and so on. These table entries are effectively classical capabilities (see Chap. 4), we will refer to them as capabilities. We will call the table containing the capabilities a **capability list**.

Each process has exactly one capability list. When a thread asks the kernel to create a port for it, the kernel does so and enters a capability for it in the capability list for the process to which the thread belongs. The calling thread and all the other threads in the same process have equal access to the capability. The integer returned to the thread to identify the capability is usually an index into the capability list (but it can also be a large integer, such as a machine address). We will refer to this integer as a **capability name**, (or sometimes just a capability, where the context makes it clear that we mean the index and not the capability itself). It is always a 32-bit integer, never a string.

Each capability consists of not only a pointer to a port, but also a rights field telling what access the holder of the capability has to the port. (All the threads in a process are equally considered holders of the process' capabilities.) Three rights exist: RECEIVE, SEND, and SEND-ONCE. The RECEIVE right gives the holder the ability to read messages from the port. Earlier we mentioned that communication in Mach is unidirectional. What this really means is that at any instant only one process may have the RECEIVE right for a port. A capability with a RECEIVE right may be transferred to another process, but doing so causes it to be removed from the sender's capability list. Thus for each port there is a single potential receiver.

A capability with the SEND right allows the holder to send messages to the specified port. Many processes may hold capabilities to send to a port. This situation is roughly analogous to the banking system in most countries: anyone who knows a bank account number can deposit money to that account, but only the owner can make withdrawals.

The SEND-ONCE right also allows a message to be sent, but only one time. After the send is done, the kernel destroys the capability. This mechanism is used for request-reply protocols. For example, a client wants something from a server, so it creates a port for the reply message. It then sends the server a request message containing a (protected) capability for the reply port with the SEND-ONCE right. After the server sends the reply, the capability is deallocated from its capability list and the name is made available for a new capability in the future.

Capability names only have meaning within a single process. It is possible for two processes to have access to the same port, but use different names for it, just as two UNIX processes may have access to the same open file, but use different file descriptors to read it. In Fig. 15-15 both processes have a capability to send to port Y, but in A it is capability 3 and in B it is capability 4.

A capability list is tied to a specific process. When that process exits or is killed, its capability list is removed. Ports for which it holds a capability with the RECEIVE

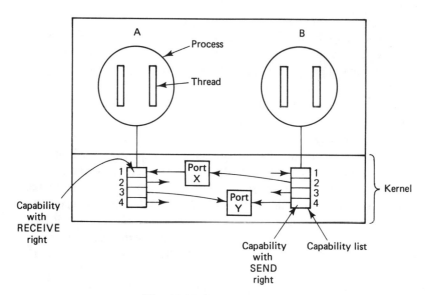

Fig. 15-15. Capability lists.

right are no longer usable, and are therefore also destroyed, even if they contain undelivered (and now undeliverable) messages.

If different threads in a process acquire the same capability multiple times, only one entry is made in the capability list. To keep track of how many times each one is present, the kernel maintains a reference count for each port. When a capability is deleted, the reference count is decremented. Only when it gets to zero is the capability actually removed from the capability list. This mechanism is important because different threads may acquire and release capabilities without each other's knowledge, for example, the UNIX emulation library and the program being run.

Each capability list entry is one of the following four items:

1. A capability for a port.

2. A capability for a port set.

3. A null entry.

4. A code indicating that the port that was there is now dead.

The first possibility has already been explained in some detail. The second one allows a thread to read from a set of ports without even being aware that the capability name is backed up by a set rather than by a single port. The third one is a place holder that indicates that the corresponding entry is not currently in use. If an entry is allocated for a port that is later destroyed, the capability is replaced by a null entry to mark it as unused.

Finally, the fourth option marks ports that no longer exist but for which capabilities with SEND rights still exist. When a port is deleted, for example, because the process holding the RECEIVE capability for it has exited, the kernel tracks down all the SEND capabilities and marks them as dead. Attempts to send to null and dead capabilities fail with an appropriate error code. When all the SEND capabilities for a port are gone, for whatever reasons, the kernel (optionally) sends a message notifying the receiver that there are no senders left and no messages will be forthcoming.

Primitives for Managing Ports

Mach provides about 20 calls for managing ports. All of these are invoked by sending a message to a process port. A sampling of the most important ones is given in Fig. 15-16.

Call	Description
Allocate	Create a port and insert its capability in the capability list
Destroy	Destroy a port and remove its capability from the list
Deallocate	Remove a capability from the capability list
Extract_right	Extract the n-th capability from another process
Insert_right	Insert a capability in another process' capability list
Move_member	Move a capability into a capability set
Set_qlimit	Set the number of messages a port can hold

Fig. 15-16. Selected port management calls in Mach.

The first one, *allocate*, creates a new port and enters its capability into the caller's capability list. The capability is for reading from the port. A capability name is returned so the port can be used.

The next two undo the work of the first one. *Destroy* removes a capability. If it is a RECEIVE capability, the port is destroyed and all other capabilities for it in all processes are marked as dead. *Deallocate* decrements the reference count associated with a capability. If it is zero, the capability is removed, but the port remains intact. *Deallocate* can only be used to remove SEND or SEND-ONCE capabilities or dead capabilities.

Extract_right allows a thread to select out a capability from another process' capability list and insert the capability in its own list. Of course, the calling thread needs access to the process port controlling the other process (e.g., its own child). *Insert_right* goes the other way. It allows a process to take one of its own capabilities and add it to (for example) a child's capability list.

The *move_member* call is used for managing port sets. It can add a port to a port set or remove one. Finally, *set_qlimit* determines the number of messages a port can hold. When a port is created, the default is five messages, but with this call that number can be increased or decreased. The messages can be of any size since they are not physically stored in the port itself.

15.4.2. Sending and Receiving Messages

The purpose of having ports is to send messages to them. In this section we will look at how messages are sent, how they are received, and what they contain. Mach has a single system call for sending and receiving messages. The call is wrapped in a library procedure called *mach_msg*. It has seven parameters and a large number of options. To give an idea of its complexity, there are 35 different error messages that it can return. Below we will give a simplified sketch of some of its possibilities. Fortunately, it is mostly used in procedures generated by the stub compiler, rather than being written by hand.

The *mach_msg* call is used for both sending and receiving. It can send a message to a port and then return control to the caller immediately, at which time the caller can modify the message buffer without affecting the data sent. It can also try to receive a message from a port, blocking if the port is empty, or giving up after a certain interval. Finally, it can combine these two operations, first sending a message and then blocking until a reply comes back. In the latter mode, *mach_msg* can be used for RPC.

A typical call to *mach_msg* looks like this:

```
mach_msg(&hdr,options,send_size,rcv_size,rcv_port,timeout,notify_port);
```

The first parameter, *hdr*, is a pointer to the message to be sent or to the place where the incoming message is put, or both. The message begins with a fixed header and is directly followed by the message body. This layout is shown in Fig. 15-17. We will explain the details of the message format later, but for the moment just note that the header contains a capability name for the destination port. This information is needed so the kernel can tell where to send the message. When doing a pure RECEIVE, the header is not filled in, since it will be entirely overwritten by the incoming message.

The second parameter of the *mach_msg* call, *options*, contains a bit specifying that a message is to be sent, and another one specifying that a message is to be received. If both are on, an RPC is done. Another bit enables a timeout, given by the *timeout* parameter, in milliseconds. If the requested operation cannot be performed within the timeout interval, the call returns with an error code. If the SEND portion of an RPC times out (e.g., due to the destination port being full too long), the RECEIVE is not even attempted.

Other bits in *options* allows a SEND that cannot complete immediately to return control anyway, with a status report being sent to *notify_port* later on. All kinds of errors can occur here if the capability for *notify_port* is unsuitable or changed before the notification can occur. It is even possible for the call to ruin *notify_port* itself (calls can have complex side effects as we will see later).

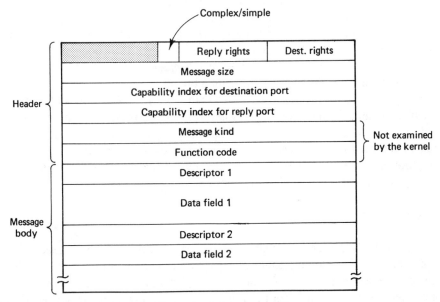

Fig. 15-17. The Mach message format.

The *mach_msg* call can be aborted part-way through by a software interrupt. Another *options* bit tells whether to give up or try again.

The *send_size* and *rcv_size* parameters tell how large the outgoing message is and how many bytes are available for storing the incoming message, respectively. *Rcv_port* is used for receiving messages. It is the capability name of the port or port set being listened to.

Now let us turn to the message format of Fig. 15-17. The first word contains a bit telling whether the message is simple or complex. The difference is that simple messages cannot carry capabilities or protected pointers, whereas complex ones can. Simple messages require less work on the part of the kernel and are therefore more efficient. Both message types have a system-defined structure, described below.

The *message size* field tells how big the combined header plus body is. This information is needed both for transmission and by the receiver.

Next come two capability names, (i.e., indices into the sender's capability list). The first specifies the destination port, the second can give a reply port. In client-server RPC, for example, the destination field designates the server and the reply field tells the server which port to send the response to.

The last two header fields are not used by the kernel. Higher levels of software can use them as desired. By convention, they are used to specify the kind of message and give a function code or operation code (e.g., to a server, is this request for reading or for writing?). This usage is subject to change in the future.

When a message is successfully sent and received, it is copied into the destination's address space. It can happen, however, that the destination port is already full. What happens then depends on the various options and the rights associated with the destination port. One possibility is that the sender is blocked and simply waits until space becomes available in the port. Another is that the sender times out. In some cases, it can exceed the port limit and send anyway.

A few issues concerning receiving messages are worth mentioning. For one, if an incoming message is larger than the buffer, what should be done with it? Two options are provided: throw it away or have the *mach_msg* call fail but return the size, thus allowing the caller to try again with a bigger size.

If multiple threads are blocked trying to read from the same port and a message arrives, one of them is chosen by the system to get the message. The rest remain blocked. If the port being read from is actually a port set, it is possible for the composition of the set to change while one or more threads are blocked on it. This is probably not the place to go into all the details, but suffice it to say that there are precise rules governing this and similar situations.

Message Formats

A message body can be either simple or complex, controlled by a header bit, as mentioned above. Complex messages are structured as shown in Fig. 15-17. A complex message body consists of a sequence of (descriptor, data field) pairs. Each descriptor tells what is in the data field immediately following it. Descriptors come in two formats, differing only in how many bits each of the fields contain. The normal descriptor format is illustrated in Fig. 15-18. It specifies the type of the item that follows, how large an item is, and how many of them there are (a data field may contain multiple items of the same type). The available types include raw bits and bytes, integers of various sizes, unstructured machine words, collections of Booleans, floating point numbers, strings, and capabilities. Armed with this information, the system can attempt to do conversions between machines, when the source and destination machines have different internal representations. This conversion is not done by the kernel, but by the network message server (described below). It is also done for internode transport even for simple messages (also by the network message server).

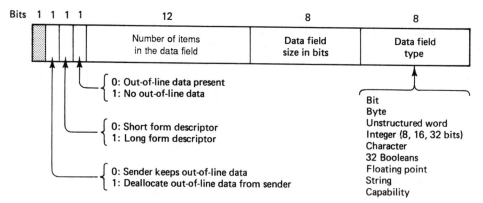

Fig. 15-18. A complex message field descriptor.

One of the more interesting items that can be contained in a data field is a capability. Using complex messages it is possible to copy or transfer a capability from one process to another. Because capabilities are protected kernel objects in Mach, a protected mechanism is needed to move them about.

This mechanism is as follows. A descriptor can specify that the word directly after it in the message contains the name for one of the sender's capabilities, and that this capability is to be passed to the receiving process and inserted in the receiver's capability list. The descriptor also specifies whether the capability is to be copied (the original is left undisturbed) or moved (the original is deleted).

Furthermore, certain values of the *Data field type* ask the kernel to modify the capability's rights while doing the copy or move. A RECEIVE capability, for example, can be mutated into a SEND or SEND-ONCE capability, so that the receiver will have the power to send a reply to a port for which the sender has only a RECEIVE capability. In fact, the normal way to establish communication between two processes is to have one of them create a port and then send the port's RECEIVE capability to the other one, turning it into a SEND capability in flight.

To see how capability transport works, consider the situation of Fig. 15-19(a). Here we see two processes, *A* and *B*, with 3 capabilities and 1 capability, respectively. All are RECEIVE capabilities. Numbering starts at 1 since entry 0 is the null port. One of the threads in *A* is sending a message to *B* containing capability 3.

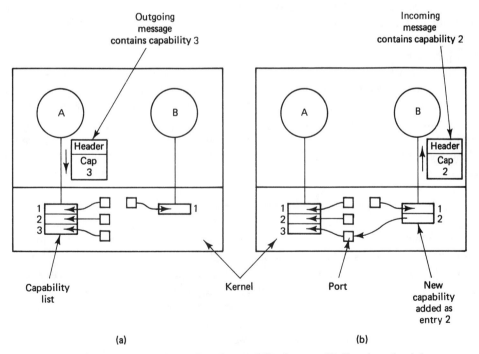

Fig. 15-19. (a) Situation just before the capability is sent. (b) Situation after it has arrived.

When the message arrives, the kernel inspects the header and sees that it is a complex message. It then begins processing the descriptors in the message body, one by one. In this example there is only one descriptor, for a capability, with instructions to turn it into a SEND (or maybe SEND-ONCE) capability. The kernel allocates a free slot in the receiver's capability list, slot 2 in this example, and modifies the message so that the word following the descriptor is now 2 instead of 3. When the receiver gets the message, it sees that it has a new capability, with name (index) 2. It can use this capability immediately (e.g., for sending a reply message).

There is one last aspect of Fig. 15-18 that we have not yet discussed: **out-of-line data**. Mach provides a way to transfer bulk data from a sender to a receiver without doing any copying (on a single machine or multiprocessor). If the out-of-line data bit is set in the descriptor, the word following the descriptor contains an address, and the size and number fields of the descriptor give a 20-bit byte count. Together these specify a region of the sender's virtual address space. For larger regions, the long form of the descriptor is used.

When the message arrives at the receiver, the kernel chooses an unallocated piece of virtual address space the same size as the out-of-line data, and maps the sender's pages into the receiver's address space, marking them copy-on-write. The address word following the descriptor is changed to reflect the address at which the region is located in the receiver's address space. This mechanism provides a way to move blocks of data at extremely high speed, because no copying is required except for the message header and the two-word body (the descriptor and the address). Depending on a bit in the descriptor, the region is either removed from the sender's address space or kept there.

Although this method is highly efficient for copies between processes on a single machine (or between CPUs in a multiprocessor), it is not as useful for communication over a network because the pages must be copied if they are used, even if they are only read. Thus the ability to logically transmit data without physically moving them is lost. Copy-on-write also requires that messages be aligned on page boundaries and be an integral number of pages in length for best results. Fractional pages allow the receiver to see data before or after the out-of-line data that it should not see.

15.4.3. The Network Message Server

Everything we have said about communication in Mach so far is limited to communication within a single node, either one CPU or a multiprocessor node. Communication over the network is handled by user-level servers called **network message servers**, which are vaguely analogous to the external memory managers we studied earlier. Every machine in a Mach distributed system runs a network message server. The network message servers work together to handle intermachine messages, trying to simulate intramachine messages as best they can.

A network message server is a multithreaded process that performs a variety of functions. These include interfacing with local threads, forwarding messages over the network, translating data types from one machine's representation to another's, managing capabilities in a secure way, doing remote notification, providing a simple network-wide name lookup service, and handling authentication of other network message servers. Network message servers can speak a variety of protocols, depending on the networks to which they are attached.

The basic method by which messages are sent over the network is illustrated in Fig. 15-20. Here we have a client on machine A and a server on machine B. Before the client can contact the server, a port must be created on A to function as a proxy for the server. The network message server has the RECEIVE capability for this port. A thread inside it is constantly listening to this port (and other remote ports, which together form a port set). This port is shown as the small box in A's kernel.

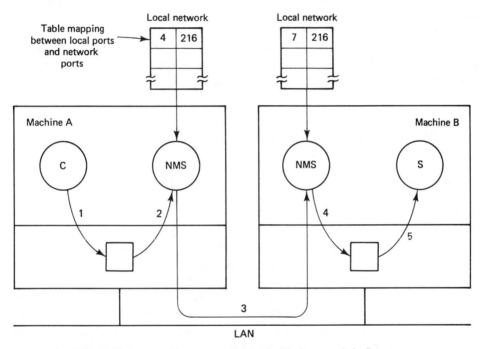

Fig. 15-20. Intermachine communication in Mach proceeds in five steps.

Message transport from the client to the server requires five steps, numbered 1 to 5 in Fig. 15-20. First, the client sends a message to the server's proxy port. Second, the network message server gets this message. Since this message is strictly local, out-of-line data may be sent to it and copy-on-write works in the usual way. Third, the network message server looks up the local port, 4 in this example, in a table that maps proxy ports onto **network ports**. Once the network port is known, the network message server looks up its location in other tables. It then constructs a network message containing the local message, plus any out-of-line data and sends it over the LAN to the network message server on the server's machine. In some cases, traffic between the network message servers has to be encrypted for security. The transport module takes care of breaking the message into packets and encapsulating them in the appropriate protocol wrappers.

When the remote network message server gets the message, it looks up the network port number contained in it, and maps it onto a local port number. In step 4, it writes the message to the local port just looked up. Finally, the server reads the message from the local port and carries out the request. The reply follows the same path in the reverse direction.

Complex messages require a bit more work. For ordinary data fields, the network message server on the server's machine must perform conversion, if necessary, for example, taking account of different byte ordering on the two machines. Capabilities must also be processed. When a capability is sent over the network, it must be assigned a network port number, and both the source and destination network message servers must make entries in their mapping tables for it. If these machines do not trust each other, elaborate authentication procedures will be necessary to convince each one of the other's true identity.

Although the idea of relaying messages from one machine to another via a user-level server offers some flexibility, a substantial price is paid in performance as compared to a pure kernel implementation, which most other distributed systems use.

15.5. BSD UNIX EMULATION IN MACH

Mach has various servers that run on top of it. Probably the most important one is a program that contains a large amount of Berkeley UNIX (for example, essentially the entire file system code) inside of itself. This server is the main UNIX emulator. This design is a legacy of Mach's history as a modified version of Berkeley UNIX. We will sketch its operation below, but for more detail see (Golub et al., 1990).

The implementation of UNIX emulation on Mach consists of two pieces, the UNIX server and a system call emulation library, as shown in Fig. 15-21. When the system starts up, the UNIX server instructs the kernel to catch all system call traps and vector them to an address inside the emulation library of the UNIX process making the system call. From that moment on, any system call made by a UNIX process will result in control temporarily passing to the kernel, and immediately thereafter passing to its emulation library. At the moment control is given to the emulation library, all the machine registers have the values they had at the time of the trap. This method of bouncing off the kernel back into user space is sometimes called the **trampoline mechanism**.

Once the emulation library gets control, it examines the registers to determine which system call was invoked. It then makes an RPC to another process, the UNIX server, to have the work done. When it is finished, the user program is given control again. This transfer of control need not go through the kernel.

When the *init* process forks off children, the children automatically inherit both the emulation library and the trampoline mechanism, so they too can make UNIX system calls. The EXEC system call has been implemented in such a way that it does not replace the emulation library, but just the UNIX program part of the address space.

The UNIX server is implemented as a collection of C threads. Although some threads handle timers, networking, and other I/O devices, most threads handle BSD

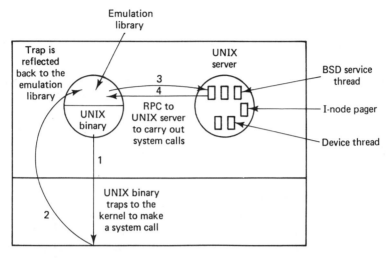

Fig. 15-21. UNIX emulation in Mach uses the trampoline mechanism.

system calls, carrying out requests on behalf of the emulators inside the UNIX processes. The emulation library communicates with these threads using the usual Mach interprocess communication.

When a message comes in to the UNIX server, an idle thread accepts it, determines which process it came from, extracts the system call number and parameters from it, carries it out, and finally sends back the reply. Most messages correspond exactly to one BSD system call.

One set of system calls that do not work this way are the file I/O calls. They *could* have been implemented like this, but for performance reasons, a different approach has been taken. When a file is opened, it is mapped directly into the caller's address space, so the emulation library can get at it directly, without having to do an RPC to the UNIX server. To satisfy a READ system call, for example, the emulation library locates the bytes to be read in the mapped file, locates the user buffer, and just does a copy from the former to the latter as fast as it can.

Page faults will occur during the copy loop if the file's pages are not in memory. Each fault will cause Mach to send a message to the external memory manager backing up the mapped UNIX file. This memory manager is a thread inside the UNIX server called the **i-node pager**. It gets the file page from the disk and arranges for it to be mapped into the application program's address space. It also synchronizes operations on files that are open by several UNIX processes simultaneously.

Although this method of running UNIX programs looks cumbersome, various measurements have shown that it compares favorably with traditional monolithic kernel implementations (Golub et al., 1990). Future work will focus on splitting the UNIX server into multiple servers with more specific functions. Eventually, the single UNIX server may be eliminated, although this depends on how the work with multiple servers develops during the course of time.

15.6. COMPARISON OF AMOEBA AND MACH

In the previous two chapters we have looked at two microkernel-based distributed operating systems, Amoeba and Mach, in considerable detail. While they have some points in common, they differ in many of the technical details. In this section we will look at the two systems side-by-side to illustrate the various choices that designers can make.

15.6.1. Philosophy

Amoeba and Mach have different histories and different philosophies. Amoeba was designed from scratch as a distributed system for use on a collection of CPUs connected by a LAN. Later multiprocessors and WANs were added. Mach (actually RIG) started out as an operating system for a single processor, with multiprocessors and LANs being added afterwards. The consequences of these differing backgrounds are still visible.

For example, Amoeba is based on the processor pool model. A user does not log into a particular machine, but into the system as a whole. The operating system decides where to run each command, based on the current load. It is normal for requests to use multiple processors and rarely will two consecutive commands run on the same processor. There is no concept of a home machine.

In contrast, a Mach (UNIX) user definitely logs into a specific machine, and runs all his programs there by default. There is no attempt to spread each user's work over as many machines as possible (although on a multiprocessor, the work will be automatically spread over all the multiprocessor's CPUs). While it is possible to run remotely, the philosophical difference is that each user has a home machine (e.g., a workstation) where most of his work is carried out.

Another philosophical difference relates to what a "microkernel" is. The Amoeba view follows the famous dictum expounded by the French aviator and writer Antoine de St. Exupéry: "Perfection is not achieved when there is nothing left to add, but when there is nothing left to take away." Whenever a proposal was made to add a new feature to the kernel, the deciding question was: "Can we live without it?" This philosophy led to a minimal kernel, with most of the code in user-level servers.

The Mach designers, in contrast, wanted to provide enough functionality in the kernel to handle the widest possible range of applications. In many areas, Amoeba contains one way to do something and Mach contains two or three, each more convenient or efficient under different circumstances. As a consequence, the Mach kernel is much larger and has five times as many system calls (including calls to kernel threads) as Amoeba. A comparison is given in Fig. 15-22.

Another philosophical difference between Amoeba and Mach is that Amoeba has been optimized for the remote case (communication over the network) and Mach for the local case (communication via memory). Amoeba has extremely fast RPC over the network, while Mach's copy-on-write mechanism provides high-speed communication on a single node, for example.

System	Kernel calls
Amoeba	30
Version 7 UNIX	45
4.2 BSD	84
Mach	153
Sun OS	165

Fig. 15-22. Number of system calls (including calls to kernel threads) in Amoeba, Mach, 4.2BSD, and SunOS 4.1.1.

15.6.2. Objects

Objects are the central concept in Amoeba. A few are built in, like threads and processes, but most are user defined (e.g., files) and can have arbitrary operations on them. About a dozen generic operations (e.g., get status) are defined on nearly all objects, with various object-specific operations defined on each one as well.

In contrast, the only objects directly supported by Mach are threads, processes, ports, and memory objects, each with a fixed set of operations. Higher level software can use these concepts to build other objects, but they are qualitatively different than the built-in objects like memory objects.

In both systems, objects are named, addressed, and protected by capabilities. In Amoeba, capabilities are managed in user space and protected by one-way functions. Capabilities for system-defined objects (e.g., processes), and for user-defined objects (e.g., directories), are treated in a uniform way and appear in user-level directories for naming and addressing all objects. Amoeba capabilities are worldwide, that is, a directory can hold capabilities for files and other objects that are located anywhere. Objects are located by broadcasting, with the results cached for future use.

Mach also has capabilities, but only for ports. These are managed by the kernel in capability lists, one per process. Unlike Amoeba, there are no capabilities for processes or other system or user-defined objects, and they are not generally used directly by application programs. Port capabilities are passed between processes in a controlled way, so Mach can find them by looking them up in kernel tables.

15.6.3. Processes

Both systems support processes with multiple threads per process. In both cases, the threads are managed and scheduled by the kernel, although a user-level threads packages can be built on top of them. Amoeba does not provide user control over thread scheduling, whereas Mach allows processes to set the priorities and policies of their threads in software. Mach also provides more elaborate multiprocessor support.

In Amoeba, synchronization between threads is done by mutexes and semaphores. In Mach it is done by mutexes and condition variables. Both support some form of glocal variables.

Both Amoeba and Mach work on multiprocessors, but they differ on how they deal with threads on these machines. In Amoeba, all the threads of a process run on the same CPU, in pseudoparallel, timeshared by the kernel. In Mach processes have fine-grained control over which threads run on which CPUs (using the processor set concept). Consequently, the threads of the same process can run in parallel on different CPUs. In Amoeba, a similar effect can be achieved by having several single-threaded processes run on different CPUs and share a common address space. Nevertheless, it is clear that the Mach designers have devoted more attention to multiprocessors than the Amoeba designers.

On the other hand, the Amoeba designers have put more work into supporting load balancing and heterogeneity. When the Amoeba shell starts a process, it asks the run server to find it the CPU with the lightest workload. Unless the user has specified a specific architecture, the process may be started on any architecture for which a binary is available, with the user not even being aware which kind has been selected. This scheme is designed to spread the workload over as many machines as possible all the time.

In Mach, processes are normally started on the user's home machine. Only when explicitly requested to do so by the user are processes run remotely on idle workstations, and even then they have to be evicted quickly if the workstation's owner touches the keyboard. This difference relates to the fundamental difference between the processor pool model and the workstation model.

15.6.4. Memory Model

Amoeba's memory model is based on variable-length segments. A virtual address space consists of some number of segments mapped in at specific addresses. Segments can be mapped in and out at will. Each segment is controlled by a capability. A remote process that has the capabilities for another process' segments (e.g., a debugger), can read and write them from any other Amoeba machine in the world. Amoeba does not support demand paging. When a process is running, all of its segments are in memory. The ideas behind this decision are simplicity of design and high performance, coupled with the fact that extremely large memories are becoming common on even the smallest machines.

Mach's memory model is based on memory objects, and is implemented in terms of fixed-size pages. Memory objects can be mapped and unmapped at will. A memory object need not be entirely in main memory to be used. When an absent page is referenced, a page fault occurs and a message is sent to an external memory manager to find the page and map it in. Together with the default memory manager, this mechanism supports demand-paged virtual memory.

Pages can be shared between multiple processes in various ways. One common configuration is the copy-on-write sharing used to attach a child process to its parent. Although this mechanism is a highly efficient way of sharing on a single node, it loses its advantages in a distributed system because physical transport is always required (assuming the receiver needs to read the data). In such an environment, the extra code and complexity are wasted. This is a clear example of where Mach has been optimized for single-CPU and multiprocessor systems, rather than for distributed systems.

Both Amoeba and Mach support distributed shared memory, but they do it in radically different ways. Amoeba supports shared objects that are replicated on all machines using them. Objects can be of any size and can support any operations. Reads are done locally, and writes are done using the Amoeba reliable broadcast protocol.

Mach, in contrast, supports a page-based distributed shared memory. When a thread references a page that is not present on its machine, the page is fetched from its current machine and brought in. If two machines heavily access the same writable page, thrashing can occur. The tradeoff here is the more expensive update on Amoeba (due to the replication of writable objects), versus the potential for thrashing on Mach (only one copy of writable pages).

15.6.5. Communication

Amoeba supports both RPC and group communication as fundamental primitives. RPCs are addressed to put-ports, which are service addresses. They are protected cryptographically using one-way functions. The sending and receiving machines can be anywhere in the world. The RPC interface is very simple: only three system calls, none with any options.

Group communication provides reliable broadcasting as a user primitive. Messages can be sent to any group with a guarantee of reliable delivery. In addition, all group members see all messages arrive in exactly the same order.

Low-level communication uses the FLIP protocol, which provides process addressing (as opposed to machine addressing). This feature allows process migration and (inter)network reconfiguration automatically, without the software even being aware of it. It also supports other facilities useful in distributed systems.

In contrast, Mach's communication is from process to port, rather than from process to process. Furthermore, the sender and port must be on the same node. Using a network message server in user space, communication can be extended over a network, but this indirection is costly in terms of performance. Mach does not support group communication or reliable broadcasting as basic kernel primitives.

Communication is done using the *mach_msg* system call, which has seven parameters, ten options, and 35 potential error messages. It supports both synchronous and asynchronous message passing. This approach is the antithesis of the Amoeba strategy of keep it simple and make it fast. The idea here is to provide the maximum flexibility and the widest range of support for present and future applications.

Mach messages can be either simple or complex. Simple messages are just bits and are not processed in any special way by the kernel. Complex messages may contain capabilities. They may also pass out-of-line data using copy-on-write, something Amoeba does not have. On the other hand, this facility is of little value in a distributed system because the out-of-line data must be fetched by the network message server, combined with the message header and in-line data, and sent over the network in the usual way. This optimization is for the local case and wins nothing when the sender and receiver are on different machines.

On the network, Mach uses conventional protocols such as TCP/IP. These have the advantage of being stable and widely available. FLIP, in contrast, is new, but is faster for typical RPC usage and has been specifically designed for the needs of distributed computing.

15.6.6. Servers

Amoeba has a variety of servers for specific functions, including file management, directory management, object replication, and load balancing. All are based on objects and capabilities. Amoeba supports replicated objects via directories that contain capability sets. UNIX emulation is provided at the source code level and is not 100 percent complete.

Mach has a single server that runs BSD UNIX as an application program. It provides 100 percent binary compatible emulation, a great boon for running existing software for which the source code is not available. General object replication is not supported. Other servers also exist.

A brief summary of some of the major points discussed above is given in Fig. 15-23.

15.7. SUMMARY

Mach is a microkernel-based operating system. It has been designed to provide a base for building new operating systems and emulating existing ones. It also provides a flexible way to extend UNIX to multiprocessors and distributed systems.

Mach is based on the concepts of processes, threads, ports, and messages. A Mach process is an address space and a collection of threads that run in it. The active entities are the threads. The process is merely a container for them. Each process and thread has a port to which it can write to have kernel calls carried out, eliminating the need for direct system calls.

Mach has an elaborate virtual memory system, featuring memory objects that can be mapped and unmapped into address spaces, and backed up by external, user-level memory managers. Files can be made directly readable and writable in this way, for example. Memory objects can be shared in various ways, including copy-on-write. Inheritance attributes determine which parts of a process' address space will be passed to its children.

Communication in Mach is based on ports, which are kernel objects that hold messages. All messages are directed to ports. Ports are accessed using capabilities, which are stored inside the kernel and referred to by 32-bit integers that are usually indices into capability lists. Ports can be passed from one process to another by including them in complex messages.

Item	Amoeba	Mach
Designed for	Distributed system	Single CPU, multiprocessor
Model	Pool processor	Workstation
Microkernel	Few system calls	Many system calls
Optimized for	Remote case	Local case
Capability based?	Yes	Yes
Capabilities for	Everything	Ports
Capabilities in	User space	Kernel space
Multithreading?	Yes	Yes
Threads managed by	Kernel	Kernel
Transp. Heterogeneity	Yes	No
Load balancing	Automatic	None
Address space	Segment-based	Page-based
Mapped object	Segment	Memory object
Demand paging	No	Yes
Copy on write	No	Yes
Distr. Shared Memory	Object based	Page based
Communication model	RPC, group commun.	Message passing, RPC
Msgs addressed to	Processes	Ports
Intermachine msgs	Kernel	User space
Low level protocol	FLIP	IP
Reliable group comm	Yes	No
Stub generator	Yes	Yes
User level servers	Yes	Yes
UNIX emulation	Source (Partial)	Binary
UNIX as a single server	No	Yes
File, dir etc servers	Yes	No
Automatic replication	Yes	No

Fig. 15-23. Some differences between Amoeba and Mach.

BSD UNIX emulation is done by an emulation library that lives in the address space of each UNIX process. Its job is to catch system calls reflected back to it by the kernel, and pass them on to the UNIX server to have them carried out. A few calls are handled locally, within the process' address space. Other UNIX emulators are also being developed.

Amoeba and Mach have many aspects in common, but also various differences. Both have processes and threads and are based on message passing. Amoeba has reliable broadcasting as a primitive, which Mach does not, but Mach has demand paging, which Amoeba does not. In general, Amoeba is more oriented towards making a collection of distributed machines act like a single computer, whereas Mach is more oriented towards making efficient use of multiprocessors. Both are undergoing constant development, and will no doubt change as time goes on.

PROBLEMS

1. Name one difference between a process with two threads and two processes each with one thread that share the same address space, that is, the same set of pages?

2. What happens if you *join* on yourself?

3. A Mach thread creates two new threads as its children, *A* and *B*. Thread *A* does a *detach* call; *B* does not. Both threads exit and the parent does a *join*. What happens?

4. The global run queues of Fig.15-6 must be locked before being searched. Do the local run queues (not shown in the figure) also have to be locked before being searched? Why or why not?

5. Each of the global run queues has a single mutex for locking it. Suppose a particular multiprocessor has a global clock that causes clock interrupts on all the CPUs simultaneously. What implications does this have for the Mach scheduler?

6. Mach supports the concept of a processor set. On what class of machines does this concept make the most sense? What is it used for?

7. Mach supports three inheritance attributes for regions of virtual address space. Which ones are needed to make UNIX FORK work correctly?

8. A small process has all its pages in memory. There is enough free memory available for ten more copies of the process. It forks off a child. Is it possible for the child to get a page or protection fault?

9. Why do you think there is a call to copy a region of virtual memory (see Fig. 15-8)? After all, any thread can just copy it by sitting in a tight copy loop.

10. Why is the page replacement algorithm run in the kernel instead of in an external memory manager?

11. Give an example when it is desirable for a thread to deallocate an object in its virtual address space.

12. Can two processes simultaneously have RECEIVE capabilities for the same port? How about SEND capabilities?

13. Does a process know that a port it is reading from is actually a port set? Does it matter?

14. Mach supports two types of messages: simple and complex. Are the complex messages actually required, or is this merely an optimization?

15. Now answer the previous question about SEND-ONCE capabilities and out-of-line messages. Are either of these essential to the correct functioning of Mach?

16. In Fig. 15-15 the same port has a different name in different processes. What problems might this cause?

17. Mach has a system call that allows a process to request that non-Mach traps be given to a special handler, rather than causing the process to be killed. What is this system call good for?

A

READING LIST
AND BIBLIOGRAPHY

In the previous fifteen chapters we have touched upon a variety of topics. This appendix is intended as an aid to readers interested in pursuing their study of operating systems further. Section A.1 is a list of suggested readings. Section A.2 is an alphabetical bibliography of all books and articles cited in this book.

In addition to the references given below, the *Proceedings of the n-th ACM Symp. on Operating Systems Principles* (SOSP) held every other year and the *Proceedings of the n-th International Conference on Distributed Computing Systems* (DCS) held every year are good places to look for recent papers on operating systems. Furthermore, *ACM Transactions on Computer Systems* and *Operating Systems Review* are two journals that often have interesting articles on operating systems. Brumfield (1986) has published a useful guide to the operating systems literature. Useful bibliographies have been assembled by Metzner (1982), Newton (1979), Smith (1978, 1981), and Zobel (1983).

A.1. SUGGESTIONS FOR FURTHER READING

A.1.1. Introduction and General Works

Brooks, *The Mythical Man-Month: Essays on Software Engineering*
    A witty, amusing, and informative book on how *not* to write an operating system by someone who learned the hard way. Full of good advice.

Corbató, "On Building Systems that will Fail"

In his Turing Award lecture, the father of timesharing addresses many of the same concerns that Brooks does in the *Mythical Man-Month*. His conclusion is that all complex systems will ultimately fail, and that to have any chance for success at all, it is absolutely essential to avoid complexity and strive for simplicity and elegance in design.

Deitel, *Operating Systems,* 2nd Ed.

A general textbook on operating systems. In addition to the standard material, it contains case studies of UNIX, MS-DOS, MVS, VM, OS/2, and the Macintosh operating system.

Finkel, *An Operating Systems Vade Mecum*

Another general text on operating systems. It is practically-oriented and well-written and covers many of the topics treated in this book, making it a good place to look for a different perspective on the same subject.

Lampson, "Hints for Computer System Design"

Butler Lampson, one of the world's leading designers of innovative operating systems, has collected many hints, suggestions, and guidelines from his years of experience and put them together in this entertaining and informative article. Like Brooks' book, this is required reading for every aspiring system designer.

Silberschatz et al., *Operating System Concepts,* 3rd Ed.

Another textbook on operating systems. It covers processes, storage management, files, and distributed systems. Two case studies are given: UNIX and Mach. The cover is an allegory, depicting operating systems as dinosaurs, but showing MS-DOS as more advanced than UNIX, OS/2, and Mach defies comprehension.

A.1.2. Processes

Andrews and Schneider, "Concepts and Notations for Concurrent Progr."

A tutorial and survey of processes and interprocess communication, including busy waiting, semaphores, monitors, message passing, and other techniques. The article also shows how these concepts are embedded in various programming languages.

Ben-Ari, *Principles of Concurrent Programming*

This little book is entirely devoted to the problems of interprocess communication. There are chapters on mutual exclusion, semaphores, monitors, and the dining philosophers problem, among others.

Dubois et al., "Synchronization, Coherence, and Event Ordering in Multiprocessors"

A tutorial on synchronization in multiprocessor systems. However, some of the ideas are equally applicable to single processor and distributed systems as well.

Silberschatz et al., *Operating System Concepts,* 3rd Ed.

Chapters 4 and 5 cover processes and interprocess communication, including scheduling, critical sections, semaphores, monitors, and classical interprocess communication problems.

A.1.3. Memory Management

Denning, "Virtual Memory"

A classic paper on many aspects of virtual memory. Denning was one of the pioneers in this field, and was the inventor of the working set concept.

Denning, "Working Sets Past and Present"

A good overview of numerous memory management and paging algorithms. A comprehensive bibliography is included.

Knuth, *The Art of Computer Programming* Vol. 1

First fit, best fit, buddy systems, and other memory management algorithms are discussed and compared in this book.

Silberschatz et al., *Operating System Concepts,* 3rd Ed.

Chapters 7 through 9 deal with memory management, including swapping, paging, and segmentation. A variety of paging algorithms are mentioned.

A.1.4. File Systems

Denning, "The United States vs. Craig Neidorf"

When a young hacker discovered and published information about how the telephone system works, he was indicted for computer fraud. This article describes the case, which involved many fundamental issues, including freedom of speech. The article is followed by some dissenting views and a rebuttal by Denning.

Hafner and Markoff, *Cyberpunk*

Three compelling tales of young hackers breaking into computers around the world are told here by the New York Times computer reporter who broke the Internet worm story and his journalist wife.

Harbron, *File Systems*

A book on file system design, applications, and performance. Both structure and algorithms are covered.

McKusick et al., "A Fast File System for UNIX"

The UNIX file system was completely reimplemented for 4.2 BSD. This paper describes the design of the new file system, with emphasis on performance aspects.

Livadas, *File Structures, Theory and Practice*

A detailed treatment of actual file systems and file structures, including BISAM, VSAM, Version 7 UNIX, MVS, locate mode, cylinder overflow areas, inverted files, timing and tuning.

Rosenblum and Ousterhout, "The Design and Implementation of a Log-Structured File System"

A new file system organization is presented here in which the entire disk is a log. This approach allows many small writes to be collected together into large transfers, yielding a much higher throughput than conventional designs.

Silberschatz et al., *Operating System Concepts,* 3rd Ed.

Chapter 10 is about file systems. It covers file operations, access methods, consistency semantics, directories, and protection, among other topics.

A.1.5. Input/Output

IEEE, *IEEE Computer*, July 1985

This special issue on mass storage has five papers on advanced disk systems, including optical disks.

Finkel, *An Operating Systems Vade Mecum.* 2nd Ed.

Chapter 5 discusses I/O hardware and device drivers, particularly for terminals and disks.

Geist and Daniel, "A Continuum of Disk Scheduling Algorithms"

A generalized disk arm scheduling algorithm is presented. Extensive simulation and experimental results are given.

Stevens, "Heuristics for Disk Drive Positioning in 4.3BSD"

A detailed study of disk performance in Berkeley UNIX. As is often the case with computer systems, reality is more complicated than the theory predicts.

A.1.6. Deadlocks

Coffman et al., "System Deadlocks"

A short introduction to deadlocks, what causes them, and how they can be prevented or detected.

Holt, "Some Deadlock Properties of Computer Systems"

A discussion of deadlocks. Holt introduces a directed graph model that can be used to analyze some deadlock situations.

Isloor and Marsland, "The Deadlock Problem: An Overview"

A tutorial on deadlocks, with special emphasis on data base systems. A variety of models and algorithms are covered.

A.1.7. UNIX

Bach, *The Design of the UNIX Operating System,*
A comprehensive tour of the internals of System V. Among other topics are the kernel, the buffer cache, the file system, processes and scheduling, memory management, I/O, and interprocess communication.

Blair et al., "A Critique of UNIX"
A discussion of areas in which UNIX is weak, including file management, process creation, process scheduling, and resource management. A useful antidote to the numerous papers and books that describe UNIX as the greatest invention since sliced bread.

Bourne, *The UNIX System*
An easy introduction to UNIX by one of the people who was part of the group that designed it.

Kernighan and Pike, *The UNIX Programming Environment*
Like Bourne's book, another introduction to UNIX written by people who were there when it happened. This one is somewhat more advanced than Bourne's. It is suitable for readers who already have considerable computer experience.

Leffler et al., *The Design and Implementation of the 4.3BSD UNIX Operating System*
Essentially the same kind of book as Bach's, except about BSD instead of System V. Both books are well written, but they are very detailed, and require a considerable amount of study to master.

Quarterman et al., "4.2 BSD and 4.3 BSD as Examples of the UNIX System"
A survey of the structure, internal organization, and algorithms used by Berkeley UNIX including processes, scheduling, paging, I/O, communications, and networking.

Ritchie and Thompson, "The UNIX Time-Sharing System"
This is the original paper on UNIX by its designers. All the key ideas are here. It is as well worth reading now as when it was first published.

Shaw and Shaw, *UNIX Internals*
Yet another "How UNIX works inside" book. It is less detailed (and thus more accessible for beginners) than Bach or Leffler et al. Dedicating the book to themselves is excusable; the use of a 7×9 matrix printer for the examples is not.

A.1.8. MS-DOS

Angermeyer et al., *The Waite Group's MS-DOS Developer's Guide,* 2nd Ed.
A hands-on guide to advanced MS-DOS programming with numerous examples. It covers memory management, TSR programming, device drivers, and disk layout and

recovery in great detail. A working knowledge of 8088 assembly language is needed to read this book.

Gookin, *DOS 5 User's Guide*
A reasonably comprehensive guide for beginning, intermediate, and advanced MS-DOS users. It starts out explaining what a computer is, proceeds through commands and the file system, and ends telling about system configuration, maintenance, and recovering from disasters.

Halliday, *Turbocharging MS-DOS*
Although this book is nominally for users wishing to maximize the performance of their MS-DOS systems. It covers so much detail about how MS-DOS works, that it is a useful reference for advanced users. Most of the emphasis is on the disk structure and performance, and on memory management.

Schulman et al., *Undocumented DOS*
This book is probably the best single reference on how MS-DOS works internally. It is nearly 700 pages long, covering the file system, memory, the command interpreter, and the debugger. It comes with two 1.2M diskettes full of programs that allow you to snoop on the system. Definitely not for the faint hearted.

A.1.9. Introduction to Distributed Systems

Champine et al., "Project Athena as a Distributed Computer System"
Athena is a network operating system at M.I.T. consisting of 1000 UNIX-based workstations. The project has developed several software packages that have become de facto standards, such as X (window management) and Kerberos (authentication). The paper gives an overview of the whole system.

Cheriton, "The V Distributed System"
V is another microkernel-based distributed operating system, like Amoeba and Mach. This paper describes communication, process management, memory management, and device management in V. In addition to telling what was done right, the paper also tells what was done wrong.

Couloris and Dollimore, *Distributed Systems Concepts and Design*
An introductory text on distributed systems. It covers network protocols, RPC, distributed file systems, and security. Case studies include Locus, Argus, XDS, the Cambridge distributed system, Amoeba, Mach, and Apollo Domain.

Duncan, "A Survey of Parallel Computer Architectures"
A tutorial on multiprocessors and multicomputers. Among the topics covered are SIMD and MIMD architectures, pipelined pipelined, systolic, dataflow, reduction, and wavefront machines.

Goscinski, *Distributed Operating Systems- The Logical Design*
A monstrous compendium (913 pages) of various topics related to distributed systems. Although the book is not especially well structured, some of the individual chapters are worth reading. Case studies of Accent, V, Charlotte, Amoeba, Eden, Locus, and Mach are given.

Mullender (Ed.), *Distributed Systems*
A collection of 20 papers on various aspects of distributed systems written by the leading experts in the field. Subjects include communication, naming and security, data storage, transactions, replication, methodology, architecture and other topics.

Ousterhout et al., "The Sprite Network Operating System"
Sprite is another workstation-based distributed operating system. Unlike Amocba, Mach, and V, it is based on a monolithic kernel, rather than on a microkernel. Among other topics, the paper discusses Sprite's file system, virtual memory, and process migration.

Tanenbaum and van Renesse, "Distributed Operating Systems"
A survey article about distributed operating systems. It focuses on those aspects of distributed operating systems that differ from single-processor systems. Four existing distributed systems are examined in detail.

A.1.10. Communication in Distributed Systems

Birman et al., "Lightweight Causal and Atomic Group Multicast"
A discussion of the ISIS system, including its protocols, applications, and performance.

Birrell and Nelson, "Implementing Remote Procedure Calls"
Remote procedure calls are commonly used in distributed systems for interprocess communication. This paper describes the implementation of a particularly elegant remote procedure call system developed at Xerox PARC.

Hutchinson et al., "RPC in the *x*-kernel: Evaluating New Design Techniques"
The *x*-kernel uses a technique similar to UNIX streams to allow protocol stacks to be assembled for handling RPC-based layered protocols. The mechanism is lightweight, using procedure calls between the layers.

Tay and Ananda, "A Survey of Remote Procedure Calls"
Despite certain fundamental similarities, RPC systems differ in various ways. This paper surveys eight different RPC systems, ranging from academic research projects to commercial systems, and compares them in various ways.

A.1.11. Synchronization in Distributed Systems

Fidge, "Logical Time in Distributed Computing Systems"
   An approach to dealing with event ordering in distributed systems that is based on causality and partial time ordering, rather than total time ordering.

Lampson, "Atomic Transactions"
   A good introduction to the concept of atomic transactions, showing how they can be built up from simple primitives.

Ramanathan et al., "Fault-Tolerant Clock Synch. in Distrib. Systems,"
   An overview of clock synchronization algorithms for use in distributed systems. Hardware, software, and hybrid methods are covered.

Raynal, "A Simple Taxonomy for Distributed Mutual Exclusion Algorithms"
   A taxonomy and bibliography of distributed mutual exclusion algorithms. The major categories defined are permission-based and token-based, with centralized algorithms occurring at the intersection of the two.

Singhal, "Deadlock Detection in Distributed Systems"
   A tutorial on distributed deadlock detection. First it looks at the issue involved. Then it goes on to discuss centralized, decentralized, and hierarchical algorithms in distributed systems.

A.1.12. Processes and Processors in Distributed Systems

Anderson et al., "Scheduler Activations: Effective Kernel Support for the User-Level Management of Parallelism"
   A new abstraction is presented for combining the best properties of user-level and kernel-level thread management. The abstraction is to give each process a virtual multiprocessor and use upcalls to inform users about relevant scheduling events.

Bershad et al., "Lightweight Remote Procedure Call"
   A method for doing fast RPC on a single processor or multiprocessor is described. It involves having the client run a preselected procedure in the server's address space, thus avoiding a context switch.

Marsh et al., "First-Class, User-Level Threads"
   A set of mechanisms and conventions are presented to allow threads to be managed in user space but still take advantage of kernel knowledge. The idea is based on upcalls.

Nichols, "Using Idle Workstations"
   A description of the Butler system for finding and using idle UNIX workstations. A registry keeps track of machines and allocates them.

A.1.13. Distributed File Systems

Gifford et al., "The Cedar File System"
  Cedar is a distributed file system for a network of workstations. The paper discusses naming, caching, performance and other aspects of Cedar.

Levy and Silberschatz, "Distributed File Systems: Concepts and Examples"
  The first half of this paper discusses principles of distributed file systems. The second half covers five examples: UNIX United, Locus, NFS, Sprite, and Andrew.

Nelson et al., "Caching in the Sprite Network File System"
  Sprite is a network file system for connecting workstations, analogous to NFS and AFS. In this paper the designers tell how Sprite handles client caching and how it maintains client consistency. Measurements of its performance are also given.

Purdin et al., "A File Replication Facility for Berkeley UNIX"
  A low-cost method for doing file replication on Berkeley UNIX is described. It is based on reproduction sets, which are collections of file the system attempts to keep identical.

Satyanarayanan, "A Survey of Distributed File Systems"
  Some basic design issues for distributed file systems are examined in this survey. Case studies of NFS, Apollo Domain, Andrew, AIX, RFS, and Sprite are also presented.

Satyanarayanan, "Integrating Security in a Large Distributed System,"
  A discussion of the Andrew and Coda file systems, both of which apply to wide area networks. The paper covers authentication and security, and for Coda, disconnected operation.

Svobodova, "File Servers for Network-Based Distributed Systems"
  A survey of file servers used in distributed systems. The emphasis is on file servers that provide atomic actions and transactions.

A.1.14. Amoeba

Douglis et al., "A Comparison of Two Distributed Systems: Amoeba and Sprite,"
  A comparison of two distributed systems: Amoeba, which has a microkernel and uses the processor pool model, and Sprite, which has a monolithic kernel and uses the workstation model.

Kaashoek and Tanenbaum, "Group Communication in the Amoeba Distributed Operating System"
  An introduction to group communication in Amoeba, especially the reliable

broadcast protocol used and its implementation. The paper also discusses fault tolerance in the protocol, and how the reliable broadcast protocol recovers from sequencer
and other crashes.

Mullender et al., "Amoeba: A Distributed Operating System for the 1990s,"
    An overview of Amoeba, emphasizing the communication mechanism, objects,
security, the file system, and process management.

Tanenbaum et al., "Experiences with the Amoeba Distributed Operating System,"
    Another introduction to Amoeba. This one emphasizes objects, RPC, servers,
wide-area Amoeba, applications, and performance. It concludes with an evaluation
of the design—what was done right but even more important, what was done wrong.

A.1.15. Mach

Accetta et al., "Mach: A New Kernel Foundation for UNIX Development"
    One of the first published papers on the Mach system. It describes the goals of
the system, the basic ideas, such as threads, ports and messages, and the implementation.

Black, "Scheduling Support for Concurrency and Parallelism in the Mach Sys."
    The Mach scheduling algorithm for multiprocessors is described here. Various
optimizations, such as handoff scheduling, are discussed, and performance measurements are given.

Boykin and Langerman, "Mach/4.3BSD: A Conservative Appr. to Parallelization,"
    The trials and tribulations of making the Mach UNIX emulator run efficiently on a
multiprocessor, something for which it was never intended. The problems encountered with I/O and the file system are described, as are the authors' solutions.

Golub et al., "UNIX as an Application Program"
    Although UNIX was never designed to run as a user program, in Mach it does pre-
cisely that. Read all about how that works here.

Rashid, "From RIG to Accent to Mach: The Evolution of a Network Operating Sys."
    A brief history of RIG, Accent, and Mach written by their author. The evolution
of the system is described, emphasizing the changes that occurred as a result of new
technology and new goals.

Young et al., "The Duality of Memory and Communication in the Implementation of
a Multiprocessor Operating System,"
    The goals, design, and implementation of the Mach memory management system,
and how it interacts with the communication system. The use of external memory
managers is described.

A.2. ALPHABETICAL BIBLIOGRAPHY

ACCETTA, M., BARON, R., GOLUB, D., RASHID, R., TEVANIAN, A., and YOUNG, M.: "Mach: A New Kernel Foundation for UNIX Development," *Proc. Summer 1986 USENIX Conf,* pp. 93-112, 1986.

AGRAWAL, D. and EL ABBADI, A: "An Efficient and Fault-Tolerant Solution of Distributed Mutual Exclusion," *ACM Trans. on Computer Systems,* vol. 9, pp. 1-20, Feb. 1991.

ANDERSON, T.E., BERSHAD, B.N., LAZOWSKA, E.D., and LEVY, H.M.: "Scheduler Activations: Effective Kernel Support for the User-Level Management of Parallelism," *Proc. Thirteenth Symp. on Operating Systems Principles,* ACM, pp. 95-109, 1991.

ANDREWS, G.R.: *Concurrent Programming—Principles and Practice,* Redwood City, CA: Benjamin/Cummings, 1991.

ANDREWS, G.R., and SCHNEIDER, F.B.: "Concepts and Notations for Concurrent Programming," *Computing Surveys,* vol. 15, pp. 3-43, March 1983.

ANGERMEYER, J., JAEGER, K., BAPNA, R.K., NARKAKATI, N., DHESIKAN, R., DIXON, W., DUMKE, A, FLEIG, J., and GOLDMAN, M.: *The Waite Group's MS-DOS Developer's Guide,* 2nd Ed. Carmel, IN: Howard W. Sams, 1989.

ARTSY. Y., and FINKEL, R.: "Designing a Process Migration Facility," *IEEE Computer,* vol. 22, pp. 47-56, Sept. 1989.

ATKINSON, R., and HEWITT, C.: "Synchronization and Proof Techniques for Serializers," *IEEE Trans. on Software Engineering,* vol. SE-5, pp. 10-23, Jan. 1979.

BACH, M.J.: *The Design of the UNIX Operating System,* Englewood Cliffs, NJ: Prentice Hall, 1987.

BAL, H.E.: *Programming Distributed Systems,* Hemel Hempstead, England: Prentice Hall Int'l, 1991.

BAL, H.E., KAASHOEK, M.F., and TANENBAUM, A.S.: "Experience with Distributed Programming in Orca," *Proc. Int'l Conf. on Computer Languages '90,* IEEE, pp. 79-89, 1990.

BALL, J.E., FELDMAN, J.A., LOW, J.R., RASHID, R.F., and ROVNER, P.D.: "RIG, Rochester's Intelligent Gateway: System Overview," *IEEE Trans. on Software Engineering,* vol. SE-2, pp. 321-328, Dec. 1976.

BARON, R.; RASHID, R.; SIEGEL, E.; TEVANIAN, A. and YOUNG, M.: "Mach-1: An Operating Environment for Large-Scale Multiprocessor Applications," *IEEE Software,* vol. 2, pp. 65-67, July 1985.

BAYS, C.: "A Comparison of Next-Fit, First-Fit, and Best-Fit," *Commun. of the ACM,* vol. 20, pp. 191-192, March 1977.

BECK, L.L.: "A Dynamic Storage Allocation Technique Based on Memory Residence Time," *Commun. of the ACM,* vol. 25, pp. 714-724, Oct. 1982.

BELADY, L.A., NELSON, R.A., and SHEDLER, G.S.: "An Anomaly in Space-Time Characteristics of Certain Programs Running in a Paging Machine," *Commun. of the ACM,* vol. 12, pp. 349-353, June 1969.

BEN-ARI, M: *Principles of Concurrent Programming,* Englewood Cliffs, NJ: Prentice Hall International, 1982.

BERNSTEIN, P.A., and GOODMAN, N.: "An Algorithm for Concurrency Control and Recovery in Replicated Distributed Databases," *ACM Trans. on Database Systems*, vol. 9, pp. 596-615, Dec. 1984.

BERSHAD, B.N., ANDERSON, T.E., LAZOWSKA, E.D., and LEVY, H.M.: "Lightweight Remote Procedure Call," *ACM Trans. on Computer Systems*, vol. 8, pp. 37-55, Feb. 1990.

BIRMAN, K.P. and JOSEPH, T.: "Reliable Communication in the Presence of Failures," *ACM Trans. on Computer Systems*, vol. 5, pp. 47-76, Feb. 1987a.

BIRMAN, K.P. and JOSEPH, T.: "Exploiting Virtual Synchrony in Distributed Systems," *Proc. Eleventh Symp. on Operating Systems Principles* ACM, pp. 123-138, Nov. 1987b.

BIRMAN, K.P., SCHIPER, A., and STEPHENSON, P.: "Lightweight Causal and Atomic Group Multicast," *ACM Trans. on Computer Systems*, vol. 9, pp. 272-314, Aug. 1991.

BIRRELL, A.D., and NELSON, B.J.: "Implementing Remote Procedure Calls," *ACM Trans. on Computer Systems*, vol. 2, pp. 39-59, Feb. 1984.

BLACK, D.: "Scheduling Support for Concurrency and Parallelism in the Mach Operating System," *IEEE Computer*, vol. 23, pp. 35-43, May 1990.

BLAIR, G.S., MALONE, J.R., and MARIANI, J.A.: "A Critique of UNIX," *Software—Practice and Experience*, vol. 15, pp. 1125-1139, Dec. 1985.

BOLOSKY, W.J., FITZGERALD, R.P., and SCOTT, M.L.: "Simple but Effective Techniques for NUMA Memory Management," *Proc. Twelfth Symp. on Operating System Principles*, ACM, pp. 19-31, 1989.

BOURNE, S.R.: *The UNIX System*, Reading, MA: Addison-Wesley, 1982.

BOYKIN, J., and LANGERMAN, A.: "Mach/4.3BSD: A Conservative Approach to Parallelization," *Computer Systems*, vol 3., pp. 69-99, Winter 1990.

BRERETON, O.P.: "Management of Replicated Files in a UNIX Environment," *Software—Practice and Experience*, vol. 16, pp. 771-780, Aug. 1986.

BRINCH HANSEN, P.: "The Programming Language Concurrent Pascal," *IEEE Trans. on Software Engineering*, vol. SE-1, pp. 199-207, June 1975.

BROOKS, F. P., Jr.: *The Mythical Man-Month: Essays on Software Engineering*, Reading, MA: Addison-Wesley, 1975.

BRUMFIELD, J.A.: "A Guide to Operating Systems Literature," *Operating Systems Review*, vol. 20, pp. 38-42, April 1986.

CADOW, H.: *OS/360 Job Control Language*, Englewood Cliffs, NJ: Prentice Hall, 1970.

CAMPBELL, R.H., and HABERMANN, A.N.: "The Specification of Process Synchronization by Path Expressions," in *Operating Systems*, Kaiser, C. (Ed.), Berlin: Springer-Verlag, 1974.

CHAMPINE, G.A., GEER, D.E., Jr., and RUH, W.N.: "Project Athena as a Distributed Computer System," *IEEE Computer*, vol. 23, pp. 40-51, Sept. 1990.

CHANDY, K.M., MISRA, J., and HAAS, L.M.: "Distributed Deadlock Detection," *ACM Trans. on Computer Systems*, vol. 1, pp. 144-156, May 1983.

CHANG, J. and MAXEMCHUK. N.F.: "Reliable Broadcast Protocols," *ACM Trans. on Computer Systems*, vol. 2, pp. 39-59, Feb. 1984.

CHERITON, D.R.: "An Experiment Using Registers for Fast Message-Based Interprocess Communication," *Operating Systems Review*, vol. 18, pp. 12-20, Oct. 1984.

CHERITON, D.R.: "The V Distributed System," *Commun. of the ACM*, vol. 31, pp. 314-333, March 1988.

CHOW, T.C.K., and ABRAHAM, J.A.: "Load Balancing in Distributed Systems," *IEEE Trans. on Software Engineering*, vol. SE-8, pp. 401-412, July 1982.

COFFMAN, E.G., ELPHICK, M.J., and SHOSHANI, A.: "System Deadlocks," *Computing Surveys*, vol. 3, pp. 67-78, June 1971.

COHEN, D.: "On Holy Wars and a Plea for Peace," *IEEE Computer*, vol. 14, pp. 48-54, Oct. 1981.

CORBATO, F.J.: "On Building Systems that will Fail," *Commun. of the ACM*, vol. 34, pp. 72-81, June 1991.

CORBATO, F.J., MERWIN-DAGGETT, M., and DALEY, R.C: "An Experimental Time-Sharing System," *Proc. AFIPS Fall Joint Computer Conf.*, pp. 335-344, 1962.

CORBATO, F.J., SALTZER, J.H., and CLINGEN, C.T.: "MULTICS—The First Seven Years," *Proc. AFIPS Spring Joint Computer Conf.*, pp. 571-583, 1972.

CORBATO, F.J., and VYSSOTSKY, V.A.: "Introduction and Overview of the MULTICS System," *Proc. AFIPS Fall Joint Computer Conf.*, pp. 185-196, 1965.

COULOURIS, G.F., and DOLLIMORE, J.: *Distributed Systems Concepts and Design*, Reading, MA: Addison-Wesley, 1988.

COURTOIS, P.J., HEYMANS, F., and PARNAS, D.L.: "Concurrent Control with Readers and Writers," *Commun. of the ACM*, vol. 10, pp. 667-668, Oct. 1971.

CRISTIAN, F.: "Probabilistic Clock Synchronization," *Distributed Computing*, vol. 3, pp. 146-158, 1989.

CRISTIAN, F.: "Understanding Fault Tolerant Distributed Systems," *Commun. of the ACM*, vol. 34, pp. 56-78, Feb. 1991.

DALEY, R.C., and DENNIS, J.B.: "Virtual Memory, Process, and Sharing in MULTICS," *Commun. of the ACM*, vol. 11, pp. 306-312, May 1968.

DAY, J.D., and ZIMMERMANN, H.: "The OSI Reference Model," *Proc. of the IEEE*, vol. 71, pp. 1334-1340, Dec. 1983.

DEITEL, H.M.: *Operating Systems,* 2nd Ed., Reading, MA: Addison-Wesley, 1990.

DENNING, D.: "The United states vs. Craig Neidorf," *Commun. of the ACM*, vol. 34, pp. 22-43, March 1991.

DENNING, P.J.: "The Working Set Model for Program Behavior," *Commun. of the ACM*, vol. 11, pp. 323-333, 1968a.

DENNING, P.J.: "Thrashing: Its Causes and Prevention," *Proc. AFIPS National Computer Conf.*, pp. 915-922, 1968b.

DENNING, P.J.: "Virtual Memory," *Computing Surveys*, vol. 2, pp. 153-189, Sept. 1970.

DENNING, P.J.: "Working Sets Past and Present," *IEEE Trans. on Software Engineering*, vol. SE-6, pp. 64-84, Jan. 1980.

DENNIS, J.B., and VAN HORN, E.C.: "Programming Semantics for Multiprogrammed Computations," *Commun. of the ACM*, vol. 9, pp. 143-155, March 1966.

DIJKSTRA, E.W.: "Co-operating Sequential Processes," in *Programming Languages*, Genuys, F. (Ed.), London: Academic Press, 1965.

DIJKSTRA, E.W.: "The Structure of THE Multiprogramming System," *Commun. of the ACM*, vol. 11, pp. 341-346, May 1968.

DOUGLIS, F., OUSTERHOUT, J.K., KAASHOEK, M.F., and TANENBAUM, A.S.: "A Comparison of Two Distributed Systems: Amoeba and Sprite," *Computing Systems*, vol. 4, pp. 353-384, Fall 1991.

DOUGLIS, F., and OUSTERHOUT, J.: "Transparent Process Migration: Design Alternatives and the Sprite Implementation," *Software—Practice and Experience*, vol. 21, pp.757-785, Aug. 1991.

DRAVES, R.P.: "The Revised IPC Interface," *Proc. First USENIX Conf. on Mach*, pp. 101-121, 1990.

DRAVES, R.P., BERSHAD, B.N., RASHID, R.F., and DEAN, R.W.: "Using Continuations to Implement Thread Management and Communication in Operating Systems," *Proc. Thirteenth Symp. on Operating Systems Principles*, ACM, pp. 122-136, 1991.

DUBOIS, M., SCHEURICH, C., and BRIGGS, F.A.: "Synchornization, Coherence, and Event Ordering in Multiprocessors," *IEEE Computer*, vol. 21, pp. 9-21, Feb. 1988.

DUNCAN, R: *Advanced MS-DOS Programming,* 2nd Ed., Redmond, WA: Microsoft Press, 1988.

DUNCAN, R.: "A Survey of Parallel Computer Architectures," *IEEE Computer*, vol. 23, pp. 5-16, Feb. 1990.

EAGER, D.L., LAZOWSKA, E.D., and ZAHORJAN, J.: "Adaptive Load Sharing in Homogeneous Distributed Systems," *IEEE Trans. on Software Engineering*, vol. SE-12, pp. 662-675, May 1986.

ESWARAN, K.P., GRAY, J.N., LORIE, J.N., and TRAIGER, I.L.: "The Notions of Consistency and Predicate Locks in a Database System," *Commun. of the ACM*, vol. 19, pp. 624-633, Nov. 1976.

EVEN, S.: *Graph Algorithms*, Potomac, MD: Computer Science Press, 1979.

FABRY, R.S.: "Capability-Based Addressing," *Commun. of the ACM*, vol. 17, pp. 403-412, July 1974.

FERGUSON, D., YEMINI, Y., and NIKOLAOU, C.: "Microeconomic Algorithms for Load Balancing in Distributed Computer Systems," *Proc. Eighth Int'l Conf. on Distributed Computing Systems*, IEEE, pp. 491-499, 1988.

FIDGE, C.: "Logical Time in Distributed Computing Systems," *IEEE Computer*, vol. 24, pp. 28-33, Aug. 1991.

FINKEL, R.A.: *An Operating Systems Vade Mecum,* 2nd Ed., Englewood Cliffs, NJ: Prentice Hall, 1988.

FLYNN, M.J.: "Some Computer Organizations and Their Effectiveness," *IEEE Trans. on Computers*, vol. C-21, pp. 948-960, Sept. 1972.

FORIN, A., BARRERA, J., YOUNG, M., and RASHID, R.: "Design, Implementation, and Performance Evaluation of a Distributed Shared Memory Server for Mach," *Proc. Winter USENIX Conf.*, Jan. 1989.

FOTHERINGHAM, J.: "Dynamic Storage Allocation in the Atlas Including an Automatic Use of a Backing Store," *Commun. of the ACM*, vol. 4, pp. 435-436, Oct. 1961.

GARCIA-MOLINA, H.: "Elections in a Distributed Computing System," *IEEE Trans. on Computers*, vol. 31, pp. 48-59, Jan. 1982.

GARCIA-MOLINA, H. and SPAUSTER, A: "Ordered and Reliable Multicast Communication," *ACM Trans. on Computer Systems*, vol. 9, pp. 242-271, Aug. 1991.

GEIST, R., and DANIEL, S.: "A Continuum of Disk Scheduling Algorithms," *ACM Trans. on Computer Systems*, vol. 5, pp. 77-92, Feb. 1987.

GIFFORD, D.K.: "Weighted Voting for Replicated Data," *Proc. Seventh Symp. on Operating Systems Principles*, ACM, pp. 150-162, 1979.

GIFFORD, D.K., NEEDHAM, R.M., and SCHROEDER, M.D.: "The Cedar File System," *Commun. of the ACM*, vol. 31, pp. 288-298, March 1988.

GOLDEN, D., and PECHURA, M.: "The Structure of Microcomputer File Systems," *Commun. of the ACM*, vol. 29, pp. 222-230, March 1986.

GOLUB, D., DEAN, R., FORIN, A., and RASHID, R.: "UNIX as an Application Program," *Proc. of the USENIX Summer Conf.*, pp. 87-95, June 1990.

GOOKIN, D.: *DOS 5 User's guide*, Redwood City, CA: M& T Books, 1991.

GOSCINSKI, A.: *Distributed Operating Systems- The Logical Design* Reading, MA: Addison-Wesley, 1991.

GRAHAM, R.: "Use of High-Level Languages for System Programming," Project MAC Report TM-13, M.I.T., Sept. 1970.

GRAY, J: "Notes on Database Operating Systems," in *Operating Systems: An Advanced Course*, Bayer, R., Graham, R.M., and Seegmuller, G. (eds.), Berlin: Springer-Verlag, pp. 394-481, 1978.

GRAY, J.N., HOMAN, P., KORTH, H.F., and OBERMARCK, R.L.: "A Straw Man Analysis of the Probability of Waiting and Deadlock in a Database System," Report RJ 3066, IBM Research Laboratory, San Jose CA, 1981.

GUSELLA, R., and ZATTI, S.: "The Accuracy of the Clock Synchronization Achieved by TEMPO in Berkeley UNIX 4.3BSD," *IEEE Trans. on Software Engineering*, vol. 15, pp. 847-853, July 1989.

HAFNER, K., and MARKOFF, J.: *Cyberpunk*, New York: Simon and Schuster, 1991.

HALLIDAY, C.M.: *Turbocharging MS-DOS*, Que, 1991.

HARBRON, T.R.: *File Systems*, Englewood Cliffs, NJ: Prentice Hall, 1988.

HARRISON, M.A., RUZZO, W.L., and ULLMAN, J.D.: "Protection in Operating Systems," *Commun. of the ACM*, vol. 19, pp. 461-471, Aug. 1976.

HAVENDER, J.W.: "Avoiding Deadlock in Multitasking Systems," *IBM Systems Journal*, vol. 7, pp. 74-84, 1968.

HEBBARD, B. et al.: "A Penetration Analysis of the Michigan Terminal System," *Operating Systems Review*, vol. 14, pp. 7-20, Jan. 1980.

HOARE, C.A.R.: "Monitors, An Operating System Structuring Concept," *Commun. of the ACM*, vol. 17, pp. 549-557, Oct. 1974; Erratum in *Commun. of the ACM*, vol. 18, p. 95, Feb. 1975.

HOLT, R.C: "Some Deadlock Properties of Computer Systems," *Computing Surveys*, vol. 4, pp. 179-196, Sept. 1972.

HOLT, R.C: *Concurrent Euclid, The UNIX System, and TUNIS*, Reading, MA: Addison-Wesley, 1983.

HOWARD, J.H., KAZAR, M.J., MENEES, S.G., NICHOLS, D.A., SATYANARAYANAN, M., SIDEBOTHAM, R.N., and WEST, M.J.: "Scale and Performance in a Distributed File System," *ACM Trans. on Computer Systems*, vol. 6, pp. 55-81, Feb. 1988.

HUTCHINSON, N.C., PETERSON, L.L., ABBOTT, M.B., and O'MALLEY, S.: "RPC in the x-Kernel: Evaluating New Design Techniques," *Proc. Twelfth Symp. on Operating Systems Principles*, ACM, pp. 911-101, 1989.

ISLOOR, S.S., and MARSLAND, T.A.: "The Deadlock Problem: An Overview," *IEEE Computer*, vol. 13, pp. 58-78, Sept. 1980.

JOSEPH, T.A., and BIRMAN, K.P.: "Reliable Broadcast Protocols," in *Distributed Systems*, Mullender, S. (Ed.), ACM Press, 1989.

KAASHOEK, M.F., and TANENBAUM, A.S.: "Group Communication in the Amoeba Distributed Operating System," *Proc. Eleventh Int'l Conf. on Distributed Computing Systems*, IEEE, pp. 222-230, 1991.

KAASHOEK, M.F., TANENBAUM, A.S., HUMMEL, S., and BAL, H.E.: "An Efficient Reliable Broadcast Protocol," *Operating Systems Review*, vol. 23, pp. 5-19, Oct. 1989.

KARLIN, A.R., Li, K., MANASSE, M.S., OWICKI, S: "Empirical Studies of Competitive Spinning for a Shared-Memory Multiprocessor," *Proc. Thirteenth Symp. on Operating Systems Principles*, ACM, pp. 41-55, 1991.

KAUFMAN, A.: "Tailored-List and Recombination-Delaying Buddy Systems," *ACM Trans. on Programming Languages and Systems*, vol. 6, pp. 118-125, Jan. 1984.

KERNIGHAN, B.W., and PIKE, R.: *The UNIX Programming Environment*, Englewood Cliffs, NJ: Prentice Hall, 1984.

KERNIGHAN, B.W., and RITCHIE, D.M.: *The C Programming Language,* 2nd Ed., Englewood Cliffs, NJ: Prentice Hall, 1988.

KLEINROCK, L.: *Queueing Systems. Vol. 1*, New York: John Wiley, 1974.

KNAPP, E.: "Deadlock Detection in Distributed Databases," *Computing Surveys*, vol. 19, pp. 303-328, Dec. 1987.

KNOWLTON, K.C.: "A Fast Storage Allocator," *Commun. of the ACM*, vol. 8, pp. 623-625, Oct. 1965.

KNUTH, D.E.: *The Art of Computer Programming, Volume 1: Fundamental Algorithms,* 2nd Ed., Reading, MA: Addison-Wesley, 1973.

KUNG, H.T., and ROBINSON, J.T.: "On Optimistic Methods for Concurrency Control," *ACM Trans. on Database Systems*, vol. 6, pp. 213-226, June 1981.

LAMPORT, L.: "A New Solution to Dijkstra's Concurrent Programming Problem," *Commun. of the ACM*, vol. 17, pp. 453-455, Aug. 1974.

LAMPORT, L.: "Time, Clocks, and the Ordering of Events in a Distributed System," *Commun. of the ACM*, vol. 21, pp. 558-564, July 1978.

LAMPORT, L.: "Concurrent Reading and Writing of Clocks," *ACM Trans. on Computer Systems*, vol. 8, pp. 305-310, Nov. 1990.

LAMPSON, B.W.: "A Scheduling Philosophy for Multiprogramming Systems," *Commun. of the ACM*, vol. 11, pp. 347-360, May 1968.

LAMPSON, B.W.: "A Note on the Confinement Problem," *Commun. of the ACM*, vol. 10, pp. 613-615, Oct. 1973.

LAMPSON, B.W.: "Atomic Transactions," in *Distributed Systems—Architecture and Implementation*, Lampson, B.W. (Ed.), Springer-Verlag, pp. 246-264, 1981.

LAMPSON, B.W.: "Hints for Computer System Design," *IEEE Software*, vol. 1, pp. 11-28, Jan. 1984.

LANDWEHR, C.E.: "Formal Models of Computer Security," *Computing Surveys*, vol. 13, pp. 247-278, Sept. 1981.

LaROWE, R.P., ELLIS, C.S., and KAPLAN, L.S.: "The Robustness of NUMA Memory Management," *Proc. Thirteenth Symp. on Operating Systems Principles*, ACM, pp. 137-151, 1991.

LEFFLER, S.J., McKUSICK, M.K., KARELS, M.J., and QUARTERMAN, J.S.: *The Design and Implementation of the 4.3BSD UNIX Operating System*, Reading, MA: Addison-Wesley, 1989.

LEVIN, R., COHEN, E.S., CORWIN, W.M., POLLACK, F.J., and WULF, W.A.: "Policy/Mechanism Separation in Hydra," *Proc. of the Fifth Symp. on Operating Systems Principles*, ACM, pp. 132-140, 1975.

LEVY, E., and SILBERSCHATZ, A.: "Distributed File Systems: Concepts and Examples" *Computing Surveys*, vol. 22, pp. 321-374, Dec. 1990.

LI, K., and HUDAK, P.: "Memory Coherence in Shared Virtual Memory Systems," *ACM Trans. on Computer Systems*, vol. 7, pp. 321-359, Nov. 1989.

LINDE, R.R.: "Operating System Penetration," *Proc. AFIPS National Computer Conf.*, pp. 361-368, 1975.

LINDEN, T.A.: "Operating System Structures to Support Security and Reliable Software," *Computing Surveys*, vol. 8, pp. 409-445, Dec. 1976.

LITZKOW, M.J., LIVNY, M., and MUTKA, M.W.: "Condor—A Hunter of Idle Workstations," *Proc. Eighth Int'l Conf. on Distributed Computing Systems*, IEEE, pp. 104-111, 1988.

LIVADAS, P.E.: *File Structures: Theory and Practice*, Englewood Cliffs, NJ: Prentice Hall, 1990.

LO, V.M.: "Heuristic Algorithms for Task Assignment in Distributed Systems," *Proc. Fourth Int'l Conf. on Distributed Computing Systems*, IEEE, pp. 30-39, 1984.

LUAN, S.-W., and GLIGOR, V.D.: "A Fault-tolerant Protocol for Atomic Broadcast," *IEEE Trans. on Parallel and Distributed Systems*, vol. 1, pp. 271-285, July 1990.

LUNDELIUS-WELCH, J., and LYNCH, N.: "A New Fault-Tolerant Algorithm for Clock Synchronization," *Information and Computation*, vol. 77, pp. 1-36, Jan. 1988.

MAEKAWA, M., OLDEHOEFT, A.E., and OLDEHOEFT, R.R.: *Operating Systems: Advanced Concepts*, Menlo Park, CA: Benjamin/Cummings, 1987.

MARSH, B.D., SCOTT, M.L., LeBLANC, T.J., and MARKATOS, E.P.: "First-Class User-level Threads," *Proc. Thirteenth Symp. on Operating Systems Principles*, ACM, pp. 110-121, 1991.

McKUSICK, M.J., JOY, W.N., LEFFLER, S.J., and FABRY, R.S.: "A Fast File System for UNIX," *ACM Trans. on Computer Systems*, vol. 2, pp. 181-197, Aug. 1984.

MELIAR-SMITH, P.M., MOSER, L.E., and AGRAWALA, V.: "Broadcast Protocols for Distributed Systems," *IEEE Trans. on Parallel and Distributed Systems*, vol. 1, pp. 17-25, Jan. 1990.

METZNER, J.R.: "Structuring Operating Systems Literature for the Graduate Course," *Operating Systems Review*, vol. 16, pp. 10-25, Oct. 1982.

MICROSOFT: *Microsoft MS-DOS Programmer's Reference*, Redmond, WA: Microsoft Press, 1991a.

MICROSOFT: *Microsoft MS-DOS User's Guide and Reference*, Redmond, WA: Microsoft Press, 1991b.

MORRIS, J.H., SATYANARAYANAN, M., CONNER, M.H., HOWARD, J.H., ROSENTHAL, D.S., and SMITH, F.D.: "Andrew: A Distributed Personal Computing Environment," *Commun. of the ACM*, vol. 29, pp. 184-201, March 1986.

MORRIS, R., and THOMPSON, K.: "Password Security: A Case History," *Commun. of the ACM*, vol. 22, pp. 594-597, Nov. 1979.

MULLENDER, S.J. (Ed.): *Distributed Systems*, New York: ACM Press, 1989.

MULLENDER, S.J. ROSSUM, G. VAN, TANENBAUM, A.S., RENESSE, R. VAN, STAVEREN, H. VAN: "Amoeba: A Distributed Operating System for the 1990s," *IEEE Computer*, vol. 23, pp. 44-53, May 1990.

MULLENDER, S.J., and TANENBAUM, A.S.: "Immediate Files," *Software—Practice and Experience*, vol. 14, pp. 365-368, April 1984.

MUTKA, M.W., and LIVNY, M.: "Scheduling Remote Processor Capacity in a Workstation-Processor Bank Network," *Proc. Seventh Int'l Conf. on Distributed Computing Systems*, IEEE, pp. 2-9, 1987.

NELSON, B.J.: *Remote Procedure Call*, Ph.D. thesis, Carnegie-Mellon University, 1981.

NELSON, M.N., WELCH, B.B., and OUSTERHOUT, J.K.: "Caching in the Sprite Network File System," *ACM Trans. on Computer Systems*, vol. 6, pp. 134-154, Feb. 1988.

NELSON, V.P.: "Fault-Tolerant Computing: Fundamental Concepts," *IEEE Computer*, vol. 23, pp. 19-25, July 1990.

NEWTON, G.: "Deadlock Prevention, Detection, and Resolution: An Annotated Bibliography," *Operating Systems Review*, vol. 13, pp. 33-44, April 1979.

NICHOLS, D.A.: "Using Idle Workstations in a Shared Computing Environment," *Proc. Eleventh Symp. on Operating Systems Principles*, ACM, pp. 5-12, 1987.

OLDEHOEFT, R.R., and ALLAN, S.J.: "Adaptive Exact-Fit Storage Management," *Commun. of the ACM*, vol. 28, pp. 506-511, May 1985.

ORGANICK, E.I.: *The Multics System*, Cambridge, MA: M.I.T. Press, 1972.

OUSTERHOUT, J.K.: "Scheduling Techniques for Concurrent Systems," *Proc. Third Int'l Conf. on Distributed Computing Systems*, IEEE, pp. 22-30, 1982.

OUSTERHOUT, J.K., CHERENSON, A.R., DOUGLIS, F., NELSON, M.N., and WELCH, B.B.: "The Sprite Network Operating System," *IEEE Computer*, vol. 21, pp. 23-36, Feb 1988.

PANZIERI, F. and SHRIVASTAVA, S.K.: "Rajdoot: a remote procedure call mechanism with orphan detection and killing," *IEEE Trans. on Software Engineering*, vol. 14, pp. 30-37, Jan. 1988.

PATIL, S.S.: "Limitations and Capabilities of Dijkstra's Semaphore Primitives for Coordination Among Processes," M.I.T. Project MAC Computational Structures Group Memo, Number 57, Feb. 1971.

PATTERSON, D.A., and SEQUIN, C.H.: "RISC I: A Reduced Instruction Set VLSI Computer," *Proc. Eighth Int'l. Symp. on Computer Arch.*, ACM, pp. 443-457, 1981.

PETERSON, G.L.: "Myths about the Mutual Exclusion Problem," *Information Processing Letters*, vol. 12, pp. 115-116, June 1981.

PETERSON, J.L., and NORMAN, T.A.: "Buddy Systems," *Commun. of the ACM*, vol. 20, pp. 421-431, June 1977.

PU, C., NOE, J.D., and PROUDFOOT, A: "Regeneration of Replicated Objects: A Technique and its Eden Implementation," *Proc. Second Int'l Conf. on Data Engineering*, pp. 175-187, Feb 1986.

PURDIN, T.D., SCHLICHTING, R.D., and ANDREWS, G.R.: "A File Replication Facility for Berkeley UNIX," *Software—Practice and Experience*, vol. 17, pp. 923-940, Dec. 1987.

QUARTERMAN, J.S., SILBERSCHATZ, A., and PETERSON, J.L.: "4.2BSD and 4.3BSD as Examples of the UNIX System," *Computing Surveys*, vol. 17, Dec. 1985.

RAMANATHAN, P., KANDLUR, D.D., and SHIN, K.G.: "Hardware-Assisted Software Clock Synchronization for Homogeneous Distributed Systems," *IEEE Trans. on Computers*, vol. C-39, pp. 514-524, April 1990a.

RAMANATHAN, P., SHIN, K.G., and BUTLER, R.W.: "Fault-Tolerant Clock Synchronization in Distributed Systems," *IEEE Computer*, vol. 23, pp. 33-42, Oct. 1990b.

RASHID, R.F.: "Threads of a New System," *Unix Review*, vol. 4, pp. 37-49, Aug. 1986a.

RASHID, R.F.: "From RIG to Accent to Mach: The Evolution of a Network Operating System," *Fall Joint Computer Conference*, AFIPS, pp. 1128-1137, 1986b.

RAYNAL, M.: "A Simple Taxonomy for Distributed Mutual Exclusion Algorithms," *Operating Systems Review*, vol. 25, pp. 47-50, April 1991.

REED, D.P.: "Implementing Atomic Actions on Decentralized Data," *ACM Trans. on Computer Systems*, vol. 1, pp. 3-23, Feb. 1983.

REED, D.P., and KANODIA, R.K.: "Synchronization with Eventcounts and Sequencers," *Commun. of the ACM*, vol. 22, pp. 115-123, Feb. 1979.

RICART, G., and AGRAWALA, A.K.: "An Optimal Algorithm for Mutual Exclusion in Computer Networks," *Commun. of the ACM*, vol. 24, pp. 9-17, Jan. 1981.

RITCHIE, D.M.: "Reflections on Software Research," *Commun. of the ACM*, vol. 27, pp. 758-760, Aug. 1984.

RITCHIE, D.M., and THOMPSON, K.: "The UNIX Timesharing System," *Commun. of the ACM*, vol. 17, pp. 365-375, July 1974.

ROSENBLUM, M., and OUSTERHOUT, J.K.: "The Design and Impl. of a Log-Structured File System," *Proc. Thirteenth Symp. on Operating System Prin.*, ACM, pp. 1-15, 1991.

SANDERS, B.A.: "The Information Structure of Distributed Mutual Exclusion," *ACM Trans. on Computer Systems*, vol. 5, pp. 284-299, Aug. 1987.

SANSOM, R.D., JULIN, D.P., and RASHID, R.F.: "Extending a Capability Based System into a Network Environment," *Proc. SIGCOMM '86*, ACM, pp. 265-274.

SALTZER, J.H.: "Protection and Control of Information Sharing in MULTICS," *Commun. of the ACM*, vol. 17, pp. 388-402, July 1974.

SALTZER, J.H., and SCHROEDER, M.D.: "The Protection of Information in Computer Systems," *Proc. IEEE*, vol. 63, pp. 1278-1308, Sept. 1975.

SATYANARAYANAN, M.: "A Study of File Sizes and Functional Lifetimes," *Proc. of the Eighth Symp. on Operating Systems Principles*, ACM, pp. 96-108, 1981.

SATYANARAYANAN, M.: "Integrating Security in a Large Distributed System," *ACM Trans. on Computer Systems*, vol. 7, pp. 247-280, Aug. 1989.

SATYANARAYANAN, M.: "A Survey of Distributed File Systems," *Annual Review of Computer Science*, vol. 4, pp. 73-104, 1990a.

SATYANARAYANAN, M.: "Scalable, Secure, and Highly Available Distributed File Access," *IEEE Computer*, vol. 23, pp. 9-21, May 1990b.

SATYANARAYANAN, M., HOWARD, J.H., NICHOLS, D.N., SIDEBOTHAM, R.N., SPECTOR, A.Z., and WEST, M.J.: "The ITC Distributed File System: Principles and Design," *Proc. of the Tenth Symp. on Operating System Principles*, ACM, pp. 35-50, 1985.

SATYANARAYANAN, M.: "Coda: A Highly Available File System for a Distributed Workstation Environment," *IEEE Trans. on Computers*, vol. C-39, pp. 447-459, April 1990.

SCHROEDER, M.D., and BURROWS, M.: "Performance of Firefly RPC," *ACM Trans. on Computer Systems*, vol. 8, pp. 1-17, Feb. 1990.

SCHROEDER, M.D., and SALTZER, J.H.: "A Hardware Architecture for Implementing Protection Rings," *Commun. of the ACM*, vol. 15, pp. 157-170, March 1972.

SCHULMAN, A: "Undocumented DOS," *Byte*, vol. 16, pp. 297-298, March 1991.

SCHULMAN, A, MICHELS, R.J., KYLE, J., PATERSON, T., MAXEY, D., and BROWN, R: *Undocumented DOS*, Reading, MA: Addison-Wesley, 1990.

SEAWRIGHT, L.H., and MACKINNON, R.A.: "VM/370—A Study of Multiplicity and Usefulness," *IBM Systems Journal*, vol. 18, pp. 4-17, 1979.

SHAW, M.C., and SHAW, S.S.: *UNIX Internals*, Blue Ridge Summit, PA: Tab Books, 1987.

SILBERSCHATZ, A., PETERSON, J.L., and GALVIN, P.B.: *Operating System Concepts,* 3rd Ed. Reading, MA: Addison-Wesley, 1991.

SINGHAL, M.: "Deadlock Detection in Distributed Systems," *IEEE Computer*, vol. 22, pp. 37-48, Nov. 1989.

SMITH, A.J.: "Bibliography on Paging and Related Topics," *Operating Systems Review*, vol. 12, pp. 39-56, Oct. 1978.

SMITH, A.J.: "Bibliography on File and I/O System Optimization and Related Topics," *Operating Systems Review*, vol. 15, pp. 39-54, Oct. 1981.

SPAFFORD, E.H.: "The Internet Worm: Crisis and Aftermath," *Commun. of the ACM*, vol. 32, pp. 678-687, June 1989.

SRIKANTH, T.K., and TOUEG, S.: "Optimal Clock Synchronization," *J. ACM*, vol. 34, pp. 626-645, July 1987.

STEPHENSON, C.J.: "Fast Fits: A New Method for Dynamic Storage Allocation," *Proc. Ninth Symp. on Operating Systems Principles*, ACM, pp. 30-32, 1983.

STEVENS, W.R.: "Heuristics for Disk Drive Partitioning in 4.3BSD," *Computing Systems*, vol. 2, pp. 251-274, Summer 1989.

STONE, H.S., and BOKHARI, S.H.: "Control of Distributed Processes," *IEEE Computer*, vol. 11, pp. 97-106, July 1978.

STUMM, M., and ZHOU, S.: "Algorithms Implementing Distributed Shared Memory," *IEEE Computer*, vol. 23, pp. 54-64, May 1990.

SVOBODOVA, L.: "File Servers for Network-Based Distributed Systems," *Computing Surveys*, vol. 16, pp. 353-398, Dec. 1984.

SWAN, R.J., FULLER, S.H., and SIEWIOREK, D.P.: "Cm*—A Modular Multiprocessor," *Proc. NCC*, pp. 637-644, 1977.

TAM, M.-C., SMITH, J.M., and FARBER, D.J.: "A Taxonomy-Based Comparison of Several Distributed Shared Memory Systems," *Operating Systems Review*, vol. 24, pp. 40-67, July 1990.

TANENBAUM, A.S.: *Operating Systems: Design and Implementation*, Englewood Cliffs, NJ: Prentice Hall, 1987.

TANENBAUM, A.S.: *Computer Networks,* 3rd Ed. Englewood Cliffs, NJ: Prentice Hall, 1988.

TANENBAUM, A.S., KAASHOEK, M.F., and BAL, H.E.: "Parallel Programming Using Shared Objects and Broadcasting," *IEEE Computer*, vol. 25, 1992.

TANENBAUM, A.S., MULLENDER, S.J., and VAN RENESSE, R.: "Using Sparse Capabilities in a Distributed Operating System," *Proc. Sixth Int'l Conf. on Distributed Computing Systems*, IEEE, pp. 558-563, 1986.

TANENBAUM, A.S., and VAN RENESSE, R.: "Distributed Operating Systems," *Computing Surveys*, vol. 17, Dec. 1985.

TANENBAUM, A.S., VAN RENESSE, R., STAVEREN, H. VAN, SHARP, G.J., MULLENDER, S.J., JANSEN, J., and ROSSUM, G. VAN: "Experiences with the Amoeba Distributed Operating System," *Commun. of the ACM*, vol. 33, pp. 46-63, Dec. 1990.

TAY, B.H., and ANANDA, A.L.: "A Survey of Remote Procedure Calls," *Operating Systems Review*, vol. 24, pp. 68-79, July 1990.

TEORY, T.J.: "Properties of Disk Scheduling Policies in Multiprogrammed Computer Systems," *Proc. AFIPS Fall Joint Computer Conf.*, pp. 1-11, 1972.

THEIMER, M.M., LANTZ, K.A., and CHERITON, D.A.: "Preemptable Remote Execution Facilities in the V System," *Proc. Tenth Symp. on Operating System Principles*, ACM, pp. 2-12, 1985.

THOMPSON, K.: "Reflections on Trusting Trust," *Commun. of the ACM*, vol. 27, pp. 761-763, Aug. 1984.

TSEUNG, L.N.: "Guaranteed, Reliable, Secure Broadcast Networks," *IEEE Network Magazine*, vol. 3, pp. 33-37. Nov. 1989.

VAN RENESSE, R., and TANENBAUM, A.S.: "Voting with Ghosts," *Proc. Eighth Int'l Conf. on Distributed Computer Systems*, IEEE, 1988.

VAN TILBORG, A.M., and WITTIE, L.D.: "Wave Scheduling: Distributed Allocation of Task Forces in Network Computers," *Proc. Sixth Int'l Conf. on Distributed Computing Systems*, IEEE, pp. 337-347, 1981.

VASWANI, R., and ZAHORJAN, J.: "The Implications of Cache Affinity on processor Scheduling for Multiprogrammed Shared Memory Multiprocessors," *Proc. Thirteenth Symp. on Operating Systems Principles*, ACM, pp. 26-40, 1991.

WITTIE, L.D., and VAN TILBORG, A.M.: "MICROS, a Distributed Operating System for MICRONET, A Reconfigurable Network Computer," *IEEE Trans. on Computers*, vol. C-29, pp. 1133-1144, Dec. 1980.

WULF, W.A., COHEN, E.S., CORWIN, W.M., JONES, A.K., LEVIN, R., PIERSON, C., and POLLACK, F.J.: "HYDRA: The Kernel of a Multiprocessor Operating System," *Commun. of the ACM*, vol. 17, pp. 337-345, June 1974.

YOUNG, M., TEVANIAN, A. Jr., RASHID, R., GOLUB, D., EPPINGER, J., CHEW, J., BOLOSKY, W., BLACK, D., and BARON, R.: "The Duality of Memory and Communication in the Implementation of a Multiprocessor Operating System," *Proc. Eleventh Symp. on Operating System Principles*, pp. 63-76, Nov. 1987.

ZAYAS, E.R.: "Attacking the Process Migration Bottleneck," *Proc. Eleventh Symp. on Operating System Principles*, ACM, pp. 13-24, 1987.

ZOBEL, D.: "The Deadlock Problem: A Classifying Bibliography," *Operating Systems Review*, vol. 17, pp. 6-16, Oct. 1983.

B

INTRODUCTION TO C

C was invented by Dennis Ritchie of AT&T Bell Laboratories to provide a high-level language in which UNIX could be programmed. It is now widely used for many other applications as well. C is especially popular with systems programmers because it allows programs to be expressed simply and concisely. All students of operating systems should have at least some familiarity with C.

In this appendix we will attempt to provide enough of an introduction to C that someone who is familiar with high-level languages such as Pascal, PL/I, or Modula 2 will be able to understand the C code given in this book. Features of C not used in the book are discussed only briefly or not at all here. Numerous subtle points are omitted. The emphasis is on reading C, not writing it.

B.1. FUNDAMENTALS OF C

A C program is made up of a collection of procedures (often called functions, even when they do not return values). These procedures contain declarations, statements, and other elements that together tell the computer to do something. Figure B-1 shows a little procedure that declares three integer variables and assigns them all values. The procedure's name is *main*. It has no formal parameters, as indicated by the absence of any identifiers between the parentheses. Its body is enclosed between braces (curly brackets). This example shows that C has variables, and that these variables must be declared before being used. C also has statements, in this example, assignment statements. All statements must be terminated by semicolons (unlike

Pascal, which uses semicolons *between* statements, not *after* them). Comments are started by the /* symbol and ended by the */ symbol, and may extend over multiple lines.

```
main()                      /* This is a comment */
{
  int i, j, k;              /* declaration of 3 integer variables */
  i = 10;                   /* set i to 10 (decimal) */
  j = i + 015;              /* set j to i + 15 (octal) */
  k = j * j + 0xFF;         /* set k to j * j + FF (hexadecimal) */
}
```

Fig. B-1. An example of a procedure in C.

The procedure contains three constants. The constant 10 in the first assignment is an ordinary decimal constant. The constant 015 is an octal constant (equal to 13 decimal). Octal constants always begin with a leading zero. The constant 0xFF is a hexadecimal constant (equal to 255 decimal). Hexadecimal constants always begin with 0x. All three radices are commonly used in C.

B.2. BASIC DATA TYPES

C has two principal data types: integer and character, written int and char, respectively. There is no Boolean data type. Instead, integers are used, with 0 meaning false and everything else meaning true. C also has floating point types, but we do not need them. (Real computer scientists never use numbers larger than 255 anyway.)

The type int may be qualified with the "adjectives" short, long, or unsigned, which determine the (compiler dependent) range of values.

The qualifier register is also allowed for both int and char and is a hint to the compiler that the variable being declared might be worth putting in a register instead of in memory, to make the program run faster. Some declarations are shown in Fig. B-2.

```
int i;                      /* one integer */
short int z1, z2;           /* two short integers */
char c;                     /* one character */
unsigned short int k;       /* one unsigned short integer */
long flag_pole;             /* the 'int' may be omitted */
register int r;             /* a register variable */
```

Fig. B-2. Some declarations.

Conversion between types is allowed. For example, the statement

```
flag_pole = i;
```

is allowed even though *i* is an integer and *flag_pole* is a long. In many cases when converting between types it is necessary or useful to force one type to another. This can be done by putting the target type in parentheses in front of the expression to be converted, as in

```
p( (long) i);
```

to convert the integer i to a long before passing it as a parameter to a procedure p, which expects a long. This construction is called a **cast**.

B.3. CONSTRUCTED TYPES

In this section we will look at four ways of building up more complex data types: arrays, structures, unions, and pointers. An **array** is a collection of items of the same type. All arrays in C start with element 0. The declaration

```
int a[10];
```

declares an array, a, with 10 integers, referred to as a [0] through a [9] . Two, three, and higher dimensional arrays exist.

A **structure** is a collection of variables, usually of different types. A structure in C is similar to a record in Pascal. The declaration

```
struct {int i; char c;} s;
```

declares s to be a structure containing two **members**, an integer i, and a character c. To assign the member i the value 6, one would write

```
s.i = 6;
```

where the dot operator indicates that a member is being selected from a structure.

A **union** is also a collection of members, except that at any one moment, it can only hold one of them. The declaration

```
union {int i; char c;} u;
```

means that u can either hold an integer or a character, but not both. The compiler must allocate enough space for a union to hold the largest member. Since it knows the sizes of all the members, it can do this.

Pointers are used to hold machine addresses in C. An asterisk is used to indicate a pointer in declarations. The declaration

```
int i, *pi, a[10], *b[10], **ppi;
```

declares an integer, i, a pointer to an integer, pi, an array with 10 elements, a, an array of 10 pointers to integers, b, and a pointer to a pointer to an integer, ppi. The exact syntax rules for complex declarations combining arrays, pointers, and other types is somewhat complex.

Figure B-3 shows a declaration of an array z, of structures, each of which has three members, an integer i, a pointer to a character, cp, and a character, c. Arrays of structures are common in operating systems, for example, for system tables. The name *table* is defined as the type of the structure, allowing `struct table` to be used in declarations to mean this structure. For example,

```
register struct table *p;
```

declares *p* to be a pointer to a structure of type *table*, and suggests that it be kept in a register. During program execution, *p* might point, for example, to $z[4]$ or to any of the other elements of *z*, all 20 of which are structures of type *table*.

```
struct table {              /* each structure is of type table */
  int i;                    /* an integer */
  char *cp, c;              /* a pointer to a character and a character */
} z[20];                    /* this is an array of 20 structures */
```

Fig. B-3. An array of structures.

To make *p* point to $z[4]$, we would write

```
p = &z[4];
```

where the ampersand as a unary (monadic) operator means "take the address of what follows." To copy to the integer variable *n* the value of the member *i* of the structure pointed to by *p* we would write

```
n = p->i;
```

Note that the arrow is used to access a member of a structure via a pointer. If we were to use *z* itself, we would use the dot operator:

```
n = z[4].i;
```

The difference is that $z[4]$ is a structure, and the dot operator selects members from structures. With pointers, we are not selecting a member directly. The pointer must first be followed to find the structure; only then can a member be selected.

It is sometimes convenient to give a name to a constructed type. For example,

```
typedef int semaphore;
```

defines *semaphore* as a synonym for int. Although the compiler does not make a distinction between the two, for human readers, the distinction may make the code clearer. It can be used as though it were a basic type. For example,

```
semaphore mutex;
```

declares *mutex* to be an int in such a way that it is clear that it will be used as a semaphore. Declaring new types with `typedef` is done for the purposes of making the code clearer to the programmer and subsequent human readers. The compiler itself does not care whether a type is given a different name or not. Good programming style, however, is to make the program as clear as possible for people.

B.4. STATEMENTS

Procedures in C contain declarations and statements. We have already seen the declarations, so now we will look at the statements. The assignment, if, and while statements are essentially the same as in other languages. Figure B-4 shows some examples of them. The only points worth making are that braces are used for grouping compound statements, and the while statement has two forms, the second of which is similar to Pascal's **repeat** statement.

```
if (x < 0) k = 3;              /* a simple if statement */

if (x > y) {                   /* a compound if statement */
      j = 2;
      k = j + 1;
}

if (x + 2 < y) {               /* an if-else statement */
      j = 2;
      k = j - 1;
} else {
      m = 0;
}

while (n > 0) {                /* a while statement */
      k = k + k;
      n = n - 1;
}

do {                           /* another kind of while statement */
      k = k + k;
      n = n - 1;
} while ( n > 0);
```

Fig. B-4. A few simple examples of if and while statements in C.

C also has a for statement, but this is unlike the for statement in any other language. It has the general form

```
for (initializer; condition; expression) statement;
```

The meaning of the statement is

```
initializer;
while (condition) {
      statement;
      expression;
}
```

As an example, consider the statement

```
for (i = 0; i < n; i = i + 1) a[i] = 0;
```

This statement sets the first *n* elements of *a* to zero. It starts out by initializing *i* to zero (outside the loop). Then it iterates as long as $i < n$, executing the assignment and incrementing *i*. The statement can, of course, be a compound statement enclosed by braces, rather than just a simple assignment, as is shown here.

C has a construction that is similar to Pascal's **case** statement. It is called a switch statement. Figure B-5 shows an example. Depending on the value of the expression following the keyword switch, one clause or another is chosen. If the expression does not match any of the cases, the default clause is selected. If the expression does not match any case and no default is present, control just continues with the next statement following the switch.

```
switch (k) {
     case 10:
          i = 6;
          break;                 /* do not continue with case 20 */

     case 20:
          j = 2;
          k = 4;
          break;

     default:
          j = 5;
}
```

Fig. B-5. An example of a switch statement.

One thing to note is that after one of the cases has been executed, control just continues with the next one, unless a break statement is present. In practice, the break is virtually always needed.

The break statement is also valid inside for and while loops, and when executed causes control to exit the loop. If the break statement is located in the innermost of a series of nested loops, only one level is exited.

A related statement is the continue statement, which does not exit the loop, but causes the current iteration to be terminated and the next iteration to start immediately. In effect, it is a jump back to the top of the loop.

C has procedures, which may be called with or without parameters. When used as a parameter, the name of an array is taken to mean a pointer to the array, making it easy to pass an array pointer. Thus if *a* is the name of an array of any type, it can be passed to a procedure *g* by writing

```
g(a);
```

This rule holds only for arrays, not for structures.

Procedures can return values by executing the return statement. This statement may provide an expression to be returned as the value of the procedure, but the caller may safely ignore it. If a procedure returns a value, the type of the value is written before the procedure name, as shown in Fig. B-6. As with parameters, procedures may not return arrays or procedures directly, but may return pointers to them. This rule is designed to make the implementation efficient—all parameters and results usually fit in a single machine word (except for structures, which may be used as parameters and results).

```
int sum(i, j)                  /* this procedure returns an integer */
int i,j;                       /* formal parameters declared before { */
{
   return(i + j);              /* add the parameters and return the sum */
}
```

Fig. B-6. An example of a simple procedure that returns a value.

C does not have any built-in input/output statements. I/O is done by calling library procedures, the most common of which is illustrated below:

```
printf('x = %d y = %o z = %x\n', x , y, z);
```

The first parameter is a string of characters between quotation marks (it is actually a character array). Any character that is not a percent is just printed as is. When a percent is encountered, the next parameter is printed, with the letter (or two letters) following the percent telling how to print it:

d - print as a decimal integer
o - print as an octal integer
u - print as unsigned decimal integer
x - print as a hexadecimal integer
s - print as a string
c - print as a single character

The combinations *ld*, *lo*, and *lx* are also allowed, for printing decimal, octal, and hexadecimal `longs`.

B.5. EXPRESSIONS

Expressions are constructed by combining operands and operators. The arithmetic operators, such as + and −, and the relational operators, such as < and > are similar to their counterparts in other languages. The % operator is used for modulo. It is worth noting that the equality operator is == and the not equals operator is !=. To see if *a* and *b* are equal, one can write

```
if (a == b) statement;
```

C also allows assignments and operators to be combined, so

```
a += 4;
```

means the same as

```
a = a + 4;
```

The other operators may also be combined this way. Some compilers produce slightly better code from these combined operators than from the straightforward form.

Operators are provided for manipulating the bits of a word. Both shifts and bitwise Boolean operations are allowed. The left and right shift operators are `<<` and `>>` respectively. The bitwise Boolean operators `&`, `|`, and `^` are AND, INCLUSIVE OR, and EXCLUSIVE OR, respectively. If i has the value 035 (octal), then the expression `i & 06` has the value 04 (octal). As another example, if i is 7, then

```
j = (i << 3) | 014;
```

assigns 074 to j.

Another important group of operators is the unary operators, all of which take only one operand. As a unary operator, the ampersand takes the address of a variable. Thus `&i` has the value of the machine location at which i is located. If p is a pointer to an integer and i is an integer, the statement

```
p = &i;
```

computes the address of i and stores it in the variable p.

The opposite of taking the address of something (e.g., to put it in a pointer) is taking a pointer as input and computing the value of the thing pointed to. If we have just assigned the address of i to p, then `*p` has the same value as i. In other words, as a unary operator, the asterisk is followed by a pointer (or an expression yielding a pointer), and yields the value of the item pointed to. If i has the value 6, then the statement

```
j = *p;
```

will assign 6 to j.

The `!` operator returns 0 if its operand is nonzero and 1 if its operator is 0. It is primarily used in `if` statements, for example

```
if (!x) k = 8;
```

checks the value of x. If x is zero (false), k is assigned the value 8. In effect, the `!` operator negates the condition following it, just as the **not** operator does in Pascal.

The tilde is the bitwise complement operator. Each 0 in its operand becomes a 1 and each 1 becomes a 0. In fact, this is the one's complement of the operand.

The `sizeof` operator tells how big its operand is, in bytes. If applied to an array of 20 integers, a, on a machine with 2-byte integers, for example, `sizeof a` will have the value 40. When applied to a structure, it tells how big the structure is. The size is in bytes.

The last group of operators are the increment and decrement operators. The statement

```
p++;
```

means increment p. How much it is incremented by depends on its type. Integers or characters are incremented by 1, but pointers are incremented by the size of the object pointed to. Thus if *a* is an array of structures, and *p* a pointer to one of these structures, and we write

```
p = &a[3];
```

to make *p* point to one of the structures in the array, then after we increment *p* it will point to *a*[4] no matter how big the structures are. The statement

```
p—;
```

is analogous, except that it decrements instead of incrementing.

In the assignment

```
n = k++;
```

where both variables are integers, the original value of *k* is assigned to *n* and then the increment happens. In the assignment

```
n = ++k;
```

first k is incremented, *then* its new value is stored in *n*. Thus the ++ (or --) operator can be written either before or after its operand, with different meanings.

One last operator is the ? operator, which selects one of two alternatives separated by a colon. For example,

```
i = (x < y ? 6 : k + 1);
```

compares *x* to *y*. If *x* is less than *y,* then *i* gets the value 6; otherwise, it gets the value *k* + 1. The parentheses are optional.

B.6. PROGRAM STRUCTURE

A C program consists of one or more files containing procedures and declarations. These files can be separately compiled, yielding separate object files, which are then linked together (by the linker) to form the executable program. Unlike Pascal, procedure declarations may not be nested, so they all appear at the "top level" in the file.

It is permitted to declare variables outside procedures, for example, at the beginning of a file before the first procedure declaration. These variables are global, and can be used in any procedure in the whole program, unless the keyword static precedes the declaration, in which case it is not permitted to use the variables in another file. The same rules apply to procedures. Variables declared inside a procedure are local to the procedure in which they are declared.

Variables may be initialized, as in

```
int size = 100;
```

Arrays and structures may also be initialized. Global variables that are not explicitly initialized get the default value of zero. Local variables that are not explicitly initialized do not get zero or any well defined value. It is up to the program to explicitly initialize them.

B.7. THE C PREPROCESSOR

Before a source file is even given to the C compiler, it is automatically run through a program called the **preprocessor**. The preprocessor output, not the original program, is what is fed into the compiler. The preprocessor carries out several major transformations on the file before giving it to the compiler. For our purposes, the two most important are:

1. File inclusion.

2. Macro definition and expansion.

Preprocessor directives all begin with a number sign (#) in column 1.
    When a directive of the form

```
#include "file.h"
```

is encountered by the preprocessor, it bodily includes the file, line by line, in the program given to the compiler. When the directive is written as

```
#include <file.h>
```

the directory *usr/include* rather than the working directory is searched for the file. It is common practice in C to group declarations used by several files in a **header file** (usually with suffix *.h*), and include them where they are needed.
    The preprocessor also allows macro definitions. For example,

```
#define BLOCK_SIZE 1024
```

defines a macro *BLOCK_SIZE* and gives it the value 1024. From that point on, every occurrence of the 10-character string "BLOCK_SIZE" in the file will be replaced by the 4-character string "1024" before the compiler sees the file. All that is happening here is that one character string is being replaced by another one. By convention, macro names are written in upper case. Macros may have parameters, but in practice few of them do.

B.8. IDIOMS

In this section we will look at a few constructions that are characteristic of C, but are not common in other programming languages. As a starter, consider the loop

```
while (n--) *p++ = *q++;
```

The variables p and q are typically character pointers, and n is a counter. What the loop does is copy an *n*-character string from the place pointed to by *q* to the place pointed to by *p*. On each iteration of the loop, the counter is decremented, until it gets to 0, and each of the pointers is incremented, so they successively point to higher numbered memory locations.

Another common construction is

```
for (i = 0; i < N; i++) a[i] = 0;
```

which sets the first *N* elements of *a* to 0. An alternative way of writing this loop is

```
for (p = &a[0]; p < &a[N]; p++) *p = 0;
```

In this formulation, the integer pointer, *p*, is initialized to point to the zeroth element of the array. The loop continues as long as *p* has not reached the address of *a*[*N*], which is the first element that is too far. On each iteration, a different element is set to 0. The pointer construction is much more efficient than the array construction, and is therefore commonly used.

Assignments may appear in unexpected places. For example,

```
if (a = f(x)) statement;
```

first calls the function *f*, then assigns the result of the function call to *a*, and finally tests *a* to see if it is true (nonzero) or false (zero). If *a* is nonzero, the statement is executed. The statement

```
if (a = b) statement;
```

is similar, in that it assigns *b* to *a* and then tests *a* to see if it is nonzero. It is totally different from

```
if (a == b) statement;
```

which compares two variables and executes the statement if they are equal.

INDEX